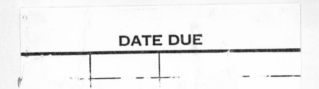

# BRITAIN AND THE
# EASTERN QUESTION
## 1875–1878

# BRITAIN AND THE EASTERN QUESTION
## 1875–1878

RICHARD MILLMAN

CLARENDON PRESS · OXFORD
1979

*Oxford University Press, Walton Street, Oxford* OX2 6DP

OXFORD LONDON GLASGOW
NEW YORK TORONTO MELBOURNE WELLINGTON
KUALA LUMPUR SINGAPORE JAKARTA HONG KONG TOKYO
DELHI BOMBAY CALCUTTA MADRAS KARACHI
IBADAN NAIROBI DAR ES SALAAM CAPE TOWN

© *Oxford University Press 1979*

**British Library Cataloguing in Publication Data**
Millman, Richard
Britain and the Eastern Question, 1875–1878.
1. Eastern question (Balkan) 2. Great Britain –
Foreign relations – Balkan Peninsula
3. Balkan Peninsula – Foreign relations –
Great Britain
I. Title
327.41′P496        D375        78–40325
ISBN 0–19–822379–X

*Text set in 11/12 pt Photon Baskerville printed by photolithography,
and bound in Great Britain at The Pitman Press, Bath*

*To*
*my parents.*

# PREFACE

THERE HAS been a great amount of writing on the Eastern crisis of the 1870s. Publications commenced contemporaneously with the course of the crisis, and some of those active in it continued to write about it down to the outbreak of war in 1914. To most of these writers it seemed to be another major chapter of an old story, the basis of which was the increasing disparity in technology and power between the Ottoman Empire and the European Great Powers, complicated by Christian–Muslim antagonism. The flow of books and articles from academic historians in the generation following the First World War became almost a torrent as the Eastern Question itself ended with the demise of the Ottoman Empire. In the last twenty-five years, with occasional significant exceptions and a small recent renaissance, a well-deserved silence has ensued.

I have disturbed this repose in an attempt to discuss the formulation and execution of British policy over the course of the crisis together with the tremendous, almost unique, domestic reaction to both Eastern events and the Government's response to those events. I have gone over much of the same ground traversed in 1935 by R. W. Seton-Watson in *Disraeli, Gladstone and the Eastern Question*, but have differed greatly in viewpoint and interpretation from that eminent scholar. The story begins in detail with the outbreak of revolt in 1875, though with considerable reference to the Eastern Question before that year, and ends in 1878 on the eve of the Congress of Berlin, though with some consideration of the results of the Congress. I have not included the events of the Congress itself in order to avoid lengthening an already long narrative. Indeed, as W. N. Medlicott has shown us, a full discussion of the Congress is as much a projection into the decade after 1878 as it is a culmination of the period since 1875. Finally, a convenient and significant resting place is with the ending of the Russian-Turkish war and the prevention of an Anglo-Russian or Austro-Russian conflict which was largely if not completely accomplished before the Congress met.

The narrative differs from those contained in previous accounts in its treatment of the Bulgarian massacres of May 1876 and in its characterization of Lord Derby, the British Foreign Secretary. It is based on evidence old and new, drawn from an exhaustive, often pleasant, and usually exhausting search among British private papers and, more suprisingly, from the superb collection of Foreign Office material at the Public Record Office. Much secondary literature was consulted and use was made of Foreign Ministry archives on the Continent, especially those of Austria, Belgium, Germany, Italy, the Netherlands, and Spain. I am overwhelmed by the generosity of many libraries, archivists, and owners of private papers, and regret that I cannot acknowledge individually the kindness and assistance of all to whom I am indebted. I can only hope that those not specifically mentioned will accept a general though anonymous thank you.

Travel to Europe and research there was made possible by research board grants from the Universities of California and Illinois and especially by the generosity of the American Philosophical Society whose support made possible the completion of this work. I am greatly indebted to a number of Continental archivists and scholars and must mention Dr. Richard Blaas, M. Pierre Desneux, M. Hugo de Jonghes, Matilde Medina, Dr. Christiane Thomas, and Dr. J. Woltring. The last-named scholar's kindness and assistance exceeded anything that this student could have expected. The staffs of the Haus-, Hof- und Staatsarchiv and of the archives of the Spanish Foreign Ministry were exceedingly helpful.

In Britain the extent of my indebtedness is, of course, even greater and I would like to thank Lord Bradford, Lord Derby, Lord Halifax, Lord Harcourt, Lord St. Aldwyn, Sir Philip Magnus-Allcroft, A. M. Broom, Patricia Gill, Sheila Sokolov Grant, T. L. Ingram, J. F. A. Mason, Mrs. J. E. Robinson, and Mr. T. L. Wragg. I owe much to the staffs of the National Library of Scotland, the Bodleian Library, St. Deiniol's Library, the libraries of the Foreign Office and India Office, and the Manuscripts Department of the British Library where I was fortunate in encountering P. H. Agrell. The publishers W. H. Smith and John Murray generously offered their assistance. I cannot say enough about the help given me by the staff of the Public Record Office where I must single out Mr. P. Fellows and Mr. L. G. Seed. Finally, I have to acknowledge the gracious kindness of Her Majesty the Queen for her permission to examine and quote from the Royal Archives at Windsor Castle.

There are three people whose expert knowledge and assistance have been extended to me over many years. There is no commensurate way that I can acknowledge the kindness of Kenneth Timings, Jane Langton, and Felicity Strong, and I am reduced to recording my great indebtedness and appreciation.

During the unconscionably lengthy period required for the research and writing of this work I have been extremely fortunate in obtaining the help of three outstanding research assistants—Yeshaiahu Cahana, Alberto Sbacchi, and Winfried Seelig. I was equally well served by the assistance of Mr. Alejandro Rodero.

Professors Roderic Davison and Otto Pflanze kindly consented to read parts of the manuscript which were improved as a result of their suggestions. A friend and former colleague, Dr. Arthur Silver, generously made available to me microfilm in his possession. I must also extend my thanks to two other friends and colleagues, Robert Conrad who provided a great number of translations of Spanish material and Marion S. Miller who heroically read the entire manuscript, which as a result was much improved. Joanne and Bill Bruce willingly gave their expertise, interest, and kindness.

The inter-library loan departments of the libraries of the University of Illinois at Chicago and the University of Pennsylvania and the reference department of the latter library were of much help. The typing ability of Rose Zubrow was used and abused.

Finally, the composition of the manuscript was made much more pleasant by those two devoted Anglophiles, Jennifer and Darby.

# CONTENTS

| | | |
|---|---|---|
| | LIST OF MAPS | xii |
| | LIST OF ABBREVIATIONS | xiii |
| 1. | Derby | 1 |
| 2. | Insurrection in Hercegovina and Bosnia | 13 |
| 3. | Bankruptcy, Rebellion, and Reform | 27 |
| 4. | The Andrássy Note | 39 |
| 5. | Anglo-German Entente | 58 |
| 6. | Winding Down the Insurrection | 74 |
| 7. | The Berlin Memorandum | 87 |
| 8. | The Spread of War | 107 |
| 9. | Bulgaria | 121 |
| 10. | Bulgaria and Britain | 146 |
| 11. | War, Mediation, and Agitation | 165 |
| 12. | Arranging a Conference | 190 |
| 13. | Two Conferences in Constantinople | 208 |
| 14. | Two Conferences in London | 232 |
| 15. | The London Protocol and War | 254 |
| 16. | War: Conditional Neutrality | 274 |
| 17. | Plevna | 305 |
| 18. | Armistice | 335 |
| 19. | San Stefano | 372 |
| 20. | Preparing for a Congress | 403 |
| 21. | At Long Last Berlin | 433 |
| 22. | Conclusion | 452 |
| | BIBLIOGRAPHY | 463 |
| | NOTES | 475 |
| | INDEX | 605 |

# MAPS

1. Bosnia-Hercegovina in 1878     14
2. Bulgaria     122
3. Constantinople and the Straits     337

# ABBREVIATIONS

| | |
|---|---|
| Anderson | Dorothy Anderson, *The Balkan Volunteers* (London, 1968) |
| BFM | Belgian Foreign Ministry Archives, Brussels |
| Cecil | Lady G. Cecil, *Life of Robert Marquis of Salisbury* (4 vols., London, 1921–32) |
| Cran. Pap. | Cranbrook Papers, East Suffolk Record Office |
| *GD* | E.T.S. Dugdale (ed.), *German Diplomatic Documents, 1871–1914* (4 vols., London, 1928–31) |
| GFM | German Foreign Ministry Documents. Microfilm copies of German documents taken by the Allies at the end of World War II |
| Glad. Pap. | Gladstone Papers, British Library and St. Deiniol's Library, Hawarden |
| Good. Pap. | Goodwood (Richmond) Papers, Chichester Record Office |
| *GP* | Ausswärtiges Amt, *Die Grosse Politik der europäischen Kabinette, 1871–1914* (40 vols., Berlin, 1922–7) |
| Gran. Pap. | Granville Papers, Public Record Office |
| Hardy | A. E. Gathorne-Hardy(ed.), *Gathorne-Hardy, First Earl Cranbrook, A Memoir, with Extracts from His Diary and Correspondence* (2 vols., London, 1910) |
| Harris | David Harris, *A Diplomatic History of the Balkan Crisis of 1875–78. The First Year* (Stanford, 1936) |
| Hart. Pap. | Hartington Papers, Chatsworth |
| HG | C. Howard and P. Gordon (eds.), 'Cabinet Journal of Viscount Sandon,' supplement no. 10 of *Bulletin of the Institute of Historical Research* |
| HHSA | Austrian Foreign Ministry Archives (Haus-, Hof- und Staatsarchiv), Politisches Archiv, Vienna |
| *Horrors* | David Harris, *Britain and the Bulgarian Horrors of 1876* (Chicago, 1939) |
| IFM | Italian Foreign Ministry Archives, Rome |
| Jelavich | C. and B. Jelavich, *Russia in the East, 1876–1880* (Leiden, 1959) |
| Lay. Mem. | Layard Memoirs, John Murray, London |

| | |
|---|---|
| Lay. Pap | Layard Papers, British Library |
| Lee | Dwight Lee, *Great Britain and the Cyprus Convention Policy of 1876* (Cambridge, 1934) |
| Mackenzie | David Mackenzie, *The Serbs and Russian Pan-Slavism, 1875–78* (Ithaca, 1967) |
| MB | W. F. Monypenny and G. E. Buckle, *The Life of Benjamin Disraeli* (6 vols., London, 1910–20) |
| NA | Netherlands Foreign Ministry Archives (Ministerie Van Buitenlandse Zaken), The Hague |
| Northc. Pap. | Northcote Papers, British Library |
| PRO FO | Foreign Office Correspondence, Public Record Office |
| *QVL* | G. E. Buckle (ed.), *Letters of Queen Victoria* (2nd ser., 2 vols., N.Y., 1926) |
| RA | Royal Archives, Windsor |
| Ramm | A. Ramm (ed.), *The Political Correspondence of Mr. Gladstone and Lord Granville, 1876–86* (2 vols., Oxford, 1962) |
| Reid | T. W. Reid, *Life of W. E. Forster* (2 vols., London, 1888) |
| Rupp | G. H. Rupp, *A Wavering Friendship: Russia and Austria, 1876–78* (Cambridge, Mass., 1941) |
| Salis. Pap. | Salisbury Papers, Christ Church Library and India Office Library |
| Seton-Watson | R. W. Seton-Watson, *Disraeli, Gladstone and the Eastern Question* (London, 1935) |
| Seton-Watson, *Slav. Rev.* | R. W. Seton-Watson, 'Russo-British Relations during the Eastern Crisis', *Slavonic Review*, iii–vi. (1924–8); xxv–xxvi (1946–8); xxviii (1949–50) |
| SFM | Spanish Foreign Ministry Archives, Madrid |
| Shannon | R. T. Shannon, *Gladstone and the Bulgarian Agitation, 1876* (London, 1963) |
| Stojanovic | M. A. Stojanovic, *The Great Powers and the Balkans, 1875–78* (Cambridge, 1939) |
| Sumner | B. H. Sumner, *Russia and the Balkans, 1870–1880* (Oxford, 1937) |
| Taylor | A. J. P. Taylor, *Struggle For the Mastery of Europe, 1848–1919* (Oxford, 1954) |
| Thompson | G. C. Thompson, *Public Opinion and Lord Beaconsfield, 1875–80* (2 vols., London, 1886) |

| | |
|---|---|
| Wantage | Baroness Wantage, *Lord Wantage* (London, 1908) |
| Wirthwein | W. G. Wirthwein, *Britain and the Balkan Crisis, 1875–78* (N.Y., 1935) |
| Zetland | Marquis of Zetland (ed.), *Letters of Disraeli to Lady Chesterfield and Lady Bradford* (2 vols., N.Y., 1929) |

# 1 DERBY

IN THE first third of the nineteenth century, a gradual but growing anxiety and suspicion towards Russian ambition permeated Britain's ruling élite. Most of the same political leaders, who were coming to view Russia with hatred and anxiety, had nothing but contempt and disgust for the Ottoman Government. Despite the unacceptability of Muslim rule over Christians to British feeling and opinion, however, the continuance of such dominion was thought necessary as a barrier to the expansion of Russia.

Ironically, in a period of rising negative feeling towards Russia, in the Greek revolt of 1826 and the Turco-Egyptian crisis of 1839, Canning and Palmerston sought co-operation and agreement with her. The Anglo-Russian protocol of 1826 led to France's joining the duo which resulted in the London Treaty of 1827. The Anglo-Russian Agreement of 1839–40 elicited Austro-Prussian adhesion and resulted in the London Treaty of 1840 and then the Straits Convention of 1841. Canning's achievement, which was interrupted by his death, replaced a congress system dominated by the Holy Alliance with another combination reflecting much more the diplomatic initiative and national interests of Britain. Palmerston's destruction of Russia's special position at Constantinople inaugurated by Unkiar Skelessi in favour of five-Power co-operation did the same.

It was the connection of the two things, hatred of Russia and defence of Turkish integrity, reinforced by the accessibility of Turkey to sea power, which transformed the hostility felt for St. Petersburg into the possibility of military confrontation with her. When the latter seemed committed to destroying Turkish independence in 1853, Britain went to war in the Crimea.

The British relationship with and attitudes towards the Porte changed significantly after 1856. Palmerstonian concern for the security of the Eastern Mediterranean and therefore the desire to preserve the Ottoman Empire continued, especially as it was now sanctified by treaty. But London's interest in Ot-

toman reform increased greatly compared with what it had
been before the Crimean War. Palmerston and the two ambassadors, Stratford and Ponsonby, had attempted to lead and
drive the Porte to military and fiscal reform before 1854 in
order to make Turkey a more viable buffer against Russia.
Stratford, admittedly, was also motivated to press reform by
the disgust he felt at the way Turkey's Christians were
governed. After 1856, when Britain had spent both blood and
money in Turkey's defence, and had with France begun the
eventually disastrous policy of granting loans to Constantinople, the English stake in Ottoman preservation seemed to have
grown. But along with this, British feelings of complicity,
having fought as Turkey's ally, in the way Ottoman Christians
were governed and the right to admonish the Porte for services
rendered it, grew even more. This concern with the necessity
for the good government of Balkan Christians was not merely a
Gladstonian guilty conscience, or humanitarian sympathy, or
Christian prejudice. It reflected a recognition that without a
serious Turkish attempt to satisfy Christian grievances in a
period of rising national feeling within the Balkans, there
would result almost constant interference in the internal affairs
of the Ottoman Empire by Russia and perhaps France and
Austria as well.

When Russia in 1870 unilaterally renounced the Black Sea
clauses of the Treaty of Paris of March 1856, Gladstone, as
Mosse has shown us, responded in a way which dissatisfied
those concerned with national interests and prestige. He
seemed to have stood up for the sanctity of treaties and the rule
of law. It was perhaps less noted that he had done so over the
carcass of the Tripartite Treaty of April 1856.

On the eve of revolt in Bosnia in July 1875 Britain's policy
continued as before to press for Ottoman reform to keep
things as quiet as possible in the East, to avoid undue interference by the Powers in Ottoman internal affairs, and to
stand up verbally for the treaties of Paris and London of 1856
and 1871. British relations with the major Powers were
generally good despite Bismarck's anger at Anglo-Russian co-
operation in placing pressure on Germany during the war
scare of April–May 1875. Central Asia and Turkey stood in the
way of good Anglo-Russian relations in spite of the slight fillip

resulting from the marriage in 1874 of the Duke of Edinburgh with the daughter of the Tsar. Italy and France were both friendly but were weak and occasionally exhibited pro-Russian leanings. Notwithstanding a mild concern for Ottoman integrity, Andrássy, the Austrian Foreign Minister, did offer the possibility of diplomatic and military support against Russia, but as would be the case over the next three years, it was a support viewed by London with suspicion.

Even before the France-German war scare of 1875 and the outbreak of revolt in Hercegovina in July, Britain's two most prominent political figures attempted to improve connections with Germany. Gladstone, in the midst of a pamphlet war against the Vatican's pretensions to infallibility, proposed to the German ambassador his aid in popularizing Bismarck's anti-Catholic legislation in England by influencing the *Guardian* and the *Daily Telegraph* to print favourable information about German church policy. Bismarck jumped to accept the offer, and Gladstone responded by sending to the German leader 'the first copy' of his second pamphlet entitled *Vaticanism* as an indication of his 'sincere adoration and admiration' for him. 'Gladstone added that the deeper he penetrated these questions the more he came to the conviction that England as well as Germany and the Protestants of the whole world should regard Bismarck as the vanguard of their cause. Gladstone has sent the manuscript [of *Vaticanism*] to a translator, for a soon to be published German translation.' Bismarck replied in English of his gratification at finding Germany and Britain, the two national champions of liberty of conscience marching together in defence of the higher interests of humanity.[1]

Disraeli, who may have been more concerned with the political dominance of the Dreikaiserbund than the threat of Papal or Catholic influence, also approached Münster, the German Ambassador, in February 1875 and told the ambassador that France could never be the 'sincere ally' of Britain. 'Germany and England', he said, 'are the two people who could go hand in hand as he increasingly realized.' The Prime Minister assured Münster that British non-intervention as practised in 1870–1 had no following in the present Conservative ministry and that for the future Germany would be able always to count upon Britain, a nation of similar race and religion. Allusion was made to Russia with whom Disraeli indicated there would be an attempt to avoid serious complications, but that if St. Petersburg did not act more cautiously 'John Bull' would become nasty.[2]

The amalgam which comprised British dislike and fear of Russia was injected in 1873 with the question of Central Asia. The addition did not lighten or tranquillize the mixture. The new Conservative Government of 1874 contained Salisbury and Derby as the Secretaries of State for India and Foreign Affairs. The latter, characteristically, as he reported to the Queen, preferred to consider the question settled.

Lord Derby did not refuse to enter into such discussion [on Central Asia] but did not especially invite it.

If Russian assurances are to be trusted, they have already been given in abundance; if not, it seems useless to ask to have them repeated.

Lord Derby thought it better to treat the question as settled: which ostensibly and formally it is.

He took the opportunity ... of respectfully hinting to the Czar the danger that might arise from the proceedings of over-zealous officers ...[3]

Derby had been Foreign Secretary before during the 1866–8 ministry of his father, the fourteenth Earl. As the nature of his personality and character were to be important during the crisis of 1875–8, some attempt will be made here to outline it.

Edward Henry Stanley was the eldest son of the fourteenth Earl of Derby, a man of great vitality who was three times Prime Minister, an outstanding orator, successful man of business, translator of the *Iliad* and a lover of shooting and the turf. It would have been a hard act for anyone to have followed, and the fact that his two sons did as well as they did is a tribute to both, even allowing for the advantages they had as Stanleys.

The future fifteenth Earl, unlike his dynamic father, was largely devoid of fire and passion, and his later Cabinet colleagues and foreign ambassadors experienced his carefulness, hesitancy, indecision, and suspicion as a lack of compassion and warmth. Disraeli, who knew him long and well, suspected the absence of any self-confidence, a lack which he attempted to repair by acting as a kind of surrogate father to the younger man. Stanley's relationship with his own father, to say nothing of his mother, apparently was an inadequate one. Blake assumes that Stanley was immobilized by a distant and forbidding father whose affection for his son was intermittent. Grant Duff tells what may be an apocryphal story concerning Stanley's being offered the Cabinet post of Colonial Secretary by Palmerston in 1855. 'He [Stanley] was much tempted by the proposal and hurried down to Knowsley to consult his father, who called out when he entered the room, "Hallo, Stanley! What brings you here?—Has Dizzy cut his throat, or are you going to be married?" . . . The offer was declined . . .'[4]

A biographer of the fourteenth Earl claims that Stanley's love and affection for his father remained intact over the years.[5] Robert Morier, the diplomatist, who knew Stanley fairly well, thought that he had a difficult childhood.

He [Stanley] is morally and intellectually incapable of shaping out an opinion of his own—and his neutral attitude is a deprecatory one to the opinion of others. The intellectual cause is the exclusively critical nature of his mind. He is totally incapable intellectually of any kind of generous impulse. . . . The moral cause has a curious history of its own. I think at least I can discern in much of his ways and character of a most unhappy youth and here I feel strong sympathy for him . . .[6]

Disraeli wrote to the Queen of the adult Derby.

Mr. Disraeli . . . adjured him, in his approaching audience, to do justice to himself, and step out of his icy panoply.

And then, even with softness, he gave Mr. Disraeli his hand, which is not his habit, and said 'Good-bye old friend.' 'Dear Friend' Mr. Disraeli assumes Lord Derby would say to no one . . .[7]

It has been alleged by Schreuder that Stanley was sent down from Eton because of kleptomania.[8] Even if the kleptomania is a myth, it is fairly clear that before Stanley reached adulthood his capacity to trust[9] and express warmth had been seriously impaired, his need to be careful and intellectually consistent had become oppressive, and his sense of self-worth and self-reliance had been significantly blunted. Driven to protect a wounded and disjoined personality, he unconsciously became its slave.

After Trinity College, Cambridge, where he did well, he travelled to the West Indies, Canada, and the United States. In 1852, while touring in India, he was given the post of Under-Secretary for Foreign Affairs in his father's first Government. Two years later he joined with Cobden and Bright in opposing entry into the Crimean War. In his father's second administration in 1858–9 Stanley was successively Colonial Secretary and Secretary of State for India. He was again offered office by the Liberals in 1865, but refused it as he had done with Palmerston's tender in 1855. In the Conservative Government of 1866, though it was generally agreed by his father, the Queen, and Stanley himself that he was not well suited for the post, in lieu of a better choice, he was appointed Foreign Secretary. In his first period of office as Foreign Secretary between 1866 and 1868 he emphasized and enlarged the self-effacement which Britain adopted toward Continental affairs and lent it a kind of dignity.

Though as Foreign Secretary he avoided the blunders of Palmerston and Russell in 1863–4, he committed some of his own, seemingly proving that between caution and impetuosity there was little to choose. His explaining away the Luxemburg guarantee before the ink was dry was embarrassing. In a speech at King's Lynn in 1864 he favoured the break-up of European Turkey, but once in office he seemed to equivocate, as may be seen from a statement he made in 1868. 'But an indifferent government is better than none. . . . I [Stanley] should say to them [the Christian population of Turkey] . . . anarchy is not progress, and that it is not wise to pull down that for which you have not provided any substitute.'[10]

But his lack of initiative and personal need to be careful meshed well with a public mood which placed a premium on sober common sense and unadventurous commonplaces. His stock suffered with neither party, especially outside Parliament. An unsuccessful attempt was made in February 1870 to have him accept the Conservative leadership of the Lords. In June the Liberals gave serious consideration to making him another offer to join them.[11]

In January and February 1872 temporary dissatisfaction with Disraeli's leadership of the party resulted in some talk, which was never acted upon, to make Derby the new leader of the Conservatives. Derby was never formally asked apparently nor Disraeli informed of the leanings of a few prominent Conservatives.[12] The usual explanation is that Derby was in his opinions or tendencies more of a Liberal than a Conservative. This is misleading because his opinions or attitudes were calculated to some extent to avoid taking action or adopting measures and reflected neither political philosophy nor class interests. His conversation was defensive and often inappropriately intended to preserve a kind of personal autonomy. Viscount Esher noted in 1873 that, 'He [Derby] is a difficult man to talk to, pausing as he does for an answer and pausing himself before he answers a question, so fearful of not expressing exactly what he means.'[13]

In 1870, the year following the death of his father, Derby, then forty-four years old, married Salisbury's widowed step-mother, Mary, Marchioness of Salisbury, who was then forty-six. Lady Burghclere has depicted their married life in glowing terms, describing the warmth she brought to a shy man and the adoration in which he held her.[14] Much of Lady Derby's energy was expended on political activity, conversation, and interference. The fact that Derby adopted a completely indulgent attitude toward his wife's behaviour, even when it was inappropriate and dangerous, allowed the Countess considerable scope for satisfaction and pleasure. The temptation to act with less than complete loyalty to her husband was sometimes not resisted.

The fact that her husband and step-son were to some extent political rivals and cool friends offered apparently no awkwardness for Lady Derby, who continued to maintain a close political relationship with Salisbury even after 1870. Both Disraeli and Salisbury were not unhappy to use her as a convenient go-between in an attempt to negotiate Salisbury into the new Conservative Cabinet being formed in 1874.[15]

The following seemingly cruel note from Salisbury to his step-mother did not terminate their relationship nor prevent future communication. 'I hope Derby is none the worse for the late hours he has been keeping—in the bedrooms of charming ladies.'[16]

As Foreign Secretary for the second time in 1874, Derby was accurately observed by the foreign ambassadorial corps resident in London. The French ambassador described an awkward and unbending Derby greeting foreign diplomats at a Foreign Office reception, while the German ambassador,[17] agreeing with the writer of an article in the *Spectator* quoted below who spoke of Derby's caution and high intelligence, emphasized the Foreign Secretary's timidity and lack of initiative:

... he sees both sides too strongly to believe in either; and that his Conservatism, therefore is due ... to the want of any adequate motive—power to induce men to alter what is. But that is almost as dangerous a habit of mind as rashness itself, for anyone who has really got to take great resolves. ... He is so timid of great professions, that he disavows the only adequate motive for his own policy, and so plays his adversaries' game. There is great wisdom in him of the negative kind, but it is not the kind of wisdom which a great leader wants ... through stormy seas ...[18]

Yet there remained general confidence in Derby as Bourke, the Parliamentary Under-Secretary for Foreign Affairs, told Dilke. 'The one thing that astonishes him [Bourke] is the confidence of the people in Ld. Derby.'[19]

Some of that confidence evaporated as the Eastern crisis of 1875–8 unfolded. Askwith, Thorold Rogers, Dilke, Grant Duff, and others became aware of Derby's indecision and inadequacy, especially after the British refusal of the Berlin Memorandum in May 1876 and the outbreak of the Bulgarian agitation in the autumn of that year. Grant Duff referred to it in an article, where he depicted a Government with no policy, having jettisoned its old and unsatisfactory compromise between support for Turkey and diplomatic coercion of her.[20] Though many of those active in the Bulgarian agitation hated him for being unwilling to threaten Turkey with physical coercion, some recognized his aversion for a strong pro-Turkish line and his association within the Cabinet with Carnarvon and Salisbury, the two ministers most vocally concerned for the welfare of Ottoman Christians. So he was criticized for being insufficiently Palmerstonian and insufficiently Christian, both of which were true.

Even within the Cabinet dissatisfaction with Derby's behaviour grew, especially after the beginning of the Russo–Turkish War in April 1877. With Ottoman military defeat, the necessity for British military precautions and an Austrian alliance grew. Derby obstructed both. Just before the war began, Carnarvon, Derby's close cabinet ally, temporarily irritated, complained to Northcote, the Chancellor of the Exchequer, about his friend's 'intemperate conduct even in the ordinary relations of daily life'. By January 1878, with the probability of a British war with Russia, Derby was prepared to stand firm against the entire Cabinet and the patriotic howls of London opinion. Hardy noted in his diary, with unintended irony, that 'Derby is so timid and irresolute that all the rest of the Cabinet cannot move him.'[21] Earlier, during the passionate blast of the Bulgarian agitation, Derby and Disraeli were the only ministers unwilling to propitiate it. The Prime Minister rightly feared the domestic political effects of doing so, but Derby was moved only by the fact that the charge of the agitators of British complicity in Ottoman atrocities was without foundation. It is true that he used the anti-Turkish outburst in Britain as an excuse to justify his unwillingness to contemplate any British military support for the Porte.

In the middle of January 1878 Derby broke down in a kind of emotional or nervous collapse, and took to his bed at the height of the crisis. After two weeks he had recovered sufficiently to return to his duties, but from January until his second and final resignation at the end of March his opposition to war and warlike measures resulted in increasing criticism by his colleagues and near public obloquy from the warlike members of his own party inside and outside Parliament. One of the rumours current was that he had given way to alcoholic excess. The charge, repeated and accepted as true by many later writers, is probably false, but the evidence is inconclusive. Part of the responsibility for this belief about Derby rests with Salisbury, who was a good hater and hated Derby especially after the two came to verbal blows in Parliament in April and July 1878.[22] In 1880 Salisbury told the young Balfour about the Foreign Secretary who recorded the following in a memorandum: 'Lord Derby, between overwork, alcohol and responsibility. . . .' At the end of January 1878 there is a short note by Argyll which may point to a drinking problem or something else equally ominous. 'I am very sorry to hear a report about the nature of Derby's late illness—if true nobody

need reckon on his lasting long in public life.' Near the climax
of a party attempt to oust Derby from office, Hammond, the
ex-Under-Secretary, confirmed the existence of the rumours.
'There are nasty, ugly stories going about Derby—who is said
to drink too much.'[23]

Shuvalov, whose testimony is suspect because he believed his
personal and political success depended upon Derby's holding
on to office, denied that the Foreign Secretary was ever in an
unfit state for business. The younger Malet, the future ambassador, who knew Derby well, agreed with the Russian ambassador. 'Public opinion is beginning to feel that it has been
too hard upon Lord Derby—now that he is out [of
office]—and people are ashamed to say that he is a drunkard
which as far as I can make out was never true . . .'[24] If Derby's
drinking is myth, called forth by inflamed and excited feeling
reacting to what was considered insufficient patriotism in the
midst of foreign crisis, there is no doubt and little by way of
defence which may be offered for his display of disloyalty
towards his colleagues and his constitutional impropriety, if
not outright national indifference.

For about a year and one half before his resignation in
March 1878, Lady Derby, who apparently successfully pumped
her husband dry of cabinet conversations and secret ministerial
decisions, repeated a great deal of this information to the Russian ambassador in their frequent and usually private meetings
with one another. The result was both embarrassing and, in a
number of instances, antithetical to the interests of the country
as defined by the Cabinet. Derby may not have first realized
that his wife was being indiscreet, and perhaps could claim that
she was never so while he was present, though this seems
doubtful. But after a while he became aware of what Lady Derby was doing, as she made so little attempt to hide it, and he
did nothing about it even after being warned. That Disraeli felt
it necessary to skirt Derby's inertia by establishing his own
private relationship with Austrian diplomatic representatives
and later with Layard, once the latter was posted to Constantinople, is hardly an excuse for the potentially dangerous and
equally disloyal conduct of the Foreign Secretary. Salisbury
was probably correct in thinking that Disraeli had been mistaken in not bringing about a reconstruction of the Cabinet in

1876 or 1877 which would have relieved him of Derby and in all likelihood of Carnarvon and Salisbury as well. Disraeli could not bring himself to ask for Derby's resignation out of feeling for him and for their long and significant relationship. The Foreign Secretary's desire for office prevented him from withdrawing unasked, though he also wished to prevent war if he remained. After his first resignation in January 1878, his desire to return was at least as strong as that of his colleagues to have him back. His abhorrence of war was powerful[25] but stronger still was the meaning, purpose, and satisfaction with which high political office provided him.

The behaviour of the Derbys had made a mockery of Cabinet government, and it had begun long before the possibility of an English war with Russia had emerged. The attempt to prevent such a war was humane, besmirched only by the means adopted for that admirable purpose by the Foreign Secretary. With his public reputation nearly destroyed, his health broken, and deriving some support from Parliamentary Liberals[26] rather than from any considerable number of Conservatives, he resigned because he felt the Cabinet's decision to exhibit firmness would further inflame an already excited opinion and lead to war. He believed in addition that the Cabinet intended the forceful occupation of Cyprus and Alexandretta, which he considered wrong. Bitter that Beaconsfield had allowed it to be thought that he had resigned only because the reserves had been called out and perhaps resentful that his brother had immediately been made Minister of war, he spoke in Parliament in April to defend his conduct and in doing so mentioned private Cabinet discussions. Such indiscreet behaviour elicited much condemnation and further lowered his reputation.

General disapprobation compelled Derby to continue to believe that he was right. 'I feel so sure of being right that I care little for what the public may think. If wanted again in Downing Street, I suppose one must sacrifice oneself. . . . What does alarm me a good deal is the tone of reckless rowdyism, among what ought to be the educated classes. . .'[27] In July in Parliament he gave the show away about Cyprus and the Indian expedition, explaining that his resignation had been due to the Cabinet's decision to adopt those two measures. He was directly contradicted by Salisbury in a heated exchange which did Derby little good. It has been said that by resigning Derby voluntarily gave up the chance to be Prime Minister as Beaconsfield was both old and ill. One might say with more accuracy that he resigned only after it was evident that few, if any, of his colleagues would serve under him and a considerable part of his own party had repudiated his conduct. Experience had taught him that there were few people that one could trust, and his search for security and safety ended only with his death in 1893. The impact of Derby's personality on Britain's diplomatic position was marked. His suspiciousness and withdrawal, manifested to preserve safety and autonomy, usually had the effect of increasing Britain's isolation from the other powers, and the resulting solitude only roused the foreign secretary's mistrust and the need to be careful.

INSURRECTION IN
HERCEGOVINA AND
BOSNIA[1]

*Nevesinje*

AT THE beginning of July 1875 an uncertain but small number[2] of Christian Hercegovinians, recently returned from Montenegro, began to stir up a revolt in the vicinity of Nevesinje, a village south-east of Mostar in Hercegovina. In this they were successful, being aided by Turkish in-decisiveness, support from Serbs and South Slav sympathizers in Serbia, Montenegro, and Austrian Croatia and Dalmatia, and a hilly and mountainous terrain which lent itself to successful guerrilla activity. Why and how the insurrection began has never been really established as the available evidence is meagre and contradictory. The reports of the con-suls of the major European Powers and newspaper stories emanated from individuals too far away from the actual events reported and perhaps too committed to the rebel or Turkish side to be able to give a convincing and trustworthy account. The British consul, William Holmes, who had been at Sarajevo since 1861, depended upon the Turkish Governor in that city for his information and was therefore distant from the rebels. Moreover, he has been accused of unregenerate Turcophilism.[3]

William J. Stillman, a former United States consul in Crete, who took the side of the Cretan rebels against the Turks in 1866, went to Montenegro and Hercegovina in August 1875 and sent reports from Ragusa to *The Times* in London with a decided bias in favour of the Montenegrins and South Slavs.[4]

Many of the contemporary observers emphasized the agrarian and fiscal conditions as causal explanations for the dissatisfaction in Hercegovina and Bosnia. Evans and Yriärte, supported by many later writers, describe an unhappy Chris-tian peasantry ground down by oppressive Muslim landowners and tax farmers.[5] It must be remembered, however, that the landowning aristocracy of Bosnia was comprised of some Turks and many Slavs who had converted to Islam in order to maintain their lands and positions. The latter were as hard on Christian Slavic peasants as were the Turkish beys. Tax farming[6] is especially singled out against a background of assumed or argued Turkish injustice and barbarism. But how does one deal with the evidence? Jelavich argues that the reports of diplomatic agents and foreign travellers usually

MAP 1. Bosnia-Hercegovina

reflect exceptional or unusual conditions. In some instances this is surely the case. Some mitigate the significance of Turkish administrative corruption by blending it with outside and foreign instigation usually ascribed to Slavs or Slav sympathizers. While many agree that outside influence acted upon indigenous discontent, they still disagree as to the identity of outside agents and the relative weight to be given to internal conditions and outside instigation.[7] Stojanovic describes the revolt as a result of Serbian preparations and propaganda for union with Serbia;[8] Sumner places more emphasis upon secret societies in Hercegovina and Montenegro; Rupp argues for the importance of Austrian Dalmatia and Holmes, the British consul, for Austrian Croatia and Serbia; Seton-Watson is impressed with the activities of Baron Rodich, the Governor of Austrian Dalmatia, and Alexander Yonin, the Russian consul in Ragusa. Langer feels that Serbs or Serbo-Croats in Serbia, Montenegro, and Austrian Dalmatia were all responsible.[9]

Intolerable Turkish administration, if such was the case, is not satisfactory as the sole explanation of the rebellion, and this for several reasons. Turkish control was resented by the Christian peasantry but not any more than in other years when there were not insurrections.[10] Temperley and Davison are unimpressed with misgovernment as the cause and argue more for Christian Slavic discontent with any Turkish or Muslim Government. It was not reform of habitual Turkish oppression, they argue, but independence which was desired in 1875.[11] Jelavich, who recognizes Ottoman rule as incompetent, corrupt, and barbaric, points out that much of the same was characteristic of the Balkan succession states without eliciting attempts to overthrow the Government.[12] Further, both Jelavich and Davison agree that inefficient and corrupt government was felt by Muslim peasants as well as Christian, and Davison goes beyond this, and perhaps too far, by saying that a greater burden was borne by Muslim Turks and Arabs than by Christians.[13] Yet the revolt of 1875 was overwhelmingly a Christian, if even a Slavic Christian, rising. One can see as well aspects of a Christian–Muslim civil war in the risings of 1875[14] and in the revolt of the Bulgarians in 1876, with peasant fighting peasant as well as Turkish regular troops going against armed insurgent bands. When the one hundred and fifty or so Christian Hercegovinans had departed for neighbouring Montenegro in October of 1874, they had declared they would not return until Turkish rule was at an end.[15] Taylor, Harris, and Jelavich seem to agree that the insurrection of 1875 was a manifestation of national (Serbian or South Slav) revolt and that in the latter's words the 'feeling of the Christian that he was a second-class citizen in a basically alien state-structure' was the motivating force for discontent.[16] Feelings of assertive self-confidence were heightened to an extreme degree by certain inequalities in the Ottoman Empire. Those mentioned most often were the closure to Christians of the higher administrative posts and the right to serve in the army,[17] as well as the disadvantages the non-Muslim faced in the Ottoman judicial and legal system and in his right to buy and own land.

Some argue that this awakening Slavic self-confidence and desire for independence were bred and nourished within Hercegovina and Bosnia from beyond the boundaries of those two provinces. Andrassy, as well as Disraeli, suspected 'international revolutionary committees'. Sumner also mentions the plotting of secret societies and Slav committees in Austrian Dalmatia and in Montenegro, but contends that it is not possible to show to what extent they planned the revolt in Hercegovina and Bosnia. Sumner, Temperley, Mackenzie, and Taylor agree that the rising was not created by Russian intrigues. This is true as far as the Russian Government in St. Petersburg is concerned, but perhaps not true regarding the independent activities of the Russian consulates at Belgrade, Mostar, Ragusa, Scutari, Fiume, Trieste, Widdin, Orsova, and Sarajevo.[18] The military group within Austria-Hungary which desired the annexation of Bosnia, the Serbian Government, and Slav sympathizers generally looked upon the rising with hopeful interest. Most students are agreed that the revolt, once started, received the support of Danubian Slavs generally but especially of those across the border in Dalmatia, Croatia, Montenegro, and Serbia.[19] With so many seemingly benefiting from the amputation or destruction of the Turks it is very difficult, if not impossible, to pinpoint the instigator, especially when it is not certain that only one instigator existed.

Even if the assumption that the national explanation—the desire for independence—is the correct one, with uncertain outside planning and instigation, many still see the trigger in the form of Turkish tax farming.[20] Stillman and others, however, emphasize the catalytic effect, especially on the Catholic Hercegovinans, of the visit of the Austrian Emperor, Francis Joseph, to Dalmatia in April–May 1875. In any case the existence of 'free' Serbs just across the frontier in Dalmatia, Croatia, Montenegro, and Serbia was a constant and frustrating reminder, as Renouvin and Stillman observe, of fellow South Slavs who spoke the same or nearly the same language, shared many of the same traditions, and often adhered to the same religion,[21] but who were free of any close or constant Ottoman supervision. The force of national attraction, though real, is not conducive to close analysis for even a chart on the behaviour of one individual so imbued with national desires would reflect an amalgam of other often unrelated feelings which also determine his conduct. Nor do we know how many individuals in Bosnia-Hercegovina actively revolted, for whatever motives, though the number was probably small. We do know that much pressure and even violence was used by the active insurrectionists to stir up their inactive brothers.[22] Most of the battles fought in 1875 involved several hundred men or less.[23] There were rival rebel chieftains and bands and Serbian Roman and Orthodox Catholics in Bosnia-Hercegovina had a history of antagonism and bitterness.[24]

The national explanation for revolt in 1875 also leaves much to be desired and at best is a partial factor. Holmes, in his report to Derby and Elliot, the British ambassador, from Mostar, where he returned after having met some of the insurgents, was very clear on this point, even allowing for any possible tendency on his part to report what he knew his superiors desired to hear.

They [the rebels] repeatedly declared that they were, and wished to remain, faithful subjects of the Sultan, taking off their caps at the mention of his name, but that His Majesty was deceived by his Pashas, and could not be aware of their condition . . .
. . .

They [the insurgent chiefs met by the Austrian, German, and Italian consuls] do not, and never have desired independence or annexation to Montenegro, but they wish to remain Turkish subjects under very extensive administrative reforms, the execution of which is to be guaranteed by Europe.
. . .

In Bosnia, almost to a man, the population would refuse to be annexed to Servia or Austria, and they have never dreamt of independence, which from the nature of the circumstances, and the state of education, is impracticable. They only wish to be Turkish subjects, but to be governed with justice, and . . . equality. . . .[25]

There were many in Serbia and Montenegro who desired to annex Bosnia-Hercegovina and some of them no doubt plotted, aided, and fought alongside the rebels. They were not bothered by Muslim tax-collectors. There were many in Bosnia-Hercegovina who hated and feared the Muslim land-owner and the local police and tax-collector, and one hundred and fifty of them fled to Montenegro. More who did not were ready to fight for a kind of local autonomy or freedom from local oppression. Some in Dalmatia and Croatia desired control over Bosnia-Hercegovina, and a few of these favoured some kind of autonomous South Slav confederation within either the Ottoman or Austro-Hungarian Empire. Some fought willingly and some were coerced, some looked to Nicholas of Montenegro and others to Milan of Serbia, some longed for Turkish land, and a few derived pleasure from the killing of Turks. There were anger and hope, greed and despair, fear and exhilaration.

Finally, the revolt maintained itself in Hercegovina and burst out in neighbouring Bosnia as a result of inadequate Turkish countermeasures, much outside support from Dalmatia, Serbia, Montenegro, and Russia,[26] and the policies of the six European Great Powers.

## The Revolt Spreads and Europe Intervenes

When a meeting between the insurgents and the two commissioners sent by the Turkish Governor in Sarajevo failed to take place, the rising continued and expanded. By the middle of August Bosnia was in revolt.[27] If Holmes's information is to be believed, the Turks had inadequate troop strength scattered in garrisons that could not be moved lest insurrection begin with the departure of the local Turkish forces. Lacking in numbers and mobility, Ottoman soldiers faced insurgent bands which dispersed on the approach of the enemy only to reassemble elsewhere, often in Dalmatia and Croatia where they were safe from Turkish pursuit.[28] The Turks found themselves too often rooted to points where they could only flail the air. When the Porte requested the British Government to intercede with Austria, Derby asked Andrássy, whose policy could be described as late Byzantine, to close the frontier to the insurgents over the border in Hercegovina.[29] Derby, automatically hypersensitive to possible complication, wanted the Turks to crush the rebellion before a local matter could become an international one; this wish was apparently shared by Andrássy and Ignatiev, the Russian ambassador. To this end Derby used English influence with Serbia to persuade her against aiding the rebels[30] on the premiss that if unnoticed the rebellion would cease to exist.[31] White, the British agent at Belgrade, spoke to Prince Milan, who had recently returned from Vienna,[32] and warned him of the danger of supporting the insurgents in Bosnia-Hercegovina. Elliot in Constantinople urged the Porte to greater vigour to stamp out the rising.[33] All this was to no avail for on 19 August the Sultan officially consented in an audience with Ignatiev to a mission of mediation by the consuls of the Great Powers. This step was to have the opposite effect from which it was probably intended, and made Derby's fears of an international complication a reality. Nor did Stillman have doubts as to the significance of the consular commission.

To it was due the reawakening of the insurrection. It was a partial recognition by the Powers of the wrongs of the Herzegovinians, and an indication that the eyes of official Europe were on his state—sufficient encouragement at any time to make him revolt, and to stimulate the spirit of combativeness in the mountain regions bordering Montenegro; and owing to this the whole aspect of the affair changed rapidly.[34]

When the Turkish Grand Vizier begged Elliot not to stand aloof but to join the other Great Powers in sending a consul to the scene of the insurrection, he indicated his willingness to do so. The consuls were to inform the rebels that no help would come to them from the Great Powers and were to advise them to end their insurrection and make known their complaints to a Turkish commissioner. The consuls were then to consider their mission finished and to leave any further negotiation to the appointed Ottoman delegate. Though Derby approved Elliot's support of the consular mission, he did not like it, and expressed his suspicions to Disraeli:

Whether the Turks are well advised in accepting this kind of mediation may be a question: but they have accepted it: and that being so, and the grand vizir asking us not to stand aloof, I conceive that we have practically no option. I propose therefore at once to signify our willingness to join.

If the apparent friendship shown by the other powers is sincere, there is no harm done, and some good, if otherwise, we shall be of more use in checking mischief by taking part than we could be if we declined to act.

I shall go on at once with the affair, unless you telegraph to stop me.[35]

It was an initiative which was typical of Derby, taken reluctantly, and then only after its safety and unavoidability had been indicated by Elliot and Tenterden, the Permanent Under-Secretary of the Foreign Office, and not contradicted by Disraeli.[36] In his official instructions to Elliot, Derby indicated what he, Disraeli, Elliot, and Tenterden were all agreed that such an intervention was not really compatible with the Sultan's independent authority, that it offered inducement to the rebels, and that it might lead to further diplomatic interference in the internal affairs of Turkey.[37] Derby's worry was not, in my opinion, due to concern for the integrity of the Ottoman Empire, but was rather how to avoid raising a serious international question which might entail British action and responsibility. Unlike Disraeli and Elliot, he manifested concern for Ottoman sovereignty because it was consistent with his desire to avoid responsibility and complication, not because he saw such concern as necessary for the preservation of British interests.

Elliot immediately instructed Holmes to take part with the other European consuls, but to act individually and to avoid any collective or united action with them even though the instructions for all the consuls were identical.[38] Elliot, though cold and shy like Derby,[39] was more in control of his personality and emotions. His concern for Turkish integrity was of the traditional kind—a reflection of British interests in the eastern Mediterranean and in India, which often required restraint of Russian ambition. But unlike Ponsonby, Stratford de Redcliffe, and Bulwer, three of his predecessors at Constantinople, his urging of the reform of abuses at the Porte was usually tempered by his recognition of the Ottoman Empire as an independent and sovereign state with a right to control its own internal affairs. Harris accuses him of being so excessively suspicious of Russia and Ignatiev that he failed to be objective about Turks or Turkey.[40] This I think is an unfair estimate. He had always condemned Turkish administrative corruption and, on his own initiative, though approved afterwards by his chief, Granville, he communicated to the Porte the substance of the injustices noticed by British Levantine consuls, with strong recommendations for remedial action.[41] As to his Russophobia, while rightly mistrusting Ignatiev, the Pan-Slav Russian ambassador, he saw the real danger to Ottoman stability and integrity coming from the tortuous policy of Andrássy who was intent on showing the Serbs in Serbia, Montenegro, and Bosnia-Hercegovina that they had more to hope for from a reliance on Austria than from trusting to Russia. Elliot regarded this attempt to bid against others for popularity among the Slav peoples as dangerous and perhaps fatal to the Porte's authority.[42] He also saw Austria's policy as playing into the hands of Ignatiev. His contest with Ignatiev for influence at the Porte was affected by feelings of personal rivalry with the Russian ambassador, but while the official policy of his own Government required the maintenance of the Ottoman Empire, Elliot used what influence he had to further that end.[43] He fought united European pressure upon the Porte as an obstruction of Turkish administration and refused to take part in the 'system recently inaugurated of having frequent and formal meetings of the heads of missions for the purpose of weighing upon the Porte by a concerted action and identical notes'.[44] He opposed such ambassadorial parliaments as inconsistent with the independent dignity of the Porte and dangerous because such a system could be dominated by Ignatiev who seemed to have the Austrian and German ambassadors under his influence. The main reason Elliot went along, albeit suspiciously, with the consular mission, was his hope that if the insurgents saw that nothing was to be gained from any of the Great Powers, but especially from Austria, they would lay down their arms and treat with the Turks.[45] He also feared the repercussions of a Turkish refusal of the consular suggestion from Austria, Russia, and Germany.

Gorchakov, the Russian Foreign Minister, seemed to prefer European non-intervention in Turkish affairs.[46] Ignatiev, who had much opportunity to essay a personal policy of his own while his superior remained away for months in Germany and Switzerland[47] taking the waters, seemed temporarily bent on not raising a crisis for which from his point of view the time was as yet inopportune. In Elliot's view therefore, towards the end of August, both the Russian Government and her ambassador were being reasonable, but Austria was another matter. The ambassador believed that the suppression of the insurrection depended upon Austria's restraining her Slavic subjects from aiding and abetting it.[48] At the beginning of September Elliot assured the Grand Vizier that if the insurgents did not disperse, England would be indisposed to interfere with the Porte in bringing the rebels into submission. When the Serbian agent in Constantinople begged Elliot to urge the Porte against irritating Serbia by concentrating troops on the Turkish–Serbian frontier, Elliot not only declined and observed that Turkey's action was prudent, but informed the Sultan of his language in response to the Serbian request.[49] He did, however, obtain the promise of the Sultan that the Porte would not invade Serbia though Serbia and Montenegro were now openly aiding the insurrection. As a Turkish war with Serbia and Montenegro had become a real possibility,[50] Ignatiev, Zichy, the Austrian ambassador, and their German colleague Werther protested to the Foreign Minister as well against any Turkish attack on Serbia. Safvet Pasha replied that no such intention existed in Constantinople.[51] The Porte had sent Sever Pasha, as a special agent, to treat with and to pacify the same rebels whom the European consuls were to persuade to peace in order to talk with the Ottoman commissioner. The consuls of the Great Powers had all arrived at Mostar in Hercegovina by the end of the first week in September. They all had considerable knowledge of Bosnia. They divided themselves into two groups of three who would each go out in search of the rebel leaders. Holmes felt there was little possibility of success, since the instructions to all the consuls were to avoid the appearance of 'united action.' Unity alone, he felt, could give sufficient weight to the consul's advice to the insurgents in order to induce acquiescence. He apparently was unaware that Elliot personally favoured the avoidance of such action even though his instructions from the ambassador had indicated the necessity of it. The consul reasonably believed that only if the rebels saw that they could not split apart the unity and co-operation which existed between the Great Powers would they lay down their arms, especially in view of his belief that only political trouble-makers from Serbia and Montenegro were keeping the revolt alive.[52]

Everyone's expectations were fulfilled. The consuls failed to persuade the insurgents to bring their complaints before Sever Pasha.[53] Holmes's group of three consuls failed to find many of the insurgent chiefs, and returned to Mostar on 22 September. The other group of three—the Austrian, German, and Italian consuls—did encounter some of the rebel leaders near Trebigné (slightly north-east of Ragusa) but were equally unsuccessful and returned to Mostar on the twenty-third. The demands of the insurgent spokesmen, who were unwilling to disarm, were for an armistice and a European guarantee of any reforms to be adopted.[54] The Turks, on 20 September, apparently decided to take advantage of the opportunity of having a sufficient number of rebels rooted in one spot waiting to meet the consuls and launched a surprise and treacherous attack on them.[55] European non-intervention to bring about pacification had in a few short weeks come full circle, and unwittingly provided the vehicle for a continuation of the fighting.

The consular commission, as Sumner writes, was a farce in both its inception and its termination.[56] Originally, it was desired by Russia in order to mediate and bring about peace; but Andrássy wished to treat the rising as an internal Turkish question, and consented to the consular mission only after changing its purpose from mediation to that of placing pressure on the insurgents to lay down their arms and negotiate with the Turks directly. The Austrian Foreign Minister wished to restrict the consular attempt to the agents of Russia, Germany, and Austria alone, in order to prevent international interference in an area where he considered Austria had special interests. This was frustrated by the Tsar's innocent invitation to France, Italy, and Britain to participate, thus extending Andrássy's plan. Even before the failure of the consuls, Ignatiev in Constantinople attempted to undercut Andrássy in order to wrest control and initiative away from him.

He arranged a new role for the consuls, further altering the proposal from Vienna.[57]

Ignatiev had worked hard to gain influence over the Sultan and his Government in order, when the time was right, to inaugurate a Pan-Slav programme calculated to destroy Austrian influence in the Balkans. To retrieve the initiative from Andrássy, Ignatiev attempted a system of having policy on the Eastern Question decided in Constantinople, where he could control Zichy and Werther, rather than in Vienna, or Vienna and St. Petersburg. The Russian ambassador suggested a permanent committee of the consuls to report on rebel grievances and to recommend reforms for the disaffected areas to the Porte where ambassadorial pressure could be used to insure Turkish compliance.[58] Ignatiev gained the consent of his Austrian and German colleagues to this but was overridden when Andrássy and Elliot refused to agree.[59] The British ambassador instructed Holmes to take no part in this consular parliament as he feared this would be the beginning of official European intervention which he desired to avoid. Even before he knew the results of the consular mission, Elliot had advised the Grand Vizier to take the initiative in remedying the complaints of Bosnia-Hercegovina before any of the European Powers did so. He intimated to him that in Christian areas, Christians might be given a share in the local administration.[60] Derby had already indicated to Decazes, the French Foreign Minister, his support for the policy which Elliot was executing—the redressing of grievances by the Porte and opposition to intervention in the internal affairs of Turkey.[61]

At the end of September Elliot still described Andrássy's policy as the great danger, and rumours of a European conference to deal with the insurrection seemed to the British ambassador even worse than having Austria, Russia and Germany impose their will on Turkey by force. In the latter case, he felt Britain would be in no way a party to any arbitrary act of the three Northern Powers.[62] Another point also troubled the ambassador. This was the use by the Turks of Bashi-Bazouks, irregular troops composed often of indigenous Muslim inhabitants armed by the Government, in fighting the insurrection. Elliot inquired of Dupuis, vice-consul at Adrianople, as to their use and received a reply in the negative.[63] It was generally believed by Europeans, even by those sympathetic to Turkey, that barbarism and cruelty were characteristics peculiar to the Ottoman Turks or Muslim rulers. In part this reflected an attitude that any military action against Christian non-combatants or even those who were actively involved in revolt was cruel. Examples of Ottoman brutality were not scarce, but at the beginning of the insurrection the brutalities were perhaps even more on the other side. Reference has already been made to the terror tactics of the active rebels to rouse their more quiescent brothers to join the insurrection. Stillman, who had much sympathy with the Serbs of Montenegro and Hercegovina and almost equal contempt for the Turks, wrote that Peko Paulovich, a Montenegrin warrior and one of the insurrection leaders in Hercegovina, captured a Turkish provision convoy killing eighty men, the heads of these dead being skewered on poles and displayed at the insurgent camp. At a fight at Utovu, he reported the insurgents brought back the noses of fifty-eight Turkish soldiers, and though Prince Nicholas had forbidden the mutilation of the dead, it was impossible to enforce this outside Montenegro.[64] Elliot, with no irony intended, wrote to his brother-in-law, Lord John Russell, that in Bosnia the Muslims were nearly as savage as the Christians, and that he feared horrible cases of retaliation against the pillage of the insurgents who cut off the noses and ears of Muslims before putting them to death.[65] Novikov, the Russian ambassador in Vienna, who had no love for either Serbs or Turks, referred to the rebels as paid brigands who slaughtered poor people for the sake of Ristich[66] who desired to dethrone Prince Milan of Serbia.[67] It should be noted that these reports and reactions occurred long before Turkish brutality had become a European issue or had excited British domestic opinion. Such brutality, had the Turks not eventually resorted to it, would have left unfulfilled an almost universal European expectation, which on the part of some in Austria and Russia reflected not so much a concern for Christian Slavs or humanity as a fear that mutilation of Slavs would excite further domestic opinion that was already stirred up. Excited opinion might pressure governments into the thing that all the major Powers wished to avoid—a military intervention within Turkey and the resulting confrontation of the Great Powers.

This is one reason why the Austrian, Russian, and British governments wished and urged the Porte to energetically crush the rebellion quickly, and why at the same time they pushed reforms on the Turks to satisfy the Christian Slavs and salve their own consciences.

At the end of September, when Elliot urged the remedy of grievances on the Grand Vizier, the latter informed the British ambassador that he was preparing a circular on that subject and requested from him a memorandum of the most pressing grievances.[68] The Ottoman imperial irade of 2 October sought to satisfy the complaints on Elliot's list. There was to be a 2½ per cent reduction in the tithe and an abandonment of the collection of taxes in arrears with special agents being sent from the Porte to the provinces to see that taxes were equitably levied. Local councils, which were to properly represent their communities, would send deputations to Constantinople to make known their wishes.[69]

Such an attempt at reform would have had a slight chance of success before July 1875, but the death, destruction, and consequent embitterment caused by the insurrection had made direct Ottoman–Slav reconciliation impossible. European intervention which aimed at producing accommodation mainly encouraged the insurgents to continue the struggle, and only a few realized that the Porte's declaration to lessen taxes would be paid for by the holders of Turkish bonds in Britain and France as the Ottoman Government had reached bankruptcy.

## 3  BANKRUPTCY, REBELLION, AND REFORM

ON 6 October the Turkish Government publicly indicated its inability to meet its financial obligations.

Elliot was apparently forewarned of the intentions of the Porte and felt that only an immediate reduction of interest could prevent a total repudiation. The ambassador agreed with this plan but had avoided intimating approval of it as this would have taken two million pounds a year from British bondholders.[1] On 6 October the Porte announced in the journals of Constantinople that for the next five years, owing to a budget deficit, it would pay only one-half the interest on its foreign debt in cash, the other half in new bonds bearing 5 per cent which would be issued to the holders of Turkish securities. Protests exploded from the bondholders and the Press. As a contemporary observer put the outraged British feeling, 'all who had lent money on the faith of Turkish solvency felt that they were being robbed for the support of a system of misgovernment, the errors of which they had not until then discovered ...'[2] Gladstone had little sympathy for the bondholders and looked upon 'this Turkish repudiation as a great political event ...'[3] The bondholders were using their influence to have the British and French governments intervene for them. Decazes, the French Foreign Minister, favoured obtaining some security for the holders of Turkish bonds that the one-half interest now promised should be punctually paid. He suggested to London that commissioners of the Great Powers superintend Ottoman finances and set aside about seven million pounds for the service of Turkish loans.[4] As the British Government had only guaranteed or partially guaranteed the Ottoman loans of 1854 and 1855, Derby felt justified in not supporting the French proposal.[5] At the moment of declared Turkish financial default, Lord Derby made the first official and public British reference to the insurrection in a speech at a banquet in the Liverpool Town Hall. 'He spoke in a tone calculated to convey the impression that he regarded the incident [insurrection] as over.'

[The] disturbances . . . have been greatly magnified in importance by popular report. . . . The armed force of the insurrection has never been considerable; indeed I fancy one of the difficulties of the consuls . . . was to find the insurgents whom they were to conciliate. . . . I don't think, therefore, that we shall hear much more of the armed insurrection. . . . It is proposed by some persons that the provinces in question should have granted to them a local autonomy like that of Roumania and Servia. . . . Local autonomy is very well where you have to deal with only one religion and race, but where Mohametans and Christians are mixed together, or not very equal in strength, leaving them to settle their own internal affairs simply means leaving the stronger of the two parties to oppress and possibly to exterminate the weaker. . . . It is only in a high state of civilization, and not always then, that two rival religions can get on side by side in the same country. . . . And now I come to a question of more immediate and direct interest to ourselves [China].[6]

Shuvalov, the Russian ambassador in London, made a trip to Knowsley, Derby's home outside Liverpool, to see the Foreign Secretary. He reported to Jomini, senior counsellor in the Russian Foreign Ministry, the preoccupation with China and the inclination of Derby and others to minimize the insurrection because of the entente of Austria, Germany, and Russia and the weakness of France, both of which isolated Britain.[7] Münster, Shuvalov's German colleague in London spent a week at Knowsley two and one half weeks after the Russian ambassador's departure. In the interval between the two visits a change had come over Derby probably as a result of the Turkish financial repudiation and the outburst of opinion it produced. Münster observed that the Balkan unrest and the latest Turkish financial measures were more upsetting to the Foreign Secretary than Shuvalov assumed. Derby seemed to the German ambassador extremely anxious that the continuance of the insurrection might lead to complications. The Foreign Secretary condemned the weakness of Turkish administration and said that it was increasingly difficult to advocate the integrity of Turkey;[8] if the British Government, he said, were to back the Turks, it would be contrary to all principles so far followed.[9] Derby seemed to have jumped, in three weeks' time, from a belief that insurrection barely existed to a feeling that Turkey would not be able to suppress it.

From almost the very beginning of the crisis, Derby and Disraeli had differed in their reaction to it, a fact not surprising as they were so unalike. They concerted any measures together without calling a Cabinet meeting, which may have been trying on both. Disraeli, like the Queen, felt the image of Britain required forceful expression with a touch of bravado,[10] and an occasion presented itself to the Prime Minister in a speech at the Guildhall on Lord Mayor's Day, approximately a month after Derby's effort at Liverpool. When the Foreign Secretary had spoken there on 7 October, he had said that Britain need only remain loyal to the other Powers as her interests in Turkey, though real, were indirect and any decisions reached there would be collective ones.[11] Disraeli's reply in the City on 9 November was not aimed at his colleague but was for the benefit of foreign Powers and the Queen who had already expressed anxiety about Derby's not keeping up the tone. At the Guildhall he admitted that Austria, Russia, and Germany had more direct interests in the Balkans than those of Britain but that this did not mean that they were more considerable. '[He] assured the nation that the Cabinet [which had not met] was "deeply conscious of the nature and magnitude of those British interests" which they were "resolved to guard and maintain".'[12] Reports of this speech and an official Russian article in the *Journal of St. Petersburg* the following day, which argued the necessity of reforms for Turkey put forward by the Great Powers, produced an explosion in Constantinople.

The incident of the day is of course the Russian official article and a very serious one it is; for it must greatly diminish the chances of a pacification of the Herzegovine and increase those of an intervention.

The Turks are very indignant and the grand vizier [Mahmoud Pasha] who used to be looked upon as devoted to Ignatiev, now speaks of him as an 'unblushing liar'—rather strong expression to use of an ambassador.

The telegraphic summaries of Mr. Disraeli's speech at the Mansion House had made a sensation which [Elliot] cannot understand. The statement that England will maintain and defend her own interests had been taken as implying that she means to secure her share of the plunder or the break up of the Turkish Empire.[13]

Turkish debt, the health of the insurrection, and now his friend's bold speech were too much for Derby who told

Shuvalov that he had been correct all along in urging Britain to associate her policy with those of the continental states. He said nothing would prevent the Cabinet from associating itself with 'wise and moderate' Russian efforts.[14]

Two weeks after the Prime Minister's Guildhall speech the Government was able, as a result of the bankruptcy of the Khedive, to buy the latter's shares in the Suez Canal. The impact of the purchase on the maintenance of Turkish integrity, as Decazes complained to Lyons, was a negative one. With Egypt and the Canal secure, the route to India was safe. The preservation of the Ottoman Empire which appeared to some in Britain as an affront to morality would be asserted by many now as unnecessary to British interests, and by others as more necessary than before. For the moment, however, the fate of Ottoman integrity seemed to be in the hands of others.

## More Reform. Andrássy Versus Ignatiev

The hopes of the Powers for pacification continued in October and November but were frustrated by lack of control and unified direction. The rebels as well seemed to be without organized leadership, and the ebb and flow of the struggle varied with the communication of Turkish or rebel reports, while the reality of the strife escaped detection.[15] The insurrection continued and even worsened as the rebels avoided major encounters with the Turks and the latter were reduced to an attempt to maintain communication among the scattered Ottoman fortresses, as the Slavic bands often hid in the mountains or crossed the frontier into Austria-Hungary and Serbia. Apart from ineffective military repression, with more and more use made of Bashi-Bazouks, Turkish policy involved promises of reform impossible to implement while guerilla fighting continued and many Christians from Bosnia-Hercegovina refused to return to their homes from Serbia, Montenegro, and Austria. Andrássy[16] had prevented Ignatiev from turning the failed consular mission into an ambassadorial directorate at Constantinople under Ignatiev's control for the purpose of persuading the Sultan to introduce Christian reforms. As it seemed to Ignatiev that his Government was leaning towards a policy of Austro-Russian suggestions for reform under Andrássy's control, he left Constantinople on 19 October for

Livadia in the Crimea to persuade Alexander II to break the entente with Austria in favour of an informal association with the Porte.[17] Ignatiev could control Russo-Turkish co-operation through his influence with Mahamoud Pasha, the Grand Vizier, and use it to bring about Turkish reform without officially implicating the government at St. Petersburg, which could maintain its freedom of action. If the Balkan Slavs came to realize that their interests were being furthered by the Russian ambassador at Constantinople, they would come to look to him and not to the man who had refused to accept him as ambassador at Vienna in 1871. For Ignatiev the important thing apparently was Russian or his own control over the Balkan Slavs, and whether they lived in independent states, autonomous units, or fully under Ottoman administration was subsidiary to their recognizing their indebtedness to Russia or himself.[18] Though he could count on Yonin and Kartzov, Russian consuls in Montenegro and Serbia, Onou, his dragoman, who had influence with Jomini, and the Austrian and German ambassadors in Constantinople as willing or unwitting accomplices, he could not persuade the Tsar to break with Austria and he returned to Constantinople at the end of October still scheming to frustrate Andrássy.

The Austrian minister, at odds with Austrian Slavic subjects who sympathized with and aided the insurrection and the military party in Vienna which chafed to annex Bosnia-Hercegovina, wished to contain and end the insurrection in order to maintain a weak Turkey which would allow Austrian political influence and economic domination over the Balkans, but especially in Serbia, Montenegro, and Bosnia-Hercegovina. The main danger was that the spread and success of the insurrection might result in the establishment of an independent Slav state or states bordering on Austrian Dalmatia and Croatia and that this would constitute a threat to Austrian integrity and Magyar dominance. Alexander II, Gorchakov, the Russian Foreign Minister, and Novikov, the Russian ambassador in Vienna, looked upon the rebels as radical scum[19] whose success would be abhorrent ideologically and potentially dangerous politically. This was the mutual basis for continued Austro-Russian co-operation and the temporary defeat of Ignatiev. The inner contradiction of Andrássy's policy was that while wishing to maintain Turkey, he felt he was forced to bid against Ignatiev for South Slav indebtedness which could end in the amputation of the Ottoman Empire. Andrássy, of course, realized this risk but thought he could blunt it by maintaining in his own hands control over Christian reform through the formulation of a specific calendar of measures which he could persuade St. Petersburg to accept, and which they could together urge on the Porte.

Ignatiev, upon his return from the Crimea, responded to this by attempting to persuade the Sultan and Grand Vizier to institute their own improvements, which he suggested, in order to forestall the collective intervention which Andrássy was organizing.[20] As this is what Elliot and Derby wished from the beginning—no European intervention and spontaneous Ottoman rectifications—the British ambassador surprisingly found himself at one with his Russian rival. Ignatiev, having failed to destroy the Austro-Russian entente, was now trying to undercut it by making it unnecessary. He attempted to show the Tsar that his policy at Constantinople was not incompatible with the façade of Austro-Russian co-operation.[21] Everyone except the South Slavs was intent on containing the insurrection and satisfying rebel grievances by forcing reform down Turkish throats.

The fact of Austro-Russian differences was no secret. Both the Porte and Elliot were well aware of it in connection with the consular mission and now over the method used to bring about Turkish reform. Ignatiev was not at all hesitant to complain to Elliot.

Ignatiev ... spoke with great soreness of the manner in which his government had placed the whole direction of the Bosnian question in the hands of Austria.

He did not understand a Government being willing, as his own appeared to be, to adopt any decision that might be come to by the Minister of another Power.[22]

Nor was it a secret that Ignatiev hoped to use England to frustrate Andrássy, which Elliot rightly regarded as travesty. But the Russian ambassador undoubtedly felt that British influence would be useful in urging the Porte to spontaneous reform.

[Ignatiev asked] whether it would not be possible for Mr. Holmes to persuade Server Pasha of the necessity of giving immediate effect to the reforms sketched in the Imperial Irade [of 2 Oct.] . . .

As I [Elliot] have always strongly felt that the course advocated by General Ignatiev was the proper one for the Porte to follow . . . I could not hesitate to telegraph to Mr. Holmes to hold, unofficially, to Server Pasha, the same language as I had here been holding to the Grand Vizier and Minister for Foreign Affairs.

Your Lordship will be struck with the strange postition in which the Russian Ambassador is at this moment placed, in being forced to appeal to his English colleague to urge the adoption of steps which shall defeat the object of the Austro-Hungarian Government, with which his own profess to be acting in strict concert.[23]

Elliot instructed Holmes by telegraph to light a fire under the slow-moving Server Pasha, the Ottoman pacification commissioner for Bosnia-Hercegovina, and to tell him officially and confidentially that the British ambassador considers it important that no time should be lost in executing the Imperial Irade of 2 October. 'He [Server Pasha] will incur much blame if he shrinks from the responsibility which his position renders necessary.'[24] When Holmes pressed the Turkish commissioner, the latter complained, not without some justification, of the difficulties in executing reforms in Bosnia-Hercegovina, referring especially to the obstacles—low pay and the lack of qualified individuals—in the way of appointing Christians to the police and the local administrative posts.[25] The Powers had little success, even with British support, in bringing about spontaneous Turkish reform. The attempt of the European governments to contain the insurrection by pressuring Serbia and Montenegro against a war with Turkey met with more success, though here the British Government followed only reluctantly.

On 4 October the representatives of all the Great Powers at Belgrade, save England, had been instructed by their governments to warn Serbia not to make war. As White, the British consul at Belgrade, had already been instructed to press neutrality on Serbia, Elliot decided not to authorize him now to repeat that advice in conjunction with the other European consuls or 'to accompany it with a threat'. The British ambassador concluded that if a warning were desirable, it would have more effect if White gave it upon official instruction from his own government.[26] When Austria asked Derby to support the warning to Serbia, the Foreign Secretary replied that this had always been the British advice. He telegraphed to White that he could join in the identic representation, indicating simultaneously that Britain had given such advice from the beginning.[27] White, fearing to intervene in Serbia's internal crisis and also wary of the language of the Powers' representation to Serbia, telegraphed to Derby that unless he was directly instructed to deliver a similar telegram, he would limit himself to supporting it generally as consistent with his previous communications.[28] The representatives of the Great Powers delivered their identic and collective warning to Serbia on 6 October and two days later White indicated to Prince Milan's Government Britain's adherence to the warning of the Great Powers, emphasizing that this had always been the advice of London to Belgrade from the beginning of the insurrection.[29]

Britain's tortuous policy of preserving the fiction of non-intervention in the internal affairs of the Turkish Empire drew a plea from Jomini, who seemed to be unaware of the extent of Elliot's efforts at Constantinople in urging the Porte to execute reforms.

His Excellency [Jomini] expressed openly his regret that Her Majesty's Government does not join with the other Great Powers in their representations to the Porte; he avows his belief that the only efficacious method to arrive at an improvement in Turkish administration for the benefit of the whole population is by placing a pressure on the Government at Constantinople by the collective action of the European Courts. Turkey is in a state which exists only by sufferance, because necessary for the balance of Europe, and, therefore, the principle of non-intervention cannot be applied to Turkey as to other States. . . . This pressure to be exercised in the interests of Turkey for her own preservation can only be used beneficially and with success when all the European Powers are agreed to act in concert. The Ottoman Government will relax its efforts and disregard its promises of better administration as soon as divergence of opinion and absence of cordiality is manifested among the Contracting Powers to the Treaty of Paris. Baron Jomini attributes the Sultan's Iradé [of October] to this beneficial pressure . . .[30]

The position of Elliot, and to some extent of Derby as well, was a disinclination to add their ayes at the last moment to a step that had previously been concerted by Austria and Russia alone, and which might further undermine the Porte's authority and lead to the disintegration of its Empire. The consular mission and the threatening representation of the Powers to Serbia lent credence to Elliot's view.

Step by step we might be drawn into participation in the disintegration of the Empire, and although there is no great discredit in recognizing our inability to resist decisions of the united military Governments of the North, the same could not be said if we were found to be acting with them.

The course latterly followed by those Governments precludes the possibility of what can fairly be called acting in concert with them.

They discuss between themselves, and to the exclusion of all others, the line that is to be taken, and when they have come to a decision, the other Powers are to be told that they may join.[31]

Elliot's reaction in one sense was both wise and practical. Since there was divergence in the views of the Great Powers on the Eastern Question, an attempt to force them always to act together would destroy or lessen the possibility of united or collective representations on those points where general agreement existed. To allow freedom of action for disagreement would tend to promote co-operation where it was possible, but to force collective action where views differed would only create conflict and mistrust. The Andrássy–Ignatiev struggle was, in part, an example of the difficulties of concerting policy without sufficient mutual interest. But the attempt of Elliot and Derby to preserve the image of Ottoman sovereignty by opposing intervention in Turkey's internal affairs, which they translated as collective advice from the Great Powers, was short-sighted where it caused them to refuse or delay British general agreement aimed—as in the case of the concerted warning to Serbia—at containing the insurrection and preserving Ottoman integrity. What seemed to St. Petersburg an ostentatious display of independence on the part of Britain further precluded the possibility of London's influencing Austro-Russian policy from within rather than merely refusing to associate with what England considered undesirable after it had been concerted.

On 9 October in a long talk with Derby at Knowsley,

Shuvalov attempted to convince the Foreign Secretary that there was no need for British isolation as the views which their respective governments took of the crisis in the Balkans were quite similar. The Russian ambassador spoke strongly of the lack of desire of his government to weaken the Porte or to raise again the Eastern Question and added that there was no wish in Vienna to increase the Slav population of the Austro-Hungarian Empire.

The wish of his Government, Count Schouvaloff said, was to induce the insurgents to lay down their arms, and to persuade the Porte to take such steps as might, without in any way endangering the unity of the Empire, prevent such outbreaks in future. They entirely repudiated the idea of local autonomy, such as had been granted to Roumania and Servia. . . . Administrative and fiscal reform . . . were wanted, and beyond this their advice would not go.[32]

Derby assented in a general way and said it was essential that any reforms should be promulgated at the initiative of the Porte and should not appear to have been elicited by foreign pressure.[33] Unfortunately, the work of Shuvalov in London was undone by Jomini in St. Petersburg. The Russian counsellor had a conversation with Loftus, the British ambassador:

His Excellency [Jomini] said that the Russian Government having full confidence in Count Andrassy, and in consideration of the importance of the question to Austrian interests which, from the closer proximity of Austria to the disturbed districts, were more directly concerned than those of Russia, had left free action to the Austrian Minister President to devise the means of attaining a satisfactory solution of the existing difficulties. Baron Jomini stated that Count Andrassy was informed that the Russian Government were ready beforehand to accept and concur in any mode of solution he might propose, and that Count Andrassy was now occupied with drawing up some plan of arrangement.

He observed that since the principle of intervention had already been exercised in behalf of Turkey by the efforts unsuccessfully made by Russia and Austria to maintain the neutrality of Servia and Montenegro, it was but just that their same good offices should now be exercised in behalf of the Christian population, and that the principal aim was to seek for some guarantee for the faithful execution of the promises and concessions now offered by Turkey to the insurgents . . .[34]

And even Derby privately admitted that it was an uncommonly

fine line between guiding the Turks and leading or dragging them forward.[35] It was becoming clearer that Andrassy intended to do the latter and was preparing the views of Austria, Germany, and Russia which would be communicated to the Porte.[36] Any doubt was dispelled in a conversation between Buchanan, the British ambassador in Vienna, and the Austrian Foreign Minister on 17 November.

He [Andrássy] said, however, that the policy of Her Majesty's Government had been to consider the Porte the best judge of its own interests in its relations with its Christian subjects, but that he cannot concur in this view, and that, on the contrary, what is now occurring proves, in his opinion, that it is absolutely necessary for the Turkish Government to act hereafter on principles which will meet with the general approval of Europe.[37]

Jomini informed Loftus, the British ambassador at St. Petersburg, on 24 November that he had just received Andrássy's newest proposal for Bosnia-Hercegovina, slightly modified from those that Austria had sent previously to Alexander II at Livadia. He would go into no details as to its content beyond saying that it established 'perfect social and religious equality' and other 'serious reforms'. He gave it as his personal opinion that these proposals would be accepted by the Tsar.[38] Derby was anxious about Andrássy's proposals and, taking advantage of a chance remark of Baron Hofmann, Austrian Minister of Finance, to Buchanan that the Austrian Government had nothing to conceal from Britain, he instructed the British ambassador to ask Hofmann about the content of the reform proposals. When Buchanan delivered Derby's request, the Finance Minister merely said he would communicate the request to Andrássy. 'I fancied, however, that he thought . . . [I] represented him [Hofmann] to have gone further in assuring me of his readiness to give me information as to the views of the Government with respect to Herzegovina than would be agreeable to Count Andrassy, as it is generally understood that Count Andrassy and M. de Novikov have agreed to keep what passes between them secret, until the two Imperial Governments have come to an agreement . . .'[39]

Unable to penetrate the veil of Austro-Russian negotiations, Derby unhappily saw the insurrection lingering on and the Turks no nearer to executing reforms than before. On this last point, it was becoming clearer to the British consuls in the Balkans that the Porte's announced intention to remedy non-Muslim grievances had stirred up a wave of Muslim opposition sufficient to frustrate the attempt of the central Government to execute its promises. When the Grand Vizier told Sandison, the British dragoman, that the Porte would execute other reforms but that it 'could not undertake to enforce the acceptance of Christian evidence in the courts', it was interpreted as a disinclination to allow the official use of the Slav language in the courts as Muslims generally could not read or write it.[40] Even more serious was the fact that in the last three months of 1875 there were reports of increased use of irregular troops by Government forces. In a number of cases local Muslim inhabitants were organizing themselves without any official requests to do so, and having taken to the field they did not usually distinguish between armed insurgent bands and peaceful Christian peasants. But even had there been an effort on the part of local Muslims to do so, the nature of the fighting often blurred any distinction between a soldier and a farmer. The necessity to end the insurrection now had a double dimension. It was not merely a question of how long it would be possible to keep Serbia and Montenegro at peace, but whether Muslim retaliation and anger could be controlled and rendered harmless. Reform imposed upon Turkey by Austria and Russia seemed calculated not to accomplish either.

# 4 THE ANDRASSY NOTE

*Bashi-Bazouks*[1]

MUSLIM BARBARISM was assumed, expected, and found. This process affected not only British ecclesiastics and middle-class Nonconformists, but England's Levantine consuls and diplomatic personnel as well. The key distinction was not whether one sympathized with the Turks as Elliot did or felt them to be a noxious form of subhuman development as did Freeman, the well-known British historian, but whether one was a Christian or not, especially a non-Catholic Christian. It was considered legitimate for the Turks to defend themselves and to destroy insurgent bands as the British Government had urged the Porte to do with vigour from the moment the insurrection began. What was condemned as insupportable was any military activity by Muslim inhabitants not in the Ottoman regular army and especially by Circassian immigrants who had been settled in the area of Bulgaria by the Ottoman Government shortly after the Crimean War.

Such activity, even allowing for the exaggerated and unreliable reports upon which the British consuls often based their dispatches, did occur. Muslim inhabitants of Bosnia and Bulgaria, stirred by proclamations of Ottoman reform for non-Muslims,[2] used the insurrection as an opportunity to get back at their Christian neighbours and give vent to repressed feelings of dissatisfaction often emanating from the same provincial maladministration under which the Christians suffered. Ottoman authorities were not loth to make use of these 'volunteers' to cow areas not yet in active revolt and to help subdue those that were. It was difficult for the bankrupt Porte, unable to pay its regular soldiers and bureaucrats, to neglect such inexpensive assistance. Often the activity of these irregular soldiers was independent of Ottoman control or knowledge and a hindrance to both the military and civil activities of the Ottoman Government.

On 4 October Dupuis, the British vice-consul at Adrianople, alerted Elliot to the activities of Bashi-Bazouks based on reports from a Bulgarian informant at Philippopolis (Plovdiv). Dupuis complained to Elliot that, stationed as he was at Adrianople, it was often impossible for him to derive trustworthy accounts of activities within the central region of Bulgaria. He stressed the importance of establishing a British consulate at Philippopolis in order to obtain accurate information from that area. The British ambassador complained to the Turkish Foreign Minister and also to the Minister of War that the activity of these irregulars would lead to incidents and provocations which might ignite general insurrection.[3] Dupuis requested Elliot to urge the Porte to dispatch regular army units in order to control any lawless irregulars. Unconfirmed reports from Serbia complained of the incursion of Turkish irregular bands into that principality and again Elliot complained to the Porte.[4]

At the end of October Holmes informed the ambassador of a massacre of some Christian refugees who were returning to their homes in Hercegovina. One aspect of Elliot's concern with this report may be seen from the following.

I immediately sent Mr. Sandison [his dragoman] to represent to Safvet Pasha [Turkish foreign minister] and the Grand Vizier the necessity of making a summary example of those who had been guilty of this atrocity.
. . .

Your Lordship will at once perceive the unfortunate results which may follow this deplorable incident; for, on the one side, the refugees will be justified in any reluctance they may show in trusting themselves to a Government which has proved so little able to protect the first of them who returned . . .

Upon the other hand, those who have maintained that a foreign force would be necessary to secure the returning fugitives from the Mussulman populations will be supplied with an argument the strength of which it is impossible to deny.

I understand that the information received by the Russian Embassy puts the number of victims of this outrage at twelve . . .[5]

Further reports from Bulgaria brought further complaints from Elliot to the Porte. 'My dragoman reports from the Yeni-Zagra [north-east of Philippopolis] that the Mussulman population of that district is committing the greatest possible disorders . . . and murdered some 260 of the Bulgarians, in-

cluding men, women and children. . . .'[6] The reply of Ottoman
ministers was always that the matter would be investigated and
the guilty would be summarily punished.

When Freeman, the British consul, recommended disarming the whole population of both religions, Elliot demurred.

The measure has at various times been recommended to the Porte as
the proper course to follow; although at the present moment there
would no doubt be much difficulty in putting it into execution; for as
long as armed bodies of insurgents are looking out for defenceless
points to attack [this was not so in the Bulgarian region], it would seem
to be hardly possible to deprive the well-affected population of the
arms which they have carried from time immemorial, and leave them
exposed to enemies who would not be slow to avail themselves of any
opportunity of falling upon them.[7]

The British ambassador, if lacking in sympathy for the victims
of the Bashi-Bazouks, was never slow to advise the Porte to
control its irregulars and punish the guilty.[8] It is true that this
latter effort was in part motivated by a fear that Muslim retaliation on non-insurgent Christians would fan the flames of
revolt, but not completely. Whatever Elliot's personal feelings
which may have affected his actions, he never lost an opportunity to warn the Turks of Bashi-Bazouk activity, even when
proof of such activity was dubious or unconfirmed. Derby approved of all the efforts of his ambassador to warn the Porte
about irregulars, but both must have realized that while they
complained of inadequate Turkish energy in suppressing the
insurrection, the expectation that the Ottoman Government
would be able to control its Muslim subjects in the Balkans at
the same time was unrealistic. The ambassador did realize that
the spread of the insurrection, which he feared would result
from uncontrolled barbarity by the irregulars, could only lead
to greater Christian–Muslim carnage, and the non-
containment of the revolt had already elicited signs of Austro-
Russian intervention which his Government was attempting to
frustrate in the interests of Ottoman integrity.

### Andrássy Versus the Porte: A Race to Reform

Having temporarily checked Ignatiev at St. Petersburg, Andrássy found that in so doing he was now faced with another
problem which was partly due to the work of the Russian am-

bassador. The Porte, having been urged by both Ignatiev and Elliot to proclaim reform as the only way to prevent mediation and intervention within Ottoman affairs by the Great Powers, was engaged in preparing such a programme to implement its previous proclamation of 2 October.[9] Andrássy feared that any spontaneous Turkish reform would be controlled and used by Ignatiev. The Austrian minister now set to work to force the Turks to drop their programme so that he could get the agreement of the Russian Government to his own scheme when Alexander II at Livadia and Gorchakov at Vevey would return to St. Petersburg.

At the beginning of December Zichy, as instructed by Andrássy, urged the Grand Vizier against proclaiming any project for reform as such a programme should be proclaimed together with the Great Powers which signed the Treaty of Paris. The Ottoman minister firmly refused and expressed his surprise at the Austrian request,[10] which was repeated a few days later but again received no Ottoman acquiesence.[11] Elliot supported the Turkish position and when his opinion was asked by the Grand Vizier he replied that Britain had always urged prompt Ottoman reforms, and unless Austria gave a good reason for desiring delay, no time should be lost by the Porte in promulgating measures of reform.[12] On 8 December the Turkish ambassador called upon Derby in London and informed him that the Porte's reforms would soon be made public.

His Excellency [Musurus Pasha, Turkish ambassador] informed me that he was instructed to add that the Porte regarded the question of reform and the administration of the Empire as exclusively within its own competence, and that the Sultan could not accept proposals for reforms from any other Powers, as it would be incompatible with the independence of the Ottoman Empire and inconsistent with the provisions of the Treaty of Paris, by which the Powers had bound themselves not to interfere in the internal affairs of this country.[13]

Derby thought this premature as the nature of the Andrássy reforms were still not known. Vienna refused to recognize Turkish non-compliance and Beust, the Austrian ambassador in London, was instructed to tell Derby that the Porte would arrange measures of a general kind while it was prepared to accept the specific reforms of the Powers for Bosnia-

Hercegovina so long as they did not adversely affect the dignity of the Turkish Empire. For Andrássy, the demise of the in-surrection and the maintenance of Austrian influence were more important than sustaining Turkish sovereignty and, in fact, the attempt to do the latter was, in his eyes, seriously delaying the former.

The Turkish ministers had hitherto directed their energies exclusively to the task of preventing anything which could be construed into an interference of any kind into the internal affairs of Turkey. This standpoint, however respectable it may be, has the disadvantage, the Austro-Hungarian Government considered, of prolonging a regret-table state of things, and therefore of aggravating the danger.

Negotiations . . . are now being carried on between Vienna and St. Petersburg, the result of which will be communicated . . . to Her Majesty's Government, not in the light of an accomplished fact, but for their consideration and for them to state their own opinions on the propositions agreed upon.[14]

Gorchakov, who returned to St. Petersburg on 3 December, indicated general acceptance of Andrássy's reform plan to Lof-tus and further said that it and the impending Turkish reforms of Mahmoud Pasha were not incompatible.[15] The Porte, however, had the satisfaction of prior publication. On 14 December a firman completed two days earlier was com-municated to all the embassies in Constantinople listing the reforms together with the order for their application.[16] Two days later Andrássy told Buchanan that the Austro-Russian programme would in no way be affected by the Turkish publication as the former merely repeated long-standing proclamations regarding Christian subjects, while the Austro-Russian plan would be of a much more practical nature. He countered the Turkish argument of interference in the internal affairs of the Ottoman Empire by reminding the British am-bassador of Austrian efforts to restrain Montenegro from war, a service which gave her a right to advise concerning pacifica-tion. 'And besides that, as the Porte had proved that her troops could not suppress the insurrection, her neighbours who were suffering from it had as much right to suggest how the country might be pacified as the occupants of neighbouring houses would have to assist in extinguishing a fire which was threatening their property with destruction.'[17] But there could be no doubt, as the Italian Foreign Minister pointed out, that the effect of the latest Turkish step would be muted as the Turkish measures would be appearing simultaneously with the completion of the Austro-Russian plan. And as the insurgents would not be likely to accept more Turkish promises to execute often proclaimed remedies, it was unlikely that they would lay down their arms.[18] Elliot, while pointing out that the reception given to the edict of reform was unenthusiastic, thought that the document was sufficient in what it proclaimed, and that the difficulty was the one of applying and executing its contents.

The course for the friendly representatives to take is to encourage the Porte to carry out, and to develop and extend, the reforms which it itself elaborates; to point out the grievances which call for remedy, and to use such pressure as may be required to obtain it; but to abstain from proposing projects which may appear plausible to those imperfectly acquainted with the people to whom they are to be applied and for whom they would probably be found unsuited.[19]

Gorchakov referred to the Turkish effort as an 'inapplicable novel' minus any required guarantee for the execution of Christian reforms.[20]

Andrássy, however, made no secret, even before publication of his note, 'that the moral guarantee of the Sultan's promise is the only one which the Porte can give or the Powers ask for'.[21] As there was almost universal agreement that such a promise would be seen by the insurgents as worthless (it was a European guarantee which the rebels had demanded of the consular mission), the fact of Russian agreement to Andrássy's proposals on 28 January seemed less promising than it might have. The Porte was fully aware that the seriousness of its intentions needed to be made more manifest in order that it might derive benefit from its own proposals, and especially to convince Austria and Russia to give up their propositions for reform as these had already been anticipated by the Ottoman Government. As a result, the Porte created a permanent commission, under the Grand Vizier, composed of four Muslims and four Christians for carrying out the edict of reform and ensuring its execution.[22] But Vienna was not to be deterred, and on 31 December the Andrássy note was sent to London, Paris, and Rome and communicated to Buchanan, the British ambassador in Vienna.

The note proposed that the European Powers should ask, by identic instructions but not in a collective note, for an official communication from the Porte of the irade of 2 October and the firman of 12 December as well as a notification of its acceptance of the points in the Andrássy note intended to pacify the insurgent provinces. There were five specific proposals in the Austro-Russian note for Bosnia-Hercegovina: complete religious liberty, abolition of tax farming, the appropriation of direct taxes in Bosnia-Hercegovina to local purposes under the control of councils as indicated by the firman of 12 December, the creation of a mixed commission of Muslims and Christians to control the execution of reforms, and the improvement of the agrarian condition of the rural population.

The note left the execution of the points to the Ottoman Government. Andrássy was treading an impossible path. Hoping still to preserve the shattered fragments of Ottoman sovereignty by leaving the application of the reforms to the Porte and by avoiding a collective European communication to the Ottoman Government, yet at the same time wishing to convince the insurgents of the reality of the proposed remedies so that they would lay down their weapons, the Austrian Foreign Minister hoped to entice everyone into a half-way house which the rebels had long since passed and which the Turks could still not see. To have made the European governments responsible for the application of reforms, which the Slavs might have accepted but which Britain and the Porte would have assuredly refused, would have complicated, if not shattered, the relations between the Powers and at the same time given the initiative back to Ignatiev. To do nothing meant the insurrection would continue into spring, when everyone, including Andrássy, expected that Serbia and Montenegro would officially go to war. If it was unrealistic to have expected the Sultan to make the reforms a reality because of a public promise to the major Powers to do so, there was even less reason to suppose that the rebels would be satisfied by reforms granted by Europe but to be executed by the Turks. But there seemed nothing else better to do.[23]

## Reception of the Andrássy Note and Britain

It was apparent from the initial communication of the

note to the other Powers that Austro-Russian agreement was limited to issuing the document; any action beyond that, especially the course to be adopted if the insurgents refused to be pacified or if Serbia or Montenegro went to war, was not clearly indicated.[24] Novikov, the Russian ambassador in Vienna and ardent supporter of Andrássy, expected some communication by the Great Powers with the insurgents on the question of pacification, but this does not seem to have been Andrássy's intention.

Beust delivered the Andrássy note to the Foreign Office on 3 January. Elliot in Constantinople immediately telegraphed his first impression of it and made little attempt to disguise the anger, frustration, and surprise which he felt.

I hardly see how a note such as proposed by Count Andrassy could be addressed to the Porte, for most of the reforms suggested by him have already been adopted by the Porte.

The Firman of 12th December was officially communicated to the Embassies a day before it was promulgated, and they could not ask that it should be communicated a second time. A proposal to appoint a mixed commission of Mussulmans and Christians to control the execution of the reforms could not be made, for one was appointed a fortnight ago, and sits daily to organize details.

Religious liberty is proclaimed, except as regards rendering Christians liable to military conscription.

The abolition of farming of the tithes is resolved upon.

The constitution and duties of the provincial councils are being defined.

The remedies required for the improvement of the position of the agricultural population will come under the consideration of the Reform Commission, but they can only be judged by persons intimately acquainted with local habits and traditions . . .

The Powers [should be] careful not to do anything likely to cause exasperation among Mussulmans, which might be the effect of an identic note such as is proposed.[25]

The initial reaction of the Grand Vizier, Mahmoud Pasha, was against receiving in any official manner European advice on reforms. Such advice he would not lay before the Sultan, who would be affronted, though the minister implied his readiness to receive friendly unofficial communications on the subject. The Turkish ambassador in Berlin agreed as to the indignity. The firman of 12 December required first the submission of the insurgents before its measures would be enacted. As the Andrássy note made no such stipulation, the Sultan could not without loss of face retract this condition which would be at least implied by his acceptance of the Austro-Russian programme.

Decazes favoured the note and thought official European disapproval would terminate the insurrection. He balked only at the proposed appropriation of direct taxes to local purpose in Bosnia-Hercegovina. As this concession, he told the British ambassador, could not be withheld from the rest of the Ottoman Empire, an already bankrupt central Government might never be able to meet its obligations to the holders of Ottoman bonds, a large number of whom were French.[26] The French Foreign Minister, however, appealed to the British Government to view the note favourably and announce their adherence to it. Though Decazes argued that the ninth article of the Treaty of Paris of 1856 was never intended to preclude European 'observations' to the Porte, de Vogué, the French ambassador at Vienna, disagreed.

The act demanded by the three Northern Courts appears to be a sequel of the campaign undertaken by Russia against the Treaty of Paris, only that in re-entering the Black Sea she assured to herself an exclusive advantage, whereas now she pursues an European interest. If she draws the signatories of the Treaty into a step which leads the Porte to subscribe to their collective will, she will virtually have destroyed the independence of the Ottoman Empire, and will have given to Europe alone the right to take a part, at a given moment, in her internal affairs; in any case, she will have assured eventually to the Christian populations the sole guarantee compatible with the at least nominal preservation of Turkey.[27]

Italy agreed with the French Government in favouring the note and saw its efficacy in the 'moral guarantee', or to use Andrássy's phrase, 'European sanction', that would persuade the insurgents to peace in lieu of the Ottoman inability to force them to submit militarily.

With France and Italy about to adhere to the note of the three Northern courts, only Britain remained to be heard from. The main anxiety of Gorchakov and Andrássy was not the stubbornness of the rebels but the anticipated refusal of the Porte, a step which was considered almost certain if London did not lend her support to the weight of the other Great Powers.[28] Derby, suspicious, timid, legalistically consistent, stubborn, and defensive, was a difficult man with whom to deal. He tended to go along with what was unanimously approved, impossible to prevent, and unnecessary to do. He only felt free in committing himself to a major step when he could first convince himself of the impossibility of doing anything else. And when he could not do this, a task to which he brought considerable intelligence, he did nothing. With the Andrássy note, a considerable amount of his own ingenuity and self-deception combined with Bismarckian reassurance and a careful Austro-Russian handling of his fears and susceptibilities enabled the Foreign Secretary to break through the web of his own personality.

As early as the preceding October Shuvalov, the Russian ambassador in London, had attempted to elicit more positive reactions from the Foreign Secretary by a campaign of friendship and openness. Andrássy reassured him of Austrian opposition to her own occupation of Bosnia, a solution which *The Times* favoured temporarily in November, and everyone, including Derby, believed that if pacification were to succeed no delay was possible as Serbia, Montenegro, and Bulgaria were only awaiting spring to join the fight against the Turks. If Beust is to be believed, Derby admitted Europe's right to intervene in Turkey at the end of the first week in December, though, if pressed, he surely would have explained this as his personal impression and not the opinion of the British Government. Andrássy's decision to leave the execution of his note entirely in the hands of the Porte, though intended to avoid the dangers of European complication and win Turkish acceptance, also reassured Derby. At the end of the first week in January the Foreign Secretary was made aware of Gorchakov's feeling that if the insurgents refused to comply with the note, then a 'second phase of the question' would have begun 'when England might abstain if she thought fit'.[29]

Derby seems to have been away when Beust delivered the Andrássy note to the Foreign Office.[30] A copy was sent to him at Knowsley which he read on the morning of 4 January. Two days later Beust travelled up to Derby's home and found him surprisingly sympathetic to the note. The probable explanation of this is the private letter and telegram he received from Odo Russell, the British ambassador in Berlin, who had had a long conversation with Bismarck on Eastern affairs in which the latter expressed a desire to come to an understanding with England.[31] During his talk with Russell, Bismarck removed the major anxiety of Derby about adhering to the Andrássy note.

> At present [Bismarck said] Prince Gorchakov, Count Andrassy and himself were agreed and acting cordially together, but there were ambitious men in Russia and Austria who might interfere. For ought he knew the late visit of Archduke Albrecht [who desired to annex Bosnia-Hercegovina], the sworn enemy of Germany, to St. Petersburg might have been the occasion of an attempt to sow discord between Russia and Germany.

> The danger he apprehended most in Austria was the down fall of the present administration. Andrassy, as a Hungarian, resisted the annexation the Slav party were urging on the Emperor, but if he fell, we must be prepared to deal with an annexation policy in Austria and its consequences in Russia. For his part he was willing to join with England in resisting it or not, as Her Majesty's Government might think best for the good of Europe. Alone without the support of England, he would not resist the annexing tendencies of Austria and Russia, in Turkey, because he did not think either of those powers would be strengthened by such increase of territory, or the interests of Germany be affected by it. On this question he would however reserve his opinion until he knew that of Her Majesty's Government and through Her Majesty's Government he also hoped to know what the French Government might be disposed to do . . .[32]

Derby distrusted no foreign statesman more than he did Bismarck, and rightly so. Yet Bismarck's words reassured him about any ulterior motives that Andrássy or Gorchakov might have had in proposing their note. Their suggestion for reform was not intended as a trap to ensnare Britain into supporting steps which would lead to the disintegration of the Ottoman Empire. This was a real fear shared by Derby, Elliot, Salisbury, Disraeli, and Tenterden, the Under-Secretary for Foreign Affairs. They could not understand Andrássy's policy which was admittedly quite tortuous. Tenterden's words to Odo Russell could have been written by either Elliot or Derby. 'What I [Tenterden] should like to have is the real secret of Andrássy—what is he driving at—Is he going in for annexation or what? and why he keeps Zichy at Constantinople and allows him to make such a display of being under Ignatiev.'[33]

At approximately the same time as his talk with Beust on 6 January, Derby received a memorandum on the Andrássy note prepared by Tenterden. Allusion was made to the fact, as was done earlier in Elliot's first reaction, that the Porte had already adopted three of the five points of the note. On point three, the application of taxation to local purposes, Tenterden wrote that this was 'only a crude suggestion' about which much more information would be required. Point five, the improvement of the condition of the peasantry, drew from the Under-Secretary a response almost identical with Elliot's, that this could only be dealt with 'after local inquiry by competent persons'. Tenterden pointed out that what the Porte needed was men not measures and ended with a suggestion that if the note were agreed to by all, Austria and the Powers should inform the insurgents and Serbia and Montenegro that the rebels could expect no more benefits and should submit.[34] If Derby received this at Knowsley while Beust was still there, it would explain his desire 'to go into the question of eventualities' with the Austrian ambassador.[35]

The following day, though the exact chronology is uncertain, Derby received letters from Salisbury and Manners, the Postmaster-General, and wrote himself to Disraeli. Manners was wary of the same two points in the note as Elliot and Tenterden.

On what grounds the Imperial Governments should prescribe to Turkey the first reform I don't know; but it strikes me that if we support the suggestion we should furnish the Home Rulers with a good argument for claiming the allocation of the Irish income tax to the development of Irish Railways, Fisheries, etc. Foreign advice, unsolicited, in matters of taxation seems, on the face of it, a clear invasion of the rights of independent sovereignty.[36]

Salisbury, while he opposed full support for the note, thought a refusal of it would encourage the insurrection, and therefore advised a more vague general acceptance which would not include assent to anything which intimated armed intervention into Turkey by Austria, Russia, or Germany.

Probably if it [an armed intervention] happened we could not stop it but if we gave our full adhesion to the note and agreed as Andrassy expresses it to instruct our Ambassador 'à agir conjoinment et d'une manière, identique auprès du gouvernement du Sultan dans le sens que nous venons de développer,' we should be committed to an approval of the policy and we should be not protesting bystanders but assenting parties. ... And the Eastern question would be settled by the gradual reduction of the Porte to the conditions of a protected principality under the three Eastern Powers. ... In short what I want is that we should give our adhesion to his [Andrássy's] reforms but not to his note.[37]

Without realizing it, Salisbury was diluting the effect of Bismarck's assurances. Apparently, the Secretary of State for India did not yet realize, though he would soon enough, that the one thing the Foreign Secretary needed not was advice to be wary of the intentions of others.

The effect on him of the reactions and advice of Bismarck, Tenterden, Salisbury, Manners, and Elliot may be seen from the letter Derby wrote to Disraeli on 7 January. He described the proposed reforms as not unreasonable and, with one exception, as remedies which the Government could support. The exception was the appropriation of revenue to local purposes. He felt it was both safer and less humiliating to join in than to hold aloof, since Britain's refusal would bring on that of the Porte and the responsibility and consequences of the failure to pacify would be England's. If, despite Britain, the Porte accepted the note, 'we stand in the foolish position of being more Turkish than the Turks'.

I assume then that in some form, and possibly with some necessary reservations, we ought to give in our adhesion. ... If we join, we ought to insist ... on some sort of pledge being given by the Austrian and Russian Governments that they will use their utmost exertions to induce the insurgents to lay down their arms. It is still possible that they may fail, and that the war may go on; but in that event we are no worse off than if the attempt at pacification had not been made. If contrary to advice, the Porte ignores the suggestion addressed to it, our hands are free; we cannot take the responsibility of results arising from a policy which we have deprecated.

It is too late to stand on the dignity and independence of the Sultan; a sovereign who can neither keep the peace at home, nor pay his debts, must expect to submit to some disagreeable consequences.

We may be dupes, but I think both Austria and Russia desire peace. Mutual jealousy, and fear of the establishment of an independent Sclave state make it reasonable and natural that they should wish to see the *status quo* maintained. Whether the old fabric is not too rotten to bear patching is another question; but a question which we cannot answer till we have tried.[38]

Derby was willing to allow others to attempt to hold the Ottoman Empire together, if that were possible, even at the expense of the Sultan's position and independence, as it seemed the only way to do it. A qualified adhesion to such an attempt was desirable because it committed Britain to very little, if indeed to anything at all, and kept her clear of any responsibility for either Turkish corruption or the continuance of the insurrection. To avoid blame for failure was as important, or more so, as to contribute unconditionally to a desirable solution for which the chances of success were problematical.

On this last point, the possibility of preserving Ottoman sovereignty, Derby was not hopeful. He disbelieved in any satisfactory solution for the question of Ottoman existence because he thought that Turkish rule and administration were too weak and rotten to be patched. And, of course, Derby had no intention of directly aiding the patching. He was not prepared to give a promise of aid in order to suppress the revolt.[39] When Odo Russell wrote on 8 January, he still suspected the possibility of a British rejection and politely pressed for an acceptance. 'Thanks for your letter of the 4th. The Austrian Note impresses me as it does you, and the five Powers having already agreed, I most sincerely hope H. M. Govt. will be able to join them as it would greatly simplify the question and facilitate the passage into its next phase. I therefore await your decision with interest and impatience.'[40]

Any impact of Russell's plea was neutralized by a letter from Disraeli on the following day in response to a request for his opinion from Derby. The Prime Minister knew his Foreign Secretary and the latter's lack of self-confidence which he continually attempted to repair by warm expressions of appreciation for Derby's great abilities. This was usually done to give Derby sufficient confidence to act and to associate with other Powers in order to avoid isolation. Now, ironically, it was Disraeli who was dragging his feet and encouraging Derby to do likewise.

You know how great is my confidence in your judgement, and, therefore, you can better appreciate the hesitation wh. I feel in differing from the course wh. you recommend.

I think it will land us in a false position, and it would be preferable to appear isolated wh. I usually deprecate, than, for the sake of a simulated union, wh. will not last many months, embarrass ourselves, when independent action may be necessary.

In declining to identify ourselves, as requested, with the note, is it necessary to appear as Turkish, or more Turkish, than the Turks? Could we not devise a course wh. might avoid that?[41]

Derby returned to London from the north and on 12 and 13 January listened to the urgings of the French, German, and Russian ambassadors who were anxious that Britain should not hold aloof.[42] He replied that he could give no official answer until the Cabinet met on 18 January.[43] On the fourteenth Beust came to the Foreign Office on Andrássy's instructions to deny the rumours, which Salisbury feared, of an Austro-Russian armed occupation of Turkey.[44] Derby's less than enthusiastic demeanour with Beust and Shuvalov was possibly intended to prepare Austria and Russia so that they would give a favourable reception to an English adhesion to the note which would be conditional and vague.

British diplomatic opinion was turning increasingly in favour of the Andrássy note. Elliot had telegraphed on the twelfth, informed by his colleagues in Constantinople that Britain would adhere to the note, that he had strongly advised the Porte 'not to be predisposed against the overtures intended to facilitate the pacification of the Herzegovina'. Derby, who had asked the opinion of Lyons, the British ambassador in Paris who had served in Constantinople and was of sound and mature judgement, received a reply that support was unavoidable and that by joining in Britain 'leaves the other powers the least excuse for interfering for their own profit'.[45]

If there had been doubt about the decision of the British Government, its adherence was made almost certain by the generally unexpected receipt on the evening of 14 January of a telegram from Elliot reporting that the Turkish Foreign Minister asked that unless the Austrian note were totally objectionable, Turkey would prefer that England adhere to it so she would not be left alone with unfriendly powers.[46] Disraeli interpreted the Ottoman request as emanating from Austrian anxiety.

Our delay so alarmed Austria . . . that Andrassy had offered all sorts of concessions to the Porte provided the Porte wd signify to England that the Porte wished us to join the other Powers. And, the day I was with D[erby], he expected this. . . . We can't be more Turkish than the Sultan—plus Arabe que l'Arabie.

I think they have only postponed the crisis; wh. will happen in spring . . .[47]

Though there is no direct evidence for it, it seems probable that Derby verbally enlightened Disraeli and Salisbury as to Bismarck's assurances or at least his own, of an Austro-Russian intention to occupy European Turkey which may have mitigated their suspicions as well.[48] Whereas a few days before, Salisbury had indicated his feeling that the Andrássy note hinted at an Austrian occupation of Turkey, he now broadcast his belief in the necessity of an English adherence to the note, but with certain qualifications.[49] Though it was not Bismarck's intention, the impact on Derby of his words to Russell, Austro-Russian assurances of innocence, together with urgings to adhere from the five Great Powers, and finally the Ottoman request that Britain join with the other Powers made it extremely difficult, if not impossible, for the Cabinet to reject the note. It did not, however, dictate the nature of the Cabinet's acceptance, or the necessity of an official reply or reaction.

The decision of the British ministers, for which Europe was waiting in agonizing frustration, was made at a Cabinet meeting held on 18 January. If Disraeli's report to the Queen is accurate, Derby advised acceptance to his colleagues and it was agreed that the note would 'be supported in its general tenor and the Porte counselled to receive it, and consider it, in a friendly spirit'.[50]

The European sign of relief which accompanied the knowledge of the British decision was premature, as the Powers had not yet agreed on the manner in which the note would be communicated to the Porte, nor had they yet received a full and official British reply which would explain what 'general support' meant.

Beust called on Derby at the Foreign Office to elicit such a

reply on the twenty-second. Vienna had heard happily the
Cabinet's decision of the eighteenth but before communicating
its note to the Porte, wished to know whether London objected
to this course or desired it to delay so as to allow time for a
British declaration. Derby replied that before formal communication was made to the Porte, Elliot would require instructions from the Foreign Office, and these he had not yet
received. Derby promised the Austrian ambassador that in
three or four days[51] he would clarify the position of the British
Government.

Some conversation followed, in the course of which Count Beust
took occasion to observe that the communication intended to be addressed to the Porte was not regarded by his Government in the light
of mere good advice. They wanted a pledge that the reforms which
they proposed should be carried into execution, failing which they
would not undertake to use their influence with the Christian population to advise them to lay down their arms.

I stated in answer that I clearly understood this. . . . [But that] we
were not prepared to do more than offer such friendly advise as the
circumstances seemed to require, but this difference between the
relative positions of the two countries need not prevent us from supporting recommendations which we believed, in the main, to be
founded on sound principles.[52]

Derby apparently told Beust that Britain refused to join the
other Powers in demanding from the Turks a written reply to
the Andrássy note,[53] for on 24 January Beust communicated a
written request left at the Foreign Office indicating the necessity of a written Turkish reply and a desire that Britain's full
and official explanations would be given by the following
day.[54]

It was given and was a fuller reply than either Beust or Andrássy could have anticipated.[55] After a lengthy discussion of
the five reforms with demurrers on direct taxation for local
purposes and agrarian legislation, the British reply concluded
with a general assent and a specific expectation.

Your Excellency [Beust] will have observed from the foregoing
remarks that Her Majesty's Government see nothing in the five
points proposed by Count Andrassy to which they cannot give a
general support; although on the other hand, the proposed reforms
relating to taxation and grants of land involve in their detailed

application to districts like Bosnia and Herzegovina many questions upon which they are not prepared, in their present state of information, to offer a definite opinion.

. . .

They reply upon the assurances contained in Count Andrassy's dispatch and upon those which Your Excellency has conveyed to me [Derby], that if these suggestions were carried into effect the Austro-Hungarian Government will, in concert with the other Powers whose united action Count Andrassy has invited, use their best exertions to prevent the spread of the movement, and to induce the insurgents to submit, or effectually to preclude them from receiving assistance from beyond the frontier, should they persist in continuing the struggle.

Her Majesty's Ambassador at Constantinople will accordingly be instructed to a give a general support to the proposals of the Austro-Hungarian Government, and to act with his colleagues for this purpose.[56]

It would seem that for the sake of suppressing the insurrection, the possibility of which appeared to be increased by the prospective closure of the Austrian frontier and Austro-Russian pressure on Serbia and Montenegro, the British Government was willing to give its 'general support' to five measures, two of which they felt to be questionable, inapplicable, and potentially embarrassing.

In the telegram of instructions for Elliot, Derby interpreted the Andrássy proposals as amounting to a request that the Porte execute the reform decrees of 1839 and 1856, together with the irade of 2 October and the firman of 12 December. He did not, he wrote, regard the note as being contrary to the Treaty of Paris of 1856 since it contained only suggestions or recommendations' and did not include foreign intervention between the Porte and its subjects.

Do not see that the Porte need feel difficulty in acting on advice, and communicating to the Powers in some form the measures proposed in consequence . . .

Essential that Porte should act vigorously and promptly in execution of reforms . . .

You should strongly impress on Porte indispensable to appoint officers of energy and determination, who will disregard local apathy and prejudice and sternly repress atrocities like murder of returning

refugees, and restore feeling of security to Christian population, otherwise no pacification can be expected.
. . .

You should conform your representations to the usual form of oral communications to Grand Vizier and Raschid Pasha [Foreign Minister] . . .[57]

All the Great Powers had now agreed to urge on the Porte the acceptance of a note to which the Porte itself had requested the British Government to adhere. The last hurdle was successfully got over when Elliot persuaded Raschid Pasha to accept a written version of the Andrássy note which would be read to him by the Austrian ambassador. As it was more normal in Constantinople than in other capitals for all important diplomatic communication to be made orally, a written communication was resented as an affront by the Turks. A solution was arranged on 31 January, when, after the note was read to Raschid Pasha, the latter requested a written copy which Zichy then gave to him. Elliot supported the note as instructed and was informed by Raschid Pasha that the only point of difficulty was the one of direct taxation used for local purposes. By 3 February all the ambassadors in Constantinople had spoken in support of the note to the Turks, though none save Zichy left a written communication. On 13 February the Porte conveyed to the ambassadors of the six Powers its answer in an official note which announced that the Sultan had issued a new iradé ordering four of the five Andrássy proposals to be immediately executed in Bosnia and Hercegovina.[58] It was hoped by Elliot, Ignatiev, and Zichy that the affirmative Ottoman response to his note would lead Andrássy to agree to the withdrawal of the consular commission, which apparently, like earlier irades, firmans, and decrees, proved the potency of illusion over reality.[59] The rebels were now faced with a new combination, a firman and a European note contained within, chronologically speaking, two irades. The question now was would they accept, or as some would have put it, would they be allowed to accept.

# 5 ANGLO-GERMAN ENTENTE

As THE insurrection continued, more and more official and self-appointed correspondents for British journals went to Bosnia. The horrors of the fighting and the terrible plight of the Bosnian refugees who had gone into Dalmatia, Croatia, and Montenegro touched the sympathies of British reporters who were already disposed to picture a Christian peasantry struggling to be free of Muslim oppression. Hostility developed, not surprisingly, between these observers and the official British Levantine diplomatic corps, especially when the sympathy of the former for the Balkan Christians led some to actively support the rebels.

W. J. Stillman, an American, whose reports were sent to *The Times* from Ragusa, was one such individual. After investigation, Monson solved the mystery of Stillman's name and acknowledged his activities.

Mr. Stillman (for such is, I am informed, the correct spelling of his name) . . . has done [much mischief] not among the educated people here but among the ignorant classes who not without some reason, regard the correspondent of the *Times* as the recognized exponent of public opinion in England, and as consequently invested with a quasi official character.

Mr. Stillman lives with the Secretary of the Russian Consulate-General; he is every day with M. Jonin, the Russian Consul-General, and ordinarily dines with him. . . . He is in constant communications with the Russian officers who are directing the insurgent operations [of these meddlers and interpreters at Constantinople]. Derby replied 'It is . . . very much to be desired that the directors of the *Times* should accede to his proposed anxiety to be relieved from his position with as little delay as possible.'[1]

Newspaper writers were not the only ones who managed to complicate affairs for the British diplomatic corps in the Balkans. Turcophiles, Slavophiles, and reasonably neutral private individuals came in increasing numbers as the insurrection continued. Lord Stratheden and Campbell, who took a great interest in the Eastern Question, left Constanti-

nople in February 1876 the bearer of a message from Raschid
Pasha to Bismarck concerning the impossibility of suppressing
the insurrection while it was fostered from abroad.[2] Two other
Turcophiles who attracted attention were Lady Strangford and
Butler-Johnstone. The latter asked Elliot to deliver to the
Sultan an address which was in fact an anti-Russian harangue,
but which he described as an expression of sympathy to the
Sultan from the Foreign Affairs Committee in England. Elliot
refused.[3]

The Queen complained to Derby of these "unauthorized
agents' who 'meddle' at Constantinople. Derby replied that
neither individual represented the government, but he guessed
at Lady Strangford's opinions. 'I fancy rather in the line of
wishing to see an exclusive English interest paramount in the
East—the *regime* of Lord Stratford made permanent which is
more easily said than done.'[4]

Humphrey Sandwith, surgeon, journalist, and agitator, was
a strong Slav partisan. Engaged in raising money to aid the
Bosnian refugees, he wrote to a fellow Slav sympathizer who
was active in a Balkan mission of mercy.

The money I gather is to be used entirely at your discretion. It is for
the use of the Bosnian refugees, a few blankets for their hunted
husbands and brothers hiding with arms in the woods would be
desirable and there would be no harm in spending an odd sum now
and then in powder if necessary. The war is strictly defensive and
every Turk shot is a benefit.

Yesterday I gave a lecture in a private house with 5 tickets. I hope I
raised about £20. . . . The day after tomorrow I am going to Oxford
to . . . make an appeal for the Christian refugees . . .

Thank God England's policy is very decidedly changing, the anti
Turk feeling is growing.[5]

For some, and Sandwith was only one, South Slav sympathy
was indistinguishable from hatred of Turks. Ponsonby, the
Queen's private secretary, noticed that there were people in
England who were agitating against Turkey and he singled out
Professor Freeman, whose bitterness against the Sultan's rule
knew no bounds.[6]

In Parliament, interest in the insurrection elicited a
governmental promise to lay papers. Before such papers were
produced there was a serious party fight, which briefly eclipsed

the Eastern Question, over Disraeli's plan to give Queen Victoria the title of Empress of India. The Liberal Harcourt made reference to the opposition which many in England felt to such a change and Münster, the German ambassador, who knew Britain well, thought the controversy over it weakened both the position of the government as well as the influence of Disraeli.[7] Disraeli felt the explosion serious enough to call in his political credit.

We are in the throes of a great party struggle the greatest we have had for some years.

The opposition . . . gave their challenge last night by Hartington himself.

Let me entreat you to be present [in Parliament]. It is an occasion I must count upon my friends.[8]

The affair was quickly over when the Government carried the measure with a large majority. Salisbury saw the resulting calm as temporary for both parties were in a combative mood and as there were too few subjects to elicit a fight there would be much noise about trifles.[9]

Behind and hidden from all of this was an attempt by Bismarck to arrange an understanding with Britain which occurred during January and February of 1876. British opinion could not express itself on what would have been a significant turning-point in the Eastern crisis as only a few knew of the secret.

### An Understanding on the East

This country [Britain] does not stand in great need of special alliances, and it ought carefully to beware lest they should bring it into special dependencies.

It is blessed with a position more independent than any State in Europe. But this independence need not imply and never has implied isolation.

Because of its independence, and because it has less temptation than others to prosecute selfish interests in Europe or the Levant, there is for the most part a disposition in Continental States to confide in it more than any one of themselves, and defer to it quite as much as it deserves.[10]

Britain's position with the Powers of Europe in January 1876 was hardly ideal. France, her Crimean partner, now relatively impotent, was intensely annoyed with England because of the latter's purchase of the Khedive's shares in the Suez Canal, and was playing up to Russia for support in Egypt against London. Italy was sympathetic, but too weak not to do the bidding of the northern courts. Germany, Austria, and Russia, though far from being in complete harmony, were sufficiently united to be able to safely ignore the British Government, and had done so.

Bismarck, for his part, had no desire for Ottoman territory, and was as ready to help preserve the crumbling Empire as he was to arrange for its demise. He knew of Austro-Russian tension and the Andrássy–Ignatiev struggle, and his great fear was the outbreak of a war, especially one between Russia and Austria in which France would ally herself with St. Petersburg. British support for the preservation of peace and her naval neutralization of France should war occur were very useful services for which the price to be paid—containment of the insurrection and the preservation of Turkish integrity—was neither great nor impossible. German and British interests seemed to mesh so well that Bismarck was ready to build on them to obviate the dangers of both an Austro-Russian bargain and an Austro-Russian fight. Either was possible, as Bismarck believed with most European statesmen that the Andrássy note would fail to bring pacification. He now decided to forsake the passive acceptance of any Austro-Russian agreement on the East for an initiative of his own. In seeking an English entente, Bismarck's purpose was not to throw over Austria and Russia but to be better able to control them.

On 2 January, at Bismarck's request, Odo Russell, the British representative at Berlin, called on the German statesman, who told him that 'he very much wished to come to an understanding with Her Majesty's Government ... [on the Andrássy note] because [at present] England and Germany were the two powers most earnestly desirous of maintaining the peace of Europe ...' Russell's report continued:

[Bismarck would] reserve the power of giving his support to Her Majesty's Government, if they wished it, by withholding at the outset an unqualified approval of the Austro-Russian scheme, which might disturb the good relations he wished to keep up with England. Indeed he would gladly find an opportunity of cementing those good relations, even more closely ... by cooperating with Her Majesty's

Government in regard to Turkish affairs, should difficulties arise in which Your Lordship would be willing to accept the friendly assistance of Germany in the general interest of peace. He did not agree with those who said things are too bad to last so any longer; in his opinion Turkey might yet be kept together with a little good will—but good will depended on mutual forbearance and cordial cooperation.

Russell's response was meaninglessly polite and slightly offended.[11] He said that his government desired friendly relations with Germany and would always join her in order to maintain European peace but that reticence had come not from Britain but from Germany.

[Russell said] that Germany having no interests in the East, left the initiative to her Austrian and Russian allies in dealing with Eastern Affairs, and would simply maintain a silent and observant attitude in regard to Turkey. Count Münster in London had been as reticent as Herr Von Bülow in Berlin, and it was not for want of good will on our part that we had been kept in ignorance of Count Andrassy's proposed policy by the Northern Allies until today.

Bismarck minimized the significance of plans for reform and referred to the importance of the intentions of ambitious Austro-Russian politicians.

On ... the administration of the Austro-Russian remedy to the sick man, he wished for a previous confidential agreement with Your Lordship. ....Having no special German interests to guard in Turkey, he was at liberty to support those of England if Her Majesty's Government wish for his support in coming events, in which case he thought his influence might be beneficially exercised at Vienna and St. Petersburg.

. . .

If he [Andrássy] fell, we [Germany] must be prepared to deal with an annexation policy in Austria and its consequences in Russia. For his part he [Bismarck] was willing to join with England in resisting it or not, as Her Majesty's Government might think best for the good of Europe. Alone, without the support of England, he would not resist the annexing tendencies of Austria and Russia, in Turkey, because he did not think either of those Powers would be strengthened by such increase in territory, or the interests of Germany be affected by it. ... If he could thus obtain for Germany the good will of England and her friends [France and Italy] he could look to the future with greater confidence. Germany could not well afford

to let Austria and Russia become too intimate behind her back—nor could she let them quarrel with safety to herself. . . . [If Germany sided with Austria] Russia . . . would then find a willing ally in France to injure Germany.
. . .

All these considerations he wished to submit confidentially to Her Majesty's Government and to solicit an exchange of views in return, in the hope of being able to cooperate with England for the maintenance of European peace. I said I would . . . bring him an answer as soon as possible.[12]

Britain was now faced with a serious offer to escape isolation on the Eastern Question. A more than fair quid pro quo was offered—British influence via Bismarck in Austro-Russian counsels in return for British intercession with France and Italy in a pro-German sense; German support for the preservation of Ottoman territorial integrity in return for an unspecified British backing of Germany; and finally, equal co-operation in the preservation of European peace.

Some historians have denied that Bismarck intended an understanding with London, and an imposing array have argued that the German minister's aim was for a European partition of Turkey in which Britain would participate. Harris assumes and Medlicott, Langer, and Stojanovic state that this was the object of Bismarck's efforts.

Harris writes that Russell's reports of his talk with Bismarck omits mention 'of the all important provisions for the future . . .' and incorrectly assumes that those prospective territorial changes were probably conveyed to London in private letters not part of the official Foreign Office material. In later years much of Odo's correspondence was destroyed by his wife. In the last few years a collection of Russell's private letters was discovered and is now deposited at the Public Record Office. Medlicott argues that, though Bismarck supported British efforts to maintain the *status quo*, 'there is no evidence that his approaches to England had any other purpose than to encourage her in a policy of partition'. I disagree with this. Attempting to interpret Bismarck's intentions is more than usually difficult because he was flexible and usually had several approaches, often contradictory, leading to the same desired end. I see no reason to question Bismarck's words to Russell that he was neutral on a partition, which he could support or not. Bismarck, though he was not above misleading others, was here speaking the truth, if only because there is no evidence that he was not. His often-quoted words to d'Oubril, the Russian ambassador, suggesting a partition, only meant, as he told Russell, that he was not averse to one, and if unsupported by England would not oppose an Austro-Russian partition. If England favoured a partition, and some were interpreting the purchase of the Canal shares as a possible intimation of this, it is probable that Bismarck would have heartily gone along with this. Langer writes that Bismarck 'was not fishing for an alliance with England. What he was after was the conversion of the English and then the Russians to the idea of a settlement based on partition of the Ottoman Empire if the reform program failed'. Bismarck was not Nicholas I, and he understood the nature of the British political system and the difficulty of its accommodating written alliances concerning prospective possibilities. But he was willing to try for a looser and less formal arrangement which would bestow on him the same degree of freedom it might give successive British cabinets in interpreting an agreement of a previous government. Stojanovic feels that Bismarck was prepared for a partition, certainly a reasonable position to take—Bosnia to Austria, Bessarabia to Russia, Egypt to England, and North African areas to France and Italy. He then writes of the German Chancellor's failure 'to attract England to a scheme for the partition of Turkey' in order to prevent an Austro-Russian war. Bismarck wished an understanding with London whether or not a war occurred, though he certainly wished to avoid an Austro-Russian conflict if possible. If British support could be bought by opposing any change in the territorial *status quo*, he was, as he explicitly told Russell, ready to do this. Only Taylor has questioned, correctly I believe, Bismarck's motivation as a desire to settle the Eastern Question by means of a Great European partition. He interprets Bismarck's object as a safeguard against a too close Franco-Russian friendship.[13]

It seems much more likely that the object of his approach to Britain was what he told Russell, an understanding with England for which he was prepared to support or oppose partition. Without British support, and again as he told Russell, he was prepared to go along with an Austro-Russian partition, but more in the sense of making a virtue of necessity—of a course preferable to an Austro-Russian war—than of an object desirable in and of itself. The German Chancellor was prepared to use partition as a means to an end—to create an understanding with England and if this failed to use it to avoid an Austro-Russian war, or not to use it at all.

Before Derby, who was still at Knowsley, could begin to formulate any reply to Bismarck's advance he received another dispatch from Russell written the day after the latter's talk with the German leader. 'The impression left on my mind by this conversation is that Prince Bismarck means what he says, and really desires a frank and cordial understanding with England . . .'[14]

Derby either misinterpreted or preferred to ignore Bismarck's offer. He composed his reply on the fifth at Knowsley, and sent it off on the morning of 6 January. 'Thank Prince Bismarck for friendly communication. Assure him of sincere desire of Her Majesty's Government to cooperate with that of Germany in regard of Turkish affairs. I will speak to Count Münster without reserve, but some days must pass before our opinion can be expressed since colleagues must be consulted.'[15]

Upon receiving Derby's answer, Russell sent a private letter to Bismarck conveying Derby's thanks for his friendly words and expressing the desire of the British Government to cooperate with Germany in regard to Turkey. The ambassador returned a private letter to the Foreign Secretary.

Bismarck's overtures to H.M.'s Govt are most gratifying and satisfactory and may be turned to good account at the proper moment. I have endeavoured to explain his secret motives in my no. 9 [see n. 2] and I see nothing in them that we need object to.

If we could interest Bismarck in the preservation of peace *with us* it would be a good thing and a great gain. An unaccountable, ambitious, irresponsible genius with a million of soldiers at his disposal like Bismarck, is a friend to cultivate . . .[16]

Russell's belief that a British connection was desired by Bismarck in the case of a European war was reinforced by Lyons, the British ambassador at Paris.

Like everyone else, he [Bismarck] feels sure that if there is a quarrel between Russia and Germany, France will side with Russia. In order to prevent his enemy being all powerful at sea, he must have the English fleet not merely neutral, but on his side. The only advantage he can offer to England is support on the Eastern question. . . . That he intends some day . . . to annex German Austria to German Empire I make no doubt . . .[17]

There was a hiatus in the negotiations for an Anglo-German Eastern understanding while attention was focused on the reception of the Andrássy note and especially on the British reaction to it. Bismarck, who had a cold, sent Bülow to tell the British ambassador of his gratification with Münster's reports of the latter's talks with Derby. 'The interest, anxiety and excitement about the adherence of H.M. Govt. to the Andrássy note has really been great and deep here, and final decision has been received with sincere satisfaction.'[18] After Britain had agreed to the note, Derby, through Münster, asked Bismarck on 26 January to delay its communication to the Porte until the Foreign Office had time to send its instructions to Elliot to associate his efforts in support of it. Berlin apparently attempted to do so, but there had already been such great delay in producing the note that Andrássy insisted upon its communication to the Porte at once.[19]

At the end of his secret telegram to Derby of 26 January, in which he reported Bismarck's regret of London's delay in requesting him to protract the delivery of the Andrássy note, Russell added another message. 'Prince Bismarck is most anxious to give his best support to the wishes of Her Majesty's Government at Constantinople as soon as he knows what they are.'[20]

It was a reasonable request. Bismarck had laid his cards on the table, though some suspected that all the meaningful ones were up his sleeve. He had asked London to tell him her desires, for further discussion perhaps, though he had indicated that whatever they were he was prepared to support them. On the back of the telegram, Tenterden wrote a note for Derby. 'Will you say anything to this. He seems to be hinting that his overtures have been scarcely met.' Derby's reply on the back of the same telegram was short. 'I will speak to you [Tenterden] as to this tomorrow'.[21]

Derby had been given a blank cheque to spend as he liked and was apparently unable to find anything to buy. Harris writes of the 'great interest' created 'in the inner circle of British politics' by Russell's dispatches, discussions going on in January and into February.[22] There seems to be no evidence, however, that until after 1 February anyone in England but Derby and Tenterden knew of Bismarck's offers. Surely Disraeli and Queen Victoria, had they known of them, would have stirred. Derby may have purposely kept Russell's dispatches from going to the Queen or the Prime Minister, as was normally the case, until February.

Near the end of January Bismarck asked Russell to come to see him and on 31 January in a very long conversation he again repeated his desire and offer of an understanding with England on the East for the third time in four weeks.

Bismarck spoke earnestly and impressively of the importance he attached to a timely understanding between our two governments. He begged I would once more explain to you that Germany having no direct interests in the East he is willing to further the interests of the friends of Germany who will support him in maintaining the peace of Europe. . . . He anxiously desires and solicits a thorough understanding with Her Majesty's Government, so as to be prepared before complications arise, to give his steady support to the policy of England in the East.

Austria and Russia have conflicting interests in the East which may at any moment lead to sudden and serious differences between them, when Germany . . . may have to take sides, and in so doing a previous knowledge of the views of H.M. Govt would enable him by adopting those views and making them his own, to secure beforehand the moral support of England in seeking to keep the peace between Austria and Russia in Turkey.
. . .

I [Russell] thought it more prudent not to go beyond the usual assurances that he would find England ever ready to cooperate with Germany for peace and 'status quo'—until I hear from you whether you wish to encourage these overtures or discourage them—If the former, it would be necessary to send him some distinct message as to what you are most prepared to sanction in Turkey—if the latter, you must expect to see him drop England and offer his services to some other Power.[23]

In typical fashion Derby slowly began to peek outside his co-

coon. He wrote to Russell privately, on 2 February, asking the ambassador how best to respond to Bismarck's friendly initiatives. Russell had already done this at the end of his letter of 1 February, as he pointed out to the Foreign Secretary in his reply. But again, the ambassador explained:

Bismarck foresees that sooner or later Austria and Russia must quarrel over the spoils of European Turkey . . .

He . . . might be dragged into a war, he wishes to avoid. To save himself from his friends . . . he would gladly espouse the views of England and declare them his own, for he thinks that the moral influence of England and Germany combined, would be sufficient to put off for some years longer the dismemberment of European Turkey and prevent the outbreak of war.

Bismarck does not propose or offer an exclusive alliance with England which he knows would be inconsistent with our modes of action, but he hopes for an understanding with England to keep Turkey together a few years longer in spite of Russia, and of Austria . . .

That is to the best of my knowledge Bismarck's present policy. If you wish to encourage it . . . it would be necessary to tell him distinctly what the views and wishes of H.M. Govt. are in respect to the future of Turkey and invite an exchange of ideas. . . . A preliminary exchange of ideas is in no way binding and serves to clear the political horizon.

If . . . you see no reason to encourage his confidence we can leave matters as they are but as Bismarck has always two strings to his bow, he will seek some other combination in his fertile brain and offer his services elsewhere.

In either case I think some *more* direct and distinct acknowledgment of his friendly contentions would be desirable as well as prudent, so as to avoid offending his susceptible nature without cause. After all, Bismarck is not an enemy we can afford to despise.[24]

Bismarck, far from enticing Britain to partition, appeared to Russell to be seeking her aid to prevent it. This was so because nearly everyone associated such a dissolution of the Ottoman Empire with the probable outbreak of a European war, which all wished to avoid, including and especially Bismarck.

It is only now, in the first week of February, that evidence exists to show that Disraeli and Queen Victoria were aware of Bismarck's overtures, a situation which may have been due to the Foreign Secretary's attempt to avoid an understanding before wider discussion could add to its significance. The Queen wrote to her private secretary after a talk with Disraeli.

This is an important letter of wh. Genl. Ponsonby shd take some note. Mr. Disraeli is very anxious that we shd act with Bismarck who evidently wishes it and wishes the Queen to urge it strongly on Lord Derby who is too cautious he says and won't act. The Queen would be glad if Genl Ponsonby cd. write her a draft of a letter wh. she wd. write in sending back [to Derby] Ld Odo's and Mr. Lumley's letters.[25]

Ponsonby replied to the Queen's letter on the same day, favouring an Anglo-German compact but pointing out that Derby's cautiousness must derive from good reasons.

At the same time . . . Your Majesty's views are so good and so likely to produce good results that Lord Derby should hear them at once.

It is evident that Lord Odo is in favour of *a cordial understanding with Germany*. And as no ambitious designs are entertained by either nation, it is very probable that Russia . . . may agree.

The difficulty seems to be to define what policy any country has as regards *Turkey*. No one (except the King of Italy) wishes to dismember it.

And yet how to support it is the difficulty which oppresses all.[26]

On general grounds, because Albert had wanted it and because her daughter was married to the German Crown Prince, the Queen was always ready for a link between England and Germany. She urged Derby to action. 'He [Bismarck] is apparently honest in his wish for a good understanding with England, and at all points the object he aims at is the maintenance of peace. This being also our object, it would seem but natural that we should act together.'

The Queen considers that the importance of establishing a link between the two countries cannot be overrated, and desires earnestly to impress upon Lord Derby the necessity of authorizing Lord Odo Russell to enter into free and unrestricted communication with Prince Bismarck upon Eastern affairs.[27]

Derby agreed with the Queen that Bismarck's offer was one to be accepted, but one had to be aware, as he wrote to Her Majesty, 'that more may be intended by this communication than meets the eye'.

He cannot possess implicit confidence in Prince Bismarck's desire of peace, remembering the events of last spring [the war scare of 1875].

And he would like to see more clearly than he does what assistance England is expected to give in return for that which is offered.[28]

Derby wrote to Russell on 7 and 9 February about the danger of being duped by Bismarck but did authorize the ambassador to an exchange of ideas with the German Chancellor. It was now over five weeks since Bismarck had first suggested such an exchange. On the eleventh Derby had a talk with Münster to whom he strongly expressed the government's satisfaction at Bismarck's overture. He explained his delay in responding to his hesitancy in laying down general principles which would govern future action when such a future was unclear and events changed daily. The Foreign Secretary informed the ambassador of two general desires—maintenance of the territorial *status quo* in Turkey and the necessity to advise the Porte, urging such advice on it strongly.[29]

Russell, who perhaps felt that he had gone as far as he respectfully could in pressing Derby to respond to the German overtures, replied in the following way.

All you say is perfectly clear to me and quite what I feel myself. All I contended for, was, not to throw cold water on Bismarck's overtures for fear of dampening his desire for a friendly understanding from which we might derive useful information without necessarily committing ourselves to any one line of action.

You have now given me the authority I required to *question* him by a direct and distinct reply to his twice repeated message. I can now tell him that you are not unwilling to exchange ideas on the whole Eastern question with entire frankness, if he really wishes it himself, and by way of a first idea I can take as a text that a disturbance of the territorial 'status quo' in Turkey would be unfavourably looked upon by the people of England [not the Government of England]. . . . I shall be careful to commit you in no way.

No one can be more alive to the difficulty of dealing with such a man as Bismarck after five years experience of his vagaries, than I am—and while I believe him to be this year peaceably disposed, I adhere to what I said last year that we can never be certain that he may not be tempted, when least expected, to mobilize the army he has at his disposal.

At present he wants peace—and what he hopes to get from an understanding with us is the power to impose peace on Russia and Austria if they should quarrel in Turkey . . .[30]

When Disraeli read Derby's draft report to Russell of his talk with Münster on the eleventh, he indicated there was a lack of warmth in the draft and proceeded to explain the nature of the German Chancellor.

You have to deal with a man who is dangerous but who is sincere and who will act straight forward with an English minister whose sense of honour he appreciates, a man, too, very sensitive and impulsive.

The step he is now taking is one wh. I believe he has long and often meditated, but he was piqued by our doctrinaire non-intervention, and all that.[31]

Following Disraeli's suggestion, Derby wrote a second dispatch to Russell incorporating the Prime Minister's idea in a letter more defensive and suspicious than the one which drew Disraeli's reaction. Derby wrote that Britain of course desired no 'exclusive alliance' but greatly wished the maintenance of European peace which combined action with Germany might promote. Such a combination could not be formally accepted until the motives which elicited Bismarck's overture were clearer and his expectations more precisely indicated. Russell was then instructed to discover the truth and to invite the Chancellor to give a complete and uninhibited expression of his expectations and desires.[32] Derby was being totally unreasonable. Bismarck had several times clearly indicated his intentions to maintain peace, to better control Austria and Russia, and to preserve Andrássy in power. The Foreign Secretary expected him to indicate his expectations of England in future and unforeseeable contingencies on which Derby was most hesitant even to exchange ideas.

In Derby's defence, his great suspicion of the German statesman, which Russell and the Queen shared, is understandable. He was believed to have caused the wars of 1864 and 1866 and to have been partly responsible for the war scare of 1875. Derby had witnessed how he had tricked Napoleon III over Luxemburg in 1867. It was generally felt by most European diplomats that in the characteristics of irresponsibility and deceitfulness he was matched only by Ignatiev. Bismarck had about himself a European credibility gap. One could not believe what he said when it was assumed that what he meant was left unspoken. The search for his hidden intentions was conducted not only by his contemporaries but by twentieth-century European historians. In the case of his attempt for an English understanding he was a prisoner of his reputation. But more usually he benefited from and used the distrust he inspired. It was assumed that Bismarck never said what he meant or really intended.

Following Derby's instructions of 16 February, Russell went to see Bismarck and delivered Derby's polite but very cool message. Bismarck cordially thanked the British ambassador and seemed to have changed tack when he said 'that all he had asked for was the faculty of exchanging ideas confidentially with Her Majesty's Government in case of danger'. Nothing was said now of any confidential understanding, only 'a frank and frequent exchange of ideas ... to prevent mischief, if things took a threatening turn'. Bismarck then said that there were two ways of 'dealing with the Eastern Question', to maintain the territorial *status quo* as at present or 'territorial modifications' if that became the only way to preserve peace. Russell thanked him for his frank communication of views and asked him if he could indicate specifically how Austria and Russia might partition the Ottoman Empire. Bismarck replied that he could not. Russell concluded the long report of his talk with the impression that Bismarck wished to be ready for any eventuality and feared a too great Austro-Russian intimacy. In his private letter to Derby of the same date there is an addition not in his official dispatch.

The upshot of his confessions is that he would prefer a division of Turkey among his friends to a war for the integrity of her territory—but with careful management that contingency can still be put off if I am not mistaken.

I will continue now and then to encourage his confidence, but not his policy, which it is our interest to know and watch.[33]

Bismarck had cooled on the possibility of an English connection, and one could not blame him.[34] He had never offered a relationship of lashing affection, but several times he manifested a desire to move close enough for a warm hug and received from Derby after a long wait only a frosty smile. Bismarck had not changed, but was only doing what he said was a possibility from the first—that, if left to himself, he would not oppose an Austro-Russian partition of European

Turkey, especially as an alternative preferable to an Austro-Russian war. Derby's distrust and lack of initiative left the German statesman no option but to accept an exchange of ideas in lieu of a co-ordination of policies. He asked the British Government for a policy he could support at Vienna, St. Petersburg, and Constantinople, but Derby had none to give.[35] Disraeli, who was certainly alive to the importance of prestige and influence and the awkward and debilitating position that isolation created for his government in Eastern affairs, did push Derby but not very hard. He did attempt to use the Queen's influence with the Foreign Secretary and then seems to have retired, save for the brief effort he made on 15 February to get Derby to respond more warmly to Bismarck. Perhaps he too came to believe that Bismarck wished for a territorial partition of the Ottoman Empire and that it was not in his interest to destroy what he meant to preserve. The Anglo-German exchange could have ended worse than it did, and for Britain an opportunity had been lost to influence Eastern affairs with the support of the strongest Continental Power. Derby was mainly responsible for the failure to move closer by dragging his feet, which action killed an Anglo-German entente. His extreme cautiousness was a result of his fear and distrust of a partnership with Bismarck, especially as it was difficult for him to believe that Bismarck meant peace instead of war. The latter, by enlightening Derby as to the intentions of Andrássy and Gorchakov, enabled the Foreign Secretary to dissipate any anxiety he felt over Austro-Russian ulterior motives in proposing the Andrássy note. Ironically, the man who convinced Derby of the innocence of others was unable sufficiently to erase the doubts of the English minister about his own.

Within a week of the end of the attempt at an Anglo-German understanding, the Porte officially accepted the Andrássy note. Though there was great doubt that the note would lead to a pacification of the insurrection, there was hope that such would be the case. As there was nearly universal belief in a still greater Balkan explosion if the insurrection continued into the spring, many eyes closely and anxiously followed the effect of the advice of Europe on both the rebels and the Turks.

## 6 WINDING DOWN THE INSURRECTION

THE PORTE, though faced with an impossible situation, did less than it could in helping itself. There was indifference, disbelief, and hostility on the part of its subjects to proclaimed reform and open aid and refuge for the rebels came from Montenegro and Serbia which the Ottoman Government was warned by the Powers not to attack. Austria could not or would not close her own frontier and Russia, equally well disposed officially, but with a Balkan diplomatic staff, with the major exception of her ambassador at Vienna, which transmitted its official instructions but at the same time gave aid and encouragement to the rebels and helped Montenegro and Serbia prepare for war. Finally, while all the Great Powers watched expectantly as a bankrupt Government with few motivated and capable provincial officials executed costly though promised reforms, Austria was to attempt to persuade the rebels to lay down their arms and return to their homes through her officials in Dalmatia and Croatia, most of whom sympathized with and were of the same ethnic stock as the rebels.

It was little wonder, therefore, that the execution of the firman and the Andrássy note was not done smoothly or effectively. One of the reforms was opposed by both the Porte and its Christian subjects; this was the adjustment of the tax on Christians for exemption from military service. To meet the legitimate grievance that such a tax should not be levied on children and old men long past the age of military activity, the firman of December restricted the tax to those who were of an age for army service. In order not to lose badly needed revenue the Porte was prepared to raise the amount to be paid by each individual of military age. The latter, of course, declared themselves unable to pay more.

The Porte drew up lengthy instructions for provincial governors-general on reforms and their manner of execution, but unfortunately often made poor appointments to these posts and then changed occupants every two or three months.[1]

Equally serious were the poor judicial appointments about which Elliot complained to the Ottoman Government, as grievances relating to the administration of justice were rife. The difficulty here was the low pay given to judges, the ambassador commenting that he gave more to his own coachman, and worse, that these insufficient salaries were usually in arrears.

Men of integrity and character will not accept these posts, which consequently fall in the hands of those who know that it will be easy for them to cover the insufficiency of their salaries by illicit gains.
. . .
The already paltry salaries have been reduced to a scale which honest and competent men can hardly be expected to accept.

The financial embarrassments cannot be fairly alleged in attenuation of this unfortunate resolution, for I am assured that sufficient salaries for the judges and officers of the courts could be provided out of the legitimate fees . . .[2]

A further difficulty faced by Constantinople in executing reform was the conflict and rivalry of three sets of Turkish officials. In Bosnia and Hercegovina there were the governor-general for each province, the chief military authority leading the fight against the rebels, and the commissioners for reform and pacification sent out from Constantinople. By the end of April the British consuls at Mostar and Sarajevo were agreed that the reforms had not been successfully applied and that the general situation was very bad if not critical.

No doubt the position of Haidar Effendi [reform commissioner] is an exceedingly difficult one. Being subordinate to the Governor-General, he cannot take the initiative in any matter. . . . The local Medjlisses [councils] have been re-elected, exactly as in former years, and without any regard to the interests and wishes of the people in general. The 'Bedel-i-askerich' or tax in lieu of military service, is being exacted as heretofore. . . . The state of the Treasury is so low that even the civil employees no longer receive their salaries, and army contractors have such large sums to receive that they refuse to deliver any further supplies . . .[3]

Ali Pasha, the Ottoman Governor of Hercegovina, was a man of some ability, but he could not control his military commander, Mouhktar Pasha. On the other hand, Ibrahim Pasha, the Governor of Bosnia, was so incompetent that Holmes, the

British consul at Mostar, urged his replacement without delay.

Holmes was almost despondent and summed up an impossible state of affairs for which he could not imagine any acceptable arrangement.

When one witnesses the incompetence of the Government as evidenced in the appointments it makes, and the confusion of the orders it issues, its total indigence, the incapacity of most of the authorities, complicated by their jealousy and conflicting pretensions, famine staring one in the face, the insufficiency of troops, and the difficulty of maintaining even those now in the country, the hopelessness of executing reforms, with a divided population regarding each other with feelings of mutual fear, hatred, and vengeance, deepened by religious fanaticism, and the continuance of political intrigues by agents of all kinds with or without the knowledge of their respective Governments, the man who can hope for any satisfactory results must be sanguine indeed . . .[4]

Holmes might have added, had he known it, one further fact to his list; Midhat Pasha and other Ottoman 'Liberals' were planning to depose the Sultan, Abdul Aziz, and create a representative Parliament for the whole of the Ottoman Empire.[5]

Prospects could hardly have been more dismal and not a few thought that the 'sick man' was at least in his dying throes. Elliot wrote that he felt that things were worse than they had ever been and the German Emperor referred to Turkey's state as beyond sickness and approaching disintegration.[6]

The failure of the execution of the reforms was met by a refusal of the rebels and refugees to be pacified, the former intent upon carrying on the fight, the latter unwilling to return to often desolated homes. Again one of the obstacles was the lack of money and provisions to repatriate the Christian Slavs who had gone into Austrian Dalmatia and another was the fear by the latter of being met upon their return by local Muslim violence and oppression. The Porte attempted to overcome this by appointing special agents to dispense protection and 'pecuniary relief' as well as by a promise to remit temporarily some taxation on those who agreed to return to their homes. Austria-Hungary had been requested to inform the refugees within her territory of these provisions.[7]

. The number of individuals to be repatriated was large,

Vienna estimating the number within Austria-Hungary alone at 65,000, but Andrássy was optimistic that promised reforms and the amnesty offered by the Sultan would succeed in bringing pacification, the difficulties notwithstanding.[8] Apart from the lack of money, it was also found that the Porte lacked the necessary troops, who had their hands full with the rebels, to ensure the safe passage of the refugees from Austria to their homes in Bosnia. The Turkish Governor of Hercegovina estimated that his Government would face the task of supporting a total of 300,000 impoverished refugees. If this were not sufficient discouragement, there was also anxiety among the refugees that if they did return home while the insurrection continued they would be driven out by the insurgents even when their villages escaped the fate of being fields of battle.[9]

The Porte did try one tactic, unsuccessfully, to attract its subjects back. In mid-February Constantinople had announced an amnesty for those who would return to their lands.

The Porte had proposed to accompany the promulgation of the amnesty with a declaration that the property of those who did not avail themselves of it would be confiscated and given to the refugees or insurgents returning to their allegiance, but Count Andrassy having represented that such a declaration would be unpolitic . . . the declaration will be amended to the effect that the property of those not accepting the amnesty will be sold, and the proceeds applied to relieve the distress of the sufferers from the insurrection.[10]

Andrássy tried another tack by asking London whether it could not assist the Turkish Government to raise the necessary money for pacification. Buchanan, the British ambassador, gave Andrássy no hope for such a request, but at least had the tact not to use the word 'loan' in reporting the step of the Austrian minister to Derby.[11]

Apart from Andrássy there was another optimist, one M. Vassilitsky, known as the 'King of Trebigñe' (a village in Hercegovina), who was being employed in Ragusa as the principal dispenser of Russian clothes, food, and money sent for the Hercegovinian refugees. His suggestion for pacification which had both some merit and much ulterior purpose was twofold. First, to remove part of the Turkish troops from Hercegovina and to concentrate the remainder in three or four fixed garrisons; then European commissioners, perhaps the consular commission at Mostar, would supervise and guarantee the supply of provisions and other aid to the refugees.[12]

As the spring approached, pacification was making small or no progress. Generals Mollinary and Rodich, respectively governors of Austrian Croatia and Dalmatia, failed to induce the refugees in Austria to return to Ottoman territory. Nor did the two Turkish commissioners fare any better. They offered not ungenerous terms to refugees and insurgents toward the end of March but the former did not comply, fearing a renewal of hostilities between insurgents and Turks from which, if they returned, they would suffer much.[13] At the end of March a meeting was arranged between Ali Pasha and Baron Rodich in an attempt at Austro-Turkish co-operation to arrange what each singly had failed to effect. Though the meeting succeeded in producing an armistice of twelve days beginning on 1 April, it created nothing but Austro-Turkish recrimination on the question of the repatriation of refugees. The attempt to order or entice a starving population to return to 'a wasted wilderness' proved impossible. By the end of the third week in April Gorchakov admitted that all hope of pacification had vanished.[14]

The non-execution of reforms and the refusal by refugees to return to their homes was matched by the failure to persuade the active rebels to lay down their arms. The insurgents, with few if any exceptions, seemed determined to fight to the end rather than again accept Ottoman authority. Yonin, the Russian consul at Ragusa, carried the Turkish offer of an amnesty to Montenegro where he met the insurgent chiefs who refused the Sultan's offer. Andrássy ordered General Rodich to arrange a conference between the insurgent chiefs and the Turkish military commander, which he was also to attend, the Porte having consented to a twelve-day suspension of hostilities for this purpose.[15]

It was agreed that hostilities would be suspended from 1 to 12 April during which time the insurgents and Nicholas of Montenegro would allow the Turks to supply their beleaguered fortress of Niksic, on the frontier between Hercegovina and Montenegro, and meet with Rodich and the Ottoman representatives. But in the meantime fighting continued with occasional Turkish defeats, and at the beginning of April a serious rising occurred in Turkish Croatia which previously had been largely peaceful. When the meeting with the insurgents occurred at Sutorina, conditions were given by them to Baron Rodich to be satisfied before the rebels would submit: Christians not to be disarmed, guarantees of reform under consular commission or foreign commissioners, precise information as to the meaning of 'supporting and installing refugees,' and finally, Turkish troops to be withdrawn into fortified places.[16]

When Andrássy heard the rebel terms he telegraphed Constantinople to inform the Turks of his disapproval of the insurgent demands and advised the Porte not to add a single concession beyond those already promised. Gorchakov disapproved Andrássy's rejection of the insurgent counter-proposals especially as the Austrian minister's reaction had been given without previous communication with St. Petersburg. Andrássy then, with British support, attempted to prolong the suspension of hostilities in the hope of submission by the rebels, but without success. A Turkish force attempted to push through to revictual Niksic and was met by insurgent bands. Fighting had thus begun again, the meeting at Sutorina having failed to bring about an agreement between the rebels and the Turks. At the end of April Mouhktar Pasha was able to reach Niksic and provision the fortress.

In Britain, Gladstone, who had been relatively quiet, gave as his personal view that which must have been in the minds of some if not nearly all of the rebels. 'If the Turks expect the Herzegovinians to lay down their arms upon a renewal of promises so shamelessly broken after 1856, I hope in God they will be disappointed. Great events seem to be drawing near in the East.'[17]

There seemed no way out of the impasse. The rebels naturally hesitated to submit and place themselves back under Ottoman authority which they had greatly damaged, without some European control which both the Turks and Andrássy opposed. On the other hand, it was apparently beyond the power of Ottoman forces to suppress the insurrection in Hercegovina as long as the fiction of Montenegrin neutrality had to be respected and the Austrian border remained open to the insurgents.[18]

There appeared to be a sincere disposition on the part of Vienna to close her border; such was not the case, however, with Austria's Slavic subjects and officials in Dalmatia and Croatia. Andrássy was not blind to this, but his own position in the government was not so secure that he could afford to stamp down too hard upon Slavic Austria-Hungary, nor did he wish to drive the Balkan Slavs generally into the hands of Ignatiev. Derby instructed Buchanan to bring formally to the attention of the Austrian Government a report of a recent skirmish on the Dalmatian border which involved men and ammunition that had come from Austrian territory.[19] When Buchanan delivered his message, Andrássy replied that measures were being taken to close the border and added that his government was very anxious to effect an end to an insurrection which was nearly as damaging to Austrian interests as it was to Turkey's.[20] Monson, the British consul, wrote of the situation to his superior in Vienna.

> Everyone agrees also that the reason . . . [the frontier is open] is the connivance of the Austrian officials. . . . From Baron Rodich down to the humblest douanier, all are more or less warmly in favour of the insurgents! All the officials are Slavs; and they take no pains to conceal their sympathies. . . . The Insurgent chiefs come and go as they please, and hold their meetings openly at a cafe in front of my hotel . . .[21]

Andrássy did attempt, unsuccessfully, to close the frontier but his efforts aroused great resentment among Austria's Dalmatian Slavs who loudly complained that Slavic interests should not be thwarted by the selfishness and arrogance of a few Magyars.[22] In spite of the official efforts of Vienna, border crossings continued, increasingly from Croatia, as did those in Dalmatia. The work of Rodich in Dalmatia and Mollinary in Croatia may not only have permitted open frontiers but also may have been partly responsible for the failure of pacification. The British ambassador in Vienna thought so. 'Count Andrássy doubtless feels that his police . . . and the efforts he is making to bring about an arrangement, are being compromised by the luke warm support of General Rodich, who apparently, while obeying the letter of his instructions has not been inspired by their spirit, or acted with the energy and firmness necessary to convince the insurgents . . .'[23]

The other serious obstacle to suppressing the insurrection was the activity of Montenegro. Any Turkish military action against the principality was prohibited by Russia, but suggestions were made that Prince Nicholas might be bought off by a Turkish recognition of his country's independence and for a cession of territory—the frontier area and the port of Spizza being most often mentioned.[24] Rumours concerning negotiations for a territorial cession to Montenegro caused a sensation in Belgrade which did not look with favour upon such a gain for her only rival for leadership of the Serbs. When Ignatiev made a strong appeal to the Sultan for a territorial cession to Montenegro, the latter gave a firm refusal.

The Ignatiev–Andrássy rivalry affected this question, as pacification resulting merely from the Andrássy note would be seen as stemming from the influence of Austria, but if Montenegro received a territorial increase this would be attributed only to Russia. At the end of March Prince Nicholas offered to help with pacification for a recognition of independence and the cession of Spizza. Derby was not completely against an extension of Montenegro.

I have not given any support to the proposed cession of territory to Montenegro under present circumstances; not feeling sure whether any such proposal might not be regarded as a proof of weakness on the part of the Porte, and so encourage rather than disarm opposition; but I think it a question well worthy of consideration whether, in the event of peace being restored, the cession to Montenegro of some territory situated in the plain might not be advantageous.[25]

Andrássy opposed a cession in return for Nicholas's honest neutrality, as he described it as a proposal with no end, with Serbia, Romania, Greece, and Croatia then making similar territorial demands. Andrássy did not say so, but Buchanan felt his objections were also due to his refusal to grant Montenegro any coastline which would allow direct Russo-Montenegrin communication.[26]

When the Turks failed to reach an agreement with the rebels at Sutorina and the insurgents fought with Montenegrin aid to prevent the revictualing of Niksic, it appeared that despite repeated warnings from the Great Powers the Porte, feeling it had been duped by Nicholas and Rodich, was prepared at the end of the third week of April to attack Montenegro. Gorchakov at once requested the other Powers to help restrain Constantinople and for this purpose called a meeting in St. Petersburg with the representatives of the other five Powers. Once assembled the Russian Foreign Minister requested the five ambassadors to invite their governments to advise the Porte against the contemplated step.

Loftus's telegram from St. Petersburg containing the Russian Government's request arrived in London on 22 April, the same day London received a telegram from the Ottoman Government denying any intention of attacking Montenegro. Consequently, Derby did not instruct Elliot to make a representation at Constantinople, and Britain was the only Great Power which refrained from the collective warning to the Porte, as the other five ambassadors delivered their communications to the Ottoman Government. On 27 April Shuvalov called at the Foreign Office and communicated Gorchakov's anxiety that England's abstention might be seen at the Porte as an objection on her part to the warning to Turkey delivered by the other five Powers. Shuvalov asked what answer to this he might give to his government. At 6 p.m. of the same day Derby telegraphed his ambassador in St. Petersburg:

Your Excellency will explain to the Russian Government that Her Majesty's Government had not declined to act in concert with the other Powers in this matter; but that, the Porte having denied any intention of attacking Montenegro, any remonstrances had been anticipated.

Her Majesty's Government believed that this was understood also by all the Governments to whom the Russian Government had appealed.[27]

When Loftus delivered Derby's explanation to St. Petersburg, Gorchakov replied that England's non-participation might be misinterpreted and give the mistaken impression that she had parted from an association with the other five Powers. The Russian minister expressed a hope that the British Government would make known to the Porte its concurrence in the views of the European concert.[28]

Gorchakov's fear that recognition by the Turks of disunity among the Great Powers would give the Ottoman Government too much of a free hand in the Balkans was in the existing circumstances curious if not deceitful. While St. Petersburg required unanimous advice to and control of Constantinople, her own advice to the South Slavs was carried out under a modified central Asian technique. This tactic allowed Russia to benefit from two lines of policy only one of which the government of St. Petersburg would accept any responsibility for. Movement by Russian governors-general into Turcoman areas was winked at by the Government, which gave simultaneous protestations of innocence to British complaints, until formal annexation had occurred. In the Balkans the Tsar, Gorchakov, Jomini, and others in the central administration looked the other way while Ignatiev, Kartsov in Serbia, Yonin in Montenegro, and the other Pan-Slav diplomatic representatives followed a line which the Government often publicly disavowed, but could, at any moment, usually control or countermand, and which occasionally provided desirable services for the Government which could always deny responsibility or complicity. The danger in the use of such a system was the constant potential of having policy escape from the control of the official formulators.[29] What was occurring was no secret, at least to Elliot.

The Course that will be taken by Russia is less certain and we are met at the outset with the question, who represents the Russian policy.

The language of the Emperor and of Gorchakov is all that could be desired but that of Ignatiev and the acts of the Russian consul at Ragusa [Yonin] are quite the reverse.

I believe him [Ignatiev] in most cases to have pretty nearly carte blanche in the policy to be followed here, and also that his govt. do not wish him to keep them too well informed about his doings.

They allow him to work with the Slavic committees and it is more convenient to them to be left in ignorance of what goes on.[30]

It was generally recognized that restraint of Serbia and Montenegro, so necessary to prevent a Balkan explosion which all feared, would depend on the pressure and influence of Austria and Russia. Pressure and influence were applied but not always with desired effect. When a pacific representation was made to Nicholas of Montenegro and simultaneously to Prince Milan of Serbia, the last on February 17 by Kartsov, the Russian consul, no noticeable result, no abatement of Serbia's warlike preparations occurred, even though the advice was supported by the Austrian consul. Milan admitted to Wrede, the Austrian consul, that military preparations were going on but that they had no aggressive purpose. When the above *démarche* was also supported by the French consul, White, the British representative, considered whether the effect of the repetition of similar admonitions would be only the production of irritation.[31]

On 17 March Wrede demanded a pacific pledge from Milan, threatening an Austrian occupation of Serbia if compliance were not made. Before the Russian consul tardily supported this demand, Serbia met Austria's requirement by declaring that there were no hostile intentions against Turkey and that only ordinary military preparations had transpired. Elliot, at Constantinople, was not impressed and referred to the blatant disingenuousness of the explanation while visible efforts had been made to buy arms and horses.[32]

Until the Sutorina meeting, though Rodich and Ignatiev were conducting unfettered and personal diplomacy, Vienna and St. Petersburg were acting in unison and appeared to be sincere in wishing an end to the insurrection. When the rebels made known to Rodich their counter-proposals for submission, Andrássy refused to consider them and wished an Austro-Russian representation to be made to Prince Nicholas for the latter to insist on the submission of the rebels according to terms previously granted them. Gorchakov disagreed, and wished to consider the counter-proposals of the insurgents as a basis for negotiation. Further, he rejected the joint representation to Montenegro, and was sorry that Vienna neglected any previous communication with Russia before taking such decided action.

Austria and Russia did agree in opposing any Turkish attack on Montenegro, Andrássy threatening to close the port of Klek if the Ottoman Government refused to desist from the contemplated action. Austro-Russian harmony had been restored, but it had never been complete, as Loftus pointed out.

I could perceive that although there is a cordial wish . . . to act and cooperate with Austria . . . there is no harmony of views in regard to the mode or basis on which such an arrangement can be come to.

Count Andrassy appears to hold an arrangement within the limit of his note accepted by the Porte.

Prince Gortchakov seems to think that this Andrassy note should be adapted and harmonized as far as may be possible with the demands of the insurgents . . .[33]

The Northern Powers were making some effort to proclaim their unity. Beust showed Derby a dispatch from Andrássy which confirmed complete agreement between Austria, Germany, and Russia, and stated that any reports to the contrary were untrue.[34]

Melegari, the Italian Foreign Minister, was unconvinced of Austro-Russian entente, if only because of the activity of Ignatiev who was pressing the Porte to negotiate with the rebels on the basis of the latter's counter-proposals which Andrássy opposed. Whether the chinks in the unity between the Great Powers were the catalyst or whether there were other factors, Melegari made an almost identical offer to the one Bismarck had made to the British Government in January.

M. Melegari . . . could not see how the Powers, who had urged the Austrian programme on the acceptance of the Porte, could now turn round, after the Porte had shown every disposition to carry it into effect, and recommend something entirely different. He believed, he said, that the interests and policy of Her Majesty's Government and of the Italian Government were identical; that both desired the maintenance of existing territorial arrangements in the East, and the preservation of general peace in Europe. He should therefore be very glad to be informed of the opinion of Her Majesty's Government in regard to the new phase of the Herzegovina question, with a view to the two Governments acting in concert respecting it . . .
. . .

Mr Melegari informed me it was his intention to communicate also with the French Government on these matters.[35]

Derby received the above communication on 24 April. Four days later, hoping apparently to make use of the friendly disposition of Italy, the Foreign Secretary telegraphed Rome, and the other Powers as well, requesting an Italian representation at Cetinje to urge neutrality on Prince Nicholas of Montenegro.[36] Eight days later Derby replied to the Italian offer, Rome being kept waiting a much shorter time than had Berlin in January and February.

I should wish you [Paget] to assure M. Melegari that Her Majesty's Government sincerely share his desire for concerted action, and will be glad to find that the line of policy pursued by the two countries is identic. At this moment, however, the state of affairs seems so unsettled and changes so rapidly, and the information received is of so partial and confused a character, that it seems difficult to form a positive opinion as to any course of action which would be productive of good results.[37]

Translated, this seemed to mean that if I had a policy I should very much like your support. Writing to Disraeli at approximately the same time about an impending Cabinet meeting, Derby thought that there was little to discuss about Foreign Office matters. 'And as to the great question of the East, there is nothing anyway urgent. Matters have come to a deadlock, and it is clearly for the Powers which initiated the policy of the Andrássy note to suggest a way out of the difficulty.'[38]

With the insurrection going strongly, the failure of the Andrássy reforms and the unwillingness of the Russian Government to hold Serbia and Montenegro in check any longer, Melegari's phrase was not inaccurate. A new chapter or phase of the Hercegovina question had begun. To devise a policy appropriate to events, a meeting was arranged in Berlin for the second week in May at which the leaders of Austria, Russia, and Germany would seek in Derby's words a new solution to a difficult problem. The Foreign Secretary's expectation was to be fulfilled, but it remained to be seen how well he would like the solution. In the meantime the British Government was content to go no further than to attempt to contain an insurrection, which the Turks could not extinguish, fearing that territorial rearrangements, which might have the desired effect, would only make the general situation worse.

ANDRÁSSY ARRIVED in Berlin on 10 May for his meeting with Gorchakov and Bismarck. He talked with the latter who failed to convince the Austrian minister of the desirability of the partition of Turkey.[1] The following day Alexander II and Gorchakov reached the German capital and two days of talks ensued during which Andrássy successfully objected, with German support, to Gorchakov's schemes for an international reform commission and autonomy for Bosnia-Hercegovina. The document agreed to by the evening of 12 May reflected largely the ideas and policy of Andrássy, as had been the case previously with the note of December and the consular commission of August.[2] The ambassadors of Britain, France, and Italy were then requested by Bismarck to meet with Gorchakov, Andrássy, and himself on the afternoon of the thirteenth.[3]

Bismarck and Gorchakov opened the meeting of the representatives of the six Powers held at the house of the German Chancellor by explaining the necessity created for Austria, Russia, and Germany to agree on a new arrangement for Balkan pacification. Insufficient results of previous efforts at reform, the affair at Salonica,[4] and the great agitation and excitement which existed at Constantinople and throughout European Turkey were given as justification for the latest attempt by the three Powers to bring peace to the Balkans. The Russian minister said that none of the previously promised reforms had been executed by the Porte but that the new proposal of the three Empires had for its object the maintenance of Turkish integrity, but with substantial changes, and that the agreement of the three Eastern Powers on the above end, as well as on the individual points of the new note, was complete. Jomini then read the new note and asked for the reaction of the Italian, French, and British ambassadors. Russell replied that he was without instructions but that he would refer the new note or memorandum to London at once. Upon Gorchakov's observation that from his own correspondence he expected Derby's support, the British ambassador said that he thought that it would be given. The three ambassadors were then pressed to obtain a quick response from their governments.[5]

The memorandum began with insistence at Constantinople upon an armistice lasting two months to facilitate direct negotiations between the Turks and the rebels based on the following five points:

1. Porte to provide for the reconstruction of houses and churches and to supply food for the refugees until they could supply their own.

2. To help with the distribution of relief, the Andrássy note's mixed commission would be used. The head of the commission would be a Christian Hercegovinian and after the suspension of hostilities the members of the group would be elected and would represent both Catholic and Orthodox Christians.

3. The Porte to concentrate its troops at some place to be settled later.

4. The Christians as well as the Turks to keep their arms.

5. The consuls or representatives of the Powers to watch over the application of reforms and return of the population.

The memorandum ended on a somewhat ominous and ambiguous note. If, after the expiration of the armistice, hostilities continued, the three Powers would sanction an accord to arrange more 'efficacious measures' as might be required to re-establish peace.[6]

In his private letter to Derby, written on the same day as his meeting with Bismarck, Gorchakov, and Andrássy, Russell hoped that Derby would be able to give it a general acceptance similar to that given to the Andrássy note as a break with the three Powers would leave Britain completely isolated in the East. Russell did not think the Berlin memorandum would bring pacification, but he felt two months of peace would be valuable. 'Both Gorchakov and Bismarck told me to assure you they wished to maintain the territorial 'status quo' in Turkey. Gorchakov added on his honour that Russia wanted nothing for herself and attached the highest importance to a cordial cooperation with England.'[7]

The ambassador's telegraphic report of the memorandum reached London late on the evening of Saturday the thirteenth.[8] That evening Tenterden, the Under Secretary, drew up for his chief a fairly long and very negative criticism of the Berlin proposal. In fact, he found much to which serious objection could be made. The five points of the memorandum were described as the same as the rebel demands at Sutorina which the Porte already had refused to consider and the wording was too strong to be used at Constantinople. Who was to pay for the feeding of refugees and the rebuilding? How could the returning refugees be protected from their Muslim neighbours if Turkish troops were to be concentrated only at given places? How could arming of the Christians lead to peace? Consular intervention would be the equivalent of governing the provinces with a foreign agency. The threat of more efficacious measures and the intervention of the Powers could only be seen by the insurgents as an invitation not to submit, but to wait for the greater gains to be achieved through their intervention.

This is as much as to say to the Porte—you shall not suppress the insurrection by arms. It looks to me as though the three Powers under the direction of Russia are menacing an intervention but cannot come to an accord—as to what it is to be and that the armistice is a mere stop gap.

What is to be said in reply to the Chancellors is a very difficult matter to determine.

An armistice . . . is not of itself unreasonable. . . . [But] an armistice will certainly one wd. suppose, arouse the Mohametans throughout the Empire if forced on Turkey by the 3 Powers . . .

. . .

That this plan is intended to assist the insurgents against the Porte and to lead to further intervention, I have no doubt.

. . .

That it may lead to a Mohametan outbreak is not impossible.

On the whole I should be disposed to say that the best reply would be that H.M. Govt. were prepared to join in recommending an armistice with a view to the return of the population but could not pledge themselves to the details of the basis proposed for negotiations . . .[9]

Derby had come to rely on Tenterden as previously he had leaned on Hammond during his earlier and first appointment as Secretary of State. His Under-Secretary's shrewd but negative response was not calculated to attract his chief's support even for the armistice alone.

Owing to a foul-up at the Foreign Office, Disraeli and the Queen did not receive copies of the Berlin note until Sunday afternoon, which under normal circumstances would have been more than sufficiently rapid, but which under the present urgent conditions was not considered so. Disraeli was furious at the delay, but the relatively trivial incident only sparked off a frustration that had been building up within the Prime Minister for a longer period of time. Since the beginning of the year Disraeli had given veiled signs, as if to hide them from himself, of his vexation and irritation over Derby's handling of affairs. He had mixed some acid in his ink when he earlier wrote to the Queen of the Foreign Secretary's habit of being away from the office at weekends. He could not bring himself to criticize Derby directly or openly. Instead the shafts of his dissatisfaction sought other and often undeserving targets. There were repeated criticisms of the want of discipline within the Foreign Office, volleys of sarcasm, worthy of Bismarck, heaped upon nearly all British ambassadors and scathing vituperation for most foreign ambassadors and statesmen. When, a week earlier, Disraeli had written to Derby apropos an Anglo-German understanding that 'Odo writes, as if it were something that had happened in a dream', it would have been more accurate to have substituted the Foreign Secretary's name for that of the British ambassador. Without frequent and safer outlets for accumulated exasperation, for which, of course, Derby was only partly responsible, the Prime Minister would have climbed up the wall. As it was, he frequently hit the ceiling. At the Cabinet meeting to consider Britain's answer to the Andrássy note, Derby had led the meeting. In a few days, when that same body was to meet to respond to the Berlin memorandum, there would be another chairman taking the lead.

Normally, Disraeli's handling of the Foreign Secretary was calculated to raise his confidence in order to enable him to act. The Prime Minister realized that criticism would only produce withdrawal in Derby and so he gave encouragement, often in the form of a prediction of public approbation for the line which Disraeli was encouraging the Foreign Secretary to take.

As this last tactic did not sufficiently overcome Derby's reserve, Disraeli was prepared to take the reins himself and to drag with him a man he could not always push from behind. In this task he enlisted the support of the Queen to bring royal pressure upon his friend.

The Queen was anxious about British isolation and professed to believe, as did some of her ministers, in the existence of a German understanding. She instructed Ponsonby to write to Disraeli about her puzzlement over the fact that Germany had not communicated its views after they had indicated a wish to work in tandem.[10] She manifested more concern than her Prime Minister over a combination of the Eastern Powers without England and directed her private secretary to seek out Disraeli and speak to him of her fears. As Ponsonby found the Prime Minister in a Cabinet meeting when he called, he left a note for him.[11]

On Sunday, 14 May Disraeli wrote to the Queen that he intended to bring before Lord Derby's attention the absence of discipline in the Foreign Office.[12] Ponsonby was also irritated at the delay in sending the Berlin memorandum on to the Prime Minister and the Queen, as time was vital. 'It is incredible that the telegram should not have been sent to Your Majesty and Mr. Disraeli at once. As he [Disraeli] received it so late it makes it most difficult for the government to come to a decision before tomorrow morning.'[13] No attempt was made, however, to hold a Cabinet meeting on Monday, 15 May, the day that Gorchakov had indicated a desire to hear affirmatively from London. Apparently, the Prime Minister was less concerned about responding than he had been about the delay in receiving. He did send a line to Derby, informing him that he had called a Cabinet for Tuesday at one as there had been pressure from colleagues to do so.[14]

Though no official reply was transmitted on Monday, Berlin received a good intimation of what to expect when Münster, the German ambassador, talked with Derby at the Foreign Office, as Shuvalov did afterwards as well.

Derby expressed only his initial reaction to Münster, as the Cabinet had not yet met, and he repeated, slightly rephrased, nearly all of Tenterden's memorandum written two days before. He omitted the only mildly positive part of it, by saying nothing about supporting the armistice.

I could not, however, but remark that the intimation contained in the last paragraph of the Memorandum [Berlin], seemed to leave the disposal of events wholly with the insurgents. It almost amounted to an invitation to them to refuse to entertain any terms that were likely or possible to be offered, since it gave them to understand that by continuing the insurrection they would secure further intervention on their behalf.[15]

To the Russian ambassador, Derby repeated his, or rather Tenterden's, words to Münster. Shuvalov attempted to retrieve something by pointing out to Derby how it was possible to decline the memorandum without refusing it.

Count Shuvaloff admitted that the proposals, as they stood, seemed open to objections in points of detail. He thought, however, that most, if not all of these, might be obviated by separating the scheme into two parts, and keeping the plan of a renewed armistice distinct from the ulterior negotiations.

If we would once succeed, he said, in getting an armistice of two months agreed to ... there would be time to consider at leisure the means of arriving at a permanent settlement, and the Powers would be freed from the necessity of committing themselves at once to the details of the project as it now stood.[16]

Elliot anticipated a telegraphic request from London for his opinion, but assumed that what was wanted was an idea of the Ottoman response to the memorandum and he had not yet been able to see the new Grand Vizier to learn it. He telegraphed the Foreign Office that he did not expect a strong objection from the Porte except to the second and fifth clauses which contained the mixed commission and supervision by the consuls.[17]

When Derby entered the Cabinet on the afternoon of 16 May, he knew that France and Italy had already accepted the Berlin proposal, that Russell was urging Britain to do the same, and that Elliot did not anticipate an outright Turkish rejection. Derby had even told the Russian ambassador that he would press for the acceptance of the armistice. On the other hand, he personally objected to the memorandum and was armed with Tenterden's negative analysis. He may also have known of Disraeli's opposition as both the Foreign Secretary and the Prime Minister were in London.[18] It is possible, though no proof can be offered, that the Berlin memorandum itself had been framed to same extent with Derby in mind, allowing him to associate or adhere to it generally, without fully accepting all the small print. If Britain would agree at least to the armistice, then, as in the case of the Andrássy note, a light glaze of British mustard might be smeared over an Austrian bratwurst.

Disraeli came to the meeting of the ministers suffering from physical decline—asthma, bronchitis, and gout—and mortification caused by wounded and outraged sensibilities. The latter were elicited by an apparent disdain by the Dreikaiserbund for the opinion and influence of Britain. While he recognized that he could not control the dreaded 'north-west blast' which made him ill, he intended to raise the image of his Government and its prestige on the Continent, and, in fact, had already succeeded in doing so to some extent. Opposition and hatred he could give back, but contempt, which was not so easy to return, was insupportable. While he exaggerated the lack of respect shown to Britain, it would be wrong to believe that it was entirely without foundation. London was not being treated like Bosnia and Montenegro, only like a recently crushed France and a new-born Italy. A combination of his own illness and Derby's timidity had muted his efforts in January and February to raise Britain's desirability through an association with Germany; he would brook no obstacles now to obtain for his country the treatment that he considered was her due.

This comes out in his heated conversation with Shuvalov on the day before the Cabinet met. Before the Russian ambassador's talk with the Foreign Secretary, Shuvalov had words with Disraeli at a social gathering in St. James's Palace. The Prime Minister said that Britain would have no response to the latest proposal since she had been treated as if she were Bosnia or Montenegro and had been given twenty-four hours to communicate a reply. Shuvalov answered that agreement to an armistice, which was an urgent necessity, did not require long consideration. Disraeli rejoined by saying that the armistice intended was for Turkey alone. At that moment the Prince of Wales arrived, and Disraeli suggested to Shuvalov that they shake hands to prevent the public confirmation of an unpleasant incident.[19]

On the afternoon of 16 May the Prime Minister opened the meeting of ministers by reading a memorandum which he had drawn up for the occasion. It was partially a rephrasing of Tenterden's original and hurried reaction. Each of the five points of the Berlin proposal were condemned as putting a knife into Turkey's heart and leading to her dissolution. Apart from not wishing to support a policy which he said he opposed, Disraeli referred in bitter terms to the cavalier treatment of England. 'It is almost a mockery for them to talk of a desire that the powers should act in concert and then exclude France, Italy, and England from their deliberations, and ask us by telegraph to say yes or no to propositions which we have never heard discussed.'

With an eye, perhaps, to Derby's plea, Disraeli allowed that were Turkey to agree he was prepared to suggest an armistice and a conference based upon the maintenance of the *status quo*. '[But] above all it is taking a leap in the dark to act in this matter before we know what Turkey herself thinks of the new programme, and it would seem that we may fairly tell the three Northern Powers, that a general concert cannot be attained by the course they are adopting.'[20] By his own report the meeting lasted one and a half hours and concluded with a general agreement to his own memorandum even though there was no attempt on his part to dominate the views of the rest of the Cabinet.[21]

Gathorne-Hardy, the Secretary of State for War, summed up the meeting in his diary on the day following. 'It is rather cool to ask it [British adhesion] by telegraph, as if they were to discuss and decide, and we only assent. To us the propositions seem impraticable in some particulars, and unfair in others, and behind all we see 'measures efficaces' which may mean armed intervention. We shall therefore, while aiming at an armistice, not adhere . . .'[22]

At 4.20 p.m., on the same afternoon as the Cabinet meeting, Derby's telegram went out to the British embassies. It was short.

Her Majesty's Government see grave objections to the plan put forward by the Three Powers, and are not prepared to press its adoption on the Porte.

A copy of the telegram was sent to Windsor and it brought forward an eruption of royal wrath, as the Queen feared the British refusal would encourage Turkish intransigence as well as lead the Porte to lean on England against the rest of Europe.

Pray cypher to Mr. Disraeli something to this effect. Viz. *why we dissent*—and whether this may *not* have a very serious effect, and if we are prepared to support the Porte if she declines to accept the proposals and saying that this ought not to have been sent without *her being told what were the reasons for separating ourselves from the other powers.*[23]

Almost as quickly, Russell's reaction to the British decision arrived from Berlin. As he had assumed some kind of British acceptance, his brief telegram, sent off at 11 p.m., was tinged with both frustration and mortification.

Am I to communicate rejection by Her Majesty's Government of the plan put forward by the three Powers officially to the German Government?
The consequences may be serious.[24]

Derby's reply asked what serious consequences the ambassador anticipated. The Foreign Secretary was puzzled as to the meaning of Russell's telegram, and Disraeli must have been as well, as he asked Derby to obtain a fuller explanation from Russell.

I am puzzled by O[do] R's [Russell's] telegram having just seen MacDonnell [secretary of the Embassy at Berlin] who tells me that he (O.R.) is quite aware of the impractical nature of the scheme, and expected us to withhold our assent . . .
I will ask as you suggest what are the dangers that Russell apprehends—but it is too late to draw back nor do we wish it.[25]

Odo's reply was dispatched on the eighteenth. He listed five serious dangers which might result from Britain's refusal to adhere: the encouragement it would give the Porte to resist; the difficulty for Britain of successfully supporting in Turkey a policy opposed by the three Eastern Powers; the more vigorous action by the three Powers it might induce in Turkey; the creating of situations that it would be desirable to postpone; and the fright it would create in financial circles.[26]

When Buchanan delivered Britain's refusal to adhere to the Berlin memorandum to Andrássy, who had returned to

Vienna, the latter defended the proposals and then 'expressed a hope that Her Majesty's Government would at least recommend the Porte to grant the proposed armistice, and that if they could not support the other proposals, they would not encourage the Porte to reject them'.[27] Beust, the Austrian ambassador in London, was instructed to make the same request to Derby. Derby's reply to the appeal for support of the armistice was negative, and seemed to contradict the Cabinet decision to support the armistice if the Porte agreed to such a cessation. The Foreign Secretary told Beust that he did not think the Porte would agree to an armistice because there would be no guarantee for its maintenance.

On the Turkish side, there was an organized government to deal with, and the generals of the Porte would not venture to break engagements into which they had been ordered to enter; but could the same thing be said of the insurgents? Had they recognized chiefs capable of enforcing obedience along the whole frontier? and if they had, could these chiefs be relied on? These were considerations which the Government of the Sultan could not overlook.

Beust then asked the Foreign Secretary if he would, at least, not oppose the Berlin proposal at Constantinople. Derby answered that he would not press his view but that it seemed silly to talk of ending the fighting while the ruler and people of Montenegro were permitted to aid and participate in the rebellion, as was now occurring.[28] The unanimity of the Cabinet decision and the nature of his own personality had apparently stiffened the Foreign Secretary's resolve to refuse the Berlin memorandum in its entirety and, as before, to continue to do nothing. The influence of Disraeli also contributed to the refusal by the Foreign Secretary.

The proposal to support an armistice, without any reference to the other propositions, is absurd. They [Austria and Russia] always argue, as if the armistice depended merely on the assent of the Turks
. . .

   I think that you will find, that public opinion will ratify your policy.[29]

After sending Russell a full explanation of Britain's non-adherence to be read to Bismarck, the Foreign Secretary sent off another dispatch to enlighten the Eastern Powers as

Disraeli wished. Derby complained that, as in the case of the Andrássy note, Britain had no opportunity of prior discussion.

Her Majesty's Government attach little importance to forms in matters of this kind, and would have readily accepted the present proposals had they appeared to them to afford a feasible plan for the pacification of the insurgent districts; but they cannot accept, for the sake of the mere appearance of concert, a scheme in the preparation of which they have not been consulted and which they do not believe calculated to effect the object with which they are informed it has been framed.

I leave it to Your Excellency's [Odo Russell] discretion how far it may be desirable that you should indicate the views of Her Majesty's Government in this respect in your communications with the German Government.[30]

As the Queen and Prime Minister still heartily favoured an Anglo-German understanding, perhaps more than ever, it is not surprising to find a further dispatch of the same date, reconfirming a telegram sent on 17 May, expressing a vague and meaningless British desire for German co-operation. Russell was instructed to tell Bismarck of the British Government's regret in having to separate from the German Government in respect to the Berlin memorandum. 'They [British government] would be glad to act in concert with the German Government in all matters so far as it may be possible to do so, since they believe that the interest of Germany and of Great Britain are equally directed to the maintenance of the territorial status quo and the preservation of European peace.'[31]

Andrássy's attempt to modify the British refusal was seconded by Germany, France, and Italy. All the Powers were trying to influence London to reconsider and support the armistice, and to refrain from advising a refusal at Constantinople.[32] Paris went so far as to indicate that it would hold off communicating the memorandum to the Turks in the hope of winning some kind of British adherence.[33] The farthest that any of the Powers seemed prepared to go in their reaction to British non-compliance was to express disappointment and a hope that London might reconsider and change its mind, at least on the armistice.

Derby's desire to escape any responsibility for a Turkish

refusal of the Berlin memorandum influenced him in giving a careful communication to the Porte of Britain's refusal. This, incidentally, satisfied the hope of the other Powers that England would abstain from advising the Porte to decline the Berlin proposals. In a conversation with the Turkish ambassador, Musurus Pasha, Derby made it clear how far he felt the Porte might count upon British support.

Her Majesty's Government had declined to join in proposals which they thought ill-advised, but both the circumstances and state of feeling in this country were very much changed since the Crimean War, and the Porte would be unwise to be led, by recollections of that period, to count upon more than the moral support of Her Majesty's Government in the event of no satisfactory solution of the present difficulties being found.[34]

Without going so far as advising the Turks to accept an armistice, both Derby and Elliot warned them to be cautious and conciliatory. 'The language I [Elliot] have been holding to the Porte is, that although Her Majesty's Government are indisposed to join Berlin proposals, they must not be considered as advising their rejection; and that the Five Powers being agreed, the Porte should rather point out what it considers objectionable in the proposals, than offend them by a summary objection.'[35]

Andrássy made a last attempt, reported by Buchanan on 26 May, to attract British support for the armistice. He decided to tell London the truth which, unfortunately for his purpose, came a bit too late to be effective. He began by defending the memorandum to the British ambassador, and touched on each one of the English sore points. He denied that an immediate reply had been asked in Berlin of the Italian, French, and British ambassadors.

[Andrássy] said, as the French and Italian Ambassadors spoke with confidence of the programme being accepted by their Governments, and Lord Odo Russell expressed a personal opinion that it would meet the views of Her Majesty's Government, Prince Gorchakov may have intimated a wish to receive an answer before his departure.

He spoke of the armistice as possibly favouring the Turks and that only by accepting it and making efforts for the return of the refugees could Serbia and Montenegro be separated. He hinted that if the armistice failed to bring pacification, the new measures to be arranged would not especially be aimed at Turkey. The Austro-Hungarian minister then told Buchanan to inform his chief confidentially what he could not write to Count Beust.

Austria can only maintain peace by effective compromises with Russia, and as he [Andrássy] failed in reconciling by telegraphic correspondence, he [Andrássy] went to Berlin, where Prince Gorchakov advocated measures he could not approve. . . . Andrassy says that he insisted on the programme adopted as the utmost concession he could make, stating his conviction that even it would be rejected by England. That it has been so he considered fortunate, as the independent attitude of Her Majesty's Government may be most useful in promoting Austrian as well as English interests. But to secure this advantage, a suspension of hostilities will, he says be absolutely necessary . . .[36]

Buchanan's two telegrams reporting his talk with Andrássy were received at the Foreign Office on 26 May. Six days were required for Derby to formulate his very polite no.[37]

On the same day as Andrássy's appeal to Buchanan to support the armistice proposal, Russell was able to see Bismarck and delivered Derby's tepid and polite desire, sent to him on 19 May, to co-operate with Germany in the interests of European peace and the territorial *status quo* of the Ottoman Empire.[38] In his reply to a distrustful London, Bismarck, as Andrássy, tried the truth and made an appeal for British support of Austria.

Prince Bismarck replied that he was gratified by Your Lordship's message, but he nevertheless regretted that Her Majesty's Government had separated themselves from the united action of the other five Powers. . . . Germany like England . . . was interested in the maintenance of peace, and peace, as matters now stood, depended on the continuance of the friendly understanding existing between Austria and Russia, which, the general concert of the six great Powers tended to confirm and consolidate; but which the withdrawal of the support of England might weaken and disturb.
. . .
If a difference of opinion arose between them [Austria and Russia], the position of Germany would become extremely difficult . . . and then would come the moment when the moral support of England might be advantageously put forward in the interest of peace. For this

reason he welcomed the proffered cooperation of Her Majesty's Government, and tendered his thanks . . .

He regretted that Your Lordship had not, in January last, when he had invited an understanding on Eastern affairs, initiated some more detailed line of policy, but he thought that the present situation might even facilitate an agreement . . . for the preservation of peace, in case of danger.

Bismarck, then, expressed his hope that England would give her moral support to Austria, as Andrássy, who was the real author of the Berlin memorandum, had been strongly checked when Britain had refused the proposals of 13 May. A friendly gesture would help Andrássy if he were 'unduly pressed by Russia'. The Chancellor indicated that Andrássy had opposed Gorchakov's plan of autonomy for Bosnia-Hercegovina. 'He [Bismarck] regretted Her Majesty's Government could not support . . . an armistice at Constantinople, but her Majesty's Government would always find him ready to consider and support any better proposals they thought more likely to bring about the pacification of European Turkey and to secure the maintenance of peace in general.'[39] The following day the British ambassador sent a private letter to the Foreign Secretary.

Bismarck is quite anxious as before for our friendship and that he solicits the cooperation of H.M. Govt. to keep the peace between his allies in the event of a quarrel . . .

If a quarrel ensues the Emperor William will be all on the Russian side—and Bismarck will have to choose between the sympathies of his Sovereign and the policy of his party [pro-Austrian]—A contingency in which the moral support of England would be very useful, he thinks, in the interests of general peace.[40]

On the same day Russell spoke to the German Emperor who told him that he was disappointed at England's refusal and hoped, as everyone did, to delay the death of Turkey for as long as possible.[41]

While the unsuccessful attempt was being made to obtain a British change of mind, the five Powers and their representatives at Constantinople stumbled towards an agreement on how the proposals of 13 May should be presented to the Porte. Only after Andrássy agreed to Gorchakov's plan of identic notes, which would contain the Berlin proposals, were the ambassadors able to collaborate, and it was arranged on 29 May to communicate the Berlin memorandum to the Ottoman Government at noon the next day. Late on the evening of the twenty-ninth and early on the following morning a bloodless *coup* in Constantinople deposed the Sultan Abdul Aziz and proclaimed his successor.[42] The memorandum remained undelivered. If a potential crisis had been averted by the nondelivery of the Berlin proposals, the spread of war had become more certain.

## The Fleets of Europe

As a result of the murder of the French and German consuls at Salonica at the beginning of May and the manifest dissatisfaction of Ottoman subjects throughout European Turkey, though most of the latter was aimed at the Porte and the Sultan rather than at Christians,[43] Britain and the other European Powers directed units of their fleets to Turkish waters to be at hand for the protection of Europeans and Christians should Muslim fanaticism make this necessary. The *Swiftsure* was ordered to Salonica and three other British ships under Admiral Drummond were to go to Besika Bay, just outside the Dardanelles, where the Admiral could be in communication with the Embassy at Constantinople. At Elliot's request, a small vessel had been sent to Constantinople itself.

The third paragraph of the Berlin memorandum had suggested that all the Powers should come to an agreement upon naval measures to be taken for the safety of foreigners and the Christian subjects of the Porte. When London received its copy of the Berlin proposals, the Admiralty was alerted by the Foreign Office. In his reply to the memorandum Derby indicated that Britain would of course co-operate to protect life and property in Turkey, but he then issued a warning. 'Her Majesty's Government do not, however, at present apprehend any necessity for such measures and they are of the opinion that care should be taken that the naval forces of foreign Powers are not employed in any manner contrary to the treaty rights of the Porte or subversive of the Sultan's authority.'[44] The warning was due to Disraeli who was anxious about British naval preponderance in the Eastern Mediterranean as well as a possible attempt by Russia to seize the Turkish fleet. In his own memorandum, read to the Cabinet meeting called to consider the Berlin proposals, he indicated his objection to having any warships at Constantinople for the excuse of protecting Christians.[45]

Apart from anxiety about a Russian seizure of Ottoman ships, Disraeli was beginning to see how a show of British naval force could be turned to good account. Ward Hunt, the First Lord of the Admiralty, was asked to ascertain the naval strength in the Mediterranean.[46]

At a Cabinet meeting held on 24 May a decision was taken to strengthen the Mediterranean fleet by sending the *Monarch,* the *Rupert,* and the *Sultan* to the Dardanelles, thus raising to 10 the number of British ironclads in the Eastern Mediterranean.[47]

With the large number of ships of the Great Powers now in the Eastern Mediterranean, the danger of some or many of them sailing through the Dardanelles had greatly increased. St. Petersburg and London quickly and simultaneously began to read old treaties. After going over the treaties of 1856 (Paris) and 1871 (London), Gorchakov determined that only the Sultan had the right to open the Straits, making it difficult for any Russian squadron to enter, except when the Porte judged it necessary, in order to ensure the execution of the Treaty of 1856. But, as Jomini and Gorchakov recognized, Russia had little in the way of ships to send through the Straits. The Tsar's approval of co-ordinating Russian maritime action with that of the other Powers was an attempt to disguise Russian naval weakness in the Black Sea.[48]

Tenterden in London duplicated the work of Gorchakov and Jomini and produced a memorandum on the subject for Derby. What he feared was a foreign fleet entering the Straits under the excuse of protecting the Christians, and the awkward position in which this situation would place the British Government.

When Sir. H. Elliot telegraphed at the instance of The British residents who were in a state of panic, to summon the British squadron from Syria to Besika Bay, I ventured to point out that ... Sir H. Elliot's example would be followed and there be a great concentration of fleets of all Powers at the entrance of the Dardanelles to be utilized for their own purposes for those hostile to the Porte's interests.

. . .

[Our fleet] arrives there [Besika Bay] today [26 May]. My supposition that the other Powers would send their fleets has been fully realized and Russia moreover has put a clause into the Berlin Memorandum that requires the fleets to protect not merely foreign residents but the Christian population throughout the Ottoman Empire.

I cannot help thinking that this is a serious state of things—Here is an immense force of ironclads congregated at the entrance of the Straits at the time when five Powers are urging proposals which the Porte, with our concurrence and countenance though not advice, is resisting—Any incident, such as a street fight in Stamboul may revive the panic and the fleets be at Constantinople. ... The Turk is, as usual, unprepared in all ways ...

Since the fleets are there at Besika Bay or will very shortly be there, what is to be done. Is any instruction to Sir H. Elliot to be given to be ready to protest against any violation of the Treaty of 1841 [Straits Convention]? If we protest, what next? Is any warning to be given to him not to summon the British fleet to Constantinople unless in the last resort?

Are any secret orders to be given to the Admiral or to the Ambassador?

Should anything be done to endeavour to get them [the fleets] to disperse?[49]

The movement of the British fleet to Besika Bay did not, of course, escape notice, nor was it desired by Disraeli that it should. Decazes unknowingly agreed with Tenterden and viewed the step as one which would only increase tension.[50]

The French Foreign Minister, who viewed France's security as being best served by a concert of the six Powers rather than of the three or five, now informally suggested to Derby the calling of a European congress or conference. The Foreign Secretary, who hated international gatherings on principle, suspected that Decazes's attempt was really a Russian proposal and he gave little encouragement to Paris. As he explained to Disraeli, he felt that unless Britain entered such a gathering with a distinct formulation of its goals, the resulting muddle would only be increased.[51]

To the Prime Minister, however, conferences were not anathema, only opportunity to be taken and used.

I have no fear of a Congress, but I entirely agree with you, that before we enter it, our scheme shd be matured. I am myself inclined to stipulate, that it shall be founded on the *status quo* but that a liberal interpretation shd be placed on that phrase so that we may create other vassal states. I think it would be better not to increase the territories of Montenegro or Servia, I fancy all the powers, except Russia, wd agree with us in this—and if secured, the defeat of Russian designs would be complete.[52]

Though he did not use the word, Disraeli was suggesting the very solution which Gorchakov had proposed at Berlin only to see it successfully opposed by Andrássy—autonomy for Bosnia-Hercegovina. With such friends the Porte did not need enemies.[53]

A fundamental change in the administration of a significant portion of European Turkey, none of which, however, touched the Mediterranean or Black Sea, did not excessively worry the Prime Minister, but a Russian violation of the Straits was another matter.

The Turkish fleet is at present in everybody's mind, a prize the possession of which may influence the fate of nations. The imminent danger . . . a few weeks ago—was . . . from the side of the Bosphorus. Had Ignatiev succeeded in inducing the frightened Sultan to admit a Russian garrison and place his fleet under the guardianship of Russia, the difficulties would have been great . . .

The danger from the Dardanelles is of another kind. The Treaty of 1841 must not be violated. That should be a cardinal principle with us. But if violated, there is but little compensation to be found in the consciousness, that we have made a protest. What if secret instructions were given to our admiral, that, if any of the naval forces assembled propose to violate the Treaty of 1841, he shd warn them . . . that he is instructed to maintain that Treaty by force?[54]

Disraeli's essential purpose was not to maintain Ottoman sovereignty but, as he conceived them, British interests. As he wrote to the Queen, 'Your Majesty's fleet had not been ordered to the Mediterranean to protect Christians or Turks, but to uphold Your Majesty's Empire'.[55]

On 1 June the Cabinet met to again consider the naval question, and, perhaps, to discuss as well the deposition of the Sultan. Disraeli explained to the Queen that this last event had temporarily interrupted diplomatic action but that its inclination would be to help forward a pacific arrangement. The British ministers decided to make a friendly request to all the

Powers who had assembled squadrons at Besika Bay. The message was that it was the intention of the British Government to observe strictly the treaties of 1841 and 1856 which prohibited warships from entering the Dardanelles while the Porte was at peace, and invited the other governments to make a similar declaration.[56]

The refusal of the Berlin memorandum seems to have caused no great debate within the Cabinet, the majority of whom must have been very imperfectly aware of the complex and fluid situation. Though Disraeli, possibly with aid from Salisbury, played the major part in the rejection, Derby was not unhappy to go along with the Prime Minister, his own Under Secretary, and the rest of his colleagues. Carnarvon, Secretary for the Colonies and closer to Derby than most of his other colleagues, wrote of a kind of opposition on the part of the Cabinet to the Foreign Secretary's acute indecision.[57] It was, at least, from this point in time, if not before, that the Foreign Secretary temporarily began to lose control over the affairs of his own department, at first to the Prime Minister and then to others in the government. Derby, who had a fairly strong personal dislike and contempt for the Turks, nevertheless defended the latter's integrity and sovereignty, because it was the policy that required Britain to do the least as well as being a course not in conflict with vital British interests. His distrust of Russian intentions, his fear of an Austro-Russian design to carve up the Ottoman Empire, and his feeling that the Berlin memorandum was unfair to the Turks, were all rationalizations in support of his doing nothing. Derby was to a great extent the prisoner of his own personality and his formulation of policy was largely an attempt at the rationalization of psychological necessity.

Disraeli's support for the preservation of the Ottoman Empire, made easier by his lack of contempt for Muslims, was also, like Derby's support, a byproduct of other desires. In the Prime Minister's case, the need was to maintain the British Empire and the prestige and image of England in Europe and throughout the world. His rejection of the Berlin memorandum was due to the humiliating contempt for Britain expressed by the three originators of the proposal of 13 May.[58] How else is it possible to explain his objection to the five points of the memorandum, as being unfair or deleterious to Turkey, and his almost simultaneous move in favour of the far more serious and significant autonomy for Bosnia-Hercegovina? The British naval demonstration at Besika Bay and the warning of potential violators of the Straits Convention also derive from his concern for Britain prestige and empire. He sought that respect for Britain which he long attempted to win for himself.

When the Prime Minister had decided that a European conference might solve the Balkan question, a conference at which he was prepared to propose and support autonomy for Bosnia and Hercegovina, he began to press for an understanding with Germany which Bismarck had indicated earlier that he too desired, in order that Britain might avoid isolation and embarrassment at the meeting of the Great Powers. As the possibility of a conference faded, and when Disraeli had become aware of Gorchakov's desire for Bosnian autonomy, he did not cool his hope for an arrangement with Germany but sought as well a Russian connection. This was not a man temporizing for want of a policy, as is usually claimed, but rather one who clearly and coolly saw that which he wished, and was prepared to employ a flexibility of means in order to obtain it. As the Prime Minister had neither the health, energy, nor inclination to run the Foreign Office himself, he was prepared to obtain his goals with a Foreign Secretary whose withdrawal seemed capable of neutralizing his own expansiveness.

A further obstacle for Disraeli was the increasing seriousness and complexity of events. Serbia and Montenegro were preparing to go to war against the Porte, and while the fleets of Europe had gathered at Besika Bay to protect the Christians, news slowly filtered into Europe of a great Muslim atrocity in Bulgaria.

# 8   THE SPREAD OF WAR

At the end of April and beginning of May 1876 Prince Milan, the ruler of Serbia, whose warlike inclinations had previously been restrained by pressure from the Great Powers, began to lean towards the war party in his own country. One of the two main restraining influences on Serbia, Austria-Hungary, had lost some of her power to persuade, as White, the British consul, explained.

The deplorable decline of Austrian influence in Servia [is undoubted].

That Power is looked upon here [in Belgrade] by Prince, Ministers, and people in the light of an enemy; her reprimands and threats are not heeded and certainly her moral influence appears slumbering.[1]

White, who was later to become ambassador at Constantinople, further noted that he had not met a single Serbian politician who did not believe in the inevitability of a war with the Porte, not for the purpose of political freedom or independence but in order to acquire Bosnia and remain under the suzerainty of the Porte, as long as European Turkey continued to exist.

It would appear that the war party here have two concurrent plans; they think that either Turkey will take the initiative of attack, or they hope that the insurrection will assume such proportions in Bosnia as to give Servia some pretext for giving open assistance to the Christians of the Province against the probable outrages of their Mohametan fellow countrymen, the latter being well armed.
. . .

Though, as I had the honour of stating above, it is believed that the mass of the Servian people is by no means disposed in favour of a war . . . and would prefer by far a pacific solution . . . [yet] their patriotic feelings are being gradually strongly aroused . . .[2]

What Austria, perhaps, could not do, Russia would not. Gorchakov made no secret now that he would no longer induce Montenegro and Serbia to remain neutral.[3] The situation in Montenegro drew a very cynical report from Holmes at Mostar.

Montenegro professes neutrality, but has really been the most active partisan and supporter of the insurrection. ... It has received immense sums of money from Russia and other quarters, ostensibly for the use of the poor and wounded insurgents but of which the greater part finds its way into the pockets of the Prince and his senators. Of this there is no doubt, and therefore Montenegro is quite content that the present state of affairs, so profitable to herself, may be prolonged. In the meantime she is prepared for war . . .[4]

At the end of May Serbia suspended liberty of the Press and General Chernaiev, a former Russian general and a Pan-Slav, came to Belgrade without the 'official' permission or knowledge of the Russian Government. Buchanan, the ambassador at Vienna, reported that it was almost certain that Serbia would open hostilities with Turkey within three weeks.[5] Derby, whose position since the deposition of the Sultan was that time needed to be given to his successor, Murad V, to consider his course, was appealed to by Austria. He agreed to Andrássy's request that Britain counsel moderation at Belgrade, and White was instructed to act in concert with his Austrian colleague in advising Milan to adopt a pacific course.[6] It was at this point that the Porte announced a general amnesty for all, and a suspension of hostilities for six weeks, appealing to the rebels to lay down their arms and bring their complaints to the Sultan.[7] While Andrássy was attempting to exert pressure from the Great Powers to quiet Serbia, Shuvalov was trying to forward his chief's plan for autonomy with London. In a conversation with Derby he tried with much ardour to win the Foreign Secretary's support for autonomy for Bosnia-Hercegovina.[8] Disraeli, temporarily, was very satisfied, and felt that all his intentions might be completely realized.[9] What he intended, as he told the Queen, was European peace coupled with British influence in the councils of Europe.

To escape isolation by consenting to play a secondary part does not become Your Majesty; and is a short-sighted policy, for, leading to frequent humiliation, it ultimately occasions wars, which are neither just nor necessary.

Mr. Disraeli looks upon the Tripartite understanding between the three Imperial Powers of the Continent as virtually extinct . . . and that no leading step will in future be taken without first consulting Your Majesty.[10]

The Queen was less happy than her Prime Minister because she was more anxious about the spread of war than he. She had an unconventional, unrivalled, and unpaid diplomatic staff to the courts of Europe which she sometimes put to use, as at Berlin during the 1860s, to warn a fellow sovereign of an unscrupulous minister. Her initiative, apparently, was taken without prompting from her ministers though she informed Disraeli of her step afterwards. It resulted in a letter to her second son, who was married to the daughter of the Tsar.

I hope and trust that peace will be maintained, but let me tell you, that if it was possible for you to tell the Emperor either directly or indirectly through Marie, he should know that Ignatieff is the cause of all the mischief there. . . . He [Russian Emperor] is not told. I am sure of the shocking falseness and intrigues of Ignatieff who is all powerful with Gorchakoff.[11]

While the Queen was attempting to make informal contact with the Tsar, Disraeli had an interesting talk with the Russian ambassador at a dinner given on the evening of Friday, 9 June. It was the first meeting between the two since their confrontation which had been interrupted by the arrival of the Prince of Wales on 15 May. Their conversation was continued on the day following the dinner, and an Anglo-Russian understanding seemed a possibility. The Prime Minister told Shuvalov that he did not distrust Russia and that an agreement could be made if St. Petersburg would convey directly to Britain, and not through Decazes, Beust, d'Harcourt, or Münster, the solution that she desired. If Russia did this, an agreement could be made. The Prime Minister arranged for Shuvalov to see Derby, after a Cabinet meeting on Monday, two days hence, to work out an arrangement.[12] Shuvalov telegraphed for instructions to Gorchakov at Ems for the official Russian reaction to this surprising British *démarche*. Gorchakov was suspicious and instructed Shuvalov only to listen and to ask the English ministers what practical proposals they could make for the pacification of the East, and then not to express an opinion but to refer any proposals back to Ems.

In their discussion Shuvalov reported Disraeli as saying that he did not distrust Russian policy in Asia or within the Ottoman Empire as long as Russia did nothing to menace Afghanistan.[13] The Prime Minister knew that Russia had no desire to precipitate events in Turkey but was wise enough to await the natural and inevitable disappearance of Turkey from Europe. Disraeli then said that Russia's great mistake was to keep Ignatiev at Constantinople as he was exciting the Christian population against Turkish control. He indicated no confidence at all in Andrássy or his proposals since the insurgents were fighting for independence and not reforms. In this situation, struggle and the shedding of blood were inevitable and could not be prevented, and it was a mistake on Russia's part to attempt to restrain Serbia and Montenegro from war. After the required bloodshed, the Prime Minister indicated, if the Christians won, then Russia and England need only register accomplished facts; if the Turks proved successful and resorted to atrocities then all the European Powers could interfere to prevent this in the name of humanity. Shuvalov objected to a policy based on bloodshed, and replied that Russia wished Christian reform without raising or reopening the Eastern Question, to which he felt Disraeli's suggestion would lead.[14]

The day before Disraeli initiated his talk with the Russian ambassador, he asked Tenterden, in a rather unusual request, to come to see him, and there transpired a general discussion of Turkish affairs at which there was agreement that the new Turkish Government should be given time to act for itself unhindered by European reforms pressed upon it. The Prime Minister then gave way to an outbreak of anger.

He [Disraeli] however specially mentioned to me that he was not satisfied that Ld. Odo Russell was sufficiently alive to the importance, indeed the necessity of securing the good will of Germany. He thought that his despatches and letters showed more of the courtier than the diplomatist . . .

He hoped that Ld. Russell wd be kept alive to the policy which H.M. Govt desire to pursue towards Germany and asked me to mention this to you [Derby].[15]

What was Disraeli up to? His critics argue, not much and all of that negative, and they may be right.[16] There is a good possibility, however, that he may have been pursuing a number of objectives, but the evidence is not conclusive. Firstly, he wanted to ensure that the Berlin memorandum was not presented at Constantinople. It had only been postponed and could still have been resurrected. This would not happen if

Russia saw she had more to gain from an English than from an Austrian agreement. In his offer to Russia the Prime Minister was also attempting to make Britain a real partner in any Balkan settlement which was made. This required more than splitting apart the entente of Austria, Russia, and Germany, it necessitated raising Britain's image and the desirability to attract the Continental Powers to her. He may have thought temporarily that he could capitalize on Gorchakov's desire for autonomy for the areas in revolt and move closer to Russia by outbidding Austria, but he saw Bismarck as the lynchpin of Continental politics and though he did not completely trust him, his basic wish was a solid and close understanding with Germany. A Russian connection might possibly reignite Bismarck's British interest. As Derby's reserve had cooled Bismarck's earlier ardour for an English connection, it had become necessary to rekindle the flame by showing Bismarck that there was now sufficient receptivity in London to warrant a real Anglo-German entente. Bismarck had indicated, after the English rebuff to his initial offer of an understanding, that purposeful Anglo-German co-operation could come in the interests of peace, when an Austro-Russian war threatened. But such a threat might never arrive, and, even if it did, how many more Austro-Russian notes and memorandums concerted without British participation would be concocted to London's embarrassment. So Disraeli needed to prime Derby without raising any higher the latter's already exaggerated suspicions; he needed to pressure Derby, without seeming to, in the hope of enticing a positive response rather than producing the usual apathy or withdrawal.

The Prime Minister well knew that it was not Russell who had destroyed a possible entente with Germany, but Derby. The ambassador, in fact, had attempted to push such an agreement which he favoured. Disraeli had used the Queen, and would do so again, to stir the Foreign Secretary. The Prime Minister now widened his indirect approach to move his friend. His outburst at Russell, which he asked Tenterden to relay to Derby, was for the purpose of showing the Foreign Secretary the great importance which Disraeli placed upon an Anglo-German understanding. To have directly criticized Derby, or to have pressured him in a straightforward manner, would have only increased his great and inpenetrable reserve and apathy.

Ironically, on the same day that Disraeli spoke with Shuvalov, Russell did the same with Bismarck, and the latter made another request for friendly English diplomatic gestures to be made to Austria.

I [Russell] said I had received no answer yet . . .

But he [Bismarck] thought that the intrigues of Gorchakov and the Russian National Party could be defeated by supporting Austria, and he most sincerely hopes H.M. Govt would lend a hand to Andrassy and support him against Gorchakov. He firmly believed that war could then be avoided.

I asked Bismarck why he did not act on his own advice . . .

Bismarck replied . . . it was simply that his policy was hampered by the Russian sympathies of Emperor William . . .

He repeated cheerfully and cordially that he was personally delighted at the attitude assumed by H.M. Govt and at the magnitude of the British squadron in the Mediterranean—'the larger the better,' he said, as no measure was more calculated . . . to intimidate Russia. . . . And if to those measures already taken H.M. Govt could add the moral support to Austria, he felt convinced that Gorchakov would not be able to disturb the peace of Europe.[17]

Rather than cow Russia, however, Derby's desire was to stir the Turks to the significance of the occasion, so they might seize the opportunity to forestall further European intervention into Ottoman affairs. The Foreign Secretary hoped to make use of the present high regard in which Britain was held at Constantinople, and informed Elliot accordingly.

The Sultan and his Ministers cannot be but aware of the serious nature of the present crisis, and of the urgent importance of taking advantage of the opportunity afforded by the change of Government to establish the administration of the country on a sound footing. Above all it is essential that no time should be lost in executing the reforms in the insurgent Provinces in a real and effectual manner.

The incapable men who as your Excellency [Elliot] has had too often reason to know have been placed in positions of authority, should be at once removed and replaced by those who can gain the confidence and respect of the people. Extortion and corruption should be promptly punished, and the reforms in the administration of justice, and the concession of full civil rights to all the religious communities vigorously proceeded with.

. . .

They [H.M. Government] feel that they are in a position, from the circumstances of the political situation, in which their counsel should carry with it peculiar weight, and they accordingly desire that your excellency [Elliot] should avail yourself of the earliest occasion to express these views to the Sultan in courteous and becoming, but explicit language.[18]

Derby liked to believe, as he told Shuvalov on 12 June, that the time for mediation between the Turks and the insurgents had not yet come; that if direct negotiation between the two sides should fail to bring pacification, Britain was opposed to using compulsion against one side or the other. He indicated that he thought such failure probable as the insurgents would only accept independence or autonomy and the Porte was ready to grant only administrative reforms. 'Nothing, I [Derby] thought, remained, except to allow the renewal of the struggle, until success should have declared itself more or less decisively on one side or the other.'[19]

Andrássy, however, still believed the insurgents would settle for less than independence, and had Beust convey this to Derby on 22 June, together with a request for active British help in connection with pacification. Derby refused to become active. 'Her Majesty's Government, I [Derby] said, are ready to take part in the work of pacification when they see a chance of doing so with effect. If they do abstain it is only because they see nothing to be done. When circumstances lead them to alter that opinion their inaction will cease.'[20] In the meantime Derby had not completely dissuaded Gorchakov and Shuvalov from the understanding which Disraeli had offered. Though there was Russian distrust of British motives, Gorchakov decided to flatter English vanity and continue in the attempt at an agreement with London. Shuvalov was instructed to suggest autonomy for Bosnia and Hercegovina. The Russian ambassador talked to Derby several times but could not move him, and to Russia, Britain's willingness to allow events to take their course seemed little calculated to prevent the crisis from worsening. After seeing Derby on three separate occasions between 18 and 21 June, Shuvalov gained the impression that he, as well as Disraeli, were unsympathetic to a new autonomous Slavic state, and that the Prime Minister was suspicious that such a state would be merely a Russian satellite.[21] The Russian ambassador then left with Derby on the twenty-first a letter Gorchakov had written to him on 17 June, in which he urged Shuvalov to impress on London the gravity of the situation and the need for united action by the Great Powers. Gorchakov further indicated his willingness to talk about any arrangement which the British Government might propose.[22]

Derby sent a copy of Gorchakov's letter to Disraeli, who met Shuvalov at dinner on the evening of 23 June. The Russian ambassador impressed upon Disraeli the need for a quick arrangement as a Serbo-Turkish war seemed imminent; 'propose yourselves,' he said, 'and we will follow you'.[23] Disraeli was favourably impressed by Gorchakov's dispatch and he sent a copy to Elliot as the ingredients of a possible compromise. But, as he complained to the Queen, Derby was out of town as he usually was over the week-end, and said he would not lay the dispatch before the Cabinet until he was prepared to lay before it the policy it should pursue.[24] On the twenty-seventh, to further allay British suspicions of Russia, Shuvalov wrote to Derby, enclosing copies of Russian diplomatic correspondence with its agents in Serbia and Montenegro, as proof that St. Petersburg was advising peace at both Ragusa and Belgrade.[25]

Though thoroughly exasperated by the British delay, Shuvalov seemed to have gained London's confidence. According to Lady Derby, Disraeli and Derby were near to agreeing to the Russian proposals, when they heard reports that Russia was secretly pressing both Montenegro and Serbia to undertake hostilities.[26] When Shuvalov called on Derby at the Foreign Office on 28 June, they discussed the three proposals of Gorchakov. On the first, additional territory for Montenegro, there was agreement; but on the second, the same for Serbia, Derby declined until Serbia and given unequivocal evidence of not meaning war. The Foreign Secretary equivocated on point three, autonomy for Bosnia-Hercegovina.[27] Derby's written reply to Gorchakov's proposals paralleled his conversation with Shuvalov save that it was much more explicitly negative on autonomy for Bosnia-Hercegovina.

Her Majesty's Government cannot, however, regard the insurrection in Bosnia and the Herzegovina as being exclusively or principally a struggle directed against local oppression, whether in religious or civil matters.

The reports which they have received show that it arose from other causes, and is now fomented and maintained for purposes ... of a general and political, rather than of a local and administrative character ...

It also appears that numbers ... are ready and willing to return to them [villages], and are deterred from doing so not by fears of their Mohamedan neighbors, but by the action of the insurgents, who drive away the cattle and destroy the goods of the returning refugees.

The insurrectionary movement must be surpressed, and order restored before any such schemes can be advantageously treated.[28]

Though there was less basis for an Anglo-Russian accord than there had been for an Anglo-German one, both foundered on British suspiciousness, for which there was some justification, and the absence of any English policy beyond leaving a clear field for the two opposing sides to fight it out. Both Berlin and St. Petersburg had asked London to name its policy and they would support it. Bismarck cared as little for the Slavic Christians as he did for the Turks, and when England failed to give him her lead, he could do nothing. Gorchakov thought the British felt embarrassed by their isolation and, according to Jomini, believed he could draw Britain into supporting more concessions for the Slavic Christians, with whom he sympathized, than the meagre Andrássy proposals allowed them. But he too failed, despite the support of Shuvalov's efforts to obtain a British commitment. He could believe now that Disraeli's only purpose had merely been to compromise Russia with her allies.[29]

In January Bismarck had wanted England to take the lead so that he might follow. In June Disraeli made the same offer to Shuvalov, and then he and Derby received the identical proposal back from Gorchakov and Shuvalov, but London declined to co-operate. In this same month Bismarck used similar language to the Crown Prince of Germany on 11 June, and the latter relayed it to his wife, the daughter of Queen Victoria, who wrote to her mother. 'I was to tell you, that Prince Bismarck said it was his wish that England should entirely take the lead in the Oriental question, and that he was quite ready to follow and back up whatever England proposed ...'. The

Crown Prince supported his wife's letter with one of his own in which he indicated that there was no German regret at the failure of the Berlin memorandum, and that Germany sincerely desired a closer association with England.[30] The Queen was impressed and sent a copy of the Crown Prince's letter to Disraeli enclosed with one of her own.

The Queen is certain that you will agree with her that a communication of this nature is of the highest importance and should stimulate the government in drawing closer to Germany whose interests are similar to ours.

Germany now looks to a union with England.

The Queen hopes that you will be able to furnish her with an answer to this communication which will encourage the German chancellor.[31]

Disraeli sent a copy of the Queen's letter to Derby and received the following reply:

The answer I think is simple enough. We are ready and willing to act with Bismarck: we have always said so: but at the present moment we have nothing to propose in the way of pacificatory measures: we have agreed that the new Sultan must have time to negotiate with the insurgents, and if he fails, and if they persist in continuing the struggle with the avowed object of achieving their independence, I don't see what kind of mediation is possible. We can in that case only see fair play.

It is not unreasonable to ask . . . why if Bismarck is so anxious for our cooperation he joined in the Berlin note without even stipulating that we should have a voice in the matter.[32]

Disraeli replied to the Queen, using almost verbatim the language of Derby in the letter he had received from the Foreign Secretary.[33]

Derby was puzzled by Bismarck's conduct and left a short note for Tenterden in which he indicated his puzzlement that Bismarck, who he felt did not confide in England, should be so concerned that he inspired distrust in Britain. In reply Tenterden gave a not uninteresting reaction.

I suspect that he is playing us off against the Russians. He is too well informed about England . . . not to know that he is safe in asking us for a programme, it being pretty notorious that an English Govt never expresses opinions in advance.

He therefore acts with entire safety. The fact of his requesting us to give him a programme shows his wish to be friendly. The fact of our not giving him one relieves him from having to do more than make fair speeches to us.

Whether he wd really act with us in a difficulty remains to be proved.[34]

In response to the anxieties of the Queen and Ponsonby over Anglo-Turkish and Anglo-Russian relations,[35] the Foreign Secretary agreed with the Queen on the hazard of seeming to be a friend of Turkey against her Christian subjects, a danger of which the Prime Minister was also aware. 'I do not believe the Czar or his responsible advisers desire to break up the Turkish empire at present. But the conduct of their agents in all places is absolutely at variance with the language held at Petersburg; showing either great duplicity or great administrative weakness ...' Derby then explained the impossibility of relying on anyone else as Russia might be lying, Andrássy changed his mind weekly, one could not confide in Bismarck, and France was Russia's plaything. It was, he wrote, impossible to be too careful.[36]

As Disraeli was fluid in reference to any particular solution for the Balkans, and especially as warmer relations had been established with Germany and Russia which seemed to preclude further embarrassing isolation for Britain, he had been influenced temporarily by Tenterden and Derby, or had so influenced them, to do nothing and allow the Turks and the insurrectionists to fight it out. In view of the impossibility, in Derby's opinion, of trusting any of the Powers sufficiently to work for a European solution to be imposed on both the Turks and the insurgents, the Foreign Secretary merely allowed himself the luxury of not preventing what seemed to Britain's diplomatic representatives to be the only realistic possibility of ending the insurrection—bribing Montenegro to peace.[37] At the end of May, just before the Sultan's deposition, Elliot asked the Grand Vizier whether he could not reach a direct agreement with Montenegro, and received the impression that the Grand Vizier intended to attempt an understanding.[38]

At the end of the first week of June Loftus, the much maligned British ambassador to Russia, offered a suggestion which exactly duplicated the one of Andrássy to the Turkish ambassador at Budapest.

If the Porte is wise she will profit of the inaction and hesitation of the two govts [Austria and Russia] to make her peace with the insurgents directly and utilize Montenegro for that purpose. She would then be able to turn her whole force against Servia—and I think that both Austria and Russia would not regret to see the Revolutionary Element of Servia put down . . .

There is much bitterness against us here [St. Petersburg] accompanied by a wholesome fear of us . . .[39]

Holmes, the British agent closest to the scene of the insurrection in Hercegovina, pointed out what he believed to be the key to the continuation of the revolt.

The war in the Herzegovina has been, and is, entirely kept up by the inhabitants of the old revolted districts, who have been virtually independent of the Porte for the last fifteen years, supported by Montenegro. These people care nothing for any concessions which may be made to the inhabitants of the Herzegovina, which would in no wise affect them, and are ready to continue to harass the Turks . . . so long as they receive orders to that effect from Montenegro and Russia, and while they are, as hitherto, protected and paid to do so, therefore, believe that no promises of reform or any amount of concession to the Christians will produce any effect until Montenegro is either persuaded or forced to give the signal for peace.[40]

Elliot again reported that the Porte was not indisposed to make concessions to Montenegro. The only British representative who did not place primacy on Montenegro's role was Monson, attached to the Embassy in Vienna but sent to Ragusa in March, and who was later to be ambassador at Paris. He saw the main problem in Dalmatia.

[The] insurrection . . . in regard to its origins and the number of *bona fide* insurgent combatants, may fairly be termed 'fictitious.' My own conviction is, that had it not been for the money spent by Russia and the Dalmatian Panslavist Committees upon certain influential Chiefs, the insurrection would have long since collapsed. The mass of the population of the revolted districts would probably from the outset have been contented if they could have obtained a hearing for the agrarian grievances under which they undoubtedly laboured. As it is, a large proportion of them have not resorted to arms . . .

It is clear that, as far as the Herzegovina is concerned, a great step in the suppression of the insurrection would be effected if the

Austrian Government would dissolve the Panslavist Committees, enforce a strict surveillance of the frontier, and would absolutely forbid and put down the export of arms ... to Montenegro.[41]

As Serbia and Montenegro made little effort to disguise their intention to go to war together, the question of pacification merged into the more serious one of preventing the spread of war or securing its outcome. Elliot, without specific instructions from Derby, acted on 23 June and strongly pressed Turkey to attempt to separate Montenegro from Serbia. The method of so doing suggested by the British ambassador was a letter from the Porte to the Prince of Montenegro alluding to the possibility of territorial increase once peace had been reached.[42] This, and a French-led European attempt to warn Serbia against war, were too late, and at the beginning of July Montenegro and Serbia declared war officially against the Ottoman Government. All the European Powers quickly announced their intentions to follow a policy of non-intervention. The time for initiatives by the Great Powers had ended temporarily.

Thompson rightfully regards the end of June and the beginning of July 1876 as an important point of demarcation in the development of British opinion on the Eastern crisis. From July 1875 to July 1876 there had been little manifested feeling and interest and this was pliable, not distrustful of the Government, inconstant, and he refers to it as the 'incubation period'. 'Throughout the whole of the Incubation Period, the volume of political opinion was comparatively small and its voice scarcely heard. During the month of June it had been growing. ... At the beginning of July the public interest in politics suddenly becomes keen ...'

The causes for the change he sees as two: the impression that the government might attack Russia, or at least attempt some *coup de main,* and news of Turkish atrocities in Bulgaria.[43] The refusal of the Berlin memorandum, reinforcement of the British fleet, and the overthrow of the Sultan produced strong anti-Russian feeling in June and made the movement of the British fleet appear as a provocative and unfriendly step. 'We note that in England the idea at once came to the front that Turkey had at last turned over a new leaf, and ought to have another chance given her ...'[44]

Ironically, at this point, reports and rumours reached Western Europe that the Turks had fulfilled a common British and European expectation by committing great barbarities upon Christian Bulgarians.

# 9 BULGARIA

DISRAELI'S HEALTH and age precluded a close and energetic control of British foreign policy. One senses this in the spring of 1876, at the very moment when the Prime Minister had become more active in international affairs than at any time since the beginning of his ministry. He could only hope that his influence on Derby, Tenterden, and the Queen would be sufficient to enable Britain to follow the correct line. Though Derby had received some of the credit with the public for the brief and temporary success of the government, the initiative behind it was Disraeli's. The Cabinet, of course, realized this. Lytton, the recently appointed Indian viceroy, referred to Britain's policy as the most vigorously successful since Palmerston's early successes. He too described it as the policy of the Prime Minister rather than that of the Foreign Secretary.[1]

Britain's partial diplomatic success occurred when it had become apparent to the Prime Minister that he could no longer continue as Leader of the House of Commons, or perhaps as an active political figure in any capacity. He apparently approached Derby on the chance of the latter's succeeding him as Prime Minister, though it is doubtful if Disraeli considered this as a serious possibility, and in any event, his tentative approach was turned down by Derby. 'He [Derby] withdraws more and more and feels his unfitness to lead men—Cairns said that he doubted if he would serve under him.'[2]

Blake suggests that Disraeli, as a result of his social and psychological relationship with the Stanley family, hid from himself Derby's incapacity for decision and action, and that in the late spring and early summer of 1876 was beginning to realize, slowly and reluctantly, the gulf between himself and Derby of which the Queen had already become aware.[3] I would agree with this save for the date of Disraeli's realization which goes back to the middle 1860s, if not before that. What he was attempting to hide or overcome was the necessity for doing anything about the quirks of his friend, which the Queen equally recognized but felt less compunction about calling to notice, though if necessary the Prime Minister was ready to attempt to overcome Derby's personality.

MAP 2. Bulgaria

In the late spring of 1876 Derby wished to bring the Turks and the insurgents into direct communication so that there would be no necessity for Europe or Britain to act. His support for the territorial *status quo* and his desire to give the new Turkish regime time to devise its own solution had the same purpose. His feeling that mediation was premature was partly a rationalization to do nothing and partly a realistic estimate of the inopportuneness of such an attempt. His distrust of all the other Powers also had some basis in reality as Ignatiev, Yonin, Kartsov, Rodich, and Mollinary, the commanding Austrian general at Agram, had not been unsuccessful in carrying a line different from the one officially espoused at St. Petersburg and Vienna.[4] He hoped and expected, as did the Prime Minister, that the Turks would defeat the Serbs militarily, but whereas Disraeli's desire could be explained on the grounds of British political interests, Derby's preference was more a product of his recognition that a Turkish victory would require less in the way of Balkan reorganization than an insurgent one.

Disraeli had no fear of acting, only the anxiety of England's being left out by Russia, Austria, and Germany, and not being treated by them as an equal partner. He had no real plan for the Ottoman Empire and was probably ready to accept any solution which, in his opinion, did not negate England's interests or prestige. Bismarck, Andrássy, and Gorchakov all recognized that Disraeli's vanity had been wounded, and this and the Prime Minister's actions produced a change and caused them to approach England more. Disraeli had succeeded in drawing Britain further into the international discussion of the Eastern question, and, in lieu of a solution for Turkey, this is all he wished to do.

Neither the Prime Minister nor the Foreign Secretary had produced a policy for Britain: Derby because of great and ingenious efforts to demonstrate that one was not necessary, and Disraeli owing to Britain's diplomatic isolation and the fact that he was usually less concerned with the substance of any Balkan solution than with the manner or method by which it was arranged and its proposed execution. When the news of Turkish cruelties in Bulgaria appeared in the *Daily News* in June 1876, both men had succeeded in their aims—the one to do nothing, the other to raise Britain's prestige and influence. Disraeli managed his achievement partly by going behind the Foreign Secretary's back, as in his talk with Shuvalov, and partly by taking advantage of fortuitous occurrences in Salonica and Constantinople. Derby succeeded because the Prime Minister's emphasis on style and tone and his flexibility on substance made it possible for Derby to convince Disraeli that the time for English mediation and intervention had not yet come.

### An Insurrection in Bulgaria

The Bulgarian Revolutionary Central Committee was established in Bucharest in 1870, the same year in which a firman was issued by the Sultan promising the Bulgarians their own church organization. A pronounced grievance prior to this firman had been the Greek exarchate under which Bulgarians were placed, and its removal in 1872 not only brought immediate satisfaction but acted as a fillip to those who desired political autonomy or independence to go alongside the religious.[5] When the Greek Patriarch formally pronounced a sentence of schism against the Bulgarian Church, Gladstone expressed his feelings about Russia and Elliot. 'I cannot help fearing that the schism may become a source of political danger as it will bring in Russia to meddle in the religious concerns of the Turkish Empire under the plea of ecclesiastical communion. . . . Sir H. Elliot's language and conduct seem to me most reasonable . . .'[6]

There were approximately three million Bulgarians, mostly peasants, and, according to Sumner, those active for political independence were few and divided. A meeting of the nationalists was held at Bucharest on 12 August 1875 and a decision was taken for revolution, the date of 28 September being fixed upon for a general rising. It became necessary, however, to defer action from the twenty-eighth, though a few rebels on that date sang a revolutionary hymn and fled to the hills.[7] Some prisoners were taken by the Turkish authorities, but there was an intention on the part of the rebels to try again as apparent conditions in Bulgaria seemed to justify dissatisfaction with Ottoman rule. The following report was sent by the British vice-consul, Dupuis.

The Bulgarians, my informant tells me, are still in great fear, and when obliged to travel generally secure a Turk as a road companion.

Frequent robberies and occasional murders take place . . .

He informs me, that no attempts at insurrection will be made soon, as the Christians feel themselves powerless but the Government

needs to institute very great reforms without delay, or a more serious attempt will be made at the first favourable opportunity.
. . .

My informant in Philippopoli ventures the opinion that the British Government does not . . . understand the necessity of caring for the Bulgarians, and adds that if England only showed them a little sympathy, English influence would be paramount . . . in Bulgaria.[8]

In December White reported that stories from Bulgaria described the local Ottoman conduct there as so immoderate and unreasonable that it was enabling political agitators there to produce seditious propaganda.[9]

A badly organized revolt occurred in Bulgaria at the beginning of May 1876.[10] As there were relatively few regular Turkish army units within central Bulgaria, local Ottoman authorities began arming and forming into irregular units the civilian Turkish and Circassian population. The nearest British consul was Dupuis at Adrianople, there being no representative at Philippopolis, the chief town in the area of the insurrection. Dupuis sent reports of the outbreak to Elliot on 3 and 4 May and on the latter day Elliot telegraphed the news to London. Within a week of the outbreak, Turkish irregulars began the work of suppressing the insurrection which ended in the killing of many innocent Bulgarians and the burning and destruction of many Christian villages.[11] Before receiving any official news of atrocities, Elliot warned of the possibility. 'Outrages committed upon the peaceful Mussulmans, and especially upon the women and children, may provoke among the Mohamedans a spirit of fanaticism and revenge likely to lead to similar acts of retaliation, which it may be very difficult to restrain . . .'[12] On 9 May Dupuis enclosed to Elliot a report sent to him by his dragoman from Eski Zagara, informing Dupuis that local Ottoman authorities were arming irregulars. Elliot sent this report to Derby on 12 May, and three days later enclosed to Derby Dupuis's dispatches of 12 and 13 May which reported hearing accounts of Bashi-Bazouk activity laying waste to the entire area.[13]

On 24 May Elliot enclosed to Derby two further dispatches from Dupuis. The first mentioned talk of 300 Bulgarian men, women, and children having been slaughtered.

Extraordinary activity is being displayed there [Adrianople] by the authorities and others in recruiting, arming, and forwarding to the disturbed districts Bashi-Bazouks and Circassians. ... I do not hear of any disorders having been committed by these troops in Adrianople, but I am assured that, once outside the city, they gave themselves up to all kinds of violence, and to the firing on women and other defenseless people in the villages and roads in this vicinity.

Three days later Dupuis sent his second dispatch.

In the surrounding country ... reports continue to reach me of acts of insubordination, excesses and disorders by the Bashi-Bazouks, Circassians and even armed gypsies, who, it is stated, rob, plunder, kill and levy black-mail on peaceable people. Unheard of cruelties and tortures, on the other hand, it would seem, are also practiced by Bulgarians on women, children, and other defenceless Musulman villages. How far atrocities said to have been committed on both sides are true or exaggerated, I have no means of ascertaining.

Upon receiving Dupuis's two communications, Elliot sent his dragoman, Sandison, who forcefully remonstrated with Raschid Pasha, the Foreign Minister, concerning the Porte's unwise use of Bashi-Bazouks in Bulgaria.

His Excellency [Raschid Pasha] stated in reply that Vizirial orders were sent yesterday directing the authorities in Bulgaria not to resort to the services of Circassians as irregulars. I [Elliot] thought proper to tell his Excellency that this was doing away with one class of Bashi-Bazouks only, and that there were just as strong grounds for giving similar orders in regard to the common Bashi-Bazouks, who were equally brutal and licentious.[14]

Derby's only response to the information was to approve Elliot's representation to the Porte against the use of irregulars.[15] The ambassador's censure of the use of such forces was sincere even if its purpose was as much to restrict the spread of revolt as to protect defenceless Christians. 'There is no excuse for the measures adopted by the Turks in arming Bashi-Bazouks, Circassians and gypsies, whose outrages are driving peaceful villagers to desperation and revolt, and I am doing what I can to have this put a stop to.'[16]

Still without reliable information, Elliot wrote on 8 June that the Bulgarian insurrection had been suppressed, but regrettably with cruelty and even at times with brutality.

There is evidence that the employment of Circassians and Bashi-Bazouks has led to the atrocities which were to be expected.

These irregulars have now been recalled ...

. . .

The indignation of the Bulgarians is now directed chiefly against the Russians, by whom they were, they say, urged, and almost forced, to rise against their Government.[17]

Eight days later Reade, the consul at Rustchuk, confirmed Elliot's suspicions that Circassians had committed atrocities, and the ambassador, hearing on 19 June other accounts of Turkish cruelties, again warned the Grand Vizier who attempted a defence.

The Grand Vizier, after alluding to the exaggeration of the reports sent here and to the omission of all mention of the horrors practised upon the Mussulmans by those who had attempted to get up the insurrection ... assured me that it would be impossible to add to the stringency of the instructions which he has sent to put an end to the disorders, and to disarm the Circassians ...

Mehemet Ruchdi Pasha added that the emergency had been so great as to render it indispensible at once to stamp the movement out by any means that were immediately available.

. . .

The Government had resorted with repugnance to the service of the Circassians, but under the circumstances they had no choice.[18]

Among the other accounts the ambassador had heard were those from Dr. George Washburn, an American ex-missionary and director of Robert College at the Bosphorus, and Dr. Albert Long, Professor of Natural Science at the college who had done fifteen years of missionary work among the Bulgarians. The news came from some of their Bulgarian students at Robert College, and they put it in a memorandum which they gave to Elliot with whom they were friendly.[19] In his dispatch to Derby of 19 June the ambassador did not refer specifically to the memorandum Washburn and Long had given him, but the information may have prompted Elliot's warning to the Grand Vizier.

Gallenga, the Constantinople correspondent of *The Times,* and Pears, correspondent for the *Daily News,* were also given copies of the same statement on 16 June, and both posted their information to their London newspapers. Pears's account was published in the *Daily News* on the twenty-third but Gallenga's, though it was received by *The Times,* was not printed.[20] Elliot not only did not transmit the Washburn–Long information to London, but did the same with the dispatch sent from Bourgas by Brophy, the vice-consul, which reached him on 20 June and with that from Dupuis of 23 June which reached him three days later. Brophy's report told of an unprovoked massacre of almost 2,000 Christians in a town in the area of Philippopolis. Dupuis's dispatch contained estimates that 12,000 Bulgarians had been massacred, that many young women had been dishonoured, and that 60 villages had been destroyed. It is not clear why Elliot did not send the above unconfirmed information to London. Harris feels that the ambassador was sufficiently rooted in prejudice to disbelieve these reports. Medlicott suggests that Elliot regarded this news merely as a recapitulation of earlier reports.[21] It has to be remembered that at this time Elliot was unaware that great atrocities had taken place in Bulgaria. I believe that if he had been more certain, he would have attempted to do more. The accuracy of unconfirmed Balkan information was minimal. The number of previous reports in the past few years announcing Bashi-Bazouk activity had been considerable. Only slightly less numerous were the warnings against such activity that Elliot had given to the Porte. Overwhelmed with other serious concerns—the Salonica murders, overthrow of the Sultan, the Berlin memorandum, and the probability of Serbia and Montenegro going to war—Elliot reported the existence of barbarous activity against Bulgarian Christians without giving credence to reports which in the past had turned out to be either exaggerated or completely false.

Even had Elliot fully believed in the accuracy of the information, and considering that the sources of most of this information were Bulgarian and Russian, it would have required an extreme degree of belief and trust on his part and would have been already too late for him to do anything to prevent the barbarous cruelties which so excited his critics. Washburn and Long gave the ambassador their news on about 16 June or a little before, and Dupuis's dispatch of 23 June reached him on the twenty-seventh. The earliest date Elliot could have acted, then, would have been in the middle of June, and by that time there was little left to prevent. The only way he might have known early enough in order to have prevented a significant part of the cruelties would have been if a British consul had been stationed at Philippopolis. Dupuis had long urged the necessity of this but the pressures for economy in London were too strong. In December 1860 the Liberal Government had removed a vice-consulate from Philippopolis. In 1871–2 under another Liberal Government a select committee recommended and the Government abolished consulates and vice-consulates throughout Europe and the Levant as a money-saving measure. Even a British consul, sent to investigate the area of alleged atrocities, could not have been sent much before 10 June. This would have been too late to have saved many Bulgarian Christians. Elliot apparently never considered sending such a representative, a lack of action which nearly matched the lack of concern shown for peaceful Muslims murdered by Bulgarian or Serbian rebels that was characteristic of many of those who manifested the greatest anxiety concerning peaceful Christians alleged to have been killed or molested. Such blindness, however, does not excuse completely the want of good judgement shown by the ambassador in this instance, even if he believed initially that all was quiet in Bulgaria, when he became alive to the fact that extensive barbarities on both sides had been committed there.

On 23 June Pears's article, dated the sixteenth from Constantinople, was published in the Liberal *Daily News*. The correspondent's name was not given and the title of the article was 'The Assassinations at Constantinople—Moslem Atrocities in Bulgaria'.

Dark rumours have been whispered about Constantinople during the last month of horrible atrocities committed in Bulgaria. . . . Cruelties are being revealed which place those committed in Herzegovina and Bosnia [?] altogether in the background. These cruelties have not been altogether (though they have in the main) confined to the side of the Turks; but that which throws the balance altogether against the latter is that the Government has been either unable or unwilling to prevent its own employees . . . Bashi-Bazouks . . . from committing these cruelties. . . . The cruelties are, from all that I can learn, still continuing . . .

The atrocities complained of are not the work of soldiers, but of Bashi-Bazouks. . . . Composed of the dregs of the Turkish and Circas-

sian population, with gipsies and gaol birds let out for the purpose
... they have been let loose upon a large portion of central Bulgaria
to put down the insurrection in their own fashion. The result is ...
the plundering of all moveable property, the burning of the houses
and villages of the peasantry ... whether the occupants have taken
part in the insurrection or not, and the almost indiscriminate
slaughter of old men, women, and children. ... It is too soon yet to
attempt to ascertain, with any degree of exactness, the number who
have been killed. An intelligent Turk ... estimates it at 18,000.
Bulgarians speak of 30,000, and of the destruction of upwards of 100
villages. I pass over the stories of the burning of forty or fifty
Bulgarian girls in a stable, and the massacre of upwards of 100
children in the village school-house ... because though they are
repeated everywhere in Constantinople, I have no sufficient authority
to enable me to express an opinion on their truth. ... I have,
however, trustworthy information of a number of other outrages,
many of which are altogether unfit for publication ...

Pears then listed the names of thirty-seven villages partially or
fully destroyed, adding that among those who managed to escape no girl over the age of ten was to be found. Singling out
Perushtitza, where he wrote that 1,500 people, mainly women
and children, were slaughtered, Pears narrated a dreary ànd
horrible account of the destruction of the village.

Every house in the village was burnt, and on the 14th of May not a
house existed. A certain number of the women and children escaped
... but a number of women were carried off as legitimate prizes by
the Bashi-Bazouks.
    Nothing but the most positive orders to the Turkish Government
will be sufficient to effect this object [the ending of the acts of cruelty].

On 26 June, as a result of this article, questions were asked
in both Houses of Parliament. In reply to the Duke of Argyll,
Derby implied that the *Daily News* story was exaggerated and
that the reports [Derby's reports] 'certainly do not bear out in
any degree the statements which the noble Duke [of Argyll] has
quoted and, in the absence of any such official confirmation, I
think we should be slow to believe those statements.'
    The Foreign Secretary did not disguise his scepticism regard-
ing the scale of atrocities reported by the newspaper and informed the House that as a result of the representations made
at the Porte by Elliot, the employment of irregulars had been

stopped. Derby reminded his hearers of the exaggerated reports of atrocity in the Cretan insurrection nine years before and indicated he would make inquiries at Constantinople.

In the House of Commons Forster, a prominent member of the late Liberal Government, put his question in this way: 'As a rule I should not think of asking the Government a question either with regard to the treatment by a foreign Government of its subjects or as regards the correctness of anonymous statements in any newspaper. ... If allegations such as I have stated are true we should be aware of them, and that if false we should not be misled by them.' He asked the Government for information. Disraeli answered that he had none to give verifying the *Daily News* story. The Prime Minister drew a picture of Turkish settlers attacked by foreigners and strangers who then had to defend themselves—sometimes ferociously. He too mentioned Elliot's warnings to the Porte about the use of irregulars and suggested that Bulgaria was now tranquil.[22]

On 28 June, two days after the Parliamentary interrogation and as he had said he would, Derby wrote to Elliot and enclosed a copy of the *Daily News* article, informing the ambassador that he had been questioned concerning it. Elliot was instructed to inquire and provide London with information as to its accuracy.[23] The ambassador had mixed feelings about the Turkish use of irregular bands, fearing their activity, but considered that the Turks were not ill advised to have recourse to such measures in view of the nature of guerilla warfare and his own Government's desire to see the insurrection quickly crushed. 'But what can be done! In a mountainous country irregulars may be more serviceable, or as much so as regulars; and in the face of such an utterly unprovoked attack [the Bulgarian rising] the Turks will retaliate with any instruments within their reach.'

Elliot dreaded the excesses of the Bashi-Bazouks, but felt that the Porte was not ill advised to make use of irregulars to crush rebellion.[24]

Before the ambassador received Derby's dispatch of 28 June, the Foreign Secretary telegraphed to him on 12 July to anticipate its arrival. As he told Ponsonby, Derby believed the *Daily News* story to be a fiction, but as he was being pressed in Parliament, he desired all the information Elliot could give him.[25] On 3 July in response to a request from Granville to lay papers generally on the Eastern Question, the Foreign Secretary agreed to do so as Serbia and Montenegro had officially gone to war. Disraeli made the same announcement in the Commons and was met by a speech by John Bright who said the country would not support a British war to maintain Ottoman integrity. Fawcett supported Bright's speech and expressed a hope that papers would be presented before the Government proceeded to act. He too deprecated any British moves against those Ottoman subjects seeking emancipation.[26] Derby was also being pressed by the Queen through Ponsonby. 'The Bashi-Bazouks shd really *not* be allowed to *outrage* the feelings of Europe. Could you write to Lord Derby or Mr. Disraeli urging him to telegraph to warn agst atrocities committed—wh wd. be too dreadful! and do Turkey and ourselves much harm.'[27] Ponsonby entirely shared the Queen's abhorrence of the use of barbaric irregulars, and as requested wrote to the Foreign Secretary.

If these were simple irregular troops no objection could fairly be made to their aiding the Turkish army. But it is notorious that they are wild bands of undisciplined men who are let loose upon the inhabitants.

Whatever sympathy existed in this country for the Turkish government is becoming weaker daily, and the atrocities reported in Bulgaria will go far to obliterate all feelings on behalf of the Turks. The Queen protests most strongly against this aggravation of the horrors of war, and considers it the duty of this country to warn the Porte that these atrocities cannot be tolerated and that if these Bashi-Bazouks are thus employed by the Turks, without restraint, it will be necessary for us to withdraw our countenance from them altogether.[28]

The Foreign Secretary felt the combined pressure of Parliament and the Queen and it may have been only at this point that he transmitted his dispatch to Elliot written on 28 June. His reply to Ponsonby contained acquiescence in the Queen's desire to warn the Turks, but at the same time defended himself for not having done so, though Elliot had given a warning without instructions from London.

We cannot prescribe to the Porte the precise nature of the troops it shall employ in defending itself against invasion [by Serbia and

Montenegro]: irregulars must be used when irregulars are not to be had: but it is quite fair to point out the mischief which the Porte does to its own cause, as well as to that of humanity, by not enforcing proper discipline among the troops whom it employs, whatever may be their character or organization.

I am afraid in this war there is not much to choose between the two sides. We have not heard as yet of such a thing as a Turkish prisoner.[29]

The Press now added to the Foreign Secretary's problems. Another discussion had occurred between Pears, Gallenga, the two Robert College professors, and Sir Philip Francis, the British consul-general in Constantinople, and the result was an exchange of information in which Francis was guilty of indefensible conduct. He gave to his friends Dupuis's dispatch of 23 June in which the estimates of 60 destroyed villages and 12,000 massacred Bulgarians appeared. On the thirtieth the two correspondents mailed their stories and they appeared in their London newspapers on 8 July.[30]

As a result, Derby telegraphed to Elliot on 12 and 13 July and sent him two dispatches on the thirteenth, in one of which he enclosed Pears's article of 30 June published in the *Daily News* on 8 July under the title 'The Moslem Atrocities in Bulgaria'.

It is stated that in the district of Philippopolis alone 25,000 innocent lives have been taken whilst by others the number is fixed at about 12,000.

It is reported that upwards of sixty villages have been pillaged and burnt ... Large numbers of Bulgarian girls and children are said to have been sold publicly as slaves at Philippopolis and elsewhere ...

In one instance ... 40 girls were seized, violated, and subsequently burnt alive in a straw-loft.
. . .

I have to instruct your Excellency to report to me how far reliance is to be placed in these statements.

Her Majesty's Government desire that you should, whenever you have reason to believe it necessary, urgently impress upon the Porte to see that its irregular forces are kept from committing atrocities which discredit the Ottoman cause.

Her Majesty's Government trust that the reports which have been circulated ... will prove to be unfounded. In a conflict such as is now taking place in European Turkey it is unhappily almost inevitable that acts of unnecessary violence and bloodshed should at times oc- cur. .... But the Porte will not deny that it is the duty of a civilized Government to use its utmost endeavours for the repression of such barbarities on the part of its own forces. The emergency of the mo- ment, or the nature of the country, may render the employment of irregular troops a matter of necessity; but unless these are kept under proper control, it is probable that the indignation which will be roused throughout Europe by the accounts of cruelties and outrages ... may go far to counter balance any material successes which the use of such undisciplined levies may secure.[31]

Large extracts of Pears's article were sent to Elliot by Derby. The article contained a scarcely veiled indictment of the Government. 'Had the Government wished to know the facts—though, of course, it is childishly absurd to suppose they did not know them—they could have sent a Commission to Philippopolis in two days.' The unnamed author of the article also writes that it is not possible to name the people who provided his evidence. Many crimes against women and children, the latter of whom it is alleged that Circassians sold or placed upon sale as slaves, are listed. Sixty villages are said to have been burnt and then the figure of 100 is given, with in- numerable young Bulgarian women carried off to harems. Worse still, the Turks, selecting the prettiest women, 'violate them before the eyes of their mothers. The wretched women scream for help, but no ones dares to go near.' The writer in- dicates that this was common practice 'on a larger scale in the towns and villages of the district' [Philippopolis]. Pears accuses the Turks of a form of genocide. 'Looking through the facts before me there are indications of a general understanding among the Turkish authorities in Bulgaria that the easiest way of getting rid of the complication arising from European in- terference or sympathy on behalf of the Christians is to diminish their number. I see no other sufficient explanation of the deliberate system of plunder and massacre which has been organized.'[32] Then, also on 13 July, Derby, who as can be seen from his letter to Elliot of the same date left the latter to judge the necessity of a warning to the Porte about the use of Bashi- Bazouks, telegraphed to the ambassador about a new charge against the Turks which appeared in the *Daily News* of that day.

In the Tatar Bazardjik district in Bulgaria [about thirty-five miles west of Philippopolis], the Bashi Bazouks have, it is said, boastfully paraded carloads of heads of murdered women and children. These exhibitions are their revenge after each defeat. Young women are now, it is affirmed, regular articles of traffic, being sold publicly in the villages by the Tatars and the Turks.

It is very important that Her Majesty's Government should be able to reply to the inquiries made in Parliament about these and similar statements of atrocities.

Inquire by telegraph of the Consuls, and report as soon as you can.[33]

Dissatisfaction in Britain increased partly out of ignorance of the government's policy and partly as the result of what seemed to be the insufficiency of that policy. A. J. Mundella, M.P. for Sheffield with strong working-class sympathies, wrote at this time to his friend Robert Leader, who owned the *Sheffield and Rotherham Independent*. 'I should hardly like to pledge myself to non-intervention. If these atrocities go on I think our Government ought to intervene to put a stop to them. If Russia violates her engagements I think the Government could hardly abstain from intervention.' In the House of Lords Derby could not give Granville any confirmed information about the atrocities in Bulgaria on 10 July, not having heard from Elliot. In the Commons, on the same day, Disraeli was asked when the Eastern Question papers would be presented and he replied they probably would be given the following week. Forster questioned the Prime Minister specifically about the atrocities and the *Daily News* report of a large number of Bulgarian girls who had been sold as slaves and an equally large number of Bulgarians tortured in prison. Disraeli answered that as yet the government had no accurate information on atrocities but he minimized reports of torture and slave-trading. In his reply he expressed a hope that when all information had been received, the number of atrocities would prove exaggerated. There then followed a brief burst of sarcasm, which later writers have seized upon, and by emphasizing out of context, have distorted the Prime Minister's expressed views. Here is the sarcasm in its context.

Elliot is not a man to be insensible to such terrible proceedings. On the contrary, he is a stern asserter of humanity. . . . We are in constant communication with those gentlemen [British consuls] and certainly no information of the kind has as yet reached Her Majesty's Government. That there have been proceedings of an atrocious character in Bulgaria I have never for a moment doubted. Wars of insurrection are always atrocious. ... I cannot doubt that atrocities have been committed in Bulgaria; but that girls were sold into slavery, or that more than 10,000 persons have been imprisoned, I doubt. In fact, I doubt whether there is prison accommodation for so many, or that torture has been practised on a great scale among an Oriental people who seldom, I believe, resort to torture, but generally terminate their connection with culprits in a more expeditious manner. ... I have no doubt there may be much to deplore in what has been done, and we may even become convinced that scenes have occurred which must bring to everyone feelings of the deepest regret. Still, I cannot but cherish a hope that some of the statements— the heart-rending statements—we have heard ... [are untrue].

Ashley asked whether the Government had any information from the consuls in the area of the reported cruelties, and Mundella implied Government laxness in informing the Commons of its policy. Watkin asked whether the Government would send someone to the Balkans to inquire into the newspaper reports. The Prime Minister ended by confirming that atrocities had been committed, and reiterated this several times, but not in the numbers reported in the Press.[34]

The Liberal leaders in Parliament, and especially Hartington, though anxious to see the Government dispatches which they had been promised, were, from a position of ignorance, not anxious to urge the Government to follow a particular line.

I think that in the present case, less even than usual, it is the duty of the opposition to be provided with a positive policy; and when the papers come out there will be probably quite enough work for us, in criticisms and in eliciting explanations. There will probably be some rather strong opinions expressed on our side, as to what our policy ought ... [and] ought not to be; and I think it decidedly desirable that you [Grant Duff] ... should point out how inadequate they ['the materials for forming a judgement'] are for enabling an opposition to provide a policy for the government.[35]

Disraeli and Derby believed in the exaggeration of the newspaper reports of atrocities though both the Prime Minister and the Queen were anxious for news which could be trusted. Disraeli referred to the *Daily News* stories as almost pure invention and asked Derby if anything had been heard from Elliot about the atrocities. The Queen telegraphed to Disraeli to 'have enquiries made as to the horrors ... in the *Daily News* of today. It is too awful. It will turn everyone against Turkey. One ought also to know what the other side have done.' The Foreign Secretary was puzzled by the Queen's reaction. 'I [Derby] don't know what has set off the great lady again—When I saw her she was quite composed on the subject, and readily agreed to my suggestion that there was immense exaggeration in all these stories, and that they were put about for a purpose.'[36]

On 15 July the Prime Minister exploded at Derby, an outburst ignited by the fact that a dispatch from Reade, the consul at Rustchuk, which reached the Foreign Office on 28 June, was communicated to him only a day or two before the fourteenth. His anger and annoyance do not seem commensurate with the stated reason for it, which was that this dispatch would have caused him to alter his words in Parliament on 10 July. If it would have done so, it is not clear from the content of the dispatch how it might have done so. Reade wrote, what Disraeli reiterated in the Commons, that 'from what has reached me, however, from reliable quarters, it appears that these people [Circassians] are committing atrocities, chiefly amongst the villages near the Balkans [mountains].'

From what I can make out, I am really inclined to think that the object at this moment ... is to diminish the number of Bulgarians as much as possible, for it is said that the Circassians seem to be doing all this with the apparent connivance of the authorities.
. . .
But to ascertain the real truth ... nothing but a personal visit to the spot would suffice ...

The consul did write that 'it is even actually said here that these Circassians are kidnapping children of Bulgarians killed in the late affairs'.[37] In other words, Reade tended to think that atrocities had been committed, but that more reliable information was required, which is what Disraeli had said in the Commons on 10 July.

Disraeli wrote a rather strong letter of protest to the Foreign Secretary.

I must again complain of the management of your office and request your personal attention to it.

It is impossible to represent F.O. in the House of Commons, in these critical times, without sufficient information. What I receive is neither ample, nor accurate.

After I had made the declarations, wh. I did, on yr. authority respecting the Bulgarian 'atrocities' I find a despatch from our consul at Rustchuk, received . . . on the 28th June, & which reached me a fortnight afterwards, wh: if it do not confirm them as facts, refers to them as rumours, wh. are probable & refers to them in some detail.

Last night Mr. Baxter gave notice of a question to be put on Monday to me . . .

I have no confidence what [eve]r. in y[our] office, & I was obliged to submit in silence to the indignity, & for ought I know, Monday may increase the pain of my position.[38]

Disraeli was not happy at being attacked in Parliament, but what rankled were two things, and it was these which were fired by the late reception of Reade's dispatch. First, there was his belief that Derby's lethargy was permitting sloppiness and want of zeal both within the Foreign Office and throughout the Diplomatic Service. Second, the Prime Minister resented the public demonstration of his own ignorance of Balkan geography and the British consular establishment, when Ashley indicated that information on any atrocities would come from Adrianople and Philippopolis and not as Disraeli mentioned from Belgrade, Ragusa, and Cetinje.[39] This explains the Prime Minister's reference in his outburst to Derby that 'this was pretty well giving me the lie'.[40] Derby must have been puzzled by the outburst and quickly asked Tenterden to provide the reply. 'I must ask you to read the enclosed. I suppose there is an explanation. You supplied the information for this answer to the Premier, and I dare say you know whether it was really imperfect.' Disraeli sent for Tenterden on the morning of 14 July and the latter quite correctly explained that until that very morning, when a dispatch from Elliot arrived, the Foreign Office had received no 'reports of the particular atrocities mentioned in the Daily News', and that Reade's dispatch was merely another unconfirmed report of suspected atrocities. Derby, of course, replied similarly to Disraeli.

I do not see that you have anything to retract or even modify. The despatch wh. you did not see did not bear on the particular subject on wh. you were questioned. Where papers must pass through various hands—mine, Tenterden's, Bourke's [the Parliamentary Under-Secretary] & then the Queen's & those of our colleagues, I don't see how it is possible to guard against the chance of a paper wh. you want at very short notice being out of the hands of the Department.[41]

The Foreign Secretary managed much better with the deputations he received at the Foreign Office on the same day. The first, headed by John Bright, presented a petition signed by over forty members of Parliament and industrialists and political associations mainly from the Midlands and the north of England, calling for British neutrality and opposing British aid for the continued authority of the Porte in the area of the insurrection. Derby made an extremely interesting reply.

I have often thought that it is one of the most difficult parts of the duty of a Minister in a Parliamentary country that, being as he is in practice the servant of Parliament and of the public, as well as of the Queen, he does not always receive his instructions from his employers before hand, but is left to guess what it is they would desire him to do . . .

I think it is the most improbable thing in the world that, in consequence of anything that is now passing within the limits of the Turkish Empire, a general European war should ensue (loud and general applause). . . . I do not see the quarter from which the war is to come.

If . . . the Turkish Empire is in a state of decay from internal causes . . . it is clear that merely external assistance would be no remedy. (Cheers). . . . We undertook twenty years ago to guarantee him against suicide or sudden death. (Cheers). . . . We shall not intervene; we shall do our utmost, if necessary, to discourage others from intervening; (Cheers) but I don't believe that under the present circumstances it will be necessary. If an opportunity of mediation should offer itself . . . we shall gladly avail ourselves of it.

The report of the Foreign Secretary's reply to the deputations appeared in *The Times* of 15 July and produced a public feeling of relief and reassurance.[42] Harris points out that Bright went away reassured and happy, a reaction which the press also reflected shortly afterwards.[43] Derby was much more successful with the Liberal opposition and the general public than with the Prime Minister.

At the end of the day (14 July), Disraeli wrote to the Queen that the opposition were 'going to work the "atrocities" as a party question'; he also reported that information had finally arrived from Elliot, whose slowness elicited his irritation, but whose report showed that there was considerable exaggeration and that the atrocities were shared by both Christians and Turks.[44]

Elliot's dispatch of 6 July enclosed two communications from Dupuis and arrived at the Foreign Office on 14 July. The ambassador wrote of quite considerable excesses, but as it was derived from Bulgarian and Russian sources, there was very great exaggeration.

Without impartial agents on the spot, I am unable to say more than I am satisfied that, while great atrocities have been committed, both by Turks upon Christians and by Christians upon Turks, the former have been by far the greatest, although the Christians were undoubtedly the first to commence them.
. . .

[that] Circassians, who have no compunction in selling the children of their own countrymen, would scruple to sell those of the Bulgarians is not to be supposed, and I have not a doubt that many such instances must have occurred.
. . .

For weeks past I have never seen one of the Turkish Ministers without insisting upon the necessity of at once putting an end to these excesses . . .

They deny that the cruelties have been upon a scale at all approaching to what they are represented. They point out that the horrors committed on Turkish women and children are passed over in silence; and they plead that they had no alternative but to use the irregular force at their disposal to put down an unprovoked insurrection fomented from abroad . . .

Dupuis's letter of 28 June contained no sure information, but the consul reported that the sale of Bulgarian children was quite likely in remote places. Nor did the consul doubt that Bulgarian girls had been supplied to Turkish harems. In his dispatch of 3 July, again without any confirmed information, Dupuis was led to conclude that the Turks were not capable of civilized conduct.[45] This time Derby reacted at once and, unlike the instructions given to Elliot on 13 July, leaving him to judge the necessity of any representation to the Porte on the use of

Bashi-Bazouks, the Foreign Secretary gave explicit instructions for one to be made at once. On Elliot's preceding dispatch, Derby minuted the following. 'Instruct Sir H. Elliot . . . to urge strongly [to the Porte] that the local authorities be directed to lose no time in repressing these outrages & punishing those concerned in them & that the sale of women and children be prohibited . . . under the severest penalties & all persons held in illegal captivity by the Circassians & others be immediately released . . .'[46] Before Elliot received these instructions he telegraphed to Derby that he could add little to the information in his dispatch of 6 July and reported that there were no British consular officials in the area of the atrocities and, consequently, those in other places could not guarantee the veracity of the reports of excess.

There can be no doubt the instigators of the insurrection began by committing atrocities on Mussulmans and burning Bulgarian villages with the view of creating exasperation between the two races. In this they succeeded, and when the Bashi-Bazouks and Circassians were called out, they indulged in every sort of misconduct, killing and outraging numbers of innocent persons.
. . .

It . . . appears . . . that the regular troops have at other times been guilty of great excess. Bulgarian children have certainly been sold, but I cannot find that there has been anything like a regular traffic in them. Until I received your telegram I had heard nothing of either cartloads of heads being paraded, or young women publicly sold, but I will make every possible inquiry. It was supposed here that the abuses had been put a stop to for some time.[47]

Elliot's telegram probably crossed one from Derby to Dupuis. The Foreign Secretary was being moved by reports of atrocities of the most barbarous kind and instructed Dupuis to visit the area of the atrocities and discover the truth, and then telegraph his findings to both himself and Elliot.[48] On 17 July Disraeli spoke in the Commons and gave a résumé of the diplomatic dispatches on the Bulgarian rising and the atrocities, reading from many of Elliot's reports. It was an attempt to reinforce the Government's position that a Bulgarian insurrection planned by outside agitators caused atrocity to Muslim inhabitants who returned it to the Christians many times over, but that the reports in the *Daily News* were exaggerated.

Four days later an extended discussion transpired in the Commons on the Turkish loan of 1856 and to what extent, if any, it had been guaranteed by the British Government. Between bankruptcy and atrocity there was an increasingly narrowing piece of ground for Turkish supporters in Britain to stand upon. But there were still some unregenerate Palmerstonians, like Hammond, the former Permanent Under-Secretary for Foreign Affairs, who were willing to do so.

Of course our thoughts are now all directed towards Turkey and her troubles, with the satisfaction of knowing that there cannot be a word of truth in the contradictory accounts that we receive. I must indeed give the insurgents credit for their inventive power, by means of which they impose on the credibility of good people in this country, and lead them to believe that the Christians are all angels and martyrs, while the Mussulmans are all fiends and demons. I see the Bishops are taking the field in that sense . . . and I suppose we shall soon have prayers of the Church in their [Christian] behalf . . .

At the other extreme there was increasing anxiety and activity, and one of the louder voices belonged to an old acquaintance and friend of Gladstone, the Reverend Malcolm MacColl.

I believe that they [atrocities] are substantially accurate & the shameful efforts of Dizzy & Lord Derby to palliate them are intolerable . . . Dizzy I regard as one of the most inveterate liars in Christendom. I feel humiliation at the thought that such a man now rules the destinies of my land. I sincerely trust you may find it convenient to speak on the Eastern question & tear away the mask from the shameful pictures of Turkey wh the government & a portion of the press have presented the public.[49]

There were others who wished Britain to side actively with the Christian rebels and they were beginning to organize themselves. A meeting was held at Willis's Rooms on 27 July. It was arranged by Lewis Farley and the League in Aid of Christians in Turkey. Farley, a Levantine banking expert and former employee of the Porte when Turkish consul at Bristol, seemed now bent on completely destroying the Turks.[50] Lord Shaftesbury presided at the meeting, at which a sympathetic letter was read from Earl Russell and a number of resolutions were moved, one by the historian E. A. Freeman which urged independence for the insurgent provinces. Though there is no evidence of it here, Freeman's feelings were so stirred by the

Turks and Disraeli, that they would cause him to lose all balance and perspective in belching forth an unremitting torrent of abuse which was embarrassing when it was not disgusting.[51] At the gathering were a sizeable number of M.P.s, but the net was spread wide and George Howell, the labour leader and organizer, was asked to serve as one of the sixty sponsors of the meeting, at which great abhorrence was expressed about the Turkish cruelties committed in Bulgaria. Shaftesbury's opening speech as chairman set the tone. 'Surely it is high time for the kingdoms of Europe to interfere and declare that Turkey is a spectacle disgusting to humanity and wholly unfit to exercise rule and authority. (Cheers).'[52]

As lines of battle were being drawn in Britain, the need to know reliably what had occurred in Rumelia caused a mild rush on the chief city in the area—Philippopolis (Plovdiv). There were only three consuls in the town—the Greek, Austrian, and Russian. The Russian consul was a Bulgarian who was strongly suspected of helping to plan the Bulgarian insurrection; the Austrian seemed only to report of villages burned by the rebels, not by the Turks, and the Greek consul denied that any Bulgarian children had been sold by the Bashi-Bazouks as slaves. But the Constantinople correspondent for the *Daily News,* Pears, was active enough with his unnamed Bulgarian sources, and he, of course, was the great disseminator of information for the British public. According to Harris, he was affronted by Disraeli's treatment in Parliament of the news of the atrocities which he supplied to his newspaper. 'He gathered information and sent it on to London with the zeal of a man engaged in a personal vendetta [against Disraeli]. His third letter published on July 19, was an even more savage reply to Disraeli than his second. He asserted that. . . . "I underestimated rather than overestimated the outrages." '[53]

As Pears was involved with his legal practice and probably suspected that the Porte would prevent his going to Rumelia, he suggested the *Daily News* send out another correspondent to Bulgaria. The man chosen was J. S. MacGahan, a young American journalist in his late twenties who had gained a measure of fame by a book describing his experiences with the Russian army in central Asia. He set out from Constantinople with a friend, Eugene Schuyler, the recently arrived United States secretary of legation and consul-general, who, like MacGahan, had also toured central Asia. Washburn, the American director of Robert College, used his influence with the United States minister in Constantinople to send Schuyler on a mission to investigate the atrocities. The latter took with him as an interpreter a Bulgarian from Robert College who also spoke Turkish, and he and MacGahan left for Bulgaria on 23 July.[54]

The two Americans had been preceded by Baring, a second secretary of the Embassy at Constantinople, who was sent out to investigate the reported atrocities a little before this. But Dupuis, from Adrianople, as instructed by Derby, had reached Philippopolis first and telegraphed to London on 21 July. 'Although great atrocities have been committed by Turkish irregulars against the Bulgarians, they have been exaggerated. As regards [district] . . . of Philippopoli, lives sacrificed below 15,000. No women or children sold as slaves here or [at] Tatar Bazardjik. Sixty villages more or less burnt'.[55]

The very act of minimizing the number of some and denying the existence of other barbarities had the effect, gradually, of overcoming one's critical capacity. Unconfirmed and second-hand reports began to acquire a general validity, especially as everyone knew that the Muslims were given to atrocity and barbarity. Elliot wrote the following to London: 'I wish it were possible for me to accept the denial of Midhat Pasha that outrages had been committed upon Bulgarian women, but the testimony of there having been many such instances is far too strong to be resisted.'[56]

The following day Elliot telegraphed to Reade at Rustchuk and asked him to report on the stories in English newspapers of murdered and beheaded women and children and men being sold as slaves. The consul's reply was that he could find little evidence for such activity. When the ambassador spoke to the Grand Vizier, concerning excesses, on 22 July, he was told that most cruelties had been committed by unauthorized bands which the Ottoman Government was doing all it could to put down. 'Three [Bashi-Bazouks] had already been hanged. A considerable proportion of the villages destroyed were, he [Grand Vizier] says, burned by the insurgents . . .'[57] Even the

French and German governments, which did not have consuls in the area of the atrocities, believed in their existence.[58]

In London, towards the end of July, the Government finally presented papers, and the thirty-first was selected for Parliamentary debate. It was to be a political summer, the like of which Britain has not often known.

AFTER THE Austro-Russian meeting at Berlin in May 1876 and the outbreak of war at the beginning of July, when Serbia and Montenegro attacked Turkey, Alexander II and Gorchakov met with Francis Joseph and Andrássy at the Bohemian castle of Reichstadt on 8 July. We shall never completely know what was said there owing to the discrepancies between the Austrian and Russian versions of the meeting, which were only afterwards written down.[2]

The public pronouncement which issued from the meeting was that Austria and Russia had agreed on a policy of non-intervention in connection with the Serbo-Turkish war. A secret verbal agreement, however, had also been arranged for the outcome of the war which would see, if Turkey won, Austro-Russian intervention to prevent atrocities and to preserve the territorial *status quo ante*, with reforms for the insurgent provinces. If the Christians won, Andrássy and Gorchakov agreed to exclude the creation of a large Slavic state, with Bosnia-Hercegovina being divided up among Serbia, Montenegro, and Austria. Because of the differences in the Austrian and Russian versions of the agreement, it is not clear if Austria or Serbia and Montenegro were to obtain the major slices of Bosnia and Hercegovina. Russia was to be compensated with that part of Besserabia lost in 1856 and areas of Turkey in Asia. If the Ottoman Empire in Europe were to collapse entirely, Constantinople was to be a free city, Thessaly was to be joined to Greece, and autonomy or independence was to be given to Bulgaria.[3]

If Rupp is correct, Gorchakov agreed to give up some of Bosnia, if not most of it, to Austria in order to make a direct agreement with her free of Germany and Bismarck who, unlike his sovereign, had clearly indicated a pro-Austrian leaning and an undisguised contempt for Gorchakov.

For Andrássy, the agreement was defensive, and the Russian recognition of Austria's right to some of Bosnia as well as a refusal to countenance the creation of a large Slavic state were potential immediate gains for Austria. Andrássy was still in control of the extremely unstable Austro-Russian partnership and his policy of maintaining Ottoman integrity if possible was now extended by protecting Austria in view of a probable Ottoman collapse. Andrássy's dominance was proving to be misdirected, however, as unofficial Russian diplomacy, supported by highly placed and outraged Orthodox and Slavic feelings in Moscow and St. Petersburg, had taken the lead from the unsteady hands of Alexander II, Gorchakov, and Jomini. The Bulgarian rising and the Serbian war were largely inspired by Russia's Pan-Slav Balkan diplomats. Ignatiev failed only in convincing the Tsar and the Russian Government to join the Serbian war against Turkey.

The war[4] continued throughout the summer and early autumn of 1876, interrupted only by a suspension of hostilities. Montenegro was able to hold her own but Serbia met with military defeat, and this brought on attempts by the Great Powers to mediate and end hostilities. These attempts at peace were exceedingly intricate and convoluted, and so the fighting continued unhampered by an all-European effort to define the meaning of autonomy.

In Britain diplomacy by the Great Powers was engulfed in a storm over the government's Eastern policy, but especially over the atrocities reported in the *Daily News*. The Government, after many requests, presented Parliament with a rather large selection of the diplomatic dispatches, and full debates occurred in both Houses on 31 July.[5]

Recognizing political circumstances, Liberal criticism of the Government in both Houses was at best indirect and at times picayune and feeble. The policy of non-intervention announced by the Government offered a divided opposition little to attack. Harris has summed up the debates uncommonly well.

The Liberal attack on the government was weak. The Opposition leaders had so fully recognized the hopelessness of trying to make an issue of foreign affairs that they had not prepared a motion that would invite a test of confidence. Indeed, the Liberal spokesmen were too much of a common mind with the ministers to wish to make an issue. . . . At the same time, the progress of the debates revealed a divergence of opinion between the two parties on Ottoman affairs.

The Liberals had joined the public in welcoming Derby's announcement [to the deputation] of a policy of non-intervention, but . . . the Liberal leaders, like the journals of their party, were not genuinely neutral. Each one of the Liberal leaders made a slashing attack on Turkish rule, and each went on to espouse active intervention on the part of the British government in favor of the Christians.[6]

Though the Government came out of the debates quite well, there had been remarks as to the atrocities in Bulgaria, and Gladstone had made a brief reference to such activity so long being covered up, as well as an unfair characterization of Baring as being prejudiced and ill suited to conduct the inquiry into the atrocities.[7] Newspapers continued to carry stories of atrocities and on 7 and 11 August two further debates were given over entirely to Turkish conduct in Bulgaria from which the Government emerged much less well.

While indignation and excitement were growing in England, Dupuis and Baring[8] had set out to investigate the truth and the extent of the alleged barbarities which were so raising the political temperature at home. Baring left Constantinople on 19 July and two days earlier Dupuis had left Adrianople; the former arrived at Adrianople on the evening of 19 July. The following morning he started out for Philippopolis and arrived there late on the afternoon of the same day, and called at once upon the Turkish provincial governor. The latter told him that while atrocities had been committed, their number had been exaggerated, and that no women and children had been sold, a statement Baring heard confirmed by others in the town. On 22 July Baring made his first report, having been in Philippopolis barely two days. He wrote that he was obtaining information in the town—he does not indicate from whom—but that volumes of contradictory statements were making his job difficult. The sale of women and children he refers to as pure fiction and the cartloads of heads being paraded in the streets as invention. 'As regards the number of killed, till I have visited the villages I hardly dare speak, but my present opinion, which I trust hereafter to be able to modify, is that about 12,000 Bulgarians have perished.' Baring does not distinguish in his figure of 12,000 between Bulgarians who revolted and fought, and innocent non-combatants, who were massacred. Nor is it clear from where this estimate came. The figure of 12,000 was being bandied about in both Adrianople and Constantinople. Other guesses which had gained currency were 20,000 and 30,000. Back in June Dupuis had reported an estimate of 12,000 to the embassy at Constantinople. The main source of information seemed to be from the American ex-missionaries who were attached to Robert College in Constantinople and who were horrified with what seemed to be happening in Bulgaria. One can only witness their revulsion and horror with sympathy and recognize their tendency to exaggerate events which excited in them such extreme feelings. Before leaving Constantinople Baring, who knew the American contingent at Robert College, was supplied by the missionaries with a special memorandum to assist him in his inquiry.[9]

As he had been in Philippopolis, and nowhere else, only two days, it is likely that Baring's estimate was derived either from their memorandum or similar reports of the kind which had reached Dupuis at Adrianople. His report of 12,000 was given, therefore, on the basis of guesses and estimates which he had been sent to investigate at first hand. It is true that in the non-Ottoman calculations of Bulgarians killed, 12,000 was the lowest or near the lowest guess, other estimates running to over 100,000. With Baring's figures, in this same report, of villages wholly or partly burned, the number of 60 is given—50 by the Turks and about 10 by the rebels. This too was given before he had seen one of the villages himself. Harris's accusation that Baring, like Elliot, was a Turcophile and that he drew his opinions from the ambassador[10] is therefore unfair, inaccurate, and, in the specific instance of the atrocities, entirely misleading. For what Baring had done was to absorb non-Ottoman estimates with little question, and to give them the patina of truth by expressing them as his considered opinion before he had gone to the actual localities of the alleged murder and destruction. Harris labels Baring, and his father-in-law who travelled with him, a Levantine by the name of Guarracino, as Turcophiles, as though this were a crime. When Ottoman authorities at Philippopolis gave the estimate of 1,000 Turks killed in the rising, Baring wrote that his investigation led him to believe that such a figure had little basis in reality, and that about half the estimated number was nearer the truth, though doubtless many of the dead had met with much cruelty. His information could only have been Christian Bulgarian or American missionary information. 'One thing is perfectly clear, viz., that the province is ruined, as the Government will discover to its cost when the tithe is collected. ... Large numbers of horses, oxen, sheep, and cows have been driven off by Pomaks [Bulgarian Muslims] and others, and it is the duty of the Government to oblige the latter to return them to their owners.'[11] Harris's accusation, then, that the British inquiry would be in the hands of the dubious Guarracino and the Ottoman officials in Bulgaria could not be further from the truth. Rather it was at the mercy of outraged American ex-missionaries, the equally disturbed administration of Robert College, and reporters in Constantinople who were supplied information by Bulgarians. Baring's error in their eyes, perhaps, was that he fixed upon the lowest of their estimates of Bulgarians killed rather than upon one of the higher guesses.

Dupuis, the vice-consul at Adrianople, sent a report approximately a month before his departure to investigate the situation at Philippopolis containing information concerning the alleged use of torture against political prisoners in Bulgaria. Upon learning this, Derby instructed Elliot on 3 August to bring this unacceptable behaviour to the attention of the Porte. Six days later the ambassador telegraphed back that after pressing the Porte to free imprisoned Bulgarians awaiting trial, he was promised by the Grand Vizier that this would be done at once except for a few of the leading insurgents.[12] On the same day the ambassador sent a second telegram:

It is impossible to use stronger language than I have employed about atrocities in Bulgaria.

Porte repeats that they were chiefly committed not by Bashi-Bazouks [presumably here meant as government-armed or paid irregulars], but by the Mussulman populations threatened with extermination and made furious by the cruelties inflicted on their countrymen by the insurgents.

No time can be fixed at which the insurrection was finally suppressed, for long after it was put down in the plains large bands of insurgents remained in the mountains, where probably some still remain. No disturbances are now going on . . .[13]

On 23 July Baring left Philippopolis and made his way to the two burnt villages of Prasadura Dervent (Klissoura in

Bulgarian) and Singirli, making a careful investigation at all villages passed along the way concerning any cruelties or evidence of looting. It is clear from the following that his information was supplied to a great extent by the Bulgarian victims of the Circassians and Pomaks rather than by the Ottoman authorities.

Everywhere I heard the same tale—their cattle and horses had been taken by the Circassians and Pomaks; if they went any distance from their homes they were sure to be plundered, and perhaps beaten . . . . . .

The village of Dervent consisted of 800 houses; every one has been burnt. At the outbreak of the insurrection the [Bulgarian] inhabitants murdered a Turkish kiatib [leader of prayers] and two Zaptiehs [policemen], and threw up some rough fortifications, consisting of a low loop-holed stone wall.

The Turkish population marched against them, and after a slight resistance, entered the village, pillaged, and burnt it. Some 250 Bulgarians are missing out of a population of between 3,500 and 4,000.

The Turkish version is, that on approaching the village they called on the inhabitants several times to surrender, and only attacked on receiving a decided refusal; and further that the villagers themselves, on taking flight to the hills, set fire to their own homes.

I am not inclined quite to accept this [Turkish] story . . .

From Dervent I proceeded to Kalofer, to find out, if possible, the truth of the awful story respecting the burning of forty-six girls in a barn . . .

I have now no doubt that the story is an invention. No one in Kalofer could tell me anything about it . . .

Singirli, a village of 177 houses is certainly burnt, the following story being told by the [Christian] villagers.

One day, quite at the outbreak of the insurrection, the priest, the school master, and some six or seven others called them and told them that the Russians were advancing, and that they must leave their villages as the Turks would attack them; those who objected were driven out by force, and twelve Mussulmans (the Turks say thirty-two) who happened to be in the village were murdered. The village was then set on fire, and the inhabitants fled. The Mussulmans, seeing part of the village in flames, went and pillaged all they could, and burnt remaining houses.[14]

Dupuis, who had been at Philippopolis since 18 July, visited a few of the Bulgarian villages in the vicinity of the town and found that they had been partly burnt down. On 19 July he made his way to Peroushtitza, a village of some size near the Rhodope mountains, and found the place completely destroyed, with scarcely a single house remaining intact. It had been burnt, he wrote, by Bashi-Bazouks under Ahmed Aga on 13 May. Dupuis complained that none of the Pomak Bashi-Bazouks was punished for the atrocities they committed unlike some innocent Bulgarians who suffered for defending themselves.[15]

On 31 July, the day of the debates in both Houses of Parliament, Baring, whose efforts in the heat of the summer had caused him to be temporarily unwell, visited Batak, having travelled there from Tatar Bazardjik, returning to the latter place on the same day. He was accompanied by Guarracino but not Dupuis. The second secretary wrote that he was met there by 'the most awful sight that could present itself to the eyes of man'.

The village consisted of 800 houses, and about 8,000 inhabitants. Of these at least 6,000 have been massacred. . . . The first thing I saw was some twenty or thirty dogs devouring human bodies, and in the place they had been feasting in I counted sixty-two skulls in about 20 yards. . . . Here [inside and around the church] the corpses lay so thick that one could hardly avoid treading on them, and the stench was so fearful, that any examination was next to impossible. . . . The women were sitting on the ruins of their houses wailing and singing the most melancholy sort of dirge, which could be heard some way from the village.

Baring reported that the perpetrator of this horror was one Achmet Agha who had been decorated by the Ottoman authorities. 'It will be a great disgrace if the Porte lets this affair pass unnoticed. The people of Batak may have had an intention of rising, and they had, in fact, erected some slight fortifications, but whatever they did cannot justify Achmet Agha's perjury and cruelty.' For the next couple of days Baring visited other villages, at times accompanied by Dupuis; he found Vetven partially burnt, the inhabitants having committed some insurrectionary acts. A similar report was made on the village of Otloukeui where a large number of women and children were killed. Baring indicates that the inhabitants of this village led and began the revolt, but that the general looting and burning were not justified here or elsewhere.

Here [Yenikeui] the people killed about thirty Turks, and left for the hills with the inhabitants of the other villages; the Bashi-Bazouks came and burnt it, and a few days later the inhabitants returned, but were attacked by the Turks, and sixty killed.

I am most anxious to finish, as it is not pleasant to hear every day and all day tales of misery and suffering. Everywhere I hear the same story: the people were told they must rise, as the Turks would otherwise kill them, and the Russian troops were crossing the Balkans. . . . It is he [Gueroff, Russian vice-consul] who has done all the mischief more than anybody.[16]

Elliot made a copy of Baring's dispatch of 1 August and sent it to the Turkish Foreign Minister whom he also went to see. The latter naturally attempted to defend Turkish barbarism to the British ambassador, but Elliot threw Batak in his face, 'seen with his [Baring's] own eyes'. 'He [Safvet Pasha, the Foreign Minister] complained bitterly, and certainly not without justice, that while the European newspapers systematically exaggerated every excess on the part of the Turks, they studiously suppressed all mention of those which had been committed by the insurgents who commenced by masacring the Mahomedans where they were in a minority . . .'[17]

Dupuis had returned to Adrianople by 7 August, from where he sent a long report to Derby of the investigation he and Baring had made. He wrote of the outbreak of the Bulgarian insurrection as the work of revolutionary committees and described the enlisting of Turkish irregulars and their destruction of Bulgarian villages, Peroushtitza and Batak being ones that he singled out.

As far as I can learn, I have reasons to believe that the inhabitants of Peroushtitza had, in the first instance, provoked the anger of the Turks by killing two Mussulmans of a neighbouring village. . . . The provocation, however . . . scarcely justified . . . the horrible loss of life and destruction of property caused by the Pomak Bashi-Bazouks.

It is said, without any attempt at concealment, that the Russian Vice-Consul in Philippopolis is solely responsible for the sad disasters which have befallen this flourishing village. . . . Peroushtitza [was burnt] on the 13th, and Batak on the 9th of May. . . . The slaughter at Batak, by the Pomak Bashi Bazouks . . . has been variously estimated to be between 2,000 and 5,000 persons of both sexes.

Otlukeui ... was attacked on the 12th of May ...

. . .

In many instances, the villages were set on fire by the Bulgarians themselves, in order to compel its inhabitants to take up arms. ... Singerli ... was, in the first instance, set on fire by the priest.

. . .

It is impossible to estimate the total number of lives sacrified. ... There are no statistical returns to show the former population of destroyed villages ... I am inclined to think that the number of lives sacrificed will not be more than 10,000 ... [in] the districts of Philippopolis and Tatar Bazardjik ...

The vice-consul estimated that 57 villages had been destroyed and that atrocities had been committed by both Bulgarians and Turks.[18]

Baring returned to Constantinople on 22 August and apparently spent some days composing his report, which he finished on 1 September, and which Elliot forwarded to London on 5 September. He gave a short history of the origins of the Bulgarian rising and its brutal suppression with lists of statistics of lives lost and villages burnt. In the district of Philippopolis 18 villages were reported as partly or completely destroyed, and of these Baring visited 4 having obtained the statistics for the others from a trustworthy Bulgarian at Philippopolis. In the district of Tatar Bazardjik 33 Christian villages were gutted, of which he visited 6; his source for those he had not visited personally being a Bulgarian and possibly the only 'highly respectable Turk of Philippopolis'.

During my journey I have heard the number of killed differently estimated at anything between 200,000 and 1,830, the latter being the Turkish official estimate ...

. . .

I think I cannot be accused of exaggeration, or of wishing to paint things blacker than they really are, if I maintain the estimate I previously made, viz., that about 12,000 persons perished in the sanjak of Philippopolis [this included the area of Tatar Bazardjik].

It is not much easier to discover the number of Mussulmans killed ... but the list I append I have received on good authority, and I think may be relied on.

One hundred and sixty-three was the figure given for Turks who were killed, with 5 Turkish villages burnt. Baring singled out Achmet Agha and his men for what they did at Batak, 'perhaps the most heinous crime that has stained the history of the present century'. But he did not forget that those who had initially reported the atrocities to the public had taken little notice of the fact that an insurrection had ever occurred.

As regards the importance of the insurrection it was neither so formidable as the Turks in their first panic thought it, nor was so utterly insignificant as many people wish to make it out to be.

The principal instigators came entirely from abroad, and without foreign intrigue no revolution would have broken out . . .. I believe the majority of the respectable Bulgarians took no real part in it.
. . .
Wherever there is Turkish rule . . . owing to its inherent faults, there will be Christian discontent . . .

The foreign agitators and those natives whom they succeeded in seducing [priests and schoolmasters] seized upon this apparently favourable opportunity to strike a blow; the peasants were deluded into leaving their villages by being told that the Turks were going to massacre them, and the population of the small towns was induced to take part in the insurrection by threats and . . . foreign aid.
. . .
The Turks gained an easy victory and abused it most shamefully, the innocent being made to suffer for the guilty in a manner too horrible to think of . . .

I can honestly state that I started with no preconceived ideas . . .[19]

Baring listed statistics for 51 villages of which he had visited 10. His sources of information were largely Bulgarian.

At the same time that he enclosed Baring's report to London, Elliot also sent a letter given to him by the United States minister in Constantinople from Eugene Schuyler, who had also made an investigative tour of Bulgaria with several newspaper correspondents, at times travelling with Baring.[20] Schuyler listed information on 63 villages in the districts of Philippopolis and Tatar Bazardjik, of which he visited 11. Schuyler stated categorically that absolutely no Bulgarian atrocities were committed on Turks and not surprisingly made no attempt to estimate Turkish or Muslim deaths caused by the rising.[21] Baring reported that the American investigator made no attempt to disguise his violent hatred for anything Turkish, and was quite open in his desire that the Ottoman Empire might disintegrate. 'During his tour in the Province of Slimnia he [Schuyler] was accompanied by Prince Tchertelew, Secretary to the Russian embassy at Constantinople, and Acting Vice-Consul at Philippopolis, whose influence did not probably weaken Mr. Schuyler's anti-Turkish sentiments.'[22] Another person who also did nothing to mitigate Schuyler's prejudices was his American friend and newspaper reporter, J. A. MacGahan, whom the *Daily News* sent out to Bulgaria as a special correspondent. MacGahan travelled with Schuyler and sent to the *Daily News* two telegrams which were printed on 7 August, one of which cast aspersions on Baring's investigation. J. A. MacGahan had strong pro-Russian sentiments. In 1872, in Paris, he had married Barbara Nicholaevna Elagin, a lady from an old Russian family whom he had met at Yalta, where he was something of a favourite with the Tsar's court. His adventurous disposition led him to events of interest which he described vividly, if not always with accuracy. He was more than able to carry the ball which Pears had put into play.

On 28 July he sent a report to the *Daily News* from Philippopolis.

When you are met in the outset of your investigation with the admission that 60 or 70 villages have been burned, that some 15,000 people have been slaughtered of whom a large part were women or children. . . . Details represented to you . . . by the different consuls at Philippopolis[23] and the German officials on the railway, as well as Greeks, Armenians, priests, missionaries, and even Turks themselves, you begin to feel that any further investigation is superfluous.

Mr. Baring, I am informed, will report that in the districts about Philippopolis and Tatar Bazardjik alone . . . nearly 15,000 people have been slaughtered. . . . There are people who put the number of killed at 100,000 . . .[24]

On 2 August MacGahan submitted his report on Batak and only the effect of the horrible sights he saw there could explain the illogicality and inaccuracy of his account.

Batak . . . was a place of nine hundred houses, and about 8,000 or 9,000 inhabitants. As there are no . . . trustworthy statistics of any other [other than census statistics of which there were none] kind in Turkey, it is impossible to tell exactly what the population of any place is or was. . . . Edep Effendi, in his report, states that there were only about 1,400 inhabitants in the village, all told. A more impudent falsehood was never uttered, even by a Turk. . . . I have always heard them [Bulgarians] spoken of as mere savages, who were in reality not much more civilized than the American Indians. . . . The percentage of people who can read and write is as great in Bulgaria as in England and France.[25]

Schuyler was as much affected by what he saw as MacGahan. 'As to outrages I am burning with indignation and rage—can scarcely contain myself. . . . Lowest estimate of Christians killed 12,000, highest of Turks killed two hundred and thirty . . .'[26] Schuyler and MacGahan, hating the Turks, found ample evidence in their tour for such feelings, and their reports justified their prejudices and contempt by the enormity of what they had heard and observed. Baring and Dupuis were less extreme than the two Americans, but their investigation was as limited and nearly as anti-Turkish. The difference was that Baring thought he was impartial, 'I started with no preconceived ideas', a handicap under which the two Americans did not labour. But Baring was wrong, if honest, and was unaware of the influence of his own Christianity. It was he who had written in his official report that 'wherever there is Turkish rule . . . owing to its inherent faults, there will be Christian discontent'.

MacGahan's report of 2 August containing news of Batak was published in the *Daily News* of 7 August and immediately elicited, on two hours' notice to the Government, a speech and discussion in the Commons initiated by Mr. Anderson, M.P. for Glasgow. He began by referring to the extreme dissatisfaction felt by many with the flavour of the Prime Minister's statements in the discussion about Bulgaria on 10 July. He considered that he has spoken with unseemly frivolity about a subject of grave importance. He criticized the Government and singled out Sir Henry Elliot for special condemnation. He finished with MacGahan's narrative on Batak.

Even allowing for exaggeration—as he [Anderson] was quite willing to do—the particularity of these statements [of atrocity] . . . showed that there must be much truth in them. But he came now to the statements in that day's *Daily News* which spoke of atrocities exceeding any previously heard of. In this case, he did not see how it was possible to throw doubt on the statements, because they were sent by a correspondent accompanying the American Commissioner, Mr. Schuyler . . .

Anderson then read from the article.

'I [MacGahan] counted from the saddle 100 skulls, picked and licked clean, all of women and children. ... The whole churchyard [at Batak] for three feet deep was festering with dead bodies partly covered—hands, legs, arms and heads projected in ghastly confusion. ... There were 3,000 bodies in the churchyard and the church. ... In the school ... 200 women and children had been burnt alive ...'

He ended with a hope that there would be some more serious statement from the Prime Minister than that which he had last made to Parliament.

Disraeli, who had been silent during the debate, rose to speak and end the discussion. He referred to Ashley's criticism of the Government and said that if the latter really believed censure of the Government's conduct was justified, he ought to have made a motion to this effect. The Prime Minister specifically defended Elliot, and on the question of the British Levantine agents he replied that there would have been better communication with European Turkey, if in past years the number of Ottoman vice-consulates had not unfortunately been reduced by the Liberal Government. He ended on a purely patriotic but probably sincere note. 'But those who suppose that England ever would uphold, or at this moment particularly is upholding Turkey from blind superstition and from a want to sympathy with the highest aspirations of humanity, are deceived. What our duty is at this critical moment is to maintain the Empire of England. Nor will we ever agree to any step, though it may obtain for a moment comparative quiet and false prosperity, that hazards the existence of that Empire.'[27]

Disraeli felt personally the criticism which was elicited by the Parliamentary discussions of 7 and 11 August. His hesitancy in crediting the newspaper reports and his apparent sarcasm in reference to the cruelties had been hurled back in his face. He naturally resented the embarrassment which he saw, a little unfairly, as the result of the inadequacy of Elliot and Derby.

We have had a very damaging debate on Bulgarian atrocities & it is lucky for us, in this respect, that the session is dying.

Had it not been for an adroit & ingenious speech by Bourke, who much distinguished himself, the consequences might have been rather serious.

But two grave results are now evident:

1. That Elliot has shown a lamentable want of energy & deficiency of information throughout: &

2nd that our own F.O. is liable to the same imputations. The F.O. misled me in the first replies wh. I gave on their voucher, & had I seen that despatch of Consul Reade, which never reached me, I wd. never have made those answers, and, what is more, shd. have pressed it on you [Derby] to follow up Reade's revelations.

. . .

It is a very awkward business, and, I fear, a great exposure of our diplomatic system abroad and at home.[28]

As before, Derby allowed Tenterden the job of defending the Foreign Office, as Disraeli left the same onus with respect to defending the Government in the Commons to Bourke in the debate on 7 August. Again, Tenterden pointed out that the information the Foreign Office supplied to the Prime Minister regarding statements in the *Daily News* was accurate, even though Reade's dispatch was not sent to Disraeli in good time.

I really do not think it necessary to defend myself in regard to the diplomatic work at the Foreign Office. Mr. Disraeli has always been so good as to express to me personally his appreciation of what I have done to assist the Government. . . . As to Sir H. Elliot I scarcely think that he can with good reason be accused of any laxity. . . . We do not even now know the truth about the extent of the murders or the number of villages burned—Every hamlet, every little collection of two or three mud and stone huts goes as a village in these countries. . . . As soon as Sir H. Elliot heard of these atrocities he remonstrated and protested time after time. What more could he have done? . . . Sir H. Elliot saw at once that the employment and arming of Circassians might lead to them [horrors] & protested in advance agst. the use of them—He . . . has since insisted on the punishment of the guilty. . . . I am not aware that any other ambassador has done so much or indeed done anything until after public excitement in Europe had been aroused.[29]

The criticism of Elliot was really elicited more by his known pro-Turkish feelings than by what he did or did not do in May 1876.[30] The British colony in Constantinople was largely against him and attempted to blacken his reputation in every way. This group included certain newspaper reporters, some junior people at the Embassy, among them the British consul-general, Sir Philip Francis, and, of course, assorted members of foreign diplomatic staffs. One example of the former category was a Mr. Hanley, the editor and owner of *Le Journal de Stamboul,* who had taken the initiative of writing to Gladstone on 28 July about the atrocities. In a second letter to the former Liberal leader he wrote, 'Since I had the honour of addressing you on the subject of the atrocities ... I have received from the Sublime Porte a communication warning me that if I continue to criticise the conduct of the British Ambassador respecting those matters my paper will be suppressed.' Shuvalov reported that Elliot's attitude on Bulgaria was not approved by Derby and that he hoped the Foreign Secretary would have the courage to recall him from Constantinople. The Netherlands' minister, writing of Disraeli's elevation to the House of Lords, also referred to Elliot.

It is whispered that it will be difficult to maintain [Elliot] in his position in Constantinople. [Bylandt, the Netherlands' representative] however, doubts whether this demand [Elliot's recall] will be satisfied, since the humiliation of England with [Elliot's] adversaries [Ignatiev] would be too great. Nevertheless, it would be very difficult for the government to deny its moral responsibility, because the atrocities are the direct consequence of the principle of non-intervention that it pursued ...[31]

When Gallenga, *The Times* correspondent in Constantinople, referred to Baring's mission in one of his reports, it drew a letter from Elliot in which the harassed ambassador referred to the tone of the report as one which must prevent anyone at the Embassy from having any further contact with the journalist.[32] The Prime Minister, however, seemed at one with the ambassador's critics. He wished to replace both Elliot and Buchanan, the latter having been at Vienna and in the public service over fifty years. 'Elliot has many excellent qualities, both moral and intellectual, but he has no energy [This was not true]. ... His conduct has seriously compromised, and damaged the Government. ... As a public servant the nation has utterly condemned him. ... He might yet remain at his post, & assist an extraordinary envoy. ... I think, myself, that Layard is the man for such a mission.'[33] (Layard was waiting anxiously at Madrid and hoping he would be asked.)

Elliot's sympathies were mixed, but he was, of course, pro-Ottoman at a very inconvenient time to be so. He had become a natural scapegoat, a function he would continue to fill until his departure from Constantinople the following year. Most of this was unfair, and to the honour of some, only the ambassador's absence from England prevented still more Parliamentary and out-of-doors jeering at his behaviour. Critical attack does not usually elicit one's best qualities, and this was also true of Elliot. He was not completely blameless and perhaps his greatest sin was his failure to take any initiative in investigating the uncorroborated reports of atrocities which first reached him. This seemed to give some substance to a desire, which it was alleged he had, of white-washing the barbarous conduct of the Turks. It seemed to make his frequent warnings to the Porte of Bashi-Bazouk of irregular activity into merely formal admonitions.

As most of the Bulgarian rising and suppression was over by the middle of May,[34] Elliot could have done nothing more than he did to save innocent Bulgarians. To many in Britain and to all at Robert College in Constantinople, all Bulgarians were innocent, even those who revolted. This sprang from the process of turning the suppression of the Bulgarian rising into a Christian myth. One can observe elements of it even in the reports of Baring and Dupuis. They both frequently and repeatedly refer to Bulgarian villages where the amount of revolutionary activity could not, in their opinion, justify the Ottoman plunder and destruction perpetrated there to contain it.

The amount of that destruction is also part of the myth. It was based almost entirely on Christian and Bulgarian evidence. Estimates of Bulgarians killed and Christian villages destroyed probably nowhere approaches a reasonable approximation to reality. We simply do not know how many Bulgarians, innocent or not, were killed by Turkish regular and irregular marauders, nor how much of the destruction of Bulgarian villages was due to them. There were no census statistics kept before the insurrection. Schuyler, Baring, and MacGahan actually visited about 10 of the 50 odd villages they list as partially destroyed or worse. It is impossible to estimate, even in the villages visited, how many of the native Bulgarian population had fled to the hills, plotting more outbreaks or fearing to return.

A railway engineer named Stoney who made a house-to-house investigation after Baring had left Rumelia indicated that many whom Baring thought were dead had fled into the hills and only returned after he had left. Stoney's estimate, which is ignored by Harris, was 'only' 3,694 Bulgarians killed, considerably lower than Baring's 12,000 and Shuyler's and MacGahan's 15,000. Stoney knew both the Bulgarians and the Turks, having worked in railway construction and then in relief and charity work in the Balkans between 1876 and 1878. According to him, the general devastation of Bulgaria, including the destruction of livestock, had been exaggerated by earlier reports. 'More particularly, the people and the countryside had shown a resilience and ability to recover that the English . . . had failed to anticipate.'[35] Baring made no allowance, nor could he have done had he realized that every spring and summer many Bulgarians migrated to Romania and Hungary for agricultural employment. They returned in autumn with their accumulated earnings. Finally, as has been indicated previously, the investigators based their figures of Bulgarian dead on the assumption of ten Bulgarians to a house. This is probably double the actual number of five to each dwelling, which is more likely, and, furthermore, even the lower estimate does not differentiate between armed Bulgarians who rose in revolt and 'innocent' villagers who remained at peace.

It seems clearer than in the revolt which had occurred in Bosnia-Hercegovina that some villages were put to the torch by the revolutionaries themselves, in order to force more active participation upon quiescent Bulgarians. It would seem that the Bulgarian rising was more got up or elicited less of an indigenous response than the insurrection in Bosnia and Hercegovina. But such fiendish reprisal overwhelmed everything else.

Ironically, it is not even completely clear who was responsible for such barbarous behaviour. It occurred at a time when central control from Constantinople was even more weak than usual, owing to the Muslim movement active there which led to the overthrow of the Sultan. Bulgarian Muslims, or Pomaks as they were called, seemed to be responsible for the worst occurrence at Batak, which first had been discovered for Europe by Baring. But some Bashi-Bazouks were probably ordinary

Turkish peasants, neither Pomak nor Circassian. Ottoman regular troops also seem to have contributed their share. The Christian myth of Bulgarian atrocities was not made up of whole cloth. There was barbarous and cruel behaviour and enough of it was committed by Muslims or Muslim sympathizers to give Christian charges a touch of truth. But it was only a touch, as most charges were consistent only with the great indignation and outraged feeling which were honestly experienced as a result of distorted information received fifth hand.

Outraged feeling and indignation were manifested on the Continent, but to only a slight degree compared to the British reaction, which was infinitely greater and which lasted far longer. It inundated the Government's official line, which had been for the Turks to display energy in quashing insurrection. Continental indignation, at least that manifested by the French and German governments, was not directed at the Bulgarian barbarities but at the murder of their consuls at Salonica and the amount of indemnity to be paid by the Porte for the outrage.[36] The Ottoman Government must have been perplexed at the official British reaction to the massacres. Throughout the revolt in Bosnia-Hercegovina the Government castigated the Turks for turning the rising into an international question by showing insufficient energy in suppressing it. Apparently too much manifested energy, as in the Bulgarian rebellion, was even worse.

After receiving and reading Baring's report on 14 September, Derby dispatched a reply to Elliot a week later, instructing him to demand an audience with the Sultan in order to communicate to him the substance of the second secretary's examination, and to give the names of officials and leaders guilty of atrocities.

There can be no doubt that the conduct of the Vali of Adrianople [district governor] in ordering the general arming of the Mussulmans led to the assemblage of bands of murderers and robbers, who under the pretext of suppressing insurrection were guilty of crimes which Mr. Baring justly describes as the most henious that have stained the history of the present century.

While 1,956 Bulgarians were arrested for complicity in an insurrection movement which was at no time of a dangerous character, only a

score or so of the murderers of unarmed men, women, and children
have been punished.

. . .

By his [Baring's] statement it appears that eighty women and girls
were taken [from Batak] to Mussulman villages . . . and that they still
remain there; that the bodies of the murdered victims were still, at
the time of his visit, lying unburied.

. . .

Ample reparation shall be afforded to the sufferers, and their
future security guaranteed.

Your Excellency [Elliot] will . . . call for reparation and justice, and
urge that the rebuilding of houses and churches shall be begun at
once . . . and above all, you will point out that it is a matter of absolute necessity that the eighty women should be found and restored
to their families.

Derby ended by suggesting a measure which had been urged
on him by Bourke. 'That the disturbed districts should be at
one placed under an able and energetic Commissioner . . .
who, if not himself a Christian, should have Christian
counsellors in whom trust could be reposed by the Christian
population.'[37]

While war with Serbia and Montenegro continued, the out-
of-doors agitation in Britain against the Bulgarian atrocities
began in earnest. Public meetings, ecclesiastical sermons, Press
exhortations, charitable relief committees to aid the Balkan
wounded and homeless created a public controversy, the extent of which has rarely ever been seen in Britain. Of added
significance, as Shannon has demonstrated, was the fact that
much of this activity and commotion occurred while Parliament was not in session. Finally, it occurred at a time when
other events in the Balkans were transpiring relatively unconnected with the rising and barbarities of May 1876.

## 11 WAR, MEDIATION, AND AGITATION

THERE WAS some surprise when, on the evening of 24 August, Serbia requested the good offices of the Powers to obtain an armistice. Derby lost no time, fearing the complications of the continuance of the war, to press upon the Porte the advantages of a quick peace. He explained his fears to Elliot in a confidential telegram.

I think it right to mention, for your guidance, that the impression produced here by events in Bulgaria has completely destroyed sympathy with Turkey. The feeling is universal and so strong that even if Russia were to declare war against the Porte, Her Majesty's Government would find it practically impossible to interfere. Any such event would place England in a most unsatisfactory situation. Peace is, therefore, urgently necessary. Use your discretion as to the language which you shall hold; but you will see how essential it is that the Turkish Ministry should be alive to the situation, and that you cannot be too strong in urging upon the Porte a conciliatory disposition.[1]

Though all the Powers indicated their assent to Serbia's request for help in an armistice, nothing was done and delay was victorious. A number of explanations are relevant. First, the mechanical difficulty of obtaining the simultaneous concurrence of the six Great Powers was considerable. The Turks were taken up with proclaiming Abdul Hamid as Sultan on 31 August to replace the alcoholic and incapacitated Murad V, who had been Sultan for only ninety days. The instructions the Powers sent to their ambassadors in Constantinople were not sufficiently precise to enable them to lay before the Porte a proposal for mediation. Finally, while most Serbs wanted peace, the Russian volunteers who had come to fight for them did not. On 1 September Derby telegraphed to Elliot to propose to the Porte a one month's armistice to include all combatants. The Ottoman ministers, knowing the near possibility of a great victory over Serbia, feared that an armistice would only favour the latter, which daily was receiving money and soldiers from Russia, and they therefore hesitated to suspend their military operations until they knew what the final terms of peace would be. Derby was near despair, and again telegraphed to Elliot to prevail upon the Turks. 'Warn the Turkish ministers that, if the proposal for armistice is rejected, Her Majesty's Government can do nothing more to prevent the ruin which they will have brought on the Empire. It is impossible to exaggerate the gravity of the situation ...'[2] Derby's fear was that a Russian attack on the Ottoman Empire might invoke an obligation under the Tripartite Treaty of 1856 signed by France, Austria, and Britain which would compel Britain to come to Turkey's support, which would be directly opposed by the anti-Turkish sympathies of the country as a result of the Bulgarian massacres. A quick moderate peace by the Porte would preclude Russian military intervention.

When Elliot received Derby's telegram of 6 September, it was too late on that day to communicate its contents to the Porte, and he telegraphed back to London that the Ottoman Government would only accept an armistice if it learned of the terms of peace Britain would be prepared to support. Derby had already heard from Vienna that in declining the armistice proposal the Turkish ministers were preparing their own peace conditions to submit to the Powers. Derby's uncharacteristic energy and initiative in pressing peace upon Constantinople, going so far as to indicate that Britain would not support Turkey if Russia declared war, was partly due to the effect upon his own colleagues of domestic opinion on the Bulgarian atrocities, a reaction which to some extent they shared, but was even more a reflection of his own personality.

Bourke, the Parliamentary Under Secretary, was naturally most alive to the Parliamentary reaction, and, in so far as the M.P.s reflected it, to popular opinion as well, on events in Bulgaria. About 25 August he sent Derby a suggestion in order to allay criticism that the British Government was somehow responsible for the massacres by its support of Ottoman integrity. His idea was to propose an investigative commission for the punishment of guilty Turks, an idea that Derby was later to propose himself. 'I [Bourke] continue to receive daily letters from members of Parliament recording the indignation of their constituents about Bulgarian atrocities—Baring's account in his letters of Aug. 1 and Aug. 4th justify everything that has been said by the Daily News correspondent.'[3] But the Foreign Secretary was much more concerned with ending the war than with punishing the Turks for massacres already committed.[4]

Disraeli was most concerned with the popularity of his Government and effective British influence in any solution to the Eastern Question adopted by the Powers. He was more flexible on the nature of the solution than on the necessity for Britain to play a major part in devising it. He believed Elliot had misled London as to the extent and reality of the atrocities, which in turn had caused immense Parliamentary and popular criticism of the Government. The resulting anger he felt at the ambassador's behaviour he blamed on the latter's lack of energy.[5] The Prime Minister also misjudged Andrássy and viewed his intricate and devious diplomacy as a sign of weakness and indecision. A strong British ambassador at Vienna, Disraeli thought, could enlighten and lead Andrássy.

It is not age which has enfeebled his [Buchanan, the British ambassador at Vienna] intelligence or dimmed his powers. He was, and ever has been, a hopeless mediocrity.

Andrassy wants a guide: a man of quick perception and iron will about him.

. . .

I wish you [Derby] success and fame—and I believe you will obtain both but in great affairs to suceed, you must not spare the feelings of mediocrities.[6]

Hence the Prime Minister's advice to Derby was neither to punish Turks nor end the war, but rather to get rid of Elliot and Buchanan. This last the Foreign Secretary was able to parry temporarily. Disraeli tended to favour a quick peace because it would restrict Russia's opportunities for making trouble and give Britain the diplomatic initiative. 'The "atrocities" will permit us to dictate to the Porte. . . . It is to be hoped, that the leading part, which England may take, in obtaining an armistice, and afterwards in the preliminaries, will make the excited 'public' forget or condone the Elliotiana.'[7]

He was not optimistic about ending the war and felt that if England could not prevail on the Turks to make peace, Russia and Austria would invade the Balkans in the spring, a step which he saw as leading to partition. He thought this could be prevented if Britain managed to obtain the diplomatic initiative.[8] He suggested this to Derby.

It is wise that we shd take the lead in it [partition]. Our chance of success will be greater because from us, it will be unexpected.

Whatever the jealousies of Austria and Russia, they would prefer a division of the Balkan spoils under the friendly offices of England to war between themselves certainly, &, probably with others. Constantinople with an adequate district, should be neutralised, & made a free port in the custody & under the guardianship of England, as the Ionian Isles were!

. . .

I write this on the assumption that the present attempt at peace will fail. God grant it may not! But if it do, I humbly think we cannot act too powerfully & too promptly. Decision and energy will render the work practicable; hesitation & timidity will involve us in infinite difficulty & peril . . .[9]

The Prime Minister's solution for the Balkans—boldness and energy —were in contrast to his designs for meeting the largely critical explosion of domestic opinion which came at the beginning of September. Many in the Government wished to offer public explanations and attempt to propitiate the outraged feelings of the country. Disraeli thought it best to wait things out quietly and advised the Foreign Secretary accordingly.

What I wish to impress upon you, at this moment as regards home is not to act as if you were under the control of popular opinion. If so, you may do what they like, but they won't respect you for doing it.

After all, all this tumult is on a false assumption, that we have been, or are, upholding Turkey—All the Turks may be in the Propontis so far as I am concerned . . .[10]

As he wrote to the Queen, when the public temporarily goes crazy on a particular subject, reason and clarification have no chance. One must wait, until repetition causes weariness, and calm reflection replaces a burnt-out meteor. Tornadoes of this sort, he indicated, were not usually dangerous in September when Parliament was not in session.[11]

In his efforts to handle and stir Derby, Disraeli used his trusted methods—pressure and suggestions from the Queen coupled with vituperative outbursts at Elliot, Buchanan, Loftus, and Russell for their weakness and incapacity.[12] To some

extent Derby responded because he did desire the approbation
of the Queen and the Prime Minister. 'Derby is behaving with
energy, and I hope will be up to the mark. It will not be from
want of bottle holding ...'[13] Disraeli also attempted direct
suggestion and encouragement. 'Ld Beaconsfield has done his
best to enbolden Ld. Derby, and he thinks not without success.
Ld. Derby is prepared to act with audacity even, if necessary,
and he wd be guided by his own powers of judgment, which
are great.'[14] He wanted Derby to be ready for the question of
partition so that Britain could take a leading part in that or any
other solution agreed to by the Powers. But for this he thought
a good understanding was necessary with Germany, an
association of which he emphasized the importance to Derby
and the Queen. Initiative and the expression of a strong lead
generally went against the grain of Derby's personality and
though his energy in the question of ending the Turco-Serbian
war was prominent, it was also misleading. Derby believed, as
did many others, that if hostilities continued, Russia inevitably
would go to war against Turkey. This could present what for
the Foreign Secretary was a horrible alternative—a British war
for Turkey or the crushing obloquy of evading treaty
obligations.

The Cabinet colleagues of Derby and Disraeli were more
troubled by domestic opinion, being less aware of the
diplomatic details. Hardy, the War Secretary and perhaps the
Conservatives' most effective and forceful debater, believed in
the extent of the atrocities and the significance of the resulting
reaction they produced at home. He attempted unsuccessfully
to persuade Derby, who wished no unnecessary obstacles
placed in the way of his attempt to convince the Porte to make
an immediate peace, that any negotiations must take into account the atrocities. He then tried to reach Disraeli by writing
to Cairns, the Lord Chancellor, because he was more referred
to on foreign affairs than the rest of the Cabinet. 'Derby is I
fear not enough alive to this [the atrocities] but I hope our
chief who generally tries the public pulse will not be unmindful
of it on this occasion.'[15] Northcote, the skilful but somewhat
gentle Chancellor of the Exchequer, who, much to Hardy's
disappointment, had been chosen by Disraeli as his successor
and Leader of the Commons upon his own removal to the

House of Lords, was even more concerned than Hardy that the atrocities should not go unpunished and should not be permitted to occur again. Northcote at this moment had the sometimes unenviable task of being the minister in attendance upon the Queen, who strongly reinforced his feelings about the atrocities.

He wrote to the Prime Minister from Balmoral that peace without better government for Turkey's Christians was unsatisfactory. But what he meant by better government was autonomy or independence, as the Porte cannot rule its Christian subjects with decency. Northcote wished the perpetrators of the barbarities punished, and he feared that British opinion, unchecked, might possibly carry the country into immediate opposition to its own best interest. He suggested that the Government should threaten the Porte with abandoning it, unless it punished the guilty and granted a form of autonomy to the Christians. Disraeli sent Northcote's letter to Derby and it may have influenced the Foreign Secretary in the threats he made to the Turks.[16] The Chancellor of the Exchequer also wrote in the same sense to Cross, the Home Secretary, and Carnarvon, the Colonial Secretary.

The [difficulties] have been considerably increased by the imbecility of Elliot and (in the profoundest secrecy be it said) that unfortunate levity of our chief, in the matter of the atrocities.

The stupid brutality of the Turks has . . . made it difficult for us to say a word in their favour; and we have insanely doubled that difficulty by allowing the idea to get abroad that we are indifferent to the cruelties which have been committed. It is now almost impossible to remove that impression, unjust as it really is . . .[17]

Carnarvon's anger, shock, and disgust with the Turks was stronger even than Northcote's. He looked upon them as crazed hyenas whose cruelties upon the Bulgarians, the full extent of which he believed true, demonstrated that the Turks had not improved for four hundred years, and the fact that no other European state would be guilty of such behaviour caused him to frankly consider the possibility of throwing them over.

We are bound at least to bring every pressure of the strongest kind to bear upon them. There are even limits beyond which political considerations ought not to be carried and we seem to me to be in danger of fast approaching that point. . . . I regret . . . that we do not take a distinct initiative in bringing about a cessation of hostilities. . . . No language can be too emphatic and no action too strong to make the Turkish government understand that we will not tolerate . . . atrocities. . . . I believe the country will condemn Turkey. . . . I do not know what is to be done . . .[18]

Like the Queen, Hardy, and Northcote, he believed that public feeling would grow unless checked, and unlike Disraeli, he wished to meet it head on with some direct step which would reassure the public on the score of the Government's real attitude towards Turkey, and at the same time exonerate the Cabinet from the charges of complicity in the barbarities.[19] He wrote to the Prime Minister, to whom he suggested the summoning of all available Cabinet members for a meeting, to Salisbury, his closest Cabinet friend at this time, and to Hardy. To the last Carnarvon also commented on Russia and Britain's foreign policy.

Russia has never in my opinion, had so favourable an opportunity to take any line she may please since the Crimean War . . .
The fact is, as we both know, that there has been too much dualism and that the combination of spirited and do-nothing policy has ended, as all such combinations do, in a muddle . . .[20]

Cross and Cairns were agreed with most of their colleagues on the need publicly to record horror at the barbarities and to express some sympathetic feelings for the Christian victims. The Lord Chancellor also favoured, as he indicated to Derby and Disraeli, the use of the greatest pressure on the Porte to force it to make a generous and non-vindictive peace. He wrote this directly to the Prime Minister, but he reached the Foreign Secretary through Lady Derby with whom he corresponded. 'I took the opportunity of impressing, through her, on D[erby] the necessity of our insisting on the Turks coming into reasonable and liberal terms [of peace], and also of recording some unqualified condemnation [of the atrocities]. . . . The more hints D. gets on the subject the better . . .'[21]
Salisbury, the India Secretary, was as livid at Elliot's behaviour as Disraeli and believed, quite incorrectly, that if the ambassador had been on top of things, the atrocities might

have been checked earlier.[22] Sympathizing with the Christians and despising the Turks as much as Carnarvon, he was surprised by signs of Ottoman vitality. He wrote of this, with a journalistic flair and a little exaggeration, to Lytton, the viceroy.

Turkey, a depotism without a despot, is governed absolutely by a set of officials who have no title to their places except that they were appointed by the man they murdered: is fighting a very costly war without money and without credit: and is maintaining with success a desperate struggle for national existence without the aid of a single man of conspicuous ability, against the hatred of more than half of her subjects, and against a growing ill will of the greater part of Europe. I shall begin soon to believe in the Hindu legend that the elephant which bore the world stood on the tortoise; and the tortoise stood on nothing in particular . . .[23]

Disraeli's refusal to trim to satisfy the public outburst, a course opposed by most of the Cabinet, was temporarily and partially seconded only by Derby. The Foreign Secretary refused to share the onus of responsibility for the cruelties. 'We have nothing to unsay or to undo and we must not make things look as if we had.'[24] But whereas Disraeli opposed protestations of governmental innocence as both bad tactics and a sign of weakness, Derby did so because he felt that that part of the agitation directed against the Government was unfair and unreasonable, and the rest aimed at the Turks was from his point of view useful. 'Bulgarian events, will be to us as much help as a hindrance: I have thought so all along. The cause of the Turks was becoming impossible to defend, and this new stupidity of theirs give us a perfectly honourable and legitimate reason for partially throwing them over. So the 12,000 (if there are 12,000) have not died in vain: they will have saved the consistency of the F.O.'[25] If necessary, Derby was prepared to use the atrocities to justify the refusal of British military aid or diplomatic support to Turkey were she to be attacked by Russia. Ottoman cruelties in Bulgaria did not lead him to throw over the Turks from whom no improvement could be expected, but rather they were convenient excuse which could be used should it prove necessary. But if a Turco-Serb peace could be quickly arranged, which was Derby's main priority, a Russo-Turkish war and a possible British treaty obligation to fight for Turkey would not arise. Further, the Foreign Secretary believed that a cessation of hostilities would also quench the domestic agitation. 'The one essential thing now is to make a peace, and for my part, I am prepared to put any necessary amount of pressure on the Porte ... Continued war means Russian intervention and their [Turkish] destruction. We could not save them, or even try it, as English feeling is now ...'[26] Though Italy and France strongly supported Derby's efforts at Constantinople to bring about an armistice, the Turkish ministers were obdurate in refusing a cessation of hostilities until peace conditions, which they now proposed, had been accepted. One of the conditions, which Elliot telegraphed to Derby on 10 September, was a money payment from the Serbs who were bankrupt. Elliot, who was unable to obtain the Porte's consent to an armistice, did manage on his own initiative to convince the Turks to agree to a suspension of hostilities upon their being told that the Powers would consider the Turkish peace conditions.[27]

Derby objected to the Turkish peace conditions and put forward his own, which included local autonomy for Bosnia-Hercegovina and similar pledges against injustice in Bulgaria.[28] Andrássy, when he learned of Derby's conditions, objected to them, as he felt autonomy for Bosnia was impractical and could only lead to an Austrian occupation, which presumably he opposed. 'He [Andrássy] also objects to stipulating for reforms in Bulgaria ... and he would, therefore, only ask, as a guarantee against future outrages against the Christians, for an engagement that regular troops should be alone employed in Bulgaria and the other European provinces of the Empire ...'[29] Austro-Russian disagreement also existed as rivalry between Ignatiev and Andrássy continued. Russia was urging an armistice on the Porte independently of peace conditions, whereas Andrássy wished the Powers to agree on the latter, and then to impose them and an armistice simultaneously. However, Andrássy modified his view before long and agreed to Russia's position. The Porte's reaction to the European pressure exerted on it was partly to give way by ordering on 15 September a ten-day suspension of hostilities,[30] which apparently was not as complete or formal as an armistice, but then no one was completely certain of the distinctions between the two.[31] During the period of the suspension of hostilities Derby had taken the lead in Europe in order to devise peace terms acceptable to all the Powers, but, as time was running out, Anglo-Austrian pressure at Constantinople for a formal armistice elicited from the Turks a prolongation of the suspension of hostilities until 2 October.

Turkish obstinacy was less an obstacle to British peace efforts than Russian-Serbian attempts to escape payment for the Serbian military débâcle.[32] Both Russian sympathy and some Russian honour were attached to the Serbian war effort as a result of the thousands of Russian military volunteers who had come to Belgrade to help their fellow Slavs. They came in such numbers, one estimate being 10,000, that Derby complained to Shuvalov about them, as each augmentation only bolstered the influence of the war party in Serbia.[33] Russia and Serbia were holding out for a prolonged formal armistice, during which time Serbia could recover from military defeat and be resupplied by Russia. The Ottoman ministers naturally desired an immediate peace, to avoid giving Serbia a respite and while a Turkish threat to overrun all of Serbia still existed. From Belgrade White wrote that Milan was entirely in the hands of Russia.

The Serbs recommenced the fighting on 27 September. Five days later the Turks formally refused the terms 'administrative autonomy' and 'protocol'[34] in the British peace conditions. On the day following the Turkish refusal Gorchakov proposed that the Powers impose an armistice or truce of six weeks on both sides, during which the Great Powers could devise peace terms. London indirectly supported this now, by returning to its original proposal made five weeks previously for an armistice of not less than a month. Derby communicated to Elliot a Cabinet decision to threaten Turkey again.

You [Elliot] will press the Porte, as an alternative, to grant an armistice for not less than a month, stating that, in case of refusal, you have instructions to leave Constantinople, as it will then be evident that further exertions on the part of Her Majesty's Government to save the Porte from ruin have become useless.

You will, however, not take this step without reference home.

You are at liberty to state that, on the conclusion of an armistice, it is intended that a Conference shall immediately follow.[35]

A prospective conference provided new opportunities for differences between the Great Powers on the procedure to be followed and the basis for the expected international gathering.

Then, on 10 October, Derby's efforts and pressure on the Turks seemed to have succeeded as the Porte indicated it had agreed to an armistice of five months. 'I [Derby] congratulate you [Elliot] on the success of your efforts to bring about an armistice. It is mainly due to your ability and perseverance. I have pressed on Russian and Austrian Governments the importance of inducing Serbia to accept the armistice.'[36] Success was brief, as Russia now refused to accept that at which earlier the Turks had balked—a long armistice. Derby's energy under conditions calculated to deter the weak was wonderful.

I have requested the German Ambassador to press on his Government strongly the importance of the armistice being accepted by Russia. German influence may do much at the present moment. The Russian Government hesitates and seems disposed to refuse.

Refusal will involve serious danger to European peace.[37]

The Foreign Secretary also warned Shuvalov not to misinterpret British opinion, which was reaching almost hysterical proportions against Ottoman atrocities.

I warned him that however strong might be the feeling of national indignation against Turkish cruelties, it would be superseded by a very different sentiment if it were once believed by the English nation that Constantinople was threatened. Rightly or wrongly, I said, the conclusion to which everyone here would come would be, that the rejection by Russia of the Turkish proposal indicated a fixed purpose of going to war . . .[38]

Russia now proposed an armistice of one month or six weeks in the face of a British and Austrian acceptance of the Turkish armistice of five months.[39] Derby was now ready to admit that he had exhausted his mediatorial efforts and suggested that Germany uncompromised might intervene to arrange some successful compromise. The Foreign Secretary requested Münster, the German ambassador, to transmit his appeal to Bismarck, but the latter refused to move,[40] and Germany was tending towards support of the Russian proposal. Britain adhered to the Turkish one, but indicated that if the Porte were willing to consent to the Russian suggestion, England would not object. On 21 October the Grand Vizier told Ignatiev that Turkey would accept a six-week armistice on condition that it could be renewed should peace negotiations require it.

Remaining on the defensive, a suspension of hostilities, a truce, and an armistice had been suggested by Britain for a period of more than one month, by Russian for one month, or six weeks, and for three months, by Italy for two months, and by Turkey for six or five months, it not being clear which. Russia and Turkey were in the process of retreating and retracing their steps from their original positions, when they backed into one another. Andrássy saw little humour in the situation, and Buchanan detected his bitterness at the vacillation by the Great Powers. The Porte and Ignatiev seemed headed for agreement, when the Turkish forces won a major military victory in Serbia on 29 and 30 October, and the Russian Government seemed to repudiate Ignatiev's efforts and instructed him to demand an immediate armistice with no conditions for prolongation.

Russian Government ... have ordered him [Ignatiev] to send in an ultimatum requiring the Porte to accept the armistice of six weeks or two months unconditionally.

If this is not accepted within forty-eight hours, relations between the two countries are to be broken off, and General Ignatiev is to leave Constantinople with all the members of the Embassy.[41]

The Porte used only twenty-four hours to reply affirmatively to the Russian ultimatum.

### British Reaction to Bulgarian Horrors[42]

During August, September, and October, against the background of war and mediation by the Great Powers in the Balkans, there occurred in Britain one of the deepest, most varied, and most prolonged outbursts of public feeling ever to manifest itself in a people not usually given to extravagant public display of private feeling.[43] It went much beyond a mere anti-Ottoman or Muslim outburst, and no simple explanation is sufficient to account for or characterize it. It arose shortly after reports of atrocities began to appear in the *Daily News* in June. Questions were asked and anti-Turkish spleens were vented in Parliament in July. In August, after Parliament had adjourned, the full force of the gale manifested itself as the vivid reports of MacGahan and Schuyler appeared in London newspapers and seemed to confirm the worst of the horrors.[44] Baring's official British confirmation of the atrocities in September was almost an afterthought as letters, speeches, sermons, pamphlets, daily newspaper reports, public meetings, and efforts at charitable and humanitarian relief work engulfed the country like a torrent.

Some relief efforts were partly elicited by the war and had little to do with former events in Bulgaria. At the beginning of August Colonel Loyd-Lindsay, a hero of the Crimean War and one of the initiators and chairman of the National Society for Aid to the Sick and Wounded, which developed into the British Red Cross Aid Society, wrote to Lord Derby to ask whether the aid society could be of help in the Turco-Serbian war. Tenterden, replying for the Foreign Secretary, suggested application to the Ottoman and Serbian governments which the Foreign Office initiated. After receiving affirmative replies, Loyd-Lindsay and two other officials, with six surgeons and several nurses, left England at the end of the third week of August for the Balkans, taking with them stores for the sick and wounded Serbians and Turks.[45]

At the same time as Loyd-Lindsay's letter to Derby, Schuyler at Tatar Bazardjik wrote to his future wife of the pressing necessity for relief and the desirability of raising money by public subscription.[46] A large number of public subscriptions and relief missions were organized in Britain which elicited much public generosity stirred on by a steady daily flow of newspaper reports recounting new and greater horrors. On 15 August Lady Strangford, who had devoted herself to nursing and hospital charity, announced the establishment of the Bulgarian Peasant Relief Fund in the memory of her husband who had been a champion of the Bulgarian people. At the end of September she departed for Philippopolis with a collection of over £5,000 for the homeless and suffering in Bulgaria.[47]

At first the London Press editorialized on Bulgaria according to political party preferences. MacGahan's telegrams reached London at the end of the first week in August and shortly thereafter Baring's 'preliminary' report was read by Bourke in Parliament. This was soon followed by publication of Schuyler's preliminary report. These seemed to confirm the atrocities and the Conservative Press now joined the editorial bandwagon of invective and censure, though it still referred to exaggeration in the reports of atrocities. On 8 August *The Times*, influenced by MacGahan's report in the *Daily News* of the previous day, condemned the Porte and the Cabinet, and for the next six weeks *The Times* thundered against Henry Elliot and the governments blue books, and defended Serbia from the charge of wantonly beginning a war. 'Even the *Daily News* was to be outstripped [by *The Times*] in the blasts of fury leveled at the Sublime Porte and the two journals were to be greatly responsible for the vehemence of the atrocity agitation which reached its peak in September.'[48]

On 16 August, and following frequently, letters were published in the *Daily News* from MacGahan. 'There are things too horrible to allow anything like calm inquiry; things, the vileness of which the eye refuses to look upon, and which the mind refuses to contemplate. These are the facts which repel and revolt. . . . Such is the nature of the facts I came to investigate.'[49] *The Times* and the *Daily News* published, also on 16 August, two letters read at a public meeting by a Liberal expert on foreign affairs, Sir Charles Dilke. One letter was from MacGahan and the other was from Schuyler. The first was an attack on Baring and Guarracino and the second dwelled on the atrocities. 'Blindings, impalements, roastings, bayoneting of pregnant women; heaps of bones licked clean by the dogs . . . the churchyard and church [at Batak] filled with reeking corpses.'[50] Six days later the *Daily News* printed MacGahan's Batak letter written in a style, as described by Shannon, calculated to raise the political temperature.

The skill and artistry of these narratives [MacGahan's letters as distinct from his telegrams] certainly helped greatly to bring the crisis of public conscience to a head. MacGahan set out deliberately to project his own sense of passionate indignation. The protest of the *Saturday Review* that this infringed the conventions of the higher English journalism was rather beside the point. MacGahan had found at least a subject for which his talent for sensationalism could do full justice, but yet not more than justice.[51]

The week following MacGahan's letter witnessed the beginning of another characteristic of the agitation, along with letters to the editor—the holding of public meetings. There had been a few before the twenty-second. One of the first, if not the first, of these protest demonstrations was called by the mayor of Manchester on 9 August in response to a signed petition and at which a letter from Bishop Fraser of Manchester, one of the leaders of the agitation movement, was read. But after the twenty-second a continuous round of protest meetings spread throughout the country and they became 'the chief forum for the articulation of England's deeply stirred feelings'.[52] Bishop Fraser, Canon Liddon, and the historian Freeman, all friends since Oxford, were prominent in this campaign but, following Shannon, the main figure was the editor of the Darlington *Northern Echo*, W. T. Stead. Beginning on 23 August, Stead joined a growing and inchoate tide of indignation which had started with Freeman and Farley and 'supplied the great national movement emerging in the last days of August with a voice, a method, and a direction'. 'It [Stead's campaign] was the most important development in the actual process of agitation before the publication on 6 September of Gladstone's *Bulgarian Horrors*'.[53]

Although unlike Freeman, Fraser, and Liddon, who represented London upper-class Anglicanism and the universities, he stood for the forces of democracy, Nonconformity, and the provinces of England, Stead shared with them at least two basic characteristics—strong religious fervour and a certain lack of balance and restraint.[54] He began after MacGahan's Batak letter and 'set in motion a series of atrocity meetings over as wide an area as he could direct and inspire by his personal and political influence, and by means of a pushing provincial newspaper'.[55] On 25 August he agitated at a public meeting held at Darlington, which issued a call for Gladstone to intervene. Stead sent to Gladstone a copy of the *Northern Echo* report of the meeting along with a letter beseeching Gladstone to allow the use of his great name by the agitators.[56] Other meetings in the North quickly followed the one at Darlington; some were party meetings, others were nonpartisan. Though the provinces took the lead in organized demonstrations, a significant and first meeting on 28 August was held in London, when more than 1,000 working men gathered at the Hackney Working Men's Club and Institute to

denounce the ministry for its support of the Ottoman Government and the latter's successful attempt to eradicate the Christian population of European Turkey. Letters were read from
John Holms, the local M.P., Gladstone, and Lord John
Russell.[57]

The same day as the Hackney meeting, the *Daily News*
published Schuyler's preliminary report which named 65
destroyed villages and estimated the dead at 15,000. The worst
was confirmed as even the ministerial dailies had to admit.
More and more angry letters to newspapers were written, and
more and more protest meetings were held; many were con-
voked by mayors in response to requests by citizens, some were
party meetings, and not a few were under the auspices of
various church groups. The gatherings usually voted
resolutions condemning the traditional policy of Ottoman
support and demanding security for the Balkan Christians.[58]
There was also a reaction against the attitude expressed by
Elliot in his dispatch of 4 September, that the atrocities or
moral issues should not be allowed to alter the protection of
British interests.[59] Liddon and Henry Sidgwick, the ethical
philosopher, took a position later dominated by Gladstone,
that foreign policy or British interests should conform to
morality and righteousness, a somewhat inconsistent position
for some individuals who displayed much religious bigotry to
adopt.

Liddon violently denounced the immoral policy of Disraeli
and on 13 August had given a sensational sermon at St. Paul's
on the topic of a '"moral, Christian humane" Eastern policy'.
Such a policy he was not unhappy to square with a Russian war
on Turkey, and he reached the same conclusion as Derby, that
it was now no longer possible for England to attack Russia, if
that country, as Liddon hoped she would, declared war on
Turkey in the name of the Lord and humanity.[60] His humanity,
however, seemed to be restricted to Christianity, a fact which
Shannon inadequately attempts to explain away on the
grounds that some individuals who attempted to bring succour
to Christians and Muslims alike really had pro-Turkish sympathies.

Liddon busied himself also in recommending Freeman's fund raising
campaign on behalf of the oppressed Slavs, at the same time warning

his fellow-clergy of funds being raised by people like Lady Strangford [who was pro-Bulgarian]. .. whose philanthropy extended to wounded Turks as well as Christians. Their first duty, Liddon pointed out, was to the 'household of faith.' This was less an expression of bigotry than an appreciation of the underlying pro-Turkish sympathies of the relief funds which made a virtue of their neutrality and conformity to the rules of the Geneva Convention.[61]

Freeman, the noted historian, was likewise outraged that Loyd-Lindsay's National Aid Society should attempt to help Christian and Turk alike. His letter to *The Times* published on 28 August expressed his conviction that he did not feel that it was necessary or proper to give relief to thieves, killers, and rapists.[62] He was blatantly anti-Semitic and violently Turcophobe, referring to Disraeli as that 'ever lying Jew'.[63] Shannon refers to his unbalanced outbursts, not hesitating short of scurrility.[64]

On 5 and 6 September Disraeli was sent two unsolicited gifts. One was from Hartington, the Liberal leader in the House of Commons; the other was forwarded by Gladstone, who had been gradually caught up in the Bulgarian agitation. From the former the Prime Minister received four brace of grouse; the latter sent him a copy of a pamphlet on the *Bulgarian Horrors* he had finished the evening before, which may be seen today in the Hughenden archives, its pages uncut.[65] When Gladstone realized that the question of atrocities was alive in the country, though Parliament was no longer in session, he grasped at an opportunity to strike at the Government. Shannon feels that his reaction was more than political opportunism, though it was that; he blends it with the attraction felt by Gladstone when he recognized 'that a stirring of truly popular moral passion was in being'.[66] At the end of the third week in August Gladstone was pondering both a speech to his Greenwich constituents and a pamphlet.

Letters arrived from MacColl, the canon of Ripon, urging the creation in the Balkans of a row of Christian states, and from de Lisle, a Catholic writer, expatiating on the atrocities; both correspondents preferred the presence of the Russians in Constantinople to the continuance of Turkish rule in Europe.[67] To the meeting of the Working Men's Club in Hackney Gladstone sent £5 and permission to read a letter he wrote to them. As he informed Granville, 'I really hope that on this Eastern matter the pot will be kept boiling.'[68]

At the end of August Gladstone received a politically disinterested and humanitarian appeal from Lady Strangford, who was preparing to go herself to Bulgaria on a mission of mercy.

Whatever we may think about the Turkish government, you have no doubt as to the calamities that have befallen the Bulgarians, and I hope you will help me to relieve their pressing needs. Pray help me. The public is apathetic—chiefly because they are shooting, or bathing or travelling—but also, because they are contented to make violent speeches at 'indignation meetings' and do nothing better than give their breath to the poor people who are in need of all our charity and generosity. . . . I want £10,000 to take with me. Give me all you can.[69]

But more of his correspondents towards the end of August, MacColl and the latter's friend, the Reverend William Denton, Hutton of the *Spectator,* and, of course, Stead, after the Darlington meeting on the twenty-fifth seemed less motivated by humanitarian concern as they urged Gladstone to make a speech in order to smite down the iniquitous Turks and their ally, the British Government. Gladstone himself was responding politically as well.

I agree with the *Spectator* that the existence of the Government should be challenged in this election [in Buckinghamshire] on the ground of the Bulgarian massacres and of their conduct about them and what hangs on to them. Good ends can rarely be attained in politics without passion: and there is now, the first time for a good many years, a virtuous passion.

I am in half, perhaps a little more than half, a mind to write a pamphlet: on the ground that Parliamentary action was all but ousted.

Does this shock you [Granville].[70]

The nature of Gladstone's reply to Lady Strangford, inferred from her reaction to it, seems to have been unsympathetic, if not completely negative.

In the first place I have no more intention of 'undertaking the organization of a system of relief for Bulgaria'. . . . The calamities that have befallen my poor Bulgarians are *chiefly* confined to a small district lying between Philippopolis and Bellova—and a few more villages in one group about half way between the mountains and the Danube.

Secondly, as to larger schemes than my own, I have grave doubts of their efficiency. . . . Remember the large sums that were collected for the relief of the poor people at the time of the Syrian massacres [1860] and remember how it was squandered and wasted by a Committee in which the responsibility was shared not concentrated . . .

I do not know from your last paragraph what large means of practical relief you are going to recommend. . . . But I am going to work simply and quietly and practically at no one's expense but my own—and I think you will hardly be able to organize anything more economical than that.

As to the political views alluded to in your letter, I could say much—but I refrain from doing so—for I wish the subject to be kept quite separate—the logic is poor that binds them together; and at any rate I have nothing to do with the causes of the calamities; my mission, such as it is, is purely one of help and healing to a suffering and cruelly used people.[71]

On 3 September Gladstone left Hawarden for London to finish his pamphlet. He was, as he wrote to Elliot, coming to favour autonomy for Bulgaria. As the number of atrocity meetings denouncing both the Government and the Turks were increasing in the first week of September, there would be a sympathetic audience for it. He completed his draft at Harley Street and had the advice and reaction of Hartington and Granville, the two official Liberal leaders, who were feeling the awkwardness of their position as a result of his re-emergence into the pit of political controversy. On the evening of 5 September the pamphlet was completed, and after it was printed the following day, its sale was tremendous—40,000 within a few days and probably over 200,000 in all. It articulated the feelings of the shocked and horrified, and released a huge burden of accumulated guilt by denouncing the Turks and demanding the end of the Turkish administration in Bosnia and Bulgaria. It also misled.

The fame of the bag and baggage phrase led to widespread misapprehension that he [Gladstone] had called for the expulsion of the Turks from Europe. This misapprehension, fostered deliberately or mistakenly, undoubtedly did the agitation more good than harm. It helped to conceal the fact that beneath the rhetoric the substance of Gladstone's programme remained moderate. Turkish territorial integrity was still the foundation, though Gladstone did not, as on 31 July, go out of his way to assert that he was not ashamed to stipulate this.[72]

The rhetoric of the *Bulgarian Horrors and the Question of the East* was florid and irresponsible, but, presumably for Gladstone himself, psychologically necessary. The double opportunity both to lead a moral crusade after his public rejection in 1874 and to expiate his feelings of guilt for supporting Turkey during the Crimean War was grasped. 'But the report of Mr. Schuyler together with the report from Berlin, and the Prologue, so to call it, of Mr. Baring, in my opinion turns the scale and makes the responsibility of silence, at least for one who was among the authors of the Crimean War, too great to be borne.'[73] At the very end of his pamphlet of sixty-four 'short' pages, Gladstone made a shrewd suggestion for the relief of Bulgaria. 'I will presume to urge that, under the peculiar circumstances of the case, there is a call upon Her Majesty's Government to take the matter in hand. I do not mean by means of a grant of public money: but by communicating with the municipal and local authorities, and submitting to them the expediency of opening subscriptions.'[74]

A semi-permanent, national, Bulgarian Sunday,[75] contained the possibilities for huge personal and political benefit for both Gladstone and the Liberal party, as it would institutionalize the agitation.

The reaction to the pamphlet, where manifested in writing, was at best mixed. Most readers, both in favour of and opposed to the pamphlet, responded more to its rhetoric and sometimes to the agitation movement itself than to its proposals of autonomy for Bulgaria and local subscriptions for charity.

There was considerable contemporary agreement that the Government's silence, imposed by Disraeli with Derby's support in the face of growing evidence of atrocities, was, even when not morally reprehensible, tactically disastrous by allowing the agitation to develop. There had been, by way of Government explanation, only Bourke's unauthorized letter read at a meeting on 31 August. Then, nothing until 7 September, the day after the publication of the *Bulgarian Horrors*, when Government representation was required at the annual Cutlers' dinner in Sheffield. Lord George Hamilton, Under-Secretary for India, spoke at the dinner and indignantly denied any ministerial responsibility for the events of May in Bulgaria. His words seemed to derive support from a speech by Hartington who also attended the dinner and who had previously consulted Granville about what to say. Hartington refused to attribute the atrocities to the Government and called for a special autumn session of Parliament. Unlike Granville, who hedged his bets and was more politically devious, Hartington was more open, almost naïvely so, and was not ready to throw over Palmerstonian orthodoxy to make political capital at home. His anxiety stemmed less from ministerial behaviour than doubts as to Gladstone's ability to exercise a reasonable degree of self-control. A week after the Sheffield dinner he left, with the Duke and Duchess of Manchester, on a trip to Constantinople, where Forster had already preceded him.[76]

On 13 September, in *The Times*, Granville publicly refused to attend an atrocity meeting at the Guildhall, but he responded affirmatively to a private appeal from Mr. J. Alfred Giles of the Workmen's Exeter Hall Demonstration Committee. This last group had exceeded their funds by about £25 at a recent Exeter Hall meeting, but were prepared to hold another if supported. Granville responded at once and sent Giles £15.[77]

On 9 September, two days after the Sheffield dinner, Gladstone, as had been arranged, spoke at Blackheath to his Greenwich constituents—a crowd of 10,000 gathered in the rain. It was a more moderate, toned-down meeting, though Shannon writes of 'the almost religious intensity of the occasion'. In the pamphlet Gladstone had advocated the withdrawal of Turkish administration from Bulgaria; in the speech he was now agreeable, out of respect for the opinion of Stratford de Redcliffe, to give to a European commission the direction over all Ottoman officials.[78]

Some felt that it was not only Gladstone who was backing off. Two days after the meeting at Blackheath, Derby received two deputations of working men at the Foreign Office, together with some agitation spokesmen. The Foreign Secretary received a last-minute suggestion from Disraeli. 'Would it be advisable to hint that the course some persons were taking was not strengthening the hands of the British Govt?'

In part Derby's remarks to the deputations were a reply to Gladstone. He denied any Government responsibility for the Bulgarian atrocities, including any indifference to them. "'Considering we never heard of them until after they had occurred, I am quite unable to understand what is the practical meaning of that charge.'" The Foreign Secretary's reply to the address of one of the deputations, that independence should be granted to the Ottoman Christians, was that the territorial integrity of Turkey was necessary as partition would lead to a European war, but that the Government did not oppose some change within the bounds of Ottoman sovereignty. Derby was purposely both vague and careful. "'There are a great many people in England under the impression that Lord Beaconsfield is the Sultan, and that I am the Grand Vizier. We have exactly the same right, and the same power of interference ... that is possessed by every other power. I do not know whether in France, Germany, Italy, and other countries people are crying out as they do here and denounce their government as being accomplices in these atrocities.'"

The reaction to Derby's words to the deputations was mixed, but more favourable than not. The Conservative Press was pleased, the provincial Liberal journals were not. *The Times* and the *Daily News*, the leading London agitation papers, chose to interpret the Foreign Secretary's address misleadingly as a partial capitulation to the agitation, as did Lewis Mallet at the India Office. Disraeli was pleased and thought his colleague's speech would dampen the agitation. '*The Times* cannot bear his [Derby's] "razing" we have not changed our policy one inch.' Salisbury, still fulminating against Elliot and the Turks, thought Derby's speech was for the present all that could be said. The Queen was also pleased but doubted whether the speech would end the agitation. Froude, the writer and historian, also liked the Foreign Secretary's declaration and felt, at this time, that Gladstone and the Liberal leaders, except for Hartington, were acting outrageously when they were not being completely unprincipled.[79]

Hardy and Cairns expressed some dissatisfaction with Derby's effort.

Derby's speech [to the deputations] is calm and clear but cold and too much addressed to the reasonable world only. At the same time it proves non complicity in fact by dates and otherwise and he was right not to answer the violent men like Freeman who impute wilful connivance. I hope his [Freeman's] histories are more impartial than his letters which are specimens of malignant calumny particularly against Beaconsfield and Derby such as one seldom has seen.

Cairns agreed with Hardy that their colleague's speech was too coolly reasonable and also too negative. 'All seems to me to be negative, like his speech, which was good as far as it went, but sadly deficient in sentiment or suggestion. ... Gladstone and Lowe are atrocious in the things they propose, which they must know could not be done, which they, in our place, could not do. And all this row at home paralyzes us ... and leaves Russia mistress of the situation.'[80]

Derby was treading water and realized it. His solution of local self government or administrative autonomy for Bulgaria and Bosnia was vague and elastic enough to seem more than it was. He denied the report of *The Times* that he suggested ending Turkish administrative authority. 'Absolute autonomy such as that of Serbia is out of the question. Even Russia does not demand it, and the Porte could not concede it without war. It would amount to the disruption of the Turkish Empire. But the question what kind of local institutions are to be granted, and how they are to be worked, is one of extreme complexity.'[81] Gladstone rightly recognized Derby's position and answered it in a letter to *The Times* and the *Daily News* on 16 September, in which he characterized Derby's speeches as the same old policy. He now came out and supported Hartington's call for an early reassembling of Parliament, and set out for a trip to the north to visit a number of country houses.[82]

The agitation continued through the end of September, though its intensity had somewhat lessened. The *Spectator* on the sixteenth named 48 meetings for the week. Disraeli now followed Derby and Northcote, with a speech before 500 county notables at the annual dinner of the Buckinghamshire Agricultural Association at Aylesbury. He met atrocity opinion head on and indicated that there would be no change in Government policy even though the ministry was not supported by the country.

Unquestionably there is a large party and a large portion of Her Majesty's Subjects whose thoughts and sentiments are attracted to . . . other matters than the maintenance of the permanent interests of this country, or the maintenance of peace.

The danger at such a moment is this, that designing politicians may take advantage of such sublime sentiments and may apply them for the furtherance of their sinister ends.

Humanitarian politicans do not always look before they leap . . .

Whereas Derby was prepared to fudge the gulf between Government policy and agitation anger and sentiment, the Prime Minister was not, and any hope Gladstone may have had for a public governmental change of policy in recognition of the agitation was not to be.[83]

The dispersal of ministers, with the prorogation of Parliament, allowed Disraeli to control the Government's reaction to the Bulgarian agitation—the main plank of which was not to appear to have changed policy as a result of public indignation. Derby was willing to go along because he believed that the Government was not responsible for the atrocities—a belief which was necessary to enable him to function. But the Foreign Secretary was affected by the uproar even when he used it as an excuse to place pressure on Turkey to end the Serbian war. It reinforced the Prime Minister's exhortations to grasp the initiative diplomatically, which Derby did during the very height of the agitation in September. His disinclination to fight for Turkey were she to be attacked by Russia would have existed without any public clamour at all, and his forcefulness with the Porte had for its object the ending of the war in order to prevent Russian military intervention which he expected if it continued.

Hartington wished the agitation to stop as it was both unseemly and unbalanced, and his call for an early session of Parliament, a call which was not affirmatively answered, was for the purpose of taking the issue back indoors, inside the more sober walls of Parliament. Granville, who took a sort of middle position between Hartington and Gladstone, wished to use the agitation to aid and abet the Liberal party. He opposed an early calling of Parliament for it would be necessary to bring foward a vote of censure which would be defeated by considerable majorities in both Houses.[84] Gladstone favoured

the calling of Parliament and also wished the agitation to continue to politically embarrass the Government and to reinforce
his public popularity.

Public commotion would go on beyond September but its
volume was diminishing. As the war had been stopped, the
agitation would now transpire against the background of a
European attempt to make peace and, it was to be hoped, to bring
better government to the Balkan Christians.

# 12   ARRANGING A CONFERENCE

BY THE beginning or middle of October the agitation within Britain, which had been in full force since the end of August, cooled down somewhat. Its impact, nevertheless, was considerable. It had, as Disraeli admitted, 'changed the bent of opinion in England as regards Turkey',[1] and this change was reflected in Government policy.

Up until the Berlin memorandum in May 1876, Derby advocated complete Ottoman sovereignty, the right of the Porte to deal with its internal problems without significant European interference. Now, in September, he was unwilling to advocate unfettered Ottoman control over Bulgarian and Bosnian Christians. As Lyons put it, 'one can hardly tell them [Turks] to their faces that they are a set of savages, who must not expect to be treated as if they were really members of the civilized community of European nations'.[2] This was a change as real as Derby's advising the Porte that Britain probably would not fight in its support against a Russian attack. An even greater contrast, however, was apparent between Britain's diplomatic position in Europe up until July 1876 with what it would be from August to the end of the year. Having been dragged in the wake of Austro-Russian manoeuvring for over a year, Derby emerged in August with a burst of energy and seized the diplomatic initiative which enabled him to play the major European role in ending the Turco-Serbian war and arranging the Constantinople Conference which followed it. The contrast is more stark when one recalls that in May and June it was the Prime Minister who called the tune which the Foreign Secretary hummed.

The fit of Stanlerian exuberance in the late summer and autumn of 1876,[3] though welcomed at first by Disraeli, soon manifested its potential to obstruct certain measures the Prime Minister considered desirable. Ironically, various ministers—Cairns, Northcote, and Salisbury—expressed dissatisfaction with Derby at the very moment he grasped the initiative in Europe. This was for the most part not the fault of the Foreign Secretary, who could not keep his colleagues scattered over Britain and on the Continent fully informed, when his steps to obtain a Turco-Serbian armistice had to be altered almost daily to meet a series of ever-changing obstacles. Before the armistice was arranged at the end of October, Derby found that it was necessary to throw his weight against the fertile and imaginative suggestions of the Prime Minister. It marked the beginning of a political estrangement, minor and muted at first, which gradually increased and ended in the Foreign Secretary's resignation in March of 1878. It involved the question of the appropriate British response to a Russian war with the Ottoman Empire, or with Austria-Hungary, which threatened British interests.

The suspicion of an Austro-Russian attack on Turkey and a Russian proposal for an Austro-Russian occupation of Bosnia and Bulgaria, together with the assembling of a fleet composed by the Great Powers at Besika Bay, resulted in the calling of a Cabinet meeting on 4 October, the first since Parliament had been prorogued in early August. The ministers decided to refuse the Russian proposal of coercive occupation and considered, with the exception of Derby, the possibility of occupying Constantinople if Russia moved into Bulgaria. The idea of a 'friendly occupation of Constantinople' was introduced by the Premier.

Disraeli's concern was that Russia, feeling that the Bulgarian agitation had emasculated London's ability to respond militarily, might attack Turkey and menace or occupy Constantinople. He believed that if Britain showed firmness, Russia would not choose war, and even if she did, he wished to prepare militarily to protect British interests. Derby was equally concerned about St. Petersburg's military intentions but desired to conciliate Russia in order to end the Turco-Serbian war and remove any excuse for Russia to attack the Ottoman Empire. He viewed English military preparations as an obstacle to peace by heightening tension and complicating or escalating response.[4]

After the ministerial meeting on 19 October, while Derby was diluting any British obligation to uphold the Tripartite Treaty of 1856, Disraeli was preparing military measures to enable Britain to maintain her dignity and interests. The Prime

Minister wrote to Derby and criticized his unwillingness to consider the military necessities and the humiliation of England which a Russian occupation of Constantinople would bring. He complained to Hardy, the War Minister. 'His [Derby's] tone was not satisfactory to me, and so far as I can judge, will not satisfy the country. The vile Crimean war might have been prevented by firmness on our part.'

On the twenty-third the Premier concerted naval measures with Hunt, the Naval Minister, and arranged with Hardy to send some officers to survey the area around Constantinople with a view to its defence.[5] Disraeli's plan to send the fleet to Constantinople was successfully opposed by Derby. 'The step of ordering a British fleet to pass the Dardanelles . . . is not one to be taken off hand, nor without the fullest consideration. I cannot sanction the order which has been suggested to you [Hunt] as matters now stand. If a Russian vessel went through—[the Straits] which I do not consider probable . . . since the passage would be resisted, and as we know the Russians have no fleet to match that of Turkey.' Upon hearing that guns were being ordered for Constantinople, the Foreign Secretary wrote indignantly and a little quickly to both Disraeli and Hardy. 'We [the Cabinet] have never sanctioned the sending out of guns to Constantinople. . . . I do not think steps of this kind ought to be taken, with the result of creating a panic throughout Europe—unless after full consideration and discussion.' Hardy was extremely annoyed by Derby's intervention as he had no intention of sending guns to the Bulair lines near Constantinople without Cabinet consent.[6]

Disraeli too was annoyed with Derby's obstruction but expressed it indirectly to the Foreign Secretary. He wrote to him that he was anxious to know whether Derby had sent off the warning to Russia about a possible occupation of Bulgaria to which the Cabinet had agreed. Derby replied that he was preparing the dispatch with Tenterden, who was as intent as he in the wish to water down the threat. The Under-Secretary thought that a weaker version would still allow the Russians to know that Britain respected the Treaty of Paris of 1856 even though she would not specify any particular step in its defence. On 28 October Derby explained to the Prime Minister the reasons for his refusing to use the strong warning to Russia that Disraeli wished and to which the Cabinet had assented.

I have carefully avoided using any expression that looks like a threat for two reasons:

The first that beyond the fact that Russia is arming, we have really no reason for imputing to the Czar a project of occupation by Russia alone; or in other words of war on Turkey. What he proposed a month ago was a joint occupation by agreement among the Powers.

The second, that at the present moment there is some reason to hope that matters will settle themselves amicably. It would be a misfortune to have this settlement [a Turco-Serbian armistice] interrupted by anything that might bear the appearance of a challenge or menace . . .

For these reasons I have confined myself to a friendly warning; enough to show that we do not mean to be consenting parties to a plan of occupation.

. . .

I am not prepared to alter the draft in that sense [of a threat to Russia] . . .

Disraeli's reaction was again oblique and consisted in a blast at Odo Russell and the suggestion of a treaty with Germany for the preservation of the *status quo* which would guard European peace and at the same time preserve Britain's empire in the East.[7] Derby also vetoed Disraeli's German alliance as the time was not favourable for arranging such a convention.[8]

Disraeli was not only not prepared to allow the dissolution or weakening of Britain's Eastern Empire, he was willing to draw upon its strength and use it. In India, Disraeli had a viceroy who was a personal friend with an expansiveness that equalled his own, and an area not under the direct control of a careful and hesitant Foreign Secretary, though Salisbury was equally unafraid to disagree. Lytton, the viceroy, followed the Balkan crisis closely and in September and October embarked on a campaign to convince London that Indian Muslim opinion was strong and growing stronger in support of the Sultan at Constantinople.[9] The Prime Minister needed little if any convincing and asked Salisbury, the India Secretary, about the possibility of striking at Russia in central Asia. When Salisbury telegraphed Lytton for his opinion, the viceroy responded almost ecstatically to a war with Russia in which the Indian Government would play a major part.[10]

When the Porte accepted the Russian ultimatum for an armistice at the end of October the division between Derby and Disraeli over the way to avoid and the need to prepare for Russian military action subsided temporarily. Disraeli had wished to scare Russia away from the steps towards which Derby desired to avoid provoking her. The Prime Minister perhaps misjudged her timing, but Derby was wrong on her eventual intention. Each man checked the ultimate extreme of the other—dangerous provocation and senseless appeasement.

There was possibly even greater disunity within Liberal ranks which included the Palmerstonian section with Hartington at one extreme, and at the other, the agitators and the historian Freeman, whom Morley thought had gone off the deep end. Floating easily over most of the area between was Granville, who had little personal sympathy with the agitation, but was quite happy to use it in order to damage the Government. 'I [Granville] admitted that we [the Opposition] were rather exaggerating their [the Government's] amount of responsibility for the Bulgarian atrocities, but that it was not our business to extenuate their conduct and that it was obvious that the feeling of the country was getting much excited on the subject.' Gladstone strongly wished the agitation meetings to continue in order to influence and control the Government, but he desired personally to remain in the shadows and not come forward as he had in early September.[11] Granville felt he wished to turn out the Government which the former opposed doing.

The agitation generally floundered somewhat in October, in part because of the impossibility of maintaining indefinitely a high level of momentum, as well as the absence of Gladstone's leadership.[12] At the end of September Henry Joseph Wilson, secretary of the Sheffield Liberal Association and Robert Leader, president of that group and co-proprietor of the Sheffield *Independent*, discussed the idea of a national agitation meeting and on 30 September met with representatives of the Liberal Associations of Darlington, Leeds, and Manchester and decided to arrange a national conference or convention on the Eastern Question.[13]

## Arranging a European Conference

The suggestion of a European meeting to deal with the

Eastern Question had been put forward while Derby was making his heroic effort to obtain an armistice and end the fighting in October. By 1 November both the Porte and Serbia had accepted Russia's armistice and Gorchakov immediately pressed Derby to initiate at Constantinople preliminary discussions among the representatives of the Great Powers using the British bases of peace earlier formulated by London. On 2 November Loftus had an interview with Alexander II in the Crimea, during which the Tsar explained Russia's ultimatum to Turkey as being necessary in order to prevent Turkish atrocities in Serbia after the Porte's victories there.

His Imperial Majesty evidently desires that the conference should meet without delay . . .

He pledged his honour that he had no views of conquest . . . of Constantinople . . . several times and in the most solemn manner.
. . .

He wished to maintain the European concert, but if Europe remained passive, he would be obliged to act alone . . .[14]

When Derby saw Shuvalov on the afternoon of 3 November, he informed him that Britain was prepared to take the initiative in proposing a conference but that some delay in doing so was desirable as complicated questions should not be settled in haste. Derby then indicated that it would be better, should a conference be held at Constantinople, if all the Powers followed Britain's lead in appointing a special plenipotentiary not bound, as the permanent ambassadors were, by previous negotiations.[15]

London's intention to send a special representative to any European conference reflected at least two things: the possibility of emasculating the potential of Ignatiev to make trouble and the undesirability of leaving British negotiations entirely in the hands of Elliot. The British ambassador's credibility had been largely destroyed in England even among Conservatives. Disraeli almost blamed the Turkish atrocities on the British ambassador's health and lethargy. After his return from Constantinople, Hartington, far from being an agitator, wrote to his father. 'I like him [Elliot] very much but he seems anxious and worried and is I should say too much tied up to the old Turkish and anti Russian policy to be the best possible adviser or organ of the English Government at this time . . .'[16]

Sir George Campbell, the former Indian administrator, wrote a letter to Salisbury from Contantinople, which the latter forwarded to Derby and Disraeli.

I do not impute direct imprudence to the ambassador [Elliot]. But I do say that if the opinion which excuses the Turks and abuses the Russians is strong in Galata and Pera, it is much stronger in Therapia in the quarter of the [British] Embassy and the English. I have myself heard male members of the English Embassy in gossip with Turkish ministers join them in saying hard things of the Russians . . .

After seeing a good deal of these people [the Turks] I am convinced that they do not realize the seriousness of the situation. . . . They will never concede to what England demands unless they see plainly that *they will be forced to do so by the Powers united*. Can we hope that they will do so when they see the English feeling here . . . going so much with them and against Russia? . . .

The Turks are unlikely to accept necessary terms here under the present English regime. No doubt the ambassador will honourably carry out the orders of his Govt. but personally he has been very much committed, As I have said, all about him are strong partisans, his health is very poor . . .[17]

Salisbury, especially, had nothing but contempt for the British ambassador. He had been critical of him in and out of the Cabinet for two years. 'But throughout his [Elliot's] feebleness and prejudice have been our stumbling block. That we might be able to settle matters between Turkey and her enemies it was essential that we should be able to manage the Turks and that is what we have never been able thoroughly to do.'[18]

The Prime Minister, of course, wished to control the Turks and suspected that Elliot's sympathy for them precluded their fearing him sufficiently to do the disagreeable things which Britain considered necessary. While Disraeli hardly minded Elliot's suspiciousness of Russia, he still unfairly blamed him for much of the criticism of the Government as a result of the Bulgarian atrocities. As he wrote to the Queen on 4 October, he had the consent of Salisbury to go to Constantinople as temporary ambassador, should it become necessary to act on London's threat to the Porte to remove Elliot if it did not consent to an armistice.[19] The initiative in asking the India Secretary to act, then as well as later, as co-representative with

Elliot to the Constantinople Conference, was apparently the Prime Minister's. The Queen and Tenterden both suggested Lyons, the reliable and clever ambassador to France who had been at Constantinople before he was transferred to Paris. If there was an advantage in having a Cabinet minister at the conference, appointing one so contemptuous of the resident ambassador who was also to be present, and one who usually was not troubled with sparing the feelings of those he opposed, was questionable. Derby never considered going himself.

Derby formally asked Salisbury to represent Britain at the conference and implied that the choice was his own.

Your tendencies are not supposed to be Turkish, and the choice would therefore satisfy the public, while your Indian experience will have shown you that Russians are not exactly the self-sacrificing apostles of a new civilization which our Liberals seem inclined to consider them. ... Your going would not humiliate Elliot ... and you would be able to help in the Parliamentary defense of your own acts.

Think it over; we shall discuss the matter tomorrow in Cabinet. I need not say that I write with the knowledge and sanction of the Premier.

Salisbury accepted with pessimistic expectations.

I am afraid there will not be much reality in the conference. I doubt the possibility now of Russia being content with any terms to which Turkey can reasonably be expected to submit. Still it is quite necessary that we should do our part as diligently as if we were assured of a successful issue. ... I will take my part in the comedy with all solemnity ...[20]

The India Secretary received a note of advice from his former step-mother, Lady Derby. 'When it was a question of asking you to go to Constantinople a few weeks ago I said I thought you were the right man to go with an ultimatum in your pocket—but this is a very different story—I am behind the scenes. I see the hideous complications of red tape and diplomacy. ... If you accept, mind you insist upon going with unfettered hands.'[21]

Salisbury was convinced, as he wrote to Disraeli, that the traditional Palmerstonian policy was no longer possible and that none of the revolted areas could be returned to the Porte's unfettered authority. His solution for a guarantee of good Turkish government was the creation at Constantinople of an officer who would be a defender of Christian subjects, nominated with the consent of the Great Powers and not removable except with their consent. He would advise the Porte and the Sultan as to any delinquencies in the protection of Christians and he would submit to the Turkish Government a list of acceptable governors for Bosnia and Bulgaria from which the Porte could make its selection. The governors would not be removable except with the protector's consent.

Our best chance of coming to a peaceful issue of these perplexities is ... to come to an early understanding with Russia. Our danger is that we should make that result impossible by hanging on to the coat-tails of Austria. Austria has good reasons for resisting the faintest approach to self-government in the revolted provinces. Her existence would be menaced if she were hedged on the South by a line of Russian satellites. But her existence is no longer the importance to us that it was in former times. Her vocation in Europe is gone.[22]

The Cabinet meeting held on 4 November approved the choice of Salisbury and recommended it to the Queen. On the same day Derby invited the other Great Powers and the Porte to a conference at Constantinople, where each Government could have two representatives. The bases suggested by Britain for the meeting were the independence and territorial integrity of the Ottoman Empire, a declaration that the Powers were not seeking territorial advantages, and the pacification terms proposed by England to the Porte on 21 September. These last were the rough *status quo* for Serbia and Montenegro, the Porte and the Powers to sign a protocol giving to Bosnia-Hercegovina local or administrative autonomy and similar guarantees to guard against maladministration in Bulgaria.[23]

No one, including Derby himself, was quite certain what local or administrative autonomy meant. It did not mean, by his definition, political autonomy or tributary status, but arrangements to give some control over local affairs to the inhabitants, as he wished, needed to be implemented in some fashion. And, as the Foreign Secretary himself admitted, the manner of doing so was not an easy question. Disraeli was

anxious to define quickly the phrase 'administrative autonomy', and Andrássy refused to take part in a conference until
this was done to his satisfaction.[24]

Count Andrassy is apprehensive lest Her Majesty's Government may
be disposed to make concessions to Russia on the point of autonomy
to be given to the Turkish provinces. He said he feared little
resistance to Russian views is to be expected from the other Powers,
and that unless Austria is supported by England she would stand
alone, and proposals would be made to the Porte which it could not
accept, and war should be inevitable.[25]

Even Russia, who gave her acceptance of the conference to
London on 6 November, had a reservation; she wished to
exclude the word 'territorial' before the phrase 'integrity of the
Ottoman Empire' in the British peace bases.

His highness [Gorchakov] observed that he could not accept that
term as it would exclude possibility of an occupation which he considers will still be necessary as a guarantee for the security of Christian population and for execution of reforms. This occupation
should bear European character as in the case of Syria . . . in 1860,
and it might be entrusted to Russia and Austria, acting in the name of
Europe.[26]

Gorchakov gave way and did not insist upon his exclusion, and
on 8 November Italy accepted the British invitation to the
conference.[27]

Disraeli did not trust either Gorchakov or Ignatiev any more
than Derby, and he further suspected a possible occupation of
the Straits or a partition of European Turkey. Failing to
achieve an agreement with Germany, the Prime Minister was
prepared to discuss a treaty with Austria before the conference
commenced.[28] Corry, his private secretary, entered into talks
with Count Montgelas of the Austrian Embassy, indicating that
he was speaking for the Prime Minister. They discussed what
Austria and Britain would agree to at the conference, the *status
quo ameliore*, as well as a possible alliance treaty in case of an
Anglo-Austrian war with Russia. Nothing came of the talks as
neither Disraeli nor Andrássy, the latter tied to Russia by
Reichstadt, was prepared for a military alliance against
Russia.[29]

On 8 November it was announced publicly that Salisbury had

been selected by the Government to attend the prospective conference along with Elliot. The appointment aroused general satisfaction. It was commonly interpreted as a defeat for Disraeli, and Gladstone described it as the best step the Government had taken since the Eastern crisis had flared up again.[30] One foreign observer commented that the choice of Salisbury was overwhelmingly favoured, especially by the Liberal party.[31] On the same day the Cabinet met. Lady Derby forwarded to Salisbury a private suggestion.

Could you at the Cabinet tomorrow invite each member to send round afterwards in a box a memorandum of their views or get Lord D[erby] at the Cabinet to give a suggestion of what he proposed, & then let each one write his own views afterwards upon that proposal. I know Ld. D[erby] will say 'wait till Turkey assents or refuses' [the conference].

But your colleagues feel that they wd. like to know beforehand what they are likely to go in for, & that when emergencies or telegrams arrive they will not be consulted.

A member of the Cabinet speaking for several others wd. be glad to know what Ld. Salisbury's instructions wd be as to the extent of the guarantee to be given to ensure the reforms being carried out, if Turkey assents to them.

Or in case of Turkey refusing—the extent to wh. England wd be prepared to go for the purpose of enforcing them.[32]

The Prime Minister also received some advice on the day of the Cabinet meeting in a ciphered telegram from the Queen at Balmoral. 'I am anxious that my views respecting the future government of the Northern Provinces of Turkey [Serbia and Montenegro] should be communicated to Lord Derby and Lord Salisbury, and should be considered by the Cabinet.'[33] The Prime Minister replied that such an arrangement was impossible, as even Russia had accepted the British bases, one of which was the maintenance of Ottoman territorial integrity. He reported the ministers as united at the Cabinet meeting, in which a discussion ensued on the sort of guarantee necessary for the fulfilment of the reforms contemplated for Bosnia and Bulgaria. Only military occupation had been ruled out. 'What Ld Beaconsfield most fears, is, that Russia may secretly advise, or encourage the Porte to refuse the conference, & then make private terms with the Turks. He has reasons to believe that such an intrigue is on foot.'[34]

Disraeli's suspicions seemed to be borne out by the objections the Porte raised to a conference, objections not communicated to Elliot, but telegraphed direct to London and delivered to Derby on the afternoon of 10 November. The Ottoman Government objected that the term 'local or administrative autonomy' was too vague and elastic, and that to give advantages to Bosnia and Bulgaria would be tantamount to rewarding insurrection. Derby was not sympathetic to the Turkish objections.

There can . . . be no question that the Powers have the right to discuss matters relating to the internal administration of the Ottoman Empire [as was done in 1860 and 1867] under circumstances like those which occasioned the present proposal for a Conference.
. . .

'Local or administrative autonomy' is 'to be understood [as] a system of local institutions, which shall give the population some control over their own local affairs and guarantees against the exercise of arbitrary authority. There is to be no question of the creation of a tributary state.'

Her Majesty's Government are disposed to agree with the Porte that administrative reforms which may be desirable for one part of the Empire, can scarcely be withheld from the rest of it; but they cannot regard this as a reason for not entering upon a Conference to determine what reforms are now required to ensure the pacification of the disturbed provinces.

Her Majesty's Government regret that they cannot accept the proclamation of these reforms as in itself sufficient; nor, were they disposed to do so, would there be any probability of the other Powers assenting to such a course.[35]

On 9 November, the day after the Cabinet meeting and the public learning of Salisbury's nomination, Disraeli spoke at the Guildhall on Lord Mayor's Day, and used words which seemed to throw down the gauntlet to public opinion, and foreign governments as well.

But although the policy of England is peace, there is no country so well prepared for war as our own. (Cheers.) If she enters into a conflict in a righteous cause . . . her resources, I feel, are inexhaustible. (Loud cheers.) She is not a country that, when she enters into a campaign, has to ask herself whether she can support a second or third campaign. (Cheers.) She enters into a campaign which she will not terminate till right is done. (Loud cheers.)

It was really the Prime Minister's answer to Gorchakov's haughty declaration to Loftus, that if the Russian propositions regarding autonomy were not accepted, Ignatiev was to leave Constantinople. Disraeli interpreted this as an announcement to England which she should not pass by in silence.[36] The Premier's words were also meant to encourage Turkey. The British response to the Guildhall speech was generally unfavourable. 'It was remarked that the tone of it was not conciliatory enough, at a moment when a conference was about to convene to try to seek peaceful solutions, and one which in his [Disraeli] language was a menace, as if any conclusions that did not take account of the specifically British interests, would be rejected.'[37]

The day after Disraeli's address Alexander II, returning to St. Petersburg, made a public speech in Moscow, a thing he rarely did, which reiterated Gorchakov's intimation of possible Russian military action unless Turkey were reasonable.[38] 'A conference is about to assemble at Constantinople, in which Russia will present her demands. If her endeavours are not crowned with success, Russia will be forced to take up arms and I count on support of my people.' The Tsar concluded his remarks by saying 'May God help us to fulfil our sacred mission.'[39]

On 12 November, two days after the Tsar's Moscow address, Shuvalov in London talked with Borthwick, the Conservative editor of the *Morning Post*. The editor described the Russian ambassador as unhappy and discouraged as a result of Disraeli's speech which he interpreted as meaning war. He said that he knew that the Prime Minister insisted on the observance of the Treaty of Paris of 1856. On the following day the two men again talked but the editor found the ambassador entirely changed as the London newspapers carried their first reports of the Tsar's Moscow address together with the news of the partial mobilization of the Russian army.[40] The Porte was still attempting to avoid a conference and had not yet given its formal acceptance. The result of this was a warning telegram from Derby.

Her Majesty's Government are greatly surprised at not receiving the

Porte's answer about the Conference. They cannot believe that after the urgent manner in which they have pressed it on the acceptance of the Porte as the only alternative left for the averting of war, the Porte will refuse. .... If this last chance is allowed to pass Her Majesty's Government will be compelled to withdraw all support and countenance from the Porte in future negotiations.[41]

In the meantime Salisbury was still the man of the hour and much of official Europe wished to see him before he left for Constantinople, or while he was on his way there. Andrássy and Decazes indicated this on 12 November. Shuvalov apparently convinced Lady Derby of his desire to see the India Secretary. 'Ct. Schouvaloff is getting fidgetty at not seeing you [Salisbury] at all. I [Lady Derby] don't think a quarter of an hour with him wd. be thrown away, & it might help to keep things straight. But you know best,—do not let me seem to press you, if you say you prefer not to see him at present I will get rid of it; the Russian Govt. have an idea that you are more hostile than any member of the Cabinet to Russia.'[42] Odo Russell wrote from Berlin of the importance of Salisbury stopping to see Bismarck and the German Emperor.[43] All seemed well, as late on the evening of 18 November Elliot informed London that Turkey had agreed to the conference. Only the Cabinet was at odds as to the formal instructions to be given Salisbury for negotiating at Constantinople, for where he planned to depart from London on 20 November.

Disraeli, Tenterden, and Lady Derby did not wish Salisbury tied closely to instructions agreed on by the Cabinet in London. They wished to allow him the freedom to negotiate and manoeuvre. Cairns, Cross, Carnarvon, and Northumberland did not favour this and wished Salisbury to take with him fairly restrictive instructions approved by the Cabinet. Within this last group, however, there was disagreement on the content of the instructions. One point of contention was whether foreign troops should be used in Bulgaria and Bosnia as a temporary guarantee of good government. Tenterden and Derby worked together to draw up the instructions for the consideration of the Cabinet on Saturday, 18 November. The Under-Secretary did not like the idea of a foreign occupation, which was mainly a Russian proposal, but was willing to consider it.

It may be that this idea of a small neutral force being used, under the name of police, is an excuse [of the Tsar's] to avoid war without seeming to retreat without having done anything.

If any force is to be employed, a Belgian wd. be better than any other. It wd. satisfy the public in England.

It is not a vital matter on which England could declare war.
. . .

On the whole therefore . . . I do not think the Govt. should refuse to entertain the idea . . .[44]

Loftus, who had returned from the Crimea to St. Petersburg, thought that only a military occupation could bring order and peace to Bosnia and Bulgaria. He was convinced that Russia meant to do this and preached to Derby the desirability of her doing so with the consent of Europe rather than by directly infringing Europe's will.[45] Andrássy wished to avoid such a course by Russia and had Beust see Derby on 17 November in an attempt to reach an unofficial understanding in opposition to a Russian occupation of Ottoman territory. Derby was sympathetic but careful.

[Beust] intimated that any such step would be viewed with disapprobation and anxiety by his Government . . .

I said that Her Majesty's Government, like that of Austria, would object in the strongest manner to any such military occupation . . . and that in the event of such an occupation being threatened I agreed with him that it would be desirable that a frank and unreserved exchange of opinion should take place between our two governments.

Derby explained that for Britain it was constitutionally not possible to go further than this as Parliament would censure any engagement of the executive, which could involve the country in a war, without the opportunity of prior consultation.[46] Two days later Derby received from Andrássy a communication with which the Foreign Secretary expressed his satisfaction. Beust reported that Austria was under no engagement to Russia and that she would not be neutral if her interests were violated and would seek to defend them were they to be threatened by Russia.[47] Andrássy hoped to garner British support to oppose a Russian occupation at the conference by scaring London with the probability that were it not prevented Austria would occupy Bosnia. The Queen wrote to Salisbury to urge the necessity of making it understood that any Russian occupation of Ottoman territory would immediately cause Britain to do the same.[48]

While Derby was carrying on official communications with the Russian and Austrian governments, he was being much assisted, probably without his being informed, by the unofficial activities of his wife and the Prime Minister. Lady Derby was providing a channel of communications between Shuvalov and Salisbury. On 18 November she informed the India Secretary of Shuvalov's plea to delay for a few weeks any British move on Khelat in central Asia, a move he admitted that London had a treaty right to make, as it might excite Russia to war. A little later it would go unnoticed.[49] Corry, Disraeli's secretary, was providing access to Austria through Montgelas and to Shuvalov through Borthwick, the editor of the *Morning Post* who was friendly with the Russian ambassador. The latter was attempting to bridge the gulf between a British preservation of the Treaty of Paris and a Russian occupation of Turkey. His suggestion, which Borthwick communicated to Corry, was for a commission supplemented by an international police force to act in Bulgaria and Bosnia.[50]

The day before the Cabinet was to meet to consider them, Derby and Tenterden completed a draft of the instructions for Salisbury. It was very long and full, but, as Ponsonby explained to the Queen, it left Salisbury much discretionary power and freedom of movement. The instructions were basically an amplification and slight modification of the British bases which had been used in inviting all the Powers to the conference. Some additional territory and the port of Antivari were suggested for Montenegro.[51]

The Porte is unable to guarantee the execution of reforms in the Provinces by Turkish officials, who accept them with reluctance, and neglect them with impunity.

. . .

Her Majesty's Government do not desire to hamper Your Excellency's discretion in the approaching discussions by any detailed plan . . . of reforms, but it may be useful to indicate generally the points in which the existing system of administration in the provinces might be strengthened and improved.

. . .

Her Majesty's Government have not endeavoured to offer more than an outline of a system of local self-government, in which they

have aimed at the establishment of provincial administration under Governors whose ability and integrity would be vouched for by the guarantee of a diplomatic veto, acting with provincial elective assemblies having control over local taxation, with permanent judges and other higher officials appointed under a similar guarantee, and with a reformed system of local militia and police, the removal of any remaining Christian disabilities, the improvement of the land laws, and the amelioration of the condition of the whole agricultural population.
. . .

Her Majesty's Government cannot countenance the introduction into the conference of proposals . . . which would bring foreign armies into Turkish territory in violation of the engagements by which the Guaranteeing Powers are solemnly bound.[52]

It is interesting to note that the amelioration of the condition of the whole agricultural population' contained in Salisbury's instructions had been one of the points of the Andrássy note to which the British government took serious objection in January 1876, when it was understood that such reform would be completely under the control of the Porte and not as now intended under the supervision of an international body or commission.

The Cabinet met on Saturday, 19 November to consider the instructions. There was a wide division among the ministers over the question of a foreign occupation of Turkish territory. One group led by Cairns and Carnarvon strongly favoured it in some form. They were opposed by another bloc led by Derby and Disraeli. A compromise of sorts was agreed upon. Discussion of military occupation was to be excluded from the conference, but it was to be left as an open possibility to be decided upon by the Powers in certain pressing circumstances. This last was to be inserted in a supplementary instruction for Salisbury to be considered by the Cabinet at its next meeting on the following Thursday.[53]

After the Cabinet meeting the instructions were sent to the Queen for her approval. When Carnarvon and Cairns learned this they were furious, for they considered that the instructions had not been passed by the Cabinet, which was to consider them at the later meeting. Derby disagreed and contended that assent had been given to the instructions.

I am convinced that this allegation of mistake is an after thought only, and I shall therefore take no step to prevent the instructions being approved [by the Queen] though of course, if you [Disraeli] think fit to do so I shall make no objection . . .

The question at issue is really serious, and I do not see how we can give way upon it.[54]

Disraeli quieted Cairns and 'the little Carnarvon', as he referred to the Colonial Secretary, and the instructions stood.[55]

At the Cabinet meeting on the eighteenth the Foreign Secretary had been very difficult in strongly opposing any occupation. He feared that which Bismarck desired, a partition of Turkey agreed upon by Europe. His anxiety resulted from his expectation that European occupation or partition would not, as Bismarck anticipated, lead to the maintenance of peace, but rather to a European war. Had not Austria already intimated as much? Derby preferred to maintain the fiction of Ottoman independence because all the Powers, save perhaps Russia, could agree to this. The Foreign Secretary hoped that the Ottoman Government would accept a limitation of its sovereignty in Bulgaria and Bosnia. It now remained to be seen whether the Porte would agree to allow Europe to force it to be reasonable in order to satisfy the Russian Government and prevent war.

# 13 TWO CONFERENCES IN CONSTANTINOPLE

SALISBURY AND his entourage left London for Paris on Monday, 20 November. With him were four gentlemen from the Foreign Office who were to provide secretarial and other aid which the special ambassador might require in Constantinople. They were Philip Currie, H. A. Lee, J. H. C. Hozier, and H. S. Northcote, son of the Chancellor of the Exchequer. Salisbury's wife and eldest son and daughter also accompanied him.

Leaving Rome by special train on the morning of 1 December, Salisbury's group reached Brindisi late that evening and departed by ship for Constantinople early the following morning. After a smooth voyage, Constantinople was reached on 5 December, at 9 a.m., the special ambassador taking up residence at the Hotel Royal in Pera. It had been one of the most unusual and significant journeys undertaken by a British minister in the interests of peace between those of Castlereagh and Neville Chamberlain. Salisbury had encountered most of the European royalty, heads of state, and executives of the foreign ministries of France, Germany, Austria, and Italy in a ten-day period from 21 to 30 November. He had departed representing a divided Cabinet, with little European diplomatic experience and good French, and arrived at his destination to face an antagonistic permanent embassy, a discordant group of foreign ambassadors and representatives, and Madame and General Ignatiev.

Within a day of his arrival the special ambassador had seen the ministers of the Porte and all the foreign representatives. It is not surprising, considering their differences, that the ambassadors of the Great Powers agreed on a series of meetings amongst themselves before entering a formal conference with the Turks. Salisbury happily reported that the Russian ambassador did not consider occupation a *sine qua non*.

The only point in his [Ignatiev's] demands which is menacing is for a force to secure the Christians from massacre during the interval of the few months till organization of police or militia agreed on at the Conference can be started. . . . I have told him that my instructions prohibited me from entertaining questions of occupation, and have given him no encouragement; but I feel that the demand in the form he puts it is awkward to break off upon.

All Ambassadors strongly opposed to occupation except Russian, and, perhaps, German.[1]

Disraeli also had occupation on his mind and decided to send to Salisbury by a private and trusted emissary some personal and unofficial instructions to supplement the official and the secret, supplementary ones which had already been sent him.

[When the question of occupation is raised] England will not say that she is unequivocally opposed to the occupation of Turkey for a temporary purpose but she cannot agree to such a step except at the instance, and with the full consent, of the Porte—as in the Syrian case [in 1860], now so quoted.

This attitude would prevent conference breaking up . . .

When ultimately submitted to the Porte, this position might be assumed by the Sultan: the Porte will consent to the occupation provided it is not effected by coterminous Powers, which will lead to war; and she may suggest that, England shd. occupy. Having taken this position, she must be inexorable.

I am prepared to propose such a measure to the Cabinet, and cannot doubt, especially with your aid and approval, that they would adopt it, and that it would be cheerfully accepted by Parliament, and be popular outside: maintaining the authority of this country.

We have a force of 40,000 men ready . . .

Of course, it must be the last card to be played, and it must be so done, that we must seem almost unwillingly to consent.
. . .

I have not, I shall not, breathe a word of . . . [this]. . . . Let it come to us if you approve it, in due course as your proposal, which I will immediately support in the Cabinet.

A joint occupation with Russia I look upon as highly objectionable . . .

We must never attempt to occupy Constantinople but at the instance of the Porte.[2]

Before the preliminary conference of the foreign representatives began, Salisbury and Ignatiev discussed together a great deal. They met twice, on 6 and 7 December. Calice, one of the two

Austrian representatives, reported that Salisbury had told him that he did not yet really understand what Ignatiev wanted. But the British special emissary understood enough to oppose Ignatiev's plan to extend Bulgaria south of the Balkan mountains and to question his suggestion of an international delegation responsible for the administration and tranquillity of the new province.[3]

Salisbury had gone to Constantinople believing Ottoman obstinancy would prove a greater obstacle to a peaceful solution than Russian demands. Upon arrival he believed that to be the case, and from inclination, therefore, as well as necessity, he went out of his way, along with his wife, to show a united front with Russia in order to induce the Porte to be reasonable. The permanent British Embassy and the Turks were naturally angry with such conduct, and even Northcote, of Salisbury's group, had doubts as to this behaviour.

The conference will clearly consist of two men [Salisbury and Ignatiev]—the others are dummies and Elliot I should say foremost amongst them. He has been most civil personally but is too thorough going a Turk for his opinion to have any weight—especially as a shy English gentleman is the last man to benefit the Ottoman cause if a champion they must have. There is an extraordinary popular delusion that we are going to back Turkey for which of course Elliot is responsible. The Salisburys male and female almost err on the other side . . .

Elliot is absurdly touchy about very trivial personal matters. Ignatieff keeps him in perpetual irritation. . . . In this he is assisted by a handsome, clever wife, and they are both absolutely unscrupulous, unscrupulous . . . to an extent that defies underlining. . . . There is much soreness at the very close personal relations he [Salisbury] has established with Ignatieff. Our Embassy are sore, and the newspaper and casual people who come daily to see me expatiate everyday more and more on this. I fancy he [Salisbury] begins to see this. . . . Madame Ignatieff calls daily to ride with or drive out Lady Maud [Lady Salisbury], and the General calls here ostentatiously at all hours. . . . Currie is ridiculously *en tete*—raves over Madame's [Ignatiev] *beaux yeux*. . . . Lady Salisbury too [as well as Salisbury] is unluckily furiously anti-Turk . . .[4]

Schuyler, who was drawing up a constitution for Bulgaria at the request of Ignatiev, confirmed Northcote's impression of

Russian flattery, with Ignatiev acting as if enthralled by Lady Salisbury.[5]

Madame Ignatiev did not limit her attentions to Lady Salisbury. At a banquet given by Ignatiev for all the foreign diplomats, Madame Ignatiev, according to Onou, the Russian dragoman, attempted to seduce Salisbury, and Onou warned her that as her prey was a man of virtue she would not succeed. Madame Ignatiev replied to Onou that did not matter. 'I shall make use of virtue to seduce him.'[6]

Russian charm in London easily matched that exhibited in Constantinople, and it had been going on for a much longer period of time. Shuvalov, the purveyor of it in London and at Knowsley, was devoid neither of political ability nor energy, and happened also to be something of a playboy. He had gained the affection of Lady Derby, who was now fifty-two years of age, and flattered her feelings of self-importance by discussing politics with her. Derby apparently kept little politically from his wife and she in turn told all to the Russian ambassador. Most Cabinet decisions and secrets were known to Shuvalov shortly after they were told to Lady Derby. One would like to feel that Derby was unaware of his wife's indiscretions. A good deal of what Salisbury reported to London and what London sent him in reply was known to Shuvalov who informed Gorchakov and Ignatiev.[7] Lady Derby obviously relished her political role and the sense of helping to direct Anglo-Russian relations.

Everybody comes to me [Lady Derby]—friends and foes—all with one story—one question. . . . Will Ld. S[alisbury] be able to disabuse the Turks of their 'belief respecting the course wh. Eng. d is likely to take in the last extremity? If they can flatter themselves with the hope that a Russian invasion will bring Eng.d to back them, they will resist, and there will be an invasion and a bloody war, whoever may take part in it.'

The promoters of the St. James Hall Conference (the moderate men) come to me and say this, members of the Cabinet say it, ask me to write it, fearing the F.O. tendencies and the Premier's . . .[8]

Derby was characteristically suspicious, as was Manners, and did not like Ignatiev's disguised occupation, though it was strongly supported by Cairns, Richmond, Northcote, and Carnarvon. Salisbury continued to stress Britain's awkward position.

If the Porte accepts the decisions of the conference and then an outbreak or massacre occurs, we shall be in an awkward position before Parliament, for Ignatiev will have left on record on the protocols of the conference his warning of danger. Then it will be impossible to resist or control the Russian occupation. England's power will be paralyzed by agitation at home and the Russians will cross the frontier and do what they like.[9]

The special ambassador supported the specific suggestion of Chaudordy, one of the French representatives, who proposed that two or three Swiss or Belgian regiments could serve as the nucleus for a native police force organized under European officers. What was more, Salisbury was angry with Derby and felt the need for cipher communications with Carnarvon.

I am disturbed that I have now for a week been urging this question [occupation] on Derby and have not received from him any expression of his own or the cabinet's opinion. Meanwhile Schouvaloff daily telegraphs to Ignatief what he states to be the decisions of the cabinet and opinions of Derby, and Ignatief shows me these telegrams. It puts me in an awkward and difficult position.

Salisbury then arranged a cipher system with Carnarvon in case of need.[10]

Carnarvon continued to press Derby to formally accept Ignatiev's proposals, and was joined by Northcote, who thought that a gendarmery with a Belgian contingent would be a safeguard against occupation. The Chancellor of the Exchequer supported Salisbury's being permitted to agree to such an arrangement, and informed Derby that if the special ambassador were not given a free rein in the matter a Cabinet meeting should be called.[11] At Tenterden's suggestion most of Britain's Balkan consuls had been ordered to Constantinople to assist Salisbury in any way they could. The latter took advantage of their presence and instructed vice-consul Calvert and Captain Ardagh to proceed to Bulgaria in order to inquire whether there was any evidence of a Muslim excitement there. This had been the justification of the Russian ambassador's desire for a foreign gendarmery.[12]

Between 5 and 11 December, the last day being the date of

the first meeting of what came to be called the preliminary conference, Salisbury and Ignatiev met every day to discuss the whole range of Ignatiev's proposals for European Turkey. The reason for the relatively quick and easy agreement between the two men, beyond any positive effects elicited by the Ignatiev campaign of charm, was that, ironically, the scheme of administrative organization contained in Salisbury's original instructions was, save on the questions of foreign occupation and the size of Bulgaria, more comprehensive and restrictive of unfettered Ottoman sovereignty than Ignatiev's proposals, which were partly based on a plan drawn up by Schuyler and Tzeretelev, the second secretary of the Russian Embassy.[13] This can be seen from a memorandum by Tenterden in the Foreign Office library.[14]

Even on the two most disputatious issues there seemed to be hope for an agreement. Ignatiev's gendarmery only awaited Cabinet sanction, which Salisbury was urging,[15] and the latter's proposal of dividing Bulgaria longitudinally into two provinces with two separate administrations in order to allow more Ottoman control over the eastern one, which was contiguous with the Straits and Constantinople, drew no insuperable objection from the Russian ambassador.[16] But Derby still feared a Russian trap and hesitated. Lady Derby was excited by the pressure which made any positive response difficult for her husband. She sent a note to the Home Secretary, whom she regarded as a political protégé of her husband and a social one of her own.

The situation grows more and more 'tendue.' I shall be free tomorrow morning at 11 or from that to 12 if you like to call, or at 6 this evening.

If there shd. linger an ambassador till 6 never mind—come in, he ought be gone by that time.[17]

The ambassador, who was seeing her husband every day, was, of course, using Lady Derby, even though the latter liked to pretend that he was in her pocket if not between her sheets.

On Monday, 11 December the first preliminary meeting of all plenipotentiaries except the Ottoman took place at the Russian Embassy. Ignatiev chaired the meeting in his position as doyen of the ambassadorial corps in Constantinople. Zichy and Salisbury co-operated in successfully blocking Ignatiev's suggested organization and procedure for the meetings, but the Russian ambassador was pleasantly surprised at an Anglo-Austrian proposal to give Montenegro access to the Adriatic. Zichy expressed a feeling that Salisbury had gone a little too far out of a wish to placate Russia.[18]

There were daily meetings of the preliminary conference following the first one. The next day Derby got around to responding to the proposal for a gendarmery. He still feared a trap and had no intention of answering officially until the Cabinet had expressed itself; so he temporized. 'What do the English Consuls who are with you [Salisbury] think of General Ignatiev's scheme, and what is their view as to supposed incapacity of Porte to maintain order in Bulgaria with its regular troops? ... What do the other Plenipotentiaries think of the scheme? You will remember ... that all propositions were to be *ad referendum*'.[19] Salisbury replied that all the plenipotentiaries except Calice approved the scheme and that White, the only consul whose opinion was asked, did as well.

General Ignatiev has communicated intimation from his Government that they will not yield on the question of providing material force to assure lives of Christians, but they do not claim that force should be Russian. The question of war or peace will probably turn on this point.

. . .

With reference to what you say about taking proposals *ad referendum*, nothing will be formally determined without reference to you. But except Belgian force all the proposals are within my instructions.[20]

At the third sitting of the preliminary conference the size and organization of Bulgaria were discussed. When Salisbury could not induce Ignatiev to reduce the proposed size of the province, he pressed its longitudinal division into two parts to which the Russian ambassador yielded. He explained his step to Derby as necessary for the Porte's independence.[21] The following day the question of occupation was discussed, and Ignatiev, dwelling upon the danger of massacre, argued the necessity of introducing a foreign military force. Russia would provide it, he said, if no other arrangement were proposed. Both Salisbury and Elliot argued against occupation and the former indicated that Russian occupation was not to be countenanced, but that he would propose the use of British troops should the conference find this acceptable. When Ignatiev strongly opposed this, the German ambassador suggested that soldiers of the Guaranteeing Powers be excluded from consideration. Chaudordy, the French representative, then proposed a small Belgian force as a kernel for the gendarmery. All except Elliot and Salisbury considered that 3,000 to 5,000 Belgian troops did not mean an occupation and were ready to assent, though the suggestion was taken *ad referendum*. Salisbury begged London for a favourable reply.

I recommend adoption earnestly, because I do not believe [Russia will] . . . give way on this, and because no possible political danger can result.

I crave, therefore, decision from Cabinet, which I hope may be summoned as early as possible for this purpose.[22]

Salisbury's telegram must have crossed one from Derby.

In reference to the project of employing a Belgian armed force for police purposes, you are fully authorized to discuss it. As a compromise between Russian occupation and the employment of a purely Turkish force, it has obvious advantages; but with our present knowledge I cannot absolutely pledge the Cabinet to its adoption. We shall meet on Monday [18 December] next.[23]

The special ambassador felt Russia was attempting to avoid a war, though he still feared Turkish obstinacy. He realized that Elliot and the British Embassy generally thought he was yielding too much and that he was being very hard on the Turks. 'But their views could not be carried out without another Crimean war for which opinion in England is manifestly disinclined . . .'[24] Disraeli was keeping in close touch with Derby as Salisbury's telegrams arrived, usually in the evening. Much more than the Foreign Secretary, he was opposed to calling an unnecessary Cabinet meeting until definite proposals, or General Ignatiev's reform bill, as Russell described it, needed to be sanctioned. He referred to Shuvalov's having told Derby that properly supervised Turkish regulars would be preferable to a small body of Belgian troops,[25] and interpreted Russian moderation as a sign of financial weakness, no fleet, and Turkish backbone.

The session of the preliminary conference on 16 December

agreed to a general organization for both Bosnia and Bulgaria which Salisbury communicated home in a long telegram which conveniently arrived in London just before the Cabinet meeting called on 18 December to consider the proposal of a Belgian gendarmery. Though the Cabinet agreed to both the proposed reorganization and the Belgian contingent, Derby's carefully worded telegrams communicating its decision left a loophole out of what he still considered a Russian trap.

The Cabinet is ready to assent in principle to the plan proposed by the preliminary Conference, viz., local reforms as stated in your telegram of the 17th instant, with a Commission of supervision for one year, such Commission to be supported by an escort not exceeding 6,000 men at the utmost, to be drawn from some minor State such as Belgium.

It must be understood that the scheme is open to modification of detail.

The Cabinet reserves absolutely the question of steps to be taken in the event of refusal by the Porte.

Thirty minutes later Derby supplemented this with a suggestion. 'It would be desirable if possible that the introduction of the Belgian force should appear to be made at the request of the Porte, and that it should be accompanied by some withdrawal of Russian troops from the frontier as a counterbalance.'[26]

At the sixth sitting on 19 December Salisbury said that Britain would agree to the use of 3,000 to 6,000 Belgian troops. The French representatives supported by the Austrians stipulated that no more than 3,000 were necessary, and this was then agreed to by all. With the major decisions taken, the foreign representatives decided to open the full conference in order to present their deliberations for Ottoman consideration and approval, as Turkish plenipotentiaries had been excluded from the preliminary meetings in their own capital.[27]

No one, including Salisbury, was sanguine about Turkish acceptance of the European proposals. Believing that the Russians meant war in the event of an Ottoman refusal,[28] the special ambassador was prepared to place pressure on the Turks.

I [Salisbury] note your [Derby] instruction that proceedings, in event of Turks refusing, are absolutely reserved by Cabinet. I must, however, earnestly call attention to fact that rapidity in dealing with Turks is essential to success, and that delay or hesitation may bring about entire failure of negotiations. I hope that if Cabinet take this decision out of my hands, they will be ready to meet and decide at shortest possible notice . . .

I know from secret source that the present orders are to declare war on January 6th (Russian Christmas day), and to cross Pruth on January 7th, and that the declaration is ready printed.

The Turks favourite weapon is delay; and unless I am able to apply the strongest pressure when required, the opportunity of effecting agreement may be lost . . .[29]

The Russians knew, probably through Lady Derby, of Derby's suggestion to Salisbury to ask for the withdrawal of Russian troops from the frontier. Before Salisbury could communicate this, Ignatiev came to him on the morning of 20 December and read a telegram from the Tsar which indicated his acceptance of the conference proposals, but also his intention to remain militarily at the ready until they had been executed. Salisbury thought it best to be quiet, and did not present the Foreign Secretary's proposal.[30]

Before the first full conference which was fixed for Saturday, 23 December, Salisbury and Chaudordy met with Midhat Pasha, the new Grand Vizier, and the two Ottoman plenipotentiaries. The day before, on Wednesday, the proposals of the preliminary conference had been privately communicated to the Sultan. At the private meeting with Midhat and Safvet Pasha, which Salisbury characterized as tempestuous and disappointing, the Turks vigorously rejected the international commission and any kind of guarantee save the Sultan's promise. The special ambassador was told that Turkey would permit herself to be pressed providing she were not suffocated, but that if there was an intention to strike off her arm she would refuse and take steps to defend herself. Salisbury interpreted all this as an opening gambit, Ottoman obstructionism, but wrote to Derby that the greatest force would be needed in order to elicit Turkish acceptance.[31] He felt that Ottoman objections and resistance were infantile and could not understand any more than he could with England's own Muslim children in India, how they might instinctively desire to maintain their own independence or sovereignty. He attributed their resistance to a belief in Russian weakness and an even stronger belief that Britain would eventually fight for them.[32]

Austria and Russia also attempted to informally influence the Turks before the first full meeting of the conference. Zichy saw Midhat on the same day as Salisbury and Chaudordy, and the Grand Vizier requested the Austrian ambassador to inform Andrássy that the Porte still counted on Austrian friendship and sympathy. Ignatiev dispatched Onou, the Russian dragoman, to warn the Grand Vizier and the Foreign Minister that it would be dangerous to reject the proposals of the preliminary conference, and that it would be impossible to change the opinions of the foreign representatives. Midhat and Safvet replied that they did not intend to threaten or provoke Russia, but that Turkey would not commit suicide by agreeing to a dismemberment of her empire. Midhat asked Russia for a little time in order to prove Turkey could carry out her own reforms.[33]

Before the cabinet meeting on 22 December to consider the British position on the use of coercive measures against the Porte in the event of Turkish intransigence, Shuvalov, d'Harcourt, and Disraeli separately met with the Foreign Secretary. The Russian ambassador expressed a hope that Britain would not encourage the Porte to resist, and that if Turkey rejected the proposals, London would give her no support. Derby replied that the British Government already had used such language and would be prepared to do so again. The French wished to learn what Britain would be prepared to do in the event of a Turkish refusal. Derby told d'Harbourt that England would strongly support the proposals of the preliminary conference, but on the question of coercion he could only give his personal view as the Cabinet had not yet met to consider this question.

Her Majesty's Government would not be prepared themselves to employ measures of active coercion in order to extort the consent of Turkey to the proposals which had been drawn up at Constantinople . . . on the other hand, they would not hold out to the Porte any hope of assistance or protection in the event of war ensuing on the refusal to entertain these proposals.[34]

Disraeli also saw Derby before the Cabinet meeting on the

twenty-second, and the two discussed verbally and in writing the possibility of suspending diplomatic relations with Turkey in certain eventualities. Derby, characteristically, was only a little more opposed to coercing the Porte than Disraeli, but the Prime Minister as well had no intention of supporting the Russian policy of coercing Turkey. He suggested to the Foreign Secretary that in the event of a Turkish refusal of the conference proposals there should be no coercion, the return of Elliot as well as Salisbury, and the maintenance of diplomatic relations. The two men were quite agreed when they attended the Cabinet meeting on the afternoon of 22 December.[35]

Salisbury was more and more convinced that only the greatest pressure on the Porte might make it give way. He angled for both the Prime Minister's agreement and Carnarvon's assistance.

The Slavs are backward and boorish. The Greeks and Musulmans have the entire monopoly of whatever ruling qualities are to be found in the population of Bulgaria. Whether I shall be able to make the stupid Turks accept this scheme [the conference proposals] I don't know. When the time comes about a week hence I shall urge you [Disraeli] to allow me to use the strongest means of pressure . . .[36]

Salisbury was notified of the Cabinet's decision by a telegram from Derby on the evening of the ministerial meeting.

Cabinet has decided that England will not assent to or assist in, coercive measures, military or naval, against the Porte.

The Porte must, on the other hand, be made to understand, as it has from the first been informed, that it can expect no assistance from England in the event of war.

In the event of the Porte persisting in refusal, and the Conference failing, you will, of course, come away; and it will be desirable in that case, that Sir H. Elliot shall also come to England, to report upon the situation, leaving a Secretary in charge of the Embassy.

These are the views of the Government. Use your own discretion as to language which you shall hold.[37]

At the Cabinet meeting itself Hardy had successfully opposed his colleagues' willingness to have Elliot ask for leave, which, in fact, the latter had already done unsolicited, as not 'a straight course'. Carnarvon fought, with some support from Northcote and less, disappointingly, from Cairns, for the free hand to pressure the Porte which Salisbury desired. '[I stood] out alone against the original proposals which wd. have left you [Salisbury] almost powerless to carry on negotiations with any chance. I at last got the telegram into the shape in which it finally was sent to you.'[38]

Disraeli had decided already that were Elliot to leave Constantinople for England, he would not be returned to the Bosphorus. The ambassador, almost universally condemned in Britain, superseded at the conference by the anti-Turkish Salisbury, found his sympathy for the Turks bypassed by a British policy which was neutral or worse. His relationship with Salisbury had broken down completely. Northcote described Salisbury, his chief, whom he liked, to his father.

The Salisbury's are very anti-Turkish—almost too much so . . .
. . .

The relations between the head of the Special and Resident Embassies are, as I have, I think, told you, about as bad as they can be.[39]

With his health as broken as his spirit, Elliot telegraphed to Derby, only minutes before the beginning of the first full conference, of his intention to leave Constantinople.

I have been unable to attend the three last preliminary meetings, and there is little probability of my being able to attend the conference with any regularity.

As, if I remained at Constantinople, my absence from them would be sure to be taken here as the result of a disagreement with Lord Salisbury, and would encourage the Turks to resist, I have determined, in the public interest as well as in justice to myself, to leave in the first week of January.

I have taken care, in making my termination known, to guard against this misinterpretation.

I . . . hope you will not ask me to sacrifice myself beyond my strength.

You will believe me when I say how painful it is to me to be obliged to leave at such a moment as this, but it cannot be avoided.[40]

When Elliot told Salisbury of his intention to depart, for reasons of health, the special ambassador telegraphed to Derby of the need to replace him with a strong man, and suggested Morier as a temporary substitute. Both Derby and Tenterden opposed Morier, the Under-Secretary suggesting Lyons and Paget. Derby's reaction to this was that Tenterden apparently had not thought of Layard. If Tenterden had not, the Prime

Minister already had, when he wrote to the Queen on the twenty-second that if Elliot were called away he hoped that Layard would succeed him. Though it may have occurred to the Foreign Secretary simultaneously, it is more probable that it was suggested to him by Disraeli.[41]

Near noon on Saturday, 23 December, the first full conference opened and Safvet Pasha, the chief Ottoman plenipotentiary, delivered the opening address at the Admiralty building near the Golden Horn. His speech was interrupted by the firing of cannon close by. Safvet explained to the assembled delegates that the cannon marked the promulgation of an Ottoman constitution which guaranteed equal rights for all subjects of the Sultan. De Moüy of the French Embassy, who served as conference secretary, has given in his memoirs the reaction of the foreign diplomats. After 'a profound silence' of several minutes, the delegates ignored the event and went on with the business of the meeting. Devereux has accurately described the moment. 'Such diplomatic rudeness can only be explained by the arrogant self-righteousness which habitually characterized Europe's dealing with the Porte.' It was personified by Salisbury who described the session to the Queen.

It [the conference] was very tiresome and very fruitless. . . . Safvet . . . a sleepy old man who can scarcely talk intelligible French, loses his places, and . . . puts to the vote the question that was decided half an hour before. . . . Edhem [Pasha] . . . is very violent; and he somewhat relieves the tedium of the sittings by insulting the plenipotentiaries all around. They, neither of them, however, show the slightest inclination to consent to any reforms, however moderate. The seance lasted four hours, and at the end of it nothing, except the prolongation of the Armistice, had been effected.

The first sitting was something of a formality but the Turkish delegates were given a copy of the project of the preliminary conference which they already had been given informally.[42]

The reaction to the Turkish constitution varied greatly. Considerable enthusiasm within Constantinople was matched by utter indifference in outlying Ottoman provinces.[43] On the European Continent and to some extent in Britain the reaction was hostile owing to blind prejudice, unfulfilled Turkish reform promises in the past, and the timing of the promulgation, which was interpreted by many as an insult and a defiance. In the meantime the Turks, according to Salisbury, delayed the next meeting of the conference while they considered the proposals of the European Powers.

Salisbury was prepared to inconvenience himself a good deal in order to win a favourable response from the Porte. As the probability of a refusal increased, particularly after the promulgation of the constitution, Salisbury began searching for something which would underline British earnestness. He considered a cancellation of the Treaty of Paris by the six Powers and complained to Elliot that British dragomans and embassy personnel were encouraging the Porte to resist by promises of eventual British support. 'I [Elliot] will take care that all the members of the embassy shall be warned that, if spoken to on the subject, they must declare that the Porte has no assistance to expect from us. Mr. Sandison [British dragoman] has several times been instructed to convey this distinctly to the Porte . . .'[44] When informed by the British admiral that the Mediterranean fleet was preparing to leave Besika Bay for Salonica, Salisbury ordered it instead to Athens and the Piraeus so that it might not encourage the Turks by the close presence of potential British protection. On 26 December Salisbury saw the Sultan for an hour, and considered him to be entirely in the hands of Midhat Pasha. 'He [the Sultan] was very plaintive, talked of his life being threatened, said that his subjects would not allow him to make concessions, but refused to enter into argument. He is a poor weak creature and counts for nothing in solution of the problem.'[45]

The Turks made little effort to mask their disappointment and anger at what they considered British abandonment.[46] This encouraged Salisbury, whom Onou described as a good Christian and a sincere believer in God and his Church. Chaudordy thought that the special ambassador was neither a statesman, nor a negotiator, nor an ambassador, but an 'apostle of early Christianity'.[47]

On 28 December, at the second sitting of the full conference, at which the proposals of the six Powers were discussed for four hours, the Turkish delegates expressed their objections to the individual points of the organization of Bulgaria and resisted any European supervision. They did suggest an armistice of two months, which Salisbury thought meant war, but as Ignatiev accepted it, he felt he could not object.[48]

Salisbury, fearing a breakdown of the conference through Turkish obstinacy, was both dispirited and disgusted, and allowed his anger to expend itself on the person of Henry Elliot.

Chaudordy, Werther, Corti, and Zichy, have all separately urged me most earnestly to procure Sir Henry's absence, as a most important addition to our chances of peace. I am of their opinion. I do not for a moment suggest any doubt of Sir Henry's loyalty. . . . But he is weak . . . and he allows it to be seen that his sympathies are with the Turks, and against the proposals of the Powers.

I wish you would let the Cabinet see this. . . . All that I can do is undone [by Elliot]. . . . I feel . . . I am bound to recommend the Cabinet on some pretext or other to get him away.

The ambassador, who had been urging Derby to permit him to leave, now seemed to want to remain to the end of the conference. He wrote to Tenterden that, in lieu of peace, the next best thing would be to make Russia appear to be in the wrong if she declared war on Turkey.[49] Salisbury appealed also to the Prime Minister to remove Elliot. Ironically, Disraeli, who was no supporter of the ambassador, was now much more annoyed by Salisbury, who seemed to him to be unaware of the necessity of keeping Russia out of the Ottoman Empire and only concerned with creating nirvana for Turkish Christians. The Premier suggested to Derby that the special ambassador needed to be advised that both Turkey and Russia were willing to compromise. In this he was influenced by a report from Elliot saying Midhat was willing to be reasonable. He also submitted a warning to the Foreign Secretary.

If Elliot is recalled, or even returns, and it gets about . . . that he has been returned or recalled thro Ignatieff, the ministry will be turned out, the first night of the session, by their own men.

Have, care! We are treading on very dangerous ground.[50]

At the third sitting of the conference, held on 30 December, the Turks announced their own counter-proposals which were being made ready for presentation. To the urging of Chaudordy, Ignatiev, and Salisbury, that the Porte accept the proposals already produced, the Turkish delegates made no reply. The Ottoman counter-proposals ignored or refused most of the original proposals of the Great Powers and Salisbury would not accept this as proof of a Turkish desire for compromise.[51] It is not clear whether Elliot informed the special ambassador of a conversation he had with Midhat on 27 December, but as Salisbury hated Midhat and was not on easy speaking terms with Elliot, the communication might not have been made. Midhat objected especially to the guarantees demanded of the Turks by the Powers.

To a Commission of Control, such as proposed, he would never consent, but he was ready to give another effectual guarantee for the execution of the reforms.

Let a year be granted in order that they may be put into operation, and at the end of that time let the Ambassadors report whether they had been fairly carried out or not.

If they report in the negative he will submit to the appointment of an International Commission, or such other control as is thought desirable.[52]

On 31 December the delegates of the Powers met to consider the Turkish counter-project. The Austrian, French, German, and Russian ambassadors were reported by Salisbury as exceedingly angry with the Porte's behaviour. 'On my proposition, it was ultimately resolved formally to 'constater' at the conference tomorrow the list of our propositions which were rejected by the counter-project, and to express an earnest hope that a more satisfactory reply might be produced without delay.'[53] At the conference on 1 January Salisbury urged the Turkish representatives, with the support of the other foreign plenipotentiaries, to reflect on the peril of their situation. Afterwards Salisbury, who believed the crisis point had come, and that all depended on scaring Turkey within the next few days, saw Midhat, who said that the Turks were unprepared to yield on most of the foreign demands.[54] At the sitting of 4 January the Turkish delegates, who had refused to indicate the reasons behind their objections to the proposals by the Great Powers three days earlier, did so in a statement which was read to the plenipotentiaries. When the meeting was adjourned the foreign representatives arranged to prepare a reply to the Ottoman reasons for the next sitting.

On 5 January the delegates met at the Russian Embassy to consider their response.[55] Salisbury had already indicated to

Derby that Turkish obstinacy had caused Ignatiev to reduce his terms in the expectation of a Turkish refusal.[56] Salisbury had decided that nothing could be obtained in dealing with the Sultan or the Ottoman plenipotentiaries, and that the only hope, and that a very small one, lay in dealing with Midhat, whom he saw for an hour and a half on the seventh.

He [the Ottoman Turk] refuses everything of importance, especially everything which diminishes the arbitrary power of the Central government, which is precisely what we wish to do . . .

I am very sorry you [Derby] have not seen your way to relieving me of Elliot . . .

. . .

Convincing the Turk is as easy as making a donkey canter.[57]

An Italian-Russian suggestion to move the conference out of Ottoman territory was opposed by both Disraeli and Derby and the German Government.

The news that the Powers were preparing concessions or reduced terms became public before they could be presented to the Turks at the conference. Germany appeared unwilling to accept the modified proposals but Derby, who like Salisbury thought that Bismarck desired a Russo-Turkish war, was pleased with them.

The Belgian *gendarmerie* scheme will disappear: and the intended commission of supervision will be cut down so as to be little more than a slight extension of the actual powers of the consuls. These are the main points.

I entirely approve these changes which seem to me to be in the right direction: but I doubt the Porte accepting them any more than it would the original scheme.[58]

Tenterden, who prepared a long memorandum on the conference, thought that the reduction of the proposals was a mistake and advanced cogent reasons for so thinking.

The fact that, directly after submitting them [the original proposals] to the Porte as an irreducible minimum, they have abandoned or watered them down to next to nothing, is a confession that the points had not been duly discussed, considered and decided upon, and, after such a confession, it will not be surprising if the Porte were to urge that the new points were open to amendment as the old ones.

In such matters regard must be had to expediency but it is quite a new thing for England to be bargaining in this way. The strength of English policy has always been that what an Englishman says, he means, and what he means he insists upon.

. . .

I do not myself see that the cabinet is in a position to come to any useful decision at present. The great thing to be avoided at Constantinople is impatience.[59]

The conference session on 8 January was not satisfactory. The Italian representative read a reply to the Turkish arguments which was followed by an excited discussion on the geographical limits of Bulgaria. The Turks maintained that it was the district north of the Balkan mountains, and upon being told that the atrocities had occurred south of that mountain range, they referred to the massacre of St. Bartholomew which until then had been absent from the discussion. When guarantees were pressed on them, it being pointed out that the Andrássy note contained a commission, the Turkish plenipotentiaries replied that they had never read the note.[60]

Midhat, with few good cards, was playing them rather well. Desiring to maintain Ottoman sovereignty and integrity, which the proposals of the Powers could only weaken or destroy, and at the same time hoping to separate France and Britain from Russia by giving proof of Turkish reasonableness, he secretly dispatched Odian Effendi, the Under-Secretary of Public Works and a trusted friend, to Paris and London. Derby informed Salisbury of the Turkish proposal presented by Midhat's emissary.

The Constitution recently decreed by the Sultan should be brought to the cognizance of the Powers in a form which should make its execution a matter of international obligation between the Porte and them, and that the organization of the provincial administration to be drawn up by the Turkish ministers should, after receiving the approval of the Powers, be made a portion of the general plan, and embodied in the same agreement.

The whole system of reforms granted by the Sultan to his subjects would thus be placed under the guarantee of the Powers, who would have a right to watch over the manner in which it was carried out.

Derby refused to discuss the suggestion and indicated that if it were to be proposed by the Turkish Government, it must be done by them on their own responsibility at Constantinople.

He pressed Odian Effendi, as he had done previously with Musurus Pasha, the Ottoman ambassador, to accept painful conditions rather than risk a war with Russia. When Odian and Musurus approached Disraeli, two days before seeing Derby, with the same suggestion, they received a similar reply. 'I [Disraeli] earnestly recommended to him [Odian] to accept the modified programme [of the Powers] as the only means of saving his country. This I put in every form and as strongly as possible, and he said he shd tel. to Midhat.'[61]

Gladstone suspected that Disraeli was working against Salisbury's efforts at Constantinople. This does not seem to have been the case. Disraeli had chosen Salisbury for the mission initially, and though the latter was more pro-Russian than Disraeli would have liked, the Prime Minister did not desire a Russo-Turkish war, which he thought would occur if the Porte did not accept Europe's terms. Disraeli made no secret of his willingness to defend Constantinople, and this and the British engineers in that city may have encouraged Turkish resistance, though it was intimated to the Porte that a British defence of Constantinople would not necessarily be in the interests of Turkey.[62] Rather it was Salisbury who was less than straightforward with Derby and Disraeli, using Carnarvon as a spy in the Cabinet. As the Powers were preparing to offer the Porte reduced terms,[63] the special ambassador feared that Derby, who approved the reduced terms, and other Cabinet ministers would demand adherence to the original propositions.[64] Seeing it as a last chance to win Turkish acceptance, Salisbury telegraphed to Carnarvon that Derby would retreat, and that the former would need to control the Foreign Secretary for there to be any hope of a Turkish acceptance.[65]

On 11 January the conference again met and listened to an apparent attempt by Midhat to detach Austria from Russia.

Ottoman Plenipotentiaries read a paper with reference to Andrassy note, and offered to put it into execution; but they continued to refuse to assent to any of our propositions; thereupon we adjourned till Monday [15 January], telling them that we should then address to them a last appeal—an intimation which discomposed them seriously. From various sources I [Salisbury] hear Midhat is now disposed to treat, I am to see him tomorrow.[66]

Salisbury's meeting with Midhat was scarcely productive.

The latter refused a commission which contained foreigners, the Powers' right to nominate governors, and a mixed Christian–Muslim militia.

He [Midhat] offered to extend Andrassy Note to Bulgaria, to forbid the carrying of arms, and the colonization of Circassians *en masse* . . . [and] to communicate Constitution to Conference . . .

I stated to Grand Vizier . . . that the nature of his present communication left me very little hope of success.[67]

Two days later Salisbury spent an hour and a half with the Sultan, who argued that the constitution made other measures unnecessary. 'He [Sultan] chiefly objected to guarantees saying that his people thought them dishonourable and would not have them. I [Salisbury] urged that they were temporary and necessary to enable him to surmount present crisis. He reserved final answer till he had consulted his Ministers. I urged him to take the authority into his own hands.'[68] The following morning, Monday, 15 January, the Sultan sent Hobart Pasha[69] with a message to Salisbury. He explained that he saw no insuperable objection to the terms of the Great Powers, but that he could not control his ministers. He begged the special ambassador to modify the two guarantees— the provincial governors and the international commission. Salisbury sent Hobart back with a written answer that he could not further reduce demands which were already greatly diminished. 'I [Salisbury] suggested, however, a formal Protocol disclaiming any interference with the sultan's dignity or authority, and stating on his part that in accepting the assistance of his allies to introduce reforms, he guarded himself from admitting any encroachment on his rights. . . . Grand Vizier is as stiff as ever.'[70]

On 15 January the conference met and the reduced terms were read to the Ottoman plenipotentiaries, who were informed that if they were not accepted at the sitting on the eighteenth, the conference would end and the representatives would return home. The Turkish delegates then requested to have until the twentieth to consider the terms, and this was agreed to.[71]

On 18 January a Turkish grand council, consisting of 237 dignitaries presided over by Midhat, met and refused both the international commission and provincial governors named with the consent of the Powers. When the conference met on 20 January, the Ottoman plenipotentiaries indicated the rejection of these two proposals as well as others. The foreign representatives then agreed that the conference was over. When Musurus communicated to Derby the Ottoman refusal, the latter advised the Turkish ambassador that the Porte should at once make an arrangement with Serbia and Montenegro[72] At this conference session Ignatiev also warned the Turks against a war on Serbia and Montenegro before the armistice expired, adding that if a single Christian were molested the vengeance of Europe would be terrible.[73]

It was perhaps somewhat naïve for the European Powers to have expected Turkish acquiescense to the terms presented them. Some Europeans, of course, did not have these expectations, but many did, and large numbers of both categories would have been willing to use military force to smash the Porte into acceptance. With Romania, Serbia, and Montenegro almost entirely independent, the arrangements proposed for Bulgaria and Bosnia seemed calculated to restrict European Turkey to the environs of Constantinople. A commission of control and governors for the above two provinces appointed by or with the consent of the European Powers, and the restriction of Ottoman troops to certain specified centres, as once had been the scheme for Serbia, would have amounted to a kind of European trusteeship for Bulgaria and Bosnia and might have caused the same kind of European rivalry as that elicited by the Polish monarchy in the eighteenth century. The Duke of Argyll, who sympathized deeply and strongly with the Slavic Christians, has accurately described the situation.

It is only fair towards Turkey to admit that the proposals of the Powers . . . were such as no Government could admit, if it pretended to real and substantial independence, and if any choice were left to it in the matter. These proposals were incompatible with the claim of independence. They invoked foreign supervision. It was, therefore, in the highest degree futile to suppose that they could be submitted to except under compulsion . . .[74]

Butler-Johnstone's[75] presence in Constantinople along with some British engineers, any Turkish sympathy exhibited by Elliot or the embassy staff, and Disraeli's supposed secret

policy are all beside the point. It is not common for governments voluntarily to commit political suicide.

It is true that Salisbury, who believed that European Turkey
was on its last legs, was denied the use of force by his own
government, and had to be content with threatening the Porte
with the bogeyman of a Russian military attack. It appears that
at least on the point of Russian readiness to go to war he was
duped by Ignatiev. The behaviour of Lady Salisbury was silly
when it was not rude,[76] and Salisbury's own treatment of Elliot
was contemptuous and counter-productive.

Had Lord Salisbury spoken at all to me [Elliot] about them [the
proposals to be offered the Porte] before arranging them with
General Ignatiev I am certain that I could easily have convinced him
that there were many parts objectionable in themselves, and others
which would never be accepted. ... When I found myself neither
consulted nor trusted, having to learn what was doing from some of
my other [foreign] colleagues, I should not have consented to remain
here a day, if I had not felt that leaving would be taken as a
manifestation which would encourage the Turks to resist what Ld
Salisbury was supporting. ... When Lord Salisbury shewed such a
marked determination to set me aside and to refuse me his confidence I had to choose between consenting to remain inactive [which
is what he did] or, by insisting on being consulted, to run the risk of a
misunderstanding which it was essential to avoid ...[77]

Salisbury differed from Disraeli to the extent that he was
willing to go in order to protect and secure the Christians in
the Balkans. He wished Britain to be prepared to take her share
of any partition of the Ottoman Empire by the European
Powers, and was much less concerned, partly as a result of
seeing no present danger, with protecting Constantinople and
the Straits from Russian attack or occupation. As Werther,
the German ambassador, informed his Government, Salisbury
did not believe that Constantinople was the gateway to India,[78]
though he certainly desired the city in Ottoman rather than
Russian or even Slavic hands. Not sharing the common British
fear of Russia, he had nothing but utter contempt for the Turks
whom he felt unfit to govern Christian civilization in the
Balkans except at Constantinople and the Straits where unfortunately it seemed politically necessary.

Disraeli was disappointed with the failure of the conference to obtain a temporary settlement of the Eastern Question. The Foreign Secretary's twin fears neutralized one another; the avoidance of coercive occupation as a Russian trap was felt sufficiently so that he was not willing to force the Porte to accept the reform proposals of the conference though he believed that Russia would go to war if the conference failed. Derby's support of the Prime Minister's refusal to coerce the Ottomans was sufficient, however, to enable both to overcome the initial willingness of Cairns, Carnarvon, Northcote, and Richmond, along with Salisbury, to do so. Derby, unlike Beaconsfield, was not unhappy at the responsibility which Europe and Britain escaped as a result of Turkish stubbornness. His feelings were reflected in a letter which Northcote sent to Salisbury.

I cannot look upon it [the conference] as an entire failure . . .

Meantime Europe is relieved of a responsibility which might well have proved an awkward one. . . . I think the tone of society here is one of moderate satisfaction at the whole affair. . . . On the other hand I think there is a good deal of sympathy with the pluck of the Turks, and a certain amount of satisfaction at our escaping the responsibility which would have attached to us if our terms had been accepted.[79]

While Europe was failing to obtain Ottoman acceptance of its programme, Russia was succeeding, secretly, in reaching agreement with Andrássy that would enable her to make war on Turkey without fear of Austrian opposition.

# 14 TWO CONFERENCES IN LONDON

SOME STUDENTS of Austro-Russian relations—Rupp and Langer, for example—feel that the Austro-Russian military convention signed on 15 January and the political convention signed on 18 March,[1] both after much wrangling and protracted negotiation, were a political *coup* for Andrássy as they permitted a Russian war on Turkey for the territorial and political benefit of Austria in the Balkans. Andrássy would not have so considered it, for he desired neither a Russian war on the Ottoman Empire nor any major change in the Balkan territorial *status quo*. From the beginning of the crisis in 1875 he had not wavered in his support of Ottoman territorial integrity. But he was not willing to fight Russia to preserve it, and if its destruction appeared imminent, he was then prepared to secure Vienna's interests in the Balkans by occupying Bosnia and Hercegovina.

Gorchakov and Alexander II hoped to use the threat of Russian military force in order to loosen the Porte's control over its Slavic Christians. War against Turkey was always a possible alternative for Russia, but was militarily dangerous unless her right, or Austrian, flank was protected by an agreement with Vienna.

Negotiations which resulted in the military convention were begun in great secrecy at the beginning of November, and thus transpired during the course of the Constantinople Conference. Austria was given the right to annex both Bosnia and Hercegovina when she so chose after war had begun. Russian troops were prohibited from entering Serbia and Montenegro and Austrian forces from Romania. Austria promised to be neutral and to give her diplomatic support to Russia. The political agreement reached in March, which rendered the above military stipulations binding, arranged for the post-war territorial settlement. By it, Andrássy excluded the creation of a large Slavic state and Russia was to gain that part of Bessarabia which was lost in 1856. Both the stiff terms required by Andrássy and the winter weather resulted in several months of futile diplomacy before St. Petersburg declared war in April.[2]

One factor which had some weight on the decision of the Russian Government to consider war was the recognized unwillingness of the British Government to fight for Turkey as a result of the anti-Turkish explosion of opinion throughout the country. The agitation had subsided to a certain extent in November and December but it did not die. At the beginning of November Mundella and his agitation friends in Parliament[3] decided to begin the process of calling together a national conference. On 6 November a circular appeared announcing a proposed meeting on the Eastern Question at an early but unspecified date, and in *The Times* and *Daily News* of 18 November a general London meeting was advertised '[to promote] the concert of the Powers ... obtaining for ... Bosnia, Herzegovina, and Bulgaria ... release from the direct rule of the Porte, with due guarantees for the equal rights of the non-Christian population ... and also of diffusing through the country [Britain] sound information on the various branches of the question.'[4]

The selection of Salisbury as a special representative and the calling of the Constantinople Conference itself were considered good signs by the agitators, but there was a feeling as well that unless sufficient pressure and vigilance were maintained the Government would slip back into a pro-Turkish position. This feeling was expressed in a letter Shaftesbury sent Gladstone.

The general sentiment, in so far as I can gather it, is that for the present, the government should be watched, jealously watched, but left alone.

Should they do well, endorse them—Should they fall short of what we have a right to expect, revive the sympathies of the people, which will, then, be found to be only dormant, but not extinct.[5]

Russophobe opinion in Britain, which was never completely silent, was growing more vocal especially as the possibility of a Russian war on Turkey increased. Lytton extolled the Asiatic brand of Russophobia, characterized as a threat to India, while others exhibited it as a Russian threat to Constantinople and a general danger to liberty and freedom. In the first week of

November a lively controversy ensued between Gladstone and the *Pall Mall Gazette*, when the latter cited examples of Russian barbarity from a recently published work on Russian Turkistan by Schuyler. Using the November issue of the *Contemporary Review*, Gladstone attacked the London newspaper, accusing it of misquoting Schuyler for the purpose of extenuating Turkish misdeeds. The *Pall Mall*, of course, replied in kind with other journals also joining in the argument.[6] Some, like Hammond, believed Gladstone to be too Russian. 'Gladstone seems resolved still to find the Russians immaculate, and he has now undertaken to white-wash them against the dirt thrown upon them by Schuyler in the part of his late book, where he reveals the orders of Kaufmann to massacre all sexes and ages, and ravage all districts in certain parts of Central Asia.'[7] Ponsonby, a warm sympathizer with Gladstone and his work, thought he was going too far in the direction of becoming Russia's champion.[8]

But Gladstone was not inclined to retreat when he felt he could not trust Disraeli and the Government.

I [Gladstone] am certain there is much ground for continued vigilance on the part of all those who are interested in the question.

Especially, I repeat, that if Russia has selfish designs in the East, no policy can so effectually promote these designs as a policy of coldness and indifference on our part toward the Christian populations, which can have no other effect than that of throwing them into her arms.[9]

Mundella asked the ex-Premier's assistance in order to attract others to the conference.

I believe that we shall have such a demonstration as England has not seen since the anticorn law days.

. . .

We intend that our conference shall only be the preliminary to our present work. Our second object 'diffusing sound information' together with providing speeches for meetings will be our chief work. But the conference and meeting will give the whole such an impetus

. . .

Carlyle's letter will be the first blow. Our demonstration of names the second, then the conference and meeting to be followed up by literature, lectures and public meetings throughout the country.[10]

He went out of his way to keep Gladstone informed of the

course of events, and indicated that his purpose was to have an Eastern Question Committee in every borough. And then on 2 December, after a recital of fifty or sixty very prominent names who had indicated adhesion to the conference, Mundella, acting as spokesman for the conference committee, asked Gladstone to take part personally in the meeting.[11]

Gladstone did not reply at once, realizing that the official leadership of the party did not favour the meeting. Hartington opposed the conference since it would be dominated by men of extreme views, speaking irresponsibly.

I feel tolerably sure that it will be a failure. . . . I object to the terms of the circular. The provinces of Bosnia, Herzegovina, and Bulgaria are not Christian. None of them are more than partially. . . . I am afraid that the tendency of anything of this kind is to drive our best men, or at all events the Whigs, to the side of the Government . . .

I am in daily dread of seeing his [Gladstone's] name in the Conference list.[12]

While making up his mind, Gladstone encouraged Mundella to set up publishing and lecturing apparatus, and sent him a list of subjects on which the country needed to be educated. He also wrote to the Prime Minister. 'All with whom I come in contact deprecate and denounce in the strongest manner the possibility of this country being drawn into war on behalf of Turkey. . . . I believe this feeling to be general with those who repudiated and condemned the "atrocities" [and] . . . based on the plain ground of British interest.'[13] By 6 December he had made up his mind to speak at the conference, and the sense of excitement he felt may be seen in a letter to his wife. 'There is a great pressure for tickets and the conference people are in high spirits . . . and I assure you that for fear of doing harm I look to the speech with fear and trembling.' Bright thought that the effect of the conference would depend on Gladstone,[14] but he was only partially correct.

The list of the conveners of the conference contained many names both well known to contemporaries and to later generations: Lord Acton, the Marquis of Bath, the Reverends M. MacColl and J. Parker, Robert Browning, Charles Darwin, J. A. Froude, J. R. Green, William Lecky, C. E. Maurice, Justin McCarthy, Thorold Rogers, Goldwin Smith, G. O. Trevelyan, Anthony Trollope, John Ruskin, William Morris, W. T. Stead,

Henry Broadhurst, Auberon Herbert, and many others. The large number of anticipated speakers at the conference held in St. James's Hall on Friday, 8 December probably dictated the decision to have two conferences, really two sittings, with an intermission in the middle. Admission to the conference was by ticket only, and of the 89 M.P.s who attended, 88 were Liberals; of the 23 peers only Shaftesbury, Bath, and Seaton were Conservatives. In one sense, however, it was not a Liberal party meeting since the leadership and many Whigs were absent, and there were present in the 700 odd gathering many who did not normally take part in political activity.[15]

The first sitting, chaired by the Duke of Westminster,[16] was held from noon to 3 p.m., followed by an intermission of one hour. The second conference or sitting, presided over by the Earl of Shaftesbury, lasted from 4 to 8 p.m., and listened to the blarings of E. A. Freeman and Canon Liddon as well as the major address of both meetings by Gladstone. Upon finishing to an out-pouring of cheers, the ex-Premier offered his arm to Madame Novikov, the Pan-Slav propagandist in England.[17]

Although the speakers varied greatly in their opinions and expressions, there were two general positions taken by most of those who spoke. Firstly, that under no condition should Britain fight for the Turks against Russia, and secondly, that the Government should co-operate with Russia to force the Porte to reform by establishing explicit guarantees.[18] Before disbanding, the conference, on a resolution by Fawcett, formed the Eastern Question Association which was a continuation in a sense of the Parliamentary and conference committees which preceded it. Its purpose and function were to watch events, spread correct information, and give further expression to public opinion. People were invited to join the association and to send contributions to its treasurer, William Morris.[19] Many pamphlets on all aspects of the Eastern Question were published by the association.

The reaction to the St. Jame's Hall conference was almost as disparate as the journals and individuals who expressed it. The Queen was both angry and upset, and asked Ponsonby to see Lord Halifax, or someone equally responsible to ascertain if they might be able to prevent further agitation. Ponsonby attempted to soothe the Queen by a sympathetic letter in which he indicated that the effect of the conference in Britain would be minimal.

The utterances of Canon Liddon and MacColl cannot be thought valuable after their extraordinary misstatements about impalement—when they were so palpably hoaxed on the Danube steamer . . .[20]

It would therefore be dangerous to say anything that might be misconstrued into the remotest hint that the expression of opinion was displeasing to Your Majesty. But in talking to Lord Halifax as a relation or some others, very confidently, General Ponsonby might hear what they think.[21]

Hammond thought the conference manifested some differences within the ranks of the agitators, but Granville felt it was a signal success and congratulated Gladstone on his speech. Hartington's impression was otherwise.

Nothing was said, even by Gladstone, to repudiate the extravagances of Freeman and one or two others, and the whole thing seems to me to be more or less discredited by them. . . . If it was intended as a demonstration that the country would not stand Ld. Beaconsfield's pro-Turkish speeches and policy, I think that it has been a failure. . . . I feel certain that the Whigs and moderate Liberals in the Houses are a good deal disgusted, and I am much afraid, that if he [Gladstone] goes on much farther, nothing can prevent a break up of the party . . .

I don't feel the slightest confidence in Russia. . . . If Russia should occupy the provinces, I doubt whether . . . the Government would be wrong in taking some steps for the protection of Constantinople and the Bosphorus . . .[22]

Gladstone, according to Hartington's brother, who was a close personal friend, considered the St. James's meeting a success. 'He [Gladstone] is very clear in his own mind that Canning's policy [acting with Russia in order to control her] which he has described . . . as the right one for us to follow, and that by it we should checkmate the designs of men like Ignatieff and secure peace and a real improvement in the condition of the inhabitants of Turkey.'[23] At the very moment when he was advocating co-operation with Russia in the matter of Christian freedom and security, the previous behaviour of Russia in Poland and elsewhere was accusingly pointed out as reason to oppose any such co-operation. Lady Georgianne Fullerton, a Catholic convert and Granville's sister, was one who did so.

You [Gladstone] have praised Russia for her humane sympathy with the victims of the Turks in a most earnest and emphatic manner; you could hardly have done so without some qualification had you believed that she was cruelly persecuting a large number of her own subjects—Thus your praise unmixed with any reference to her inconsistency seemed like a sort of acquittal on your part in the face of Europe—The ill treatment of Poland has been so notorious that it drew some years ago strong remonstrances from the English Govt. which read very much like those now addressed to Turkey.[24]

Gladstone was, however, prepared to act on his opinion. On the first day of the new year he was sent a letter by Madame Novikov which contained a request.

Could you not write me a letter in wh. you would say, that Russia *cannot, must* not give up the idea of the real guarantees in favour of the Slavs, that a serious occupation of Bulgaria wd. be useful, etc. etc.

I should *send your letter* to the *Winter Palace*: You are so trusted by our Emperor that yr. opinion might be *most* useful.

A second letter followed the next day. '*If I were allowed by you to show some remarks of yours,* your name might do what is beyond *our power.* . . . A letter, though simply written to me (*but* with *your consent* to its being shown) is absolutely necessary. Oh, let me have it . . .'[25] Gladstone was as ready to prevent the Russian Government from failing in its Christian duty as he was his own. Fearing to excite the public mind by writing to Olga too often, he entrusted some letters to his wife to be handed to her directly. 'I think your seeing Madame Novikoff will be useful. She writes to me a great deal, and I do not want to write too often to her. She seems to have had a scruple about using my letters. But she is perfectly entitled to make a discreet and guarded use of them.'[26] Mrs. Gladstone fulfilled her mission as may be seen from the following note. 'I [Olga Novikov] saw Mrs. G. this m. ing, and I received yr. most important and welcome letters. I sent at once one of them, and there may be no doubt as to its usefulness.'[27] One of the letters Gladstone sent to the Pan-Slav temptress read as follows:

Any plan that retains Turkish authority, within the geographical limits to be affected, as the source or sanction of administration, is in my view worthless.

. . .

A guarantee dependent on the Turk for its execution therein, becomes no guarantee at all. Whether the Porte should have any and what voice, or veto in regard to the composition of the new authority . . . is another question; but of course it could not be the ruling voice. . . . Anything that leaves performance either as to civil acts or as to the force behind them, in his [Turks] hands, is in my view a sheer mockery.[28]

Gladstone, who felt Disraeli was against Salisbury's efforts at the Constantinople Conference as a result of his Jewish sentiment,[29] was prepared as a result of his own Christian sentiment to encourage the Tsar, who apparently feared to tread a path where there was room for both Ignatiev and Gladstone. It is not unlikely that Lady Derby's information of her husband and the Cabinet, which reached St. Petersburg via Shuvalov, mitigated in part the effect of Gladstone's letters to Madame Novikov. And almost at this very moment, Salisbury's attempt to co-operate with Ignatiev at Constantinople was much criticized by the British Press.

Shannon, a recent student of the Bulgarian agitation movement, allows his sympathy for Nonconformity and High-Church Anglicanism (Anglo-Catholicism), which was largely responsible for the agitation, to permit less than fairness to Turkey or to those who opposed the agitation. Harris, in an earlier study of the same movement, also shares this partial view. It is well to remember that many, if not most, in Britain who did not take part in the agitation, or those who opposed it, were as appalled and sickened by the Bulgarian tragedy as the agitators. The Queen was a good example. Further, the non-agitators were as much victims of the conditioning of Western Christianity as the agitators. Thompson, who wrote almost as a contemporary, recognized this nearly from the beginning.

The conception of the Turks as different in religion, and of the Turks as alien in civilisation from the Europe to which the men of the subject provinces belonged, practically always went hand in hand to reinforce one another.

Sometimes the phrase 'the Turk cannot reform' [meant that the Turk was non-European]. The meaning was that the root of the evil

was not so much Turkish misgovernment as Turkish government
over a people of European stock and religion.

Reform in this sense was equivalent to becoming European by
adoption.[30]

The most extreme members of the agitation, and many from
both political parties, Gladstone, Carnarvon, Cairns, Salisbury—in other words, almost the whole range of British
Christianity—could not imagine meaningful Turkish reform
which did not give autonomy or independence to Turkey's
European Christians. Christianity was equated with progress,
whereas Muhammadanism meant stagnation and perversity.
Only a few, Derby and Hartington among them, considered
the question of the appropriateness of intervening into the internal affairs of a sovereign state. Gladstone, Salisbury, and
many others considered such intervention justified by the fact
that the Porte had reneged on its promise to reform which it
had given to Europe in 1856. But evil does not reform, it only
attracts condemnation. At the height of the agitation, near the
end of the third week of September, the Duke of Argyll spoke
at an atrocity meeting in Glasgow. 'I begin with this proposition, that the Turkish Government is bad, so execrably bad,
that any and every rebellion against it on the part of its Christian subjects is presumably just and righteous . . .'[31] Even so-
called pro-Turks, Palmerston, Disraeli, and Layard, would
only admit that Ottoman existence in Europe was a temporary
expedient until the Christians could be educated towards
self-government. Hardly anyone in Britain really liked the
Turks, and Ponsonby succinctly summed up the reasons for
supporting a necessary excrescence.

I doubt if any real feeling of friendship ever existed in this country
for Turkey. Some persons supported what they believed to be an oppressed nationality—some had material interest . . . some believed
that the friendship of the Sultan, the Caliph of the faithful all over the
world strengthened our position in India and some were moved by
the attitude of rivalry between ourselves and Russia—the object of
wh. is believed to be the possession of Const ple.

Besides wh. statesmen recoiled from encountering the inevitable
difficulties which must arise on the dissolution of the Turkish Empire
in Europe . . .[32]

Shannon is impressed with the moral seriousness and

greatness of spirit of the agitation, and refers to it as a manifestation 'of the highest refinement of Victorian moral sensibility'. Part of the agitation undoubtedly was. Those aspects of it which reflect on or diminish this moral sensibility—religious bigotry, prurience, morbidity, anti-Semitism, and uncontrolled emotionalism—are given no significant role in a wave of dissent against the Government's foreign policy in the East. Even the political aspects of the agitation are somewhat minimized when compared with an overwhelming expression 'of an intense moral sensibility in public life'.

In a six-week period spanning the month of September there were, according to Shannon's count, nearly 500 meetings of public protest against the Bulgarian horrors. Those most active in this outburst were High-Church and Nonconformist ecclesiastics. The petitions which were addressed to the Government—Shannon tells us of 455 from identifiable sources—show the major contribution of Nonconformity and High-Church Anglicanism. Many of the leaders of the agitation demonstrate this as well. Stead, Samuel Morley, who controlled the *Daily News*, P. W. Clayden, and Joseph Chamberlain were all either Congregationalists or Unitarians. Gladstone, Freeman, Liddon, MacColl, Pusey, and R. W. Church were Anglo-Catholic Anglicans, as well as the Marquis of Bath, who was a political Conservative. Shannon allows a lesser part in the atrocities movement for Radicalism as some Radicals—Dilke and Cowen were the most prominent—opposed the agitation. He explains the close relationship of Nonconformity to the agitation in this way:

Nonconformists could more easily (even eagerly) identify themselves with a form of religion legally discriminated against by the state . . .
. . .
   The Bulgarian affair evoked a profound and distinctive response from Nonconformists as matters related integrally to their moral system and their political traditions.[33]

Even those who had not been subjected to discrimination and prejudice could feel horror and revulsion at barbarism and inhumanity, but those who had been so subjected were sometimes prepared to respond more deeply and without qualification.

Thompson, who was less concerned with, and perhaps also less aware of, the prominence of Nonconformity, describes the agitation more as an outpouring of energy than an expression of conscience or moral sensitivity. 'It is this great outburst of energy, primarily with a definite political object but also secondarily benevolent and to some extent perhaps merely emotional, which constitutes the most striking phenomenon of the whole epoch.' The political object according to Thompson was to help or to force the Government to change its Eastern policy without the intervention of Parliament or a change of ministry.[34] The most satisfying description, because it allows for all the evidence, is the one given by Dorothy Anderson.

It [the agitation] could never be described simply as a political gesture, an outcry in public (because Parliament was in recess), against the government's policy; it was much more an emotional reaction. People were concerned sincerely for the sufferings of the Bulgarians, were distressed, if titillated, by the descriptions of the barbarities inflicted ... and were indignant that the British government should continue to support a regime that permitted such outrages to take place.[35]

It seemed that more of the moral indignation expressed was done so on behalf of tortured, raped, and murdered female Bulgarians than on their male counterparts. W. T. Stead, one of the leaders of the agitation, as well as Gladstone, were especially sensitive to outrages on female honour and recognized this feeling in others as a spur to generous action.[36] Shannon will allow for no more than an 'underlying current of ... sensuality'.

Fitzjames Stephen ... accused the agitation of appealing to prurience as well as bigotry. The atrocities certainly tapped an underlying current of rather morbid sensitivity, perhaps even sensuality. ... Freeman and Sandwith ... exploited in a crude though minor way the Turkish reputation for pederasty. ... But essentially the shock to Victorian sexual sensitivity was quite contrary to any tendencies to prurience. It was the pudic reaction of an outraged puritanism overlaid with perhaps excessive sentimentality on the honour of women ...[37]

There were attempts to keep up the public excitement by making the barbarities committed in Bulgaria graphically real.

F. Villiers, the Balkan sketch artist for the weekly *Graphic*, gives the following account.

I immediately jumped up and hurried outside, where I discovered several old ladies gathered together in front of the hospital [at Batak], holding out their capricious aprons, each containing two or three heads. At first I was much shocked—even horrified—at the grimness of this wholesale fulfillment of my request. But I reflected that business was business, so I commenced negotiating with these ancient female ghouls by picking and choosing. At last I decided on three fine specimens.
. . .

The heads were packed and sent on their way to London via Constantinople addressed to my surgeon friend at King's College Hospital, labelled 'Bulgarian atrocities.'

They safely arrived in England and, for all that I know, may have figured on many a platform at those indignation meetings which at the time set the whole civilized world agog.[38]

During August and the first part of September the rash of public meetings owed little if anything to the national party chiefs, but rather, as Thompson and Shannon agree, to local leaders—magistrates, newspaper editors, ecclesiastics, M.P.s, and mayors. 'It is clear that the impulse of this great movement originated in the ardent desire now felt by vast numbers of people ... and that it was not communicated from any authoritative quarter. ... The impulse came from below, not from above.' Then, about the middle of September, a change in the nature of the meetings was noticeable as some national leaders joined the movement.

There was no diminution in the amount of attention engrossed by the question at issue. ... Many of the later meetings were significant rather as defining the position of particular statesmen, than as irrepressible expressions of Public Opinion bursting spontaneously into voice. But the distinction is by no means a sharp one, and the characteristics of both types of meeting were often exhibited by the same specimen.[39]

The local meetings culminated in the conference at St. James's Hall on 8 December where the proceedings were dominated by national figures rather than the leaders of local opinion, though many of the latter were present. Shannon marks this as the end of his story, though admitting that popular criticism of the Government's policy and the Turks continues down to the Congress of Berlin in 1878. He sees the agitation as fundamentally an outburst while Parliament was in recess, of Parliamentary excess, and the opening of Parliament in February 1877 and the establishment of the Eastern Question Association, which institutionalized some of the functions of the public meetings, as bringing a different environment.

The agitation spawned more than a plethora of public meetings; an outburst of charitable work was also elicited by the Turco-Serbian war and the agitation movement; the relief activity which emanated from Britain continued throughout 1877 and 1878.

For many the emotional wave was easily expended in speeches and meetings and resolutions; for most there was the necessity to show in some practical way their concern, by giving donations of money or clothes; and for some smaller proportion of the population to talk and to give was not enough. More positive action was necessary, to show that not everybody supported the government, to show that England as a Christian country cared for other Christian races . . . to show the Christian subject races striving to shake off the yoke of the unspeakable Turk had sympathy an support from . . . England.[40]

Individuals and organizations were soon competing to bring medical aid and assistance to the suffering in Bulgaria, Bosnia, Serbia, and to the Turks as well.

Some of the leaders of the agitation movement were outspoken in their refusal to consider that Christian charity should cater for other than Christians. Canon Liddon at St. Paul's . . . was adamant that the first duty of the Christian was to be the household of faith. Lechmere, writing to Liddon . . . was prepared to admit that the sympathies of the promoters of the Eastern War Sick and Wounded Fund were with Serbia and Montenegro, although in theory aid must appear to be given to both sides . . .[41]

Some of this philanthropic and well-meant relief activity was resented by its intended beneficiaries who greeted British agents with distrust and at times even anger. It is difficult to bring assistance without imparting values, and some opportunities to proselytize were not neglected. 'The Bulgarians stared sullenly at the hospitals that were being built and saw entry within the walls only as an inducement to change their faith.'[42]

Though he came to it late, Gladstone's association with the agitation gave it additional weight and significance, and as Blake tells us introduced a rancour into British politics rivalled only by that exhibited during the Corn Law debates.[43] Disraeli's refusal to acknowledge the agitation publicly or to appear to have changed policy as a result of it, together with his provocative speeches at Aylesbury and the Guildhall, led Gladstone and many others to suspect that he intended to follow a pro-Turkish line which included, if necessary, a war against Russia. Gladstone attributed Disraeli's Eastern policy to his Judaism, which was only slightly true, as it allowed Disraeli to view the Ottoman Turk more dispassionately, rather than as the oppressingly evil and decadently voluptuous figure and sterotype which had lingered in the Christian imagination since the medieval crusades. Disraeli had no great affection for the Turks, and part of his unhappiness with Elliot, and in great measure the final straw in his decision to replace him at Constantinople, was that the ambassador was not able to scare the Porte into doing that which Britain found desirable. His sympathy for the struggling Christian nationalities of the Balkans equalled Bismarck's, in that it was almost nil. The absence of sympathy was not due to resentment at the cruel and inhuman treatment that the Jews were sometimes subjected to by the Serbs and Romanians, rather it reflected a belief that Russia would use Slavic discontent in the Balkans as a screen behind which an attempt to grab Constantinople and the Straits would be made. It was his concern for the greatness and strength of the British Empire and the influence and dignity of the British Government that explain a great deal, if not most, of what he did.

Gladstone, of course, would have maintained in all sincerity that this was also his work. But Gladstone was frequently affected and inundated by great gusts of passion and energy which were often stimulated by his Christian and ethical sentiments. Such a storm broke in 1876, and the Liberal statesman made a valiant attempt to have British policy conform to the demands of his moral and ethical feeling. But as he found during the relatively minor squall of 1870–1, when he wished Britain to protest against the Prussian absorption of Alsace-Lorraine, it was not always easy successfully to equate the two for others. His attempt to do so in 1876[44] and 1877 did not lead him, as it did Freeman and Liddon, to displays of intense religious bigotry, but several times he came quite close to the place where religious sensitivity ends and prejudice begins. To an unsympathetic contemporary, like the well-known positivist Frederic Harrison, and to many others, the attempt to square policy with a personal sense of morality caused Gladstone to act with a peculiar inconsistency. 'He was constantly dominated by racial, accidental, personal, and even religious sympathies . . .'[45] One of the personal ones was his increasing hatred of Disraeli. He could forgive the Prime Minister for being mistaken but not for being wrong.

The agitation was partially successful in its object because it reflected some of the humane feelings that were shared by most people everywhere in Britain who learned of the tragedy in Bulgaria. Northcote, Carnarvon, Salisbury, Cairns, Richmond, and Cross were all revolted by the news of the massacres, and this national feeling of revulsion along with the threat of war by Russia resulted in a significant alteration in Britain's Eastern policy. Because the full change was not readily apparent, most were unaware of all of it. There was a general recognition that Britain could not, as she had done in 1854, go to the military aid of the Porte were it attacked by Russia. No one felt this more strongly than Derby. But perhaps even more fundamental was the Government's modification of its attitude toward Ottoman sovereignty. From the consular commission of 1875 through the Berlin memorandum the British position was a frank opposition to measures which seemed inconsistent with the Porte's authority. But in November and December 1876 the Government strongly pressed on the Porte the acceptance of arrangements which were designed to limit, restrict, and partially remove unfettered Ottoman control over its European provinces. The leaders of the agitation, or at least those of them who had formulated a political object beyond expressing their revulsion, wished to see the entire removal of Ottoman sovereignty and administration in Europe. This nearly came at San Stephano and Berlin in 1878.

*Turco-Serbian Peace and Russo-Turkish War*

Gorchakov proclaimed, upon the close of the Constantinople Conference, that Ottoman obstinacy was an affront to Europe and that a Russian circular was in preparation. On 4 February his circular to the European Powers was published and communicated. It stated that St. Petersburg still considered European co-operation and unity vital but that the Porte's refusal at the Constantinople Conference struck at the dignity and repose of Europe. 'The Emperor [of Russia], desirous of acting as far as possible in common with Europe, wishes before taking a decision, to ascertain views of the other Great Powers as to meeting this refusal of the Porte, and ensuring execution of their wishes.'[46] Though some in Britain and on the Continent interpreted this document as a sign of Russian weakness and as a desire to erect a golden bridge for the purpose of retreating from an awkward and dangerous position, others saw it as an attempt to outflank any European opinion opposed to a Russian war on Turkey.[47] Disraeli, whom many Liberals and some Conservatives suspected of desiring and working for a war, actually wished to provide Russia with such a golden bridge in order to avoid a Russo-Turkish conflict. But, as he wrote to Derby, if such a war occurred, Britain must be prepared for a partition of Turkey to take at the appropriate moment what was required for the security of the British Empire. He also thought that if the Porte could be made to concede certain reforms—Christians in the police and militia, some control over taxation to lie with the provincial assembly, and provincial governors to be appointed for a fixed term—then Russia might be able to back down and demobilize.[48]

The Prime Minister's estimate of Russia's peaceful intentions received a boost when on 9 February Shuvalov called upon Derby to ask London to influence the Porte to adopt some of the reform proposals of the Constantinople Conference. The Russian ambassador thought that by such a step the peril of conflict would recede.[49] Two days later Derby made such a request to Edhem Pasha, the new Grand Vizier. The Turkish reply to Britain's request was quickly given by the latter. He said that some of the most significant of the reforms were being executed already, but that a number of them could not be applied until considered by the Chamber of Deputies which would meet in a month's time.[50]

In the meantime Serbia and Turkey were discussing peace arrangements while Montenegro and the Porte were attempting discussion. When it seemed to Derby on 14 February that Nicholas of Montenegro was being unreasonable, he telegraphed to the British consul in Montenegro to suggest that Prince Nicholas should not raise difficulties during the course of the negotiations for peace.[51]

Salisbury, upon his arrival in England from Constantinople, was met by Lady Derby and the two had a long conversation, part of which the latter wrote of to Cross.

The 3rd point I cd not remember was the police or militia—a very important one.

I have written down the three points as mentioned to me by Ld. Salisbury. He told me these on the first night of his arrival—very confidentially—& asked if I thought they wd. be listened to here; it is his opinion a bridge might be made if we offered these & if the Porte wd consent. But what an *if!*[52]

Lady Derby undoubtedly told Shuvalov of Salisbury's view, causing the Russian ambassador to make the request of Derby that Britain induce the Turks to accept reform. But she also kept Salisbury informed of Shuvalov's opinions or at least those opinions he wished her to have.

Ct Shouvaloff came yest y to urge strongly that there shd be no delay in answering the circular. He said he had kept—or tried to keep his Emp r & Govt quiet for the last five days on the ground that the Govt. here was entirely occupied with the opening of Parlt. But this would not last forever, & he hoped Ld. D[erby] wd see the importance of time now.

I promised to push with my small efforts in the same direction & have done so . . .[53]

After Derby saw Shuvalov on 14 February, he sent a telegraphic dispatch to Loftus.

I told the Russian Ambassador yesterday that as circumstances had changed since the receipt of the Russian Circular. . . . Her Majesty's Government . . . with an earnest desire to meet the views of the Emperor [of Russia] in a friendly and conciliatory spirit, had determined that it would be better to defer their reply to it until events should have developed themselves, and it was seen what was the effect of the change of Government at Constantinople, both with reference to the new administrative reforms and the negotiations for peace between the Porte and Montenegro and Servia.[54]

Salisbury was unhappy with the draft of the above dispatch which was sent to him, but it had been sent off before his criticism could reach Derby.

I think the draft you have sent round ought to be considered in Cabinet before it is sent.

It strikes me as open to attack . . .

The kind of criticism which I fear is that which would charge us with insouciance & inactivity—with having no definite policy—with deferring any definite determination to a more convenient moment, just at the time when matters are the most critical, & therefore a clearly defined policy is the most required.

I quite admit the question, what to do, is no easy one . . .[55]

While Salisbury was suggesting more accommodation for Russia, in order to prevent war and Parliamentary criticism, Tenterden was desirous also of avoiding Parliamentary sniping by placing more pressure on Turkey.

I do not feel happy about the position as regards our recent overtures to Turkey. Ct. Shouvaloff suggested that you should try and get the Porte to accord of its own good will some of the measures upon which the plenipos. of the powers had insisted in their final demands at the conference. . . . It was done. The result has been that the Porte instead of offering any friendly opening for negotiations has tendered the execution of some points in its own Counter Project which the conference rejected as insufficient—moreover it has tendered these in a modified form and Musurus has accompanied this rebuff by an intimation that the Porte cannot execute capital punishment on the atrocities chiefs— . . . an intimation wh. if published wd. arouse public outcry—Shd we remain unremonstrating under such rebuffs—Silence may be mistaken for acquiescence.[56]

For Bismarck the Eastern Question was important only in so far as it produced alignments of the European Powers which were favourable or not for the security of Germany. Bismarck was anxious before the Constantinople meeting that the Dreikaiserbund would be weakened or destroyed by Anglo-Austrian opposition to Russia at the conference, opposition which would cause the latter to look with more favour upon French support. During the conference, and after it had ended,

Bismarck was aware of the French attempts to draw closer to Russia by supporting her against Turkey. What Bismarck had not been prepared for was the close Anglo-Russian co-operation carried on by Salisbury and Ignatiev. Once again Britain's position had become significant for the German leader, and he attempted, by again offering an understanding to Britain, to separate her from both France and Russia.

On 27 January Bismarck saw Odo Russell and told him that if Britain meant to join further with Russia on the basis of Gorchakov's circular, he could say no more.

But if not, he would be glad to be allowed to follow the example of Her Majesty's Government in answering the Russian Circular and assuming a neutral though benevolent position in company with England.

An early hint after reading the Circular as to the answer Her Majesty's Government intended to send to Russia, would be gratefully received by him, so far as to frame his own accordingly, if possible
. . .

The second question . . . he wished to submit to you was, 'could Germany reckon on the benevolent neutrality or moral support of England for the maintenance of peace if a coalition were formed by France, Russia and other Powers against Germany?'

Russell would not take what he considered a form of Bismarckian paranoia seriously and indicated to the German Chancellor that his fears were groundless.

Bismarck said he hoped I might be right, he wished to be wrong, but he would feel less apprehensive, if he could be sure of the support of England for the maintenance of peace.

I should be very glad if you could send me a soothing message of peace and friendship to calm his nerves.[57]

When Russell next saw Bismarck, the latter asked him if Britain no longer felt bound by the Treaty of 1856, and the ambassador answered that his Government did so feel itself bound.

I said that . . . respecting the prospect of a Franco-Russian coalition against Germany I could assure him that H.M.G. would always place their good offices and moral support at the disposal of Germany for the maintenance of peace and would do what they could to avert war, but that it must be distinctly understood that England did not undertake to go beyond moral support given to the cause of peace . . .

Bismarck became grave and silent after a while and said that one of his foremost political dreams had been an active and intimate alliance with England ... [for peace] but that dream could not be realized by good offices and moral support only which appeared to be all England had to offer him in return for the intimate alliance of Germany. It was a good deal and he was grateful for it, but it was not enough when other Powers were actively preparing for war ...
...

I reminded Bismarck that if the conclusions he alluded to included the possession of Constantinople [by Russia], a conflict with England would become inevitable. Bismarck said he was glad to hear me say so, because it gave him some control over Russian appetite ...[58]

A Cabinet meeting was held on 10 February to consider Bismarck's approach to Russell. Apart from the absence of any British belief in a French or anti-German coalition, there was the usual English suspicion of Bismarck's motives and sincerity. The Queen's reaction to the attempt of the German leader to elicit support from London may be seen from her journal. 'That monstrous Bismarck is again at his tricks, wanting us to go with him & is getting up the same cry as before against France, accusing her of the intention of attacking Germany. It is just what he did 2 years ago ...'[59] Derby, who thought that Bismarck wished Britain to take on an Egyptian protectorate so as to embroil her with France, was willing to humour him. 'Lord Derby will lose no opportunity of endeavoring to explain away his [Bismarck's] misunderstandings and will use good offices whenever he sees a chance of their being effectual: but this is all he can do and it is not much.'[60] Russell, in Berlin, reported Bismarck as believing Russia intended war on Turkey, and now that he knew that an English alliance was not possible he had decided to offer his moral support to Russia.[61]

Disraeli, whether convinced by Salisbury or Bismarck, also decided on about 20 February to give his moral support to Russia in a move similar to the one he had made to Russia the previous summer. He told Shuvalov that Britain wished an accord with Russia and the failure to reach one on the previous attempt had not been his fault. As before, he told the Russian ambassador that the  days of the Ottoman Empire were numbered but that to precipitate its fall would be dangerous. It would be best, he said, to give the Porte some time to execute reforms. Shuvalov replied that Russia, with 500,000 men mobilized, could not wait very long.[62] The Prime Minister also pressed Derby to help with the making of the golden bridge to permit Russia to draw back from war. The solution, he informed the Foreign Secretary, was to obtain Turkish reform as this would enable Russia to demobilize.[63]

Derby responded to the advice of both Disraeli and Tenterden and strongly pressed upon the Porte the necessity to grant reforms.

The answer of Grand Vizier as to reforms . . . is far from satisfactory. . . . Her Majesty's Government would have wished to hear . . . that the Porte is now of its own accord proceeding to carry out the measures proposed by the Powers in Conference, at least in their substantial features. An announcement of this kind in reply to the Russian Circular might go far to avert the danger of hostilities on the part of Russia which will otherwise become imminent as soon as the weather admits of military movements.[64]

Shuvalov was also pressing the Foreign Secretary to provide Russia with a golden bridge. He told Derby on 21 February that Russia could not demobilize unless a specific advantage were granted her.

Count Schouvaloff . . . [then suggested] that a fixed time, say a year, should be granted to the Porte for carrying out the reforms, and that if at the end of that period it were found that fair progress had not been made, the Turkish Government would be ready to submit to the appointment of an International Commission or such other form of control as might be held desirable.

His Excellency [Shuvalov] seemed to think favorably of the idea . . .[65]

Disorder had occurred in northern Albania in December and Derby feared that Turkish retaliation there would excite Russia. He sent another warning to the Porte.

Press strongly upon them [the Turks] the expediency of avoiding any steps that may be likely to lead to a renewal of bloodshed in any part of European Turkey.

The moment is most critical. . . . A prudent and conciliatory attitude on the part of the Porte, and an encouragement to hope for real progress and reform, is absolutely necessary to enable the Emperor to satisfy Russian public opinion. An error or even a mishap in the conduct of the Turkish authorities towards the population may produce results which will be irrevocable.[66]

But all was not dark as Serbo-Turkish negotiations were on the point of resulting in a peace treaty, and, thanks to Monson's influence, Montenegro had agreed to negotiate with the Turks at Constantinople, also for the purpose of concluding a formal peace agreement. On 1 March, partly due to British pressure on the Porte to be conciliatory, peace was concluded between Serbia and Turkey. It was at this point that the Russian Government decided to send Ignatiev to London and the other European capitals, in order to arrange a satisfactory answer from the Great Powers to the Russian circular.[67]

Before informing Derby of Ignatiev's impending visit, Shuvalov consulted Lady Derby who advised the ambassador to see Salisbury before telling her husband. Both Lady Derby and Salisbury, whom Shuvalov saw, advised against Ignatiev's coming as it would produce a bad effect on British opinion and cause pro-Turkish feeling to become more vocal.[68] Lady Derby was quite active, especially with Salisbury, in negotiating with Shuvalov behind the back of the Foreign Secretary.[69] Salisbury should have exercised better judgement. His efforts, along with those of his stepmother, failed to keep Ignatiev in Russia. Further, Derby's pressure on Turkey to reform or face a Russian war was proving unsuccessful as the Grand Vizier told the Austrian chargé d'affaires that he regarded war as inevitable.[70] The Foreign Secretary, who had produced in draft an answer to the Russian circular, was asked by Shuvalov to delay delivering it as Ignatiev was coming to London.

Spring had almost arrived and it remained to be seen whether Ignatiev could elicit an Anglo-Russian arrangement that would prevent a Russo-Turkish war. The British Government was also concerned with defending its behaviour in Parliament, which had convened in February. As the Conservatives had a strong Parliamentary majority, the latter task proved easier than building that golden bridge which some in Russia had little desire to use.

## 15  THE LONDON PROTOCOL
AND WAR

WHEN IGNATIEV left Russia for the West on 2 March, he took
with him a draft protocol. His first stop was Berlin, where he
saw Bismarck and had a six-hour discussion with him, showing
him the protocol. The content of the protocol was telegraphed
to Münster in London, who was instructed to inform Derby.
The Foreign Secretary was also apprised of the document by
Russell. Derby's first reaction was that the Russian proposition
was too vague for a response, and that he would need to see the
Russian text.

This draft was said to enumerate the chief proposals of reform put
forward at the conference [Constantinople]; to demand binding
assurances from the Porte as to their execution; and to conclude with
a declaration on the part of the Powers that, if the Porte should
refuse or neglect to fulfil their engagements, they would come to a
common agreement.
Prince Bismarck stated that he personally saw no strong objection
to the proposal, and that he would probably be willing to sign the
Protocol, as he did not consider that it involved any undertaking to
use coercive measures against Turkey.[1]

Success in Berlin propelled the General and Madame
Ignatiev on 6 March to Paris, where Shuvalov had gone to
meet them. Ignatiev spoke with Lyons and Lady Salisbury,
asking the latter to communicate to her husband in England
the necessity of the protocol to enable Russia to disarm.[2]
Shuvalov returned to London and called upon Derby on 11
March to leave with him a copy of the draft. The Foreign
Secretary informed the ambassador that he would bring it
before the Cabinet as soon as possible.

The British reaction to Ignatiev and the Russian protocol
was as usual mixed. *The Times* and the *Daily Telegraph* wished to
aid Russia in an honourable retreat, especially if she agreed to
demobilize. The *Daily News* thought the protocol useless as it
was far too mild, and the *Pall Mall Gazette* saw it as a trap.[3] The
Queen also was suspicious when she learned of Ignatiev's mis-

sion, and the news of Bismarck's approval of the protocol only increased her anxiety and distrust. She decided to warn the Foreign Secretary. 'Beware of a trap of Russia and Bismarck and *do* not join in any demonstration against Turkey . . .

It is of course very difficult but we must not be dragged into any joint action by which we shall drift into war . . .'[4] Derby was prepared to do relatively little, and his moat of distrust was capable of infinite expansion in order to preclude any British action which might be dangerous or undesirable. Salisbury and Disraeli, however, unlike the Foreign Secretary, were concerned more with the dangers of inaction.

Salisbury, since his return from Constantinople, had gained the ear and approbation of the Prime Minister, whose health had taken a turn for the worse. The India Secretary was prepared for partition, a position which Disraeli had always been ready to support.

I [Salisbury] feel convinced that the old policy—wise enough in its time—of defending English interests by sustaining the Ottoman dynasty has become impracticable: and I think that the time has come for defending English interests in a more direct way by some territorial arrangement . . . a *pied à terre*. . . . English policy is to float lazily down stream, occasionally putting out a diplomatic boat hook to avoid collisions.[5]

Salisbury thought the Russian protocol was extremely moderate and strongly urged its acceptance upon the Prime Minister, arguing that if Britain refused it and Russia went to war, the responsibility would, in part, be England's.[6]

Even before hearing from Salisbury, Disraeli was hopeful of arranging something with the Russians. 'The great transaction will probably be concluded, & under circumstances singularly honourable to England. It will appear entirely as the consequence of Yr. Majesty's influence, & the note of settlement is to be signed, & dated, from St. James.'[7] Even Derby was mildly favourable to the Russian protocol; Disraeli quoted the Foreign Secretary's words to the Queen.

The document meant to be signed seems to me, on a first reading, studiously inoffensive: nothing is said of the Conference [Constantinople] proposals; the Turkish Reforms are accepted instead; no date is fixed for their execution; there may be something behind, wh.

I don't yet see, but, on the face of it, there is nothing that one can even plausibly object to. Not a word which savors of coercion . . .[8]

A Cabinet meeting was quickly held on 13 March to consider the Government's answer to the protocol. Disraeli described it in somewhat grandiose terms to the Queen as the most crucial Cabinet meeting of the present Government. Derby presented two possibilities to the assembled ministers; one, that Russia needed a way to retreat, and the other, that the protocol represented a conspiracy of Austria, Germany, and Russia to entrap England into an informal alliance for the partition of Turkey. The Foreign Secretary ended by saying he favoured acting with the other Powers subject to altering some of the wording of the protocol. Salisbury said that if they accepted the policy they should not quibble over words. Hardy and Carnarvon favoured concert with the Powers, as did Hunt, the latter stipulating the necessity of obtaining security for Russian demobilization. Salisbury replied and opposed making difficulties; he stated that Shuvalov had told him that demobilization of the Russian army would be immediate. Beach, Manners, and Cross all favoured the protocol, as did Cairns, but the latter felt that the fine print of the document required a very close and careful reading. Disraeli also supported it because the possibility of Turkey disintegrating should not occur while Britain was isolated. 'The Cabinet unanimously agreed to join in the Protocol subject to certain modifications of language, the adhesion of Austria, & the undertaking of Russia to demobilise her army.'[9]

Derby saw Shuvalov on the afternoon of the Cabinet meeting and told him that Britain was ready to agree in principle to the protocol subject to some modifications. He further added three necessary stipulations: a formal pledge of Russian demobilization, that the Porte should not to be asked to sign the protocol, and the agreement of the other Powers to it.[10] Shuvalov communicated Derby's reaction to his Government and to Ignatiev in Paris, and informed Lady Derby on 14 March that he was exceedingly disturbed at the number of alterations in the protocol required by the Cabinet, and the impact this would have on his Government. Lady Derby communicated this to Disraeli without her husband's knowledge.[11]

On the morning of 16 March Ignatiev left Paris for London,

taking advantage of Salisbury's invitation to him to visit Hatfield and his Government's permission for him to go to England. On the following day he and Shuvalov called on Derby and discussed the protocol with him. Disraeli was not happy with Ignatiev's arrival, and told the Queen his presence might result in difficulties.[12] Complications did arise, and they were probably due to the General, who wished a great diplomatic success in order to obtain Gorchakov's position for himself. Shuvalov, who was working for peace, had held out the prospect of Russian demobilization for a British agreement on the protocol. Ignatiev, for whatever reasons, was not inclined to guarantee demobilization, and he and Shuvalov presented Derby with Russian counter-proposals which necessitated the calling of another Cabinet meeting to consider them. Tenterden was urging the Foreign Secretary to obtain in writing the Russian conditions for demobilization, and the Foreign Secretary informed Ignatiev that the protocol and demobilization must go *pari passu*—no demobilization, no protocol.[13]

In the meantime Ignatiev went to Hatfield, where he had a long talk with Tenterden who repeated Derby's admonition in the form of the old English proverb 'no song, no supper'. The Under-Secretary's advice to the General not to pressure England too much left the latter displeased.[14] Forster, the Liberal politician, had also been invited to Hatfield, and he was sought out by the General for a conversation, which he reported to both Salisbury and Northcote. Ignatiev stated three conditions which were necessary before his Government could demobilize: peace with Montenegro, a beginning of (Turkish) reform, and a beginning of (Turkish) disarmament.[15]

He [Ignatiev] wd give Lord Derby as many times as he liked the freest personal assurance that the army would be demobilized—but his Government could not openly engage to demobilize—in fact, they could not demobilize except on three conditions.
  1. Peace was made with Montenegro
  2. The Porte Accepted the Protocol
  3. The reforms were executed
  . . .
I [Tenterden] asked how he could expect that Europe could ask the Porte to disarm in the face of the Russian army.
He said as for that he wd leave that out of the Protocol. I said that I could merely express a personal opinion . . . that what he had said

was contrary to the understanding under which the British Govt. had entered into the negotiation of the Protocol, viz. that the Porte should not be called upon to accept it . . .

He seemed much put out at this . . .[16]

On the same day as the conversation between Ignatiev and Tenterden, the Cabinet met for one hour and resolved not to consider amendments to the protocol until the prior issue of demobilizing the Russian army on Turkey's border was arranged.[17] The Cabinet's firm decision, which was strongly supported by the Queen,[18] seemed to have only one mild dissenter, that being Carnarvon, who declared the improved status of the Porte's Christian subjects to be the main British object.[19]

Ignatiev, together with Shuvalov, again called upon Derby in London as soon as the Cabinet dispersed, and the Foreign Secretary communicated to them the decision of his colleagues. Both Russians argued against the decision, and again presented the three necessary conditions for Russian disarmament, which Derby said he would report to his colleagues.[20] Tenterden thought that the Russians were squeezable, and Disraeli believed that they would give way if the Cabinet were solid and united. But the Prime Minister had doubts as to Salisbury and Carnarvon.

Lord Beaconsfield is more afraid of Lords Salisbury & Carnarvon than he is of Ct Schouvalow & Genl. Ignatieff.

Ld. Beaconsfield thanks Yr. Majesty for Yr. Majesty's generous & gracious offer of writing to those two members of the Cabinet, but a letter from Yr. Majesty is always the last, & most precious, weapon in his armoury . . .

In the meantime Ld Carnarvon will be the Minister attendant on Saturday, & some occasion may offer to brace his mind a little, at present, morbidly relaxed by the company of Lyddon, Lord Bath & a strange sacerdotal crew . . .[21]

That same evening, the twenty-first, Disraeli had the Ignatievs to dinner in a party which included the Prince of Wales. He informed Ponsonby of the affair, and indicated that he had remained firm to Ignatiev's arguments, again repeating his request to the Queen to remonstrate with Carnarvon.[22] Another Cabinet meeting was held on the morning of 23 March, described by the Prime Minister as the most critical meeting of the present ministry. He opened the meeting and spoke for thirty minutes, comparing 'the two policies now in conflict; the Imperial Policy of England, & the Policy of Crusade'.

> He [Disraeli] sketched what must be the consequences of a nation indulging in sentimental eccentricity . . .
> There was, a pause, & then Lord Salisbury spoke. . . . He said, however strong, or the reverse, the party of crusaders were in the country, he hoped, that the P. Minister did not believe there was any crusader in the Cabinet. But the religious sentiments of bodies of our countrymen could not be disregarded. . . . Still he was prepared on this vast question to bow to the opinion of the majority of his colleagues, & he had recognized, at the last meeting of the Cabinet, that the majority of his colleagues was in accordance with the views of the Prime Minister.

Cairns and Hardy followed, both strongly supporting Disraeli. Carvarvon then spoke. He harped much on the phrase 'sentimental eccentricity' . . . found great fault with the policy of the government from the beginning, said we had changed our policy, & all the disagreeable things, that are said by Lord Bath, & Canon Lyddon, & Lord Dudley. Nevertheless, after venting fully his spleen, he announced his determination to act with his colleagues. Northcote and Ward Hunt backed the Premier, and Derby declared he had nothing to say that Disraeli had not already mentioned. The Duke of Richmond and then the rest indicated their assent, resolving to sign no protocol without demobilization.[23]

Shuvalov came to Derby after the meeting, Ignatiev having departed for Paris. The Foreign Secretary communicated to him the decision of the Cabinet.

> I said that it was not our wish to break off the negotiations; that, on the contrary, we were not only willing, but anxious to find a practical solution; but that we could not accept the proposal made to us in the conversation which I had had with his Excellency and General Ignatiev on Wednesday last, according to which demobilisation on the part of Russia was made dependent upon the three conditions of Turkish reform . . . of Turkey taking the initiative in disarmament, and . . . peace . . . [with] Montenegro.
> I dwelt on the unfairness—not to say the absurdity—of its being expected that the Porte should begin to disarm while still menaced by an army on the frontier superior to its own.

Shuvalov then offered a compromise suggestion: if the Porte were willing to disarm and undertake serious reform, and to send an envoy to St. Petersburg to treat on mutual demobilization, the Tsar would then consent to disarm simultaneously with Turkey.[24]

The following day Shuvalov saw Derby again, and when the Foreign Secretary suggested that no protocol should be signed until the Porte and Montenegro made peace, the Russian ambassador seemed to assent and indicated that if peace were made, his suggestion of the previous day could be implemented.[25] The Porte and Montenegro were negotiating in Constantinople, and though they had agreed to prolong the armistice, progress in the making of peace was foundering on the territorial demands of Prince Nicholas and the extent to which the Porte was willing to satisfy them. Further complicating this issue was Andrássy's veto on some of Montenegro's territorial demands, especially that of a port, and the latter's knowledge that Russia would not allow her to be vanquished by the Turks. Loftus thought that since Nicholas had given up his demand for a seaport, the Porte would be well advised to grant Nicksich and the plain around it to Montenegro.[26]

On 26 March Shuvalov came to Derby and again pressed for the protocol, saying that the relatively minor question of Nicksich must not be allowed to result in a European war.[27]

The Russian Government have proposed that the drafting of a Protocol should be proceeded with, and urge that its signature should not be delayed. They agree that before its signature, the Russian ambassador should make a declaration in the name of his Government, and leave with me [Derby] a Memorandum, to be used publicly if necessary, to the effect that if the Porte accepts the advice of the Powers, and shows itself ready to replace its forces on a peace footing, and to take in hand seriously the reforms mentioned in the Protocol, the Sultan may send a special Envoy to St. Petersburgh to treat on the question of disarmament, to which disarmament the Emperor of Russia will also on his side consent.

Count Schouvaloff added a proviso that if a recommencement of massacres took place similar to those in Bulgaria, then the engagement on the part of Russia to demobilize would no longer hold good.[28]

Derby told the Russian ambassador that he would submit his

proposal to the Cabinet. Before the ministers met on 28 March, the Foreign Secretary received the following worried telegram from Loftus, which arrived at noon.

It is my duty to inform your Lordship that the present crisis here is one of serious gravity. I am privately informed that if the condition for [Russian] demobilization is maintained . . . [by Britain] war is certain. Emperor of Russia regards it as one of humiliation, and will prefer war to its acceptance.

Unless difficulty as regards the demobilization can be solved and the Protocol signed it is my conviction that the Russian army will cross the Pruth in about three weeks . . .[29]

The Cabinet met for two hours and agreed to sign the protocol without waiting for the conclusion of peace between Turkey and Montenegro. Derby, however, was so suspicious of a Russian trap that he informed Shuvalov that if armament and war were not avoided, the protocol should be considered invalid.[30] It was understood that Shuvalov's earlier suggestion of an Ottoman envoy proceeding to St. Petersburg so as to discuss and elicit Russian demobilization would be carried out. Derby's presence at Keston, a country house about fourteen miles from London, caused Shuvalov to commute for several days between the Foreign Secretary and the telegraph in London by which he communicated with Gorchakov in Russia. According to Lady Derby, the Russian ambassador received his Government's consent to the above arrangement on the evening of 29 March.[31]

On 31 March Derby, Shuvalov, Münster, Beust, d'Harcourt, and Menabrea signed the protocol which had been agreed between the Foreign Secretary and the Russian ambassador. The Russian declaration to Britain, suggested by Shuvalov, was read by him to the Foreign Secretary.

Let the Porte send to St. Petersburg a Special Envoy to treat of disarmament, to which His Majesty the Emperor [of Russia] will consent also on his side.

If massacres such as those which have occurred in Bulgaria took place, that would necessarily put a stop to the measures of demobilization.

It is understood beforehand that, in the event of the object proposed not being attained, viz., reciprocal disarmament on the part of Russia and Turkey, and peace between them, the Protocol in question shall be regarded as null and void.[32]

Derby, as he wrote to the Queen, was not sanguine as to the success of the protocol, but as both he and Disraeli agreed, Britain was protected against a Russian trap.

Lord Derby never has been, and is not now, sanguine of the success of the document in ensuring peace, but as it is now worded, it can do no harm even if it fails to do any good; and it will at least prevent the Russian Government from throwing the blame on England if war ensues, which assuredly would have been done if signature had been refused. If the Russian Emperor is sincere in his alleged desire for an excuse to enable him to disarm, he has got what he wants: if not, we are only where we were . . .[33]

Bismarck's concern was that a Russo-Turkish war might draw in others, and was anxious over what Britain might do if Russia crossed the Pruth. He asked Odo Russell if England would then declare war. The ambassador replied that his Government had declared that they would neither go to war for or coerce Turkey. Bismarck then asked if England would act should Russia reach the Balkan Mountains. Russell responded indirectly and gave it as his personal opinion that Britain would not permit a Russian occupation of Constantinople. The German leader then gave Russell his view as to the possibility of peace. 'A peaceful solution was quite possible if Turkey did what was expected of her in the Protocol—it rested with the Porte to deprive Russia of any further excuse for interference. . . . Much would of course depend on the ultimate fate of the Protocol both in London and later at Constantinople. . . . Here ended our conversation.' Russell then added his own opinion of Russia and, as it came to be called, the London Protocol. 'The advantages the "conspirators" expect to derive from the protocol are: 1st, in the first instance to make England responsible for war if we reject the protocol and if we do not, 2nd, to transfer the responsibility from our shoulders on to those of the Porte and 3rd, to obtain the right hitherto denied them by the Treaty of Paris of permanent interference in the internal administration of Turkey.'[34]

Andrássy pressed the Porte to accept the protocol for he did not wish a Russian invasion of the Balkans. Herbert, the Austrian chargé at Constantinople, was instructed to inform Turkey that her acceptance of the document would affect neither the esteem nor the sovereignty of the Porte. 'Do not leave the Porte in any doubts about the weight Austria attaches to the document and to the goal of peace that has come about after such difficulties.'[35] Neither the Turks nor the Russians, however, were prepared to make sacrifices for peace, suspecting the martial intentions and devious desires of each other. On 18 March Austria had been squared by the signature of the second part of the Budapest Convention. The Tsar himself, proud of his reputation as a lover of peace, seemed prepared to embrace war. Gorchakov and Jomini now favoured it. Loftus saw the former on 6 April.

Should the Porte [Gorchakov said] reply verbally, or in unsatisfactory and evasive language, war will result, as Russia cannot longer bear the heavy pecuniary sacrifices of prolonged profitless negotiation.
. . .

Prince Gorchakov replied that Your Lordship's [Derby's] declaration rendered the Protocol null and void in event of non-fulfilment of reciprocal disarmament and peace. His Highness said that it was a question of days, and that a decision must be taken by the 13th of April. The Emperor would not withdraw; a manifesto was prepared; answer of the Porte would decide for peace or war.[36]

On 9 April Shuvalov saw Derby and informed him that if war were to be averted it would be necessary for Turkey to send an envoy to St. Petersburg to treat on disarmament. The Foreign Secretary informed the Porte of the Russian message.[37] On the same day Musurus Pasha, the Turkish ambassador in London, also came to see the Foreign Secretary.

His Excellency [Musurus Pasha] said that the Porte felt that the contents of the Protocol were derogatory to the Sultan's dignity and independence and that rather than accede to its provisions it would be better for Turkey to face the alternative of war, even if an unsuccessful war . . .

I [Derby] asked him whether he meant seriously to contend that it would be better, in the interests of the Porte, that the Turks should be driven out of Europe than that the Sultan's Government should tacitly acquiesce in a document to which they were not required or requested to give any formal or express assent, which had been drawn up and signed without their being consulted, for which, therefore, they were in no way responsible, and which, after all, called upon the Porte, as I understood its tenor, to do no more than it had either already expressed itself ready to do, or than it might be presumed willing to do, with a view to the well-being and security of Turkey.

Musurus replied that the Protocol was a virtual abrogation of the IXth Article of the Treaty of Paris . . . and that this was a humiliation to which his Government would not at any risk submit.

I said that I very much regretted to hear him express this view, which I could not conceal from him was, in my opinion, a very unwise one.[38]

A Turkish council met on the ninth in Constantinople and decided to issue a circular dispatch to all the European Powers. It contained the Porte's objection to the protocol, which it wished the Powers to annul, as well as its refusal to send a representative to Russia to discuss disarmament, which was proposed in the Russian written declaration made by Shuvalov and attached to the protocol.[39] To make matters worse, Montenegrin–Turkish peace negotiations at Constantinople had broken down on Cetinje's demands for territory and the Ottoman refusal to comply.

The Turkish circular was communicated to the Russian Government on 12 April, the same day that London received it. Six days before this Gorchakov had told Loftus that unless Turkey consented to send an envoy to St. Petersburg to discuss mutual disarmament, Russia would go to war.[40] After receipt of the Turkish circular at the Russian capital, war was considered by most to be only a matter of time. When the Italian chargé called on Derby on 18 April and asked what more might be done to prevent a Russo-Turkish war, the Foreign Secretary could make no suggestion. Both he and de Martino agreed on the necessity of limiting the extension of the war to any other European Powers, and the former added that Britain could not permit Constantinople to be in the hands of Russia.[41]

Some effort was made to prevent war by Austen Henry Layard, the new special ambassador who arrived in Constantinople on 20 April,[42] and was the only ambassador of the Great Powers in the city. The other European governments had maintained only chargés since the end of the Constantinople Conference as a mark of their displeasure with the Porte.[43] Layard lost no time, and the same day he reached Constantinople, he went to see Edhem Pasha, the Grand Vizier. The latter felt it was too late to prevent hostilities, though Layard told him that Britain would not help Turkey should they occur. After a conversation lasting two hours Edhem Pasha agreed to submit to his colleagues that which Layard urged—an appeal to the Powers for mediation, spontaneous disarmament if mediation were accepted, punishment of those guilty of Bulgarian atrocities, and a satisfactory arrangement with Turkey's creditors. 'The repudiation by the Porte of his foreign debt having been, I [Layard] reminded Edham Pasha, one of the principal causes of the change of feeling in England with regard to the Turks.'[44]

The following morning Layard called on Safvet Pasha, the Ottoman Foreign Minister, who seemed much more favourable than the Grand Vizier to the idea of appealing to the Powers for mediation. The ambassador also urged the necessity of full punishment for those who committed the atrocities. Safvet replied that this would be difficult as Muslim opinion would view the Bashi-Bazouk leaders as martyrs.[45] Layard also talked with Nelidov, the Russian chargé, and appealed to him to attempt to win over Gorchakov and Nicholas II to a peaceful accommodation.[46] On the twenty-fourth the ambassador had an audience with the Sultan, who insisted, with tears in his eyes, of his desire for peace. Layard thought him sincere, and was impressed with his manner and bearing. During the conversation a telegram from the Ottoman ambassador in St. Petersburg arrived informing the Turkish Government that he had received from Gorchakov a note containing a declaration of war. It was the fourth Russo-Turkish war of the nineteenth century.[47]

Italy, Austria, and France had actively made last-minute attempts to prevent hostilities. Germany had done nothing. Though Layard tried for peace, Derby surprisingly, after his much earlier attempts to prevent such a confrontation, accepted the end with a kind of fatalistic resignation. He may have honestly believed that nothing could have been done, for such belief precluded the necessity to do more than observe. He expended much more energy in avoiding any Russian trap to coerce Turkey to reform in the name of Europe. Disraeli, who was suffering from bad health, did no more than his

Foreign Secretary to prevent war. The Prime Minister translated war as partition of Turkey, and he intended that England would get a share in the latter transaction.

In Russia, the existence of a war party, inflamed public opinion, and an exceedingly favourable diplomatic situation—Austria snarled in the bounds of Reichstadt and Budapest and Britain bound by the outburst of humanitarian sentiment—caused a decision for war to be reached rather than continuation of a fruitless and embarrassing negotiation with the Turks. The latter, refusing to compromise dignity or independence, banking on Russia backing down short of war, and believing that even if war came, British interests would not allow an overwhelming Russian victory, caused the Porte to stand up against Europe at the Constantinople Conference and in its reaction to the London Protocol. Muslim opinion, as well, was growing as intemperate as that of Russia's Pan-Slavists. Finally, the financial cost of continued mobilization by Russia and Turkey, while negotiations proceeded in an attempt at peaceful compromise, was ironically deemed too expensive by both Governments, one almost, and one completely, bankrupt.

The Russian excuse for war was Turkey's refusal of the London Protocol, which St. Petersburg had previously agreed, as a result of London's demand, would not require a formal Ottoman acceptance or signature. Turkish refusal of the protocol was therefore somewhat gratuitous, but her objection to sending an emissary to Russia to discuss disarmament, which would have amounted to the same thing as her refusal of the protocol, arose from wounded dignity and tactical considerations. Nor could Russia back down without great loss of face before both domestic opinion and foreign Powers.

Herbert, the Austrian chargé in Constantinople, believed that Layard's attempts to prevent war were exercises in British self-interest rather than sincere efforts for peace. As Layard had been dispatched to Constantinople without receiving real instructions from Derby, a somewhat extraordinary omission considering the circumstances under which he took up his post, the ambassador was left to some extent to intuit the desires of Disraeli, Derby, and Salisbury.

Before considering the reaction of British opinion to the

outbreak of war, it is necessary to look at that opinion as it developed after the St. James's Hall meeting of December 1876.

## After the Deluge: British Opinion

The anger of the autumn had subsided before the end of 1876 and the public and Press were now left to digest the failure of the Constantinople Conference, to estimate the possibility of a Russo-Turkish war, and to await the reaction of Parliament which was to open in the middle of February.

On the day before Parliament was to convene, many of the Liberal front-benchers met at Granville's London residence. Among those present were Harcourt, Argyll, James, Gladstone, Hartington, and Forster. Harcourt, Argyll, and Gladstone argued to press the Government to act with Russia and to coerce Turkey. In the end there was agreement that Granville and Hartington should support a European —meaning all the Great Powers—demand on Turkey, with a threat of coercion and this to be acted upon if Turkey did not comply. Forster argued the necessity of England avoiding acting alone with Russia.[48] It was difficult to know which was worse; allowing Russia in the name of Europe to act alone in Turkey, or Britain's acting alone with Russia, owing to the absence of the other Powers, and finding herself constrained to support an undesirable policy in order to deflect St. Petersburg from even worse steps.

On the same day as the opposition had gathered, 7 February, the Conservative ministers had their own meeting in order to prepare for Parliamentary combat. The latest blue book, containing those diplomatic dispatches worthy of being printed and those it was not awkward to publish, had already been prepared, but Cairns, the Lord Chancellor, objected to the production on the ground that it represented no distinct and understandable policy and that in its desire to proclaim abstinence from coercive action upon Turkey it would provoke feeling to act with her, which he apparently opposed. A letter from Cairns to Disraeli may have helped to bring about one from the latter to Derby.[49]

The Prime Minister, in part to dissipate the increasing criticism that he was leading the country into a war with

Russia, and in part to show that the Government had not changed its policy, presumably of neutrality, wished the new blue book to highlight Derby's dispatch to the Porte that Britain would not resort to war for Turkey's sake. 'This could not be published at the time but now the objections to its publication no longer exist.

It is the key note of our position. Nothing shd. prevent its appearance, & in a striking shape.'[50]

He and the Chancellor of the Exchequer were still intent upon respecting what Disraeli referred to as 'this famous phrase'.

When we speak of maintaining the integ.[rity] of a Kingdom, we mean the integrity as then existing . . .

Then again as to independence, we mean . . . that we acknowledge and contemplate the continuity of its sovereign power, even while we may be suggesting limitations of that power for a temporary purpose.

Prussia was subject at the beginning of this century to far more humiliating conditions, than those proposed for Turkey . . .

When one adds Northcote's words to the Premier's, it is clear that Ottoman integrity and independence were consistent with what in Western eyes was Turkey's special and peculiar position.

Of course we only use those words [integrity and independence of Turkey] in the sense in which they were used in the original treaties, where they occur side by side with provisions which we should not put into a treaty with France or Germany—Such measures, therefore, as those proposed at the conference [Constantinople] . . . must be held to be consistent with the maintenance of the Porte's independence; and undoubtedly the spirit in which they were proposed was that of a desire to save its territory from being broken up by internal convulsions . . . [51]

The Netherlands ambassador described the party situation as a political deadlock. 'It can be said (and in fact is said) that if the government has a majority strong enough in Parliament to resist all pressures for engaging in a coercive action against Turkey, the opposition and public opinion outside of Parliament are strong enough to make a war for Turkey impossible and if there were the least possibility of that, the dissolution of Parliament would become inevitable.'[52]

Thompson has described accurately the tactics adopted by

the opposition from this point on, for a considerable period of time, and the Government's response to them.

Instead of distinctly . . . challenging the Government to accept it [the coercion of Turkey] or repudiate it, the Opposition began to engage in a guerilla warfare of questions and criticisms founded on the Blue Books. The Government, while deprecating a general debate on the ground that negotiations were still on foot, maintained strenuously that their policy had not undergone any change, and referred all enquirers to the Blue Books.

At first, probably the desire to draw from the Government a definite statement of the actual attitude which they intended to adopt predominated; but when the Government . . . resented every attempt of this kind, no doubt the desire came in to discredit them by convicting them of that inconsistency which they so strenuously denied. . . .

The whole of the early part of the session was characterized by skirmishing of this kind; a vast number of questions were put to Ministers. . . . There were also a few reconnaissances in force, but there was no decisive battle. These tactics . . . only served when unduly prolonged . . . on the whole . . . to reinstate in public confidence a Cabinet against whose present policy . . . there was after all nothing substantial which could be urged . . .[53]

On 16 March Forster gave notice that three days hence he would ask if Elliot were to be returned to Constantinople. Hartington put a question, answered by Northcote, as to the present state of the Anglo-Russian negotiations. The latter indicated that a Russian draft protocol, embodying the views of all the Great Powers, had been considered by the Government which had proposed some modifications, and that negotiations were still transpiring.[54] A meeting of Liberal front-benchers took place at Granville's London house on 19 March to discuss the most effective way of bringing on a resolution. Gladstone, Forster, and Hartington favoured doing so and Granville, almost alone among the Liberal leaders, opposed a motion. The possible return of Henry Elliot to Constantinople was also discussed.[55] In the three days before the anticipated debate on 23 March, division in opposition ranks manifested itself within the leadership and among the Radicals as to whether to propose a motion and which among several (by Dilke, Courtney, Fawcett, and Ryland) to support.[56] It did not bode well for Liberal effectiveness in Parliament.

The long-anticipated discussion developed in the House of Commons on 23 March in a protracted and acrimonious set-to. Northcote described it to the Queen.

Mr. Fawcett, who had given notice of a motion on the Eastern question, which was intended to furnish an occasion for speeches only and not for a division, has been forced to make a serious debate upon it . . .

This he did in a rather bitter speech [in which he moved a resolution favouring the Great Powers' right to demand guarantees for Turkish reform] . . .

As soon as he sat down Lord Hartington rose, and in a very statesman like speech . . . [said the present was a bad moment to propose such a resolution]. He [Hartington] considered it most unopportune while negotiations [with Russia on the protocol] were still proceeding; and said the proper time for discussing the policy of the Government would be, when those negotiations were at an end.[57]

Gladstone rose and made one of his most eloquent orations—but it really was in parts like the speech of a madman. He opened every possible subject . . . [and supported Hartington in deprecating a forced division] . . .

. . .

After he [Northcote] had concluded[58] an attempt was made to adjourn the debate, in order to escape from the necessity of a division which would show the weakness of the minority. . . . The division on the adjournment showed a Government majority of about 170; and this would have been much larger had the division been on the main question.

After two and a half hours wrangle, and several divisions on repeated motions for adjournment of the debate, the House has at length adjourned (2:30 a.m.) and the motion is at an end [with no division taken on it].

The result is considered very satisfactory to the Government.[59]

But, if the Government were satisfied, the Parliamentary sniping and hit-and-run tactics of the Liberals continued.[60] Had the Liberals known of the disharmony within the Cabinet concerning Elliot's return to his post, they might have forced a Parliamentary vote on that issue and hit harder at the ambassador than they were doing already. After Elliot had repaired to England, Derby decided as a departmental matter that, once rested, the ambassador would return to his post. But on 16 March Forster gave a hostile notice in the Commons concerning Elliot, which brought the matter before the

Cabinet on the following day. Derby was stolid and unwavering about the necessity for Elliot's return. He was followed by Salisbury, who spoke with intensity and gravity, and argued that it was not merely a departmental matter as the Cabinet's reputation and existence were at stake. Every member of the Cabinet opposed the ambassador's return, especially the ministers in the House of Commons, but Derby refused to give way, as he had already arranged with Sir Henry that he should return. 'Lord Salisbury then said, "if the retirement of Lord Derby is in question, then I am prepared . . . we must sanction & support the return of Sir H. Elliot, but I think, our [the Cabinet's] general retirement will be the consequence."' Disraeli, who had been silent, then interposed:

that after the expression of feeling on the part almost of an unanimous Cabinet, & the report of the temper & prospects of the House of Commons given by its leader, it was impossible not to see that the matter was grave; that we could not ask Ld. Derby to withdraw from a position, wh. he felt was a just one, & in the maintenance of wh. his personal honour was concerned; & Lord Beaconsfield, therefore, suggested that he should, himself, see Sir H. Elliot, & make that gentleman aware of all the circumstances of the case, & while assuring him, that the Cabinet would uphold the decision of the Foreign Office, leave it to his own discretion to decide as to his course

The Prime Minister saw Elliot the same day and the latter at once saw Derby, and gave as his desire that he should not be immediately returned to his post.[61] This enabled Northcote on 19 March to indicate in the Commons that for reasons of health Elliot would remain on leave.[62] And so was avoided an issue upon which the government probably would have met defeat in a Parliamentary vote.

On the last day of March the public learned of the signing of the London Protocol and the appointment of Layard as temporary ambassador. To the first the Press responded with moderate favour; the second was seen by the journals along party lines.[63] At this point there was an interruption of what Thompson calls the 'parade debates', when the opposition, through Hartington, who on 9 April gave notice of a question on the Russian draft protocol, seemed decided to challenge and censure the Government.[64] But the expectation was premature. 'Much interest had been excited this evening by a report that Lord Hartington intended to give notice of a vote of censure. . . . But he disappointed all expectations by simply giving notice to move . . . for a copy of . . . the Protocol. . . . This will be enough to supply what Mr. Gladstone calls "a peg to hang speeches on;" but can hardly lead to a serious debate.' The difficulty for Hartington and Granville was one of finding an issue upon which all the Liberals would unite to censure the Government.[65]

The Liberals decided to avoid a direct vote of censure, and Hartington informed Gladstone that he did not think it necessary for the latter to speak at the debate unless he felt so disposed.[66] Dilke gave a marvellously accurate prediction of the course of the debate to Hill of the *Daily News*.

For the information of your leader writer I may tell you what is likely to happen to-night. Hartington will make a regular fighting speech & a very strong attack on the Government, a speech in short more appropriate to a vote of censure than to a request for papers. He will criticise the Protocol but on the whole approve of it, strongly denounce Lord Derby's declaration [that the protocol would be null and void if reciprocal Russo-Turkish disarmament failed]. . . . He [Harcourt] will repeat and reinforce the request which Hartington will previously have made for information as to what passed . . . between January and March. . . . I [Dilke] shall speak . . . & . . . reinforce the arguments [of] . . . Hartington & Harcourt. . . . Which came first—our declaration, or the Russian declaration? I mean which was first communicated to the other government? . . . But Lord Derby rather likes declarations that destroy the force of documents he signs. Refer to the Luxembourg case 1867. Repeat that there is no evidence as to which declaration was decided first; that we ought to know, & that this justifies Hartington's motion for further papers . . .[67]

Hardy followed Hartington with a telling oration, deprecating forcible European coercion of Turkey. Dilke and Goschen spoke and both charged that the Government had made Russia mistress of the situation as well as having increased the possibility of war. Northcote ended by repudiating forcible coercion of Turkey, only to be followed by Hartington who withdrew his motion.[68] The debate had turned out well for the Government.

In the Lords there transpired a short but interesting discussion involving Granville and Derby on 16 April. To Granville's charge of Government inconsistency and back-tracking, comparing similarities between the Berlin Memorandum and the London Protocol, the Foreign Secretary made the following reply.

There is the widest possible difference between the one document and the other. . . . The 'efficacious measures' of the Berlin Memorandum really meant . . . military occupation [of Turkey] . . . [whereas the London protocol says] that if certain things [reforms] are not done by the Turkish Government—we [the Powers] being the judges whether they have been done or not . . . we will proceed, in common with the other Powers, to see what we will do.[69]

As it became clear that a Russo-Turkish war was about to occur, the Liberal sniping seemed more irrelevant and less damaging. But in view of the impending conflict, increasing Cabinet disunity, which had previously never been continuous nor so serious, was a bigger worry to Disraeli and the Queen than the Parliamentary tactics of the opposition. Derby had already exhibited a willingness to oppose all his colleagues, as he did on the question of Elliot's recall. Carvarnon and, at times, Salisbury, inconveniently expressed with Liberal fervour their concern for improved conditions for Turkey's Christians. And the Prime Minister himself, interpreting war as the beginning of the European partition of the Ottoman Empire, wished Britain to anticipate such partition, or, at least, to prepare militarily to take part in it and to defend her interests. With the outbreak of war the stresses and tensions within the Cabinet found greater scope for their expression and the possibility of Conservative self-destruction increased as the fissures within the Liberal camp increasingly made united Liberal attack more and more unlikely.

# 16 WAR: CONDITIONAL NEUTRALITY

THE OFFICIAL outbreak of war between Russia and Turkey on 24 April 1877 had already been anticipated by both Disraeli and Gladstone, who, each in his own way, were ready for active measures. The Prime Minister was concerned that, unless prepared, Britain would be left out of a partition of European Turkey, which he and others saw as the likely end of Turkish military defeat; nor was he prepared to watch while Russia marched unhindered to Constantinople. This reflected no sentimental feeling for Britain's Crimean War ally, but rather a desire to maintain British supremacy in the Mediterranean and British prestige in the East. He had, as he informed the Queen, adequate and appropriate proposals ready, but there was so much weakness and 'false religionism' that he had avoided summoning a Cabinet meeting until he could reconcile or overcome the varied and opposing opinions of his colleagues. Otherwise, he anticipated chaos would be the result.[1]

On 16 April Disraeli had a satisfactory talk with Hardy whom he called upon at the War Office and to whom he suggested an occupation of Gallipoli to secure the Dardanelles against Russia. The War Secretary recognized this as an idea of Colonel Home's with whom Disraeli had been conferring. Hardy, who believed the country would condemn the Government were Russia allowed to obtain Constaninople unchecked, urged the Premier to call a Cabinet meeting.[2] On the day following his talk with Hardy, Disraeli had separate and unsatisfactory parleys with weakness and 'false religionism'.

This morning, a torturing hour with Ld. Derby, who was for doing nothing, & this afternoon, with Lord Salisbury, who evidently is thinking more of raising the Cross on the cupola of St. Sophia, than the power of England.
. . .

Tomorrow [18 April] Ld Beaconsfield hopes to see the Lord Chancellor [Cairns], who generally helps him much in Cabinet.[3]

In his conference with Salisbury, Disraeli expressed anxiety that Russia might reach Constantinople before England could establish herself at the Dardanelles. It was estimated by the British military that it would take the Russians about twelve weeks to reach Constantinople. He therefore favoured at once asking the Porte's permission to occupy Gallipoli, giving it a promise to restore it at the end of the war.

I [Salisbury] objected to this proposal very strongly—insisting that such a course would be in effect an alliance with Turkey . . . [and argued] that there was no necessity for taking any action till Russia had passed the Balkans [mountain range]. . . . I added that I doubted Russia's intention to attack Constantinople. . . . He [Disraeli] told me that Derby was equally anxious for delay—so I have not much fear for the result. . . . I was with him for an hour—and when he saw he could make no impression on me, he was almost rude. Of this I took no notice, and left him.[4]

In his report to the Queen of his talk with the India Secretary, Disraeli said that Salisbury did not oppose the occupation providing that it was not executed with the consent of the Porte, as it would then seem that Britain was Turkey's ally and in his opinion England would never accept that.[5] Certainly, Salisbury's Christian conscience considered such an alliance a personal affront.

Hardy, who was more favourable to the Premier's plan, believed, on the contrary, as did the Foreign Secretary, that such an action should be taken only with the concurrence of the Porte. In the Prime Minister's discussion with Derby, the latter could be brought only to admit that such an occupation might eventually become necessary, but even then he considered the Porte's consent an indispensable requirement. If it were not obtained, according to the Foreign Secretary, such an occupation would mark the beginning of a scramble for the spoils of Turkey, which it ill became Britain to begin.[6] Cairns, who apparently approved of the Premier's forceful plan, considered Salisbury's objection legitimate and suggested that such an expedition might be preceded by an announcement which would clarify the country's mistaken impression which Salisbury apprehended.[7]

Despite his previous explanation to the Queen, the Prime Minister called a Cabinet meeting for 21 April knowing that Derby, Salisbury, and Carnarvon would oppose him. The dangers of delay, the lack of agreement between Salisbury and Derby, and the expectation of support from Hardy, Cairns, the Queen, and various war office memorandums account for his change of mind.[8]

Disraeli opened the meeting and presented to the assembled ministers a bleak picture for Turkey, based on British military information. Three to four months after crossing the Pruth Russia would be at Constantinople, and in Asia there appeared to be no adequate Turkish means of defence. He informed his colleagues that Russia's Baltic fleet had been ordered to the Mediterranean, where British investments and interests in Alexandria, Port Said, and the Suez Canal could be endangered and even destroyed.[9] Disraeli then asked how Britain might act, and his question ignited a two-hour discussion during which Carnarvon expressed his opposition to any expedition, indicating that the presence of the fleet at the Bosphorus would suffice. The Prime Minister's plan was temporarily saved when Hardy read a military report, which stated that the Russians intended upon reaching Adrianople to occupy the Dardanelles before advancing on Constantinople. This shocked the Cabinet into reconsidering Disraeli's plan, and when the meeting dispersed there seemed to be general agreement that some step or action was required, but what and when were left undecided.[10]

The meeting had been, for Hardy, surprisingly harmonious and Carnarvon, who wrote of this time in August 1879, was disappointed at Cairns's abrupt change of course in advocating the seizure of Gallipoli. The Colonial Secretary, who since the Bulgarian atrocities had been slightly paranoid about the Prime Minister's intentions, believed that Disraeli wished Britain to go to war. Such a desire, Carnarvon recorded, was also believed by Northcote with whom he talked on the day following the meeting. The latter wrote a long letter to Disraeli in which he argued that as British opinion prevented an Anglo-Turkish alliance, the seizure of Gallipoli was not compatible with a position of neutrality. On the other hand, if England delayed, she would be waiting until it had become too late to stop Russia. The Chancellor of the Exchequer then made two proposals; one was to concert with the other European Powers to see that the war was localized and limited. 'I also strongly urge the consideration whether we ought not to be prepared to take bodily possession of the Suez Canal in order to keep it open.'[11]

There was to be another Cabinet meeting four days later on 25 April ostensibly to consider Disraeli's suggestion of the occupation of Gallipoli or some other form of action to protect British interests. The news that the Russian and French consuls in Egypt were threatening the Khedive lest he send military aid to the Sultan, and the presence in London of Nubar Pasha, the Khedive's former minister, who privately was seeking Cabinet support for the establishment of a British protectorate there, induced Northcote to seek Cairns's help before the meeting.

Supposing Egypt to be threatened, what can we do to protect our undoubted interest in her safety and in the keeping open of our communications with the East? Can we, without a breach of neutrality, take precautions for the safety of the canal?

I think we are likely to be pressed for some decision tomorrow.

The Prime Minister reported to the Queen that the ministerial gathering on the twenty-fifth was both prolonged and turbulent, but generally acceptable. He proposed, and after resistance from Derby and Salisbury was overcome, the Cabinet agreed to order the Mediterranean fleet to Alexandria, leaving at least one ship there, before proceeding to Besika Bay. 'This is as much as Ld. Beaconsfield cd. have hoped on this occasion, but he is resolved to proceed. The Cabinet is to meet again tomorrow, to consider a reply to P[rince] Gorchakov's fraudulent & impertinent manifesto.'[12]

The following day the Cabinet met again to consider its answer to Gorchakov's circular, which was a Russian attempt to disguise its invasion by presenting it as an attack on Turkey in the name of Europe. After a fair amount of agreement the ministers decided for the preparation of a draft answer. Cross, the Home Secretary, described his colleagues as unanimous on the point of not allowing Gorchakov's haughty circular to go unanswered. One of his colleagues, at least, Salisbury, while having no confidence in Russian intentions or promises, equally saw no reason to dread or fear St. Petersburg.

There is nothing in their [Russia's] history . . . to explain the abject terror which deprives so many Anglo-Indians, and so many of our

military party here, of their natural sleep. Except in conflict with bar-
barians, Orientals, or the Poles who were little better, their military
history has been one long record of defeat. Their only trophies have
been the repulse, on two occasions, of civilized invaders after a long
course of victories had brought them to the heart of the Empire—at
Moscow and Poltowa. Their finances, never good, are now desperate.
Their social condition is a prolonged crisis threatening . . . socialist
revolution. . . . Their officials [are] corrupt. . . . And yet we are asked
to believe that their presence in the Black Sea or the Bosphorus
would be a serious menance to England in the Mediterranean. . . .
We shall have probably to defend Constantinople if attacked for
reasons of prestige, which those who govern Oriental nations cannot
afford to overlook.[13]

And Northcote, who had been pushing to take over the Canal
rather than occupy Gallipoli, now suggested an occupation of
Crete with the Porte's assent, again as an alternative preferable
to Gallipoli.[14]

The ministers met again on 28 April and agreed to an
energetic response to Gorchakov's circular, as well as settling
the declaration of British neutrality. Cairns, who like Northcote had begun to take a prominent part in foreign affairs
along with Hardy, Salisbury, Derby, Carnarvon, and Disraeli,
then made a strong statement in favour of occupying the Dardanelles as the best measure to secure Britain's interests. The
Foreign Secretary replied with a substitute; Russia to be informed that an occupation of Constantinople would bring
England into the war. His colleagues reacted negatively to this,
realizing that once Russia had occupied the Dardanelles and
Constantinople, it would be very difficult for Britain then to
have recourse to war measures against her. Salisbury reluctantly accepted occupation of Gallipoli, but desired to put it off
until the necessity for it was absolutely clear. 'The Ld.
Chancellor replied that according to the statements of the
military authorities, we had only now a fortnight in our favour,
& that delay was impossible. Finally it was agreed that the
Cabinet shd meet again on Tuesday [1 May] at eleven o'ck., &
that Genl Sir Lintorn Simmons shd. attend it.'[15] Before the
meeting on 1 May Northcote continued his attempt to
galvanize support against adopting what he considered to be a
war policy without allies. He now suggested to Derby what he
thought was England's true policy.

I would ... address a categorical though friendly question to Russia as to the objects she proposes to aim at ... warning her at the same time that we should feel ourselves obliged to take measures to protect our own interests if we should consider them to be endangered by the course of the struggle. ... Secondly, I would ask Austria frankly to join us in guaranteeing that none of the six powers should occupy Constantinople. ... Thirdly, I would lose no time in taking bodily possession of the Suez Canal. ... If he [the Khedive] required a bribe I should not mind ...[16]

Outside the Cabinet, both the Queen, whom Ponsonby and Biddulph were attemping to soothe, and Loftus were proposing bold measures. The ambassador in St. Petersburg reported to Derby the necessity for immediate steps to prevent a Russian occupation of Constantinople. Lady Derby presumably told Shuvalov of Loftus's suspicions of Russian intentions, and the Russian ambassador advised Gorchakov of the need to quiet and calm Loftus. Layard in Constantinople was prepared to go much farther than Loftus. He asked Derby on 24 April whether he should get the Porte to request the sending of the fleet to Constantinople as provided for by article 2 of the Treaty of London of 1871.[17] Derby, of course, replied that such a step would be inappropriate at the present time. The ambassador, who was alarmed that the Turks were doing nothing to fortify the land defences around Constantinople and the Dardanelles, then made another suggestion which was adopted by the Government.

If her Majesty's Government thought it possible and desirable to send some English officer of experience and weight out here, who might influence Turkish counsels before it is too late, it might be of great importance to do so.

I venture to mention the name of Sir Collingwood Dickson ...[18]

The Cabinet meeting of 1 May was the fifth in eleven days and rumours of ministerial disunity were rampant. Carnarvon wrote of them to Salisbury. 'There are reports current of schisms in the Cabinet—oddly enough combining your North-cote & my names. It is serious: but it may perhaps do no harm under the circumstances.' On 30 April the official British proclamation of neutrality was issued, and the Cabinet on the first adopted an answer to Gorchakov's circular. It also agreed to communicate with Austria, France, and Italy with a view to preserving freedom of navigation in the Mediterranean. The question of occupying the Dardanelles was left open, but Russia was to be told that any one of the following would bring Britain into the war: the occupation of Constantinople, an attack on Egypt, or the obstruction of the Dardanelles.[19]

On the same day as the Cabinet meeting, 1 May, Loftus was instructed to communicate Britain's official answer to Gorchakov's circular.

Her Majesty's Government have received this communication with deep regret. They cannot accept the statements and conclusions with which Prince Gorchakow has accompanied it, as justifying the resolution thus taken.
. . .

Her Majesty's Government cannot therefore admit, as is contended by Prince Gorchakow, that the answer of the Porte [to the London Protocol] removed all hope of deference on its part to the wishes and advice of Europe, and all security for the application of the suggested reforms . . .

It cannot be expected that Her Majesty's Government should agree in this view [that Russia 'has resolved to undertake the task of obtaining by coercion that which the unanimous efforts of all the Powers have failed to obtain from the Porte by persuasion']. They have not concealed their feeling that the presence of large Russian forces on the frontiers of Turkey, menacing its safety, rendering disarmament impossible, and exciting a feeling of apprehension and fanatacism among the Mussulman population, constituted a material obstacle to internal pacification and reform. They cannot believe that the entrance of those armies on Turkish soil will alleviate the difficulty, or improve the condition of the Christian population . . .
. . .

The Emperor of Russia has separated himself from the European concert hitherto maintained, and has at the same time departed from the rule to which he himself had solidly recorded his consent [in the Treaty of London of 1871 'that no power can liberate itself from the engagements of a Treaty', in this case the Treaty of Paris of 30 March 1856, 'unless with the consent of the Contracting Parties']

As Prince Gorchakow seems to assume in a declaration addressed to all the Governments of Europe, that Russia is acting in the interest of Great Britain and that of the other powers, they feel bound to state in a manner equally formal and public, that the decision of the Russian Government is not one which can have their concurrence or approval.[20]

This dispatch and other signs convinced Shuvalov that it would be dangerous for Russia to aim at totally crushing the Turks, and he decided to return to St. Petersburg to urge Nicholas II and Gorchakov of the need to placate Britain and to be satisfied with a negotiated peace once the Danube had been crossed and a victory or two won.[21] Before departing, the Russian ambassador was given a dispatch, approved by a Cabinet meeting on 5 May, to carry back with him to his Government. The friendly warning was described by the Prime Minister as 'spirited, & tho cautious, & even conciliatory, most decidedly unmistakeable'.[22]

It represented the most which the members of the Government could unite upon, as that group would not or could not carry out a straightforward pro-Turkish line or court the ignominy of allowing an unrestricted Russian destruction of Ottoman Europe.

I [Derby] take this occasion of placing before them [the Russian government] some considerations of importance to the future good understanding between Great Britain and Russia.
. . .

Should the war now in progress unfortunately spread, interests may be imperilled which they [H.M. Government] are equally bound and determined to defend, and it is desirable that they should make it clear, so far as at the outset of the war can be done, what the most prominent of those interests are.

Keeping open the Suez Canal, no occupation of either Egypt or Constantinople, no changes in the present international regulations of the Bosphorus and the Dardanelles, and protection of the Persian Gulf were the enumerated interests.[23]

On the eighth, before he left for Russia, Shuvalov personally expressed himself well satisfied with the Foreign Secretary's note to him of 6 May. He told Derby that England need not be apprehensive about any of the British interests mentioned. The only reservation the ambassador made had to do with a desire expressed in Russia to be rid of the restrictions presently limiting the navigation of the Bosphorus and the Dardanelles.[24]

On 11 May Shuvalov called on Derby to announce his departure for Russia, indicating his absence from London would not exceed twenty-five days. He gave it as his earnest desire that the British Government would avoid any decisive act pending the satisfactory explanations he hoped to make.

I asked Count Shuvalov what he meant by a decisive step.

His Excellency replied that he referred to such measures as the putting of the British army on a war footing or the sending of our fleet up to the Dardanelles.

I told His Excellency that I could make no promise on such a subject, and, indeed, he had not asked me for one, but that I thought it in the highest degree improbable that either of the steps to which he referred would be taken.[25]

Just before Shuvalov left for St. Petersburg and during his journey there[26] and back to London, secret Anglo-Austrian negotiations were taking place. It is not clear who initiated them. Beust informed Derby that he asked Andrássy whether, in view of the outbreak of war, it would not be expedient to concert ideas with London. Andrássy replied that the two countries should closely discuss together their present problems. As the Cabinet meeting of 30 April had agreed on the desirability of an approach to Austria, Derby requested Beust to call upon him a few days after the note of 6 May had been given to Shuvalov. Britain's need for Austrian military co-operation had been stressed in a memorandum written by Simmons and read by both Hardy and Disraeli. He expected Turkey to be quickly routed by Russia, and argued that England alone could then hold Gallipoli but could not prevent Russia from taking Constantinople without an Austrian alliance. When Beust and Derby met, the latter gave him a copy of the British note of 6 May and amplified and explained its meaning. Beust replied that he would need to communicate with Vienna before he could give any official reaction.[27]

Derby, pressed by his colleagues, prepared a draft dispatch for Austria. The Cabinet had apparently agreed to offer Austria a military alliance for the protection of Constantinople.[28] Derby chose to ignore this, and drew up a draft containing an invitation to Austria to discuss rather than to conclude such an agreement. The Foreign Secretary then submitted the draft to all of his colleagues individually for their suggestions, and found that he stood alone. Salisbury made the following comments:

The wording of this draft does not seem to me to carry out, what (I understood) was the unanimous wish of the Cabinet, that a formal offer should be made to Austria. It is only an invitation to discuss. I believe that our only chance of moving Austria will be an offer to cooperate in taking measures to secure that Constantinople shall not fall into Russian hands.

Carnarvon's reactions were similar to Salisbury's.

The last part of the draft does not seem . . . to express with sufficient distinctness our readiness to combine with Austria in a joint naval & military operation . . . in certain events. Looking to the shortness of time available and the timidity of Austria, I think our offer should be unequivocally clear, and that it should be an offer rather of joint action than of discussion, to produce any good.

Hardy, Manners, Hicks-Beach, Cairns, Cross, Northcote, and Ward Hunt agreed with Carnarvon and Salisbury. The Home Secretary and Disraeli suggested a subsidy for Austria.[29]

The Foreign Secretary, even more than in the previous case involving Elliot's recall, ignored his colleagues' united recommendation and made a few inconsequential changes in his draft. He sent it together with the opinions of all the ministers to Disraeli. He also enclosed an explanation. 'I do not see what more is necessary. Nobody ever yet made such an offer of joint action without first sounding a little to see how it would be taken: if Andrassy means, or wishes to go with us, the language is plain enough; if he does not, a more abrupt procedure will not alter his decision.' Beust was called to the Foreign Office by the Foreign Secretary.

I [Derby] informed him [Beust] of the desire of Her Majesty's Government to enter into confidential communications with that of Austria on the subject of the steps to be taken in the advent of a Russian advance on Constantinople. I told him that I would place in his hand a written memorandum or letter embodying the ideas of the British Government. . . . I then proceeded to state verbally the contents of the document in question explaining that the purport of it was in strict accordance with the warning already conveyed to the Russian Govt in my note to Count Schouvaloff of the 6th of May.

Count Beust promised to lose no time in reporting to his government what I had said.[30]

The unity of the Cabinet was not deep, and even agreement to defend Constantinople reflected real differences. Northcote,

Cross, Carnarvon, and perhaps Salisbury favoured it as a step preferable to a British Gallipoli expedition, the existence of which would be sufficient it was hoped to restrain Russia without any need to resort to military measures. The above four with Manners and Beach considered and hoped that Austria might accept a directly offered English alliance. Cairns, Hardy, and Disraeli wished to take some positive step to defend Constantinople and the Dardanelles. The Prime Minister and Lord Chancellor preferred an occupation of Gallipoli, and Disraeli, who did not believe there was much chance of Austria accepting an alliance with Britain, was willing to seek one any way because some of his colleagues believed it might succeed. Then, perhaps, agreement would follow on a British occupation of Gallipoli. Derby, even more than Disraeli, thought that Andrássy would refuse any English offer, that Austrian interests were along the Danube and those of Britain were in Asia, and that neither he nor Austrian statesmen would believe that Constantinople was presently threatened.[31] He undoubtedly hoped that a positive Russian answer to his note of 6 May would preclude the necessity of a military compact with Vienna. Northcote still leaned towards occupying Egypt if it could somehow be justified internationally.[32] Only Disraeli's poor health and affection for Derby, and the deep differences within the Cabinet, explain the absence of any move to get the Foreign Secretary to resign.

Disraeli, Cairns, Carnarvon, and Salisbury were much disturbed by Derby's handling of the Austrian negotiations. The Prime Minister warned him that a failure to protect British interests would lead to a fall of the Government. 'A Government can only die once: it is better to die with glory, than vanish in an ignominious end. The country would still rally round British interests: in three months' time, Brit. interests will be in the mud.' Carnarvon talked to Montgelas of the Austrian Embassy about the British proposal to Austria to defend Constantinople. He wrote of that conversation to Salisbury.

The clear understanding of the Cabinet was ... that Derby shd. in conversation supplement his note by intimating our readiness to undertake for Austria the transport of her troops to Gallipoli or Constantinople and even further to indicate our readiness to give what Disraeli called a *buono-mano*.

Derby however seems to have remained absolutely silent and to have said nothing on either of these points. ... [The British] offer, wanting in all 'practical point' as Montgelas termed it, will probably fail of real acceptance. It is really despairing ...

Cairns complained strongly to the Premier that the Government was doing nothing to protect those interests which had been defined as British. Salisbury replied to Carnarvon's letter. 'It is as you say quite despairing. It seems to me we must give up all hope of any positive action on foreign policy. We may prevent evil; but we can do no more. The result will be an emasculate, purposeless vacillation; but perhaps it is what suits our nation best.'[33]

Derby defended his indisposition to act, and explained it to the Premier, who had argued that inaction would bring Parliamentary disapproval. He said that he believed that the middle classes were so greatly opposed to war that the seizure of an important strategic position would not justify the support lost by the necessity of asking for money for an expedition. Disraeli replied that 'nothing can justify isolation on the part of England but a determination to act'. Carnarvon's memory of this time in August 1879 was that as Derby grew more inflexible in his determination to avoid military measures, Salisbury was sliding closer to Disraeli. Realizing that it was neither possible to make Turkey strong, nor in view of the majority feeling of both the Liberal and Conservative M.P.s to assist in destroying her, Salisbury disclaimed on the question of Russian weakness and convinced himself of the necessity of defending British interests by artificially separating them from the maintenance of Ottoman integrity. He wrote to Lytton in India: 'We cling to the shred of an old policy after it has been torn to pieces. And to the shadow of the shred after the rag itself has been torn away.'[34]

One of the reasons that Disraeli and Cairns stressed the Parliamentary need to defend British interests was that Parliament had left them in the Government's hands by returning a majority of 131 against resolutions of Gladstone which were critical of the ministry. 'The country has left us to guard "British interests": & if anything miscarries as to them, no mercy will be shewn us either by foes or friends on the score that we were hampered by the H. of C. [ommons]. With a

majority of 130, it will be said, we might have done anything.'[35]
If the Cabinet could not unite sufficiently to act, neither could
the Liberals reach adequate agreement to mount an effective
attack on the Government. Gladstone made an attempt to do
the latter in May which resulted in nearly destroying the
Liberal party.

### Gladstone's Resolutions and Birmingham

On 16 April Chamberlain wrote to Gladstone on behalf of
the Birmingham Liberals to invite him to attend and speak at a
great meeting there on 31 May before an assembled gathering
of Liberal associations formed along the lines of the Birmingham model. 'The occasion too, will be one of exceptional
interest, as it is the inauguration of an effort to secure greater
unity of aim & action on the part of Liberal organisations; &
also to make these bodies more thoroughly representative of
all sections of the party.' The outbreak of war led Gladstone
not only to respond favourably to Chamberlain but to prepare,
against the advice of Granville and fifteen other prominent
Liberals, some anti-Government resolutions for presentation
to Parliament. Bright was asked to see Gladstone to attempt to
dissuade him from his resolve of acting alone, but the latter indicated that his conscience and sense of responsibility would
not allow him to remain quiet.[36]

Argyll, one of the few supporters of Gladstone's intended
action among the Liberal leadership, warned him of a potential danger. He was anxious that the framing of Gladstone's
motion, which he assumed would be defeated, might be such
as would aid the war party in the Cabinet or the growth of opinion to aid Turkey outside it. 'Such an inference . . . will be
very serious. . . . The value will be in your speech—not in the
motion itself.' Chamberlain recognized the same danger.

If as is probable the resolution is defeated by a large majority, this
will strengthen the anti-Russian party in the cabinet & the H. of C. &
may lead to the very results we deprecate.

Yet I am tired of nothing done & am glad that something like a
definite issue is contemplated.

Except for Cowen, the Radicals—Dilke, Fawcett, and Chamberlain—despite the possibility of splitting the Liberal party into
two factions, were prepared to support Gladstone. On 29 April

the latter showed his resolutions to Argyll who thought that they avoided the apprehended danger.

> If the Liberal Party voted together the minority wd be too formidable to allow any warlike action on the part of the Government—with any safety.
>
> I write this to you [Hartington] simply to express the opinion I strongly hold that Gladstone shd. be supported if it is at all possible . . .[37]

On 30 April Gladstone gave notice of his five resolutions in the House of Commons. They proclaimed that until the Porte gave good Government to its Christians, the moral and material support of Britain would be withheld from it. Further, that the Government should help promote a 'concert of the European powers' which would require the Porte to grant local self-government to its European provinces. The ambiguity of the resolutions was calculated, and the first one, condemning the Porte for the Bulgarian atrocities, was so placed because it would attract general agreement. Brand, the Speaker of the House, thought the second resolution highly objectionable. Hartington was naturally upset because Gladstone's behaviour was a challenge to his authority as Liberal leader and because the Whig magnates had already decided not to challenge the Government. Forster, Hartington, and others decided to meet the resolutions by moving the previous question.

> That . . . means that we think they [the resolutions] are out of time, and ought not to be proposed at this present crisis.
>
> For myself [Forster], the meaning of Gladstone's resolutions . . . is just what I should have liked before Russia declared war; but now that there is war, I think the time for them is past . . .

Northcote reported to the Queen, whose anger at Russia and Gladstone was very great, that the latter had lost any kind of self-control. 'There is a general impression that Mr. Gladstone has become so much excited by a morbid idea that he is partly responsible for the Bulgarian outrages, on account of his support of the Crimean War, that he does not know what he is doing. His late colleagues have done all they could to stop this last act, but have failed.'[38]

A meeting of Gladstone's ex-colleagues occurred at Gran-

ville's house on 2 May and the Liberal leadership agreed to
support the previous question. Dilke counted 110 Liberal
M.P.s who would vote with Gladstone. It appeared that the
Liberal party would destroy itself before the Cabinet dis-
integrated. Chamberlain, like Dilke and Brand, thought the
party would split, but was not so unhappy at this prospect. He
wrote to Stead commending him for rousing the North in
favour of the resolutions. Stratford de Redcliffe now moved
away from Gladstone. Both men wanted a concert of the European Powers, but whereas the latter wanted it in order to
coerce Turkey to reform, the former saw it as an opportunity
to check Russian ambition. On 5 May Granville with Hartington arranged a scheme with Gladstone to avoid a party
split. Forster also helped to arrange the compromise by which
Gladstone agreed to withdraw the last three resolutions, which
raised the issue of the coercion of the Porte, and restricted
himself to the first two, the second of which he altered. The
Whig front bench correspondingly agreed not to move the
previous question.[39]

The five-day debate began on 7 May. As the Liberal compromise had been arranged only at the last moment, it was impossible to hide it from the Conservatives who greeted the
Liberal discomfiture with jeers and laughter. Two hours were
taken up in a technical discussion over points of order during
which Radical disenchantment with Gladstone's withdrawal of
three of his resolutions was made manifest. After such a dis-
piriting beginning, Gladstone, with immense courage, great
eloquence, and almost inexhaustible energy, made one of the
most moving speeches ever heard in the House of Commons.
He charged that nothing had been done by the Porte to punish
the guilty for the Bulgarian atrocities, and that the Government, preoccupied with the Russo-Turkish conflict, had ignored the controversy between the Porte and its subjects in
revolt. 'I do not hesitate to say that the cause of the revolted
subjects of Turkey against their oppressors is as holy a cause as
ever animated the breast, or as ever stirred the hand of man.'
He spoke of Cabinet disunity and the inexpediency of allowing
unfettered Russian coercion of Turkey. Cross spoke for the
Government and made an impressive and effective reply.
'What he [Gladstone] means is this—"If you will only say you

will go to war if they [the Turks] don't do these things, although you don't mean to go to war; if you will only bark loud enough, though you don't mean to bite, Turkey will give way." Well, I call that conduct utterly unworthy of us. (Cheers). Yes, you [the Liberals] tried that policy once in the case of Denmark.'[40]

The debate was resumed the following day and one of the speeches was by Roebuck who criticized Gladstone for pushing England into a war for humanity with a Russian ally who was as guilty as the Turks. He argued that wars for humanity tend to be endless crusades as all nations at times commit acts which are abhorrent to humanity.

Is not that [the conduct of the white man to the Indians in America] as atrocious as anything which has been recited in these debates? ... And are we going in our crusade of humanity to address the Government of Washington and say—'Your conduct now to the Red Man is such as we humane people cannot possibly in any way permit. We intend to go to war with you because you have been inhuman?'

Sandon made a very effective speech for the Government.

He noticed that Mr. Gladstone had said that Lord Derby's despatch of September 21 on the subject of the Bulgarian atrocities ought either to have been followed up by action or to have been torn to shreds as a vague insult to Turkey. But, said Lord Sandon, what we are now asked to do is, to repeat by a vote of the House of Commons, the despatch of Lord Derby. It follows that our vote must either be treated as an impertinence or be followed up by action,—that is, by war against Turkey. The speech was highly successful; and that, and Mr. Cross' speech of last night, have given the Government a great advantage in the debate.[41]

As the debate entered its third night, after a one-day respite, on 10 May, the Liberals were divided into four camps: the front bench, those who supported Gladstone's emasculated resolutions, those who stuck to the entire five, and the group which wanted peace at any price. A large number of M.P.s rose in order to speak, but the quality and interest of the discussion were not sustained by the number of speakers. On the fourth night of the debate Goschen made a speech in support of Gladstone, arguing that as the maintenance of the integrity and independence of the Ottoman Empire was no longer a

British interest no moral or material support should go to Turkey. He underlined Gladstone's contention of British responsibility for the situation of Turkey's Christians. 'It was because we had maintained that Power [Turkey] by our arms, our treasures, and our Treaties, under whose sway the Christian populations were now placed, and were now suffering . . . and it was because the country felt its responsibility that it was so excited.'[42]

On the last night of debate, on 14 May, Hartington spoke with vigour and cogency. He indicated that in comparison with Turkish misrule, Russian misdeeds were not endangering the peace of Europe, and therefore were no argument against those who deprecated Ottoman cruelty. On the other hand, as war had broken out, the coercion of Turkey, which might have prevented that war, belonged to a time that was past. 'The Turkish domination is a lifeless trunk, the struggling nationalities are the living tree; and this House is asked tonight to assert that with these nationalities, and not with the remnant of a sad and shameful past, are the sympathies of the British nation and its destinies to be associated.' Northcote then spoke, relatively ineffectively, for neutrality and Gladstone finished the debate he had begun, not pressing his second resolution. The House divided at 2.10 a.m. on Gladstone's first resolution with 223 in favour and 354 opposed, giving the Government a majority of 131. The following amendment was then agreed to without a division being taken:

That this house declines to entertain any Resolutions which may embarrass Her Majesty's Government in the maintenance of peace and in the protection of British interests, without indicating any alternative line of policy.[43]

The coercion of Turkey was now buried, and as Seton Watson has pointed out, considering the fact of the outbreak of war, the whole debate seemed remote from the actual events in the Balkans. But the discussion was useful, as Brand noted at the time, in manifesting the negative opinion of the House towards Turkey, mistrust for Russia, and the firm decision to maintain the interests of England. Those who believed the Government was preparing for war listened to the official line of neutrality with relief. Granville, who was satisfied with the way his party voted, temporarily interpreted the Government's speeches as an indication that Disraeli, and presumably a war policy had been defeated. Though weakness and division in Liberal ranks was made obvious, the disinclination to help Turkey as an ally was equally manifest.[44] Finally, though the House did not realize it, the praise for Cross's speech, even from the Liberals, was an endorsement of Derby's note to Shuvalov of 6 May.

Immediately after the debate Gladstone wrote and accepted Chamberlain's invitation to speak at Birmingham, a course deprecated by Hartington and Granville, as well as others, who suspected that Chamberlain's only intention was to destroy Whig dominance in the leadership of the Liberal party. The reasons for Gladstone's decision, which he gave to Granville, were to help repair the rents in the Liberal ranks and to keep the Government straight by means of continuous pressure. Disraeli especially, he felt, needed to be watched round the clock. His state of mind, which may be seen from a letter to Arthur Gordon, had become feverish.

I have never known the country so excited upon any question. No small portion of excitement finds its way to me personally, in the shape of a kind of idolising sentiment among the people such as I never before experienced. ... The master and main spring on the other side is Lord Beaconsfield, backed I fear ... though it is most sad to write this, by the Queen ... with the aid of the anti-Russian sentiment now sustained at fever heat in London by the action of the Anglo-Turkish newspapers. ... I have watched very closely his [Disraeli's] strange & at first sight inexplicable proceedings on this Eastern Question: and I believe their fountainhead to be race antipathy, that aversion which the Jews, with a few honourable exceptions, are showing so vindictively towards the Eastern Christians. Though he has been baptized, his Jew feelings are the most radical & the most real, & so far respectable, portion of his profoundly falsified nature.

Hartington rightly felt that Gladstone's continued prominence in leading the party on the Eastern Question could only result in future party splits, unless and until the ex-Prime Minister either formally assumed party leadership or got down from the pulpit.[45]

On 31 May Gladstone arrived in Birmingham to a tumultuous welcome and helped to inaugurate the newly organized Liberal Federation which represented the Liberal associations throughout Britain. In the evening he addressed some 30,000 people at Bingley Hall, explaining the necessity of opposing both the Cabinet and the House of Commons.

[The Government] 'steadily and constantly watching its opportunity for the slightest appearance of division or tacit remission in the manifestation of public feeling, turning its course directly to the old sense of virtual assistance to the Turk, like the dog returning to his vomit, or the sow to her wallowing in the mire. . . . You have the House of Commons against you . . .

'We have a great responsibility in working upon a matter of foreign policy . . . against the Executive Government, and against the sense of the House of Commons. It is a thing that is rarely done, and it is a thing which I hope will rarely have occasion to be done again . . .'

The meeting then adopted a resolution almost identical to the one the House of Commons had just defeated. The Queen asked Hicks-Beach his opinion of all this. The latter deeply regretted Gladstone's systematic agitation on a question of foreign policy against both the executive and the House of Commons. '[He also regretted that Gladstone] should appeal to popular meetings against "the Government" . . . and demand a dissolution of Parliament because both Houses, constitutionally representing the people, differ from his peculiar views and are in complete accord with your Majesty's Government.' A great deal of public opinion supported Gladstone against the Government and the House of Commons.[46] Unfortunately for the Radicals and Gladstone, anti-Russian sentiment in pamphlets, in the Press, and in Parliament was increasing, and with the end of the five day debate a kind of party truce in Parliament on the Eastern Question came about which was to last until the end of the session.[47]

## The Cabinet

Whether, and how long, the Government was prepared to adhere to the neutrality which Parliament applauded was dependent upon Shuvalov's success in St. Petersburg in winning the Tsar over to a limited war, Andrássy's response to talks on alliance with Britain, and the events of the war itself.

There seems little doubt that in St. Petersburg Shuvalov argued for a quick and moderate peace to be made by Russia after crossing the Danube and obtaining a military victory. Bismarck, who had seen Shuvalov on his way to Russia, told Odo Russell on 21 May that such were the ambassador's intentions. In a private letter to Ponsonby, Loftus wrote that Gorchakov had told him that Shuvalov was England's best advocate. Loftus himself had completely changed his opinion, however, as to Russia and her intentions, warning Derby that Gorchakov's object was to lull England into maintaining a passive policy until it was too late to prevent a Russian occupation of Constantinople. The ambassador believed that Britain should at once occupy the Dardanelles and Constantinople. Derby was impatient for the Russian answer to his note of 6 May, and on the twenty-third requested the Russian chargé to press Gorchakov not to delay the Russian reply.[48]

Layard, worried by Kemball's[49] pessimistic reports of a complete Ottoman collapse in Armenia, and wishing to put Russia's intentions to a test, suggested to Derby on 24 May that an attempt at mediation be made while Russian forces had not yet been able to cross the Danube. In a second telegram on the same day Layard informed the Foreign Secretary that the Sultan had hinted to him on that very morning that if Britain would undertake to arrange a peace with Montenegro, he would make some territorial concession to her so long as too much were not asked. To this the ambassador replied that he feared that Montenegrin demands would now be greater than the Porte could admit. Ironically, Derby was of the same opinion concerning the possibility of a successful mediation between Russia and Turkey, thinking the step premature. 'Personally I am not inclined to be hopeful of the success of an attempt to bring the combatants to terms at present. Even supposing the Sultan and his advisers to be favourably disposed, I doubt much whether the Russians would as yet consent to conditions such as could be accepted at Constantinople.'[50]

In Constantinople Layard had established a much closer and more intrusive relationship with the Sultan than his predecessor had done. He saw it as part of his task to win a personal ascendancy over the Ottoman ruler, and in his advice and interference went far beyond the normal behaviour of an ambassador at a foreign court, even at Constantinople. Questions in Parliament and British opinion elicited frequent warnings from him to the Porte about suspected Circassian or Muslim cruelties and the need to punish or at least not to employ people like Chefket Pasha who were responsible for earlier atrocities in Bulgaria. He pressed strongly for freedom to be granted to the Bulgarians still in Ottoman prisons as a result of the rising in May 1876. He continually urged the necessity to erect fortifications to defend Constantinople and the Dardanelles, and kept the Sultan informed of the real military situation which he was not told about. He did not hesitate to criticize to the Sultan the inefficient or undesirable conduct of his civil and military officials. It is small wonder, therefore, that even though Layard always indicated when the occasion arose, that Turkey could expect no military assistance from Britain, the belief persisted in Constantinople that such assistance eventually would come. At the end of May the ambassador privately informed Derby of his frustrating situation.

Being without any definite instructions from you as to the course I should pursue here, I have thought that the best, and only thing that I could do, under present circumstances, is to prepare the mind of the Sultan and his Ministers for peace should there be an opening for mediation—I hope that I have acted in accordance with the wishes of yourself and Her Majesty's Government . . .[51]

On 3 June Loftus telegraphed that Shuvalov would leave St. Petersburg the following day with the Russian answer. The latter indicated to Loftus that he thought and hoped that it would meet with the approval of the British Government. Before the contents could be delivered to Derby on 8 June, Andrássy's reply to British overtures arrived on the first. As Beaconsfield reported to the Queen, the Cabinet, which met on 2 June, was satisfied with the Austrian answer and agreed to carry into effect the combined views of the two governments. The Queen was at Balmoral and asked Hicks-Beach, who was in attendance, to impress upon the Cabinet the necessity of taking firm measures and keeping the Anglo-Austrian negotiations secret. The minister commented upon the Austrian answer.

That despatch is as satisfactory . . . as could have been expected . . .
It defines the points which, in the interests of Austria-Hungary,

cannot be consented to. Among those points is (not only the possession, but) the *occupation* by Russia of Constantinople: and it is stated
that the 'free passage of the Bosphorus & the Dardanelles for Russian
shipping' is comprised in that question . . .

Having defined Austrian interests, Count Andrassy states the
determination of Austria-Hungary to 'stand up for them, if necessary, by force of arms': and adds that 'there remains for a further
exchange of ideas the question of coming to an understanding as to
the means by which these interests can be most securely protected.'

It therefore appears that Austria-Hungary is prepared to join
Great Britain in something more than diplomatic action.

The main point therefore now is, that no time should be lost in
deciding what the joint action of the two powers . . . should be, in the
event of the necessity for action arising.

Sir M. Hicks Beach expects that the Cabinet will agree . . . to accept
the 7 points named by Count Andrassy, and to discuss with Austria-
Hungary the means for giving effect to them. Some of them appear to
him to be matters of interest to Austria rather than to England . . .

Disraeli was not only urging Derby to come to an agreement
with Austria, but was prepared, if this negotiation ended
successfully to concert as well with Italy, Greece, and others.[52]

On 8 June Shuvalov communicated to Derby Gorchakov's
reply to the dispatch of 6 May, which reassured the British
Government that Russia would touch neither Egypt nor the
Suez Canal. As to the Straits the Russians implied the need for
a new arrangement there, but one to be reached by all the
Powers. The question of the ultimate disposal of Constantinople was also described as one of common interest. The issue of
a temporary Russian occupation of the city, which might be
required by the events of the war, was side-stepped, as was occupation of the Straits. This therefore remained a possibility,
the existence of which was unsatisfactory to London. Shuvalov
explained to Derby that Russia could not bind herself
beforehand to the course of military operations. The note
described Russia's object as the termination of the misery of
Turkey's Christians.

The Russian ambassador also communicated to the Foreign
Secretary the peace terms his Government would accept if the
Porte could be brought to sue for peace before Russian forces
crossed the Balkan Mountains. These were an autonomous
Bulgarian principality under European guarantee extending

only to the Bulgarian Mountains, an increase in territory for
Serbia and Montenegro, good administration for the other
parts of European Turkey and for Bosnia-Hercegovina, part of
the latter going to Austria if it became necessary to give her
compensation, independence for Romania or else her acquisition of the Dobruja, and Batum and the part of Bessarabia
ceded in 1856 for Russia. Shuvalov then asked Derby if, having
made these communications, his Government could depend
on British neutrality. The Foreign Secretary replied that a
Cabinet meeting would be necessary before he could reply.[53]

A long meeting was held to consider the Russian communications. The reply to the note of 6 May, as Disraeli
reported to the Queen, was not well received. 'The general
conviction was, that it contemplated the "occupation" of
Constantinople, & that, if the Russians were once there, altho
only in a "military" sense, they would not evacuate it until they
had made terms highly advantageous to themselves, & probably highly prejudicial to England.' Derby then verbally stated
the substance of Russia's confidential peace terms which at first
Disraeli described as reasonable and not inconsistent with
English interests. The Cabinet decided to meet again to consider them, and in the meantime resolved to urge Andrássy on
the pending negotiations, losing no time in offering her an
alliance. Disraeli upon reconsideration of Russia's peace offer
did not feel it to be satisfactory. He interpreted the Russian
requirement of neutrality as prohibiting any British expedition
to Constantinople or the Dardanelles.

The probable result . . . would be, that Russia would take care, that
Turkey would decline to make peace, & then Russia would march
into Constantinople, having previously occupied the Dardanelles, &
would dictate her terms to Europe.

Lord Derby seems for peace at any price, & Lord Salisbury seems
to think, that the progress of Russia is the progress of religion &
civilisation.

Lord Beaconsfield does not believe, that this is the feeling of the
British people, & that if they woke one morning to hear, that the
Russians are in Constantinople, they will sweep the Ministers . . . off
the board of public life altogether.

He still hopes to bring the Cabinet to a unanimous resolution
. . . & he counts entirely on Yr. Majesty's support on which all must
depend.[54]

As in the past, it was to the Queen to whom Disraeli now appealed for support, asking her to write to the Foreign Secretary in the hope of overcoming his fears. The Queen did so, counselling Derby to be firm and energetic in the face of Russian perfidy. Hesitation and delay, she wrote, could be fatal. Derby replied to the Queen on 11 June that though burdensome and even humiliating he did not think Turkey could obtain any better peace terms from Russia. He wrote that an English war, except one in self-defence, would be unpopular, and that Gorchakov's reply to his note of 6 May concerning British interests he found on the whole acceptable. Northcote, however, was not reassured by Russia's answer as it left the latter free to occupy Constantinople and to arrange a peace from that city. Manners was also unsatisfied and could not understand Derby's complacency, and wrote to Disraeli opposing any advice to the Turks to make peace on these terms.[55]

On 12 June Derby telegraphed the Russian peace terms to Layard and asked him whether he thought the Porte might consent to them. Layard replied that the Porte would refuse to consider such terms and that they were so harsh and dangerous that were Britain to mediate for peace on the basis of them, she would lose all her influence in the Ottoman Empire and among the Muslims in India as well. The ambassador saw in them both a Russian trap and the abandonment of Turkey, which would be most dangerous for British interests. Disraeli was not prepared to trust Russia and warned Derby that she would say anything to obtain a promise of British neutrality. He also impressed on the Foreign Secretary the importance of keeping the negotiations with Austria from Shuvalov. The Prime Minister, without the Foreign Secretary's knowledge, had written to Layard secretly on 6 June asking whether he thought it possible to obtain an Ottoman request for a British occupation of Gallipoli and for the calling of the fleet to Constantinople. He had also attempted a few days later to outflank Derby's sabotage of Austrian negotiations with Beust by conducting them secretly and directly with Andrássy, using Montgelas of the Austrian Embassy to do so. In this way both Beust and Derby would be avoided. However, Montgelas refused to go behind Beust's back unless Disraeli expressed such a request in writing.[56]

The suspicion of Russian intentions and appetite by Disraeli, the Queen, and Loftus received some reinforcement when Shuvalov was informed of a change in the peace terms which he had just communicated. Alexander II, who was present at Russian army headquarters in Wallachia, allowed the military to sweep away the more moderate influence of Gorchakov and Jomini. The Tsar decided that the autonomous Bulgaria must extend south as well as north of the Balkan Mountains, going all the way to the Aegean. Shuvalov told Derby of the change on 14 June. Being aware from Lady Derby of the Anglo-Austrian talks on alliance, the ambassador also attempted to convince the Foreign Secretary of their futility by telling him that Austria was securely tied to Russia. Derby replied that he thought Russia's original proposals would hardly be considered by the Turks until reduced to total defeat; the addition to them of such a large Bulgaria which to a considerable extent would become a client of Russia's was even less calculated to win Turkish acceptance. The Foreign Secretary justified British inaction to Layard. 'I understand the disappointment produced as you say by our "abandonment of the Turkish cause" but opinion here was practically unanimous and no other decision was possible. Dislike of war is just now the strongest feeling—and the outcry of last Autumn ... derived most of its strength from the apprehension that we were about to be involved in another Crimean struggle.'[57]

Disraeli pressed Derby to earnestly propose an active alliance to Austria and attempted by using the Queen's influence to stir Salisbury as well. He told the Foreign Secretary not to believe anything that Shuvalov had to say on the subject.

It is all part of a system of ceaseless mendacity, to convince us, that Austria is bound hand & foot to them [Russia].

Lord Beaconsfield regrets, that it was not more distinctly stated, in the conversation with Count Beust, that H.M. Government, while prepared to act in alliance with Austria to prevent the Russian occupation of Constantinople, was ready at the same time, to combine to secure all those objects, peculiarly Austrian wh. were originally stated by Ct. Andrassy in his answer to our first despatch.[58]

Andrássy, of course, was tied to Russia by the Budapest Convention and had no desire for a British alliance, but he wished to keep alive the possibility of one in case Russia violated her agreement with Austria. It was also useful as pressure on Russia which could be used, if necessary, to keep her loyal to the treaty. Though Derby suspected this, it does not explain his deliberate attempt, in violation of the Cabinet's decision, to prevent an Anglo-Austrian alliance. The Foreign Secretary thought that by maintaining the isolation of his own Government he could prevent active measures—such as an occupation of Gallipoli—which he felt certain would lead to war. An Austrian alliance he probably believed would induce the Cabinet to go along with Disraeli to take measures to defend Constantinople and the Dardanelles. Derby apparently had given little thought as yet to resigning, though it would have been best for himself and the Government if he had done so.

On the fourteenth, after much talking with both Derby and Salisbury, the Prime Minister gave the Queen reason to hope. 'His impression is, altho there are, & will be, great difficulties to encounter, he shall succeed in keeping the Cabinet together, & prosecuting a policy of which Yr. Majesty will not be ashamed.' Two days later, after a Cabinet meeting on the sixteenth, he dashed some of that hope. 'He [Disraeli] proposed a vote of credit and increase of the army. Violent opposition from certain persons. Lord Salisbury scarce concealed he wished Russia to occupy Constantinople. Adjourned cabinet to Wednesday [20 June] that Lord Beaconsfied might confer with them in detail and have the immediate advantage of Your Majesty's presence and advice. He is not daunted'. Salisbury, as he explained to Lytton, preferred to believe that nothing could resurrect Turkey and that Russian power was a myth. 'I would have devoted my whole efforts to securing the water way to India—by the acquisition of Egypt or Crete: and would in no way have discouraged the obliteration of Turkey ...' Disraeli wrote to Derby asking for his support at the next Cabinet meeting and maligning Salisbury, indicating that the latter's succession would not weaken the Government. The Prime Minister was careful to explain that the Cabinet's consent to the vote of credit he intended to ask for would not bind ministers to any particular course beyond the vote itself.

How grievous would be to me the blow, that severed our long connection & faithful friendship. ... All I want now is to reassure the country, that is alarmed and perplexed; to show, that we are in a state not of puzzled inertness, but of preparedness for action so to assist negotiation, wh. will be constantly cropping up & place ourselves in a position, if there be eventually a crash, to assume a tone wh. will be respected.

The Foreign Secretary replied that as no active step was contemplated his support would be given.

As far as you and I are concerned, I do not think we shall have any difficulty in agreeing, at least in the present stage of the affair. It seems to me, that the vital question is not yet raised. No doubt Salisbury's language was ominous, but he did not absolutely declare himself against preparation. I need not add that a political separation between us too would be as painful to me as it could possibly be to you.

Having won Derby's support, Disraeli worked upon Salisbury, who on the eighteenth consented to drop his opposition, and upon Northcote, who gave his adhesion though he preferred to buy from the Porte some Egyptian territory. The Prime Minister asked Hardy to be prepared to explain to his colleagues how the vote would be presented to Parliament. 'I will no longer take the responsibility of affairs and do nothing.'[59]

The critical meeting of 20 June drew only a short telegram from the Prime Minister. 'Cabinet satisfactory but technical reasons will occasion some little delay in bringing forward measures.' Another ministerial meeting was quickly called by Disraeli two days later and it allowed him to be satisfied that both Salisbury and Derby would support the vote when it was brought forward. In between the two meetings Disraeli met the Queen who recorded the encounter.

A new & alarming feature was 'that the Cabinet does not keep its secrets'. . . . He then went on to talk of the serious difficulties confronting him, once the present ones are overcome, for he will get the Vote of Credit agreed to. But when it comes to sending troops to hold Gallipoli, & the Fleet to Constantinople, a necessity if we are not 'to kiss the feet of Russia,' then both Ld. Derby & Lord Salisbury are sure to refuse, if not even resign, the former wanting peace at all price & the latter in favour of Russia going to Constantinople in the interests of Christianity. What should Ld. Beaconsfield do in such a contingency? I replied 'certainly go on,' as he has an immense majority & the Country would be with him.

The Queen was sure that affairs would be improved if Lyons replaced the Foreign Secretary, and she asked the Prime Minister if timidity and false religionism could not be told, that if they wanted to resign, the Queen would accept their resignations at a later time. Disraeli explained that the two men were not thinking of doing this at present, and asked the Queen instead to write to the Foreign Secretary that it was her earnest wish that Russia should not be allowed either to enter or to occupy Constantinople. In the meantime Disraeli had not given up on a Gallipoli expedition and instructed Hertslet to produce a memorandum on international law and the Straits.[60] One difficulty in the way of such a step was that it would require the consent of the Porte, which would be withheld unless Britain agreed to a Turkish alliance. All obstacles, Beaconsfield wrote, could be overcome if England declared war on Russia, but there were no three men in the Cabinet prepared to support this.[61]

Anglo-Russian relations had become almost as awkward as those within the Cabinet, and Derby and Shuvalov, who were working for Anglo-Russian accommodation and a localized war faced as many obstacles as the Prime Minister. The negotiations for a Russian promise to respect British interests and a British pledge to remain neutral were in that unsatisfactory state of suspended animation. Disraeli, Layard, and the Queen considered the Russian peace terms to be a trap, and the Russians felt disinclined to restrict their military operations by a promise not to move on Constantinople. Wellesley, the British military attaché in Russia, was gratuitously insulted by the Russian military commander in the Balkans, the Grand Duke Nicholas. The incident was smoothed over and Wellesley was removed from the headquarters of the Grand Duke and attached to those of the Tsar himself. Unfortunately for Shuvalov and Derby, Russian policy had escaped from the more moderate hands of the Foreign Ministry, Gorchakov and Jomini having been left in exile in Bucharest, into the grasp of Ignatiev and the military who surrounded the Tsar. Reading the Anglo-Austrian correspondence for an alliance as a bad sign for the future, the Russian ambassador was as near despair as the Queen. Furthermore, as Bylandt, the Netherlands minister has described, he believed that British policy was now the policy of Disraeli.

I received a visit from Shuvalov, who seemed very worried and preoccupied and told me that despite the differences of opinion within the
English cabinet, Beaconsfield's influence was preponderant, that he
held in his hands the question of peace . . . and that he feared that
soon he would ask Parliament for extraordinary credits to prepare
for the eventuality of a war, which would be voted by an immense
majority. Once the preparations were made, Shuvalov added, the
temptation to make use of them might become irresistible. If, for
example, English occupied Gallipoli and the Dardanelles, it would
be doubtful that she would ever leave that position. . . . This,
however, would in turn necessitate a Russian occupation of a position to protect the access to the Black Sea, probably on the Asiatic
side of the Bosphorus.[62]

The Foreign Secretary's cool passivity belied his extraordinary
behaviour. His conduct in the negotiations with Austria and
his relationship with Shuvalov[63] were deceitful and disloyal to
his colleagues. By comparison, Disraeli's use of the Queen and
Corry and his secret correspondence with Layard, though
hardly excusable, are made to appear simple and almost
straightforward. It is possible that the Foreign Secretary
preferred to pretend that he was unaware of his wife's political
indiscretions with the Russian ambassador and justified
everything on the ground that Beaconsfield's desire to
demonstrate, in order to protect British prestige, might lead to
a war with Russia.

Events in central Asia were further hampering Shuvalov's
and Derby's desire for accommodation. The ruler of
Afghanistan had come under the influence of Russian military
authorities, and was refusing to allow a British agent into his
country. When Layard[64] and Lytton, the viceroy, encouraged
the Sultan to send an envoy there in order to stir up Muslim
feeling and make trouble for Russia, Salisbury was furious, as
the India Office had not given its assent to such activity.[65] Anti-
Russian feeling, however, was building in Britain, and what
seem to have been exaggerated fears of a rapid Russian
advance were based on a realistic estimate of Turkish
preparations for resistance.

In Armenia, though the Russians had captured Ardahan, a
combination of bad weather and difficult geography with some
Ottoman resistance had temporarily checked any great advance.

In the Balkans the Turkish strategy apparently was quickly to defeat the Montenegrins, where some victories were won, and to transfer the bulk of their forces from Hercegovina to the Danube to meet the main Russian invasion. The Turks were strung along almost the whole length of the river. The Russian crossing, when it came at Sistova and in the Dobruja, was almost unopposed. Floods and the level of the Danube had prevented a Russian crossing for two months after war had been declared and the Pruth negotiated. The Turks made little use of this time save to prepare a few fortresses. Passage of the river in force took place on 27 and 28 June, and it elicited a worried telegram from Layard and the calling together of the Cabinet. The ambassador telegraphed the following. 'The aspect of affairs is consequently very serious, and I venture to think Her Majesty's Government should come to some decision as to the course to be pursued, and should give me as soon as possible some definite instructions.'[66] Ministers met on 30 June and the Prime Minister, whose health was quite bad, made three proposals, all of which were accepted by his colleagues. First, it was decided to invite Austria to agree to a protocol in order to frustrate a Russian occupation of Constantinople. Second, the Mediterranean fleet was to be increased, and third, it was to go at once to Besika Bay. After the meeting Richmond told the Queen that Derby was more alive to the necessity for some action than he had previously been. Hardy recorded that there was ministerial unanimity on policy.[67]

Derby telegraphed the results of the meeting to Layard, whose previous telegram had been shown to the Cabinet. 'It is decided that the fleet shall go again to Besika Bay. Probably, also, the naval forces in the Mediterranean will be strengthened. The difficulty of your position is fully understood here. Your despatches have been read with great interest. It is impossible to have done more than you have, or to have done it more judiciously.'[68] The Foreign Secretary also saw Beust and told him of the protocol request, and, to demonstrate England's seriousness, of Besika Bay and the augmentation of the fleet.[69]

Partly because of an unfavourable diplomatic situation[70] and partly because of the temper of British opinion, only Russian military victories could galvanize the Cabinet sufficiently to prepare to defend British interests if necessary. Ministers were on a kind of diplomatic treadmill, and after much activity, they found their position relatively unchanged with Constantinople and the Dardanelles still unprotected.

THE news that the fleet had been sent to Besika Bay at the end of June was publicly known almost at once. Layard reported that though the sultan expressed pleasure at the step, general Ottoman opinion in Constantinople, which looked upon Britain's neutrality as an exhibition of narrow selfishness, was negative, fearing a British participation in a European partition of Turkey. Decazes, who wished to avoid a confrontation between the Great Powers almost as much as Bismarck, saw Lyons on the morning of 4 July and expressed mixed satisfaction to the British ambassador. 'Decazes said to me this morning that he had heard with great pleasure that the English fleet had been ordered to Besika Bay because he hoped that this would be regarded in England as a sufficient demonstration, and that Her Majesty's Government would not take any further steps.' Lyons interpreted the Foreign Minister's remarks on the Russian terms of peace in a sense which did not give much reassurance to Britain.

She [France] is comparatively indifferent to Russian progress in the East, and would view with quite as much jealousy an increase of English as an increase of Russian influence in the eastern part of the Mediterranean.

    She has no inclination to give any assistance, moral or material, to England in resisting Russian encroachments or in obtaining a counterpoise to them.[1]

Bismarck, when questioned by Russell, indicated that any peace terms agreeable to Britain, Russia, and Austria would be acceptable to Germany. Hoping to avoid an Anglo-Russian military confrontation, though he was suspected in London to be pushing Russia towards a war with England, Bismarck looked at the movement of the fleet as premature.

Prince Bismarck replied that such a measure would greatly facilitate peace later on, when the belligerents were exhausted and ready to treat; but at present . . . he thought it might encourage the resistance of Turkey, and prolong the war.

Turkey was not yet beaten, and Russia flushed with the success of her passage of the Danube, would not be satisfied without a victory. Until then he looked upon all attempts at a pacification as hopeless.

He had ... heard with surprise from Count Münster that Her Majesty's Government were averse to taking possession of the road to India through Egypt, which in the interest of Great Britain and the commercial world, should, in his opinion, be now transferred from the suzerainty of the Sultan of Turkey to that of the Empress of India.[2]

Alexander II at Russian army headquarters on the Danube was anxious concerning both military operations and, since the sending of the fleet, with Anglo-Russian relations as well. He talked with Wellesley, the British military attaché, on the morning of 3 July.

His Majesty, who seemed very nervous, and whose voice faltered a great deal ... [spoke about Anglo-Russian relations].

The Emperor said that there was no use attempting to disguise the fact that these relations were now of a most delicate nature, and he was at loss to know the reasons on which English suspicions were founded.

'Lord Beaconsfield [the Tsar said] appears at the present moment to have "aggressive" ideas, why I cannot say.'

The Emperor went on to say that he had ... [already given his word on India and the Suez Canal].

With regard to Constantinople, His Majesty had already stated to Lord Augustus Loftus at Livadia, that he had no wish or intention of acquiring, and since that time he had in no way changed his mind.

His Majesty thought that his word of honour as a gentleman should be sufficient, and conceived it to be beneath his dignity to repeat the same thing so often.[3]

The Queen, her temper fully roused, wished as did Beaconsfield and Layard to prepare for a British occupation of Gallipoli. She was revolted and angered by Russian cruelties and destruction and described Gladstone as a great enemy to his country. She addressed a plaintive question to Disraeli. 'Is there no friend who could get him [Gladstone] away for his own sake?'[4]

In Parliament ministers were questioned about the fleet going to Besika and the perfunctory replies of Northcote in the Commons and Derby in the Lords well satisfied both Houses.[5] This was fortunate for the Government was divided as ever about what to do. It was not as Elliot thought, that the ministers were separated into two groups, with the party of in-action led by Salisbury and Derby. Rather, the Cabinet represented a broad spectrum of opinion on the Eastern Ques-tion which was united on very little, and, depending upon the specific issue before it, was capable of assuming various shapes and forms of agreement or the absence of it. The slightest change in events or information would produce a new kaleidoscopic arrangement of ministers which would often dis-appear with the next day's news. The Prime Minister found that time after time the disunity of his colleagues and the necessity to maintain neutrality forced him to be satisfied with much less than he wished. It is clear that he did not desire war with Russia though he was willing to occupy Gallipoli as a material guarantee and send the fleet to Constantinople. In lieu of obtaining what he desired he was restricted to getting what he could.

Jettisoning an earlier intention of asking Parliament for a vote of credit, the Prime Minister explained to the Queen an alternative. 'He thought he knew a mode in which the vote of Credit could be avoided, viz: by largely increasing our garrisons in the Mediterranean, which could be done without asking for money, as there were more men than we required at home; that then if any increase was required he would come for a supplementary vote next year . . .'[6] A Cabinet meeting was called on 11 July to consent to strengthening the Mediterra-nean garrisons to enable the dispatch at any time of ten thou-sand men to some desired point in Turkey. It was felt that British earnestness needed to be manifested for Andrássy's rep-ly on 9 July to the British request to sign a protocol embodying the Anglo-Austrian talks was in the negative. The Prime Minister, however, still hoped that if Britain exhibited a greater manifestation of vigour an Austrian agreement would yet be possible.[7] Derby's scepticism about and aversion for such a partnership caused him to refuse to take the talks seriously when he did not attempt to prevent them from leading to any successful issue.

According to Richmond ministers unanimously adopted the Prime Minister's proposal for an increase of the garrisons at their meeting on 11 July.[8] Somewhat encouraged, Disraeli, as he informed the Queen, now planned to drag his colleagues a considerable step further. He did so under the impression that a crisis was at hand as a result of a secret telegram from Layard.

The Russians may soon cross the Balkans [Mountains] and advance upon Adrianople. If H.M. Govt have decided upon occupying Gallipoli Peninsula not a moment should be lost in getting the Sultan to consent to our doing so. The very fact of our being there even if marines & sailors were to be landed provisionally from the fleet would raise the Turks from their present state of depression and encourage them to resistance in Bulgaria . . .[9]

The Prime Minister proposed to put it to the next Cabinet meeting to be held on 14 July that Russia be told that the British Government would look upon the occupation of Constantinople as a *casus belli*. He was, as he informed the Queen, prepared for dissenters.

It is possible, that this decided course may deprive Ld. Beaconsfield of the services of Lord Derby, &, more than probable that Ld. Salisbury & his friend [Carnarvon], will resign.

Lord Salisbury, tho a very able man has no following in the country or Parliament; both of them look with dissatisfaction on his conduct of the Conference [at Constantinople].

Lord Derby has a great following in the country, tho little in Parliament. Ld. Beaconsfield had a long interview with him this morning.[10]

Currie, following events from within the Foreign Office, had no faith in the Government's adopting any vigorous course. 'Ld. B[eaconsfield] is much broken in health. His colleagues are apathetic and in a very few weeks they will be scattered to the ends of the earth, which will be an additional reason for doing nothing. . . . I am convinced that we shall not get by on demonstrations . . .'[11]

The important Cabinet meeting of 14 July, which took place while a Russian force under General Gurko was crossing the Balkans near the Shipka Pass into Rumelia, followed what had now become a pattern. Unable to obtain ministerial sanction for an announcement to Russia that an occupation of Constantinople would cause Britain to declare war, the Prime Minister took what he could get, describing it to the Queen.

We [the Cabinet] have decided to address a note, of a very formal &

authoritative character, to Russia. . . . The occupation of Constantinople, or attempt to occupy it, will be looked upon as an incident,
which frees us from all previous engagements, & must lead to serious
consequences. The phrase *casus belli* is not used, but reserved for a
subsequent occasion, if necessary.

Cairns has also left a report of this meeting and the impression
it gives is much different from the one given by the Prime
Minister's account. The Lord Chancellor indicates that the
main topic before his colleagues was the proposal to move the
fleet upon the Sultan's request from Besika to Constantinople,
a journey of about twelve sea hours. The *casus belli* threat to
Russia is treated as a minor offshoot of the main discussion. 'It
would be rash—& when all the materials now in our possession
came to be known, it would be esteemed to be rash—to pledge
ourselves absolutely, at this moment, to a rupture with Russia,
merely on a strategic contingency which has not yet become
sufficiently imminent to justify a step so serious.' The Cabinet
also considered the question of whether it was safe for the fleet
to go to Constantinople without physical control of the
Gallipoli Peninsula which flanked one side of the passage to
that city. If British ships were anchored at Constantinople and
the Russians took Gallipoli, passage out to the Mediterranean
could be obstructed or prevented by artillery facing the water-
way. It was decided to ask the opinion of Admiral Commerell,
who was being sent out to the Mediterranean with the fleet
augmentation that had previously been ordered.[12]

The Queen found the accounts of the above meeting indiges-
tible and exploded to the Prime Minister with anxiety and
alarm caused by what she felt to be the weakness and
pusillanimity of her ministers. She protested strongly against
reported Russian atrocities in Bulgaria and stressed the absolute necessity of preventing Russia from occupying Constantinople before it was too late to do so. Disraeli replied with the
difficulty in attempting to lead a disunited and unwilling
Cabinet. He explained that at the Cabinet meeting on the
fourteenth he was ready to accept the resignations of Derby and
Salisbury had they been the only obstacles.

But when he found the Lord Chancellor, hitherto his right arm in
affairs, followed by the Duke of Richmond and every other member

of the Cabinet except Lord John Manners and Sir Michael Beach, shrink from the last resort [the *casus belli* warning to Russia], he felt it best (waiting to the very end before he spoke) to bring about the arrangement ultimately agreed to—which was still a step in advance, and which may lead to all that is required . . .

The news of the passage of the Balkans by a Russian force, and the reported atrocities attributed to the Russians, confirmed the Queen in her exasperation. She telegraphed and wrote to Beaconsfield to inform the Cabinet meeting to be held on 17 July of her shock and disappointment that a decision to send the fleet to Constantinople had not yet been taken.[13]

If the Prime Minister shared, used, and sometimes controlled the Queen's excitability and alarm, he found it exceedingly difficult to deal with Derby's withdrawal and Lady Derby's vain indiscretions. Evidence that the secret Anglo-Austrian alliance talks were generally known, Andrássy having just informed London that Austria was under no binding agreement to Russia, caused the Prime Minister to speak to the Foreign Secretary after the ministerial gathering on 14 July concerning Cabinet leaks. Derby replied by letter.

Any one professing to have seen notes of mine or to have been made acquainted with their contents is either lying or has been hoaxed by someone else. Notes which I generally take at Cabinets have never been seen except by Lady Derby or by my secretary [Sanderson]. They have been kept merely for the purpose of convenient reference. Those of old date have been from time to time destroyed and all will be.[14]

It is not clear whether Derby was totally ignorant of his wife's indiscretions with Shuvalov, whether he pretended to be, or whether he found them useful. He did tell the Russian ambassador on 17 July, as agreed in Cabinet, that a temporary Russian occupation of Constantinople would destroy good Anglo-Russian relations and leave Britain free to take any step which she considered necessary for the security of her interests. 'This communication, I said, was strictly confidential, and the Cabinet were convinced that it would be received by the Russian Govt. in the spirit in which it was intended—not as a menace but as a friendly warning of danger threatening both Govts., which it is most desirable they should avoid.'[15]

No sooner had the Foreign Secretary delivered this communication than a Cabinet meeting held on the same day
reverted almost to Disraeli's previous desire of threatening war
itself to stop the Russians from advancing on Constantinople.

The Cabinet had finally agreed that, in the event of Russia not leaving
Constantinople again on a given day, Lord Beaconsfield would have
to advise declaring war, and if the Cabinet again changed their
minds, then he would have to find another. The Turks were to be advised to hasten their fortifications ... [at Gallipoli] for should
Gallipoli be in possession of the Russians, our fleet can no longer go
up to Constantinople! But, if the Turks held it, then we should be
safe and able to support them ...

Surprisingly, the Premier received Salisbury's support at this
meeting in overcoming the opposition of the military committee of the War Office and Hardy to reinforcing the
Mediterranean garrisons. As sometimes occurred, the military
experts were divided in their advice as to the possibility or
desirability of holding Gallipoli. Dickson, a military attaché at
Constantinople, was inspecting with the chief Turkish
engineers the plans to improve and strengthen the Bulair lines
which had been erected in 1854 to protect the Gallipoli Peninsula. Admiral Hornby, who commanded the Mediterranean
fleet at Besika, wanted the peninsula to be occupied in order to
safeguard the fleet were it to be ordered to Constantinople.
Simmons felt it was too late for such a step before the Russians
reached it. Admiral Commerell thought that no occupation
was necessary and that it could be secured by the fleet alone.[16]
The Netherlands minister in London noted that military
events in Bulgaria had produced violent attacks on Russia in
the metropolitan Press. Questions were asked in both Houses
of Parliament about Russian and Bulgarian atrocities carried
out on non-combatant Muslims. The rising Russophobia
resulted in requests that Gladstone denounce the Russian barbarities publicly. Bothered by his own conscience and afraid
that anti-Russian opinion would seduce the Government from
its neutrality, Gladstone wrote to Shuvalov, who may not have
been the best Russian diplomatic representative ever sent to
London, but was surely the best informed.

Even a few verified cases of barbarity, however intelligible, however probable under the circumstances, will do an amount of mischief here [England] such as can hardly be measured . . .

I hope yet more earnestly that rapid and condign punishment will be inflicted by way of example on some of the authors of these [Russian] misdeeds when detected.

I am sure that special pains in proving guilt will be worth while, and that decisive punishment, made widely known will be of enormous advantage.

I have laboured to demonstrate, in print, that the most important part by far of the question raised last year by the Bulgarian massacres is the conduct of the Porte after the fact, in concealing, in denying, and in giving immunity. . . . The mischief may be without limit, unless . . . the action of the Russian authorities shall be, as I believe it will be, the direct reverse of the conduct of the Turkish Government.[17]

On 19 July in a letter from Russian army headquarters Wellesley expressed his belief that the Russians intended to occupy Constantinople. The following day, as the Russians were being defeated at Plevna, a telegram from Layard confirmed this. 'The state of affairs is very critical, and I venture to suggest that Her Majesty's Government should lose no time in coming to a decision as to the course to be pursued.' At a three-hour Cabinet meeting held on 21 July Salisbury renewed his newly found support for the energetic policy of Beaconsfield. The ministers ordered immediate steps to be taken for the sending of 3,000 men to Malta, and unanimously agreed, no one more emphatically than Salisbury, that Britain should go to war with Russia if she occupied Constantinople without declaring her intention to quickly retire from the city. Whether it was the Russian passage of the Balkans or the behaviour of the Foreign Secretary or some other reason propelling the India Secretary is not clear.[18] Only two weeks earlier he had written the following, though perhaps only to quiet Lytton. 'At present I think we are justified in hoping for two good results from the war: first, that we shall have done with our impossible Turkish client: second, that Russia's financial exhaustion will be so extreme as to bring about at an early date a political revolution . . .'[19]

The decisions of the Cabinet on 21 July produced the resignation of Lord John Manners, the Postmaster-General, the serious dissatisfaction of Hardy, and a muddle in the tortuous and continuing Anglo-Austrian talks. Manners was now something of a hawk on the Eastern Question and wished an unambiguous declaration of war if Russia entered Constantinople. By implication the decision of his colleagues would have permitted a temporary Russian occupation of that city, which he regarded as the equivalent of Russian paramountcy in the East. Disraeli, who received the letter of resignation with shock and surprise, asked Manners to keep his desire secret and then managed to persuade his old friend to withdraw it.[20]

The Prime Minister's struggle to drag his colleagues with him step by step to the point of taking the measures to defend Constantinople and Gallipoli which would cause Russia to stop short of those places, needed to be militarily credible in order to be effective. Reinforcing the fleet and the Malta garrison were intended to accomplish that, as well as rendering an occupation of Gallipoli more easily manageable if the Cabinet could be brought to the point of sanctioning it. Hardy, who like Manners generally supported Disraeli, was concerned that a useless demonstration, which he considered the sending of 3,000 men to Malta to be, as once there they would be without transport, would embarrass the Government as the step could not satisfactorily be justified in Parliament. Though he wrote privately to the Premier of his misgivings, he gave way as the orders for the demonstration had already been given.[21]

The talks with Austria had assumed the proportions of a travesty.[22] Their ostensible purpose, which was to formally commit both countries to a common defence of their mutual Balkan interests, was an agreement which neither Andrássy nor Derby yet desired. The negotiations took place on at least two levels, Derby with Beust and, behind the back of the Foreign Secretary, Disraeli and Corry with Montgelas. They were continued because all except Derby favoured doing so. The Prime Minister, who desired an Austrian alliance as the easiest way to deny Constantinople to the Russians without a war, wrote privately to the Foreign Secretary. 'A defensive treaty with Austria for a term of years, say seven or ten, might yet put all right, & even the Emperor [Francis Joseph] might accept it. Austria is terribly afraid of the Italian navy, from which we shd. protect her, & she is not a power, like Germany, who would convert her defensive into an offensive alliance.'[23] On 24

July the Queen read a telegram from Buchanan in Vienna reporting that Andrássy had been informed by Beust that Derby had told him that Britain did not object to a temporary Russian occupation of Constantinople. She telegraphed to Disraeli who informed the Foreign Secretary. The latter denied having said this, a denial supported by Beust. 'The best answer to the telegram [of Buchanan's] is the draft [dispatch] which you [Disraeli] have with you, in which I [Derby] ask Andrassy what length of occupation he would be prepared to treat as justifying war ...' The Queen was only partly mollified because however much the matter was only an honest mis-understanding, there was, as she wrote to the Prime Minister, the larger question of Derby's general behaviour.

She felt very painfully impressed with the conviction (which Lord Salisbury [who was in attendance] she found shared) that Lord D. did not truly and properly carry out the decisions of the Cabinet, and still more did not conduct foreign affairs as they ought—for the Cabinet must do that. The time is come when our policy must be clear and decided ... [passivity] is disastrous, and injures the Government in the eyes of the country and makes us contemptible in the eyes of Europe ...[24]

On 27 July Layard, who was faithfully and loyally following a course with which he had no sympathy, and who was not being clearly informed of the military situation in Bulgaria by Lennox, the military attaché, communicated an extremely worried telegram to the Foreign Office.

The Russians are making serious progress on this side of the Balkans, and may be soon at Adrianople, from whence a few short marches would take them to the Gallipoli Peninsula.

I venture once more to urge upon Her Majesty's Government to take into their most earnest consideration the occupation of this most important position, not as a threat to Russia, or as a step towards war, but in the interests of peace and humanity, and as a guarantee for the interests of England. If we told Russia clearly and decidedly that we will not consent to her taking possession of Constantinople she might ... make peace at Adrianople.

This matter is of such a vital and urgent importance that I trust that your Excellency will forgive me for again bringing it before you.

As a result of this excessively pessimistic prognosis a Cabinet meeting was quickly called for the twenty-eighth; the Queen made a record of the meeting in her journal.

It [the Cabinet] was very difficult, but Lord Salisbury & all, excepting Ld. Derby, saw the great danger & it was decided to send a telegram expressing alarm & readiness to send up Fleet with Sultan's approval to Constantinople; but there would be great danger if we could not secure its safe return, & unless Gallipoli was safe, this would not be the case. Col. Home of the Engineers had suggested that the guns might be spiked and rendered powerless, & this is to be done,—also to ask & sound the Porte as to terms of peace they would consent to. Ld. Derby had at first been inclined to say we could on no account go to Gallipoli, but this was prevented. Then a communication is to be made to Ct. Schouvaloff . . . that . . . we should be ready to help . . . in obtaining an honourable one [peace] . . . & . . . that the state of affairs at Constantinople might become so alarming, that we might be obliged to send the Fleet up there, though that would not be departing from our neutrality . . .[25]

Hardy recorded in his diary the prominence of the Foreign Secretary. 'Derby was strange, and seemed to shrink from any action, diplomatic or other, but he made our communication to Schouvaloff eventually, and the rest of us were more in earnest . . .' Richmond confirms Hardy's impression. 'Our friend's conduct is quite inexplicable. I cannot understand him. There never was anyone who gained a reputation so easily.'[26]

In answer to an anxious telegram from the Queen advocating the occupation of Gallipoli, the Foreign Secretary denounced the war party.

Lord Derby cyphered that it would be too late to occupy Gallipoli, even if that step were desirable. Lord Derby is quite aware that there will be an outcry, indeed there is one already—from the party which does not conceal its wish for war with Russia. But he believes that party to be small in numbers, though loud and active. He is quite satisfied that the great bulk of the nation desires nothing so much . . . as the maintenance of peace . . .

Though sent to the Queen, the Prime Minister saw himself as the unnamed recipient, and indicated to the Queen that if it were necessary he would not shrink from advocating war, in which case he had serious doubts that Derby, despite his angry and sullen expressions, would resign. Disraeli drafted a reply to Derby for the Queen, and the latter sent it off to the Foreign

Secretary. 'The Queen does not know from what sources Lord
Derby gathers his opinion, that the British people are in favour
of Russian supremacy. She is convinced of the contrary, and
believes there will soon be no controversy on the subject.'[27]

On 28 July Layard was sent a telegram from the Cabinet,
perhaps to prevent sabotage by the Foreign Secretary, to sound
the Sultan on requesting the fleet to come to Constantinople in
order to protect Christian lives and property. Layard also
received a telegram from Derby. 'You [Layard] are authorized
to sound the Sultan as to possible terms of peace. Her
Majesty's Government are not disposed to take the initiative in
proposing conditions, but the Sultan may rely on their friendly
offices with a view to obtain the most favourable terms possible
under the circumstances, if he is disposed to open
negotiations.' Disraeli supplemented the Cabinet's telegram by
his own secret telegram to the ambassador alluding to
England's old and sage policy, along with the assurance of his
deepest trust in Layard's energy and skill. The Queen, angered
by Derby's immovability, wished the Tsar to know that
England would never allow him Constantinople, and poured
out her anger to Beaconsfield.

Ld Derby & his wife *most likely* say the *reverse right & left & Russia goes
on!* It maddens the Queen to feel that all our efforts are being
destroyed by the minister who ought to *carry* them out. The Queen
must say she *can't* stand it! For Russia *will* have her own way & *we* be
humiliated if not ruined. Ld Beaconsfield spoke *so decidedly* of *not
standing* it any longer, that she fears some fresh change has taken
place again amongst the others [other members of the Cabinet]! All
can be set right if he [Disraeli] will devise a cypher to be *sent* to Mr.
Layard to the effect that, *while wishing to maintain* a policy of neutrality,
*circumstances may arise to render this impossible* . . .

After receiving the above Beaconsfield reassured the Queen
that there had been no alteration in the Cabinet's opinion, and
that Derby had only attempted to obstruct.[28]

The second Victory of Osman Pasha over the Russians at the
second battle of Plevna on 30 July[29] and Ottoman gains in
Armenia temporarily ended what seemed to have been a
serious crisis for Turkey and Britain. As a result of this success
Layard telegraphed to Derby that the Sultan would not

presently either propose or receive peace conditions. The ambassador wrote privately to Disraeli and his chief that suspicion of Britain and anti-English feeling, especially among most of the Sultan's ministers, encouraged by Reuss, the German ambassador, required him to be very careful else the Turks might join the side of Russia, bag and baggage. To Beaconsfield alone, Layard warned that if the fleet came to Constantinople the Turks must be told that it had been sent for their security against Russian appetite.

Nor could we, I believe, induce them to ask us to send the fleet for the protection of the lives & property of Europeans & Xtians. .... I have had the means of sounding the Sultan indirectly on this subject [the occupation of Gallipoli]. He wd. not, I have reason to think, object to it, but amongst his min[ister]s are some who wd oppose it strongly. Urgent & vitally important as I consider the possession of the Bulair lines [at Gallipoli] by us to be I do not think that it is absolutely necessary that we should hold them until Constantinople were seriously threatened; but we should be prepared to do so.[30]

At the beginning of August Wellesley left Russian headquarters on a mission entrusted to him by the Tsar before the news of the Russian defeat at the second battle of Plevna was known. Alexander's purpose was probably to reassure the British Government after their warning to him of 17 July concerning the occupation of Constantinople. Wellesley arrived in London on 5 August and was met at the station by Bourke and taken at once to Disraeli, Derby being out of town. To the Prime Minister and the Queen, whom he saw on the eighth, the attaché delivered the Tsar's message, which conveyed his intention to make peace on the terms which Shuvalov had brought to London on 8 June, along with the modification of extending Bulgaria south of the Balkan Mountains. It was stipulated that the Porte would have to be induced to solicit peace from Russia, presumably by Britain. Wellesley described the Russian Emperor as a well-meaning but weak man who needed help to arrange an end to the war. The attaché was given two messages to take back to the Tsar. One was the cool but polite official reply drawn up by Derby and modified, which indicated the Government's desire for peace and their intention not to depart from their position of conditional neutrality. It was explained that British influence at Constantinople was not now what it was, nor did it appear that the present moment was a favourable one for the purpose of initiating peace negotiations. Both the Queen and Prime Minister, however, wished the Tsar to have a personal message from themselves, a secret one, which would not be known to Derby or the rest of the Cabinet, and which, ironically, was almost the opposite of the official reply. Both Disraeli and Queen Victoria realized that a written communication to the Emperor would be sent to Shuvalov, who would tell the Derbys. So with Ponsonby's help it was decided that Wellesley would give the secret message verbally, not as officially communicated by the Prime Minister and the Queen, but as from himself as to what they had distinctly informed Wellesley in conversation was their policy. The substance of this message was as follows.

The Queen and Her Majesty's Government sincerely trust that peace may be concluded this year in a manner satisfactory to the Emperor.

At the same time the Queen and Lord Beaconsfield fear that the neutrality of England could not be maintained if the war is not soon terminated, and that if a second campaign occurred [in the spring of 1878] England must take her place as a belligerent. . . .[31]

The official, non-secret reply to the Tsar, drafted by Derby, and amended, was considerably different from the secret message given him.

It is the earnest desire of Her Majesty's Government to contribute to the reestablishment of peace, and in the meanwhile they have no intention of departing from that attitude of strict, though conditional, neutrality which they have hitherto observed. . . . It does not appear to Her Majesty's Government that the present juncture is one which offers a favourable opening for the commencement of [peace] negotiations. The military events . . . will have necessarily indisposed the Turkish Government to entertain any propositions of peace except on conditions such as it is unlikely that the Russian Government would accept.[32]

The two messages to the Tsar together seemed to indicate that while London saw little hope for peace presently, its policy of conditional neutrality would be maintained, unless hostilities continued too long, in which case Britain would be forced to go to war. While the two communications could with effort be made compatible, they were, to say the least, ambiguous.

The behaviour of Beaconsfield and the Queen in going behind the backs of Derby and the rest of the Cabinet was highly irregular and disloyal. They felt, however, that such conduct was both necessary and justifiable because they knew or suspected that Lady Derby, if not the Foreign Secretary himself, was giving the Russian ambassador privileged information and that Derby was opposing what they considered necessary for British interests. Disraeli's admonition to the Foreign Secretary about his Cabinet notes and the Queen's letters to the Prime Minister of 1 and 14 August show this. In the latter, printed in *The Letters of Queen Victoria,* the editor gives the Queen's communication as follows. 'Anyhow the Emperor will tell Gortchakoff, who will telegraph to Shuvalov . . . and so on.' The original in the archives at Hughenden without ellipses reads as follows. 'Anyhow the Emperor will tell Gortchakoff, who will telegraph to Shuvalov, who will tell Lady Derby, and so on.'[33] Beaconsfield was not prepared to ask for Derby's resignation which might have straightened out an extraordinary situation, nor, as may be seen from his letter to the Queen of 29 July,[34] did he believe the Foreign Secretary would resign if Britain was required to resort to war. He was prepared, with a secret line to Layard, Wellesley at Russian headquarters, personal emissaries in Vienna, and his own monarch's support, to outflank, surround, and render impotent the efforts of Lord and Lady Derby. That Beaconsfield did not follow Queen Victoria's repeated desire to appoint another Foreign Secretary seems in retrospect very sad.

Disraeli's belief that Derby would not resign even were Britain to go to war reflected the former's suspicion that his friend wished to be Prime Minister. It was more than apparent to contemporaries that Beaconsfield's age and bad health would force him to step down even if he did not soon die. It also seemed that the Government's majority and term in office were safe. The two most likely candidates to replace the Prime Minister were Salisbury and Derby, and the obvious recent shift of the India Secretary to support the line of his chief and the desires of his sovereign[35] perhaps reflected his recognition of his possibility for political advancement as well as a concern about the Russian threat to Constantinople.

No one in the Cabinet was working to produce war. Derby's

efforts to avoid the provocation and tension which could elicit it were impelled by an attempt of which he was unaware to preserve the nature and autonomy of his own personality. Not as fortunate as his Cabinet colleagues, who maintained a degree of control over their emotions, the Foreign Secretary was an unwilling and almost complete prisoner of his own. He had started in the spring of 1877 on the course which would only end in March 1878 with an inability to function and his resignation. The certainty that his countrymen wanted nothing more than the preservation of peace provided the justification for disloyal behaviour towards his colleagues. His gradually increasing emotional withdrawal was manifested by his physical absence from London at Keston or Knowsley, where he went weekly, if not more often. His inability to trust Bismarck, Gorchakov, and Andrássy, in which he was not alone, had now progressed to the point where he found it impossible to depend or rely on his oldest personal and political friends in the Cabinet. His high and discriminating intelligence was placed in the service of a tortured personality, and his control over the formulation, though not the execution, of policy was being reduced to the point where he was the holder of the proverbial rubber stamp. His cool and outwardly unexcitable nature, which had given Beaconsfield such pleasure when it was directed at the wild absurdities of the atrocitarians, belied a threatened personality under total attack. When further withdrawal would prove impossible there would remain only that last refuge of safety, suspended animation. His colleagues, who often sympathized with his efforts to avoid war, eventually, save for Carnarvon, balked when such efforts resulted in doing nothing.

During Wellesley's brief but busy stay in England before his departure on 17 August for the Tsar's headquarters with the two messages from Britain, ministers met on the eighth, tenth, thirteenth, and fifteenth. Such concentrated activity was largely the result of the necessity of arranging for affairs now that Parliament was about to take recess and the Cabinet consequently to disband and scatter. On 8 August the ministers considered relations with Austria and, led by the Prime Minister, who feared a Serbian attack on Turkey, asked Derby to communicate at once with Beust. On 10 August the ministers agreed that, while Derby and Beaconsfield would remain in London or near by, the rest of the Cabinet must be ready to reassemble quickly and frequently. On the thirteenth England's offensive potential in India was considered in case of a war with Russia, and two days later two very serious discussions ensued on the British response to a renewed Russian threat to Constantinople or a Russian attempt to commence a second campaign in the spring of 1878. Cross introduced the question of what his colleagues were prepared to do in order to meet the first embarrassing danger. Hardy replied that he assumed they would do what had already been decided and dispatch the fleet to Constantinople. When Carnarvon asked whether this would be done with or without the Sultan's consent, there was general assent that it would be with such consent. The two men, whose personal religious feelings were most affronted by a Turkish alliance or association, balked. Carnarvon most strongly, but even Salisbury indicated that he did not think the country was presently prepared to ally with Turkey. The only dissenter to interference recorded by Disraeli, if Russia again threatened Constantinople, was the Colonial Secretary.

The Premier introduced the second important question considered by his colleagues on 15 August, that of a second Russian campaign, which he argued ought not to be permitted. He proposed that when it was obvious that a single campaign would not be decisive, the Cabinet would meet to decide on the necessary steps to take in order to prevent the war's reoccurrence in the spring. There was, Disraeli wrote to the Queen, a general, if not unanimous decision in spite of Derby's rejoinder that England had no allies, to oppose a second Russian campaign. Beaconsfield's impression of near unanimity is not borne out by Northcote.

We are not agreed on the major points and so continually arrive at absurd conclusions. One man holds that we ought to support Turkey; another that we ought to keep at peace; another that, accepting the defeat of Turkey as certain, we ought to look out for compensation to ourselves. Each of us, when a particular step is proposed, consider how it will agree with his own view, or how it can be made to do so. The proposal is modified accordingly, and modified so often that at last it suits nobody; and then some unmeaning step is decided on; after which it is taken in a manner which was not exactly what anyone expected; and lastly it is explained according to every man's separate theory.[36]

With the end of the Parliamentary session in the middle of August the pressure on Derby was lightened somewhat, but Disraeli and especially the Queen continued to pursue him. The latter forced him to remonstrate against Russian atrocities, and also to make an appeal, albeit fruitless, to the other Powers to join Britain in urging Serbia against war. Fortunately, the Parliamentary opposition had made little attempt to embarrass the Government in the last two and one half months of the session, adhering to a kind of patriotic co-operation.[37]

Wellesley had arrived back in Bulgaria towards the end of August with the problem of delivering the message from the Queen and Beaconsfield so that it would be believed by the Tsar but would not be further communicated by him. The attaché explained to the Emperor that he was authorized to make the communication confidentially, so that its contents would not be viewed as a threat to Russia and an encouragement to Turkey. Alexander promised to keep the secrecy of the message, and though distressed by it, thanked its communicator for his efforts. This secret move by Beaconsfield and the Queen may have been counter-productive in causing Alexander II not to suspend military operations over the winter in the hope of achieving victory without the necessity of a second campaign in 1878. It also may have been naïve to have expected Russia to seriously desire peace until the loss of prestige from the military disasters in Armenia and Bulgaria had been made good. The Russian decision to fight through the winter, however, was probably due more to the military situation, the increasing numerical superiority of her forces, and the domestic situation at home than to the secret British threat. No reply was made by the Tsar to the latter and the hopes of Disraeli and the Queen were unfulfilled. 'I have never told you before but I was perplexed & astonished at the silence of Col. Wellesley. Never can a business on wh. Y.M. & himself took more pains & precaution & never was there so sterile a result.'[38]

In September the Queen was at Balmoral with Hardy in attendance. The latter reported her to be angry with Serbia,

Russian atrocities in Bulgaria, and Derby's procrastination, as well as concerned with the necessity of preventing a second Russian campaign. She urged Beaconsfield to bring the latter before the Cabinet and not be deterred if one, or two, or even three colleagues resigned. She drew up a memorandum, which she sent to Disraeli, advocating that the other Powers be asked to join Britain in ending the war, and, if Russia refused reasonable peace terms, for Britain to become Turkey's ally. The Prime Minister replied that it would be undesirable to pledge the Cabinet to decisive measures until it became clearer that a second campaign was intended. The Queen explained that she had written her memorandum to prevent a second campaign and because the Prime Minister had asked her to speak strongly to the ministers she would see.[39]

The Queen's sense of urgency reflected her anger and frustration rather more than the military situation. On 10, 11, and 12 September the Russians were again defeated after heavy losses and for the third time, in an attempt to take Plevna. News of the capitulation of Niksich to the Montenegrins on 8 September was ignored. When Osman Pasha's third victory was learned of in London it was greeted by a chorus of exultation in most of the British Press.[40] The objects of the Queen's displeasure were sufficiently numerous, however, to maintain a steady level of anxiety and anger. When Cross was to take his turn in attendance in the middle of September, replacing Hardy, the latter and Disraeli wrote to warn him of the storm he might encounter at Balmoral. Beaconsfield sent him a copy of the Queen's memorandum of 7 September, which he had not circulated to the Cabinet for reasons which he thought would be apparent to Cross.[41] The Prime Minister emitted his frustrations, using his old technique of directing his anger at Odo Russell and the other principal ambassadors to the Foreign Secretary. He must have realized that it was not Loftus, Buchanan, and Russell who were making difficulties. Having already spoken with Hardy and Cross, the Queen was asked by Beaconsfield to talk fully and often with Cairns, as the Prime Minister intended to convene a Cabinet in October.[42]

On 28 September, after a talk with the Prime Minister at Hughenden, Hardy made a suggestion which so pleased Disraeli that he indicated he would bring it before the Cabinet.

As Beaconsfield described the plan to Derby, Britain would come forward as a mediator and propose reasonable and honourable peace terms to Russia. One set of these terms included the Porte's acceptance of the London Protocol, Bessarabia to Russia, Romania to Austria, and Montenegro to be given what she was able to occupy at the end of the war. If St. Petersburg refused them the Government would end its neutrality, and tell Russia that England would give assistance to Turkey were Constantinople to be threatened. 'This is a clear & precise policy: it gets us out of all the embarrassing distinctions bet[wee]n temporary & permanent occupation wh. harassed & nearly humiliated us last session & if rejected by Russia, would put her more in the wrong in the eyes of Europe . . .'

The Prime Minister had decided to take timidity by the flank, and asked Derby to introduce this proposal to the coming Cabinet meeting. Having recently learned that at their Salzburg meeting Andrássy and Bismarck considered mediation presently impossible, the Foreign Secretary returned a straightforward reply. 'I am not prepared to support the proposal which you suggest, still less to put it forward; but a preliminary discussion will be of use as showing how far . . . there is likely to be agreement among us as to the course which we ought to take.' Besides Derby, Disraeli also wrote of the proposal to Richmond, Manners, Cairns, Northcote, and Salisbury. Strong letters of acceptance and support came from Cairns and Manners, an equivocating reply from Northcote, and no reply at all from Salisbury who was in France. Beaconsfield, who had asked the Queen to use her influence on any ministers she saw, explained that the Cabinet was still divided, but he thought that with the exception of Derby, and also Salisbury and Carnarvon whose opinions he did not know, the rest of the ministers favoured some action. The following day, however, the Prime Minister wrote from Hughenden that he expected serious conflict when the Cabinet met. His ally at Balmoral used her influence on Cairns and found him opposed to a second Russian campaign. She communicated a *sine qua non* to Disraeli for the ministerial meeting on 5 October. 'Ld. Beaconsfield must insist on the decision of the Cabinet not being communicated to wives, above all, not to foreign ambassadors. This must be insisted on.'[43]

The Prime Minister introduced his proposal to his colleagues by explaining that it was probable that there would be a second Russian campaign which he wished to prevent, as its object would be the capture of Constantinople. He then outlined the plan of mediation, which some were willing to adopt, but to which others raised objections.[44]

It was said that the time for mediation had not yet come, & that it was inexpedient for us to force or anticipate it. . . . It was said that the definition of the terms to be offered by Turkey would be a work of great difficulty & controversy. . . . Further it was argued [by Salisbury] that if we made our intervention for Constantinople conditional on the refusal of these terms, we should be asking the country to engage in war, not for the maintenance of British interests, but in order to enforce a particular mode of settling the dispute between Russia & Turkey.

The question of defending Constantinople was then separated from the one of mediation, and discussed. It was proposed that when the present campaign ended Britain should propose to the Russians only an understanding on Constantinople. 'We wd. continue to do so [remain neutral], provided Russia would assure us that she would not advance upon or occupy Constantinople, even temporarily. . . . If this assurance should be refused, we should hold ourselves free to take steps to intervene for the protection of the Turkish Capital.' Disraeli reported that while the Cabinet generally was opposed to joining mediation with anything like a threat, all save Carnarvon seemed to concur in the proposal to Russia, which was to be discussed at the next Cabinet meeting.[45]

Though he attempted to reassure the Queen, the Cabinet meeting of 5 October was hardly a victory for the Prime Minister. Ministers could not even be brought to the point which they conceded at their meeting on 17 July, though Carnarvon now was the only vocal dissenter. The latter appealed to Salisbury for some counter-proposal to defeat Beaconsfield. 'I conclude that the interval between our last, & our next Cabinet will be employed in an attempt to win over the hesitating element amongst them—and to secure a distinct and overwhelming majority. When that is accomplished I shall not be surprised if *extreme* pressure is supplied . . .'

The Colonial Secretary, incapable of agreeing out of

religious feelings even to a remote association with the Ottoman Turks, was described by Beaconsfield as a weak enthusiast pining over the celebration of High Mass in St. Sophia. Lady Derby, however, wrote to encourage Carnarvon.

'Is it not quite certain that even a majority of the Cabinet could not prevail against you and Cranborne [Salisbury] and Lord Derby? Northcote and Cross, though they may have seemed somewhat "trimming" on Friday, would not desert the three most powerful men in the Cabinet.

I think Lord D[erby] is quite as strong as you are against the proposal [of Beaconsfield], and seems to hope that a kind of dogged resistance will prevail against the wonderful chief.'

The positions within the Cabinet would not change greatly from those held at the meeting of 5 October, with the exception of Northcote's, until the end of the fighting. Carnarvon and Derby, the latter not propelled by religious scruples, would not fight the Russians, the former because it meant support for the Turks. Salisbury's religious feelings, magnified by those of his wife, were as strong as Carnarvon's, but at the appropriate time he was prepared to threaten war to secure the independence of Constantinople. Northcote was not so prepared because he believed British interests lay at Suez rather than Constantinople. Cross and Smith, the latter a recent replacement for Hunt at the admiralty, occupied as yet no firm position. The former felt he could not ostentatiously break with Derby and the latter was too new to adopt a decided line. Manners, Cairns, Hardy, Richmond, and Beach were ready to follow their leader and the Queen.[46]

The Queen could not abide 'a miserable cotton-spinning, milk & water, peace-at-all-price policy', and saw the Foreign Secretary as the main culprit. Earlier in September she had Ponsonby put a request to Derby to look into the matter of Cabinet leaks. The latter blamed them unfairly on the treacherous Andrássy, who, he said, had broadcast the secret Anglo-Austrian talks, which was not true. Beaconsfield, perhaps moved by Derby's strong public position in the City as well as in Lancashire and the North, would not break with the Foreign Secretary. To the Queen's admonition about wives and foreign ambassadors on the eve of the meeting of 5 October, Disraeli replied that it required to be kept only between the two of them.[47] While Beaconsfield solicited the Queen's pressure on a timid and vacillating minister, and found that he could depend on her energy and friendship, he did not abuse it. His theatrical flattery of her, which was partly a matter of his style, represented his own deep and sincere feelings of devotion. He was prepared to use the real political advantages the Queen's support provided, but the affection she gave, which helped to sustain a physically broken man, was even more basic. Victoria sensed his need for her support and approbation, and it must have been rarely if ever withheld. But her personal affection for him did not require a slavish abdication to her friend's political plans in order to be sustained. She remained her own woman, and in both of them that glint of steel was only rarely tarnished.

A good deal of October was spent by Derby and Disraeli in squaring what seemed to London to be a double Austrian policy on the issue of offering mediation. Zichy was saying that Austria was ready to mediate in Constantinople while Beust indicated the contrary in London and was supported by Andrássy. The Foreign Secretary also was active at this time, partly as a result of petitions from Manchester and Leeds, to save the lives of the two Geshoffs, who were involved in the Bulgarian rising of 1876 and whom the Porte was preparing to execute. Layard and White were striving to persuade Serbia and Greece against war, the latter country complaining about the Porte's use of Albanian irregulars on the Graeco-Turkish frontier, where the Greeks were attempting to incite a rebellion against Turkey. A Russian victory was won in Armenia,[48] and Todleben was attempting to starve Osman Pasha into surrender at Plevna. The number of civilian refugees, sick, starving, and destitute had alarmingly increased as the fighting continued. The Prime Minister had gone to Brighton in October, an unlikely place to seek 'some days as warm as Egypt & as soft as Sicily'.

Towards the end of October Beaconsfield informed the Queen of his intention to call a Cabinet meeting for 5 November to pick up the threads left dangling on 5 October, and also to consider the measures to be submitted to Parliament, and what should be spoken on Lord Mayor's day. Upon leaving Brighton on 29 October the Prime Minister met Cairns and Hardy, as arranged, in order to prepare for the expected disagreements at the coming meeting. The three agreed completely as to the course to follow. Back in London, Disraeli saw most of his colleagues, including Derby, to whom he explained his intended proposal to inform Russia that continued British neutrality would require a secret written promise from her that she would not occupy Constantinople or the Dardanelles. The Foreign Secretary would only promise not to oppose this, but admitted to Beaconsfield that it gave a better hope of keeping the Cabinet together than any scheme mentioned so far. The Prime Minister, with a certain amount of characteristic exaggeration and inaccuracy, described his colleagues to the Queen on the day before the Cabinet meeting as representing seven separate policies,[49] but indicated his belief that the above proposal would receive unanimous support except for Carnarvon, who would likely resign. Disraeli consciously avoided the course to be followed upon a Russian refusal, because it would quickly destroy the Cabinet.[50]

The meeting held on 5 November, the results of which Disraeli communicated with obvious satisfaction, did not particularly please the Queen who was not even mollified by Carnarvon's isolation. The Prime Minister sent a telegram of the result of the meeting immediately it was over. 'I proposed the policy agreed upon which Lord Carnarvon immediately opposed, but as to his evident surprise it was supported both by Lord Salisbury and then Lord Derby he was routed. Otherwise the Cabinet unanimous.' The Queen feared that a Russian promise on Constantinople and the Dardanelles would leave unprotected other vital places such as Batum and Erzeroum in Armenia. She urged instead that the government revert to the position originated by Beaconsfield and taken in the secret warning communicated to the Tsar by Wellesley that there should be no second campaign. Now, in November, the Prime Minister, fearing a Russian move on Constantinople without the necessity of closing the present campaign, changed back to the Queen's position of August, thus reversing the stands adopted by monarch and minister at that time.[51]

Though prepared for firm action, the Queen desired to avoid exciting or fomenting agitation for a peace at any price, and advised Beaconsfield, who was to speak on 9 November at the Lord Mayor's dinner, not to be provocative. Just before this occasion, Hartington, the opposition leader, made two mild anti-Ottoman speeches in Glasgow in which he defended Gladstone. Münster, the German ambassador, thought these efforts might be an attempt to reunite the fragmented Liberal party. Whether because of the Queen's appeal or not, the Prime Minister's speech was mild and innocuous, unlike his 'bellicose effusion of the previous year on the same festive occasion'. When Shuvalov complained to Derby about Disraeli's reference in his speech to the Tsar's pledge repudiating the desire for any increase of territory, which the ambassador denied had been promised since the outbreak of war, the Foreign Secretary objected.

I said in reply that without denying his [Shuvalov's] statement I thought he would admit that any declarations such as those in question would not be affected by the circumstance that they were made either before or after the outbreak of hostilities, and that the language of the Emperor Alexander had throughout been to the effect that he was not waging a war of conquest, but that the conflict had been begun and was carried on by Russia for other objects.
To this remark Count Schouvaloff took no objection.[52]

In the middle of November the Queen's alarm grew, stirred by what she considered an inadequate response by the Government to a Turkish appeal for mediation and to telegrams from Layard and Wellesley reporting the Ottoman situation in Bulgaria as critical. She bombarded Disraeli with ciphered telegrams and letters containing criticism of the Government's inaction. The Prime Minister's defence for the absence of a warning to Russia to make peace was a weak and puzzling one, namely that it was useless because premature. 'We have information that any appeal, at this particular moment to Russia would not be listened to, scarcely received, & might create so much irritation & ill-feeling that the future might be prejudiced—the fact is Russia will say nothing, until she has ascertained whether Plevna will fall or not . . .'
The Queen replied, 'We *shall* be *too* late!' She criticized Disraeli and the Government for not communicating to Russia a request for a written promise to keep out of Constantinople, which presumably the Cabinet meeting on 5 November passed

when Carnarvon was routed. The Prime Minister explained that Russian peace terms on Bulgaria were ambiguous and dangerous. 'It was thought that if our predetermined application to Russia, limited, as it necessarily was, to Constantinople and the Dardanelles, were made at this moment an interpretation . . . would be put upon it, that we were prepared to accept the Bulgarian scheme.'[53]

An alarming telegram from Layard on 13 November resulted in one from the Queen two days later in which she warned the Prime Minister with great earnestness. A telegram from Wellesley reporting the fall of Plevna as shortly inevitable caused the Queen to complain against delay in attempting mediation and extracting a promise from Russia about Constantinople. Disraeli was forced to bring his sovereign down to earth with a careful and unheroic letter explaining that Plevna was not Constantinople.

Unquestionably the fall of Plevna . . . would be a calamity to this country, but it would not be a disgrace. . . . Now, we have adopted and announced a different policy [from the one of 1854]: one of neutrality, conditional on no British interest being menaced or attacked. We have defined those British interests. The occupation by Russia of Constantinople, or the Dardanelles, would assail one of those interests.[54]

While most people in London and Constantinople were waiting to hear news from Plevna, word was received on 18 November from Armenia that Kars had fallen to the Russians. The Queen, upset at Disraeli's inaction, suggested she might write to the Tsar in the interests of peace. Northcote still advocated a British appeal to Germany, Austria, France, and Italy for a combined attempt at mediation by the Great Powers. Cairns, shaken by the fall of Kars, wrote to Beaconsfield favouring some attempt at mediation. The Prime Minister now pressed Derby to draw up the request for a Russian promise not to occupy Constantinople and the Dardanelles which the Cabinet had approved. It elicited the following reply from the Foreign Secretary. 'I will see what I can do about the draft. . . . But it is a very awkward paper as matters now stand—I don't believe the Russians would care to go further than Adrianople, where they stopped in 1828, and where they are near enough to over awe the capital, without entering it. We shall have to take care that we don't seem to give them [the Russians] more freedom of action than we desire.' Disraeli received Derby's draft, and made some changes, omitting one paragraph. The Foreign Secretary accepted the changes but objected to the deletion.

You propose to omit the paragraph in which we promise continued neutrality to Russua in the event of her not going to Constantinople, retaining at the same time the . . . demand that she shall not go there.

Now the omission of what was intended to be held out to Russia as an inducement to agree to our requirements changes the nature of the whole proceeding. It differs so widely from what was decided in Cabinet that if we adopt this course we ought to consult our friends again. It is either a threat or nothing. As the draft stood, we proposed to bargain, offering and receiving an equivalent. As it now stands, we ask something and offer nothing. Moreover, the present memorandum would be a mere repetition of that which we gave to Schou. six months ago, when we warned him of the danger to our relations that would arise if a Russian force occupied Constantinople. It may be well to repeat our warning, but we should do it less formally, and with a reference to our former proceeding, which otherwise we should seem to have forgotten. . . . What I would suggest is that no memorandum [to Russia] should be given in: but that I should see Schou. and remind him of what passed at the beginning of the war: afterwards embodying our conversation or at least that part of it, in a secret despatch. This will satisfy our colleagues, and be a precaution against Parliamentary attack.

Disraeli disagreed, and replied that the Cabinet had never sanctioned the paragraph he desired to omit, and as proof offered in support Cairns's recollection. Nor did the Prime Minister like Derby's suggestion of an informal talk with Shuvalov. The Foreign Secretary maintained the correctness of his recollection, and suggested that Beaconsfield and he have a private talk, which took place on 27 November.[55]

While the disagreement continued between the Prime Minister, who was attempting to break Derby's obstructive tactics, and the Foreign Secretary, who was attempting to prevent an Anglo-Russian war arising from British provocation, the latter sought to arouse the favourable sentiments of the Queen. Hearing, probably from Northcote or Ponsonby, that the Queen was greatly incensed by his behaviour, Derby took what was for him the highly unusual step of writing an unrequested political letter to Ponsonby and suggesting that the latter show it to Queen Victoria. The content of the letter, recounting a private conversation with Shuvalov, had for its purpose to prove to Her Majesty that her Foreign Secretary lacked neither loyalty nor energy. At this very time, Beaconsfield was extolling to the Queen the latter two qualities of Derby, whom he was seeing every day, in the hope that such evidence of collegial loyalty would get back to the Foreign Secretary and elicit the same from him. His hope remained unfulfilled.

Manners, Hardy, and Cairns were disturbed by the inactivity of the Government, though by no means agreed upon what to do about it. Manners desired an immediate Russian reassurance about Constantinople, and if not given, to aid Turkey with 40,000 British troops. Hardy, afraid of drifting and the irresolution of the Foreign Secretary, wished to offer mediation, a step also strongly supported by Cairns. Disraeli was contemplating a possible British purchase of Ottoman territory, which would give the Porte the necessary funds to carry on a second campaign. Layard was still begging Derby, and now Disraeli as well, for definite instructions on a decided line of policy in order to maintain British influence in Constantinople, an object to which he had devoted so much energy since April. Derby and Disraeli met by appointment on 27 November, and when the latter would not give way on the dispatch to Russia, the former only acceded when Disraeli agreed to call a Cabinet meeting to consider the communication.[56]

Before the meeting of the Cabinet Derby received several jingo deputations at the Foreign Office on 28 November, and listened to appeals for a bolder course on behalf of the Turks to bring about peace. The Foreign Secretary remained un-moved, as he had to the appeals of agitation groups he had heard the year before. The *Daily News* was now much happier with his efforts than it had been in 1876, and reported with satisfaction Derby's bracing shower of common sense which he sprayed over the deputations. The effect of his words caused a general rise in City stocks the following morning. On the eve of the ministerial gathering Manners reported the Queen's sentiments for a clear and unambiguous message to Russia. 'She is quite prepared for war, but believes the surest way of avoiding it is to take, *now,* a bold and decided course.'[57]

The Cabinet meeting of 4 December discussed the communication to Russia during which Cairns and Derby indicated
their opposite recollections to what the Cabinet had previously
agreed. When Disraeli suggested that an indication to Russia
that Britain was prepared to mediate be coupled with a warning to her, all save Derby agreed. The latter slipped a note to
Beaconsfield at the meeting suggesting that mediation had no
chance of success. Forced to give way, Derby was instructed to
draw up a new note to Russia to be considered at the next
meeting on 8 December. He did so on the same day, leaving
out any assurance concerning continued British neutrality if
Russia agreed not to menace Constantinople. The key
paragraph of the draft read: 'It is with a view of avoiding what
might endanger seriously the good relations happily maintained
between the two countries that Lord Derby has been charged
by the Cabinet to express to the Russian Govt that the Russian
armies ... will not attempt to occupy Constantinople or the
Dardanelles.' Tenterden wrote a memorandum on the draft for
his chief, implying that it might be best to inform Austria of
the intended communication, as Russia surely would, once it
was delivered.[58]

During the meeting of 4 December Derby apparently made a
distinction between a Russian occupation of Constantinople
and a threatened occupation of the city, declaring that only the
former would elicit the *casus belli* for Britain. The following day
he received a letter from the Prime Minister. 'I hope I mis-
understood you. I hold myself, both this event [a Russian oc-
cupation], if impending, as well as the simultaneous opening of
the straits to Russia ... should decidedly be *casus belli* for this
country, with or without allies ... and ... we should
remember, that Turkey herself is now a powerful ally ...'

Salisbury, who, according to Hardy, would not have been
unhappy at Ottoman disintegration, especially if Britain obtained her share of that empire, was now consulted by the
Prime Minister, in an open attempt to solicit his support
against the Derbys. He now informed the India Secretary of the
Queen's letter to him of 4 October,[59] warning against the
communication of Cabinet secrets to wives and foreign
ambassadors.[60]

After consultation with Salisbury, Disraeli went to see Derby on the morning of 8 December, as he explained to the Queen.

His [Disraeli's] first impression was to read Yr Majesty's letter to the Cabinet, but on consulting Lord Salisbury he thought it better privately to communicate its contents to Lord Derby, which he will do in the course of the morning.

Lord Salisbury said Lord Derby would bow to any suggestion made by his Sovereign, but that he might be seriously offended, if such delicate matters, touching himself, were brought forward to be discussed by Mr. Smith, Mr. Cross, etc etc

Lord Derby brought the subject, as he announced, very formally before the consideration of the Cabinet, & with impression produced.

Ld Salisbury as the husband of the only other wife, who cd interfere in such affairs, expressed himself without reserve.

The unanimous decision of the Cabinet on 8 December was to approve the amended note to Russia, with the omission of the passage which Derby finally did not insist upon.[61] Before it could be delivered to the Russian Government, however, news arrived that on 9 December Osman Pasha attempted to break out of Plevna. Failing to accomplish this, he fell back into the town and capitulated to the Russians on the tenth. Most of the efforts of the Cabinet for the past two and a half months had been rendered superfluous. The road to Adrianople was almost undefended, and for London a bad dream had become reality.

# 18 ARMISTICE

THE IMMEDIATE effects of the capitulation of Plevna were not unexpected. The Porte sought mediation for an armistice, the Russians hoped to delay any such attempt in order to advance closer to Constantinople, Serbia and Greece were anxious that the war might end before they were able to join it, and Montenegro sought to occupy as much territory as she could in the hope of being able to keep what she possessed once hostilities ceased. Alarm in Britain now reached serious proportions. The Queen in despair urged Beaconsfield, not for the first time, to be firm. The London Press called for mediation and peace, though the *Pall Mall Gazette* desired to see a British demonstration in order to save Constantinople, while the *Morning Post* advised a British declaration of war if hostilities were not terminated at once. As Giers, the Russian Assistant Minister for Foreign Affairs, informed Jomini, patriotic joy reigned in St. Petersburg.[1]

Approximately 30,000 Ottoman troops were taken prisoner when Plevna fell on 10 December. It was intended to march them across the Danube, which was now or would soon be frozen, through Romania and back to Russia. The prisoners, many of whom were wounded or suffering from smallpox, typhus, frost-bite, and starvation, were made to walk over frozen ground covered with snow in bitter sub-zero weather; many, if not all of them, had little clothing. Individual Englishmen, through the National Aid Society and the Russian Sick and Wounded Fund, attempted to help, but there were too many who required care. According to *The Times* correspondent there, the terrible suffering which ensued was not due to Russian cruelty but to disorganization and incapacity. As Anderson describes it, a bullet or sharp blade would have been more humane for many of the captured. 'Out of each convoy [of approximately 4,000 prisoners each] a quarter fell along the way; it was truly 'a march of death.' No attempt was made to look after the prisoners, to organise their march, even to allocate basic rations of food for them.'

A handful of the Ottomans managed to get to hospitals and the remaining survivors had reached Bucharest by the time of the conclusion of the armistice on 31 January.[2]

On the day following the fall of Plevna the Turks discussed with Layard an appeal to the Powers who had signed the 1856 Treaty of Paris for their mediation to end the war. The ambassador, who thought the draft of the appeal was moderate in language,[3] asked the Foreign Secretary whether London had any objection to its being made. Derby thought it a wise proceeding, and the step was taken by the Porte on 13 December. The Foreign Secretary wrote privately to Layard that obviously it was better that all the Powers be requested to assist in a settlement, rather than accept a purely Russo-Turkish arrangement. The ambassador, who was irritated by his chief's excessively careful behaviour, interpreted his words to mean that it would be against the best interests of the Government to permit an isolated Ottoman–Russian peace negotiation.[4] An opportunity to prevent this occurred on the same day as the Ottoman appeal to the Powers, when the Sultan made a personal request to the ambassador. 'Whether they [H.M. Government] would ascertain, without delay, whether the Emperor of Russia would agree to an armistice for about three months. If the Emperor would consent to an armistice, an official request will at once be addressed to Her Majesty's Government to employ their good offices in obtaining one.'[5]

Russia had no intention of allowing outside mediators to interfere for Turkey in the process of making an armistice and devising peace terms, even though many of the latter would eventually require the assent of all the Powers who had signed the treaties of 1856 and 1871. Nor was Derby anxious to interpose Britain in such a capacity, especially after he was informed by Loftus that a cessation of hostilities by Russia would require a direct Turkish appeal to that country, which was indisposed to accept any foreign mediation. After the Cabinet meeting of 8 December and before any news of Plevna, the Foreign Secretary alerted Shuvalov to the warning the Government would soon make to Russia. The Russian ambassador was given a copy of the memorandum upon which the Cabinet had agreed and which the Foreign Secretary had attempted to weaken. It contained a polite and conciliatory warning.

MAP 3.  Constantinople and the Straits

The occupation of Constantinople by Russian forces, even though it should be of a temporary character and for military purposes only, would be an event which it would on all accounts be most desirable to avoid.

If such an occupation appeared imminent, public feeling in this country, founded on a just appreciation of the consequences to be apprehended, might call for measures of precaution on the part of Great Britain from which they have hitherto felt justified in abstaining.

It is with the view of avoiding what might endanger seriously the good relations happily maintained between the two countries that Lord Derby has been charged by the Cabinet to express to the Russian Government their earnest hope that should the Russian armies advance to the south of the Balkans, no attempt will be made to occupy Constantinople or the Dardanelles.[6]

A Cabinet meeting had been called for 14 December and the usual urgings of the Queen to the Prime Minister were now supplemented by the opinion of Shuvalov given to Borthwick, the London newspaper editor, who sent it to Corry. '[Shuvalov] begged me not to repeat what he said—as he was not here to criticise the English Cabinet which had failed—"through its own dissensions to take obvious precautions."' The Queen advised the Prime Minister to take immediate and energetic action, to use the Queen's name to the Cabinet in any way he might desire and not to hesitate about asking for Derby's resignation, as she would personally request Lyons to succeed him as Foreign Secretary. The consequences of inaction, she wrote, would render England a 'subservient, second-rate, cotton-spinning power'. Beaconsfield informed the Queen of his intentions, Hardy having suggested to him already the need to call Parliament early and ask for an increase of force if mediation were refused by Russia.

He [Disraeli] is inclined to propose [to the Cabinet], that Parliament shd. meet as soon as practicable, & that the speech from the Throne shd. announce a large increase in Your Majesty's armaments, & also the undertaking on the part of Your Majesty, at the solicitation of the Sultan, to mediate between the Belligerents. He thinks such a combination may bring about peace, & on terms less injurious to Turkey, than would otherwise be enacted.

Bylandt, the Dutch minister, was sure the divided Cabinet would do nothing and that Beaconsfield, weary of the struggle, might resign. Cowley, the retired ambassador, also predicted a resignation, of which he wrote to Layard. 'Your chief [Derby] is, I believe determined to resign rather than convey a menace. The Queen wd. be delighted were he to do so. She hates him & this hatred is amply returned ...'[7] On the same day as the Cabinet meeting, 14 December, Serbia declared war on the Porte. Many in Britain and Layard in Constantinople resented this declaration, and saw it as a kind of gratuitous stabbing of a dying man with a borrowed knife.

In the words of the Queen, the meeting on the fourteenth had indeed been stormy. Buckle correctly notes a change in the Prime Minister's tactics. Previously Beaconsfield had attempted to secure prior support for the proposals he planned on introducing in Cabinet. Now he did not do so. Disraeli opened the meeting by proposing the immediate summoning of Parliament, a large military increase, and the adoption of a mediatorial position between the two belligerents. The proposals were greeted with that unanswerable reaction—dead silence—broken finally by Manners who supported them, and then also assent from Cairns, Hardy, Cross, Beach,

Richmond, and Smith. Northcote, who formerly had not been a strong supporter of Beaconsfield, and had opposed provocative measures, now altered his position, as Cairns had done much earlier in the year, and his two giant steps forward effectively covered Salisbury's half-step in retreat.

Ld. Salisbury saw no abstract objection to Ld. B's proposals, but practically they would lead to an alliance with Turkey, to which he could not assent. The Chancr. of the Exchequer asked what was the alternative? Some course must be taken & he knew of no other. No one could answer. The Chr. of the Exq. said he was not only for a vote of men & money but for a large vote as the best means of securing peace . . .

Carnarvon objected and asked for whom England was to hold Constantinople. He was strongly answered by Cairns.

Then Lord Derby spoke at length. He had been taken by surprise, & had not had time to give due consideration to the proposals, but as at present advised, he entirely disapproved of them. We had sent a note to Russia [the Cabinet memorandum given to Shuvalov on 13 December warning Russia about Constantinople], & shd. await her answer. There was no *casus belli* in that note. And he wished distinctly to say, that he was not prepared to look upon the occupation of Constantinople by the Russians as a *casus belli*. Ld Derby spoke at some length, & with unusual fire . . .

There was a good deal of sharp remarks, from several members of the Cabinet, as he spoke, & after he had concluded.

Beaconsfield terminated the two-hour gathering, saying that he did not wish to hurry his colleagues, and another meeting was called for 17 December when he hoped a conclusion would be reached.[8]

Northcote wrote to the India Secretary immediately after the meeting about his concern over the Foreign Secretary. 'I am afraid of the most serious consequences if Derby cannot rouse himself to take a lead and give us a line of his own. We would find a good backing in the Cabinet if he would do this, but we cannot go on without a policy or with nothing but a *non possumus*: and a break up in the present state of affairs may lead to chaos and to war . . .' Derby's lethargy caused even Tenterden to remonstrate against any delay in answering the Sultan's request through Britain for a three months' armistice.

I venture to point out: 1. That Servia having declared war, the Porte cannot afford to wait even for a day in applying for an armistice—Unless the war can be stopped forthwith Greek troops will be on the Turkish frontiers also. 2. That the Porte will be forced, if we do not speedily act, to apply direct to Russia. This will probably result in our being excluded from the discussion of the terms of peace. 3. That the hesitation to assist the Porte in this matter . . . will weaken Mr. Layard's influence proportionately.

Surely something ought to be said at once.

No one recognized the dangers of immobility more than Salisbury, yet even he could not force himself to adopt a clear-cut policy of helping the Turks without coercing them. He explained his reasons to Northcote, who was attempting to find a bridge to maintain a semblance of unity between Derby, Carnarvon, and Salisbury with the rest of the Cabinet.

It is proposed to summon Parliament in great haste to ask for money . . .

Before the mess, the money might have been obtained as a measure of precaution, without any full exposition of policy. But money which is so urgently wanted that we cannot wait three weeks [when Parliament normally would have reassembled] to have it in the usual session of Parliament, must be wanted for a special purpose. Parliament will insist on knowing what that special purpose is. Your reply, I presume, will be 'The defence of Constantinople'. But, if you want money so urgently for this purpose, you must, in consistency, use it without delay. You must come at once . . . to Constantinople at the earliest possible date. . . . The Turks will abandon all idea of negotiation, & prepare for a desperate defence. . . . Such a proceeding, taken at this time must end in cooperation with the Turks. It will be a Crimean War: only postponed until our allies have been half destroyed.

The proposal of yesterday seems to me therefore to place us on the steep slope which leads to war. . . . Austria has pledged herself not to suffer any Russian possession of Constantinople . . .

I hold, therefore, that Constantinople is in no real danger: & that a call to arms, hasty & urgent, may have the effect, & probably proceeds from the wish, of involving us in war to uphold Turkey.

This would be difficult enough to swallow . . .[9]

Nor could Carnarvon stomach a war alliance with Turkey, as he too explained to the Chancellor of the Exchequer.

I do not oppose proposal for an increase in armaments because I oppose all war and am anxious to maintain peace at any cost: I have both in private and in the Cabinet on former occasions advised very strong measures: I desired that we should consider the occupation of Egypt ... but [this] ... has ... been always put aside because competing with the insane scheme of undertaking the defence of Constantinople: and as a consequence a Turkish alliance. My opposition therefore ... results from a conviction that in the course which is now proposed to us for adoption there are nine chances of war as against one of peace. ... We shd. go into it not only with inadequate resources and without allies ...

It [the Ottoman Empire] is breaking to pieces past all remedy. ... I cannot therefore knowingly be a party to the idea of a war with Russia and a Turkish alliance. ... I believe this to be Derby's view and holding it to be the right one I cannot see any reason for refusing any support to it ...

The Colonial Secretary still thought that a compromise was possible. 'If indeed any formula could be devised which would give me a *sufficient assurance* that the increase of armaments would not be applied in direct support of Turkey and more particularly in the impossible scheme of a defence of Constantinople ... I should be ready at all events to consider whether some increase of our forces might not be made ...'

Carnarvon wrote to Lady Derby who described her husband as holding the fundamental position and believing that he could deliver the country from war by holding on to office. The Foreign Secretary, apparently in conversation with Northcote on 15 December, did suggest a compromise, which was to put off the calling of Parliament from the middle of January as now desired by Beaconsfield, to the end of the month. Both Northcote and Salisbury liked the idea for it demonstrated the Government's concern without the manifestation of any panic. The former feared, however, that Derby would continue to sit on his hands which Parliament would condemn. The Chancellor of the Exchequer, unlike the Foreign Secretary, desired Britain to become a mediator and to protect her interests by annexing Egypt in case Russia took Constantinople and Armenia and controlled the Black Sea.[10]

Many of the Queen's ministers thought that their differences were so irreconcilable that the Government must break up and the stormy meeting on Monday, 17 December of two and a half

hours tended to corroborate this expectation. The Prime
Minister believed that what had fragmented ministers was not
his three proposals, but the fact that neither Carnarvon, Derby,
or Salisbury ever really meant either to oppose Russia or to
assist Turkey. But the three were supported at this meeting by
Northcote, Cross, and Smith, and a heated discussion arose
over making even a temporary Russian occupation of Constantinople a *casus belli*. When the Prime Minister refused to retreat
and announced that he would give in his resignation to the
Queen, Cairns proposed that the meeting be adjoined until the
following day.[11]

After the meeting the Lord Chancellor journeyed to Hatfield
in an attempt to soften Salisbury's stand on the three
resolutions, and reported his success to Disraeli on the
following morning. Manners, who expressed surprise at
Smith's defection, presumably on the issue of making
Constantinople a *casus belli,* indicated to the Premier his intention of working on him, and suggested that Beaconsfield inform the Foreign Secretary of Manners's previous tender of
resignation. Northcote also appealed to the Prime Minister
and indicated that Derby's resignation would be followed by
those of Carnarvon and Salisbury. To prevent this he suggested
a compromise proposal be made to the Foreign Secretary: to
give up the idea of defending Constantinople and instead make
all arrangements for occupying Gallipoli were it to be
threatened. Disraeli must have been enraged that a suggestion
he had been making periodically and unsuccessfully for the
past eight months was now being proposed by one who had
previously always rejected it. The Foreign Secretary came to the
Prime Minister one hour before the Cabinet meeting of 18
December, and made his own proposal in the hope of keeping
the ministers together. 'That he [Derby] wd. agree to earlier
meeting of Parliament, say 24th January, "some" increase of
force, but, under no circumstances, any attempt at mediation
which must fail. Ld. Beaconsfield held out no hope of accepting this plan, but Ld. Derby . . . said he shd offer it to the consideration of his colleagues before an absolute rupture was
decided on.'

When the Cabinet met at noon Cairns reintroduced a version of Disraeli's three proposals, and Derby then made his

compromise suggestion, but when Salisbury replied that he preferred the Prime Minister's proposals, the Foreign Secretary gave way to the unanimous opinion of his colleagues.

Then Ld. Carnarvon, who had hitherto been silent, screamed out, that altho he accepted these resolutions, he begged it to be understood that their acceptance, on his part, involved no assent to any expedition to any part of the Turkish Empire, or any alliance with the Porte.

The Prime Minister replied that no such question was now before the Cabinet . . .

Cairns and Salisbury strongly urged that the announced early meeting of Parliament be accompanied by a communication to Russia regarding mediation. This Derby strongly opposed but ultimately accepted.[12]

The morning papers of 19 December announced the Cabinet decision to summon Parliament for 17 January. Though the news excited many in Britain and produced a great commotion in the City, there was no agreement as to whether the step meant war or peace. Liberal front-benchers were puzzled over what to make of the move, and saw it with irritation as either an empty threat or a step towards hostilities. Solvyns, the Belgian minister, reported that the most general interpretation in London was that the war policy of Disraeli and Hardy had defeated the pacific views of Salisbury and Derby, which he was happy to indicate was not actually the case. Soon, however, public meetings were arranged by people like Mundella to protect against any drift towards war. Gladstone welcomed such a response and busied himself giving instructions to the Press and Birmingham.

I am confident that every non-Turkish paper will do well at once & constantly, to sound the note of resistance to war or measures tending towards war, & to threaten a stout & lively resistance North South East & West.

It is also I think not only allowable but right & needful to point distinctly & speedily to the Prime Minister as the root of all this mischief & scandal.[13]

As usual, Hartington and Granville were less ready to foment a public outcry than Gladstone. Granville wrote to the latter:

H[artington] & I think that it will be better to wait a little to endeavour to find out really what is the policy of the Govt. Not to take any active steps in getting up meetings, which if they should take place, as they probably will, should be only a short time before the meeting of Parliament—& that the object of these meetings should be as much as possible to deprecate war, encreased taxation, the rise of prices, and encreased industrial distress, and not to be too violent against Gov . . .[14]

The Continental reaction to the Ottoman appeal to intervene in order to stop the war was not favourable. The response of the German Government, which refused to budge on the matter, preferring a direct Russo-Turkish negotiation, influenced and justified the inaction of Paris and Rome. Even Andrássy thought that Anglo-Austrian good offices would be ill advised, apparently preferring as did Bismarck to interfere only after a Russo-Turkish treaty had been completed, when the guaranteeing Powers could discuss those clauses of the agreement which pertained to questions of European interest. Wellesley, who saw the Tsar on the latter's return to Russia, reported Alexander as favourable to peace but much opposed to mediation.

The communication to Russia concerning British mediation decided on by the Cabinet on the eighteenth was never delivered, at least not in the anticipated form. Derby informed Layard in reply to the Ottoman request, that it would be hopeless to ask the Tsar for a three months' armistice, but that the Cabinet was seriously considering the question of mediation. Afraid that the Porte and the ambassador might misinterpret the early recall of Parliament, the Foreign Secretary sought to explain it. 'In view of the reports which are likely to be current here, it is desirable that you [Layard] should be aware that the unusually early meeting of Parliament does not imply any intention on the part of Her Majesty's Government to depart from the policy of conditional neutrality which they have announced.'

Before communicating to Russia the British mediation appeal, it was decided to obtain Andrássy's reaction to it. The latter, without as yet any Russian action to justify a public violation of the pacts of Reichstadt and Budapest, and also upset at the possibility of an Anglo-Russian bargain which would leave Vienna isolated, strongly advised London to drop its mediatorial attempt if it still desired to maintain the Anglo-Austrian understanding of the previous August. Andrássy was especially upset that Britain was prepared to use Russia's peace terms of June, which he opposed, as a starting-point for negotiation.

We [Austria] were not clear whether it was the intention of England to negotiate in the first instance with Russia on the basis of the Russian conditions communicated in June, or whether England, according to the agreement between us, was going previously to come to an understanding with us [Austria] on the conditions of peace. In the former eventuality . . . we could also . . . sound Russia and . . . draw nearer to her. . . . Russia would, in that case, easily have turned our mutual isolation to her profit, in order to exact her most sweeping conditions. If, on the contrary, England stands fast by our agreement, we can both of us, to our own good and that of Europe, prevent Russia from bringing about a situation which would either establish Russia's preponderance in the East or lead to war.[15]

Without intending disloyalty to Vienna and perhaps sensing how little right she had to complain, Derby explained to Beust that Britain could not neglect an opportunity for peace, but that out of consideration for Austria she would modify her intentions.

In deference to the opinion of Count Andrassy, they [Britain] would be prepared to adopt a different course to that which had been contemplated . . .

I observed that his Excellency [Andrassy] would see that in thus avoiding any reference to the [Russian] conditions of peace mentioned in June, Her Majesty's Government were following the policy recommended by Count Andrassy, and I trusted that this would afford . . . a proof of the earnest desire of Her Majesty's Government to act in hearty cooperation with the Austrian Government in accordance with the understanding arrived at between them.

This was not completely what Andrássy wished, as initially he preferred the Porte to address itself directly to Russia. Derby now telegraphed Constantinople, and received an immediate and favourable reply to his question, as to the Porte's desire for London to ask Russia if she would entertain overtures for peace.[16] On 27 December the Foreign Secretary telegraphed the following instructions to Loftus:

Her Majesty's Government consider that the time has arrived when it has become their duty to make an effort to bring to a close the war unhappily existing between Russia and the Porte.

In the communication made to Her Majesty's Government on the 26th . . . the Turkish Government have signified their readiness to ask for peace . . .

With this view, they have to instruct Your Excellency to inquire of the Russian Government if the Emperor will entertain overtures for peace.

Two days later Loftus telegraphed the Russian answer to London.

His Highness [Gorchakov] charged me to reply to your Lordship's inquiry 'that Russia desired nothing better than to arrive at peace; but for that purpose the Porte must address itself to the Commanders-in-chief in Europe and Asia, who will state conditions upon which an armistice can be granted.'
(Confidential)
From what Prince Gorchakow said I am convinced that no foreign mediation will be accepted.[17]

Though rumours were flying in London more thickly and faster than usual, and many believed that Beaconsfield was working only to bring Britain into the war, in fact, with a fair prospect of maintaining the existence of European Turkey, which he favoured, he wrote secretly to Layard on 20 December to urge the Porte to lose no opportunity of concluding an honourable peace. With this in mind, and wishing to temporarily avoid further Cabinet squabbles, the Prime Minister prepared with Cairns a memorandum which was sent to Derby for a mediatorial appeal to Russia on Turkey's behalf. Disraeli suggested that the Foreign Secretary might consult Salisbury as Hatfield was so near. The communication to Russia, which was made eventually after Austria had been informed and squared, was left in the hands of the Foreign Secretary. Derby disliked acting without the knowledge of his colleagues, and though the Cabinet had assented already to the step it had not done so in its altered form as a result of Andrássy's objections. The Foreign Secretary felt that Cross and Northcote, at least, should be consulted as they would bear the burden of defending the initiative in the Commons.[18]

The Foreign Secretary's efforts to keep the Cabinet fully informed were, as he explained to Salisbury, a defence against Disraeli's desire for demonstration and the Queen's desire for war, the latter attribution being Derby's angry response to the Queen's effort to enforce some discretion on the communications which Lady Derby, and perhaps her husband as well, were making to Shuvalov. Derby was not, and perhaps never had been, on good terms with Salisbury. He did not write to him often and only the gravity of events and the paucity of people he felt he could trust account for his letter to the India Secretary.

I am fully convinced—not indeed that he [Disraeli] wishes for war—but he has made up his mind to large military preparations, to an extremely warlike speech, to an agitation in favour of armed intervention (recollect that he said in Cabinet 'The country is asleep and I want to wake it') and if possible to an expedition that shall occupy Constantinople or Gallipoli.

Now I am not inclined to any of these things . . . but if we don't take care . . . we may find ourselves in a position which none of us either expected or would have accepted beforehand.

His [Disraeli's] views are different from mine, where such matters are concerned, not in detail but in principle. He believes strongly in 'prestige'—as all foreigners do. . . . We are in real danger and it is impossible to be too careful. . . . I know what the pressure of the Court is on our chief, & am convinced that the queen has satisfied herself that she will have her way (it is not disguised that she wishes for war): and the conviction is universal among the diplomatists that she and the Premier will leave no stone unturned to accomplish their purpose.

Derby finished his letter by listing three necessities: Cabinet consultation on any step to be taken, to limit military preparations, and to be prepared for a fight on the speech from the throne.[19]

On 24 December, the day following Derby's letter to Salisbury, the Prime Minister also attempted to influence the India Secretary in a manner he had been ready to adopt on 8 December but had then postponed until now. He informed Salisbury in a slightly distorted fashion of Wellesley's secret warning to the Tsar in August about a second campaign, and enclosed a letter from the attaché indicating Shuvalov's detailed reports of Cabinet differences to the Tsar.

What I [Disraeli] wish to show you [Salisbury] is, that, if the present system of the Cabinet is persisted in, & every resolution of every council regularly reported by Count Schouvaloff, it seems inevitable that our very endeavours to secure peace, will land us in the reverse.

I have endeavoured to arrest this evil by some remarks I made in Cabinet, & I have been told, that Lady Salisbury with the wise courage which distinguishes her, has, socially, expressed her sentiments to the great culprit [Lady Derby]. But more decisive means are requisite.

We must put an end to all this mischievous gossip about war-parties & peace-parties in the Cabinet & we must come to decisions which may be, & will be, betrayed, but which may convince Russia that we are agreed & determined. You & I must go together into the depth of the affair, & settle what we are prepared to do—I dare say, we shall not differ when we talk the matter over together . . . but unless we make an effort to clear ourselves from the Canidian spells environing us, we shall make shipwreck alike of our reputations, & the interests of our country.

Salisbury sent to the Prime Minister three paragraphs against the inexpediency of going to war in reply to Wellesley's one sentence suggesting that if it were necessary for Britain to wage war against Russia, now, because of Russian exhaustion, was a good time to do so. On the difficulty of Cabinet leaks, Salisbury sympathized with the Premier but saw no remedy for it as he indicated in a letter to the Prime Minister. 'Throughout the last anxious year, the apparent ease with which a knowledge of our councils has leaked out has placed us at a constant disadvantage. I hardly see what way you [Disraeli] or the Cabinet as a body, can do anything to check the evil. It is a question of honour for each member of the Cabinet individually; but the public mischief . . . is enormous.'[20]

Previously Salisbury was happy to use Derby's incapacity for normal behaviour as a safeguard against any sudden urges of the chief. This, the fact that Lady Derby was his stepmother, and the awkwardness of the problem left the India Secretary bereft of a solution for it. It is surprising that more was not done to check the conduct of a silly and vain woman who revelled in gossip. Disraeli's efforts on 8 December had no discernible effect save to damage further his relationship with Derby. A dispatch from Wellesley on 24 December and one from Buchanan two days later, both of which were forwarded to the Queen, reported more evidence of Cabinet leaks to the satisfaction of the Tsar and the dismay of Andrássy. As Blake informs us, the Queen was prepared to do more, and had Wellesley write to Lady Derby, after which he reported his expectation that no further information would be obtained from her. Lady Derby replied unsatisfactorily to Wellesley, using a tone of one who was aggrieved. The Queen sent the countess' letter to Beaconsfield who was not prepared to do more.[21] The Prime Minister apparently informed Cairns who told Hardy, and the latter recorded his reaction. 'I dined with Richmond & Cairns at the Carlton. The latter told me some curious things about Lady Derby's leakage to Schouvaloff & Her Majesty's message by the Dean of Windsor. It is clear that she has been most indiscreet even to the revelation of discussions in the Cabinet wh. ought not to have been even known to her.'[22]

A Cabinet meeting was held on 27 December which sanctioned the sending of the note of mediation to Russia. Knowing it would be resented at St. Petersburg, anxious that it would encourage the Turks to anticipate British help, and fearing that more would be made of the step than intended, Derby explained to the Prime Minister the incorrectness of any public announcement that Britain was going to mediate.

As the word is understood in diplomacy, what we are now doing is not mediation.

It may be a preliminary step to 'mediation' but it is nothing more.

We are only asking the Russians whether they are prepared to treat for peace. The overture will probably end there, in consequence of a Russian refusal.

[Mediation] would imply giving advice, and the discussion of conditions of peace.
. . .

You may say with truth that we are 'taking the initiative in bringing about negotiations for peace.'

The negative reaction by Russia to Britain's preliminary step has already been indicated.[23]

Halifax, Harcourt, Granville, Bright, Bath, Gladstone, Lowe, Hartington, Mundella, Selborne, and Argyll were pumping their sources and each other for information, and were uncertain as to what the Liberal response should be to the early

Parliament and the anticipated request by the Government for money. Finally, on 20 December a decision was reached, as Granville explained to Selborne.

We agreed last Thursday to deprecate premature agitation which would discourage sensible Conservatives & even moderate Liberals—to do whatever would strengthen the prudent members of the Cabinet—that there was no objection to action on the part of non political bodies such as Chamber of Commerces and that those who have to express their opinions, should argue in favour of neutrality, against war, increased taxation, damage to revenue, & increased depression of trade.

Gladstone agrees for the moment—But is more inclined to put Birmingham in motion now than we are.

When Harcourt ran into the ubiquitous Shuvalov on the street on 30 January and saw him again the following day, he obtained news sufficient 'to scribble 12 sheets to Granville'. Upon the Russian ambassador informing Harcourt that his country had no intention of acquiring Constantinople, the latter urged him to most conspicuously state this. Shuvalov replied that this had already been done, and gave Harcourt the latest information of the British mediation appeal and the Russian refusal, as well as Russian peace terms. The ambassador indicated that Beaconsfield's behaviour was only prolonging the war by preventing a separate Russo-Turkish peace. After their first two encounters Shuvalov became a frequent visitor at Harcourt's London home at Stratford Place, where the ambassador supplied this prominent member of the opposition with news of Cabinet discussions and decisions which were then sent on to Granville and Hartington. It may have been the only time that Her Majesty's opposition was given secret Cabinet information by the ambassador of an unfriendly foreign Power, which was derived in part from the wife of the Foreign Secretary. If Derby had been unaware before of the use to which his wife was putting the news which he gave her, that was no longer the case, for he was made aware from too many sources of what was transpiring. His extraordinary conduct is only partially explained by his inability to exercise very much control over his personality.[24]

As the year drew to a close tempers in England were getting out of control in a public confrontation between opposing groups. The National Federation of Liberal Associations, the London Peace Society, and the Eastern Question Association, the last headed by Shaftesbury and the Duke of Westminster, were clamouring for peace and the maintenance of British neutrality. Public meetings advocating the same position multiplied at the beginning of January. But there was, as Thompson informs us, something of an opposing counter-agitation on the part of the anti-Russian party. On 29 December the National Society for the Resistance of Russian Aggression and the Protection of British Interests in the East attempted to hold an anti-Russian demonstration in Trafalgar Square, calling on the Government to aid Turkey. A counter-demonstration was organized afterwards by leaders of working men's political and trade groups for the same place at the same hour. There was some violence, but in the midst of separate fights which dotted the square, the two opposing groups passed appropriate resolutions. Ollier maintains that the crowd campaigning for neutrality was more violent and energetic than the group which favoured an English war for Turkey.[25]

The negative reply by Russia to British good offices was quickly given to Loftus who telegraphed it to London on the twenty-ninth. The Russian answer to Britain's warning of 13 December about a temporary occupation of Constantinople was not given to Loftus nor telegraphed by Gorchakov, and though dated 16 December, Shuvalov was only able to present it to Derby on 2 January. The reply was that nothing was more likely to bring about the situation which Derby was working to prevent than Turkey's acquiring the knowledge that a threat to, or attack on, Constantinople would cause London to depart from its neutrality. Such information would lead the Porte to prolong uselessly its military resistance and thus induce Russia to continue its advance to Constantinople. It would be otherwise, Gorchakov argued, if the Cabinet would persuade the Porte that it could expect absolutely no British aid or assistance. Gorchakov's reply and an enclosed Russian memorandum, which were given to Derby, were couched in both friendly and polite language, but contained no promise of ruling out a military occupation of Constantinople as distinct from a political annexation of the city which was again proclaimed as unintended and undesired.[26]

If one can believe what Shuvalov told Harcourt, Derby was unhappy with the Russian reply to London's inquiry about her readiness for peace, which the ambassador took up to Knowsley. Disraeli had not given up on a British expedition to Gallipoli and, though this was unknown to Harcourt, the latter felt the situation to be as grave as it could possibly be and expected the Cabinet meeting on 2 January to decide the question of peace or war. On that occasion an answer to Russia was devised by ministers and the amount of money Parliament was to be asked for was discussed;

& then Lord Salisbury raised the question what we shd. say we were going to do with the money?

Thereupon a discussion took place wh. was highly satisfactory [to Disraeli]. Even Twitters [Carnarvon] did not cavil. And Lord Salisbury got into an argument as to the respective advantages of occupying Gallipoli or Constantinople . . .

It would soon be apparent to the Prime Minister why the Colonial Secretary did not cavil. Another Cabinet meeting was held on 3 January which settled the reply to Gorchakov, part of which is given below.

It is evident that the projected armistice, if it is to be effectual, must include operations in Asia, as well as in Europe, and would not be complete without the concurrence of Servia and Montenegro. But in this case it is clearly indispensable that the conditions on which it is to be granted should be discussed between the two Governments, and not merely between Generals commanding a portion of the contending forces.

Her Majesty's Government invite the consideration of Prince Gortchakow to this modification of his Highness' views.

When Loftus communicated the above on the morning of 5 January, he received the following reply.

His Highness [Gorchakov] replied that he maintained the answer given to me on the previous occasion, namely, that the Porte must address itself directly, through some one of note and confidence, to the Commanders-in-chief in Asia and Europe. His Highness observed that he had not asked for an armistice, but had indicated this mode of arriving at peace, and the military commanders were instructed to state conditions on which an armistice would be agreed to. I found his Highness immoveable on this point.

A Cabinet meeting on 7 January considered the above and agreed on the answer given below, which was wired to Russia on the eighth. 'Under these circumstances, the conditions which seemed to Her Majesty's Government essential are practically fulfilled, and they are ready to convey Prince Gortchakow's message to the Porte, and to advise the latter to send delegates to Russian head quarters similarly commissioned to negotiate an armistice.' The instructions which the Russian military received from the home Government satisfied London, and the Porte was advised on 8 January to send delegates to the Russian headquarters.[27]

On 2 January, before the meeting of the Cabinet on that day, the Colonial Secretary went to the Colonial Office to meet a deputation ostensibly on colonial policy. Carnarvon had arranged beforehand with the leader of the deputation to be asked a question on foreign policy for which he had drafted a prepared speech. In a memorandum written in August 1879 Carnarvon tells us that he was moved to take such disloyal action by his fear that Beaconsfield intended a Turkish alliance and a Russian war, which he felt to be unjust, immoral, and impolitic. The Colonial Secretary was a High-Churchman, his mother being the niece of the twelfth Duke of Norfolk, very friendly with ecclesiastics such as Liddon and MacColl, and the brother of Auberon Herbert, one of the leaders of the Bulgarian agitation movement in 1876. An ardent imperialist, unafraid of war, what Carnarvon could not swallow was a Muslim alliance arranged by Disraeli. He had championed the Druses in 1860, but it was an Anglo-Turkish alliance which was the act of injustice and immorality that caused Carnarvon to embarrass the Government of which he was a member at a time that hardly could have been worse for British interests in the Mediterranean and Near East.[28]

His speech to the deputation, which was printed in the morning papers on 3 January, was a compound of reasonable common sense and tactless stupidity. His plea for the public to remain calm, his denial that Russia's reply to Britain's peace tender was an insult, and his claim that there were European issues involved in the East and that Britain had a right to have a distinct voice in their final resolution were points well and rightly taken. This, however, was followed by a poorly timed, inaccurate, and insensitive reminder. 'I apprehend that there are very few people now who look back upon that war [Crimean] with satisfaction, and I am confident that there is nobody insane enough in this country to desire a repetition of it.'

The *Daily News, Spectator,* and *The Times* praised or accepted Carnarvon's plea for peace. Foreign observers, such as the German and Dutch ministers in London, but also the Crown Princess of Prussia, pointed out that it clearly and publicly demonstrated the split in the Cabinet. While Münster reported the general feeling that Carnarvon's remarks were tactless and unlucky, Bylandt thought that they well expressed the feelings of the majority of the people. Most Liberals were pleased, Childers being an exception. Ponsonby found the speech calm and thought it would do immense good. Hammond, surprisingly, wrote that it was quite sensible and would produce a good reaction. Tenterden noted the great success of the Colonial Secretary's words; Gladstone was happy with the tranquillizing effect of them, but desired the meetings and declarations of opinion to continue in order to pressure the Government to maintain its neutrality. The funds went up.[29]

Beaconsfield opened the Cabinet meeting of 3 January by referring to Carnarvon's speech and describing it as one that Gladstone might have given. After the grave censure by the Prime Minister Carnarvon indicated the possibility of his resignation. There followed a period of silence, until Cairns, in a conciliatory tone, expressed his regret with Carnarvon's speech. Derby spoke and expressed a hope that the Colonial Secretary would not retire in the present crisis as a mistaken impression of his conduct would result. Salisbury defended the Colonial Secretary, especially on the point of his feeling the Crimean War to have been an insane policy. But Manners, Hardy, and Northcote expressed their regret with Carnarvon's action. The matter was left unresolved as the Colonial Secretary had to leave the meeting early and repair to Osborne as minister in attendance, where the Queen became angry and scolded him. Victoria, not without justification, hoped he would resign, and the Prime Minister was willing to accept his colleague's withdrawal. But between the meeting on the third and the next one on 7 January, great efforts were made by Salisbury, Northcote, Derby, and Smith to prevent the resignation which Carnarvon indicated would be given unless Disraeli retracted his censure. To Salisbury he wrote the following. 'I [Carnarvon] not only do not wish you to leave with me—if it comes to this—but I doubt whether it is wise for you to do so. The point is quite sufficient for one person to stand upon; but perhaps not large enough for three.' While Beaconsfield and Carnarvon were each waiting for an apology from the other, Salisbury appealed to his friend not to resign except on a general point of policy. 'Do not renounce such a task ["of keeping the country from entering on a wrongful war"] on account of a rude phrase by a man whose insolence is proverbial.'

It was a clear case of the pot calling the kettle black. Most of the considerable effort made by colleagues to prevent Carnarvon's resignation was done because it probably would be regarded as tantamount to a declaration of war on Russia. Beaconsfield's decision not to bring it about, which at this point would not have been difficult, was due to his realization that the public would think that war was intended and Parliament would therefore refuse funds to be so used, funds which the Prime Minister hoped to obtain in order to successfully influence Russia before she violated British interests. In fact, as Northcote pointed out, Carnarvon's speech would facilitate the Government's getting their vote of credit from Parliament.[30]

At the Cabinet meeting on 7 January both the Prime Minister and the Colonial Secretary were prepared to compromise. Before the meeting a note from Derby reached Carnarvon. 'I repeat what I have said. Don't weaken your own side. . . . Don't strengthen the war-party by secession. . . . No new member will be allowed in the Cabinet who is not hot for war.' At the opening of the meeting Carnarvon made a mild and conciliatory apology and then read a memorandum which he had prepared on the advice of the Foreign Secretary. Disraeli replied that he was happy that Carnarvon had not retired and requested a copy of the paper read by the Colonial Secretary. There the issue terminated to a chorus of general relief and 'some incoherent but well meant expressions from Lord Derby'.[31]

The soothing-over of the Carnarvon incident did little to cement ministerial unity. A Cabinet meeting was held on 9 January to consider a draft of the Queen's speech for the opening of Parliament. The draft was attacked by Derby, Salisbury, and Carnarvon, who were supported even by Cairns. Only Northcote loyally came to the defence of the draft and the Premier along with Manners. The rest were neutral or opposed. The ministers then retreated from all the positions which they had accepted for the past three weeks. There followed a half hour of sharp exchange leading eventually to agreement on three points—peace negotiations, meeting of Parliament, and increase of armaments. Beaconsfield informed the Queen that his colleagues—save for Manners and Northcote who supported him—were much influenced by the commercial depression. According to Carnarvon, the draft speech was strongly pro-Turkish and ministers were successful in significantly altering the wording. 'But it was the last success gained by the dissenters in the Cabinet, and it was also the last time Salisbury acted with Derby and myself. After that he was acting openly and consistently with the Prime Minister.'[32]

One possible reason for Salisbury's easing towards Beaconsfield was the military situation and an apparent Russian disinclination to negotiate with Turkey for peace despite indicating a readiness to treat at military headquarters. At the beginning of January Sophia fell to the Russians and by the middle of the month Philippopolis as well, as Ottoman resistance was disintegrating. Adrianople was reached on the twentieth, and towards the end of January the Russians could see Constantinople itself. In the fifty-one days between the fall of Plevna and the Adrianople armistice, Russian forces marched nearly 400 miles through deep snow and sub-zero temperatures. One writer has correctly observed that this brilliant success was largely the result of 'the almost boundless patience and endurance of the Russian soldier'.[33]

The Turks, desperate for British military support, allowed Layard's sympathy[34] and Beaconsfield's communications to Musurus in London to encourage their hope that by delaying peace negotiations with the two Grand Dukes long enough they could elicit active intervention of London.[35] It took the Porte from 8 to 15 January to dispatch two plenipotentiaries from Constantinople, the latter date being the time of their departure from the capital. They only arrived at the headquarters of Grand Duke Nicholas on 19 January. Ottoman hesitation bred from desperation out of hope was exceeded by Russian delay, when the latter realized that there was little or no Ottoman resistance left, and only the weather and the question of supplies could impede military advance. Consequently, it was decided to advance as far as possible before agreeing to a suspension of hostilities. Around 3 January peace instructions from St. Petersburg were sent by courier—not telegraph—to the two Grand Dukes, which only reached Nicholas on the fourteenth. On the morning of 19 January, a few hours before the arrival of the Ottoman plenipotentiaries, a telegram from the Tsar informed his brother to continue military operations and to delay the communication to the Turks of the peace bases by asking them for their proposals which it would be necessary to refer back to St. Petersburg. In anger Nicholas smashed the telegraph lines and unknowingly established a Russian precedent. Having informed Constantinople that Ottoman delegates must be sent to him to receive Russian terms, he was now instructed to ask them for their terms.[36]

On 10 January Layard telegraphed to London that in view of the Russian advance it would be politic to bring the fleet nearer to Constantinople. The following day the ambassador suggested that he be instructed to induce the Porte to bring troops to the Bulair lines in order to defend Gallipoli. As the fleet could not safely anchor at Besika at this time of year, Layard was prepared to request the Sultan's permission to anchor within the Straits. The Prime Minister, who was nearly as worried as his sovereign, induced Derby to complain to Russia about her delay in armistice negotiations, and informed the Queen of his intention to call a Cabinet meeting for 12 January and propose to his colleagues the occupation of the Dardanelles.[37]

Beaconsfield commenced the meeting of 12 January, a violent one of three hours, by reading a spirited memorandum from the Queen urging her ministers to decide what steps to take as a result of the Russian military advance. The Prime Minister then proposed to send the fleet within the Dardanelles and a military force to the Bulair lines, which were a few miles above Gallipoli, if the Porte would give its assent. Derby strongly objected, and the Prime Minister again, as on 17 December, indicated that it would be necessary to prorogue Parliament so that a new Government might be formed. Then a new point was raised, debate ensued, and the Cabinet was found still to have life. Ministers were learning that a completely fragmented Cabinet sometimes has a longer life than one which contains a mere two-sided division, as the former's potential for coalescing or resuscitation is nearly total. Salisbury averted disruption by proposing that Layard be instructed to obtain the Sultan's permission for the fleet, and that Gorchakov be asked for a pledge that Russia would not occupy Gallipoli.

After long reflection, & extreme stubborness, Lord Derby rose from his seat, & said that he could not sanction any projects of the kind, & that he must retire from the ministry.

Lord Salisbury said then, that if Ld. Derby retired, he must retire too, as he felt the difference of opinions in the Cabinet were insurmountable ... [and] hopeless; that he had only suggested the compromise ... as he felt it wd be disastrous ... to break up now.

Cairns asked the Foreign Secretary what he would propose as an alternative but Derby had nothing to suggest. 'He opposes everything, proposes nothing. The P. Minister said that Ld. Derby, & those who agreed with him, ought to have retired three weeks ago, & not consented to the summoning of Parliament ...'

As everyone except Carnarvon, who violently protested against Salisbury's compromise proposal, supported the Prime Minister, even Derby accepting in the end, two telegrams were sent off at once from the Cabinet room. In one Loftus was instructed to ask for assurance that Russian troops would not be sent to the Gallipoli peninsula. The other to Layard is given below.

Ascertain whether any objection would be offered by the Sultan ... to the British fleet, to anchor within the Dardanelles, it being clearly understood that this step is no departure from the attitude of neutrality hitherto maintained, but merely a precaution to keep the channel from being closed.

You had better not interfere as to the lines of Boulair, or in any way with the disposition of Turkish forces.[38]

Salisbury had supported the Prime Minister against Derby, as he had done at the Cabinet meeting of 18 December only then to relapse, but the India Secretary was finding that a combination of advance by the Russians and withdrawal by Derby left him little alternative. The Foreign Secretary, now finding Beaconsfield openly criticizing him to colleagues, as was done in Cabinet on the twelfth, was nearing physical and emotional breakdown. After the meeting on 12 January he told Smith he was opposed to occupying Gallipoli, and upon bumping into Delane of *The Times*, indicated to the latter that 'if Parliament desires a coercive policy they must get someone else to carry it out'. Ponsonby was startled by the decision regarding the fleet, as he told Carnarvon. 'So I went to church with a curious heart, and joined in the war psalm "Let God Arise" including the words "there is little Benjamin their ruler."'[39]

In the midst of great excitement, and a belief in Vienna, Constantinople, and London that Russia was being deceitful and, having no intention of making peace, was merely stringing out negotiations so her military might reach Constantinople, Derby became ill and took to his bed. The Foreign Secretary, according to Carnarvon, broke down from overwork and nervous exhaustion.[40] Overwork was not the main culprit as the Foreign Secretary's physical efforts were not particularly excessive. He was not lazy, but he was much at Keston and Knowsley, even now, and a considerable part of his work was delegated to Tenterden. The Queen suggested again that Beaconsfield accept his resignation and himself become Foreign Secretary. 'Lord D. will *do nothing, originate nothing,* and besides is indiscreet & leaves our Ambassadors *abroad* without instructions. . . . What can be the *cause* of Lord Derby's incredible conduct?' On the fourteenth the Cabinet met and, in the words of Beaconsfield, unanimously approved sending the Queen's telegram[41] to the Tsar, proving that consensus was still possible. On the same day, however, Carnarvon, dwelling upon the Cabinet's decision on 12 January to obtain the Sultan's consent to bring the fleet within the Dardanelles, decided he would resign if Ottoman permission were given, and so informed Derby whose illness kept him from the meeting.[42]

The Foreign Secretary was too unwell to meet with his colleagues even at home on 15 January, and wrote to the Premier of his opposition to sending the fleet past the entrance to the Dardanelles.

Both my doctor and my own sensations tell me that I cannot hope to appear in the House of Lords for the next week or ten days. I have passed most of the time since our last Cabinet [12 January] in bed, and though picking up, am very weak and pulled down. After the next two or three days, I could manage to attend a Cabinet, but not to make a speech.

More I think of the Dardanelles business, less I like it. Will not negotiations supersede such a step.

The Foreign Secretary was able to receive at home Carnarvon, Shuvalov, and Tenterden, the Under-Secretary having loyally replaced his chief as an obstacle to any provocative Cabinet action, as well as a means of communication between the Foreign Secretary and the rest of his colleagues. The ministerial council of 15 January also lacked the presence of Manners, Richmond, and Cross, who were with the Queen at Osborne, but Tenterden was invited into the meeting to give his views, which he did, deprecating moving the fleet by pleading the violation of international treaties. All except Carnarvon, who was silent while Tenterden was present, favoured asking Austria to join Britain in sending ships within the Dardanelles, none more strongly than Salisbury who argued that as the Porte was under constraint, its rights could be ignored. The orders to the fleet to move were suspended until Austria could reply to a British request for naval co-operation, but even a negative answer from Vienna was not to change the British orders for the Mediterranean squadron to enter the Dardanelles. As soon as the meeting ended Carnarvon wrote to Beaconsfield requesting his resignation be submitted to the Queen once final orders to the fleet were sent. Smith informed Northcote of his desire to delay the naval action if Derby objected as the latter's loss would be a greater evil than a delay involving a few hours of sailing time. Northcote, who was as eager for action now as Salisbury, alerted Disraeli to the possibility of Tenterden's using his influence with Derby to stop the sending of the telegrams. Apart from the telegram to Vienna, the ministers had decided to press Russia again for an assurance against invading Gallipoli.[43]

On the morning of 16 January the third consecutive Cabinet meeting was held at which the Premier read a memorandum from Derby as requested, which strongly opposed sending up the fleet as being without object or need. The receipt of two telegrams upon the preceding evening, however, rendered further efforts by Tenterden, Carnarvon, and the Foreign Secretary temporarily unnecessary. One telegram from Loftus seemed to have made Gallipoli safe. 'Russian Government has no intention of directing their military operations on Gallipoli, unless Turkish regular troops should concentrate there. They hope further that in putting the question, Her Majesty's Government do not contemplate an occupation of Gallipoli, which would be a departure from their neutrality, and would encourage Porte to resistance.' Information from Layard conveyed an Ottoman request that the contemplated naval action be postponed in view of the possible Russian retaliation against the Turks which it might cause. 'I [Layard] have not thought it desirable to do more than ask question, as there is much force, I think, in the Grand Vizier's objection, and there is nothing at this moment which renders the presence of the fleet in the Dardanelles of urgent necessity.'

As a result of the Ottoman refusal to consent, the Cabinet which met on the sixteenth dropped the contemplated naval action and confined itself to responding to Austria by expressing cordial co-operation with her. The Colonial Secretary still thought it necessary to inform the rest of his colleagues of his previous request to resign, occasioning further cool correspondence with Beaconsfield.[44]

The differences in the Cabinet reflected to some degree those in the country. Opinion aroused by people like Chamberlain, Mundella, Gladstone, and Liddon resulted in petitions, speeches, and articles deprecating a British resort to arms. Other Liberals less anti-Turkish or more anti-Russian—Dilke, Lubbock, Grant Duff, and most of the Liberal front bench—wished equally for the restoration of peace as probably did a large portion of those who were politically aware but silent. It was difficult to forget the conflict of 1854 and it was believed by many that the Queen and Beaconsfield desired war, and all realized that Britain had no European allies. Slightly less strong than the desire for peace was the growing hostility towards and suspicion of Russia, especially when it seemed that she did not wish to end the war, or to end it only in a manner harmful to British interests. But the feeling for peace, as Cowley wrote, was strongest. 'It was a fatal day for England when Lord D. took the seals of the Foreign Office. Still he is backed up by the country at large, or at least by that part of it which speaks.' The increasing Russophobia could not still the Christian steadfastness of the Freemans and the Liddons.

'To me [Liddon] the cause of Russia in this struggle appears plainly to be the cause of Righteousness. . . . Between Russia . . . taken at . . . [its] worst, and Turkey, the difference is enormous. It is the difference which Christianity alone can make. Christianity always carries with it the germs of a progressive improvement; whereas Mohammedanism condemns the races which it curses to stagnate in evil. . . . But Russia contains the true secret of improvement and her advance in Central Asia has been as great a blessing to humanity as has our own in India.'

On the day before the convocation of Parliament two meetings were held in London. The Committee in Favour of the Free Navigation of the Straits, formed by Freeman, Liddon, Auberon Herbert, Humphrey Sandwith, and C. Maurice, held a meeting at Willis's Rooms for the purpose of opening the Straits to all countries. Though a resolution was passed to this effect, there was an apparent difference of opinion among those present. At Exeter Hall, filled with working men, with Mundella, Broadhurst, Auberon Herbert, and Malcolm MacColl on the platform, cries and protests against a war policy were uttered.[45]

The Queen suspected that one of the reasons the Government and the country were not, in her view, up to the mark, was due to the debilitating effect of material desire and satisfaction. Northcote attempted to reassure her about the pursuit of wealth and proper public spirit.

But the people now claim, and exercise, a much larger and more direct share in the conduct of public affairs than was formerly the case, and they look at questions of foreign policy from new points of view. . . . They are liable to be much misled by one-sided appeals to feelings and principles which are in themselves highly creditable.

The cause of any unwillingness on the part of the people to act energetically at the present time is, not that they are too much absorbed in meaner pursuits . . . but that they are not convinced that they would be doing right in fighting for what they would consider the cause of Turkey, and therefore of mis-government; and their suspicions have been so artfully awakened that it is most difficult to make them see that there is no intention to lead them blindfold into a position which they would so much dislike and from which they might find it difficult honourably to retreat.

When Parliament was opened on 17 January both Hartington and Granville made reference in their speeches to the depression in trade and industry. But the news that all waited to hear was the reason for the early calling of Parliament and the intentions of the Government. The crucial part of the Queen's speech which was read to Parliament was relatively mild and indirect. 'But I cannot conceal from myself that, should hostilities be unfortunately prolonged, there is danger that some unexpected occurrence may render it incumbent on me to adopt measures of precaution. Such measures could not be effectually taken without adequate preparation, and I trust to your liberality to supply the means which may be required for that purpose.'

Hammond correctly extracted the meaning of the address from the throne. 'Porte has nothing as Porte to expect from England; the Vote of Credit is only to provide against negotiation breaking off and our interests being compromised.' It was, in other words, a mild warning to Russia. Münster, the German ambassador, thought that both political parties were dissatisfied with the declaration, the Conservatives finding it too weak, the Liberals disliking an unspecified money appropriation. Within Parliament Ponsonby and Northcote reported to the Queen that opinion was behind the Government. Of those who spoke Salisbury was the most interesting.

We had in past times pursued a policy of which the maintenance of the Turkish Empire was the life and soul. That time had passed. Opinion had changed. . . . But I am not prepared to accept the new gospel which I understand is preached—that it is our business, for the sake of any populations whatever, to disregard the trusts which the people of this country and our Sovereign have reposed in our hands.

The last sentence is exactly the position expressed by both Elliot and Layard, on which some contemporaries and later commentators and historians heaped stinging denunciation. It is true that Salisbury put the point more gracefully and delicately, and did not use the phrase British interests. And if Elliot and Layard exhibited more sympathy for the Ottomans, their behaviour was less selfish than that of the India Secretary and less naïve in artificially separating interests which London and Constantinople shared.[46]

After the address was carried by a vote of 301 to 253 on 18 January, there would be no real Parliamentary conflict until the debate on army estimates at the end of the month. As earlier intended and anticipated, the Government did not ask Parliament for an immediate vote of credit, and it fell to Northcote to explain this lapse to an irritated sovereign. The Russian promise not to invade Gallipoli together with the opinion of the British military authorities given immediately before the opening of Parliament, that a dash there on the part of Russia had only a fair prospect of success, were part of Northcote's explanation.

We could not tell what the Russian [peace] terms would be, nor whether they would be such as to justify our taking measures pointing to our active participation in hostilities. If, while it was still uncertain whether these terms would be moderate or extravagant, we had come to Parliament for a vote we should have been met with the objection that we had as yet no case ...

But, by announcing that we wait to see her terms, before declaring our own action, we place her [Russia] in a position which must convey to her a warning without a provocation ...

There was another reason why we could not ask for an immediate vote. We had advised the Porte to ask for terms of peace; and if, while it was so asking, we had begun to arm ourselves we should have encouraged the Turks to be unreasonable, and should thus have made ourselves morally responsible for their continuing the war. This would have been cruel to them, unless we had been prepared to come to their assistance.[47]

At the same moment that the Government's mild intentions

were made known to Parliament, an attempt was made to put to use and even formalize the understanding with Austria. Both Vienna and London had good reason to distrust each other's motives, and each party hoped to induce the other to take some action to moderate Russian pretentions without drawing Russian hostility or anger down upon itself. Andrássy went so far as to suggest to Buchanan that the British fleet, which was at anchor near Smyrna on the Anatolian coast, should proceed to Constantinople in order to resist Russian appetite. Within hours there was another request for the fleet, this time from the Porte; not indeed for it to come to Constantinople, but to Besika Bay so that it might reach Gallipoli should the Russians make a move towards that place or Bulair. The Queen also desired the fleet to be at Constantinople, partly for any humanitarian service it might afford,[48] and her concern surprisingly drew a demurer from Beaconsfield on the grounds that the fleet could not prevent the Russians from occupying Constantinople, and if the latter occupied Gallipoli, the Sea of Marmora would become a mousetrap.[49]

At the Cabinet meeting held on 21 January Disraeli proposed to his colleagues that Austria be offered a defensive alliance. 'If necessary, a pecuniary aid; provided she would mobilize a sufficient force upon her frontier, & join us in an identic Note to Russia. Our fleet, of course, to go up to Constantinople.' After an awkward and disagreeable discussion, all the ministers agreed to the proposal save for Derby and Carnarvon, but eventually the Foreign Secretary gave way to the identic note alone, and it was wired at once to Vienna. Andrássy was asked for an immediate answer to a joint Anglo-Austrian prohibition of a Russian occupation of Bulgaria, the shores of the Straits, or the Sea of Marmora without their consent. When the Cabinet met on the following day, Andrássy's answer had not yet been received, so the ministers disbanded, but agreed to be ready to meet at an hour's notice on the following day, the twenty-third. The Austrian reply was not a great surprise. Andrássy expressed his disappointment that Parliament had not been asked for money, that Gallipoli had not been occupied, and that the fleet had not been sent to Constantinople. Both Beust and Buchanan reported Andrássy's disinclination to accept the British proposal. 'The

Austrian Government ... would not find any support in making a demonstration in going diplomatically hand in hand with England so long as the British Government have not given a visible sign of their determination to protect at least their maritime interests, and so long as they have not by so doing created confidence in their being able to act.'

On the evening of the twenty-second Beaconsfield sent Corry, his private secretary, to see Beust. The Austrian ambassador indicated that only after the British fleet had gone to Constantinople would his country agree to give an order for mobilization. Borthwick was seen by Shuvalov, who, aware of the British negotiations with Austria, attempted to reassure London by stating that Russia would make peace at Adrianople and not advance further. But on the morning of 23 January another telegram reached London from Buchanan, reporting Andrássy's desire for the fleet to go to Constantinople and the latter's unwillingness to act jointly until Britain proved by some active and material step that she was in earnest.[50]

A crisis point was reached on the morning of 23 January. Reports had come to Layard, which were sent on to London, that the Russians were advancing on Gallipoli, and the Government still had no information concerning Russian armistice terms or the position of Russian negotiations with Turkey. Andrássy's expectations were reinforced by a letter Disraeli received from Hart-Dyke, the Conservative whip, who indicated that the party and the House of Commons expected the Government to take decided action to protect British interests. Disraeli would read this letter to his colleagues as evidence of the indignation with the Government's indecision.

Austrian pressure, Ottoman collapse, Parliamentary expectations, and suspected Russian perfidy convinced Beaconsfield and nine of his colleagues at a Cabinet meeting held on the afternoon of 23 January to order the fleet to Constantinople. Carnarvon and Derby objected, as Beaconsfield anticipated, having already obtained the Queen's permission to accept any resignations. Immediately after the meeting Smith went to the Admiralty and sent the following telegram to Admiral Hornby who was near Smyrna. 'Sail at once for the Dardanelles, and ... Constantinople. Abstain from taking part in the contest between Russia and Turkey, but the waterway of the Straits is to be kept open, and in the event of tumult at Constantinople you are to protect life and property of British subjects.' When Carnarvon left the meeting he stopped on his way home at Derby's residence in St. James's Square. At Derby's request Carnarvon agreed to suspend his letter of resignation until the following day. Both men then dispatched to Beaconsfield their resignations which the latter received reasonably early on 24 January. Carnarvon's letter was polite but cool; Derby's was friendly and sad, with almost a touch of relief that he had been able finally to break the political umbilical cord that had long tied him to the Prime Minister, though 'no lapse of time' could alter his 'feelings of private friendship'. 'I may add that the incessant anxiety of the last two years has made me often doubt of late—all questions of political difference set aside—whether I should long be capable of even moderately efficient service in an office which at times like these admits of no rest from responsibility and labour.' Disraeli quickly replied to his friend's letter, touched by their impending political separation and anxious over the impact of Derby's explanation to Parliament on the vote of funds which was soon to be requested:

I can't trust myself at this moment to make any remark on your letter [of resignation] just received & would willingly let four & twenty hours elapse before I attempted to do so, but it is my urgent duty to remind you, that no explanation or statements can be made in the House of Lords till I have received Her Majesty's pleasure on your resignation, & her permission for your remarks.

The Prime Minister sent no such reply to the 'little Carnarvon's' letter of resignation.

Shuvalov was quickly informed of the orders to the fleet. With much anxious energy he had been attempting to reassure Derby and Disraeli that Russian peace terms were moderate, and to convince Gorchakov of the danger from London. It was, Seton-Watson writes, Lady Derby who provided the Russian ambassador with the Cabinet decision to send the fleet as well as having urged him to use every means to avert the crisis.[51]

At 5 p.m. on 24 January Hornby with the Mediterranean fleet left Smyrna for Constantinople. At approximately the same time, Northcote announced to the House of Commons, as decided by the Cabinet meeting of the day before, that a supplementary vote for naval and military services would be moved on 28 January. 'The statement was received with a fair amount of cheering on the Government side, and with silence on the Opposition side. Its gravity seemed to be fully comprehended.' Hartington asked the reason for the Government's departure from its announced intention of the seventeenth, that they would take no action until they had received the Russian terms of peace. 'Sir Stafford pointed out that this was said under the impression that the terms would be made known within a few days, but that a week had now elapsed, the terms were still unknown, and meanwhile the Russian forces were still rapidly advancing. It was impossible any longer to abstain from taking some measures of precaution.' Half an hour before the Commons met Shuvalov had informed Derby that he had not yet received his Government's peace terms. Within an hour of Northcote's reply to Hartington, a telegram arrived from Layard with the terms of peace. The last line of this telegram ran, 'I am informed that the [Ottoman] Plenipotentiaries will be instructed to accept them [peace terms] this afternoon.' As Northcote explained to the Queen, the ambassador's cipher was unclear and too uncertain to be completely relied upon. 'Mr. Layard's telegram is couched in language which he sometimes employs when he does not wish to be held responsible for the accuracy of his information,—"I am informed" etc so that implicit reliance cannot be placed on his intelligence.' What was unclear or uncertain was the exact nature of the terms, not whether they existed or whether the Turks were about to accept them. Having just informed the House of its intention to ask for money in lieu of the absence of Russian peace terms, the Government felt it could no longer justify the far more serious step of the fleet, once having obtained a version of those terms and news of their probable acceptance. At 7.15 p.m. the following instruction was sent to Layard.

On the receipt of your telegram no. 102, stating that the Porte had accepted the Russian conditions of peace, Her Majesty's Government have telegraphed to the Admiral not to enter the Straits, but to anchor at Besika Bay.

You should also telegraph to Admiral . . . to stay at Besika Bay.

The telegram from the Admiralty ordering Hornby to remain at Besika was dispatched at 7.25 p.m. Hornby, reached in the nick of time, telegraphed to London: 'Received your [Admiralty] telegraphic communication to anchor at Besika Bay when abreast Dardanelles Forts. Firman received there [from Ottoman authorities] for passage of Straits. I returned to Besika Bay immediately as ordered.'[52]

On 25 January Shuvalov gave to Derby the Russian peace conditions and, in addition, read part of a telegram from Gorchakov. 'We [Russia] repeat the assurance that we do not intend to settle by ourselves European questions having reference to the peace which is to be made.' It is not clear, however, to what extent Russian assurances concerning a European agreement on the Straits could be believed, for on the same day London received from Layard a fuller version of the Russian terms according to which Turkey and Russia were 'to come to a separate understanding as to [the] Dardanelles and Bosphorus'. Even a verbatim text of the Russian conditions, which Beust received from Vienna and left with Derby on 27 January, was ambiguous on the Straits. The Queen, consequently, still desired to send the fleet to Constantinople, and Layard was pressing Derby to modify conditions so disastrous to Turkey, and to the interests of England. The ambassador was convinced that the Russians were grossly deceiving Britain and the Porte, and the fact that Grand Duke Nicholas's forces continued to advance on Constantinople even after the armistice terms were signed at Adrianople on 31 January seemed to provide proof for his charges.[53]

A Cabinet meeting held on the twenty-fifth determined, notwithstanding the halting of the fleet, to ask Parliament for the vote of credit. When Northcote announced the Government's intention to the Commons on 24 January, a not inconsiderable movement against the vote and in favour of continued British neutrality manifested itself. The National Federation of Liberal Associations, the *Daily News,* the Eastern Question Association, more town meetings, and committees whose purpose was to preserve Britain from war took part. Added to this was Carnarvon's resignation and his statement to Parliament on the twenty-fifth. He was followed in the Lords by Disraeli who attempted to justify sending the fleet to Besika

Bay by reason of the continued Russian advance, the danger to Christians in Constantinople from panic erupting there, and potential Russian interference with the free passage of the Straits. Northcote was much cheered when he made the same announcement in the House of Commons. The Chancellor of the Exchequer indicated that the Government intended to ask for £6,000,000, but on the question of ministerial resignations he would make no statement.[54]

Carnarvon's wishes were quickly granted, and it seemed that Disraeli at first was almost equally ready to accept Derby's resignation as well.[55] But Dyke, the party whip, and Northcote feared the effect of the Foreign Secretary's retirement on Lancashire and Cheshire Parliamentary elections. Salisbury was concerned that Derby's leaving would be misinterpreted by Parliament and the country as meaning that the Government intended war. Some, such as Cross, wished Derby to remain on personal grounds. He, Northcote, and Tenterden attempted to persuade their friend to withdraw his resignation as the reason for it had disappeared with the halting and recall of the fleet. Personal affection, even now, for his colleague and political calculation caused the Prime Minister to request the Foreign Secretary to put off any Parliamentary explanation on 25 January, the day on which Carnarvon gave his, and to delay any public statement until the twenty-eighth. As Northcote explained, many in Parliament put down Carnarvon's behaviour to personal ill feeling with Beaconsfield; such would not have been the interpretation if Derby had resigned, for his long and friendly connection with the Prime Minister would have precluded such a belief. There was even a possibility, which Disraeli credited, that his friend's resignation would result in a Parliamentary defeat for the Government on the vote of credit.[56] Having delayed Derby's resignation by not communicating to him its formal acceptance, the Prime Minister unsuccessfully attempted to persuade the Foreign Secretary to take another Cabinet post instead of his present one. Derby was not unwilling to return, but only to his old post. Consequently, on 27 January, shortly before the Cabinet meeting on that day, Disraeli surrendered, as Blake puts it, to 'electoral alarmism' and announced to Derby that the Queen had approved of the withdrawal of his resignation.[57]

The inability of the Government to formulate and execute a clear and straightforward policy was due to many causes. The hesitation and vacillation with the orders to the fleet was almost pathetic,[58] and did nothing to enhance respect and confidence for the British ministers. Fortunately for Britain, for its excited and spirited monarch, and its tired but undaunted Prime Minister, Russian policy was as hamstrung, uncoordinated, and poorly conceived as its London counterpart. On 30 January the Ottoman plenipotentiaries gave their acceptance of Russian terms which were signed on the following day at Adrianople. It remained to be seen to what extent these terms would meet with the approbation of Austria and England.

# 19 SAN STEFANO

In January 1878 Carnarvon's departure,[1] Derby's emasculation, and Salisbury's support for Disraeli's anti-Russian policy united the Cabinet to a degree that had not been possible for over two years. It is not clear why the Secretary of State for India threw his support unreservedly behind the Premier. He may have felt there was no other desirable alternative in view of Russia's advance on Constantinople. The enticing nature of his future political prospects as a result of Derby's increasingly apparent unfitness and the old age and physical breakdown of Beaconsfield may have influenced him. He knew that he had the approbation of the Queen, a fact which the Prime Minister used because he thought it had its effect, even on a Cecil.[2]

Unlike the Queen, irritated by what she considered Austrian procrastination and prepared to act without allies, the Prime Minister still sought the reality of an alliance with Vienna. He was banking on the Parliamentary acquiescence in a £6 million vote of money to convince Andrássy of London's seriousness, though he was equally desirous of an Austrian connection in so far as it would act positively to elicit Parliamentary approval of the Government's request for money. Elliot, who reached his new ambassadorial post in Vienna on 26 January, saw Andrássy on the evening of his arrival and urged him so as to enable the Government, when they asked Parliament for money, to indicate that they were acting in concert with Austria. Andrássy was understandably suspicious of British intentions, having just witnessed the recall of the fleet and a flurry of English peace meetings.

Suspected Russian treachery and the possible occupation by her of Constantinople had a surprisingly negative effect on Anglo-Austrian relations. The growing Slavic danger, instead of throwing Vienna and London into each other's arms, only highlighted their distrust of one another as the necessity for combined action increased. On 29 January Andrássy feared that Britain might repudiate their understanding of 14 August and informed Elliot that were Austria to be abandoned by England she would concert with Russia and obtain some compensation in Bosnia. On the thirty-first, in answer to Derby's question concerning Austria's reaction to a Russian attack on Constantinople, Andrássy's reply was not very encouraging.

He said that a Russian entry into Constantinople was not one of the points on which the two Governments had agreed to support each other, and that although he shared the objections to it of Her Majesty's Government, it would be necessary for England to be 'one length' in advance of Austria in any steps to be taken.

The case would be reversed in regard to a proposed Russian occupation of Bulgaria after peace, about which also there is no agreement between our two Governments, but which Austria must oppose even if not supported by us [Britain].[3]

On 31 January London had not yet learned of the conclusion of a Russo-Turkish armistice. Disraeli had to explain to the Queen that Britain alone had not the means to prevent the Russians from entering Constantinople as it would require a large military force. Many in Parliament were as anxious as Queen Victoria about Constantinople and even Derby was forced to admit in the House of Lords that there might be circumstances when it would be appropriate for the fleet to be sent to Constantinople. Political uncertainty and suspicion of Russia were producing more and more irritation both in Parliament and throughout the country. When on 28 January Northcote moved for additional supplies, Hartington asked for and obtained a three-day adjournment on the vote for the £6 million. The Liberal leaders, however, despite some misgivings,[4] decided to challenge the Government's request for money. On 31 January Forster moved an amendment opposing the Government's resolution for what he termed unnecessary supplies, as Britain's neutrality had not been infringed. He said that there was nothing in the reported Russian terms to which the Government could reasonably object and that its appeal for funds must therefore be considered a war vote.

I do not think the Government ought to be supported in any attempt by force to prevent the temporary occupation by Russia of Constantinople. . . . There is . . . another interest which is . . . an English interest. . . . That is the good government or better government of the

people of Turkey—the interest of the freedom of the Christian subjects of the Porte from the cruel bondage and the senseless tyranny
which, until it ceases, makes . . . European peace impossible . . .

Cross answered Forster and denied that the vote of supplies
was a war vote. He defended Beaconsfield from the personal
attack which Forster had made, and indicated that any delay in
signing the armistice was due to Russia, and implied that her
reason for such delay was to give her time to move closer to
Constantinople.[5]

On 1 February Northcote in the Commons and Derby in the
Lords announced that an unconfirmed Ottoman report given
by the Turkish ambassador indicated the signing of the armistice on the previous day. This had the effect of making the
continued Russian advance on Constantinople seem even more
unjustifiable and in violation of the cessation of hostilities. The
Foreign Secretary heard from the Queen, who feared for the
safety of British subjects in and around Constantinople, and
from Disraeli, who wished to dismiss Shuvalov and send him
home. Derby defended the Russian ambassador and implied
that any deceit or treachery was emanating not from him but
from St. Petersburg.[6] A pro-war crowd, including many
working men, gathered and created a disturbance for several
hours near the Cannon Street Station, and had to be dispersed
by the police. The crowd then marched to the Guildhall waving
Union Jacks and singing patriotic songs. The lord mayor permitted them to meet within the building where a resolution
was passed in support of the Government and a deputation
dispatched to Parliament which was received by Lord John
Manners.[7] In Parliament, debate on the Government's motion
for funds continued on 1 February, a discussion which both
the Commons and London's newspapers found dull.[8]

Beaconsfield, believing that the Russians were duping both
London and the Turks in an attempt to grab the almost
defenseless Constantinople, was stirred by hope from Italy and
his own deep aversion to England's becoming an object of
general indignation and contempt should that city fall.[9] The
Foreign Office received the following secret telegram from
Paget in Rome at 5.50 p.m. on 1 February.

I have just seen M. Depretis [the Italian Premier]. He is convinced

that Russians intend to occupy Constantinople, and he would regard humiliation of doing so, even temporarily, as most seriously menacing to Italian interests, which he considers identical with those of England. . . . He wishes to act entirely with us, but deems the consent of Austria and, if possible, of France indispensable. . . . I feel convinced that if . . . Austria alone, will join England, we may rely upon Italy.
. . .

Please telegraph as soon as possible the language I am to hold.

At a Cabinet meeting on the following day it was decided to telegraph Vienna and Rome and to seek the adherence of the latter to a combined naval entry into the Sea of Marmora in case Russia approached or occupied Constantinople. Disraeli, as he informed the Queen, was not particularly buoyant, especially as to Austria's reaction.

Austria will not act until she finds herself in conference,[10] but Italy seems disposed to adopt earlier & immediate measures. . . . Lord Derby did not seem adverse to this plan [a united appearance of the British and Italian fleets in the Sea of Marmora], and appears less scrupulous now, that the country begins to speak out. He had evidently persuaded himself, that the country was adverse to any interference.

Lord Beaconsfield suspects, that the whole affair of the armistice is a comedy, & that Russia will advance . . .[11]

The ending of the fighting was complicated by Russian secrecy and delay as well as by other problems. The Greek Government, encouraged by Russia, though restrained by Britain from attacking European Turkey during the war, was now afraid that unless it did so by moving into Thessaly, it would lose to the Slavs Ottoman territory inhabited by Greeks. Athens was in despair at reports of an armistice, and on 2 February Greek army units crossed over the frontier into Ottoman territory. Greeks, unconnected officially with the Greek Government, had attempted to stir up an insurrection in the area which the Greek army was now invading in order to protect life and property. British newspapers were even more unanimous in condemning such action than they had been in castigating Serbia for attacking the Porte after Plevna. The Government joined France in warning the Greeks and urging the recall of its troops.

Equally dangerous and more terrible was the misery endured by the thousands of largely Muslim inhabitants in Bulgaria and Macedonia who fled their homes as the Russians advanced, in the dead of winter, with insufficient clothing and little and sometimes no food. They collected in their thousands in Varna and Constantinople—sick, cold, hungry, and frightened. Many died on the journey or upon reaching the two cities which were ill prepared to care for the needs of so many refugees. There was concern in England for them and even more was expressed for the safety of British subjects in the East, and upon Derby's request for statistics, Layard reported that there were approximately 3,000 British nationals in and around Constantinople.[12]

One hopeful report was the Russian willingness to attend a European conference that Austria also desired in order to give European sanction to any Russo-Turkish peace terms. Believing that only a Russian refusal or acceptance of such a conference would enable Andrássy to consider taking active steps against St. Petersburg, London on 2 February indicated to Vienna that it favoured an immediate conference to be proposed by Austria to be held in Vienna. The following day Depretis, the Italian Premier, replied to London's request for a combined naval passage of the Dardanelles if Russia moved on Constantinople. He told Paget that the necessity for such a step no longer existed as the signature of the armistice had been confirmed. Waddington, the French Foreign Minister, also made a vague but negative response to the British suggestion. Depretis did announce acceptance of any proposal for a conference at Vienna and a desire to concert a full understanding with Britain previous to its convocation. Andrássy lost little time, and on 4 February formally invited Britain and the other Powers to a conference at Vienna. France, Italy, and England quickly accepted the invitation.[13]

The strain of events was telling upon the leaders of both parties in England. Disraeli had become irritable, unfairly criticizing Layard, and his health had deteriorated, forcing him to take to his bed. Gladstone, in an intemperate speech at Oxford on 30 January, admitted that for the last year and a half he had worked ceaselessly 'to counterwork ... what I believe to be the purpose of Lord Beaconsfield'. Privately he told Liddon that he thought that the Government would obtain a large Parliamentary majority, but that the debate then occurring would prevent the Government from posing before Europe as representing a united country in favour of what is virtually a war policy. His questionable eloquence at Oxford elicited much negative comment even among the university undergraduates who thought it fashionable to be Turkish. Hartington, foreseeing the possibility of naval action in light of continued Russian military advance, tardily asked the advice of Selborne, the former Liberal Lord Chancellor, on a question of international law.

I [Selborne] still think that it is impossible to maintain, that it is a *violation of the treaties* . . . for a British fleet to enter the Straits, upon the invitation or with the consent of Turkey, during the war between Turkey & Russia.

The question whether such an act might justifiably be treated as a *casus belli* by Russia is . . . one . . . depending upon . . . the circumstances. If (as is possible) its motive should be to enable Great Britain, in contemplation of impending events in which she would act as the ally of the Porte, to take up an advantageous position for future belligerent operations . . . and if the practical effect would be to encourage Turkey to continue the war . . . then I have no doubt that it is in substance a step inconsistent with neutrality . . .[14]

In both Houses of Parliament debate on the vote of credit and the Eastern crisis continued on 4 and 5 February. On the fourth Derby and Northcote, in reply to questions, were able officially to affirm that an armistice had been signed, though the exact terms were still not authenticated. Earl De La Warr spoke against a Russian occupation of Constantinople and, as Wirthwein points out, criticism of the vote of credit was rapidly diminishing. There were increasing numbers of public demonstrations throughout Britain expressing support for Her Majesty's ministers, and Gladstone and the Liberal frontbenchers seemed to have backed off in their Parliamentary speeches before the wave of patriotism.

Mr. Gladstone opened the debate . . . in a remarkably ingenious speech, with studied moderation, and great professions of a desire to bury all past differences, to support and strengthen the Government . . .

Then he came to his proposal, which was that we should adjourn the discussion on the £6,000,000 vote for the present . . . and should instead ask both Houses of Parliament to join in an Address to the Crown, tendering their support to the Government. . . . Although the effect produced was considerable, and if the speech had not been answered instantly it might have done a good deal of mischief among the weaker of our own friends and of the moderate Liberals.

Fortunately Mr. Hardy replied at once, and in a very firm and vigorous tone, contrasting Mr. Gladstone's out-of-door speeches with his speech of this evening. . . . Mr. Hardy's speech was excellent and most effective.[15]

Preaching moderation to Parliament, Gladstone held the scales evenly, and did the same to Russia. He requested Stead to place his views, but not to use his name, before a Muscovite audience. His Kiplingesque plea was for Russia to work for the Balkan Christians and not to be diverted by the possibility of territorial gains for herself. 'If she [Russia] can, in this supreme moment of her history, when she has been doing a great work of duty, still make the voice of duty her law, and prefer fame to flash, her position will be magnificent.' Stead sent off an article to the *Moscow Gazette* describing Gladstone's views on the terms of peace. In Parliament meanwhile debate on the vote continued. On 5 February Trevelyan and Hardy engaged in a personal argument which was followed by an effective speech by Derby's younger brother, Frederick Stanley, who answered the criticism of Childers and Gladstone, as well as explaining the necessity for the vote of credit. Northcote wrote to the Queen that it was the best speech of the debate. Harcourt followed and urged ministers to give up the scarcely hallowed independence and integrity of the Ottoman Empire at the forthcoming Congress. He argued that Britain should adopt the cause of nationalities. It had become clear to the participants in the debate that the opposition was disunited sufficiently—Radicals, Whigs, Irish, and Liberals—that it had no chance to defeat the government, and had with the help of Russia succeeded only in rousing the patriotic fervour of the country behind ministers. While Chamberlain castigated those 'weak-kneed Liberals [who] have deserted us', the Liberal leadership met in order to devise a way to avoid an embarrassing Parliamentary vote.[16]

On 6 February telegrams from Layard and Lyons arrived in

London and the information which they contained created great excitement and near panic in the British capital. From Paris came the word that Gorchakov had objected to Vienna as the seat for the conference and that Andrássy was adamant against the conference convening elsewhere. Much more calamitious news arrived from Constantinople, telegraphed by Layard who had been informed by the Turks that the Russians were continuing to advance despite the signature of armistice. His words bespoke Russian treachery.

Notwithstanding armistice Russians are pushing on towards Constantinople. . . . Although five days have elapsed since signature of bases of peace and the Convention of Armistice, Protocol had not yet reached the Porte, which is kept in ignorance of real terms. . . . Telegraph with Europe cut off, except through Bombay. State of affairs very grave. . . . One of the conditions of the armistice [is] that the Chekmedje lines should be abandoned, and Turks have been compelled to retire quite, thus leaving Constantinople completely undefended. Russians have occupied Tchataldja in considerable force
. . .

An official version of the protocol containing the Russian terms only arrived in Constantinople on the fifth or sixth of February, so that, consequently, London did not have this information when various versions of Layard's telegrams reached the Press and were printed on the evening of the sixth and the following morning. Exaggerated rumour had it that the Russians were already in Constantinople. *The Times* attempted to calm the public but other journals such as the *Morning Advertiser* and the *Morning Post* did the opposite and reported the fall of Constantinople. The former paper referred to it as the gravest news to arrive in England for fifty years, but that it was to be hoped that the country would defend its honour regardless of the cost.

As the day [7 February] advanced the excitement became more intense. Stocks, especially the Russian tumbled heavily. . . . Huge throngs centered in the neighborhood of Parliament. The palace-yard was so crowded that the gates had to be closed and the entrances guarded by large bodies of police. . . . The majority of the members of the ministry were enthusiastically cheered as they arrived, and the immense concourse of Londoners amused themselves, in the intervals, by singing patriotic songs.[17]

The blow at Britain's self-esteem was felt equally by the Queen, Layard, and Beaconsfield. The ambassador, acutely feeling the decline of British influence wrote to the admiral of the Mediterranean fleet. 'Altogether no great country was ever placed in such a position as England now finds herself. I very much fear the consequences, as there is a point of humiliation & disgrace to which the English people will not submit to descend—notwithstanding all the efforts of Mr. Gladstone, the Greeko-Anglicans & our ... politicians.' Beaconsfield also desired to escape ignominy as he explained to Derby.

We shall have French & perhaps Italian squadrons at Const[antinople] before England.

This won't look well. I believe you will see a burst of indignation in this country that has not been equalled since – 32.

The entry of the Russians will be an act of wanton duplicity, & may lead to infinite confusion.

Derby agreed as to the gravity of affairs because of the effect of a Russian occupation of Constantinople upon British opinion. Notes from the Prime Minister and Salisbury crossed. Disraeli's message was short—'Ought we not to act?' Salisbury's response was to move the fleet to Constantinople if it were possible. Even Northcote desired to send up the fleet as crowds cheered and shouted in the Foreign Office courtyard. The Queen urged the Prime Minister to use force to drive the Russians from Constantinople in order to preserve the country's honour and interests. She was, as she informed Disraeli, 'utterly ashamed'.[18]

At 11 a.m. on the morning of 7 February the Cabinet met and decided in theory to send the fleet up to Constantinople should it be necessary for the protection of British life and property. France was asked to do the same, and Austria was informed of the Russian advance and queried as to her intention of taking any measures as a result. Russia was reminded of former promises in respect to Constantinople. The Queen, though concerned about the danger to life in that city, was filled with mortification, anger, and near despair at receiving Beaconsfield's report of the Cabinet meeting and his admission that Britain lacked the means to prevent Russia from entering Constantinople. Derby explained to the Queen his agreement with the Cabinet decision. 'The war being over, he is quite willing to concur in the sending up of ships for the protection of British life and property . . . should it be decided upon that such a step is necessary. . . . His objection to it on a recent occasion does not apply now when the proceeding cannot possibly be supposed to intimate an intention of taking part in the war.' After the ministerial meeting a huge crowd lined the route between Downing Street and the House of Lords to cheer and accompany the Prime Minister, who was 'guarded by the Duke of Abercorn & Lord Abergavenny'.[19]

On the afternoon of the seventh anxious questions were asked of the Government in both Houses of Parliament. Derby and Northcote then read Layard's telegrams reporting the Russian occupation of Tchataldja and the Ottoman evacuation of the Chekmedje lines. In the Commons, in accordance with the agreement of the Liberal front-benchers, Forster rose and gave notice that he would withdraw his amendment. Hartington indicated that if the House attempted to bring on a vote his party would abstain. Some confusion ensued during which Northcote was called out and handed a note sent by Derby containing Gorchakov's denial of unauthorized Russian advance communicated to the Foreign Secretary by Shuvalov. It had been read by the Foreign Secretary to the Lords moments before, and Northcote now read it to the Commons.

The order has been given to our [Russian] military commanders to cease hostilities along the whole line in Europe and in Asia.

There is not a word of truth in the rumours which have reached you [British Government].

Greater confusion and wrangling occurred, finally ending in a division being taken on the motion that the Speaker leave the chair. The Government obtained a majority of 199 with 295 yes votes and 96 negatives. The Liberal leaders and many of their followers, along with most of the Irish, abstained from voting. A few Liberals and independents—Joseph Cowen and John Walter—voted with the Conservatives whose ranks were unbroken. Brand described the sitting as sensational and Northcote reported it as one of the most extraordinary sittings of the Commons that he could remember. The Times, which patriotically rallied behind the Government, editorialized as follows.

This has been the first real discussion of the Ministerial policy since the debate on Mr. Gladstone's resolutions [May 1877]. . . . It is good policy for the Liberals to stand aside [and permit the Government its £6 million] if for no other purpose than to spread a feeling of security. . . . Russia is profoundly distrusted, and not without reason. She is profoundly disliked, and not without reason also . . .[20]

Excitement continued in London throughout 8 February as it seemed that even if the Russians had not entered the city, there was nothing to prevent them from doing so when they pleased. Northcote uncharacteristically attempted to galvanize both Salisbury and Derby.

We should at once, openly, send orders to our fleet to go up to Constantinople to protect life and property, and invite the other maritime powers to do the same; and I would openly announce this in the House tonight. We shall do no good by confidential communications, and shall only make ourselves contemptible. A bold move of this sort is really the safest, for Russia cannot with any decency object . . .

The Cabinet met at 2 p.m. and agreed to send part of the Mediterranean fleet to Constantinople for the protection of British life and property. 'Her Majesty's Government presume that a further Firman [in addition to the one obtained in January] is not required; but procure one if you [Layard] consider it desirable.' France and Austria were informed of the British decision and asked to follow her lead. Russia was also told. Derby explained the decision to the Queen. 'While in no sense an act or a menace of hostility, [it] will in his belief do much to satisfy the feeling of those who are complaining of inaction on the part of the Government.' After the Cabinet meeting and the dispatch of the necessary telegrams Derby explained to an anxious House of Lords that the Russian advance was in pursuance of the Russo-Turkish armistice conditions, which he admitted left Constantinople absolutely undefended.

There can be no doubt that the public excitement in Constantinople is great, and that it is not likely to diminish. . . . After full consideration, we [the Cabinet] have thought it right that a detachment of the Fleet—not the Fleet itself—should go up to afford protection in case of need—first to our own subjects, and next, if it be required, to others who may be in danger from an excited population.

After Northcote made a similar announcement to the Commons, the House went into committee on the vote of money. Hartington rose and supported the sending of the fleet but effectively criticized the Government's request for money as it had not made clear the purpose for which the money was asked. Nevertheless, he indicated that he personally would not oppose the request.[21]

Northcote answered the Liberal leader, and indicated that the policy of the Government had three objects.

1, To maintain the commercial freedom of the Black Sea[22] . . . 2, to prevent any power from establishing itself in a position dangerous to our route to India; and 3, to promote a peaceful and durable settlement of the Turkish provinces. . . . He [Northcote] said the Vote was required in order to enable the country to take its own line in the Congress . . .

The Chancellor of the Exchequer concluded by saying that the money would be used, if it became necessary, for both transport and supplies for a small expeditionary force. Gladstone followed and supported the sending of the fleet, but strongly criticized a vaguely defined need for additional money. After an intemperate criticism of Austria, Gladstone indicated that he intended to vote against the proposed grant of money.

Immediately after Mr. Gladstone's sitting down some words passed between him and Lord Hartington which seemed to cause much excitement. Lord Hartington was apparently telling him that he should not vote, on which Mr. Gladstone sprang up, interrupting Mr. Hubbard, who was addressing the House, and said that he wished it to be understood that he meant to oppose the Vote. Lord Hartington immediately went out, looking very angry.

When the vote was taken in committee the Government received a majority of 204 with 328 ayes and 124 noes. The ineptness of the Government's request for additional money was a compound of no allies and inadequate leadership. Ministers were saved, however, by a combination of Liberal disunity and a patriotic aversion to Russia exemplified below by General Garnet Wolseley in a letter to his brother.

I do not dare to say this openly [the necessity of a war with Russia], for being a soldier, the curs of England would sneer out, oh he wishes for war from personal motives. In my own heart I know this is not the case: I wish it because I love my country before all earthly things, and am prepared . . . to . . . giving up my life for her, which some of those who cry out for peace . . . want ease and quiet . . .

Gladstone in the debate on the eighth gave the minority feeling in answering Cowen, who had suggested the submersion of party divisions when the welfare of the country was at stake.

It [Cowen's plea] amounts to this—that in questions of foreign policy we are to have no regard to right and wrong; that we are all to be Englishmen; and that, whatever proposal is made . . . in the name of England, we are to make no inquiry as to how far it is right or wrong. . . . In my opinion, such a proposition as that is most shallow in philosophy and most unwise in policy.[23]

Since the uproar in Britain at news of the Bulgarian massacres in the summer of 1876, Gladstone had adopted the position of a political agitator. It was at times a lonely and unpopular position, which alienated him from the official leaders of his own party and made him the object of public anger elicited by the absence of a certain kind of patriotism in the face of foreign danger. Most of Britain's political and social establishment in both parties found his conduct inexplicable and even outrageous. It was not so much Gladstone's appeal to out-of-door's opinion to counteract the work of the country's elected representatives in Parliament, to say nothing of the Cabinet, which excited so much wrath; even Gladstone admitted that such behaviour had implications so serious that it should be undertaken only infrequently and then never lightly. It was rather the affront to accepted standards of largely aristocratic behaviour, which by his conduct he ignored and transcended, that brought criticism and obloquy down upon him. The constitutional implications of an attempt to force Parliament and the Government to conform to the opinions of the vocally dissatisfied in the parishes and the towns was seen by the political élite essentially as an attempt which was socially unjustifiable rather than as something which was constitutionally questionable. The aristocracy criticized his unfairness to Hartington, the official leader whom he refused to follow, and some of the masses were angered by what seemed to them his unconcern for country. Even Chamberlain, seemingly a political ally, considered him erratic. On the evening that the vote for £6 million was passed, Gladstone dined with Shuvalov at the table of the well-known Liberal hostess, Countess Waldegrave. The latter noted that Gladstone was 'more odd and more impossible to manage than ever'.[24]

Three days after the vote was passed, Joseph Cowen, a Tyneside Liberal, rose to deny Gladstone's criticism of his own over-abundant patriotism and to point out Gladstone's questionable agitation.

He said I upheld the doctrine of allowing the Government of the day to have uncontrolled authority in foriegn affairs ... [this] may flourish in the arbitrary atmosphere of the Russian Court, but it cannot live in England.
. . .

But the policy having been assented to, its execution must be left to the Executive. If they blunder, you may censure them, dismiss them, or impeach them; but in a moment of national peril do not paralyze their movements by unnecessary complications.

Cowen then answered Gladstone's intemperate remarks about Austria with some questionable accusations against Russia and a reasonable defence of Turkey.

I admit that the rule of the Porte in the past has combined every evil that can be covered by civil government. ... [But] it is only right to add that the Government of Turkey is no worse than that of other Asiatic and African states with whom we hold close if not cordial relations. ... That of Egypt, which is propped up by English capitalists, is worse ...

When we recall the ferocity ... with which Ireland was, and with which Poland is, ruled, we should manifest some moderation in our denunciation of the Turks. ... It is true that the Christians in Turkey have been denied any participation in the civil administration, just as the Catholics and Jews were in this country till recently, and as our Hindoo and Mohamedan fellow-subjects are in India today ...

Cowen ended by emphasizing the difficult if not impossible task, ardently favoured by Churchill, Harcourt, Gladstone, and others, of planting nationalism in European Turkey, an area of conflicting creeds, races, and tribes. A few moments later Parnell, the Irish nationalist, introduced a touch of levity in an attempt to clarify the need of the Government for £6 million, that sum being totally inadequate for any real

preparations for war. 'He could conceive one reason why the
Vote was asked for. The Straits were narrow, and any Power
that held them might easily prevent the Fleet from coming
back. Perhaps these £6,000,000 were to bribe the Russians to
let the Fleet back again.'[25]

Gladstone was not the only prominent Englishman seriously
and adversely affected by the rise of British patriotic fervour.
The Foreign Secretary, whose presence in the Cabinet was
deemed a political necessity by Conservatives within and outside the Cabinet only two weeks before, and who in the past
often found his urging a fair treatment for the Porte unpopular
and in conflict with Britain's Christian conscience, now faced
criticism even from within his own party because his desire to
avoid a conflict with Russia was not sufficiently firm and
pugnacious to satisfy the public and anti-Russian outburst
throughout the country. The biographers of Disraeli and
Salisbury—Buckle and Lady Cecil—write that after Derby's
return to the Foreign Office at the end of January the formulation of policy escaped from his hands into those of an inner
Cabinet composed of Cairns, Salisbury, and Beaconsfield who
devised the course to be followed, which Derby then merely
initiated in a semi-comatose state. The Spanish minister in London adds testimony to Derby's growing unpopularity with his
own colleagues and the Press.

The peaceful attitude of this country has been considerably modified
and it is going to be modified even more in the same direction [a demand for more energetic political action].

Another important symptom of the situation is the irritation which
ministers manifest toward the language used by Lord Derby. . . . The
Ministers describe the language . . . as timid, cautious and insufficiently dignified for the language of England. [This was with
special reference to the words Derby used in announcing to Parliament the sending up of part of the fleet.]

In spite of the importance given a few days ago to the resignation
of this minister and to his remaining in the Cabinet, at this moment
. . . judging from what one hears . . . and [what is] in the newspapers
. . . one doubts that there is in the character of Lord Derby the
strength and qualities that the situation desperately demands.[26]

Lady Cecil and even Buckle, though to a lesser degree, over-
emphasize the so-called inner Cabinet and the part Derby

played in the formulation of policy after his first resignation at the end of January. Disraeli was only intermittently well enough to take an active and continuous part in affairs. Salisbury was consulted when in London but was often out of the city, and both he and Cairns were greatly consulted well before Derby resigned in January. In February the formulation of policy was undertaken by those members of the Cabinet who were near the Prime Minister or who took the initiative in placing themselves in his presence. In connection with the instruction to the fleet, after the refusal of the Ottoman Turks for it to enter the Dardanelles, Beaconsfield, Smith, and Northcote devised and settled the issue with help from Tenterden.[27]

The orders to Hornby and the fleet at Besika, which were dispatched on 8 February, instructed him to proceed if possible the next day for Constantinople. Layard, instructed by the Foreign Office to inform the Porte of the fleet's orders and to obtain its consent for British entry into the Dardanelles, acted on a telegram from London which reached him late on the afternoon of 9 February. The Ottoman ministers reacted badly to the request and, fearing Russian vengeance if it were granted, refused to give permission for British passage. When Hornby arrived at the entrance to the Dardanelles, he was denied permission to enter, and this, together with the absence of any firman and any instructions from Layard, caused him to return to Besika Bay and await further orders. As he told Layard, Hornby now favoured a joint Anglo-Ottoman occupation of the lines at Gallipoli, which the ambassador reported now contained 22,000 Ottoman troops.[28]

Layard also telegraphed to London for instructions. Wishing to avoid a Russian occupation of Constantinople, which he like the Turks thought would occur if the fleet came up and anchored off the capital, the ambassador reported to London on the morning of the tenth that there was no reason to fear at present any menace to British lives or property. If Nigra, the Italian ambassador, is to be believed, the Tsar intended such an occupation even before he learned of Britain's intended naval action, and indicated to Nigra that the Russian occupation would not be permanent, but would last only until the anticipated congress concluded its deliberations.[29] Upon learning British intentions, Gorchakov telegraphed to

Shuvalov that as Britain and apparently the other neutral Powers as well were sending their fleets to Constantinople in order to protect their subjects, the Russian Government would send into Constantinople part of its army, also for the purpose of protecting Christian life and property. As instructed by his chief, the Russian ambassador communicated the telegram to Derby on 11 February. Rarely had the Christians of Constantinople been so threatened by the near presence of Christian Europe which claimed it had come to protect them. During the course of Sunday, 10 February, Layard apparently changed his mind about the fleet coming to Constantinople and early in the evening telegraphed to London.

If Her Majesty's Government think it absolutely necessary that the fleet should come to Constantinople, I judge from what [Ottoman] Prime Minister tells me, that the Porte will limit itself to protesting and informing Russians that fleet entered the Straits in spite of such protest. The fear of an immediate Russian occupation of Constantinople prevents the Porte giving the Firman.

Ponsonby has accurately and picturesquely described Britain's position. 'We are in an awkward position just now with our fleet at the entrance of the Dardanelles sniffing like a dog at a hole hesitating for fear he may find a badger instead of a rabbit inside.'[30]

Salisbury, as he wrote to Beaconsfield, was worried lest Britain should appear utterly ridiculous, as a result of the fleet once again returning to Besika Bay. He also feared the impotence of Britain's position at the coming conference if Russia had uncontested control of Constantinople, and urged Disraeli to brook no delay in ordering the fleet to force its way in. The Cabinet met on 11 February and instructed Layard to continue to press the Porte for the necessary firman for the fleet, which would go through with or without it. 'But whatever action the Porte might take the Admiral [Hornby] was ordered to sail up the Straits at daylight on Wednesday morning [13 February].' The Admiralty's instructions to Hornby continued.

If fired upon by Forts [along and at the entrance to the Dardanelles] and ships struck, return fire—but do not wait to silence Forts, unless absolutely necessary to insure passage into the Sea of Marmora. Take what force you consider necessary, and take up position near

Constantinople—safe from surprise & attack.
Princes Island Anchorage suggested.
One or two ships may be left near Gallipoli to observe Straits.[31]

For the third time in as many weeks the fleet had been ordered through the Dardanelles, though nearly everyone believed Russia would use this as an excuse to occupy Constantinople. *The Times* rightly criticized the Government's transparent insincerity in claiming that its intention was to protect British subjects instead of plainly and justifiably admitting that its purpose was to assert British interests at Constantinople and the Straits. The Birmingham town hall was the site on 12 February of a stormy confrontation between the Conservative and Liberal associations of that city. Hartington, who thought that things appeared about as bad as they could, and that hostilities in a few days were a real possibility, nevertheless felt that no more Russian falsity could be countenanced. Forster agreed that affairs were very critical, but hoped that Liberal support for the Government would strengthen the position of Derby, calm the Cabinet, and prevent the latter being swept along by hotheads who desired war. Hardy, like Smith and Admiral Hornby, feared for the position of the fleet if the Russians occupied Constantinople, or worse Gallipoli, from where the fleet could be entrapped within the Sea of Marmora. Derby also saw war as a disturbing possibility blaming its cause on the folly of foreign governments and domestic opinion excited by the Press. 'I am puzzled to judge whether anti-Turkish or anti-Russian agitation is more vituperative or more foolish. There must be an end to the *imbroglio* within the next few months; if not, it will make an end of me. "The Foreign Secretary was reacting both to strain and to open public criticism which the Spanish minister in London characterized as unseemly. On the evening of the twelfth dissatisfied Conservative M.P.s met and agreed to withhold any further confidence in the Foreign Secretary, unless he adopted the tone of Beaconsfield.[32]

In Constantinople there were those who took some pleasure at British discomfiture. Posters were plastered about the city, one was even affixed to the door of the British Embassy, containing a mock advertisement. 'Lost—Between Besika Bay and the Sultan's Palace, a fleet of six fine iron clads, bearing the English flag. Anyone communicating to Lord Beaconsfield in-

formation as to their whereabouts will be suitably rewarded!'
Neither Layard nor the Porte found any humour in the
situation. The ambassador, like *The Times*, was amazed by the
excuse of protecting British lives and property and felt an open
declaration of purpose by London would have been more
dignified. As it was he could only record in his memoirs confusion and consternation. 'Were we going to war with Russia or
Turkey or with both, or against Turkey as the ally of Russia? I
could not say and I don't think the English cabinet could
either.' The Porte had not given up in its attempt to dissuade
the British from sending the fleet. At 3 a.m. on 13 February
Layard received such a request, which he refused, and another
was made when the Sultan appealed by telegraph to the
Queen. It was too late. At 7.50 a.m. Hornby set sail with six
ironclads, stopping at the entrance to the Dardanelles, where
the Turkish commander delivered the Porte's protest, and
proceeded eventually to the Princes Islands some twelve to fifteen miles from Constantinople and outside of the Bosphorus.
As the journey took place in the midst of a north-east gale and
snowstorm, one of the six British ironclads went aground at
the entrance to the Dardanelles and the squadron anchored
during the night within the Dardanelles. At least five ships,
however, made it through in the morning, but the transparen-
cy of the stated reason for their so doing was underlined by the
refusal of Germany, France, and Italy to ask for a firman to do
likewise since they felt there was no evidence of any danger
to European life and property. Nor did Andrássy take naval
action, though his former excuse for hesitation—a lack of
confidence in England's resolution—now seemed less
appropriate.[33]

Having already intimated to London two days before the
possibility of a Russian occupation of Constantinople,
Shuvalov communicated to Derby on 13 February a telegram
from Gorchakov indicating again the same thing. It is not clear
who determined Derby's reply to St. Petersburg as there is no
evidence that a Cabinet meeting took place.

Express to Prince Gortchakow satisfaction of Her Majesty's Government at declaration that Russian Government do not regard despatch
of a detachment of British fleet to Constantinople as partaking of any
hostile character, but that they cannot acknowledge that cir-

cumstances are in any way parallel or that the despatch of British ships for the purpose indicated justifies entry of Russian troops into Constantinople.

There is a marked difference between the two proceedings. In the one case the ships of war of a friendly Power are sent into the proximity of the city to afford protection which British subjects are entitled to require of their Government in case of need. In the other troops of a hostile army are to be marched into the town, in violation of the existing armistice, and at the risk of provoking disasters and causing the very danger to the Christian population which Russian Government deprecate.

The Foreign Secretary gave an additional warning to the Russian ambassador about any move towards Gallipoli.

I have expressed to Count Schouvaloff earnest hope that Russian Government will not make any movement of troops towards Gallipoli or of such a nature as to threaten the communications of the English fleet. I said any such movement would be regarded in England as compromising the safety of the fleet, and in the actual state of public feeling I could not answer for the consequences which might be most serious.

Your Excellency [Loftus] should hold similar language.

Shuvalov informed St. Petersburg that a favourable reply to the British requests, especially the second concerning Gallipoli, was necessary in order to prevent Derby's fall from the Cabinet. There was much evidence of the Foreign Secretary's declining popularity. In a matter of days he had fallen in the estimate of his own party from one whose presence in the Government was politically indispensable to something little short of a public embarrassment. A meeting was held in the Carlton Club for the purpose of forcing Derby to resign and of persuading Beaconsfield to become Foreign Secretary. Only the recognition of the need to present a solid front in the midst of a foreign crisis induced the warlike tail of the Conservative party to desist from its object. Shuvalov thought he saw Derby exhibit a new calm in the midst of the passionate excitement of public opinion, not realizing at first that this reflected an almost complete loss of control rather than an effort of will and determination. When the Foreign Secretary blamed British public excitement on the silence Russia maintained between 31 January and 6 February on the armistice and the bases of peace, Shuvalov answered that the sending of the fleet was no humanitarian gesture but a demonstration. This Derby readily admitted. In Parliament on the fourteenth, after Forster indicated that the entry of Russian troops into Constantinople was an insufficient ground for war, Robert Montagu denounced Alexander II as a tyrant.[34]

Peace between Russia and Britain hung by a slender thread in the middle of February. Gladstone, who now required police protection from patriotic mobs, shrewdly denounced Austria at every public opportunity, knowing that without an Austrian alliance Britain would hesitate before making war on Russia. According to Childers, the majority of the Liberal front bench did not follow him, and Brand, Speaker of the House, delivered a warning about him to Hartington.

My object was to call his attention to a danger . . . that Gladstone would inflame the country against Austria as he already had against Turkey, and that thereby we might lose the advantage of an Austrian alliance, which was to be encouraged, *provided Austria would join us in objects of which we should both approve* . . .

While Andrássy still managed to hold London at arm's length, an art in which he had become the world's foremost expert, an attempt was being made by the Cabinet to conciliate the Porte after ignoring its repeated pleas not to send up the fleet. In part the attempt reflected a British fear that the Turkish fleet by agreement or treachery would fall into Russia's hands. The Sultan was informed that at the conference which was still anticipated, England would attempt to secure for him the best possible terms. Following quickly upon this was a secret British offer to buy the four best Ottoman ironclads. 'Should you [Layard] succeed, you might suggest that means should be found to send the ships away on a mission or special service with secret orders to go to Malta where the money would be paid on transfer [of the ships].'

Along with this, and after Cabinet meetings held on 14 and 15 February, Derby handed Shuvalov a memorandum which reiterated in a more formal manner his verbal warning given on the thirteenth.

They [H.M. Government] could not but regard any attempt on the part of Russia to occupy the peninsula [of Gallipoli] or the Forts of the Dardanelles as an act which . . . must be designed to interfere with the navigation of the Straits, and, therefore, a direct breach of the conditions on which the attitude [of neutrality] hitherto maintained by Great Britain has depended.

Hardy was making all preparations for the sending of an expeditionary force from England, if it should prove necessary, which he hoped would not be the case. At the same time, Smith sent orders to Hornby to dispatch some ships to the Gulf of Saros, with orders to watch the Russians and warn their commander, if preparations were being made by him, that the fleet had been ordered to use force to oppose any Russian occupation of the Gallipoli Peninsula. Hornby or a deputy was to proceed to the Saros Gulf leaving Admiral Commerell near the Bulair lines within the Sea of Marmora. The latter was not to assist in the defence of the Bulair lines, but was, if the lines fell, to do all he could to destroy the heavy guns in the fortresses at Gallipoli.[35]

The Cabinet was meeting every day now as the possibility of war continued, and the Foreign Secretary, inner Cabinet or no, used his position for the maintenance of peace through his friendship with Shuvalov, the words by which he conveyed instructions to Layard, and his occasional criticisms within the Cabinet. Most of his colleagues also wished to avoid a military conflict, ironically none more so than Smith and Hardy who headed the fighting departments. Salisbury, Beaconsfield, and perhaps Northcote were less careful about the potential effects of British action on opinion at home and within Russia. The Queen, feeling deceived and humiliated, was urging them on. Neither London nor St. Petersburg desired to fight each other, but the danger of such a war was very real because each hoped that by intimating their readiness for it the other would back down. It was not the first time that war, which few desired, threatened to occur as a result of a game of bluff. The Spanish minister wrote from St. Petersburg that people there felt, or were allowing it to appear that they felt, that war was inevitable. Loftus remained indoors and no Russian entered his house.[36]

On the morning of 15 February the British ambassador delivered to Gorchakov Derby's telegram to the fleet of the thirteenth and the Gallipoli warning.

He [Gorchakov] considers that it [the sending of the fleet] is an act of political demonstration against Russia. ... I [Loftus] referred to question of Gallipoli ... saying that your Lordship [Derby] could not answer for consequences of any movement of troops toward Gallipoli. His Highness curtly replied that he would ... give ... [no] more assurances in regard to this subject. His Highness considers present position very grave. He was calm and anxious, but very determined.[37]

Russia continued to threaten the Porte with an occupation of Constantinople unless the British fleet departed. Consequently, in answer to the pleas of the Porte to remove the fleet, Layard and Hornby, on their own responsibility, moved the fleet from the Princes Islands to Mondania Bay about ten miles further distant from Constantinople.[38] The Turks, however, refused to sell Britain the four ironclads. Instead on 15 February in a meeting with Layard the Sultan suggested an alliance.

Sultan has personally requested me [Layard] to state ... that if England will come to his assistance with men, money or any other way, he would still be ready to defend his capital against the Russians; that he has troops and guns left which would enable him to do so especially with such assistance. ... He renewed his offer of placing his fleet at the disposal of Her Majesty's Government. ... I only undertook to transmit this message without giving him the least reason to hope that he could expect any help from England.

Shortly afterwards Layard, Hornby, and General Dickson, the latter being a hero of the Crimean War and attaché to his old friend the ambassador, all suggested versions of the same thing—military co-operation with the Porte. The Admiral reported that his ships at Gallipoli could not without Turkish consent destroy the heavy fortress guns. He considered the situation there to be critical and felt that only a quick understanding with Turkey could alleviate matters. Layard telegraphed that the Dardanelles could be secured by holding the Bulair lines, which he thought was possible with the aid of Turkish troops and ships. 'Captain Fife suggests that we should take the Turkish commander and troops now at Gallipoli Peninsula into our pay, with guarantee for pension and six months' pay in advance.' General Dickson agreed that the Bulair lines, which were above Gallipoli, could be defended by the Ottoman force already there, provided that British officers and about 1,000 men from the fleet could be attached to the Turkish troops. One would not have guessed that negotiations for final peace had opened at Adrianople between the Ottoman Empire and Russia, the latter being represented there by Ignatiev, who had come for that purpose from Russia.[39]

Shuvalov was working feverishly to maintain peace, and it seems likely that he and his friend Derby, whose courage and belief in peace he attempted to sustain, were working to some extent in harness to douse the ardour for war in London and St. Petersburg. The two men talked on 16 February and the content of their conversation was reported to Loftus and Gorchakov.

Count Schouvaloff talked at some length and earnestly on the absence of any desire on the part of Russia to go to war with England. He dwelt on the financial embarrassments of his own Government . . .

I [Derby] thought it advisable to state to his Excellency [Shuvalov] my conviction . . . that in the event of a rupture the Government of Austria would be ready to act with that of England.

Shuvalov informed Gorchakov that Derby's words had impressed him and that he believed in the sincerity of the Foreign Secretary's warning about Austria.[40] Neither Derby nor Shuvalov had a strong belief in Austria's intention to go to war. But they hoped to use the possibility of it to moderate St. Petersburg and to elicit a Russian reassurance to leave Gallipoli alone. This would deprive England of an excuse for hostilities and prepare the way for peaceful accommodation.

The dangerous gamble worked, brought off by a skilled and purposeful Russian intriguer, who saw his country's interests and his own abetted by the avoidance of an English war, and a nearly immobile English aristocrat reacting to the great and incessant pressure of emotional danger and finding it not inconvenient to go along with the ambassador, justifying his own devious and extraordinary behaviour by attaching it to a righteous cause. On the afternoon of 16 February Derby resurrected what had been only a shadow when he sent the following telegram to all British embassies.

State to Government to which you are accredited that the immediate assembling of the Conference seems to Her Majesty's Government to promise the only satisfactory issue from the present political complications, and urge that all the neutral Powers should join without delay in pressing on the Russian Government that it should be forthwith convened.

Italy, France, and Austria lost little time in responding, and pressed the Russian Government to accept a congress, Andrássy suggesting Baden-Baden as the site for the meeting. In the midst of a Cabinet meeting on 18 February word arrived from Shuvalov that a telegram from Gorchakov would be delivered that afternoon. The Cabinet adjourned to await the news which the ambassador brought to Derby.

Prince Gortchakow authorizes me [Shuvalov] by telegraph to declare to your Excellency [Derby] that the Imperial Cabinet maintains its promise not to occupy Gallipoli nor to enter the lines of Bulair.

The Imperial Cabinet expects in return that no English troops should be landed on the Asiatic or European coast [of the Straits].

The British Government quickly acceded to the quid pro quo and the danger of war seemed to have been averted, though Russia continued to threaten the Porte with occupation of Constantinople unless the fleet departed from the Dardanelles.[41]

With the possibility of a European congress being revived, there was something of a contest between Russia and Britain for each to improve her own and prevent the improvement of the other's military position. This occurred not necessarily in anticipation of war, as Sumner assumes, but in order to solidify and enhance bargaining positions at the conference table. Only in retrospect does the crisis seem to have abated, for over the next two months, even after the signing of the definite Russo-Turkish peace at San Stefano on 3 March, the possibility that miscalculation would erupt into war continued. That it did not was due only in small part to the energetic efforts of Shuvalov and the sad but supporting immobility of Derby. Uncoordinated and confused Russian policy as a result of the animosity existing between the Grand Duke and Ignatiev at Adrianople and the absence of a solid lead from the Tsar in St. Petersburg also helped, though at the same time Russian wavering increased British distrust.[42] Most important of all was the failure of London to induce Andrássy, who was probably personally ready, to mobilize and co-operate militarily with England. Here Bismarck's efforts to lean neither to Russia nor Austria were fundamental in moderating Austria's response to British solicitations.[43] German neutrality enabled the court in Vienna to overcome Andrássy's anger at what he, along with the British, considered to be Russian duplicity.

On 16 February Elliot had been instructed to communicate to Andrássy the Government's readiness to propose to Parliament a guarantee for a loan to Austria in order to facilitate Austrian mobilization. Andrássy manifested interest but refused to bite. Elliot correctly estimated that Andrássy would wait upon the outcome of the conference before taking steps to mobilize. Shuvalov conveniently informed Gorchakov of the offer of a loan and its refusal. The ambassador had assumed from the Tsar's attitude that Russia would still occupy Constantinople. He had in fact told Derby this and reported to Gorchakov his opinion that such a step, unlike a move on Gallipoli, would not provoke a rupture with England. Grand Duke Nicholas, despite the urging of Ignatiev, could not bring himself to enter Constantinople, but he did summon the courage to force the Turks to permit the movement of Russian headquarters to the fishing village of San Stefano which was only five or six miles from the city. For Turks, like Server Pasha, the recently dismissed Foreign Minister, who believed that England had thrown them over and that accommodation with Russia was both necessary and desirable, there was hope that the advance to San Stefano might satisfy the desire of St. Petersburg for an occupation of the capital. Needless to say, for London, the move only increased the already considerable British suspicion of Russia. Layard, who was kept informed by the Sultan of Russian peace proposals offered to the Ottoman plenipotentiary, was quick to telegraph them to London where terms such as a demand for the Turkish fleet and occupation of Bulgaria and Constantinople convinced those who still had any doubt of Russian duplicity. Tenterden especially was so affected, believing the Russians were using the conference as a means of delay in order to bring up reinforcements, and pressed the Foreign Secretary that he should not be fooled from taking a decisive attitude.

If H.M. Govt look on unconcerned waiting for a Conference they will find themselves as deluded as Austria, without even such compensation as Austria can grasp in Bosnia.

If one ever had any trust in Russia's moderation it must now be dispelled.

Tenterden's not completely unjustified paranoia was supported by Loftus, Elliot, Hornby, Currie, and, of course, Layard, who believed that a Russian occupation of Constantinople or her taking the Ottoman fleet while the British navy looked on would have serious effects on Britain's Muslim subjects in India as well as generally making England appear ridiculous.[44]

Though most of the London Press favoured the Anglo-Russian agreement on Gallipoli and the landing of troops as a step towards peace, the consensus of opinion, as represented by the *Daily Telegraph, Pall Mall Gazette*, and *Morning Post* considered the quid pro quo degrading for England. The Spanish minister as well as Münster reported that many in London thought the arrangement favoured Russia, and that the feeling for a war against Russia was strong. *Punch* felt called upon to offer up a 'parody for the prudent'. 'We don't want to go to war; for, by jingo, if we do, we may lose our ships, and lose our men, and what's worse, our money too.' Hammond summed up the nature of much English feeling for the benefit of Layard.

There is certainly a very ugly feeling getting up in this country where the exorbitancy of Russian pretensions and demands have startled people from the state of dreamy security. . . . Her [Russia's] reported claim for the cession of the [Ottoman] Ironclads . . . has touched our people to the quick, and the proceedings of Russia in the neighbourhood of Constantinople, her extravagant pretensions about Bulgaria, and her exorbitant demands for compensation for expenses . . . have certainly raised a state of feeling in this country, the consequences of which it would be scarcely safe to calculate upon. . . . The Liberal Party here is very much subdued in tone. . . . There is much dissatisfaction in the ranks of their own party [Conservative] with Ld. Derby. . . . For such an eventuality [war] we are making rapid preparations in this country. . . . In a few weeks, we might probably have in the field, between 40,000 and 50,000 men . . .

There are nasty, ugly stories going about Derby, who is said to drink too much, about Lady Derby, who is said to be in

Schouvaloff's pocket. It is no new story as to Madame Novikoff and Gladstone—the latter is evidently getting alarmed at the demon he has raised up. He abandoned his threatened demonstration at the Agricultural Hall [at a meeting for the purpose of preserving British neutrality] on the representation of the police that it would lead to a frightful riot. . . . Gladstone's windows suffer occasionally. . . . The result of the battle royal in Hyde Park was amusing enough . . .[45]

A Cabinet meeting on 21 February, after receiving Layard's telegram reporting a Russian demand that the Turks surrender the entire Ottoman fleet or else face a forceful occupation of Constantinople, decided upon the following warning which Derby delivered to Shavalov on the same day. 'In the event of the Russian troops entering Constantinople without the consent of the Sultan, Her Majesty's Government would feel themselves compelled to withdraw their Ambassador at St. Petersburg, and, in that state of things, they must decline to go into Conference.' Currie, as he explained to Layard, was not impressed with the threat. 'The ways of the Govt. are past finding out. They have threatened today to withdraw Loftus . . . & as far as I can make out have taken no step to meet the contingencies which such a withdrawal may lead to. . . . Our rulers have no nerve, I fear . . .'

New orders to the fleet seemed to confirm Currie's complaint. Hornby was ordered to use the fleet to aid in holding the Bulair lines if Russia attacked them, but he was to avoid any forceful prevention of a Russian entry into Constantinople. The Channel fleet, it is true, had been ordered into the Mediterranean. Bismarck, according to the French ambassador, Saint Vallier, thought the situation grave because at issue between Russia and England was a question of honour and such questions were never easily resolved. The German leader suspected, like Currie, that though disunited, confused, and ashamed, Britain would not go to war. Preferring a peaceful partition of Turkey to a European war, Bismarck suggested to Russell that before resorting to war England should occupy Egypt and other Mediterranean real estate.[46]

The occupation by Britain of an island in the eastern Mediterranean was talked of in London drawing-rooms and mooted in the Press during the fourth week in February. Shuvalov noticed the rumours and attempted to use them in order to win a diplomatic point from the Foreign Secretary, who he knew was desperately attempting to prevent the anti-Russian outbursts in Parliament from leading to war. When the ambassador told Derby on 26 February that such an acquisition would allow Russia to consider herself not bound by the engagements she had previously contracted with England, the Foreign Secretary replied that the Government had no intention of this kind. A draft of the above remarks which was in preparation for a dispatch containing them to be sent to Loftus was seen by all members of the Cabinet who were dining with the Duke of Cambridge except Disraeli, Derby, Hardy, and Smith. Northcote wrote in near horror to both Beaconsfield and Derby.

Our [the eight Cabinet members'] uneasiness arose from the inferences which we feared the Russian Govt. might draw from his [Derby's] language. It appeared to us that Schouvaloff was advancing a pretension to release Russia from all her engagements to us (including that against the occupation of Galipoli) in case we seized a Turkish island, and that Derby did not repudiate that pretension.
Whether we should, or should not occupy an Island. . . . I have not . . . made up my own mind. But . . . if we did so it would [not] in the slightest degree absolve Russia from her engagement to abstain from occupying Gallipoli and the Straits so long as we also abstained.

At the objections of the Cabinet, the dispatch to Loftus was not sent. Disraeli explained to the Queen that no treacherous conduct or disloyal leak was involved in the conversation described in the intended dispatch which was dated 26 February.

Now it was only yesterday the 27th, that the plan for occupying an island in the Aggean, & other places was first mentioned in cabinet. So there has been no treachery in imparting information to Russia. The fact is, the occupation of some base in the vicinity of the Dardanelles is so reasonable, that it is in the air, & in the conversations of the street.

After cancelling the dispatch Derby wrote in great irritation to Northcote.

I am sorry that drafts on important foreign questions are sent round and received at dinners where necessarily others besides our colleagues are present. . . . It is easy to understand how so little of

what we do or say is left secret. . . . I certainly think that the seizure of
a Turkish island . . . would be an act so violent . . . that the Russian
government might not unreasonably treat it as absolving them from
the Gallipoli engagement. That they would treat it so is nearly certain: and I am not prepared to say that they would be wrong.

The Foreign Secretary, almost childlike, resented being caught
out and criticized by his colleagues in a way they would not
have done, and did not do, even six months before. The
Foreign Secretary's anger was unjustified and seemed misdirected. Currie, a Foreign Office official, informed Layard of
Derby's unsatisfactory position. 'There is a very strong feeling
against Lord Derby who is denounced by his own side as a
traitor & leans for support to the Opposition. He will be
thrown overboard by his colleagues if he gives them a
chance.'[47]

Criticized by his own colleagues, his party, and the Press and
used by Shuvalov, the Foreign Secretary was now attacked by
Beaconsfield for sending civil messages to Russia. On 27
February Derby asked Shuvalov for the terms of peace which
were being negotiated at San Stefano. 'I have to-day stated to
the Russian Ambassador that, in the opinion of Her Majesty's
Government, it is essential that they should be informed, with
as little delay as possible, of the terms of peace now being
negotiated.'[48] Derby replied to Beaconsfield's criticism with
some sharpness.

I pressed Schouvaloff as strongly as courtesy allowed, not to keep us
in the dark. But we cannot demand as a right . . . to be made
acquainted with the terms of a treaty not yet negotiated. I did not understand that it was the desire of the Cabinet to shape their enquiry
so as to bring about a refusal to answer it; nor does that seem to me
good diplomacy.

Even Münster, the German ambassador, noticed the Foreign
Secretary's efforts to avoid war and the way in which he was
ceaselessly attacked by the war party. In response to Lytton's
description of British policy 'as being intelligible only to a man
"who has the head of a pin, and the heart of a hen"'', Salisbury
put forward in explanation the lack of a large army and the
difficulties of arranging sufficient harmony among the
ministers in the Government especially during emergencies.

An example of the latter occurred at the beginning of March when Smith refused Disraeli's request, unless directed by the Cabinet, to ask Hornby if he could enter the Black Sea should Russia occupy the forts along the Bosphorus. Fortunately for the Cabinet the crisis, as Thompson explains, quieted criticism of its policy or lack of one.

When a Government is moving fleets and armies, or is in the crisis of a dangerous negotiation, it is too late for public opinion to be considering to what objects the diplomacy of the country should be directed.

Domestic opposition seems to savour of treason. Thus adverse critics . . . must perforce hold their peace. At such a time a Government acquires an immense ascendency and accession of authority at home.

Before obtaining an official reply to the request for Russian peace terms, or the threat delivered on the twenty-first of removing Loftus if Constantinople were occupied without the Sultan's consent, peace by the Porte and Russia was signed at San Stefano on 3 March.[49] Layard, as he informed Hornby, was nearly mortified that Russia was to be free to have entirely her own way. 'I see nothing but humiliation to my country & the loss of that position amongst the Powers of the world which she once held.'[50] The ambassador's fears, as it turned out, were premature, or at least only temporary, as the embarrassments of February would give way to the accomplishments of June. It was far from clear, however, at the beginning of March that the Treaty of San Stefano would be followed by a congress. Any reasonable man viewing the situation in European and Asiatic Turkey along with the relations of the Powers of Europe would have given very long odds against a peaceful accommodation.

## 20 PREPARING FOR A CONGRESS

THE IMPENDING restructuring of European and Asiatic Turkey created a huge international mess of the sort expected by European diplomats and often put forward by them as reason for not raising the Eastern Question. That the mess was resolved at all was a minor miracle. Over the next three months Albanians prepared to rise at the prospect of an enlarged Montenegro. Montenegrins as well were getting ready for war in order to acquire as much of Hercegovina, Albania, and the Adriatic coastline as circumstances would permit. Austria made repeated and unsuccessful efforts to reach an agreement with the Porte for the acquisition of Bosnia-Hercegovina and then mobilized to improve her bargaining position at the coming congress. Serbia, bitterly frustrated, was trapped between an Austrian veto on Bosnia and the Bulgaria created by the Treaty of San Stefano. Muslim, Greek, and Jewish inhabitants of Bulgaria and Rumelia made repeated appeals to the British Government against the reality and prospect of Bulgarian rule. Russian and Bulgarian repression caused a rising of Muslims in the region of the Rhodope Mountains which Russian troops could not stamp out despite much bitter fighting. Neither Britain nor Austria was prepared to allow the autonomous Bulgaria of the San Stefano treaty to stretch to the Aegean. Romania talked of war rather than cede to Russia that part of southern Bessarabia which the latter had lost in 1856. Greece was igniting and fuelling insurrection in Thessaly and Crete lest the congress mistakenly leave those areas to the Porte. In Ottoman Armenia another Muslim insurrection erupted at the prospect of Russian incorporation and Persia demanded a boundary rectification from the Porte.[1] In the meantime the British fleet remained within the Sea of Marmora and Russian troops inched towards the walls of Constantinople, while late on the afternoon of 3 March the Treaty of San Stefano was signed against the backdrop of repeated Russian demands for Ottoman acquiescence to her entry into the capital and offers to buy Turkish ironclads.

The Treaty of San Stefano, which Sumner describes as a victory for Ignatiev in his struggle with Gorchakov for political influence,[2] was known in London well before it had been ratified, unlike the tortuous emission of the armistice of 31 January. Anglo-Russian tension was only minimally reduced, if at all, by its signing and patriotic feeling in London still ran high, often dangerously and disagreeably so. Derby remained the target of a great deal of it, as Mundella bore witness.

They [the war faction in Parliament] abuse Lord Derby in the most shameful manner and, not content with attributing to him sundry vices, libel his wife in ribald verses, which they report in the Lobbies. Old members say they have never witnessed such disgraceful conduct on the part of a section of the party towards one of its most respected members. Their lines charge the countess with infidelity to her husband with Count Schouvaloff, etc.

The criticism and loss of respect manifested among his colleagues and his party inside and outside Parliament not surprisingly caused the Foreign Secretary to seek protection in withdrawal. When Beaconsfield introduced the desirability of forming a Mediterranean league with Greece, Italy, Austria, and France and the necessity of acquiring Eastern or Mediterranean real estate, a topic which according to Disraeli was first broached in Cabinet on 27 February, all supported it except Derby.

Ld Beaconsfield feels convinced, that Lord Derby will retire, perhaps not immediately, but in a week's time or so.
The Cabinet has sent for Lord Lyons, that they may consult as to temper of French Government about Egypt etc etc.

Northcote attempted to convince the Foreign Secretary of the need for one or the other—an island or a league, but Tenterden influenced his chief against the second.[3]
Gorchakov, possibly as a step to reassert his position at home against Ignatiev, sounded the German and Austrian governments on the possibility of holding at Berlin the congress which had once again been resurrected. Neither Andrássy nor Bismarck objected, and when Austria on 7 March issued the formal invitation Britain provisionally accepted, for, as Derby explained in Parliament on 8 March, such acceptance

was based on the submission of the entire Treaty of San Stefano to the congress. A portion of the Press and British opinion manifested distrust, fearing that the congress would only rubber-stamp a previously concerted arrangement made by Austria, Germany, and Russia. But many saw it as a sign of peace and the proper forum in which to concert a new international agreement to replace the Treaty of Paris of 1856, which even Hammond indicated in Parliament was dead for all practical purposes. Münster and others were fooled by Beaconsfield's pretence of reluctance to enter such a meeting. His reluctance was manifested so that Britain's demand that the entire Russo-Turkish treaty be brought before the congress might be accepted, rather than a consideration of those parts of it only which affected the Paris treaty of 1856 and the London treaty of 1871 as Gorchakov and Bismarck thought appropriate.[4]

While the bases for the congress remained undecided, the Cabinet, not very successfully, was groping for a policy. Layard attempted to outline one for Disraeli; it included the building of a railway between Constantinople and the Persian Gulf with the development of British commerce throughout the Tigris–Euphrates Valley. Lyons, who had come to London in possible preparation for his role as Britain's representative at the congress, was asked for and gave his opinion. Whereas Layard was prepared to recognize the futility of the Porte's recovering its authority over Balkan Christians, Lyons saw the modification of the terms of San Stefano as a possibility with Austrian co-operation. But he rated Bismarck's inclination for a partition of Turkey among the Great Powers with Austria taking Bosnia as equally probable. The status of Egypt and Bulgaria and the rules for the Straits were listed by him as important British concerns.[5]

On 7 March ministers sat through a 'stormy' meeting of two hours without agreement as to the course to be followed. Disraeli, with support from Salisbury and Cairns, attempted to obtain concurrence for a league with France, Austria, Italy, and Greece in order to preserve common Mediterranean interests.[6] Hardy, Derby, Lyons, and Tenterden thought such a combination would be either impossible to arrange, or awkward to maintain, or restrictive on British behaviour. The

Prime Minister thought the moral effect of the league would counterbalance inconvenience, and he also pressed for the taking of a naval station in the eastern Mediterranean should the Russo-Turkish peace treaty or the congress compromise the maritime interests of Great Britain in the Mediterranean. Derby disagreed with this also, but Beaconsfield, as he informed the Queen, had discounted his friend's presence and indicated Cabinet agreement on the acquiring of a naval station. With characteristic exaggeration he wrote that the Cabinet had taken over the management of the Foreign Office.[7]

Ironically, at the very moment that Britain was working to have Greece admitted to the congress, the Negroponte affair exploded in Parliament. Negroponte was a Greek merchant resident in Constantinople, who Layard believed was active in stirring up revolution in Thessaly. Partly through the ambassador's efforts the Constantinople correspondent of the *Daily Telegraph* was made aware of the brief correspondence between Gladstone and Negroponte and wrote a sensational article published in his London paper on 28 August 1877, accusing the former Prime Minister of inciting the Greeks to rise against the Turks. After the antecedents of the story became known, Evelyn Ashley, on 12 March, moved a vote of censure on Layard for using his public position to damage a political opponent. A debate followed and ended in a vote favourable to Layard and the Government, 132 for the censure motion and 206 against it. Gladstone's momentary contact with Negroponte only confirmed for those like Henry Reeve, the editor of the *Edinburgh Review,* the opinion that the former Prime Minister was 'a most mischievous lunatic'. Layard, as he himself admitted, had been somewhat indiscreet, but perhaps not more so than Gladstone. Brand has fairly summed up the result of the debate. 'The motion [for censure] was negatived by a large majority, and rightly for, although Mr. Layard may have acted without discretion, his offence was not of that character to call for a vote of censure.'[8] Ashley, who had been prominent in hounding Elliot when the latter was ambassador at Constantinople, had chosen a poor time for his action. Several of Layard's Parliamentary defenders made reference to the political crisis and the inexpediency of the motion because of it. Feeling was growing again that the congress would not meet and that war would be the result.

The Spanish minister in London noted the increasing disbelief in the congress, especially as there was no obvious plenipotentiary to represent England in view of Lyon's rank, Salisbury's performance at the Constantinople Conference, Derby's unfitness, and Disraeli's lack of French. Further, the two British conditions, whose fulfilment alone would permit her to attend a congress and which were communicated to Austria on 9 March, as well as to the other Powers, had elicited as late as 18 March no formal response. The two British requirements were that the entire Treaty of San Stefano must be open to discussion by the congress and that no alteration of previous treaties—1841, 1856, and 1871—would be regarded as valid until it had been approved by the treaty Powers. Bismarck's suggestion of a preliminary congress and Gorchakov's desire to separate those articles in the San Stefano treaty touching European interests from those which did not, only the former to be discussed by the congress, did not satisfy London or mitigate Derby's distrust. Gorchakov's position in fact had been communicated to Austria but not to England, nor as late as the beginning of the third week in March had the official version of the Treaty of San Stefano signed on 3 March been given to Britain. Most serious of all, British preparations for war increased. On 15 March Salisbury privately informed the Governor of Bombay to be prepared for the possibility of a call at short notice for twenty or as many as fifty thousand troops and the necessary transport for them. A Cabinet meeting on 16 March considered a list of proposals not untypical of Beaconsfield. 'They discussed corps d'armeé, new Gibraltars, & expeditions from India, in great fullness. Lord Derby said nothing.'[9]

Another Anglo-Russian crisis had arisen in the third week of March similar to the one of February in that the outbreak of war was not unlikely. The responsibility for the tension was divided as Gorchakov, who wished to avoid placing his country in the awkward position of defending or explaining the treaty with Turkey in a European congress, attempted to refrain from giving Britain a direct answer to her two demands and negotiated with London through Andrássy, which only added confusion and heightened British distrust. This last was increased by news that Ignatiev was to accompany Gorchakov to the congress as Russia's second plenipotentiary. Disraeli was strongly supported by Derby in both requiring freedom for the congress to discuss the entire San Stefano treaty and the necessity for sanction by all the Great Powers for any changes from the treaties of 1856 and 1871. But whereas the Foreign Secretary wished to minimize tension, which was growing also in St. Petersburg, the Prime Minister added to it, convinced that only firmness would cause Russia to back down short of the war which he wished to avoid, but not at any price.

Though Disraeli had informed the Queen on the eighth that policy had been taken out of Derby's hands by the Cabinet, the latter body in this instance being a euphemism for himself, such a report was taking characteristic poetic licence in stretching the truth partly to satisfy the Queen's hatred for the Foreign Secretary and his wife. Beaconsfield again could not bring himself to ask for Derby's resignation, expecting that it would be given when more active measures were taken to which the Foreign Secretary had objected already in discussion in Cabinet. But it was obvious that though Disraeli was leaning on Cairns and Salisbury in Cabinet formulations, the difficult negotiations with Russia conducted with and through Shuvalov were performed by Derby. Mutual suspicion increased the difficulty of reaching accommodation.

Temporarily fearing a secret Russo-Turkish treaty, the Government almost added a third demand to be satisfied before accepting a congress, namely a Russian declaration that the San Stefano treaty contained all of the agreements between Turkey and Russia.[10] Shuvalov attempted to convince London that his Government would never accede to Britain's two original requirements. Russia's formal answer to them was delivered by Shavalov on 19 March. It was, as Tenterden accurately described it, both evasive and unsatisfactory, as it was still a refusal of London's preliminary conditions and was all the more irritating because it was an irrelevant reply. 'The Russian Government reply that Russia reserves to herself the same liberty of appreciation and action at the congress that the English Government claims and that it would restrict her, if alone among the Powers, she were to contract a preliminary engagement.' Cabinet meetings were held on 18 and 20 March, the latter to consider Gorchakov's answer. Derby bitterly complained to Disraeli that ministerial decisions taken on the eighteenth had been leaked to and appeared in the *Daily Telegraph* on the nineteenth. He suspected, as he wrote to Beaconsfield, that several of his colleagues wished to produce a war. 'Now it was a condition insisted upon and agreed to in Cabinet that whatever communication we made to Russia should be kept entirely secret, in order that it might retain the character of a friendly warning, and not assume that of a public defiance.' Derby's concern was not completely paranoic as Münster reported to William I that great excitement existed in England and that war was not unexpected.[11]

Shortly before the Cabinet meeting on 20 March, Derby saw Shuvalov to indicate that England would not recede from its two requirements and to complain of a Russian request to disembark its troops from Buyukdere, a suburb of Constantinople on the Bosphorus which controlled the city's water-supply. The ambassador, striving to save peace by saving the congress, did not report Gorchakov's answer on Buyukdere which was to ask what the British fleet was doing in the Sea of Marmora, nor Gorchakov's refusal to accede to London's conditions regarding the congress. He asked Derby to delay any provocative Cabinet decision while he attempted, although without success, to find ground for a Russo-British accommodation at St. Petersburg. The Cabinet, according to Hardy, adopted a proposal by Cairns in answer to Russia's communication of the nineteenth.

I [Derby] have informed Count Schouvaloff ... that Her Majesty's Government cannot recede from the position already clearly defined by them, that they must distinctly understand before they can enter into Congress that every article in the Treaty between Russia and Turkey will be placed before the Congress, not necessarily for acceptance, but in order that it may be considered what Articles require acceptance or concurrence by the other Powers and what do not.

Her Majesty's Government are unable to accept the view now put forward by Prince Gortchakow, that the freedom of opinion and action in Congress of Russia, more than of any other Power, would be restricted by this preliminary understanding.[12]

While awaiting Russia's answer to the above and its official communication of the contents of the Treaty of San Stefano, the Cabinet still struggled to find a policy and continued its preparations for war. Arrangements and costs had been prepared for sending out a corps of 36,000 men within one month, and shortly afterwards a second corps of equal size which would entail full mobilization. Plans were being formulated to send the fleet through the Bosphorus into the Black Sea. Salisbury, who was ready for either a war or a congress, suggested a policy to Beaconsfield, part of which at least the Prime Minister himself had always favoured. It included restricting Bulgaria or the Slavs north of the Balkan Mountains, effectively securing passage of the Straits, acquiring two naval stations at Lemnos and Cyprus along with the temporary occupation of a place like Scanderoon on the Syrian coast, and the reduction of the indemnity Turkey was to pay to Russia. The younger Malet, the future ambassador at Berlin who was in London, has left a picture of Derby and Lady Derby in the midst of crisis. The countess, despite the growing public criticism, continued her private tête-à-tête with Shuvalov. Her husband did not manifest the same excitement or anxiety. 'He was decidedly not looking well. . . . He has become thinner and his eyes have a heavy look which they had not before.' Disraeli described to the Queen that during a brief discussion of foreign policy in the Lords on the twenty-first the Foreign Secretary spoke with both discretion and sufficient firmness.[13]

In Parliament and throughout the country anti-Russian feeling had become less restrained and had to a considerable extent diminished the desire to remain at peace. Chamberlain thought that any agitation for peace would only elicit an outburst of rowdy patriotism which would force the Government to go farther than they intended. A writer in the *Spectator* summed up British xenophobia. 'The average Englishman has his fixed ideas about every race, and just as he regards a Frenchman as essentially volatile, and a Spaniard as the embodiment of intolerance, and a German as an unrefined Englishman, and an American as an Englishman always taking advantages, so he regards a Russian as tyranny incarnate.'

Official communication of the Treaty of San Stefano on 23 March did not soothe the excited. Layard, Elliot, and Loftus had already indicated their repugnance for the treaty, but even

Tenterden had to admit that it created Russian dominance throughout the Balkans and Asia. Disraeli counted on British firmness to induce Russia to moderation. 'People are very alarmed and think war instantaneous. I do not—I am not at all alarmed. I hold it is much more likely, that as Russia finds England firm, and preparing for conflict, she will end by opening separate negotiations with us. This will be a great triumph after all . . .'

Gladstone also hoped for Russian moderation and told his constituents on 23 March in the rooms of the Central Liberal Association of his opposition to the size of Bulgaria and the seizure of Bessarabia from Romania. But he added that he saw no reason for England to go to war to overturn the wonderful effects of the Russo-Turkish conflict. When Lyon Playfair complained to a distinguished Conservative that if war ensued the country would reap the result for having a leader such as Disraeli, his listener replied that he preferred 'our scoundrel to your maniac'.[14]

Despite Beaconsfield's hopes for a direct Russo-British accommodation which would satisfy England's requirements, this was not to be, at least not yet. On 24 March Ignatiev left St. Petersburg for Vienna in an attempt to square Andrássy on the Treaty of San Stefano, thereby isolating England, and on the same day Russia's negative answer to London's conditions for the congress arrived. Instead of the Russians, as Beaconsfield desired, the Turks made an attempt through Layard to arrange a private understanding with England regarding the concessions to be demanded of Russia at the congress. The Porte indicated that it especially wished to restrict Bulgaria to the north of the Balkan Mountains, to retain part of Armenia, and to reduce the amount of the indemnity. Gorchakov's firm refusal of London's repeated conditions, which Shuvalov communicated to Derby on 25 March, produced neither accommodation nor war. Both Powers were being unreasonable. Russia wished to be free to prevent parts of the Treaty of San Stefano from being considered by the congress, even those parts which altered previous European treaties. Britain aimed to remove beforehand the possibility that any clauses of the treaty might be placed beyond consideration by the congress, even those parts of it which did not significantly affect previous

European treaties. Britain's insistence on the acknowledgement that all of the San Stefano treaty be open to discussion was to prevent isolation in the congress on points that were more important to England than to the other Powers. Andrássy, who was trying to save the congress, attempted to influence London to give up its conditions for entry by promises of Austrian support should Russia attempt to evade considering at the congress points which altered previous arrangements stipulated in earlier treaties. Beust was instructed to reaffirm Vienna's loyalty to London despite Ignatiev's mission and a hint was dropped to Elliot that an Austrian occupation of Bosnia-Hercegovina might prove necessary.[15]

When Shuvalov verbally communicated to Derby Gorchakov's refusal of Britain's conditions on 25 March, the Foreign Secretary requested a written reply as the English conditions had been given in writing. The Russian ambassador complied and delivered the Russian answer to Derby on the evening of the twenty-sixth. 'Russia leaves to other Powers liberty to raise in Congress such questions as they think should be discussed, and reserves to herself the liberty of accepting or not the discussion of those questions.' Beaconsfield, after being informed of this answer, decided on further and more dangerous pressure on Russia and called a Cabinet meeting for 27 March to announce his plans to his colleagues. He informed the Queen of the content of the communication he intended to make to the Cabinet.

He will recommend immediately calling out the Reserves, which will place immediately at our command two *corps d'armée*,[16] and at the same time direct the Indian Government to send out a considerable force . . . and occupy two important posts in the Levant, which will command the Persian Gulf . . . and entirely neutralize the Russian conquests and influence in Armenia . . .

The Prime Minister knew he would have the support of Cairns, Northcote, and Salisbury and appealed for the same from Hardy shortly before the meeting, telling him that he thought it would be possible to maintain both peace and the empire. Except for Derby, all ministers supported, or at least did not object, to Beaconsfield's dangerous gamble on 27 March. It was questionable whether outraged national sentiment, pique, and wounded feeling, which had captured St. Petersburg, would be restrained by military exhaustion and financial embarrassment from demanding war. Gorchakov's continued refusal of Britain's conditions for the congress was calculated to avoid a review of Russia's dirty linen by eliciting a refusal on Britain's part to enter a congress, and thus throw on London the onus of that responsibility. Neither of the two men desired war, but both were playing with a fire that could have engulfed all. Derby was not prepared to gamble on peace by bluffing war, and as soon as the Cabinet meeting on the twenty-seventh ended he asked Northcote to give in his resignation to Beaconsfield who fully anticipated its arrival.[17]

After the meeting the Foreign Secretary saw Shuvalov and told the ambassador that he had resigned from the Government partly over the Anglo-Russian impasse caused by London's demand for a consideration by the congress of all of the Treaty of San Stefano, a demand which he supported along with his Cabinet colleagues, and partly because of measures resolved on by the Cabinet which he was not at liberty to tell the ambassador. It was not necessary to add that the Foreign Secretary's reputation as a safe, skilled, moderate, and discerning minister had been largely but not completely destroyed by the absence of patriotic ardour which caused many to see only his weakness and inadequacy. This fact and the breakdown of his health caused the Foreign Secretary to seek withdrawal from office with a sense of relief. Derby explained to the ambassador—and we have only Shuvalov's word for this—that his colleagues did not desire war and that a Russian proposal for direct negotiations with Britain which would allow for the acquisition of a naval station by the latter would succeed and secure peace. Whereas Derby threw out a suggestion for direct negotiations between the two Powers in the hope of avoiding war, Beaconsfield desired it as a safeguard against the destruction of British influence by a revived Dreikaiserbund, which Ignatiev was seeking in Vienna, and which could ignore Britain's full weight in any final arrangements. The Prime Minister, even at such a moment, could not mask his positive feelings for a friend whom he had long attempted to encourage. He explained to the Queen that the resignation would be kept secret until Derby's announcement to Parliament the following day, the twenty-eighth, as a Foreign Office reception was to take place on the evening of 27 March at which Lord and Lady Derby were to be the hosts. Malet, who thought that Lady Derby's meddling in public affairs had unintentionally caused great harm to her husband's reputation, has left a description of the couple at the reception. 'Lord and Lady Derby stood next each other just inside the door-way and received their guests as Royalty do. They both looked in good spirits . . .'[18]

Derby was leaving the ministry with a sense of relief and without bitterness toward his colleagues, as he explained to Northcote. 'I hope the Premier understands that my sole reason for treating this matter [his resignation] through you was the desire to avoid what can never be otherwise than a painful interchange of communications with a very old friend, to whom I owe much, and of whom I shall never think otherwise than with kindness.'

Feelings of personal friendship for Derby were also manifested in writing by Hardy, Cross, Manners, and Beaconsfield, the latter indicating that he had hesitated writing on things which infinitely distressed him. The Foreign Secretary's announcement to Parliament of his resignation on 28 March, in contrast to Carnarvon's of January, was done without recrimination and without compromising the ministry. He merely said that the Cabinet had decided on measures with which he could not agree. Beaconsfield followed and spoke of Derby with feeling and dignity, referring to his great abilities and regretting that they would no longer be in the service of the present ministry. The Prime Minister also announced the calling-out of the army reserves which led many to assume that this was the sole cause of the Foreign Secretary's resignation, and many, like the Spanish minister in London, concluded that a withdrawal based on this measure alone was inadequate justification and indicated a want of courage.

Unfortunately for Derby's reputation nothing could be said of the Cabinet's favourable consideration of an Indian expeditionary force to be sent to the Mediterranean. The public and the Press, while surprised at the news, generally approved of Derby's withdrawal and the firm front shown by the government, only the Radical journals and a few Liberals demurred, seeing the spectre of war. The majority of the London ambassadorial corps, Berlin governmental opinion, and many people in Britain thought Derby's retirement was the beginning of a British declaration of war, though Disraeli continued to deny any such intention. Part of the reason for this conclusion, as the Belgian minister Solvyns informed his Government, was the general feeling that calling out the reserves was not sufficient reason for resignation.

It was difficult to allow that this single measure had been sufficient to cause Derby to separate from his colleagues. I regret having to add that from the explanations of Disraeli, nearly everyone concluded that Derby had resigned only because he criticized the resolution that had been taken by the other members of the Cabinet to seize the first favorable occasion to declare war on Russia.[19]

Derby's leaving resulted in a reconstruction of the Cabinet, with Salisbury going to the Foreign Office, Hardy replacing him at the India Office, and Frederick Stanley, Derby's younger brother, filling Hardy's shoes as Secretary of State for War. Sandon, who replaced Adderley as President of the Board of Trade in April, was invited by Beaconsfield to join the Cabinet at the beginning of May. From Derby's resignation until the end of the Congress of Berlin the Cabinet was to be relatively harmonious, after having gone through two years of deep division and disharmony. Added to unity within the Cabinet was the failure of Russia to isolate Britain as a result of Ignatiev's lack of success with Andrássy in Vienna over arrangements for Bosnia and Bulgaria. Taylor refers to this as the demise of the Austro-Russian entente. Both Bismarck and Andrássy informed London that they would not take part in a congress if Britain refused to do so. Finally, the Government began to enunciate a policy to replace the now shattered support for the independence and integrity of the Ottoman Empire. Ministerial harmony, Anglo-Russian division, firmness, and a new formulation of British interests were to be fundamental over the next four months in enabling the Government to retrieve influence and prestige after months of hesitation and near disaster.

The possibility of an Anglo-Russian war, however, remained. Layard and Admiral Hornby desired to take steps to prepare for it. The ambassador, who met the Sultan at the end of March, was told that if given some advance notice the Porte was prepared to fight Russia alongside Britain. He telegraphed to London the Turkish readiness for a secret military arrangement and asked if this disposition should be encouraged. The Admiral, who was still under orders to use the fleet if Russia attacked the Bulair lines, telegraphed the same to the Admiralty, and Admiral Commerell with part of the fleet at Gallipoli was preparing to act in conjunction with the Turkish army should that be necessary to prevent a Russian march down the Gallipoli Peninsula to the Dardanelles. Even Salisbury, who refused to believe that the edge of war had been reached, was forced to admit at the beginning of April that matters were grave.[20]

It was in such a threatening atmosphere that Salisbury composed the well-known circular of 1 April which defended Britain's diplomatic position on the congress and the submission to it of all of the Treaty of San Stefeno, and which was communicated to all the European Powers and to both Houses of Parliament. With Russian troops ringed around Constantinople and close to Bulair and Gallipoli and with the British fleet within the Sea of Marmora, it was a dangerous moment to tell the truth in public. After recapitulating previous Anglo-Russian negotiations on a Russo-Turkish peace, Salisbury justified the legality of England's position in a European sense.

By the Declaration annexed to the first Protocol of the Conference held in London in 1871, the Plenipotentiaries of the Great Powers, including Russia, recognized 'that it is an essential principle of the law of nations that no Power can liberate itself from the engagements of a Treaty, nor modify the stipulations thereof, unless with the consent of the Contracting Powers by means of an amicable arrangement.'

It is impossible for Her Majesty's Government, without violating the spirit of this declaration, to acquiesce in the withdrawal from the cognizance of the Powers of Articles in the new Treaty [of San Stefano] which are modifications of existing Treaty engagements [Paris of 1856 and London of 1871] and inconsistent with them.

But no pretence was made that San Stefano was compatible with Britain's interests, which the circular indicated to be the Straits, the Persian Gulf, and the Suez Canal. It was then argued that the cumulative effect of the treaty would be the suppression of the political independence of the Porte and the substitution of the influence and control of Russia alone in the Balkans and Near East. Negative mention also was made of specific clauses in the treaty such as the proposed size and administration of Bulgaria, the Russian annexations of Bessarabia and Armenia, and the amount and manner of payment by Turkey of the war indemnity. The reasonableness and directness of the circular's language which were possibly the contributions of Salisbury, and its quick appearance in newspapers all over the Continent and its communication to Parliament, brought it a wide and popular reception, especially in England, which reacted favourably to a fusing of humanitarian and patriotic concerns. Thompson has indicated this.

The tenour of the despatch [the circular] indicated that while the Government were willing to allow that the object of providing for the good government of the Christian populations was worthy of approval in the abstract, yet that they regarded the practical question as confined to the alternative of rehabilitating Turkey, or of seeing Russia in a position of ascendency which they were unwilling to tolerate.[21]

There were some of course who were not pleased by the circular, and Shuvalov was one of these. Having lost his close association with Derby and his knowledge of Cabinet affairs which derived from Lady Derby, the ambassador now found that Salisbury was polite but cold and that Beaconsfield was angry with him, having received reports of Shuvalov's communicating official matters to members of the opposition during pending negotiations between Russia and Britain. The ambassador, in order to save his position, lied and denied that he had ever done this. He also attempted, unsuccessfully, according to Reeve, to find a new source for Cabinet information. 'Schouvaloff has made an attempt on the virtue of Lady Cairns, by attempting to persuade her that he wanted her assistance and instruction in reading the Bible. "Car je suis un peu Bibliste aussi" was his expression. But my Lord Chancellor heard of it and stopped his biblical education.' On 3 April he came to Salisbury at the Foreign Office and implied that the latter's circular was possibly a peaceful document but that it

might be equally a warlike one. 'I [Salisbury] assured Count
Schouvaloff that the Circular was not an instrument of war, but
declined to enter at present into the nature or extent of the
modifications which England might desire to make in the
Treaty.' Andrássy also complained that while Salisbury had
pointed out what was objectionable in the Russo-Turkish treaty, he had not sufficiently indicated how those undesirable portions should be changed or what new measures would replace
the offensive ones. Much of the Russian Press saw the circular
as an insult and called for war, and though the national sensibilities of Alexander II and his ministers had been wounded
by it, Andrássy's unfriendly communications to Ignatiev in
Vienna made a recourse to arms by Russia unrealistic if not
dangerous.[22]

Though at first it appeared that Salisbury was content, as
Derby had been, only to make objections without formulating
any proposals which would indicate what Britain desired as
distinct from what she wished to prevent, the new Foreign
Secretary soon erased this appearance. He enlightened Elliot,
Layard, Loftus, Lyons, and Russell not only as to policy but
with suggestions for its implementation. A guiding, self-
confident direction had replaced a fearful, self-protective cir-
cumspection. Having decided to restrict the new Slavic
Bulgaria north of the Balkan Mountains, he appealed for
Andrássy's support to maintain Ottoman control over the area
to the south of those mountains and explained to Layard that
compensation for Britain, though at the Porte's expense,
would better enable her to aid the reduced Turkey to resist
further Russian encroachments.

I have not invariably concurred in all the views you have expressed;
but .... I have admired the skill, and the unsparing energy with which
your very arduous functions have been performed.

Turkish break water [against Russian preponderance] ... is now
shattered. ... Another dyke may have to be established behind it. ...
To us the idea of additional territory is repellent. ... But ... the plan
of counterpoise ... cannot but be at the expense of the Porte. ... Yet
the stronger we are in those seas, the stronger will the Porte be to
resist further invasion.

The Foreign Secretary told the Greeks to cease fuelling
rebellion in Thessaly and the Turks to stop committing

cruelties there, and suggested to Münster that mediation by Germany might successfully enable Britain and Russia to exchange ideas. When Münster repeatedly referred to the danger to peace from the nearness of the British fleet and the Russian and Ottoman armies, Salisbury instructed Russell to enlist the help of Bismark.

Each [Britain and Russia] is deterred from being first to propose a simultaneous retreat by fear that enhanced pretensions would thereby be encouraged on the other side. A friendly suggestion from Prince Bismarck to both that, pending negotiations, the fleet should retire below the Dardanelles and the army retire the same number of miles from Constantinople, would evade the difficulty . . .

Bismarck happily grasped Russell's request and proposed a simultaneous withdrawal to London and St. Petersburg, which both accepted. Encouraged by Bismarck's inclination for peace, Salisbury left to Russell's discretion the opportunity to give the German leader a frank description of British policy. The latter was divided into two categories, points for which Britain might fight and others for which she would be prepared to negotiate. In the first category were opposition to a Slav state on the Aegean or near Constantinople, Russian acquisitions in Armenia without the acquisition by England of a port to safeguard her Asiatic interests, and either the neutralization of the Straits or the recognition of the validity of blockading them in wartime. Objection was also made to the extent and nature of the indemnity, the Russian annexation of Bessarabia and her occupation and influence over Bulgaria, but for these Britain was willing to negotiate. Salisbury made clear, however, that if necessary Britain would fight. 'We hope for peace—but prepare for war; and are taking every necessary precaution.'[23]

The growing threat of war galvanized those who were willing to agitate to prevent its occurrence. Resolutions and petitions were presented, especially by the Radicals, in Birmingham, Darlington, and Manchester. In Manchester a deputation introduced by Chamberlain and Bright, and appealing to the leaders of the Liberal party in Parliament to oppose what was believed to be the Cabinet's war policy, was received by Hartington and Granville. The latter did not cheer his listeners by saying that wars had previously been averted only by the wisdom of the ministers, not by the influence of the opposition. Auberon Herbert, Carnarvon's brother and a dispirited partisan of peace, admitted to his wife that Granville was correct in pointing out the impossibility of resisting the Government. As Thompson points out, those who pleaded for peace, unlike the self-confident, horrified, and titillated individuals in the agitation of September 1876, were pessimistic and doubtful of being supported by the country. Chamberlain, like Herbert, did not excessively blame the Liberal leaders since party unity was so rent that any step taken by the leadership would remain unsupported by a great part of their followers. Dilke supported Salisbury's circular and Earl Grey feared that weakening the ministry might see it replaced by a Government under Gladstone, whose absence of patriotism was seen by some Liberals under the circumstances of foreign crisis as a lack of sanity. On 8 April the Queen's message to Parliament calling out the reserves provided the occasion for a debate in both Houses.[24]

Despite the lack of encouragement from the party leaders, the Radicals in the Commons courageously forced a division, which even Gladstone apparently wished to avoid, when Wilfrid Lawson moved an amendment expressing regret that the reserves had been called out. During the debate both Hartington and Gladstone appealed to Lawson to give up his amendment and thus avoid a vote. The main argument, and a weak one, made by the Liberal leaders in the debates in both Houses was that the Treaty of San Stefano was not greatly different from the terms which Russia had communicated to the Government in June 1877, when no objection had been made to them. Henry Richard, 'the apostle of peace' from Wales, supported the amendment and argued that the possibility of war was entirely due to English xenophobia—in this case the unreasoning hatred and fear of Russia. British complaints about Russia's suppression of Poland and other nationalities was, he said, ironic coming from a people who ruled Ireland, India, Ceylon, and Jamaica. Complaints about Russia's being excessively aggrandizing were in Richard's opinion curious emanating from Britain. Inside a glass house, he pointed out, was not the ideal location from which to throw stones at others. Lawson refused to drop his amendment and a vote came after two nights of debate, the government winning by a large majority of 255 as many Liberals withdrew, some fearing for their seats and others not wishing to encourage either Russia or pro-war opinion in England.[25]

In the Lords, after Beaconsfield had stressed the necessity of maintaining the British Empire unimpaired, Granville made an effective speech in which he questioned the Government's decision to make public Salisbury's circular instead of privately communicating it to Russia. Derby then rose and attempted to justify his resignation. Stung both by previous public charges of vacillation and cowardice and the injustice he felt in his colleague's allowing it to be thought that only the calling-out of the reserves caused his decision to leave the Government, he referred to matters which were normally never alluded to outside the Cabinet, and was rebuked by Salisbury for having publicly referred to Cabinet discussion. Though he spoke with some force, his argument, when not indiscreet, lacked conviction.

If I could from this place address the English people, I would venture to ask them how they can expect to have a foreign policy—I do not say far-sighted, but even consistent and intelligent—if, within 18 months, the great majority of them are found asking for things directly contradictory? When we might have saved Turkey if we had chosen, not a voice was raised in favour of that course; and now, when the enemy—if you choose to call him so—is inside the fortress—when the Russian army is at or near Constantinople—nearly everybody is crying that we ought to turn them out. I venture to ask whether a war for the sake of influence would be a war worthy of us?

In the Lords, after Derby's speech, the Queen's message was voted without an amendment. Gorchakov made an unsuccessful attempt to influence the course of the debate by communicating his answer to Salisbury's circular to both Parliament and the London Press. Harcourt was derided for having rushed a copy of Gorchakov's reply from *The Times* to the Commons.[26]

While British preparations for war continued along with German mediation to work out the tortuous details of an Anglo-Russian military withdrawal from the vicinity of Constantinople, Austria, following Bismarck's advice for partition and failing to reach a private agreement with Russia on the San Stefano treaty, began a secret negotiation with the Porte for the purpose of obtaining Bosnia. On 6 April Zichy, as instructed by Andrássy, offered the Porte Austrian diplomatic support in attempting to revise the terms of the San Stefano treaty if it would agree to give up Bosnia-Hercegovina to Austria. The German Government was informed of the step, though Britain was not, and supported it at Constantinople. Even Elliot at Vienna thought this a good arrangement for Turkey as it would be better for the Porte to lose Bosnia in return for some advantage than none at all. Layard, however, did not so think. The Ottoman ministers who kept him informed of the negotiation hesitated to comply as they feared that such acquiescence would only lead to further demands for territorial cession. When Zichy pressed the Porte for an answer, the latter asked for London's views and advice, especially as Russia was simultaneously demanding that Turkey evacuate Shumla, Varna, and Batum which she still occupied partly on English advice to hold those places as long as possible. Before receiving any official answer from London, the Ottoman council of ministers decided on 14 April to refuse the cession of Bosnia, but then before communicating their decision to Austria, the Turks indicated to London that they would await her opinion. On 15 April Reuters reported the Ottoman rejection of Austria's request, enabling Salisbury, who until then had not been told of it by Andrássy, to question Vienna about its reported step.[27]

Bismarck had responded quickly to Salisbury's suggestion of Germany's mediating an Anglo-Russian military and naval withdrawal from Constantinople because he, like Salisbury, wished to avoid a war, in this case one arising accidently from the near proximity of the Ottoman and Russian armies and British fleet. Salisbury, of course, desired to remove Russian troops as far as possible from the Bosphorus and the Dardanelles. The Russians agreed to negotiate a simultaneous withdrawal but had no faith in it because they believed that London intended Russian humiliation or war. Having failed to convince the Porte to make an alliance, Russia still hoped to square Austria after Ignatiev's failure with Andrássy at the end of March. So she strung out the withdrawal negotiations in order to gain time to reach an agreement with Vienna on a modification of the Treaty of San Stefano. On 12 April Salisbury, informed of Russia's willingness to negotiate through Berlin, told Münster that the fleet would be withdrawn to Besika Bay if in return the Russian army would retire behind a line following the railway from Dedoagatch (Alexandroupolis) to Adrianople and then in a straight line to Midia (Midye) in the Black Sea and about sixty-five miles north-west of Constantinople. While displaying their distrust of each other's sincerity for peace, London and St. Petersburg continued preparations for the possibility of war, thus providing fuel for each other's suspicions. Around the middle of April Russia began an attempt to buy four United States steamers for the purpose of arming them in order to destroy British commercial vessels.[28] Britain learned of the attempt and reacted with concern. For its part the Cabinet continued its secret preparations to send a force from India to the Mediterranean. There was a great attempt to keep this step secret until 18 April, when Parliament would recess for Easter and the psychological impact of the move would not be lessened by criticism of it from either House. Naturally Russia found fault with Britain's specific suggestions for withdrawal and the two Powers continued to debate the question. The Cabinet was also attempting to maintain secrecy on the negotiations so that there would be no public pressure on Salisbury, but word of them leaked out into the newspapers on 17 April, the same day that the Press announced that an Indian expeditionary force was to come to the Mediterranean.[29]

Mutual Anglo-Russian distrust caused the negotiations to drag on without agreement into the fourth week of April, when Bismarck, suffering from a nervous attack, retired from Berlin into the country and announced that his mediation for withdrawal was over. He and Münster agreed that Russian conditions and behaviour were unreasonable and that she must from then on negotiate directly with England through Shuvalov. In the meantime attempts were made to revive negotiations for the meeting of the congress and also to give life to that old phantom, the Anglo-Austrian agreement of August 1877. Salisbury, slightly disgusted by Andrássy's secret attempt to get the Porte's consent for an Austrian annexation of Bosnia, told Beust on 15 April of 'the impolicy of separate action which, it would appear, was being pursued by Count Andrassy, and ... that it was an unwise waste of force, when our interests were common, to pursue a parallel instead of a common action'. The following day Beust brought to Salisbury 'a renewed proposal' from Andrássy for the purpose of reassembling a congress. The Foreign Secretary 'deferred any reply' to Andrássy's invitation to arrange a 'new formula' to facilitate the meeting of the congress until Austria made her position clearer. Salisbury explained to the Queen that 'our view ... of the importance of a Congress must be affected by the disposition of Austria toward us, & from Austria we can obtain nothing definite'. When Shuvalov telegraphed home that German aid in pressing for a congress would be useful, the German ambassador in St. Petersburg informed Berlin and Bismarck instructed Münster, who asked Salisbury on 18 April whether England was prepared to join a congress once the matter of military withdrawal had been arranged. Salisbury was in no hurry for an international meeting because until Russia and Britain moved closer to one another on the Treaty of San Stefano a congress would only call public attention to the divergence and make retreat by either side a loss of honour. Until an exact understanding had been made with Austria, the possibility of being isolated at a congress also worried the Foreign Secretary. He explained to Loftus that England was most concerned with three points: Russia being established on the Aegean, Slavic absorption of the Greeks, and the transformation of Asiatic Turkey into a Russian satrapy. On 19 April Beust communicated to Salisbury a long dispatch from Andrássy, which had been promised to the Foreign Secretary, giving Austria's views on San Stefano, which turned out to be not greatly different from England's. Andrássy, perhaps circumscribed as Elliot thought by Francis Joseph's lingering loyalty to the Three Emperor's League, was wary in his long explanation of policy and saw it only as an exchange of ideas which might lead to combined action with Britain. He again pressed for a congress and emphasized Austria's opposition to any Russian occupation of Bulgaria or Romania after the final treaty modifying San Stefano had been arranged.[30]

With the double failure to achieve Anglo-Russian military withdrawal or to find a satisfactory formula in order to hold a congress, the crisis had barely diminished as Britain continued military and naval preparations and Russia added to Austria's pressure on the Porte to cede Bosnia with a demand by her for the surrender of Shumla, Varna, and Batum, fortified places which were still occupied by Ottoman forces. The Turks asked London's advice for a reply to the Russian demand. In a telegram on 23 April Salisbury stressed the desirability of holding the three places as long as possible, but cautioned Layard against informing the Sultan that Britain would send material help or go to war on this issue. Salisbury was temporarily infected by Derby's old diseases of suspicion and distrust, though there seemed to be more of a basis in reality for it than in Derby's case, where it was usually a reflection of his personality than of the political situation. The Foreign Secretary suspected that France would see with pleasure an Anglo-Russian war in order to weaken Britain in Egypt, that Germany would be neutral in such a conflict but would lean towards Russia, that Austria was in the process of throwing over Britain for a Balkan agreement with Russia which would divide that area longitudinally, Russia in the east controlling the Danube and Austria in the west with a commercial outpost on the Aegean at Salonica. Shuvalov had to admit to Salisbury the absence of any guiding direction at St. Petersburg with Gorchakov ill and Ignatiev, powerful since January, losing influence rapidly as it was seen that his policy could only lead to war. Fearing the effect on the Turks of an excessively patriotic embassy at Constantinople, perhaps a memory of his frustrations at the Constantinople Conference, Salisbury asked the younger Malet, who was anti-Turkish and pro-Greek, to go out to Constantinople as an embassy secretary in order to have a moderating influence there. Andrássy, caught in the coils of a difficult domestic situation and an agreement with Russia—the pacts of Reichstadt and Budapest—based on an absence of mutual interest, seemed to London as slippery as an eel. Having to admit to Salisbury only on 24 April of her attempt with the Porte to obtain Bosnia, Beust not having been initially informed of the step, Austria sought to keep an English connection alive. The Foreign Secretary was still attempting to pin

Vienna down to an agreement on modifications of the San Stefano treaty, going so far as to indicate that there would be no British objection to an Austrian expansion into Bosnia-Hercegovina if Andrássy would join with Britain on the other main issues. Bulgaria was one of these, but Vienna seemed mainly interested in limiting the duration and extent of a Russian occupation, while London was more concerned with restricting the boundary of the new Bulgaria north of the Balkan Mountains. Unfairly blaming Anglo-Austrian difficulties on the not particularly reliable Beust, the Foreign Secretary wrote in frustration to the Queen. 'On the whole, the state of things is less satisfactory, not because there is any definite resolution to bring war on Europe, but because there seems no decision or clearness of perception sufficient to avoid it.'[31]

Andrássy's reluctant decision to acquire Bosnia-Hercegovina was similar to the Cabinet's plan to grab a port or island in order to concentrate on Asiatic Turkey. Both resolutions were based on the impossibility of maintaining any longer Ottoman control over all its European territories. Andrássy naturally was most concerned with Bosnia, Serbia, and Montenegro, none of which was fundamental for England, while Britain's concentration on Armenia was hardly vital for Vienna. Though neither was prepared to see complete Slavic or Russo-Slavic control over what once had been Ottoman Europe, Andrássy would or could not reach a definite accord with Salisbury. Nor, at the end of April, had Austro-Russian negotiations for the modification of the Treaty of San Stefano been concluded successfully, though Russia like Britain acquiesced in Austrian control over most of Bosnia. The territorial extent of Montenegro, the duration of the occupation of Bulgaria, and the disposition of Novibazar, an area which connected Serbia with Montenegro, stood in the way of agreement between St. Petersburg and Vienna.[32] Salisbury, convinced that if he remained firm Russia would give way and that any concession would be read as weakness, was rewarded when the Tsar and his ministers gave Shuvalov permission to discuss the San Stefano treaty directly with the Foreign Secretary.[33] This, of course, had always been Beaconsfield's position—that firmness would drive St. Petersburg to seek accommodation with London. Consequently, on 29 April

Shuvalov came to Salisbury with a proposal for England to indicate her objections and requirements and he would take them back to St. Petersburg. At the same time Münster and Bismarck reopened the negotiations for simultaneous withdrawal and General Todleben replaced Grand Duke Nicholas as commander of the Russian forces which were still encamped before Constantinople, as Nicholas returned to Russia.[34] A break in the fever of war had occurred, but Salisbury remained cautious and suspicious, as he explained to the Queen. 'Count Schouvaloff proposes shortly to go back to St. Petersburg, nominally to discuss with the Russians the English view of the Treaty of San Stefano; really to look after his own chances of succeeding Prince Gorchakoff [who was ill].'[35]

As Sumner informs us, Shuvalov had attempted to keep alive the possibility of political accommodation by not communicating to London his Government's request for Batum, Shumla, and Varna as preconditions for an agreement on concurrent Anglo-Russian retirement from Constantinople. Not wishing to endanger a possible political agreement and his own political prospects at home, he managed to convince St. Petersburg of the desirability of not exciting London, which he expected a Russian occupation of Batum would do. There is evidence that London wished him success in his quest to replace Gorchakov and outbid Ignatiev for the Russian chancellorship.

Salisbury explained to Russell his anxiety for Shuvalov to leave for Russia because it was vitally important that the chancellorship should be given into pacific hands. Before he departed the ambassador had four or five conversations with Salisbury and Disraeli, the former communicating a memorandum of British conditions. Three were listed: removing Bulgaria from the Aegean, preserving the Greeks, and maintaining the Sultan's independence. Desire was expressed in regard to the above conditions to limit Bulgaria to the north of the Balkan Mountains, to diminish Russian annexations in Armenia, and to clarify the vagueness of the Russian demand for indemnity in the Treaty of San Stefano. In their last talk on 6 May, two days before Shuvalov's departure for St. Petersburg, the ambassador gave hope to Salisbury of

Russian acquiescence in limiting Bulgaria to the north of the Balkan Mountains if the autonomy given it was sufficiently large. The Foreign Secretary replied that England would make no objection to proposals whose only object was to secure people from oppression, whereupon Shuvalov suggested a new formula to enable the congress to meet. Salisbury indicated that there should not be much difficulty about the gathering of a congress, if the above British conditions were satisfied. The ambassador then made a plea that during the two weeks he would be away from London England would do nothing to cause excitement. 'On being pressed for an explanation, Ct. Schouvaloff instanced the sending of a corps d'armée from England to Malta. Lord, Salisbury promised to mention this matter to his colleagues.'

This request on Shuvalov's part was also made in a conversation which he had with Beaconsfield after his talk with Salisbury. The Prime Minister's reply was far less conciliatory as he indicated that Britain could not even slightly defer her preparations and that they would continue even if a congress should meet.[36]

Even before Shuvalov had departed from London, Salisbury was moving in other directions, and again attempted to capture Andrássy's agreement for limiting Bulgaria at the Balkans in return for British support for Austria's concerns about the length of Russian occupation and her lack of objection to an Austrian annexation of Bosnia. He prepared Layard on 2 May for a future defensive alliance with the Porte.

If we can protect the Asiatic empire [of Turkey] from disintegration, and procure a more reasonable frontier in Europe, there will be a fair chance of the Ottoman Government retaining Constantinople for a considerable period . . .

I think that we might very properly enter into a defensive alliance with the Porte, undertaking to join in defending his Asiatic empire from any attacks of Russia. . . . But to give any strength or value to such an understanding some port in the Levant would be an absolute necessity . . .

Do not take any definite action on what I have written here until you hear more from me.

Ironically, at nearly the same moment that the Foreign Secretary considered that the Porte had failed as a ruler of

European Christians, though presumably being still quite fit to rule its own Asian subjects, Layard, who earlier was ready to write off European Turkey and concentrate on Asia, now made a prophetic plea to Salisbury for the maintenance of Ottoman Europe under British control.

I believe that even now she [Turkey] would offer a stronger bulwark against Russia than any state or combination of states that could be formed out of Turkey in Europe. As for the idea of forming Greece into a counter balancing Power I believe it to be utterly impracticable of execution *at the present time*. . . . What we now see going on amongst the various rival races and creeds [of the Balkans], their hatred of each other, their readiness to persecute each other & their already vowed intention to fight over the spoils proves that they require a very firm hand to keep them in order & that dangerous as the condition of Turkey in Europe may have been to the peace of the world, the state of things which, unless great care be taken, is likely to succeed to it will be far more so. . . . If we are led in the end to give material support to Turkey in our own interest we must make our conditions. We must insist upon a thorough reform & cleaning out & in fact take the govt. practically into our own hands. . . . It would be better to make the attempt [to help Turkey justly administer the empire] than to allow a general break up of the Ottoman Empire & a general scramble for its fragments . . .

In another private letter to the Foreign Secretary the ambassador took up the same theme.

The attempt to divide European Turkey according to 'nationalities' will probably be in the end as successful as would be an attempt to make autonomous states out of English counties according to the predominance in them of the Celtic, Saxon, Danish or Norman element.

I have constantly been thinking over the subject referred to in your last letter. The possible necessity for us to occupy some strong position either in the Persian Gulf or in some part of the Eastern end of the Mediterranean. You ask me whether any proposal or measure to that effect wd. be acquiesced in. I think that it probably would but only on condition that we come to a clear & definite understanding with Turkey and establish a real community of interests with her . . .[37]

During the Easter recess of Parliament between 18 April and 6 May and while Shuvalov journeyed to and from St. Petersburg between 8 and 22 May, there was a continuation of Press coverage and out-of-doors speeches and activity. On 29

April Hardy ventured into a strong-hold of Nonconformity to
open a new Conservative club in Bradford in the West Riding
of Yorkshire. Taking his cue from Salisbury's circular, the new
India Secretary spoke and made a plea for the sanctity of
the treaties of 1856 and 1871. Referring to the Bulgarian
massacres of 1876, he argued that the policy embodied in the
treaties of 1856 and 1871 was not to be destroyed by an occurrence, however terrible or destructive. His words were
similar to those of Elliot when the latter was ambassador at
Constantinople in 1876. Elliot's plea at that time for significant
British interests despite the atrocities had found a new respec-
tability disguised as European international law. The possibility of an evil war had aroused John Bright in a manner reminis-
cent of a time twenty-five years earlier. Having spoken at
Rochdale, he now spoke again at Manchester on 30 April
before 1,800 delegates of Liberal organizations of the North of
England. He criticized Hardy's speech and what he felt to be
the Government's war policy, and expressed his disgust with
the use of half-savage Muslims from India against Russian
Christians. But his bitterest and most violent fulminations were
reserved for Beaconsfield. Bright referred to the horrible
effrontery of the Prime Minister who was willing to spend
English blood when he himself had 'not one single drop of
English blood in his veins'. One contemporary was disgusted
by Bright's violence of language. 'Too many of our public
speakers have of late adopted a tone of personal rancour which,
if it be not discouraged, will soon degrade their utterances to
the lowest levels of the worst oratory of New York or California
. . .' Chamberlain spoke against war at Birmingham and Cross
in an address at Preston denied that such was the intention of
ministers, which, again taking the lead offered in Salisbury's
circular, he described as the desire for good government for
former and present subjects of the Ottoman Empire. At the
end of April and the beginning of May demonstrations for
peace occurred in Birmingham, Liverpool, Edinburgh,
Glasgow, and Leeds. The by-elections were not conclusive as a
gauge of public opinion, but a writer for *The Times* did not
doubt that most in Britain backed the Government.

'The Government, however wrong headed their policy, and however
malign their purposes, still have . . . the substantial support of the

country. . . . The Eastern Question is the controversy above all others which does not so much divide class from class and party from party as household from household and friend from friend. If the Government are wrong in the policy they have pursued, they are wrong with a very large party in the country . . .'[38]

When Parliament reconvened on 6 May, Hartington questioned the Government as to the reason why Parliament was not informed of the Indian expedition to Malta before the recess on 18 April. When Northcote replied that the movement of Indian troops lay within the constitutional prerogative of the Crown and therefore the Cabinet did not think it necessary 'nor . . . according to practice' to do so, a debate ensued in which Fawcett, Sir George Campbell, Harcourt, and others questioned the step and its non-communication beforehand to Parliament on constitutional grounds. Even Hammond, the former Under-Secretary at the Foreign Office, who did not oppose the expedition, thought that the Government were deserving of censure for delaying the communication of their intention to Parliament. But on grounds of Liberal party disunity, his sense of the appropriate, and an appeal from Northcote, who repeated Shuvalov's request for quiet until his return from Russia, Hartington decided to avoid raising any real attack on the Government. Despite this, on 7 May Chamberlain, unencumbered by the above restraints, gave notice of a vote of censure on the Government which Hartington was disinclined to support but admitted the impossibility of forecasting what an unstable party might wish to do. The Liberal leader appealed to Gladstone.

Northcote has told me that they are anxious that there should not be any general discussion on the Eastern Question during the negotiations on which Count Schouvaloff has gone to St. Petersburg, and that he will therefore not bring forward the vote for the Indian troops for a fortnight or three weeks. I do not think we can object to this . . .

The lawyers are considering the constitutional question . . . and I think it probable that we shall take some action on this point.[39]

Despite the general popularity of the Indian expedition in Britain, the Liberals and Radicals pressed the constitutional issue to two votes on 13 and 24 May, the second resulting in a defeat of a motion by Hartington by 347 to 226 in the Government's favour. The disunity of the Liberals and the growing possibility of a peaceful arrangement with Russia, which seemed to have justified the Government's preparations for war, only solidified the position of the Cabinet within Parliament and to a slightly lesser extent throughout the country. The question of peace or war itself rested temporarily in the hands of a skilful, ambitious, and mildly unscrupulous ambassador, who, having seen Bismarck in Berlin on 9 and 10 May, arrived at St. Petersburg on the twelfth armed with the British objections to the San Stefano treaty as well as his own. It was approximately two years before that Shuvalov had been first approached by Beaconsfield for a direct Russo-British agreement which had foundered on the suspiciousness of Russia and of Derby. Such an agreement would now prove to be the key which would overcome the previous inability of Britain and Austria to co-operate effectively and at the same time pave the way for the congress and, presumably, peace.

DURING THE second week of May the three series of negotiations continued, two of them badly. A British proposal to Austria offering to influence the Porte to agree to an Austrian occupation of Bosnia in return for Vienna's assent to support England in obtaining the Balkan Mountains as the southern border of the new Bulgaria failed to capture Andrássy. The latter also was unhappy with the latest Russian offer as it gave Novibazar to Serbia and Montenegro, thus connecting Belgrade with Cetinje and blocking Austria to the south and west. Andrássy indicated that the Russian consent to divide Bulgaria into two parts was merely a trivial concession as a Slavic state would be replaced by a Slavic confederation. Bismarck informed Stolberg, the German ambassador in Vienna, of his surprise at the Russian proposal and his unwillingness to support any such sealing off of Austria. Bismarck had clearly indicated his disinclination to see Austria weakened as a result of Slavic expansion, a tendency which was to lead to the Berlin–Vienna alliance of 1879. Ironically, it was such a division of Bulgaria, which Andrássy found wanting on 9 May, that Shuvalov was hurrying with to St. Petersburg, as a British condition that he was prepared to support with the Tsar.[1]

Shuvalov arrived at St. Petersburg on 12 May to attempt to overcome with British support those willing to go to war in order to maintain unimpaired the Treaty of San Stefano. Upon his arrival he found a patriotic campaign in full blast to raise privateers and a volunteer fleet against the British trading marine. The ambassador quickly went to Loftus, who had been instructed not to interfere in the negotiations unless directly appealed to and then only to support Shuvalov, and asked the British ambassador to explain to London. 'Count Schouvaloff begged me to inform you [Salisbury] that publication of the appeal issued by Committee for the purchase of cruisers and inserted in the "Official Gazette" . . . was done without the knowledge of the [Russian] Government, and they deplore it.'[2] Despite such bellicose manifestations Shuvalov was able to make headway with Alexander II, Gorchakov being sick and even Ignatiev suffering from Bulgarian fever. On 14 May he instructed Loftus to telegraph to London that if England would agree not to oppose the San Stefano provisions for Serbia and Montenegro, Russian agreement to Britain's conditions would be made more certain. A Cabinet meeting on the fifteenth considered the request with favour, agreeing that no promise had been made to Austria on these points,[3] and the following reply was transmitted to St. Petersburg. 'Inform Count Schouvaloff in answer to his message of yesterday that in case the Imperial Government should accept modifications proposed by England he may rely on Her Majesty's Govt not contesting the advantages which the Treaty of San Stefano grants to Servia and Montenegro.'

On the following day Andrássy, fearful of being isolated by his two allies, though not by Germany, informed Elliot of his readiness for a direct understanding with England based on his support for limiting Bulgaria at the Balkans. He added that he had just refused a Russian attempt to reach an agreement with Austria alone, implying that he had done so in order to maintain a good association with Britain, and that he hoped that he would have London's support on Serbia and Montenegro.[4]

Beaconsfield and Salisbury had decided it was now time to arrange an Ottoman understanding in order to obtain Cyprus and protect Syria and Asia Minor. At a Cabinet meeting on 11 May the proposal was introduced of a defensive alliance with Turkey to protect her from Russian attacks on her Asiatic possessions, and for this purpose Ottoman consent to a British occupation of Cyprus. There was general agreement to the plan with only the Duke of Northumberland expressing doubts. Salisbury now alterted Layard to be ready at any moment, but not quite yet, to communicate the proposal to the Porte, apparently wishing to wait until it was clearer whether or not agreement would be reached with Russia. With the major pieces about to fall into place for Britian, an incident occurred at Constantinople of the type which Salisbury had always feared and which might have brought on war. On 16 May the Russian army before Constantinople moved forward, closer to the capital, and took up new positions alleging sanitary necessity. Near panic occurred as a result in Constan-

tinople and both Admiral Hornby and Layard feared that
Russia was preparaing to seize the city and wished to take
precautions, the ambassador requesting Cabinet permission to
bring the fleet closer from its present anchorage at the Bay of
Ismid, about forty miles away, to the Princes Islands approximately fifteen miles from the city. His hope was that the
nearness of the fleet would encourage the Turks to defend the
capital if necessary. But Salisbury, impressed by Shuvalov's
efforts for peace, thought otherwise and, not wishing to give
the Russian war party at St. Petersburg any excuses for conflict,
directed Layard on 19 May, after a Cabinet discussion on the
previous day, to keep the fleet where it was. As negotiations for
simultaneous military and naval withdrawal between England
and Russia had not been broken off, events seemed to point to
the probability of withdrawal beginning only upon completion
of simultaneous occupation.[5]

Before he left St. Petersburg on 18 May Shuvalov had been
able, according to the German ambassador there, to overcome
Ignatiev's influence and win the Tsar to a division of Bulgaria
and its removal from the Aegean. Stopping in Berlin on 20
May on the way back to London, the ambassador asked Bülow
to press Bismarck to find an acceptable formula for the convocation of the congress. Bismarck was willing to do so on the
basis of a 'free discussion of the entire Treaty of San Stefano'
and informed Austria to this effect, giving Shuvalov a draft invitation for Salisbury.[6] Andrássy quickly accepted the opportunity for a congress but indicated to Bismarck his fear of
isolation at the meeting and his desire for German support of
Austria's policy at London. Salisbury did not hide from Beust
or Andrássy that if Russia were to be reasonable about
Bulgaria, England could not threaten war in Austria's support
for the purpose of keeping an Adriatic port from Montenegro
or preventing the latter's territorial expansion. On the other
hand, should Russia not give way on Bulgaria, the Foreign
Secretary thought that territorial addition for Montenegro
could be included as part of an Anglo-Austrian package on
which Britain might insist.[7]

Apart from attempting to secure London's support for an
occupation of Bosnia, Andrássy also angled for French
acquiescence. Waddington, who was now Foreign Minister in

place of Decazes, indicated to Lyons that while France was not prepared to go to war on the Eastern Question neither was she prepared to consent to an Austrian occupation or appropriation of Bosnia before the meeting and consent of the congress, as such a step would be in violation of the European guarantee of Ottoman territory contained in the treaty of 1856. He did not add that it was upon such a basis—the sanctity of European treaties—that Britain had objected to any part of the Treaty of San Stefano being withheld from consideration by the congress, an argument enunciated in Salisbury's circular of 1 April. Knowing that the French would not be overjoyed at the intended British occupation of Cyprus and the attempt to place the shaky financial condition of Egypt into steady English hands as a beginning of the process 'of taking civil possession of the Country—by means of filling all the offices with our men', London was careful not to unnecessarily disturb French *amour propre*.[8]

Shuvalov arrived back in London late on the evening of 22 May with two memorandums and a draft invitation to the congress; the latter was given officially to Salisbury by Münster. The following morning Shuvalov saw Salisbury and indicated the Russian concessions or alterations to the Treaty of San Stefano, which included removing Bulgaria from the Aegean, limiting its westward extent so as not to include essentially non-Bulgarian peoples, and dividing it at the Balkan Mountains but prohibiting Ottoman troops from the southern province, which unlike the northern one would be under Turkish control.

[The Tsar] would further consent generally the term of occupation by Russian troops should be more closely limited; and he did not object to the proposal that, in organizing the administration of Bulgaria, European should, to some extent, be substituted for Russian machinery; that the reforms in the Greek provinces should be submitted to Europe instead of to Russia alone; that Bayazid and the road from Trebizond to Persia should be given back to the Turks; & that security should be taken that the indemnity to be paid by Turkey should not be used as a pretext for further annexation of her territory.

Before taking the Russian memorandums to his colleagues for

their consideration, Salisbury in his conversation with Shuvalov alluded to a possible Anglo-Turkish alliance.

He had prepared Shuvalov for some such scheme, and found that 'he had not winced at all' when he hinted at some sort of defensive alliance between England and Turkey . . . and he [Shuvalov] accepted the idea of such being needed if Russia was strengthened in influence over Armenia, and Mesopotamia etc. Schouvaloff said they would be only too glad that we should share with them the burden of *managing this country*—and would object to nothing and to no acquisitions provided they were not within the Sea of Marmora—(or some such expression—I [Sandon] cannot remember).

At a Cabinet meeting held on 24 May the Russian propositions were discussed; the only major objection was to the Russian prohibition to permitting Ottoman troops in the new southern Bulgaria. The Prime Minister, rather hopelessly, also desired to do away with the money indemnity. Ministers then accepted Germany's invitation to the congress, assuming of course that prior agreement would be reached with Russia concerning Anglo-Russian negotiations over the Treaty of San Stefano. Finally, this momentous Cabinet meeting sanctioned a telegram to Layard to propose a defensive alliance to the Sultan if Russia kept parts of Armenia, which Salisbury knew already was likely to be the case, and for which Britain would require the occupation of Cyprus. The copies of the Russian memorandums distributed to the Cabinet were then given up to Salisbury who burnt them over the grate. Smith with un-derstandable exaggeration referred to the offer to the Porte as 'the most important move since the days of Pitt'.[9]

Shuvalov came to Salisbury immediately the Cabinet meeting of the twenty-fourth was finished and the two men had a long and animated discussion during which the Foreign Secretary explained the nature of the Cabinet's objections to the Russian memorandums. These included the vagueness of the boundaries for the new Bulgaria, exclusive promises to Russia concerning the Armenians, the excessive amount of the indemnity, and a surprisingly mild veto on Russian insistence that Ottoman troops be excluded from southern Bulgaria.

I [Salisbury] observed that the withdrawal of the Ottoman Troops from the southern province of Bulgaria might be accepted by England in principle. . . . But it would be necessary that Congress should define the mode and the emergencies in which the entry of troops to protect the province . . . should be permitted, and England would contend for the right of the Sultan to place garrisons in the passes of the Balkans [Mountains] & on the littoral of the Black Sea.

Shuvalov remained firm but did indicate that he would telegraph to the Tsar for instructions on Bulgaria. The Foreign Secretary then mentioned other English conditions or reservations, which were less fundamental, so that an absolute agreement on them prior to going into congress was not necessary. These included the duration and manner of Russian occupation, the use of European instead of Russian officials in the organization of the two Bulgarian provinces, the duration of open rights of passage through Romania for Russia, and a promise to Europe to respect the rights of monks of all nationalities on Mount Athos, not merely Russian monks. When Shuvalov departed, Beust, the Austrian ambassador, came in order to ascertain what had occurred. 'Lord Salisbury was unable to betray the secrets of the negotiations, but assured him [Beust] . . . that, excepting Montenegro, England was working as hard for Austrian points as for her own.' Before a busy day had ended the Foreign Secretary sent off to Layard a proposed alliance with the Ottoman Empire to be concluded in written form by the evening of 26 May. The ambassador was instructed to maintain the strictest secrecy in the negotiation[10] and, if necessary, to threaten the Porte with throwing it over at the congress in order to win its adhesion.[11]

On 25 May the Cabinet discussed the Shuvalov–Salisbury conversation of the previous day, especially Russian insistence upon the absence of Ottoman troops from southern Bulgaria.

We had great discussion on this—Lord Beaconsfield, almost alone, strongly against giving this up, as he said it was the 'outward and visible sign' of the Turkish power in S. Bulgaria, and without it we should have another Servia there. Salisbury explained that the numerous Greeks and Mussulmans in that district, with their hatred of the Sclaves would prevent this, and lean to the Sultan—and that Adrianople would be the center of Turkish military power—later he said when a permanent settlement was alluded to, that that was hopeless, the most we could hope for was one to last for 10 to 15 years.

The question came to this, could we refuse to go into Congress on

the ground that Russia would not allow the Turks to garrison the new
S. Bulgaria, the very scene of the atrocities (such as Batak, etc.) . . .
General agreement after Lord Beaconsfield left that we could not
(that it was in fact utterly impossible) refuse to go into Congress on
the ground of Russia refusing to have Turkish troops in S. Bulgaria.[12]

The distance between the Prime Minister and the Foreign
Secretary was still apparent, as it had been, but even more so,
in 1876 and 1877, but neither was prepared to discard compromise. Disraeli, realizing the significance of Ottoman
military power allied to England's financial and naval
resources, was seeking an arrangement which could permanently maintain the Porte in Europe as the best barrier to
Russia. Salisbury, feeling that continued and unfettered
Muslim rule over Christians was inhumane and unacceptable,
was reaching for a temporary half-way house in Europe on the
road to complete Christian emancipation—of Greeks and
Slavs which he hoped and thought would come eventually and
completely replace Ottoman power in what he felt was civilized
Europe. If the Foreign Secretary was prepared to swallow his
Muslim prejudice by making an alliance with Turkey for the
sake of British possessions in Asia, especially India,
Beaconsfield's sympathy for the Porte had always been given
only as a handmaiden for British interest and prestige and such
were not necessarily nor always identical with Ottoman integrity and influence. Both men wished equally for a congress
rather than war, Salisbury perhaps allowing such feeling to
manifest itself more than did the Prime Minister.

Bismarck, still fearing the possibility of an Anglo-Russian
war, was doing all he could to avoid it by pressing for the congress. He used his influence with Britain to push her towards
Austria and support for Vienna's Balkan interests,
simultaneously advising Andrássy that any prolonged delay in
the meeting of the congress because of disputed questions with
Russia over San Stefano, which Bismarck believed could be left
for the congress to settle, would only allow more time for
bellicose feeling in England and Russia to re-emerge or an
Anglo-Russian entente to solidify, effectively isolating Austria.
While promising to promote Austria's interests at the congress,
Bismarck indicated that such support was limited by the need
for Germany to avoid any break with Russia. On 25 May

Münster, the German ambassador, mentioned to Salisbury Bismarck's anxiety and his hope that England would make no agreement which would strike at the interests of Austria. Two days later, in order to dissipate the fears of Bismarck and Andrássy, Salisbury sent to Vienna an agreement which Britain was prepared to sign. The agreement ran:

Austria and England will together urge at Congress that the autonomous Principality [of Bulgaria] shall not extend south or south-west of a line to be drawn along the summit of the Balkans, and thence due west to the Morava River. . . . England reserves her right to urge in Congress provisions for the protection of the populations.

They agree to urge that Russian occupation south of the Danube shall be limited to six months from definite treaty, and passage through Roumania to a corresponding period, say nine months, and that occupying army shall be limited to 20,000 men.

In Articles VI, VII, XI of Treaty, European to be substituted for Russian Commissaires.

England will support any proposition with respect to Bosnia which Austria shall make at Congress.[13]

The day before Salisbury's offer was made to Vienna, agreement for an alliance had been reached with the Porte on 26 May. The original impetus for a port or island in the eastern Mediterranean was probably Beaconsfield's, though Salisbury equally supported it, and the plan for an Ottoman alliance probably was his as well. Compensation for England in view of a breakup of the Ottoman Empire had been spoken of for a year and a half and Cyprus was one of many possibilities mentioned and investigated by the military and naval experts. Home's influence may have been decisive in the choice of Cyprus. By 5 May, if not before, the proposal for what would become the Anglo-Turkish convention was fully matured. Salisbury had prepared Layard for the making of the proposal and on 25 May, the same day as he received the Foreign Secretary's order, the ambassador went to the Sultan who was in a depressed and unstable state, having just passed through an unsuccessful attempt to remove him and set the ex-Sultan Murad in his place. Before he could complete his communication, the Sultan withdrew and directed Layard to continue the negotiation with the Prime Minister and with Safvet Pasha, the

Foreign Minister. The Ottoman ministers then met in council and accepted the English proposal, the Sultan's sanction being given at 8 p.m. on 26 May though the formal convention was not signed until 4 June. The ambassador was able to obtain Ottoman acquiescence without using Salisbury's threat to throw them over if they raised difficulties. On the following day the Queen through Salisbury offered Layard the Grand Cross of the Bath in grateful recognition of his services.[14]

Salisbury's negotiations with Shuvalov had continued while Britain came to an agreement with the Porte, the ambassador having sent home a telegram of eight pages after his interview with the Foreign Secretary on 23 May. A reply was sent to him from St. Petersburg accepting all the British modifications save the one asking for Ottoman troops to be stationed in Rumelia. Despite the opposition of Beaconsfield, the Cabinet which met on the twenty-fifth felt that the country would not sanction refusing the congress, the meeting of which was the purpose of the Anglo-Russian agreement, on this point. For his part, Shuvalov was pleading with St. Petersburg to allow him to sign any agreement with London without referring it home, as this would save time and delay, he argued, might kill the congress and bring on war. He was supported in this by the Foreign Secretary who feared that an incident at Constantinople might still cause war with military forces so near one another. The ambassador's request was refused, and though he and Salisbury were generally agreed on the content of an agreement by 28 May, nothing could be done until Shuvalov received authorization to sign from home which he requested on that day. One point upon which there was yet disagreement was Salisbury's expectation that the coming of the congress would lead to withdrawal of the Russian military and of British naval forces from the vicinity of Constantinople. This the Russians refused to promise until the Porte had agreed to evacuate Varna, Shumla, and Batum, which St. Petersburg was still pressing the Turks to do. The unsettled question of Ottoman military presence in southern Bulgaria was left to be decided in congress. Shuvalov received permission from St. Petersburg to sign the agreement with Britain on 29 May and on the evening of the thirtieth signatures were exchanged on two memorandums.[15]

The first memorandum, which dealt largely with Bulgaria, removed that province from the Aegean, protected non-Bulgarian peoples on its western edges, divided it into two provinces with political autonomy going to the northern and administrative autonomy to the southern half, and removed Ottoman troops from southern Bulgaria except for the purpose of resisting insurrection or invasion, this last being a distinct British concession.[16] No agreement was reached on England's desire to permit the stationing of Ottoman troops on the frontiers of southern Bulgaria, nor was any attempt made to define precisely the boundaries of either of the two Bulgarian provinces. The remainder of the first memorandum gave Europe as well as Russia a voice in the administrative organization of Thessaly, Epirus, and the remainder of Ottoman Europe left to the Porte, indicated the Tsar's intention not to convert the indemnity into a territorial annexation, reserved the rights of British holders of Ottoman bonds and loans, and returned the Alashkert Valley with Bayazid to the Porte, thus preserving the well-known caravan trade route to Persia. In return Britain promised not to oppose the remaining articles of the Treaty of San Stefano.[17]

The significance of the Anglo-Russian agreement was the extent to which it would clear a path to the congress, which, though the German invitations were at hand, Salisbury was now hesitating to accept until Russia was prepared to guarantee a removal of her army from before Constantinople. It was the presence of such a force that gave St. Petersburg hope that a trade could be arranged and that for its removal the Porte would evacuate Shumla, Varna, and Batum. The Russians appealed for German support to be used with the British, but Shuvalov's assurances to remove his country's army caused Salisbury and the Cabinet to give way and to agree on 1 June to accept a congress invitation even before St. Petersburg's official promise to evacuate its forces from around Constantinople.[18] The Cabinet which had so agreed on 1 June was addressed by Beaconsfield who proposed that Britain be represented at the congress by Salisbury and himself.

If he [Lord Beaconsfield] and Salisbury were there they could say decisively that English feeling would not stand such and such things and that thus they could hope to be of much greater service [than

Odo Russell and Lord Lyons]. He [Beaconsfield] added that he should only go for the beginning . . . [of the congress].

Cabinet looked grave. . . . Salisbury said he thought it very important, as it would stop all the gossip of Europe and England as to he and Lord Beaconsfield representing different policies, that you must have men from the Cabinet who knew all the ins and outs of these recent negotiations, and that he and Lord Beaconsfield respectively would satisfy the 2 different views—and that as 'in England people were very much guided by authority,' the philo-Turks would accept necessary concessions to Russia from Lord Beaconsfield which they would not from him.

He spoke most strongly in favour of Lord Beaconsfield going with him.

Any doubts about Disraeli's going were not pressed in the Cabinet though when the public learned of the decision, a minor sensation erupted. Another occurred when the *Globe*, an evening paper, published on 30 May a summary of the Anglo-Russian agreement which Shuvalov and Salisbury, the latter having gone to great lengths to preserve secrecy, were at that very moment signing.[19]

Until the revelation by the *Globe* and the announcement of Beaconsfield's intention to go to the congress, most public attention, or rather Parliamentary interest, focused on the novelty, some said unconstitutionality, of the expedition from India to Malta. Debate, which had been postponed for several weeks, opened in both Houses on 20 May. While Chamberlain and some of his friends were ready to attempt a vote of censure on the Government, Hartington was not. He introduced a motion which carefully questioned the constitutionality of the expedition but not the policy which it represented and from which he somewhat artificially separated it. Debate in the Lords lasted for the whole of one night where Cairns confronted Selborne in a lengthy, and for some listeners boring, constitutional argument. In the Commons debate continued into the early hours when Gladstone spoke eloquently to a very thin House. A division was taken on 23 May on Hartington's motion which was defeated by a vote of 347 to 226, giving the Government an unexpectedly large majority of 121, with 11 Liberals and 8 home-rulers voting with the majority. Foreign crisis continued to ensure a safe and large ministerial majority even when the

Liberals were united upon a motion framed to attract the votes of those who would have drawn back from anything like a direct censure of the Government. The German ambassador interpreted the Liberal attack as an attempt to calm 'the constitutional ... conscience through a theoretical three day rhetorical tourney'.[20]

Anticipating further discussion on the supplementary estimate required for the Indian expedition, Salisbury obtained the prior consent of Shuvalov and Münster in order to inform Parliament that the prospects for a congress had materially improved. This announcement made on 27 May was received with general satisfaction in both Houses, but debate was not forestalled and a vote favourable to the Government occurred. Gladstone, who spoke of the illegality of the expedition, did not vote and Hartington, who supported the Government's motion for supply, also abstained. Many like Reeve, a Liberal, were pleased with the Government's Parliamentary success and its spirited policy which had challenged Russian pretensions. Chamberlain and others were unhappy with the game of brag practised by the Government which had run the risk of war, even when this un-English behaviour was exhibited by a Cecil. Most of those, and there were many in both parties, who feared the possibility of war, were reassured on the evening of 30 May by a rare journalistic scoop which appeared in an 'Extra Special Edition' of the *Globe* giving a largely accurate reproduction, though in summary form, of the Anglo-Russian agreement which had only just been signed. It had been supplied to the *Globe* for money by Charles Marvin, a temporary copying clerk hired by the Foreign Office. Beaconsfield and Salisbury at first thought the information had been given out by someone in the Russian Embassy as the Foreign Secretary had gone to great lengths to keep the agreement secret even from the staff within the Foreign Office. When the Porte and Andrássy excitedly asked for explanations and when questions were raised in Parliament concerning the accuracy of the *Globe* report, Salisbury, undoubtedly mortified by the leak, was not candid in denying the exactness of the article, leaving the impression, even when not stating it explicitly, that the *Globe* story was myth. Derby, who was now offering his services to the Liberals, learned the truth, probably from either Shuvalov or

Tenterden, and reported it to Granville. 'The terms lately published in the *Globe* . . . are substantially accurate. I have this from authority which I cannot doubt, though the mystery of how the story got out is still unsolved.'[21]

The scoop by the *Globe* prepared the public for the announcement made to Parliament on 3 June that the congress would meet on the thirteenth. But neither Parliament nor the public was fully prepared, though rumours abounded, for the additional news that Britain would be represented at Berlin by Lord Beaconsfield, as well as by the Foreign Secretary and Odo Russell, as was expected. Why did the Prime Minister, who was nearly seventy-three and in poor health,[22] choose to go, if only, as he informed the Queen, for the first session of the meeting—was it to reap the full and final fruits of victory and the plaudits which would follow as Münster thought, to punctuate a long career with a fitting and successful close as many suspected, or to watch over the behaviour of Salisbury as Hammond, the former Permanent Under-Secretary for Foreign Affairs, felt?

Such an arrangement [the Prime Minister as a congress plenipotentiary] has never yet been made, and it is open to innumerable objections. On the other hand, however, it has doubtless a recommendation in that he will be on the spot to counteract any Russian leaven which may still be seething within Lord Salisbury's bosom: but one may be astonished that Lord Salisbury should consent to abrogate his proper functions, and to undertake a mission under surveillance and tutelage, admitting to all intents and purposes, that his former adventure at Constantinople [Conference] disqualified him from the implicit confidence which should be reposed in a sole plenipotentiary.

The Liberal leadership—Hartington and Granville—who raised objections in Parliament to Disraeli's intention to go to Berlin, as well as to that of the Foreign Secretary, feared not Salisbury's inexperience or Muslim prejudice but the effect of the heat of Berlin upon the unpredictable Semitic instincts of a demonstrated political adventurer. But as every other Power was to be represented by its Premier or Foreign Minister, the matter was allowed to drop.[23]

On 4 June, after some delay, Layard was able to conclude the formal convention with the Porte embodying the Anglo-

Ottoman agreement of 26 May. In a long and revealing dispatch to the ambassador, drafted perhaps with Parliamentary perusal in mind, Salisbury explained his motives for the convention.

If the populations of Syria, Asia Minor and Mesopotamia see that the Porte has no guarantee for its continued existence, but its own strength, they will after the evidence which recent events have furnished . . . begin to calculate upon the speedy fall of the Ottoman domination and to turn their eyes toward its successor.

The mere retention of them [Batum, Ardahan, and Kars] by Russia will exercise a powerful influence in disintegrating the Asiatic Dominions of the Porte. . . . The Asiatic population . . . [will become devoted] to the power which is in the ascendant, and desert . . . the power which is thought to be falling into decay.

The only provision which can furnish a substantial security for the stability of Ottoman rule in Asiatic Turkey . . . is an engagement on the part of a Power strong enough to fulfil it, that any further encroachment by Russia upon Turkish territory in Asia will be prevented by force of arms . . .

They [Britain] should be formally assured of the intention of the Porte to introduce the necessary reforms . . . in those regions.

It is not impossible that a careful selection . . . of the individual officers to whom power is to be entrusted in those countries would be a more important element in the improvement of the condition of the people than even legislative changes. But the assurance required to give England a right to insist on satisfactory arrangements for these purposes will be an indispensable part of any agreement to which Her Majesty's Government could consent. It will further be necessary in order to enable Her Majesty's Government efficiently to execute the engagements now proposed, that they should occupy a position near the coast of Asia Minor and Syria . . .

The convention itself provided the following.

If Batoum, Ardahan, Kars or any of them shall be retained by Russia and if any attempt shall be made at any future time by Russia to take possession of any further portion of the Asiatic territories of the Sultan . . . England engages to join the Sultan in defending them by force of arms. In return, the Sultan promises to England, to introduce necessary reforms (to be agreed upon later between the two powers) into the government of the Christian and other subjects of the Porte in those territories, and, in order to enable England to make necessary provision for executing her engagement, the Sultan further consents to assign the island of Cyprus to be occupied and administered by England.

Though Salisbury made considerable efforts to maintain the secrecy of the Cyprus Convention until the appropriate moment at the congress, he had intimated something very like it to Shuvalov in the negotiations leading to the Anglo-Russian agreement of 30 May. It is possible that the Russian ambassador never told his Government as he was anxious for an Anglo-Russian compromise enabling the congress to meet, and even a veiled English intimation of such a convention with the Porte might have provoked a negative reaction in Russia, thus spoiling his chances beforehand. Zichy, the Austrian ambassador at Constantinople, also managed to obtain information of the convention which he telegraphed to Andrássy. '[Zichy] was notified by a thoroughly reliable person who has immediate access to the Sultan that there is an agreement between England and Turkey which provides for an English occupation of Cyprus. ... The agreement—which gives England, though allegedly only provisionally, such an important base in the Mediterranean—will ... not be submitted to the congress.'[24]

Two days later, on 6 June, the last of Britain's arrangements in preparation for the congress was concluded when Andrássy accepted Salisbury's offer of 27 May[25]—an agreement by Austria on Bulgaria for British support for any Austrian proposal on Bosnia. With the compromise with Russia already concluded, the significance of the pact with Austria was much reduced, though the lingering fear that she still might close with Russia gave it validity in Salisbury's eyes, pressed as he was by the Queen not to throw over Vienna for treacherous Russia. It was an agreement between two cool friends who had many reasons for distrust in a tortuous and frequently interrupted attempt to close with one another begun in 1876. The Foreign Secretary had instructed Elliot not to communicate to Andrássy a considerable part of the agreement with Russia, and reiterated to the Austrians the impossibility of England's threatening war at Austria's side over Serbia and Montenegro. Ponsonby expanded on this in an explanation to the Queen. 'But if war unfortunately broke out [during or after the congress] and Austria came to an understanding with England these subjects [Serbia and Montenegro] might be inserted in the agreement of the object of the war. Austria consented to this view—partially.' Though not satisfied as much as he would have wished by London, Andrássy knew that he still might need British influence with the Porte in order to obtain its acquiescence to an Austrian occupation or annexation of Bosnia which he was attempting to arrange. The secret Anglo-Austrian agreement signed in Vienna by Elliot and Andrássy provided that both would support at the congress the restricting of northern Bulgaria to the north of the Balkan Mountains and to the east of the Morava River. Southern Bulgaria was to be removed from the Aegean and the Porte was to be permitted the necessary military and political jurisdiction in it in order to respond to insurrection or invasion. The Russian occupation of the northern province was to be restricted to six months and 20,000 men and its rights of administration in European Turkey were to be replaced by a European administration. England's promise to support the Austrian position on Bosnia at the congress was for Andrássy a paltry consolation prize as he desired to occupy that province before the meeting of the congress.[26]

The reasons for Britain's three agreements with Austria, Turkey, and Russia were evident, at least on the surface. The purpose of the pact with St. Petersburg was to scale down the clauses of the San Stefano treaty in order to allow the Porte an independent existence in Europe. Salisbury's support for, or lack of objection to, an independent Romania, Serbia, and Montenegro, an Austrian occupation of Bosnia, a Russian annexation of Bessarabia, and a Greek expansion into Thessaly and Epirus would have left the Porte with part of Macedonia and Rumelia and Albania. What the Foreign Secretary meant by the Porte's independent existence, a concept in which he did not believe, being certain that the Turks' days in Europe were numbered, was temporary security for the Ottoman control over Constantinople and the Straits. To keep the latter out of the hands and safe from the threat of Russia was what lay behind his futile attempts, until it was largely unnecessary, to seek Austrian support for the line of the Balkan Mountains as the southern boundary for northern Bulgaria. But even for this more limited goal Salisbury's support was only lukewarm since it would have meant stationing Ottoman troops in southern Bulgaria (Rumelia) which contained the area where the Bulgarian massacres had occurred. He admitted as much to Elliot. 'The channel between the duty of keeping the Porte strong enough to keep Russia back, and that of saving the subject populations [Christian Slavs] from abuse is . . . a hard one to find and steer through.'[27] Finally, seeing the Greeks as the eventual inheritors of Ottoman rule over Constantinople and the Straits, he attempted to preserve a Greek independent existence through territorial expansion before a tidal wave of Slavs, albeit a Christian tidal wave. Layard attempted to disabuse him of such a hope, certain that the Greeks would not be capable of preserving such a charge for a long time to come.

Salisbury gave lip-service in both his pact with Russia and the convention with the Porte to preserving civilized government for Ottoman subjects in both Europe and Asia. He went so far in the Cyprus Convention to insist upon Britain's right to make satisfactory arrangements for the improvement of the condition of the people. Since, however, the convention itself depended for its existence and application upon Russia keeping part of Armenia, her failure to do so, which admittedly was not likely, would have lessened or obliterated Britain's right to interfere for the sake of the Porte's Asian subjects. But Salisbury's interest in the welfare of those subjects had a double motivation which only incidentally included any real concern for the subjects themselves. A reasonably satisfied citizenry would improve Ottoman stability in Asia as a bulwark against Russia. Negative British opinion, which would be mollified only partially by the acquisition of Cyprus, had to be anticipated and disarmed by the insistence upon and responsibility for good government.

Neither the public, nor the Cabinet, nor the Foreign Secretary manifested much sympathy for the welfare of the Muslim nor even some of the Christian citizenry of the Porte. When the Cabinet meeting on 5 June considered the congress instructions to be sent to Odo Russell and Sandon suggested inserting 'an allusion to Mohammedans requiring to be protected, where at end of paper we allude to looking after Greek populations', the Foreign Secretary objected. 'But Salisbury would not hear of it, as he said there were special reasons for pushing forward the Greeks.'[28] Layard had bombarded London with dispatches reporting Russian and Bulgarian atrocities to the inhabitants in Rumelia and forwarded appeal after appeal from the Muslim and Greek citizenry of that province and Macedonia which only elicited a cool politeness from London. Appeals and protests also were addressed to the Cabinet from Pomaks at Mount Rhodope, Jews in the Balkans and London, the Laz in Armenia and the Caucasus, Albanians fearing incorporation by Montenegro, and nearly all ethnic and religious groups in Bulgaria and Rumelia except the Bulgarian Christians. Britain's Christian conscience, however, was assuaged by the prevention of war and the triumph of nationalism in the Balkan peninsula at the expense of what was incorrectly assumed was unique Muslim barbarism.

Salisbury's justification for the Cyprus Convention was the necessity of preventing Ottoman disintegration in Asia following upon Russian gains in Armenia. This made little sense, even less than preserving an independent Ottoman existence in Europe, which had largely disappeared. Russian acquisition of Batum or Kars or Ardahan would not be a serious threat to the Ottoman Empire in Asia and Turkish control of these three places would not secure Ottoman Asia. This last offered just enough justification, however, for what was desired for its own sake—independent of Ottoman security or stability in Asia—an occupation of Cyprus. Britain's three agreements, though inconsistent and disingenuous, had removed her from a position of diplomatic isolation and placed her in the mainstream of the decisions to be made at Berlin. Further, the meeting of the congress itself, made possible by the bargain with Russia, was to be called under a compromise formula which did not prohibit the consideration of any part of the Treaty of San Stefano. Though Salisbury could not claim sole credit for either accomplishment, his recognition of what he wanted, his firmness in pressing for it, and his courage in not flinching before the possibility of war were decisive for success. Derby was capable of the first two things and perhaps it is to his credit that the third was so repugnant as to be impossible for him to do it very easily, if at all. Stojanovic has summed up the situation fairly. 'The proportion of power of the Great Powers had to be preserved in the East despite the transformations which were taking place there. To this principle all other interests were subordinated: the destiny of the Christians as well as that of Turkey.'[29]

The Cabinet meetings of 5 and 7 June agreed on the instructions for Russell, the Prime Minister, and the Foreign Secretary. A proposal for the withdrawal of the Russian army at Constantinople to be made at the opening of the congress was approved by all the ministers as was the offering of strong support for the admission of Greece to the congress and the pleading of her cause. After some discussion the Cabinet agreed to disclose publicly the convention with Turkey when Russia refused, as it was expected that she would, to give up Batum, Ardahan, or Kars. If the course and decisions of the congress left room for surprises and disagreements, the major results had been arranged beforehand. Outnumbered by Britain and Austria on Montenegro, Bosnia, and Bulgaria, Russia would have to content herself with Bessarabia and Armenia while her opponents obtained Bosnia and Cyprus. Within the Cabinet, in London, and throughout the country there was satisfaction mingled with relief that the crisis was over and the prospects for peaceful accommodation likely. Beaconsfield left London on 8 June in high spirits, perhaps already aware of the admiration felt for him by many of his countrymen. Arthur Grote, the younger brother of the historian, wrote to Layard of both the relief and admiration.

Indeed I cannot recollect for a long term . . . any public questions on which so widespread an interest has been felt by the English people. The last three weeks were weeks of even *painful* anxiety & I am sure that *you* must have undergone as much mental strain as it was well possible to experience. Accordingly, the prospect even, of a solution of our difficulties comes upon us as an ineffable relief. The prodigious admiration now felt for Lord Beaconsfield's direction of the English policy knows no bounds.

The *coup de tete,* in bringing the Indian troops upon the stage produced a movement of surprise and admiration among all classes, except the section of Liberals who own the leadership of W.E.G. [Gladstone].[30]

## 22  CONCLUSION

BRITISH SUPPORT for Ottoman sovereignty and integrity in the fifty years prior to 1875 was manifested most strongly, as in 1839–40 and 1854–6, when the threat to Ottoman integrity was the result of action undertaken by Britain's two main rivals in the Near East and eastern Mediterranean, France and Russia. After the Crimean War, which represented the ultimate exertion on the part of England to maintain such integrity, further British military effort for this purpose became less realistic, though the threat to continued Turkish control of her European territories was becoming nearly total. The difficulty with manifesting such an effort was due to diplomatic isolation partially self-imposed, the absence of an army of a size equal to those of the Continental Powers, and an increasing disinclination to help maintain what was considered to be the corrupt tyranny of Muslim rule over Christian subjects. The emergence of a nearly independent Romania and the remilitarization of the Black Sea elicited little in the way of real English action for Ottoman integrity.

The treaties of 1856 which enshrined in international form the British obligation to maintain the independence and integrity of the Ottoman Empire, the large amount of British money invested in that empire, and the desire to protect interests in the Near East which could be more effectively secured under Ottoman preservation all combined to cause British governments to continue to proclaim respect for Turkish sovereignty.

Such was the case when insurrection occurred in Hercegovina in 1875 and London urged the Porte to deal quickly with the revolt before European intervention could compound and complicate it. Until August 1876, when Britain learned of significant atrocities in Bulgaria, Derby continued to manifest support for complete Ottoman sovereignty as that tended to minimize British responsibility and intervention by the Great Powers. He did not believe in the efficacy or justice of Turkish rule, but its continuance was preferable to doing anything about it.

Disraeli had only the most elastic conceptions of Ottoman integrity, conceptions which were altered to meet for him the more important requirements of British prestige. He saw clearly the necessity to escape diplomatic isolation if England were to play the part which her interests and position made necessary. Consequently, he, with support from Derby, organized the rejection of the Berlin memorandum because he considered it insulting and the following month, June 1876, attempted a direct agreement with Russia when he offered Shuvalov an arrangement which foundered on the suspiciousness of Russia and the distrust of Derby. In January and February of the same year Bismarck had offered London German friendship and diplomatic support. Derby naturally found the offer suspect, fearing the entrapment of British support for a German attack on France. Disraeli also misinterpreted Bismarck's motives or was not initially made aware of his offer by the Foreign Secretary. Buying the Khedive's shares in the Suez Canal in November 1875 and sending the fleet up to the entrance to the Dardanelles in May 1876 were moves typical of Disraeli as they increased the self-confidence and manifested the might of England.

News of Turkish atrocities in Rumelia reached the British public at the end of July 1876. The resulting feelings of moral outrage and sympathy for Bulgarian Christians were sincere and strongly humane even though the intensity of the reactions of some slipped out of control and became unworthy. The public commotion and the affronted feelings of members of the Cabinet—especially Salisbury, Carnarvon, Cairns, Northcote, and Derby—caused a change in the Government's official line toward the Porte. Derby now supported local autonomy for Bosnia-Hercegovina and reforms for Bulgaria. The Foreign Secretary, fearing a Russian entry into the war if it continued, then threatened the Porte with removing Elliot from Constantinople unless it would make peace at once with Serbia. The change in attitude is best seen in the instructions the Cabinet drew up for Salisbury to guide him at the Constantinople Conference. These contained restrictions on unfettered Ottoman control over its own subjects which were far in advance of anything the Cabinet was willing to accept down to August 1876. Salisbury did not require any justification in order to despise Muslim rule except its existence, the same rule which the Duke of Argyll argued always legitimized insurrection and revolution against it. While Derby used the atrocities as an excuse for the refusal of British military support should Turkey be attacked by Russia, Salisbury desired to coerce Turkey to agree to reduce her own sovereignty and regarded any sort of association with the Turks as a kind of personal affront.

Disraeli, whose flexibility on policy was nearly total, was prepared for any Ottoman sacrifice consistent with British prestige. Well before any news of Bulgarian massacres reached England, the Prime Minister proposed autonomy for Bosnia and attempted a direct agreement with Russia. In September 1876 he suggested that Derby propose to Andrássy and Gorchakov a partition of European Turkey and at the end of the same month proposed, if Russia attacked Turkey, a British occupation of Constantinople as a material guarantee. Though health and age had diminished his energy, his imaginative fecundity continued unabated.

With the beginning of a Russo-Turkish war in April 1877 and after a momentary burst of official panic, the government defined the price for its continued neutrality in Derby's dispatch of 6 May. As well as remaining outside the Persian Gulf, Egypt, the Straits, and the Suez Canal, Russia was asked not to threaten or occupy Constantinople. Gorchakov and the Tsar refused to give an absolute promise not to do so, alleging that if the Porte knew that Russia would remain outside Constantinople and the Straits it would never make peace. In fact, during January 1878 the Turks desired peace which Russia delayed until she first could reach and occupy the city. After 6 May 1877 there were repeated English requests or warnings to Russia to remain outside the Ottoman capital. They were given on 17 July, 13 December, 30 January, and 21 February, with a further warning against a move on Gallipoli delivered on 13 February. When Russia continued to advance nearer the city, an advance which seemed to violate the armistice concluded on 31 January, the fleet after several embarrassing failures was sent up to Constantinople on 13 February.

Barbara Jelavich has written that the importance of Constantinople stemmed from the belief, however mistaken, that whoever controlled it would have also dominion or command over the entire Ottoman Empire. For Britain there was on the part of some people anxiety over the expectation that a Russian occupation of the capital would mean her control over the Dardanelles and Bosphorus. A Russian fleet would be safe from within or behind the Straits to sally forth and interrupt and menace British naval communication in the eastern Mediterranean. Others feared that sufficient Russian sway or influence over European Turkey would result in the imposition of a Russian tariff policy which would exclude British commerce. One estimate made in 1877 indicated that were British trade to be excluded from European Turkey the loss would be £12,000,000 a year.[1] Finally, and perhaps most fundamentally, a Russian occupation of Constantinople would have been a serious blow to British prestige in the Near East, India, Europe, and London.

Disraeli especially was sensitive to this consideration, though Derby informed Salisbury that for his part he did not think it important, as he considered it a factor which appealed mainly to foreigners, in which category he placed the Prime Minister. When the Constantinople Conference ended in January 1877 without result, Derby, unwilling either to fight for or to coerce the Porte, could devise no policy or clear-cut purpose and was reduced to making a careful, suspicious, and unsuccessful attempt to avoid a Russian war on Turkey with the London Protocol.

Disraeli's sense of expansiveness and theatrical style or manner resulted in providing the ideas and initiative which were beyond the careful and distrustful Derby, who in some instances opposed or sabotaged those which he was aware of. In November 1876 the Prime Minister disloyally began secret and unofficial talks with Austria for an alliance or understanding and in December secretly suggested to Salisbury at Constantinople an English occupation of European Turkey. In February 1877 he made another attempt with Shuvalov for a Russian understanding and in April he unsuccessfully suggested to the Cabinet an occupation of Gallipoli. In June he secretly asked Layard if the Porte would request the fleet to come to Constantinople and unsuccessfully proposed a vote of credit and military increase. In July he obtained Cabinet agreement to strengthen British garrisons in the Mediterranean and in August, with the Queen, secretly warned the Tsar against a second campaign. In December the Cabinet was asked to summon Parliament early, make a request to it for money, and assume mediation between Russia and Turkey, and in February 1878 he attempted unsuccessfully to inflate a Mediterranean league and broached the acquisition by England of a Mediterranean port or island.

No wonder that the Foreign Secretary increasingly manifested distrust towards the ideas of his chief, especially to those which he associated with the possibility of an English war. Apart from the disclosures which he and Lady Derby made to Shuvalov, he sabotaged the desire of the entire Cabinet to offer Austria an alliance in May 1877. The Prime Minister went to great and unjustifiable lengths to undercut or bypass the inertia of his friend: secret communication with the Austrian Embassy in London, a secret cipher with Layard, and in August 1877 the secret warning to the Tsar carried by Wellesley. Immobilized by the prospect of war after the fall of Plevna in December 1877, the Foreign Secretary faced for the first time serious, continued, and general criticism of his political and personal behaviour. He justified his political conduct and sustained himself against public criticism by belief in the worthy objective of preventing a recourse to war.

With Russian troops at the walls of Constantinople and a British fleet within the Sea of Marmora, it was no longer possible, by devious means or no, to square the requirements of British prestige with the desire to avoid war. As a result the Prime Minister made a successful attempt to elicit the cooperation of Salisbury in order to emasculate the Foreign Secretary. The India Secretary's Christianity, his concern for Balkan Christians, and his contempt for the Turks, as manifested at the Constantinople Conference, had brought critical reactions from both Derby and Disraeli. During 1877 it had seemed more likely that Salisbury would resign rather than the Foreign Secretary.

Unlike Derby, Salisbury could contemplate the possibility of war, though like Disraeli he did not wish to provoke military conflict. What the India Secretary could not stomach was an alliance with, or a war for, Ottoman rule over European

Christians. From the middle of 1877 he opposed in Cabinet on at least three separate occasions measures which might lead to an association with the Porte. During a discussion to consider the early summoning of Parliament in December and previously when Disraeli had proposed to him in April a British occupation of Gallipoli, Salisbury objected on this ground.[2] When the Cabinet was discussing the possibility of sending the fleet through the Dardanelles in January 1878, he opposed asking or obtaining the Porte's prior consent to do so. But in the accommodation he reached with Beaconsfield at the beginning of 1878, an accommodation made possible by his own concern for Britain's image and prestige and the conclusion of a Russo-Turkish armistice on 31 January, he and the Prime Minister were able to agree on preparations for war, the protection of British interests, and even, ironically, a Muslim alliance.

Lady Cecil in her biography of her father suggests, mistakenly I believe, that the decision for his conversion to support Beaconsfield's policy had been taken as early as July 1877. While Salisbury recognized the probability, long before January 1878, that it would be necessary for the Government to resort to war if Russia attempted to occupy or refused to leave Constantinople, the danger of a resulting Turkish alliance if Britain did so caused him to see a resort to force under such conditions as undesirable, if not inadmissible. After the armistice of 31 January any British military effort would not be besmirched with the Ottoman cause. Even Derby, after his first resignation in January on the decision to send the fleet through the Dardanelles, agreed on such action in February after the conclusion of the Russo-Turkish armistice, though in his case the purpose was to avoid a step which might complicate and prolong the war.

If Salisbury had been willing previously to coerce the Porte and to restrict or destroy Ottoman sovereignty in Europe, he had always shared a willingness with Beaconsfield for a European partition of Turkey. This possibility provided the basis for their co-operation. Carnarvon's opposition and Derby's obstruction after April 1877 of measures tending towards an alliance or military co-operation with Turkey had been the foundation of Salisbury's Cabinet alliance with the Foreign and Colonial Secretaries. But with complete Turkish military defeat imminent it became possible at the end of 1877 to separate a protection of British interests from any partnership with the Porte. In December he explained as much to Northcote. 'An active policy is only possible under one of two conditions—that you shall help the Turks, or coerce them. I have no objection to the latter policy or to a combination of the two. With the former alone I cannot be content. But as you know, neither the Queen nor the Prime Minister will have anything to do with the latter.'[3]

Salisbury's Christian exclusivity was sincere and represented some of the highest humanity and idealism of which nineteenth-century Britain was capable. He never hid his aversion to British support for Ottoman integrity, though such support was associated with the name of Palmerston and war in the Crimea. He was open and honest in his distaste for the Turks and was successful finally in associating British interests with a policy of coercion and partition in so far as that proved possible. What he and some others objected to in the Treaty of San Stefano was not the further and considerable diminution of Ottoman authority in the Balkans but the replacement of Turkish control there by Russian. His opposition to a Bulgaria on the Aegean and his attempt to restrict it to north of the Balkan Mountains reflected his belief that Bulgaria would merely be an extension of Russia and by restricting the extent of the former he would be denying Russia proximity to the Mediterranean and Constantinople. The necessity to refer the terms of this peace treaty to a congress of all the Powers and the refusal of Britain to attend such a meeting save upon the two bases which she proposed temporarily united the Cabinet to a greater degree than had been possible for the past two years.

Even Derby was in agreement with his colleagues not to attend a congress unless Russia agreed to submit the entire Treaty of San Stefano for consideration by the congress and unless any changes from previous treaties received the assent of all Powers who signed those agreements. This represented more proof, if any were needed, that even his great desire to prevent war, the outbreak of which was probable with the failure of a congress and with a Russian army and a British fleet around Constantinople, was exceeded by the distrust of Derby for others, a distrust often inappropriately aroused by the need felt to protect the autonomy of his own personality.

Impasse and war were avoided by the Salisbury–Shuvalov agreements of May 1878. Twice previously, in 1876 and 1877, Disraeli had attempted unsuccessfully to reach a direct agreement with Russia and Salisbury had achieved close harmony and co-operation with Ignatiev at the Constantinople Conference. Salisbury's willingness to deny at Russia's insistence the stationing of Ottoman troops within Rumelia, where the Bulgarian massacres had occurred, reflected a compound of Christian sentiment, humane feelings, and concern over the necessity of defending the settlement of Bulgaria in Parliament.

The Cyprus Convention with the Porte demonstrated Salisbury's diplomatic skill at its finest as well as his Christian bias at its most obvious. The manner in which he prepared Layard, a strong-willed Turcophile, for the presentation of the alliance to the Sultan, was masterly. In a series of dispatches he stressed to the ambassador the benefits the convention would confer upon the Porte. Layard was also instructed to inform the Sultan that unless his agreement were quickly given to the offer of an alliance, he would be left by Britain completely to the tender mercies of St. Petersburg. Salisbury may have thought that his agreement with Turkey, as well as those with Russia and Austria, had broken with the old Palmerstonian policy and replaced it with a new and less sympathetic Turkish policy. Such was not the case. What he had done was to provide Palmerston's association of British interests and Ottoman integrity in Europe with a new geographical locus. From now on Turkey in Asia was made synonymous with British interests to the extent that he pledged Britain to a war in alliance with the Porte should Russia attack its Asian dominions. It was such a military partnership that he had fought against in Cabinet for the past two years.

If the new Foreign Secretary fooled himself as to the nature of his policy, it was because it was necessary to do so in order for him to carry it out. Further support for what he believed to be the cruel and corrupt rule of Muslim over Christian in Europe had long since become insupportable for him. In Ot-

toman Asia there were few Christian subjects and he preferred
to believe that the great mass of Muslim inhabitants there were
more content with the Sultan's rule and less desirous of separation from it in the form of autonomy or independence than
Balkan Christians. At the very moment that most in Britain
viewed, some with joy others with sadness, the end of British
advocacy and maintenance of the independence and integrity
of the Ottoman Empire, the government had promised to
engage in war should the integrity of Turkey in Asia be
attacked by the Power most likely and willing to do so.

In one sense there was a break with Britain's Palmerstonian
and Crimean heritage which occurred near the end of the
Congress of Berlin. A British declaration was issued to the
effect that she no longer considered herself bound by the
closure of the Straits, a principle long enshrined in the treaties
of 1841, 1856, and 1871. Taylor has already pointed out the
significance of this repudiation of the aforementioned international agreements. Within the context of the crisis of 1875–8
the declaration was, to say the least, highly curious. In June
1876 Disraeli had underlined the importance for England of
maintaining the Straits Convention. In Derby's dispatch to
Russia of 6 May 1877 it was implied that any alteration in the
present international regulations of the Bosphorus or Dardanelles might result in Britain's going to war. In Salisbury's
circular of 1 April 1878 and also as one of the two English conditions for entering a congress, it was stipulated that any unilateral abrogation of a European treaty required the assent of
the other parties to that agreement in order for such an alteration to be considered valid. No European consent was obtained for the British declaration at Berlin which was
energetically opposed by Russia.

The Congress of Berlin was in a way a fitting climax to the
career of the Prime Minister. From the beginning of the
Eastern crisis he had fought for his image of the greatness of
Britain. Though not lacking the confidence which afflicted
Derby nor so affected by a deeply ingrained Christianity which
inhibited Salisbury, he was seriously influenced by a lifelong
battle for acceptance that the 'foreigner' often faced. If, as a
result, he became too nationally narrow and too sensitive to
the slights, disdain, and lack of respect to which Britain was oc-

casionally treated by foreign governments, his sense of country was as strong and deep as perhaps any feelings he had. The enthusiasm and affection with which he was received in England upon his return from Berlin was a partial recognition of this. If he and Salisbury had not exactly brought back peace with honour they had secured peace with prestige. It marked the end of a period of fifteen years during which the policy and position of England were too often marked by self-effacement, embarrassment, and ignominy. For many, a bracing assertion of national strength and purpose was welcome nectar after so long a drought. In so far as this assertion was the work of any single individual, it was the contribution of Beaconsfield.

# BIBLIOGRAPHY

I MANUSCRIPT MATERIALS

*A Diplomatic Archives*

Austrian Foreign Ministry, Haus-, Hof- und Staatsarchiv, Vienna, political archives VIII/83–92, XII/114, 115, 118–22, 126–30

Belgian Foreign Ministry, Brussels, general series, Britain; vols. 51–2; Turkey; vols. 14–17

British Foreign Office, Public Record Office, London

Danish Foreign Ministry, Copenhagen, dispatches from London, 1875–8

German Foreign Ministry (microfilm)

Italian Foreign Ministry, Rome, dispatches from Berlin, London, St. Petersburg, and Vienna, 1875–8

Netherlands Foreign Ministry, The Hague, dispatches from London, Constantinople, and Berlin, 1875–8

Spanish Foreign Ministry, Madrid, dispatches from Berlin, Constantinople, London, St. Petersburg, and Vienna, 1875–8

United States State Department, Washington, dispatches from Constantinople, London, and St. Petersburg, 1870–8

*B Private Papers: correspondence, diaries, memorandums*

ACLAND, H. W., Bodleian
ACLAND, T. D.–Gladstone correspondence, Bodleian
ALDENHAM, Guildhall Library
ALI PASHA, British Library
ARDAGH, Public Record Office
AVEBURY (Lubbock), British Library

BALFOUR, British Library
BLACKIE, National Library of Scotland
BRAND, House of Lords Record Office
BRIGHT, British Library
BROADHURST, London School of Economics
BRYCE, Bodleian
BURDETT-COUTTS, Lambeth Palace Library

CABINET LETTERS, Public Record Office
CAIRNS, Public Record Office
CAMPBELL-BANNERMAN, British Library

CARDWELL, Public Record Office
CARLINGFORD, Somerset Record Office
CARNARVON, Public Record Office
CHAMBERLAIN, University of Birmingham Library
CHILDERS, Public Record Office and Royal Commonwealth Society
CHURCHILL, R., East Bergholt, Suffolk
COLVILLE OF CULROSS, Montrose, Scotland
COURTNEY, London School of Economics
COWEN, Newcastle Central Reference Library
CRANBROOK (HARDY), East Suffolk Record Office
CROMER, Public Record Office
CROSS, British Library

DELANE, *The Times*
DERBY, Lancashire Record Office
DILKE, British Library
DISRAELI, Hughenden Manor
DISRAELI–Bradford letters, Weston Park, Shifnal

ELLICE, National Library of Scotland

FOREIGN OFFICE PRINTS AND MEMORANDUMS, Foreign Office Library

GALWAY, University of Nottingham
GLADSTONE, British Library and St. Deiniol's Library, Hawarden
GOODWOOD (Richmond), West Sussex Record Office
GRANT DUFF, Orford, Suffolk
GRANVILLE, Public Record Office
GREY, University of Durham
GROTE, British Library
GUEST, British Library

HAMBLEDEN (W. H. Smith), Strand House, London
HAMILTON, British Library
HAMMOND, Public Record Office
HARCOURT, Stanton Harcourt
HARRISON, F., London School of Economics
HARROWBY, Sandon Hall, Stafford
HARTINGTON, Chatsworth
HERRIES, British Library
HICKLETON (Halifax), Garrowby
HICKS BEACH, Gloucester Record Office
HORNBY, National Maritime Museum

IDDESLEIGH (Northcote), British Library

JOMINI–ONOU, British Library

KILBRACKEN, British Library

LAYARD, British Library
LAYARD, Lady, British Library
LAYARD MEMOIRS, John Murray
LIDDON, Keble College
LOFTUS, Edinburgh University Library
LYONS, West Sussex Record Office
LYTTON, India Office Library and Hertfordshire Record Office

MALET PAPERS, B. Weinreb, London
MILNE, National Maritime Museum
MORIER, Balliol College
MÜLLER, Bodleian
MUNDELLA, Sheffield University Library

NIGHTINGALE, F., British Library
NORTHBROOK, India Office Library

PAGET, British Library
PAKINGTON, Worcestershire Record Office
PATTISON, Bodleian
PLAYFAIR, Imperial College of Science and Industry
PONSONBY, Public Record Office and British Library
PUSEY, Pusey House, Oxford

RIPON, British Library
ROSEBERY, National Library of Scotland
ROYAL ARCHIVES, Windsor
RUSSELL, John, Public Record Office
RUSSELL, Odo, Public Record Office

SALISBURY, Christ Church and India Office Library
SANDERSON, Baron, Public Record Office
SANDERSON, P., Public Record Office
SCOTT, British Library
SELBORNE, Lambeth Palace Library
SHAW-LEFEVRE, Haddo House, Tarves, Scotland
SIMMONS, Public Record Office
SPENCER, Earl, Althorp, Northampton

SPENCER-WALPOLE, Gladstone correspondence, Bodleian
SPENCE-WATSON, House of Lords Record Office
ST. ALDWYN (Hicks Beach), Gloucester Record Office
STANLEY, A. P., Lambeth Palace Library
STANMORE, British Library
STEAD–NOVIKOV correspondence, Bodleian
STUART, Public Record Office

TEMPLE, India Office Library
TENTERDEN, Public Record Office

WARD HUNT, Delapre Abbey, Northampton
WELLESLEY (Cowley), Public Record Office
WENTWORTH, British Library
WHITE, Public Record Office
WOLSELEY, Hove Central Library
WORDSWORTH, Lambeth Palace Library

## II PRINTED BOOKS

ALDER, G. J., *British India's Northern Frontier, 1865–95*, Longman, London, 1963
ANDERSON, DOROTHY, *The Balkan Volunteers*, Hutchinson, London, 1968
ANDERSON, M. S., *The Eastern Question, 1774–1923*, Macmillan, London, 1966
ARGYLL, DUKE OF (G. S. Campbell), *The Eastern Question*, 2 vols., Strahan, London, 1879

BAILEY, F. E., *British Policy and the Turkish Reform Movement*, Harvard University Press, Cambridge, Mass., 1942
BALFOUR, LADY ELIZABETH EDITH LYTTON, *The History of Lord Lytton's Indian Administration, 1876–1880*, Longman, New York, 1899
BASSETT, A. TILNEY (ed.), *Gladstone to His Wife*, Methuen, London, 1936
BLACKFORD, FREDERIC LORD, *Letters*, John Murray, London, 1896
BLAKE, ROBERT, *Disraeli*, St. Martin's, New York, 1967
BLOCH, CHARLES, *Les Relations entre La France et La Grande-Bretagne, 1871–78*, Les Éditions internationales, Paris, 1955
BRIDGE, F. R., *From Sadowa to Sarajevo. The Foreign Policy of Austria-Hungary, 1866–1914*, Routledge & Kegan Paul, London, 1972
BRIGHT, JOHN, *Diaries*, William Morrow, New York, 1930
BUCKLE, G. E. (ed.), *The Letters of Queen Victoria*, 2nd ser., 2 vols., Longman, New York, 1926

CAMPBELL, SIR GEORGE, *A Handy Book on the Eastern Question*, John Murray, London, 1876
CAVENDISH, LADY FREDERICK, *Diary*, 2 vols., F. A. Stokes, New York, 1927
CECIL, LADY GWENDOLEN, *Life of Robert Marquis of Salisbury*, 4 vols., Hodder & Stoughton, London, 1921–32
CHILSTON, VISCOUNT E., *W. H. Smith*, Routledge & Kegan Paul, London, 1965
CLAYDEN, PETER WILLIAM, *England Under Lord Beaconsfield*, C. Kegan Paul, London, 1880
CLAYTON, G. D., *Britain and the Eastern Question*, London University Press, London, 1971
CROSS, A., *A Political History*, Privately printed, 1903

DAVISON, RODERIC H., *Reform in the Ottoman Empire, 1856–76*, Princeton University Press, Princeton, 1963
DENTON, REVD. WILLIAM, *The Christians of Turkey*, Daldy, Isbister, London, 1877
DERBY, COUNTESS OF, *A Great Lady's Friendships. Letters to Mary, Marchioness of Salisbury Countess of Derby, 1862–90*, Macmillan, London, 1933
DEVEREUX, ROBERT, *The First Ottoman Constitutional Period*, Johns Hopkins Press, Baltimore, 1963
DJORDEVIĆ, DIMITRIJE, *Révolutions nationales des peuples balkaniques 1804–1914*, Institut d'histoire, Belgrade, 1965
DUGDALE, EDGAR T. S. (ed.), *German Diplomatic Documents, 1871–1914*, Methuen, London, 1928–31
DUNN, W. H., *James Anthony Froude. A Biography*, Clarendon Press, Oxford, 1961–3
DWIGHT, HENRY O., *Turkish Life in War Time*, Scribner's, New York, 1881

EDWARDS, H. SUTHERLAND, *Sir William White. His Life and Correspondence*, John Murray, London, 1902
EGERTON, F., *Sir Geoffrey Phipps Hornby*, W. Blackwood, Edinburgh, 1896
ELIOT, SIR CHARLES, *Turkey in Europe*, Edward Arnold, London, 1908
ELLIOT, ARTHUR D., *Life of G. J. Goschen*, 2 vols., Longman, London, 1911
ELLIOT, G. E. (ed.), *Some Revolutions and other Diplomatic Experiences*, John Murray, London, 1922
ESHER, REGINALD VISCOUNT, *Journal and Letters*, ed. M. V. Brett, 2 vols., Ivor, Nicholson, and Watson, London, 1934

EVANS, ARTHUR J., *Through Bosnia and the Herzegovina on Foot During the Insurrection, August and September 1875*, Longman, London, 1877

FADNER, FRANK, *Seventy Years of Pan-Slavism in Russia*, Georgetown University Press, Washington, 1962
FARLEY, JAMES LEWIS, *Turks and Christians. A Solution of the Eastern Question*, Simpkin, Marshall, and Co., London, 1876
FEUCHTWANGER, E. J., *Disraeli, Democracy and the Tory Party*, Clarendon Press, Oxford, 1968
FIFE-COOKSON, Lt.-Col., *With the Armies of the Balkans and at Gallipoli in 1877–78*, Cassell, Petter, Galpin, and Co., London, 1879
FITZMAURICE, LORD E., *Life of Granville*, 2 vols., Longman, London, 1905
FORBES, ARCHIBALD, *Memories and Studies of War and Peace*, Cassell and Co., London, 1895
—— *Czar and Sultan*, Scribner, N.Y., 1894
FREEMAN, EDWARD A., *The Ottoman Power in Europe*, Macmillan, London, 1877
FUUNEAUX, RUPERT, *The Breakfast War*, Crowell, N.Y., 1958

GALLENGA, A., *Two Years of the Eastern Question*, 2 vols., Samuel Tinsley, London, 1877
GARDINER, A. G., *The Life of Sir William Harcourt*, 2 vols., Constable, London, 1923
GATHORNE HARDY, ALFRED E. (ed.), *A memoir of Gathorne Hardy*, 2 vols., Longman, London, 1910
GAVARD, CHARLES, *A Diplomat in London. Letters and Notes 1871–7*, Holt, New York, 1897
GLEASON, JOHN H., *The Genesis of Russophobia in Great Britain*, Harvard University Press, Cambridge, Mass., 1950
GORIAINOV, SERGE, *Le Bosphore et Les Dardanelles*, Plon-Nourrit, Paris, 1910
GREEN, JOHN RICHARD, *Letters*, Macmillan, New York, 1901
GWYNN, STEPHEN AND TUCKWELL, GERTRUDE M., *Life of Sir Charles Dilke*, 2 vols., John Murray, London, 1917

HAMLIN, CYRUS, *Among the Turks*, Sampson Low, London, 1878
HARDINGE, SIR ARTHUR, *The Life of ... Fourth Earl of Carnarvon, 1831–90*, 3 vols., Oxford University Press, London, 1925
HARRIS, DAVID, *A Diplomatic History of the Balkan Crisis of 1875–1878. The First Year*, Stanford University Press, Stanford, 1936
—— *Britain and the Bulgarian Horrors of 1876*, University of Chicago Press, Chicago, 1939

HAYWARD, ABRAHAM, *Selections From His Correspondence From 1834 to 1881*, 2 vols., London, 1886

HEWETT, O. W., *Strawberry Fair, A Biography of Frances, Countess Waldegrave, 1821–79*, John Murray, London, 1956

HOLLAND, BERNARD, *Life of Spencer Compton, Eighth Duke of Devenshire*, 2 vols., Longman, London, 1911

JELAVICH, BARBARA, *The Ottoman Empire, the Great Powers, and the Straits Question, 1870–1887*, University of Indiana Press, Bloomington, 1973

JELAVICH, CHARLES AND BARBARA (eds.), *The Balkans in Transition*, University of California Press, Berkeley, 1963

—— *Russia in the East, 1876–1880*, E. J. Brill, Leiden, 1959

JOHNSTON, JOHN O., *Life and Letters of Henry Parry Liddon*, Longman, New York, 1904

KENNEDY, A. L., *Salisbury, 1830–1903*, John Murray, London, 1953

KNIGHTLEY, LADY LOUISA MARY, *The Journals of Lady Knightley of Fawsley, 1856–84*, ed. Julia Cartwright, John Murray, London, 1915

KOFOS, EVANGELOS, *Greece and the Eastern Crisis 1875–1878*, Institute for Balkan Studies, Thessalonika, 1975

LANG, ANDREW, *Life, Letters, and Diaries of Sir Stafford Northcote*, 2 vols., Blackwood and Sons, London, 1890

LANGER, WILLIAM L., *European Alliances and Alignments, 1871–90*, Knopf, New York, 1950

LEE, DWIGHT E., *Great Britain and the Cypress Convention Policy of 1878*, Harvard University Press, Cambridge, Mass., 1934

LEPSIUS, J. *et al.* (eds.), *Die Grosse Politik*, Auswärtiges Amt, Berlin, 1922–7

LEWIS, BERNARD, *The Emergence of Modern Turkey*, Oxford University Press, London, 1968

LOFTUS, LORD AUGUSTUS, *Diplomatic Reminiscences*, 2 vols., Cassell and Co., London, 1894

LUCAS, REGINALD, *Lord Glenesk and the Morning Post*, John Lane, New York, 1910

LUCY, HENRY W., *A Diary of Two Parliaments*, Cassell and Co., New York, 1885

MACCOLL, MALCOLM, *Three Years of the Eastern Question*, Chatto and Windus, London, 1878

—— *Memoirs and Correspondence*, Smith, Elder, London, 1914

MACDERMOTT, MERCIA, *A History of Bulgaria, 1393–1885*, London, 1962
MACGAHAN, J. A., *The Turkish Atrocities in Bulgaria*, Bradbury, Agnew, and Co., London, 1876
MACKENZIE, DAVID, *The Serbs and Russian Pan-Slavism, 1875–78*, Cornell University Press, Ithaca, 1967
MACKENZIE, LADY G. MUIR and IRBY, A. P., *Travels in the Slavonic Provinces of Turkey-in-Europe*, 2 vols., Daldy, Isbister, London, 1877
MAGNUS, PHILIP, *Gladstone*, E. P. Dutton, New York, 1964
MARRIOTT, J. A. R., *The Eastern Question*, Clarendon Press, Oxford, 1924
MEDLICOTT, W. N., *The Congress of Berlin and After*, Methuen, London, 1938
MILLER, WILLIAM, *The Ottoman Empire, 1801–1913*, Cambridge University Press, Cambridge, 1936
MONYPENNY, W. F. and BUCKLE, G. E., *Life of Benjamin Disraeli*, 6 vols., John Murray, London, 1910–20
MORE, ROBERT JASPER, *Under the Balkans. Notes of a Visit to the District of Philippopolis in 1876*, Henry S. King, London, 1877
MORLEY, JOHN, *Gladstone*, 3 vols., Macmillan, London, 1903

NEWTON, LORD LYONS, 2 vols., Edward Arnold, London, 1913
NOVIKOV, OLGA, *The M.P. for Russia*, 2 vols., Putnam, New York, 1909

OLLIER, EDMUND, *Cassell's Illustrated History of the Russo-Turkish War*, 2 vols., Cassell, London, 1877–9
OVERSTONE, LORD, *Correspondence*, 3 vols., Cambridge University Press, Cambridge, 1971

PAUL, HERBERT, *Life of Froude*, Pitman and Sons, London, 1905
PETROVICH, MICHAEL B., *A History of Modern Serbia 1804–1918*, 2 vols., Harcourt Brace Jovanovich, New York, 1976
PLATT, D. C. M., *The Cinderella Service. British Consuls Since 1825*, Archon Books, Hamden, Connecticut, 1971
PONSONBY, ARTHUR, *Henry Ponsonby*, Macmillan, London, 1943
PURCELL, E. S., *Life and Letters of Ambrose Phillipps de Lisle*, 2 vols., Macmillan, London, 1900
RAMM, AGATHA, (ed.), *The Political Correspondence of Mr. Gladstone and Lord Granville, 1868–76*, 2 vols., Royal Historical Society, London, 1952
—— *The Political Correspondence of Mr. Gladstone and Lord Granville, 1876–1886*, 2 vols., Clarendon Press, Oxford, 1962
—— *Sir Robert Morier*, Clarendon Press, Oxford, 1973

RATH, R. JOHN, (ed.), *The Nationality Problem in the Habsburg Monarchy in the Nineteenth Century*, vol. iii, Austrian History Yearbook, Houston, 1967.

REID. T. WEMYSS, *The Life of the Rt. Hon. William Edward Forster*, 2 vols., Chapman & Hall, London, 1888

RENOUVIN, PIERRE, *Histoire des relations internationales*, vol. 6: *Le XIX Siècle*, Librairie Hachette, Paris, 1955

ROBERTSON SCOTT, J. W., *The Life and Death of a Newspaper*, Methuen, London, 1952

RUPP, G. H., *A Wavering Friendship: Russia and Austria, 1876–78*, Harvard University Press, Cambridge, Mass., 1941


SARKISSIAN, A. O., *History of the Armenian Question to 1885*, University of Illinois Press, Urbana, 1938

SCHUYLER, EUGENE, *Selected Essays*, Scribner, New York, 1901

SELBORNE, EARL OF, *Memorials*, 2 vols., Macmillan, London, 1898

SETON-WATSON, R. W., *Disraeli, Gladstone and the Eastern Question*, Macmillan, London, 1935

SHANNON, R. T., *Gladstone and the Bulgarian Agitation, 1876*, Nelson, London, 1963

SHUKLA, RAM LAKHAN, *Britain, India and the Turkish Empire, 1853–1882*, People's Publishing House, New Delhi, 1973

SMITH, PAUL, (ed.), *Lord Salisbury on Politics*, Cambridge University Press, Cambridge, 1972

STEAD, W. T., *Truth About Russia*, Cassell, London, 1888

STILLMAN, W. J., *Herzegovina and the Late Uprising*, Longman, London, 1877

—— *The Autobiography of a Journalist*, 2 vols., Houghton, Mifflin, Boston, 1901

STOJANOVIC, M. A., *The Great Powers and the Balkans, 1875–1878*, Cambridge University Press, Cambridge, 1939

STRATFORD DE REDCLIFFE, VISCOUNT, *The Eastern Question*, John Murray, London, 1881

SUMNER, B. H., *Russia and the Balkans, 1870–1880*, Oxford University Press, Oxford, 1937

TAFFS, WINIFRED, *Ambassador to Bismarck. Lord Odo Russell*, F. Muller, London, 1938

TAYLOR, A. J. P., *Struggle for the Mastery of Europe, 1848–1918*, Clarendon Press, Oxford, 1954

TEMPERLEY, H. and PENSON, L. M., *Foundations of British Foreign Policy*, Barnes and Noble, New York, 1966

THOMPSON, GEORGE CARSLAKE, *Public Opinion and Lord Beaconsfield, 1875–80*, 2 vols., Macmillan, London, 1886

VILLIERS, FREDERIC, *His Five Decades of Adventure*, 2 vols., Hutchinson, London, 1921
—— *Pictures of Many Wars*, Cassell, London, 1902

WANTAGE, H. S. L., *Lord Wantage. A Memoir*, Smith, Elder, London, 1907
WASHBURN, GEORGE, *Fifty Years in Constantinople and Recollections of Robert College*, Houghton Mifflin, New York, 1909
WATERFIELD, GORDON, *Layard of Nineveh*, Praeger, New York, 1968
WHIBLEY, CHARLES, *Lord John Manners and His Friends*, 2 vols., Blackwood, London, 1925
WIRTHWEIN, WALTER G., *Britain and the Balkan Crisis, 1875–78*, Columbia University Press, New York, 1935

YOUNG, KENNETH, *Arthur James Balfour, 1848–1930*, G. Bell, London, 1963
YRIÄRTE, CHARLES, *Bosnie et Herzégovine—Souvenirs de Voyage pendant l'insurrection*, E. Plon, Paris, 1876

ZETLAND, MARQUIS OF (ed.), *The Letters of Disraeli to Lady Chesterfield and Lady Bradford*, 2 vols., D. Appleton, New York, 1929

III ARTICLES

BAYLEN, JOSEPH O., 'Bishop Strossmayer and Mme. Olga Novikov', *Slavic Review*, xxvi, no 3 (Sept. 1967), 468–73
—— and WALTON, GERALD, 'The Froude-Stead Correspondence, 1877–91', *Huntington Library Quarterly*, 30, no. 2 (Feb. 1967), 167–83
BURKS, R. V., 'Roumania and the Balkan Crisis of 1875–8', *Journal of Central European Affairs*, ii, nos. 2 and 3 (July, Oct. 1942), 119–34, 310–20

DAVISON, RODERIC H., 'Turkish Attitudes Concerning Christian-Muslim Equality in the Nineteenth Century', *American Historical Review*, lix, no. 4 (July 1954), 844–64
DWYER, F. J., 'R. A. Cross and the Eastern Crisis of 1875–78', *Slavonic Review*, 39 (June 1961), 440–58

GAULD, WILLIAM A., 'The "Dreikatserbündnis" and the Eastern Question, 1871–6 and 1877–8', *English Historical Review*, 40, 42 (Apr. 1925; Oct. 1927), 207–21, 560–8

ISEMINGER, GORDON L., 'The Old Turkish Hands: The British Levantine Consuls, 1856–76', *Middle East Journal*, xxii, (summer 1968), 297–316

JELAVICH, BARBARA, 'The British Traveller in the Balkans: The Abuses of Ottoman Administration in the Slavonic Provinces', *Slavonic Review*, xxxiii, (June 1955), 396–413
—— 'Austria-Hungary, Roumania and the Eastern Crisis, 1876–8', *Südost-Forschungen*, 30 (1971), 111–41

LAYARD, A. H. and SMITH, WILLIAM, 'The Eastern Question and the Conference', *Quarterly Review*, cxliii, (Jan. 1877), 276–320
LEE, DWIGHT E., 'A Turkish Mission to Afghanistan, 1877', *Journal of Modern History*, 13, no. 3 (Sept. 1941), 335–56

MACKENZIE, DAVID, 'Panslavism in Practice: Cherniaev in Serbia, 1876', *Journal of Modern History*, 36, no. 3 (Sept. 1964), 279–97
MARDER, ARTHUR J., 'British Naval Policy in 1878', *Journal of Modern History*, 12, no. 3 (Sept. 1940), 367–73
MEDLICOTT, W. N., 'Vice Consul Dupuis "Missing" Dispatch of June 23, 1876', *Journal of Modern History*, iv, no. 1 (Mar. 1932), 33–48
—— 'Bismarck and Beaconsfield', *Studies in Diplomatic History in Honour of G. P. Gooch* (London, 1961), 225–50
—— 'The Near Eastern Crisis of 1875–78 Reconsidered', *Middle Eastern Studies*, 17, no. 1 (Jan. 1971), 105–9

ONOU, ALEXANDRE, 'The Memoirs of Count N. Ignatyev', *Slavonic Review*, 10, 11 (1931–2, July 1932), 386–407, 627–40, 108–25

PENSON, DAME LILLIAN M., 'The Principles and Methods of Lord Salisbury's Foreign Policy', *Cambridge Historical Journal*, 5, no. 1 (1935–7), 87–106

SANDON, VISCOUNT, 'The Cabinet Journal of Dudley Ryder, Viscount Sandon', *Bulletin of the Institute of Historical Research*, no. 10 (Nov. 1974), 58 pp.
SETON-WATSON, R. W., 'Russo-British Relations During the Eastern Crisis,' *Slavonic Review*, vols. 3, 4, 5, 6, 25, 26, 28 (1924/5, 1925/6, 1926/7, 1927/8, Nov. 1946, April 1947, April 1948, November 1949, April 1950), 423–34, 657–83, 177–97, 433–62, 733–59, 413–34, 423–33, 216–41, 538–61, 543–62, 218–28, 504–15
SUMMER, B. H., 'Lord Augustus Loftus and the Eastern Crisis of 1875–8', *Cambridge Historical Journal*, 4, no. 3 (1934), 283–95

TEMPERLEY, HAROLD, 'British Policy Towards Parliamentary Rule and Constitutionalism in Turkey, 1830–1914', *Cambridge Historical Journal*, 4, no. 2 (1933), 156–91
—— 'The Bulgarian and other Atrocities, 1875–8, in the Light of

474    BIBLIOGRAPHY

Historical Criticism', *Proceedings of the British Academy*, xvii (1931), 105–46

YRIÄRTE , CHARLES, 'Une Excursion en Bosnie et dans l'Herzegovine pendant l'insurrection', *Revue des deux mondes*, xlvi, (1 Mar. 1876; 1 May 1876; 1 June 1876), 167–200, 177–99, 596–631

*IV Dissertations*

BELL, KEITH, 'The Constantinople Embassy of Sir Henry Bulwer, 1858–65', Univ. of London Ph.D. dissertation, 1961
BJORK, KENNETH, 'Count G. H. Münster and Anglo-German Relations, 1873–85', Univ. of Wisconsin Ph.D. dissertation, 1935
MARSHALL, PHILIP RAY, 'France and the Congress of Berlin', Univ. of Pennsylvania Ph.D. dissertation, 1969
PRESTON, ADRIAN WILLIAM, 'British Military Policy and the Defence of India: A Study of British Military Policy, Plans and Preparations During the Russian Crisis, 1876–1880', Univ. of London Ph.D. dissertation, 1966

# NOTES

# CHAPTER ONE

[1] Münster to Bismarck, London, 24 Feb. 1875, German Foreign Ministry documents, A1133; Bülow or Bismarck to Münster, Berlin, 24 Jan. 1875, ibid. Unless otherwise noted, the source of these documents, largely diplomatic letters, is microfilm copy of the German Foreign Ministry documents 'captured' by the Western Allies at the end of World War II. Hereafter cited as GFM.

[2] Münster to Bismarck, London, 28 Feb. 1875, ibid., A1259.

[3] Derby to Queen Victoria, 23 May 1874, Derby Papers, Lancashire Record Office. Salisbury was uncertain over the policy to be followed in Afghanistan, but he had already written off Persia, though not publicly, believing there was no way to prevent its absorption by Russia (Salisbury to Derby, 10 Nov. 1874, ibid.). Northbrook, the Viceroy, was of the school of masterly inactivity as opposed to the forward school of Anglo-Indians.

[4] *Encyclopaedia Britannica* (11th edn., N.Y., 1910), viii. 68–9. Blake repeats this story, slightly altered, in R. Blake, *The Conservative Party From Peel to Churchill* (N.Y., 1970), p. 113.

[5] W. D. Jones, *Lord Derby and Victorian Conservatism* (Athens, Georgia, 1956), p. 214.

[6] Morier to Jowett, 1 Mar. 1878 (A. Ramm, *Sir Robert Morier*, Oxford, 1973, pp. 141–2).

[7] Disraeli to Queen Victoria, 21 Mar. 1875 (W. F. Monypenny and G. E. Buckle, *The Life of Benjamin Disraeli*, 6 vols., London, 1910–20, v. 418; hereafter cited as MB).

[8] D. M. Schreuder, *Gladstone and Kruger* (Toronto, 1969), p. 308. The article on Stanley in vol. xviii *of the Dictionary of National Biography* makes no mention of this, indicating only that 'he was at school under Arnold, though not much influenced by him' (p. 948). Schreuder gives no evidence of proof for his assertion. His source may have been Randolph Churchill. The latter wrote that 'in his youth the fifteenth Earl had been expelled from Eton, supposedly for kleptomania' (R. S. Churchill, *Lord Derby. King of Lancashire*, N.Y., 1960, p. 9). Maxwell, the biographer of Clarendon, the well-known Foreign Secretary, after being refused access to the Derby Papers, wrote that he 'learnt some years later . . . that her ladyship [the Countess of Derby] had very good reasons for not giving me a free run among the late Earl's letters' (Sir H. Maxwell, *Evening Memories*, London, 1932, pp. 270–1). Maxwell does not tell us what he learned.

[9] Münster, the English-educated German ambassador, thought that 'mistrust' was 'his [Derby's] overwhelming characteristic' (Münster to Bülow, 29 Mar. 1878, *Die Grosse Politik der europäischen Kabinette, 1871–1914*, 40 vols., Berlin, 1922–7, ii. 249–52; hereafter cited as GP. Same to same, 29 Mar. 1878, E. T. S. Dugdale, *German Diplomatic Documents, 1871–1914*, 4 vols., London, 1928–31, i. 88–90; hereafter cited as GD).

[10] G. C. Thompson, *Public Opinion and Lord Beaconsfield, 1875–80* (2 vols., London, 1886), i. 205–6; hereafter cited as Thompson.

[11] Bessborough to Granville, 24 June 1870, Granville Papers, Public Record office, 30 29/71; hereafter cited as Gran. Pap. and PRO; Hardy to Cairns, 22 Feb. 1870, Cairns Papers, PRO 30 51/7. Bessborough saw two reasons for making the offer to Derby. One was to break up the Conservative majority in the Lords, and 'the [other] ground for it would be—the kudoes he got (more than he deserved) for his conduct of For. Aff' (Bessborough to Granville, 24 June 1870, Gran. Pap., PRO 30 29/71). With the death of his father in 1869, Stanley had become the fifteenth Earl of Derby.

[12] Hardy mentions a political gathering on 23 January at Burghley, the seat of the Marquis of Exeter, at which Cairns, Pakington, Hay, Hunt, Manners, Marlborough, Eustace Cecil (Salisbury's younger brother) Noel, the chief whip, and Hardy were present. Northcote is described as arriving the following day and a further meeting held on 1 February at which no one would volunteer to inform Disraeli (A. E. Gathorne-Hardy (ed.), *Gathorne-Hardy, First Earl Cranbrook, A Memoir, with Extracts from His Diary and Correspondence*, 2 vols., London, 1910, i. 304–6; hereafter cited as Hardy). Lady Knightley mentioned others who attended a gathering, as she did, on 31 January. In this list was Corry, Disraeli's private secretary (Lady L. M. Knightley, *The Journals of Lady Knightley of Fawsley, 1856–84*, ed. Julia Cartwright, London, 1915, pp. 226–7). Corry's presence and the fact, as Blake informs us, that 'the newspapers were full of it' would seem to indicate that Disraeli was aware of the gatherings where discontent with the present leadership was expressed (R. Blake, *Disraeli*, N.Y., 1967, p. 521). Bernstorff, the German ambassador, thought that Derby would only accept the Conservative leadership if pressed to do so by Disraeli; Derby apparently told the ambassador that Disraeli 'should have it [the leadership] again' (Bernstorff to William I, London, 9 Mar. 1872, GFM, A676).

[13] Viscount R. Esher, *Journals and Letters*, ed. M. V. Brett (2 vols., London, 1934), i. 9. Reid, the political journalist, interpreted Derby's manner positively, but this estimate was made before the Eastern crisis began in 1875. 'His mode of speech—the slow, deliberate utterance of carefully-weighed words—he shows that he possesses above all things the judicial mind ...' (T. Wemyss Reid, *Cabinet Portraits. Sketches of Statesmen*, London, 1872, p. 31).

[14] Lady Burghclere (ed.), *A Great Man's Friendship. Letters of the Duke of Wellington to Mary, Marchioness of Salisbury, 1850–52. With a Biographical Sketch of Lady Salisbury* (N.Y., 1927), p. 37. The sketch indicates that Lady Mary had always been interested in the ways of politics.

[15] Lady Derby to Salisbury, 9 and 12 Feb. 1874, Salisbury Papers, Christ Church Library; hereafter cited as Salis. Pap. Salisbury wrote to his wife about his dinner with the Derbys. 'I gathered that they [the Derbys] had not quite given up the idea of his having the first place. As far as I could, I encouraged it—for it would undoubtedly solve many difficulties' (Salisbury to Lady Salisbury, 8 Feb. 1874, Lady G. Cecil, *Life of Robert Marquis of Salisbury*, 4 vols., London, 1921–32, ii. 43–4; hereafter cited as Cecil). In July 1878 O. T. Burne, army officer and India administrator, wrote of Derby, whom he did not like, to Lytton. 'There is a report today that at the time of the Bulgarian atrocities he [Derby] was at Manchester and raped a little factory girl of 15, to hush up which he has to make the mayor a knight' (O. T. Burne to Lytton, 19 July 1878, Lytton Papers, India Office Library, E218/517/6).

[16] Salisbury to Lady Derby, 15 Oct. 1874, Salis. Pap., vol. 16.

[17] Münster to Bismarck, London, 8 May 1874, GFM, A1746; Gavard to [?], 25 Feb. 1874 (Charles Gavard, *A Diplomat in London*, N.Y., 1897, p. 182).

[18] David Harris, *A Diplomatic History of the Balkan Crisis of 1875–78. The First Year* (Stanford, 1936), p. 22; hereafter cited as Harris. Derby was capable of initiative when he saw it as necessary to avoid great danger. Such was true between September and November of 1876 when he believed Russia would attack the Turks if the latter did not make peace with the Serbs and make reforms. He then led Europe both in an attempt to end the Turco-Serbian war and to arrange for the Constantinople Conference.

[19] Dilke diary, [?] July 1876, Dilke Papers, British Library, Add. MS. 43903, xxx. Hammond, the retired Permanent Under-Secretary, who knew Derby well, wrote in 1877 'but I cannot say I place the least reliance on Lord Derby taking any decided course until its utility has passed away' (Hammond to Layard, 25 July 1877, Layard Papers, British Library, Add. MS. 38955, xxv; hereafter cited as Lay. Pap.).

[20] M. E. Grant Duff, 'The Situation', *Nineteenth Century*, iii. (Jan.–June 1878), 571–90. Salisbury tended to agree with Grant Duff's analysis that the Government's foreign

policy 'lacked a bold initiative and a settled plan. So many different people have pulled unnecessarily at the strings. . . . But the worst of our policy has been that it has not been a consistent whole on either side [support for or coercion of Turkey]. A bit of each train of thought has been imbedded in it surrounded by a thick mass of general inertia' (Salisbury to Lytton, 15 June 1877, Salis. Pap., C4, letter-book).

[21] Hardy diary, 22 Jan. 1878, Cranbrook Papers, East Suffolk Record Office, HA43/7501/297; hereafter cited as Cran. Pap. Carnarvon to Northcote, 30 Mar. 1877, Northcote Papers, British Library, Add. MS. 50022, x; hereafter cited as Northc. Pap. Granville wrote of his apprehensions to Gladstone. 'I am always trustful of Derby's good sense, but I do not feel so confident as to his resistance to any sudden pressure, which appears to represent public opinion—& there may be at any time a reaction in his cabinet against his cautious policy' (Granville to Gladstone, 5 Nov. 1875, A. Ramm (ed.), *The Political Correspondence of Mr. Gladstone and Lord Granville, 1876–86*, 2 vols., Oxford, 1962, ii. 471–2; hereafter cited as Ramm).

[22] 'You [Layard] have had Parliamentary passage of arms with Lord S[alisbury]. Recollect that he is not a forgiving man, and that when he chooses to do a thing he will not care for anything or anybody' (Cowley to Layard, 29 May 1878, Lay. Pap., Add. MS. 39020, XC).

[23] Hammond to Layard, 23 Feb. 1878, Lay. Pap., Add. MS. 38956, XXVI; Argyll to Gladstone, 28 Jan. 1878, Gladstone Papers, British Library, Add. MS. 44104, XIX (hereafter cited as Glad. Pap); Balfour memorandum, 1880 (K. Young, *Arthur James Balfour, 1843–1930*, London, 1963, p. 44). Rupp refers to 'Lord Derby, the sybarite' and Blake mentions Derby's 'drinking heavily' (Blake, *Disraeli*, p. 638; G. H. Rupp, *A Wavering Friendship: Russia and Austria, 1876–78*, Cambridge, Man., 1941, p. 372; hereafter cited as Rupp). Neither offers any evidence for his description.

[24] Malet to mother, 3 Apr. 1878, Malet Papers, London, bundle A; Shuvalov to Gorchakov, 12 Mar. 1878 (R. W. Seton-Watson, 'Russo-British Relations during the Eastern Crisis', *Slavonic Review*, xxvi. (Apr. 1948), 554; hereafter cited as Seton-Watson, *Slav. Rev.*).

[25] In February 1878 he wrote the following. 'The most justifiable and inevitable war is at best a stupid and wasteful business; yet the folly of foreign states, and the ease with which the popular mind here is stirred by newspapers, may force it upon us' (Derby to Grote, 12 Feb. 1878, Grote Papers, British Library, Add. MS. 46691).

[26] Derby's resignation was announced on 28 March. Only two months were to elapse before he would offer his services to the Liberals. On 2 June he told Granville that the report in the *Globe* of the Salisbury–Shuvalov agreement was correct, and that he would be available to come up to Parliament should the Liberals decide to raise a debate on the Government's foreign policy. On 5 June he advised Granville on the line to take in attacking the Government. 'The point to make will . . . be the disproportion of means to ends—eight millions spent, great armaments prepared, Indian soldiers brought to Europe, and all to obtain what we could have got for *nothing*, if we had been prepared from the first to be content with the result actually secured' (Derby to Granville, Knowsley, 2 and 5 June 1878, Gran. Pap., PRO 30 29/26a). He would only formally announce his resignation from the Conservative Party in March 1880.

[27] Derby to Grote, 19 Apr. 1878, Grote Pap., Add. MS. 46691.

# CHAPTER TWO

[1] On the nature and causes of the revolt see D. Harris, *A Diplomatic History of the Balkan Crisis*, the most detailed and best study. M. A. Stojanovic, *The Great Powers and the Balkans, 1875–78* (Cambridge, 1939); B. H. Sumner, *Russia and the Balkans, 1870–1880* (Oxford,

1937); Rupp, *A Wavering Friendship*; David MacKenzie, *The Serbs and Russian Pan-Slavism, 1875–78* (Ithaca, 1967). The books by Stojanovic, Sumner, and MacKenzie will be cited hereafter as Stojanovic, Sumner, and MacKenzie.

² Harris says 'One hundred and fifty or more', which he takes from the first Austrian red book (Harris, p. 1). Holmes, the British consul in Sarajevo, gave the number 164 (Holmes to Derby, 2 July 1875, PRO FO 146/1797, no. 4). Bridge writes that 'by June there were 4,000 rebels under arms in Herzegovina', but gives no source for this (F. R. Bridge, *From Sadowa to Sarajevo*, London, 1972, p. 70). In a recent history of Serbia Petrovich indicates that the rising in Hercegovina occurred when Ottoman authorities used force to gather excessive taxation (M. B. Petrovich, *A History of Modern Serbia 1804–1918*, 2 vols., New York, 1976, ii. 381). Djordjević writes that the revolt began on 9 July 1875 and that ten to twelve thousand participated in it (D. Djordjević, *Révolutions nationales des peuples balkaniques 1804–1914*, Belgrade, 1965, p. 129; hereafter cited as Djordjević).

³ Iseminger refers to Holmes as a 'notorious Turcophile' and the information generally from British Levantine consuls as 'scanty, misleading . . . [and] false' (Gordon L. Iseminger, 'The Old Turkish Hands: The British Levantine Consuls, 1875–76', *Middle East Journal*, xxii, summer 1968, 311–12). Sumner says that Taylor, the British consul at Ragusa (Dubrovnik), had been there only a few months when revolt began and was not well informed (Sumner, pp. 580–2). Holmes maintained that the best information on the rebellion was to be gained not at Mostar, but where he was in Sarajevo, especially as he was on friendly terms with the Turkish Governor-General there (Holmes to Derby, 6 Aug. 1875, PRO FO 146/1799, no. 10). In February of 1876, while in Constantinople, Holmes at the request of Elliot drew up a lengthy memorandum on the causes of the insurrection. It is probable that his report was influenced by both the views of Elliot and the events of the insurrection itself which was almost of nine months duration when the consul composed his memorandum. Holmes wrote that 'there can be no doubt that the insurrection was first brought about, and afterwards supported by foreign influence'. The consul refers to those in Nevesinje, who left for Montenegro, as living in 'the richest and most prosperous district of the Hercegovina, and which might naturally have been considered the least likely to revolt' (Holmes Memorandum, 29 Feb. 1876, PRO FO 425/40, no. 423). I think Iseminger is wrong about Holmes. He did not hate Turks, but was reasonably objective about conditions in Bosnia-Hercegovina, and his prescription for that area was precisely the one which the Porte refused to consider at the Constantinople Conference in December 1876—a competent, provincial Governor, chosen with the consent of the European Powers and whose tenure of office should be guaranteed for six years (Holmes to Derby, Sarajevo, 30 June 1876, PRO FO 424/42, no. 115).

⁴ William James Stillman, *Herzegovina and the Late Uprising: The Causes of the Latter and the Remedies* (London, 1877); id., *The Autobiography of a Journalist* (2 vols., Boston, 1901).

⁵ Arthur John Evans, *Through Bosnia and the Herzegovina on Foot During the Insurrection, August and September 1875* (London, 1877); id., *Illyrian Letters* (London, 1878); Charles Yriärte, *Bosnie et Herzegovine—Souvenirs de voyage pendant l'insurrection* (Paris, 1876); id., 'Une Excursion en Bosnie et l'Herzegovine pendant l'insurrection,' *Revue des deux mondes*, xlvi. (1 Mar. 1876, 1 May 1876, 1 June 1876), 167–200, 177–99, 596–631; Sumner and Stojanovic tend to agree, as do J. A. R. Marriott (*The Eastern Question*, Oxford, 1924) and M. S. Anderson (*The Eastern Question, 1774–1923*, London, 1966). Ffrench, a British minister in Vienna, wrote 'that the so-called rising in the Hercegovina was nothing more than one of the agrarian outbreaks which generally take place whenever the Agas present themselves among the Christian population to levy taxation . . .' (Ffrench to Derby, 15 July 1875, PRO FO 7/851, no. 236). Monson, the British consul, reported that his Italian counterpart, Durando 'has invariably maintained that the agrarian grievance lay at the root of the question; that it had been, far more than the religious disabilities, the cause of discontent' (Monson to Derby,

Ragusa, 11 Apr. 1876, PRO FO 424/40, no. 609). This was confirmed by Major Gonne, the British military attaché at Vienna (Gonne to Buchanan, Ragusa, 30 Apr. 1876, ibid., no. 792).

⁶ On Ottoman tax farming see Barbara Jelavich, 'The British Traveller in the Balkans: The Abuses of Ottoman Administration in the Slavonic Provinces', *Slavonic Review*, xxxiii. (June 1955), 396–413.

⁷ R. W. Seton-Watson, *Disraeli, Gladstone and the Eastern Question* (London, 1935); E. von Wertheimer, *Graf Julius Andrassy* (3 vols., Stuttgart, 1910); Pierre Renouvin, *Histoire des relations internationales*, vol. 6: *Le XIXᵉ Siècle*, pt. ii, *1871–1914. L'Apogée de l'Europe* (Paris, 1955); W. L. Langer, *European Alliances and Alignments, 1871–90* (New York, 1950). All of the above will be cited hereafter as Seton-Watson, Wertheimer, Renouvin, and Langer.

⁸ Renouvin does as well (Renouvin, p. 65).

⁹ Langer, pp. 64–71. Monson, the British diplomat, reported in September of 1876 that both Austrian and Russian Balkan officials encouraged and aided the insurrection. 'The Russian Consul-General [Yonin] kept open house for all those of his compatriots who frequented the insurgent camps, and who fought in the rebel ranks; that the Consulate has been the Treasury into which the Russian subscriptions have poured; that the money so received, nominally for the relief of the refugees, has been largely expended, according to admissions made to me by M. de Wessilitzky and the Secretary of the Consulate in the purchase of provisions and munitions of war for the insurgents' (Monson to Derby, Ragusa, 20 Sept. 1876, PRO FO 424/43, no. 925).

¹⁰ The last previous major outbreak had occurred in 1861–2, and before that in 1858, both in Montenegro and Bosnia-Hercegovina. In August of 1876 Maynard, the American minister in Constantinople, reported on the origins of the insurrection. 'How far the insurrection was occasioned by a sense of intolerable oppression and how far by a spirit of lawlessness and impatience of all governmental authority, it is not quite clear. I am inclined to think that it was set on foot by a few restless and daring spirits, who soon rallied an over-burdened and discontented population' (Maynard to Fish, Constantinople, 10 Aug. 1876, United States State Department, Washington, vol. 29, no. 89).

¹¹ Harold Temperley, 'The Bulgarian and other Atrocities, 1875–8, in the Light of Historical Criticism', *Proceedings of the British Academy*, xvii. (London, 1931), 105–46; Roderic H. Davison, *Reform in the Ottoman Empire, 1856–76* (Princeton, 1963); hereafter cited as Davison. Elliot, the British ambassador at Constantinople, agrees that rebel grievances were just a pretext for the national Slav movement (Elliot to Derby, 3 Sept. 1875, PRO FO 146/1800, no. 512).

¹² Jelavich, *Slavonic Review*, xxxiii. 401. Lord Lyons, a former British ambassador at Constantinople and both a sane and perceptive observer, felt that the Turkish administration would never be good and, 'were it ever so good, it would not reconcile the Christian subject populations to the Turkish yoke' (Lyons to Derby, 24 Aug. 1875, Lyons Papers, West Sussex Record Office).

¹³ R. H. Davison, 'Turkish Attitudes Concerning Christian–Muslim Equality in the Nineteenth Century', *American Historical Review*, lix, no. 4 (July 1954), 845.

¹⁴ Elliot to John Russell, Therapia, 11 Sept. 1875, PRO FO 30, 22/17a.

¹⁵ Harris, p. 1.

¹⁶ Jelavich, *Slavonic Review*, xxxiii. 401; A. J. P. Taylor, *Struggle for the Mastery of Europe, 1848–1918* (Oxford, 1954), pp. 232–3 (hereafter cited as Taylor); Harris, pp. 14–17. Davison describes the Christians as being looked down upon 'as second-class citizens both by the Muslim public and by the government' (Davison, *American Historical Review* lix. 845).

¹⁷ In lieu of military service the Christians paid a tax which according to Elliot was regarded by them as more of an advantage than a humiliating disqualification (Elliot to Granville, 19 July 1873, PRO FO 78/2269, no. 252). But in Bosnia-Hercegovina

nearly all tax farmers were Muslim.

[18] See Sumner, pp. 580–2; Rupp, pp. 3–10. Mackenzie contends that while foreign agents operated in Hercegovina 'there is no evidence that the insurrection was organized or directed by an outside power. On the contrary, it appears that revolts were spontaneous protests by the Christian merchants and peasants against heavy taxation and oppressive rule ...' (Mackenzie, p. 31). The bulk of Balkan and Danubian trade with foreign lands was largely with Austria and Britain. In 1873 only 25 Russian vessels of 6,800 tons cleared the Danube compared with 85 Austrian ships of 40,000 tons and British steamers with 193,000 tons (Derby to Elliot, 20 Nov. 1874, PRO FO 146/1737, no. 222). Russia had therefore many more consuls than her trade required and, like British Levantine consuls, much of their work was political. Taylor, the British consul in Ragusa, wrote that the cousin of Nicholas of Montenegro, who was President of the Montenegrin Senate, had arrived a few days ago with Yonin, the Russian consul, and remained 'some days' in the latter's house (Taylor to Derby, 26 Feb. 1875, PRO FO 146/1790, no. 1).

[19] See Rupp. pp. 77–9. He calls Dalmatia the 'provision chamber' of and safe haven for the rebels.

[20] Renouvin mentions this, peasant seignurial grievances, and a bad harvest in 1875 (Renouvin, 64).

[21] Statistics here are unreliable but most estimates for Bosnia-Hercegovina number about 500,000 Orthodox inhabitants, 450,000 Muslim, and 200,000 Roman Catholics. Serbia and Montenegro were largely Orthodox but Croatia was Catholic and Dalmatia, like Bosnia-Hercegovina itself, was a mixture. Holmes, who had been in Bosnia for over sixteen years, thought there was little desire in Bosnia for close association with Serbia. 'The fact is that no contiguous countries could possibly be more completely estranged, and have fewer relations with, or more ignorance of each other than Bosnia and Serbia. There is no commerce, and no inter-marrying, and scarcely any intercourse at all between the two countries. Little or no sympathy ever existed between them; and the Orthodox Christians of Bosnia, though in general disliking the Turks, have little desire to be annexed to Serbia, and would prefer infinitely their present state, if a happier condition and better government could be assured them. In no case have the Christian inhabitants of Bosnia risen in arms against the Turks unless they have been absolutely forced to do so, and even now, when Serbia has declared war with Turkey, there is not the slightest response to her invitations to revolt and accept her government, except from those who have been made to take up arms, and lost all their property, and who dread to return to their allegiance, even if they were able, from fear of vengence of the Turks. ... Roman Catholics ... hate the Serbs, and side entirely with the Turks ... [are] absolutely hostile to any annexation to Serbia' (Holmes to Derby, Sarajevo, 25 July 1876, PRO FO 424/43, no. 64).

[22] Holmes, who derived part of his information from Devrish Pasha, the Turkish Governor at Bosna Serai (Sarajevo), wrote that detached bands of insurgents were trying to force others to join them by burning houses (Holmes to Derby, 9 July 1875, PRO FO 146/1797, no. 5).

[23] As late as 16 August Elliot reported that the Porte had sent from Constantinople only 2,000 men to quell the rising (Elliot to Derby, teleg., 17 Aug. 1875, PRO FO 146/1799). In February 1876 Decazes, the French Foreign Minister, said that on good authority there were less than 6,000 rebels, divided into two groups and antagonistic to one another (Lyons to Derby, 14 Feb. 1876, PRO FO 424/40, No. 262). Towards the end of April 1876 a Vienna newspaper estimate put the insurgent number in Hercegovina at 4,500 and the Turkish force at 23,000 (Buchanan to Derby, 21 Apr. 1876, ibid., no. 647). Holmes, the British consul, wrote at the beginning of March that the number of insurrectionists then was what it had always been—between five and six thousand (Holmes to Elliot, 5 Mar. 1876, PRO FO 424/41, no. 20). In September of 1876 Monson was to report as follows. 'As for the insurrection itself, during the whole

of the winter [of 1875–6] it was perfectly fictitious, was sustained by artificial means, and might have been suppressed by the simple withdrawal of those means' (Monson to Derby, Ragusa, 20 Sept. 1876, PRO FO 424/43, no. 925).

²⁴ For Catholic Croatian and Orthodox Serbian bitterness see Sumner, pp. 127–9; also chapters by Jelavich, Vucinich, and Djordevic in the *Austrian History Yearbook. The Nationality Problem in the Habsburg Monarchy in the Nineteenth Century* (Houston, 1967), iii. 24–5, 70, 83–104.

²⁵ Holmes to Elliot, 28 Sept. 1875, PRO FO 146/1802, no. 7.

²⁶ Stillman, *Herzegovina and the Late Uprising*, pp. 506–7. Lord Morley on a trip to the scene of the insurrection emphasized the importance of Austrian Dalmatia to the rebellion (Lord Morley's memorandum, 18 Nov. 1875, PRO FO 146/1803; minute by T. V. Lister, 19 Nov. 1875, ibid.).

²⁷ Mackenzie, who feels the rising in Hercegovina in July was a 'spontaneous protest' against 'heavy taxation and oppressive rule', refers to the revolt in Bosnia as the work of Bosnian *émigrés* in Serbia in close touch with the Serbian Government (Mackenzie, pp. 31, 43–8).

²⁸ Holmes to Derby, 6 Aug. 1875, PRO FO 146/1799, no. 22.

²⁹ Derby to Ffrench, 12 Aug. 1875, PRO FO 146/1798, no. 183.

³⁰ Derby to Elliot, ibid., no. 235; White to Derby, 18 Aug. 1875, PRO FO 146/1799, no. 30. The Foreign Secretary was to write to Carnarvon three weeks later. 'News from Turkey confused, indecisive, and probably inaccurate. The insurgents are better hands at burning villages, and murdering unarmed people than at fighting: the Turks have by their laziness and apathy allowed the disturbance to become serious, when in the first instance it might have been crushed with ease' (Derby to Carnarvon, 13 Sept. 1875, A. Hardinge, *Fourth Earl of Carnarvon*, 3 vols., London, 1925, ii. 326; hereafter cited as Hardinge).

³¹ Bylandt, the experienced Dutch ambassador in London, wrote home that Derby remains in the country away from London 'so that he does not have to speak about the subject with the few diplomats that remain in London' (Bylandt to Willebois, 17 Aug. 1875, Ministerie Van Buitenlandse Zaken (Netherlands Foreign Ministry Archives), The Hague, no. 262; hereafter cited as NA).

³² Milan had gone there out of financial difficulties and to arrange his marriage to a wealthy Romanian. While in Vienna, Andrássy and Novikov, the Russian ambassador, urged him to remain neutral (Mackenzie, p. 32).

³³ Elliot to Derby, teleg., 17 Aug. 1875, PRO FO 146/1799.

³⁴ Stillman, *Herzegovina and the Late Uprising*, pp. 14–15.

³⁵ Derby to Disraeli, 22 Aug. 1875, Derby Pap.

³⁶ Elliot to Derby, teleg., 20 Aug. 1875, in Derby to Lyons, teleg., 21 Aug. 1875, PRO FO 146/1799; Tenterden memorandum, 21 Aug. 1875, PRO FO 78/2385 (Harris, p. 88); Derby to Disraeli, 22 Aug. 1875, Derby Pap.

³⁷ Derby to Elliot, 24 Aug. 1875, PRO FO 146/1799, no. 258.

³⁸ Elliot to Homes, 24 Aug. 1875, PRO FO 146/1800.

³⁹ A. Gallenga, *Two Years of the Eastern Question* (2 vols., London, 1877), i. 108.

⁴⁰ David Harris, *Britain and the Bulgarian Horrors of 1876* (Chicago, 1939), pp. 26–7; hereafter cited as *Horrors*. Radowitz, while German minister at Constantinople, also felt Elliot was too Turcophile because the latter favoured Ottoman equality with other European Powers (Radowitz to Bismarck, 3 Feb. 1872, GFM, A396). There is other support for Harris' contention that Elliot's excessively Turkish attachment blinded him to Ottoman shortcomings; for this see A. W. Ward and G. P. Gooch, *The Cambridge History of British Foreign Policy, 1783–1919* (3 vols., New York, 1923), iii. 93–5.

⁴¹ Elliot to Granville, 18 Mar. 1871, PRO FO 78/2174, no. 120; same to same, 8 May 1871, ibid. 2175, no. 201; same to same, 11 Sept. 1871, ibid. 78/2177, no. 329; same to same, 21 Sept. 1871, ibid., no. 339; same to same, 6 Feb. 1873, ibid. 498, no. 36; same to same, 10 Oct. 1873, ibid. 120/500, no. 361; Elliot to Derby, 18 Oct. 1874, ibid.

78/2332, no. 244.

[42] Elliot to Granville, 19 July 1872, PRO FO 120/493, no. 97; same to same, 3 Mar. 1873, ibid. 498, no. 66; same to same, 7 Aug. 1873, ibid. 146/1657, no. 276; same to same, 12 Oct. 1873, ibid. 120/500, no. 363; same to same, 8 Dec. 1873, ibid. 507, no. 450; Elliot to Derby, 22 May 1874, ibid. 244/277, no. 19; same to same, 13 Oct. 1874, ibid. 146/1736, no. 288; same to same, 26 June 1874, ibid. 78/2331, no. 58; same to same, 11 Dec. 1874, ibid. 2333, no. 343.

[43] Elliot to Derby, 12 Aug. 1874, PRO FO 146/1732, no. 120; same to same, 23 Jan. 1875, ibid. 1788, no. 40.

[44] Elliot to Derby, 12 June 1874, PRO FO 78/2331, no. 37.

[45] Elliot to Holmes, 25 Aug. 1875, PRO FO 146/1800.

[46] Andrássy also favoured non-intervention, but unlike Gorchakov, who wished to associate Italy, France, and Britain with the three Northern Powers, Andrássy wished his non-intervention to be exercised by Austria, Russia, and Germany alone.

[47] Loftus, British ambassador in St. Petersburg, reported the Tsar's annoyance with a Foreign Minister '8 months in the year out of the country' (Loftus to Derby, 27 Oct. 1875, Derby Pap.).

[48] Elliot to Derby, 25 Aug. 1875, PRO FO 146/1800, no. 474; same to same, ibid., no. 476. After official British consent to the consular mission had been given, Elliot learned from the Grand Vizier that Turkey had only consented to accept the proposal because she had been told that Britain had concurred in it. The belief that the proposal had come from all the Powers may have been insinuated to the Sultan by Ignatiev and may have caused the former to agree to the consular mission and request Britain's support of it. See MacDonell to Derby, Berlin, 9 Sept. 1875, PRO FO 64/829, no. 382.

[49] Elliot to Derby, 3 Sept. 1875, PRO FO 146/1800, no. 511; same to same, 4 Sept. 1875, ibid., no. 515.

[50] Stojanovic maintains that it was the concentration of Turkish and Serbian troops on their common frontier and the danger of a war between them that induced the Great Powers to intervene through their consuls (Stojanovic, pp. 21-3).

[51] Elliot to Derby, 7 Sept. 1875, PRO FO 146/1801, no. 526.

[52] Holmes to Elliot, 10 Sept. 1875, ibid. 1802, no. 58.

[53] Sumner describes the insurgents as a 'half-terrified, half-exultant' group in no condition or position to treat with the Turks (Sumner, pp. 143-4).

[54] Holmes to Derby, 24 Sept. 1875, PRO FO 146/1802, no. 6.

[55] Holmes reported that six insurgents were killed and many were wounded (Elliot to Derby, 28 Sept. 1875, ibid., no. 607).

[56] Novikov, the Russian ambassador at Vienna, in the absence of Gorchakov in Switzerland and Ignatiev at Bad Ems, both taking the waters, suggested a vague consular mediation.

[57] Sumner, pp. 143-5; Stojanovic, pp. 23-5; Harris, pp. 66-7, 72-80, 88-98.

[58] Jomini to Tsar, 13 Sept. 1875, Jomini-Onou Papers, British Library, Eg. MS. 3184, 69-70; Harris, pp. 88-98, 132-9. The Jomini-Onou Papers in the British Library Manuscripts Collection do not seem to have been used, or if used, not cited by previous students. They are indexed under Egerton MSS. 3166-243 and Add. MSS. 45526-33. They include copies of dispatches, private letters, and memorandums for long periods of the nineteenth century in French, Russian, and Turkish.

[59] Elliot to Ignatiev, 25 Sept. 1875, PRO FO 146/1802, no. 597; Elliot to Derby, 26 Sept. 1875, ibid., no. 596. The Turks, of course, refused as well when the proposal was put to them for a conference between themselves and the consuls in Ragusa. Andrássy would only agree to Ignatiev's proposals if modified to allow initiative to come from Vienna and not Constantinople (Harris, pp. 140-54).

[60] Elliot to Derby, 21 Sept. 1875, PRO FO 146/1801, no. 577. Even before this Elliot advised the Porte to redress any grievances in peaceful Balkan areas as a preventive measure (same to same, 31 Aug. 1875, ibid. 1800, no. 506). Elliot was undoubtedly in-

fluenced in suggesting Christian participation in local affairs by the report of Holmes after the latter had met some of the insurgents. As part of the consular mission, Holmes wrote that the insurgents did not desire to be annexed to either Montenegro, Serbia, or Austria but wished only relief from Turkish landowners, local police, and local tax collectors (Holmes to Elliot, Mostar, 28 Sept. 1875, ibid. 1802, no. 7).

[61] Derby to Adams, 18 Sept. 1875, PRO FO 146/1800, no. 590.

[62] Elliot to Derby, 28 Sept. 1875, ibid. 1802, no. 608.

[63] Elliot to Derby, 29 Sept. 1875, ibid., no. 612, and enclosure from Dupuis.

[64] Stillman, *Herzegovina and the Late Uprising*, ii. 527–30.

[65] Elliot to Lord John Russell, 11 Sept. 1875, PRO FO 30 22/17a.

[66] The Serbian minister was disliked and maligned by many inside as well as outside Serbia.

[67] Novikov to Jomini, 27 Sept. 1875, Jomini–Onou Pap.

[68] Elliot to Derby, 30 Sept. 1875, PRO FO 146/1802, no. 614.

[69] Same to same, 2 Oct. 1875, ibid., no. 621.


# CHAPTER THREE


[1] Elliot to Derby, 30 Sept. 1875, Derby Pap.

[2] E. Ollier, *Cassell's Illustrated History of the Russo-Turkish War* (2 vols., London, 1877–9), i. 4–5. For the Turkish repudiation and repercussions see W. G. Wirthwein, *Britain and the Balkan Crisis, 1875–78* (N.Y., 1935), pp. 25–6 (hereafter cited as Wirthwein); D. C. Blaisdell, *European Financial Control in the Ottoman Empire* (N.Y., 1966), pp. 80–5. Münster, the German ambassador, wrote that the 'default has created a tremendous sensation in commercial circles here, and it will strike a severe blow at the traditional English policy with respect to Turkey' (Münster to William I, 12 Oct. 1875, GFM, England 64, VI, K. Bjork, 'Count G. H. Münster and Anglo-German Relations, 1873–85,' Univ. of Wisconsin dissertation, 1935, p. 79.

[3] Gladstone to Thomas Gladstone, 19 Nov. 1875, Glad. Pap., St. Deiniol's Library, Hawarden. The Queen's secretary thought that 'the desire of maintaining the Turkish Empire is changing, and here in England it is curious to observe how rapidly people are adopting new views about Turkey' (Ponsonby to Queen Victoria, 18 Nov. 1875, Royal Archives, Windsor, H6/164; hereafter cited as RA).

[4] Lyons to Derby, 15 Oct. 1875, PRO FO 27/2115, no. 849; same to same, 19 Oct. 1875, ibid., no. 855.

[5] The German ambassador reported that Britain recognized any entente with France as 'artificial' and that London saw Anglo-French interests in the East as opposed, especially in Egypt (Münster to Bismark, 29 Oct. 1875, GFM, A5100).

[6] Thompson, ii. 227–8. See also Stuers to Willebois, 9 Oct. 1875, NA 303; Brincken to Bülow, 8 Oct. 1875, GFM, A4762.

[7] Shuvalov to Jomini, 14 Oct. 1875 (Seton-Watson, *Slav. Rev.* iii. [1924–5], 427–30).

[8] The Secretary of State for India talked of retribution. 'I am afraid the want of courage shown a quarter of a century ago in refusing to face the fact of Turkish decrepitude is coming back to us now with a heavy punishment' (Salisbury to L. Mallet, 17 Nov. 1875, Salis. Pap., vol. 7).

[9] Münster to Bismarck, 29 Oct. 1875, GFM, A5100. Münster felt Derby and his colleagues were undecided on any action now that the policy of maintaining Turkey no longer had unanimous public support.

[10] Disraeli to Lady Bradford, 4 Nov. 1875 (Marquis of Zetland (ed.), *The Letters of*

*Disraeli to Lady Chesterfield and Lady Bradford*, 2 vols., NY., 1929, i. 393; hereafter cited as Zetland; Disraeli to Queen Victoria, 6 Nov. 1875, MB vi. 16.

[11] Thompson, i. 227–8.

[12] Wirthwein, pp. 28–9.

[13] Elliot to Derby, 12 Nov. 1875, Derby Pap.; Loftus to Derby, 10 Nov. 1875, PRO FO 65/912, no. 340.

[14] Shuvalov to Jomini, 13 Nov. 1875 (Seton-Watson, *Slav. Rev.* iii. 432–3). It should be added that Elliot's reports from Constantinople emphasized Ignatiev's and Russia's desire both to contain and end the insurrection.

[15] Both consuls Holmes at Mostar and Freeman at Sarajevo agreed as to the impossibility of obtaining correct information as to what was passing in Bosnia-Hercegovina (Holmes to Elliot, 21 Oct. 1875, PRO FO 146/1803, no. 144; Freeman to Derby, 22 Oct. 1875, ibid., no. 20). See also same to same, 9 Oct. 1875, ibid. 1802, no. 19. Holmes indicated that Turkish reports were even more untrustworthy than those the rebels issued (Holmes to Derby, 1 Nov. 1875, ibid. 1803, no. 15).

[16] The next few pages are based on Sumner, pp. 145–50; Harris, pp. 66–71, 132–9, 140–54; Jomini–Onou Pap.; and Mackenzie, pp. 68–70.

[17] He also instructed Onou, his dragoman and assistant in Constantinople, to work upon Jomini, a counsellor in the Russian Foreign Ministry, whom Gorchakov had left in control while he was in Switzerland (Onu to Jomini, 3 Nov. 1875, Jomini–Onou Pap., Eg. 3225; same to same, 13 Nov. 1875, ibid.). Novikov was also influencing Jomini, but to follow Andrássy's lead (Novikov to Jomini, 27 Sept. 1875, ibid., Eg. 3174; same to same, 15 Oct. 1875, ibid.). According to Buchanan, Novikov's Secretary of Embassy at Vienna arrived at Livadia simultaneously with Ignatiev to support Andrássy's proposals with the Tsar (Buchanan to Derby, 17 Nov. 1875, PRO FO 146/1804, no. 386).

[18] Harris and Sumner agree that Ignatiev thought it the wrong time to reopen the Eastern Question, but they do not explain why.

[19] Novikov to Jomini, 27 Sept. 1875, Jomini–Onou Pap., Eg. 3174.

[20] In a secret meeting with the Grand Vizier, the latter told the Russian ambassador that he was prepared to follow his advice. Later Ignatiev saw the Sultan, Abdul Azziz, who said that it was necessary to be careful about reforms for Christians so that it did not alienate his Muslim subjects. Ignatiev suggested to the Sultan the need for administrative decentralization within the Ottoman Empire in place of the French system of centralized control, and the use of Christians as administrators, police, and tax collectors. When the Sultan replied that his Slavic subjects really desired independence, Ignatiev said that only a small number, who were influenced by the revolutionary ideas of Napoleon III, were so disposed, that the masses wished to live in peace within the Empire but under better conditions. Ignatiev advised the Sultan to keep Mahmoud Pasha as Grand Vizier and to withdraw Turkish troops from the Serbian frontier. For the Tsar's benefit, the Russian ambassador wrote that the Sultan would never accept the intervention of the Great Powers and that after Ignatiev's audience Abdul Azziz instructed Mahmoud Pasha to prepare a programme of reforms which would satisfy Russian requirements. Then upon agreement with the Grand Vizier Ignatiev told Werther and Zichy that the Sultan had told him about a programme of reforms which the Porte would soon announce (Ignatiev to Alexander II, 4 Nov. 1875, Jomini–Onou Pap., Eg. 3186).

[21] My view tallies here with that of Mackenzie, pp. 68–70. As Mackenzie implies, it was to be a Russian salad eaten on Dreikaiserbund China.

[22] Elliot to Derby, 24 Nov. 1875, PRO FO 146/1804, no. 781. Earlier Elliot had written that 'Austria is at a disadvantage at Constantinople by being practically without a representative of her own policy, her Ambassador [Zichy] being so greatly under the guidance and direction of the Ambassador of Russia' (same to same, 14 Nov. 1875, ibid., no. 755). Ignatiev was not above lying to Elliot about Andrássy (Elliot to Derby,

teleg., 8 Oct. 1875, ibid. 1802). Half-truths, distortions, and misrepresentations were also part of Ignatiev's diplomatic technique (same to same, teleg. 6 Nov. 1875, ibid. 1803). See also same to same, 28 Oct. 1875, ibid., no. 714.

[23] Same to same, 15 Oct. 1875, ibid. 1802, no. 666. Elliot might have added, while using the Austrian ambassador in Constantinople to oppose the policy of his own Foreign Minister who was hand in glove with the Russian ambassador in Vienna to counteract Ignatiev.

[24] Elliot to Derby, teleg., 15 Oct. 1875, ibid. Holmes considered Server Pasha devoid of courage, energy, and competence (Holmes to Derby, 22 Nov. 1875, ibid. 1805, no. 18).

[25] Holmes to Derby, 22 Oct. 1875, ibid. 1803, no. 13.

[26] Elliot to Derby, 5 Oct. 1875, PRO FO 146/1802, no. 635; same to same, teleg., 6 Oct. 1875, ibid. Buchanan, the British ambassador at Vienna, reported that the Austrian Government believed 'that Prince Milan, in appealing personally to the Skupstchina [Serbian legislature], was convinced that Mr. Ristich and his colleagues were not only encouraging the war party in Serbia, but were also intriguing for His Highness' expulsion from the Principality, and the establishment of a Republican Government under the Presidency of Mr. Ristich' (Buchanan to Derby, 21 Oct. 1875, ibid., no. 351). The threat to Serbia was to allow a Turkish occupation of it, if she did not refrain from menace and war.

[27] Derby to White, teleg., 6 Oct. 1875, ibid.; Derby to Adams, teleg., 7 Oct. 1875, ibid. 1801, no. 621.

[28] White to Derby, teleg., 7 Oct. 1875, ibid. 1802.

[29] Same to same, 8 Oct. 1875, ibid. 1803, no. 64. In view of preventing difficulties for the Porte and to further contain the insurrection, Derby encouraged a disposition shown by the Greek Government for friendly relations with Turkey (Derby to Malet, 11 Oct. 1875, ibid. 1802, no. 48; Derby to Elliot, 11 Oct. 1875, ibid., no. 319).

[30] Doria to Derby, 12 Oct. 1875, ibid. 1802, no. 308.

[31] Elliot to Derby, 12 Oct. 1875, ibid., no. 660.

[32] Derby to Elliot, 16 Oct. 1875, PRO FO 146/1802, no. 326. Buchanan supported Shuvalov's contention that Andrássy wanted no more Slavs within Austria, but indicated that Austria might still annex Bosnia-Hercegovina to prevent the creation of a greater Serb state on her borders (Buchanan to Derby, 2 Nov. 1875, ibid. 1803, no. 368).

[33] Ibid.; Derby to d'Harcourt (French ambassador in London), 20 Oct. 1875, ibid.

[34] Loftus to Derby, 26 Oct. 1875, ibid. 1803, no. 321.

[35] In a minute to Tenterden, Derby wrote: 'But for the interference of the Powers the whole north of the empire would be in revolt. Therefore we can hardly say that no opinion of ours, in the sense of approval or of criticism, on the subject of internal reforms is opportune . . .' (on the back of Lyons to Derby, 21 Oct. 1875, ibid. 27/2115, no. 859).

[36] Buchanan to Derby, teleg., 14 Nov. 1875, ibid. 146/1803.

[37] Same to same, 18 Nov. 1875, ibid, 1804, no. 390.

[38] Loftus to Derby, 24 Nov. 1875, ibid., no. 356.

[39] Buchanan to Derby, 30 Nov. 1875, ibid., no. 402; Derby to Buchanan, 20 Nov. 1875, ibid., no. 271.

[40] Elliot to Derby, 20 Nov. 1875, ibid. 1805, no. 767; Dupuis to Elliot, 20 Nov. 1875, ibid. 1804, no. 773; Freeman to Derby, 24 Nov. 1875, ibid. 1805, no. 23.

## CHAPTER FOUR

[1] This designation meaning leaderless or unattached was first applied to the homeless from the Ottoman provinces who came to Constantinople to seek a livelihood. During the Crimean War the term was attached to individual volunteers, especially Albanians, Kurds, and Circassians, who formed bodies and attached themselves to the Ottoman army (*Encyclopedia of Islam*, new edn., Leiden, 1960, p. 1077). During the crisis of the 1870s a typical Bashi-Bazouk was an armed peasant supplied by Muslim landlords or Government requisition. In accordance with feudal custom, landlords often forfeited their land on failing the Government's request for troops at time of need (Major Gonne to Buchanan, 30 Apr. 1875, PRO FO 424/40, no. 792).

[2] Freeman to Derby, 30 Dec. 1875, PRO FO 424/40, no. 56; Elliot to Derby, 4 Jan. 1876, ibid. no. 87.

[3] Dupuis to Elliot, 18 Sept. 1875, PRO FO 146/1802, no. 632; Elliot to Derby, 14 Oct. 1875, ibid., no. 662; Dupuis to Elliot, 4 Oct. 1875, ibid.

[4] Elliot to Derby, 23 Oct. 1875, ibid. 1803, no. 694.

[5] Same to same, 26 Oct. 1875, ibid., no. 702.

[6] Dupuis to Elliot, 13 Oct. 1875, ibid., no. 703; Elliot to Derby, 4 Nov. 1875, ibid. 1804, no. 724; same to same, 12 Nov. 1875, ibid., no. 743.

[7] Same to same, 15 Nov. 1875, ibid.; same to same, 15 Nov. 1875, ibid., no. 759.

[8] Same to same, 23 Nov. 1875, ibid. 1805, no. 775.

[9] Next to atrocities, the Turks had come to symbolize in the European imagination the proclaimers of reform measures which would never be implemented. Freeman, writing from Sarajevo, considered the Irade of 2 Oct. a dead letter as the 'police force continues to be recruited from the scum of the population' (Freeman to Derby, 24 Nov. 1875, PRO FO 424/39, no. 542).

[10] Elliot to Derby, teleg., secret, 3 Dec. 1875, PRO FO 424/39.

[11] Same to same, teleg., 8 Dec. 1875, ibid. In a letter filled with unconcealed bitterness toward Andrássy, Ignatiev defends himself as working against entente with Austria and agrees with Jomini that the Turks would execute reforms only if they see that Austria and Russia are united. In this regard, the Russian ambassador pointed out that Andrássy's attempt to force the Turks to drop their own reform plans was done alone, and not with Russia and Germany. Further, the language used to the Turks was 'immoderate', and they no longer believe in the sincerity of the entente. Ignatiev describes Andrássy's attempt to act in isolation a great failure which has underlined for the Porte Austro-Russian division. He again urged initiative to be left in the hands of the ambassadors at Constantinople rather than being allowed to reside at Vienna. He promised to be quiet and to follow Gorchakov's instructions (Ignatiev to Jomini, 13 Dec. 1875, Jomini–Onou Pap., Eg. 3172, 50–3). A snippet of this long letter is printed in Alexandre Onou, 'Correspondance inédite du Baron Alexandre de Jomini', *Revue d'Histoire Moderne*, x (Sept.–Oct. 1935), 386. Ignatiev's letter to Jomini of 20 December in which he promises to stick to his instructions is also reproduced in part in the *Revue d'Histoire Moderne*, 386–7, and in full in Eg. 3172, 54–5, in the Jomini–Onou Papers.

[12] Elliot to Derby, teleg., 8 Dec. 1875, PRO FO 428/39.

[13] Derby to Elliot, 8 Dec. 1875, ibid., no. 551. The ninth article of the Treaty of Paris prohibited the right of the Powers to interfere in the relations of the Sultan with his subjects or in the internal administration of the Ottoman Empire.

[14] Derby to Buchanan, 11 Dec. 1875, ibid., no. 554. As Harris points out, once Gorchakov capitulated to Andrássy on 8 December by letting Andrássy decide if Turkey's reforms were sufficient, the Austrian minister was no longer worried by the Sultan's reform firman (Harris, pp. 165–9).

[15] The Turkish ambassador at St. Petersburg telegraphed that Russia urged the Porte to issue its reforms as soon as possible. Andrássy had telegraphed to postpone these measures. Constantinople was confused by Austro-Russian 'unity' and, as Harris points out, 'secure in their belief that Austria and Russia were divided', arranged to promulgate their own reforms (Harris, pp. 154–465; Elliot to Derby, 10 Dec. 1875, PRO FO 424/39, no. 581).

[16] Raschid Pasha to Musurus Pasha, teleg., 14 Dec. 1875, ibid. It was a long list and included use of Christians in provincial administration and in the police, more voice to be given to the people in provincial administration through the use of elected provincial councils, the unification of taxation, Christian equality in regard to the holding of land, and the curtailment of the jurisdiction of religious courts, which did not receive Christian evidence. Elliot's advice on the reform programme was asked and given on two points—the employment of Christians in provincial administration and the manner in which the reforms should be communicated to the Powers (Elliot to Derby, 10 Dec. 1875, PRO FO 424/39, no. 822). It is not improbable, however, that the major portion of the Turkish reform firman contained the ideas of Ignatiev. In support of this see Davison, pp. 315–16. The fact that Ignatiev was involved in the Austro-Russian negotiations leading to the Andrássy note and the way in which the Turkish firman of 12 December anticipated the specific proposals of the Austro-Russian note, would seem to indicate an enlightenment of the Turks by that rascal, Ignatiev.

[17] Buchanan to Derby, 16 Dec. 1875, PRO FO 424/39, no. 585. Andrássy thanked Derby for his advice to the Turkish ambassador, to wait to see what the Andrássy reforms were before condemning them.

[18] Paget to Derby, 16 Dec. 1875, ibid., no. 590. Visconti Venosta did not think the rebels would accept any guarantee except one from Austria and Russia, and he did not think the latter two governments would make themselves responsible for any projects not of their own devising (same to same, 22 Dec. 1875, ibid., no. 595).

[19] Elliot to Derby, 22 Dec. 1875, ibid., no. 620. William I of Germany 'censured the Sultan's Government for publishing the Firman of Reforms, after having been repeatedly requested by the Austrian and Russian [not by Ignatiev] Governments to withhold it until Count Andrassy's plan been communicated to the Porte and to the Powers' (Odo Russell to Derby, 21 Dec. 1875, ibid. 64/831, no. 523).

[20] Loftus to Derby, 22 Dec. 1875, ibid., no. 598. Elliot impressed on the Sultan that everything depended on his firmness of will in executing the firman (Elliot to Derby, 19 Dec. 1875, ibid., no. 615).

[21] Buchanan to Derby, 27 Dec. 1875, ibid., no. 599. He told the British ambassador that he would only ask for 'an engagement on the part of the Porte to carry out such reforms as might be recommended by Europe. . . . He [Andrássy] was equally confident that, if Europe intimated to the insurgents that all they could reasonably require would be secured to them, they would be satisfied with the concessions granted to them' (same to same, 24 Dec. 1875, ibid., no. 627).

[22] Elliot to Derby, 23 Dec. 1875, ibid., no. 623.

[23] According to Novikov, Andrássy felt the greatest difficulty would be to obtain a Turkish commitment to the Great Powers as he felt the Porte would create difficulties and agree only very slowly (Novikov to Jomini, 21 Dec. 1875, Jomini–Onou Pap., Eg. 3174, 137–9).

[24] Buchanan to Derby, teleg., 3 Jan. 1876, PRO FO 424/40, no. 6; Mackenzie, pp. 70–1. Gorchakov would only say that these would be issues that could be discussed after Turkish acceptance of the note (Loftus to Derby, teleg., 7 Jan. 1876, PRO FO 414/40, no. 40).

[25] Elliot to Derby, teleg., 3 Jan. 1876, ibid., no. 9. When Elliot studied the note at leisure, he addressed a dispatch on it in more detail which he rightly anticipated would reach Derby (on 27 January) after the British Government's decision on the note was made. Elliot wrote that Andrássy had somewhat exaggerated conditions in Bosnia-

Hercegovina by stating the condition of the Christians there as one of slavery. Again he repeats his view that conditions which need redressing were not the cause of the insurrection and that the position of Christians had improved in recent years. General abuses need remedies, he argues, not merely in Bosnia-Hercegovina but throughout the Ottoman Empire, and he feels the note is inconsistent when it implies that pacification must precede the execution of reforms and yet proposes reforms to pacify the insurrection. Elliot ends by saying that if the Andrássy proposals are supported by Britain and if communicated with respect for the dignity of the Sultan, they will be accepted by the Porte (Elliot to Derby, 18 Jan. 1876, ibid., no. 150).

[26] Lyons to Derby, 5 Jan. 1876, ibid., no. 24. The Turks balked at this as well. The Turkish Foreign Minister estimated that four-fifths of all taxation in Bosnia-Hercegovina was direct taxation (Elliot to Derby, 25 Jan. 1876, ibid., no. 128).

[27] Decazes to d'Harcourt, 4 Jan. 1876, and enclosure, Vogué to Decazes, 1 Jan, 1876, both communicated to Derby on 13 Jan. 1876, ibid. Loftus, in St. Petersburg, agreed with de Vogué in interpreting Russia's support of the note to her desire to further destroy the Treaty of Paris.

[28] The French ambassador in St. Petersburg, Le Flô, wrote of the anxiety of Alexander II over what Derby would do and the possibility of an Anglo-Turkish deal—Egypt to go to England for British support of a Turkish refusal of the Andrássy note (Le Flô to Decazes, 9 Jan. 1876, Documents diplomatiques français, Paris, 1930, ser. 1, vol ii, pp. 38–40; hereafter cited as DDF).

[29] Harris, pp. 183–209; Seton-Watson, Slav. Rev. iii. 431–2; Loftus to Derby, teleg., 7 Jan. 1876, PRO 424/40, no. 40.

[30] Seton-Watson implies Derby was at Knowsley and would remain there until 12 January. Harris says Derby was at Knowsley or in the North from mid-December until 12 January (Seton-Watson, Slav. Rev. iii. 657; Harris, pp. 202–3). According to the FO dispatches and his private correspondence, Derby was back in London by 12 January. Seton-Watson writes that Derby's duties as a colonel of the volunteers and other local business necessitated his presence in Lancashire until 12 January.

[31] Russell to Derby, secret, 2 Jan. 1876, Derby Pap. Bismarck expressed himself according to Russell as saying that 'Turkey might yet be kept together with a little good will' (ibid.).

[32] Ibid.

[33] Tenterden to Odo Russell, 5 Jan. 1876, Odo Russell Papers, Public Record Office.

[34] Tenterden memorandum, 6 Jan. 1876, Foreign Office Library, confidential print, 2734. Derby thanked Tenterden. 'Your memo is extremely useful; it came just at the right moment and must have cost you a great deal of labor' (Derby to Tenterden, Knowsley, 7 Jan. 1876, Tenterden Pap., PRO FO 363/1). On the Tenterden memorandum see p. 490, m. 56.

[35] Harris, p. 203.

[36] Manners to Derby. Southampton, 7 Jan. 1876, Derby Pap.

[37] Salisbury to Derby, 7 Jan. 1876, Derby Pap.; same to same, 7 Jan. 1876, Salis. Pap., vol. 16. The Andrássy note was a very long letter of explanation and intention, a small part of which contained the five suggested reforms for Bosnia-Hercegovina (Andrássy to Beust, 30 Dec. 1876 [Communicated to Derby, 3 Jan. 1876], PRO FO 424/40, no. 4).

[38] Derby to Disraeli, Knowsley, 7 Jan. 1876, Derby Pap.

[39] Derby to Manners, Knowsley, 9 Jan. 1876, Derby Pap.

[40] Odo Russell to Derby, 8 Jan. 1876, ibid.

[41] Disraeli to Derby, 9 Jan. 1876, ibid.; same to same, 9 Jan. 1876, MB vi. 18–19. Disraeli did not give an outright negative but suggested the Government 'pause' before giving any assent. His reasons were those shared with others; the effect on Ireland, the similarity with what the Porte had already decreed, and the feeling that the note would not affect the insurrection and might be used as an excuse for Austro-Russian interven-

tion within Turkey.
[42] Shuvalov wrote to Gorchakov on very good authority that Derby's initial view of the Austrian note was favourable but that some of his colleagues had influenced him to the contrary (Seton-Watson, *Slav. Rev.* iii. 657–9). This is a possible early intimation of Lady Derby's work of explaining the Cabinet to the Russian ambassador.
[43] Derby to Elliot, 13 Jan. 1876, PRO FO 424/40, no. 55.
[44] Derby to Elliot, 14 Jan. 1876, PRO FO 424/40, no. 58. Salisbury saw Russia, at least temporarily, as abandoning the Christians, thus neutralizing Britain's only weapon in dealing with the Turks—the threat of Russian anger. He also believed Germany was encouraging Russia to take some of Turkey (Salisbury to Mallet, 11 Jan. 1876, Salis. Pap., vol 12). Salisbury let it be known, at least to deMartino, the Italian chargé who spread the word, that he objected to the Austrian proposals and especially to the paragraph which he felt 'intimated an intention of an armed Austrian occupation' (Tenterden memorandum, 13 Jan. 1876, Derby Pap.). Beust saw Tenterden on 12 January to deny this (ibid.). The Austrian ambassador told Derby that Andrássy categorically authorized him 'to declare that the note contained nothing which could induce the belief that an armed intervention was intended. . . . That if the insurgents did not submit then the Porte would be left to subdue them by the force of arms, and that they would be prevented from obtaining the support derived by them from exterior aid' (Derby to Buchanan, 18 Jan. 1876, PRO FO 424/40, no. 72).
[45] Elliot to Derby, teleg., 12 Jan. 1876, PRO FO 78/2454; Lyons to Derby, 14 Jan. 1876, Lyons Pap., RA 1. Lyons added a PS. that Decazes implored 'me to conjure you not to separate England from the rest of Europe' (ibid.). Italy also pressed England to join in (Paget to Derby, teleg., 16 Jan. 1876, PRO FO 424/40, no. 70).
[46] Elliot to Derby, 9 p.m., 13 Jan. 1876, ibid. The Porte was confused about Russian advice. 'The former [Gorchakov] strongly urges a favourable reception, while the latter [Ignatiev] represents the project as preposterous' (same to same, teleg., 9.40 p.m., 13 Jan. 1876, ibid.). Ignatiev openly opposed the note but hoped for England's adherence as a way to break Andrássy's directorship of the three Northern Powers (Elliot to Derby, 9 Jan. 1876, ibid., no. 137).
[47] Disraeli to Lady Bradford, 18 Jan. 1876, MB vi. 19. Few People had real belief in the success of the note. 'I don't believe much in the efficacy of the Note . . . but if accepted it will put Austria on her mettle to try to bring about the end of the insurrection without crossing the frontier' (Lyons to Derby, 17 Jan. 1876, Lyons Pap., RA1).
[48] In Derby's letter to Salisbury of 9 January where he explains why, unlike Salisbury, he did not fear an Austro-Russian occupation of Turkey, the Foreign Secretary wrote of the Austro-Russian fear of the creation of an independent Slav state and of Andrássy's dread and perplexity rather than of his ambition. 'I could explain all this fully in conversation, but it is a long story to write' (Derby to Salisbury, 9 Jan. 1876, Salis. Pap.; same to same, 9 Jan. 1876, Derby Pap.). Disraeli writes of 'the day I was with D[erby] in explaining Andrássy's efforts' (Disraeli to Lady Bradford, 18 Jan. 1876, MB vi. 19).
[49] The Belgian ambassador wrote 'that Lord Salisbury has not hidden his opinion of the necessity of British adherence . . . but with reservations' (Solvyns to d'Aspremont-Lynden, London, 17 Jan. 1876, Belgian Foreign Ministry, Brussels; hereafter cited as BFM). The Queen saw Salisbury on 14 January and talked with him about the Andrássy note. She, however, gives no indication of Salisbury's opinion (Queen Victoria's Journal, 14 Jan. 1876, RA).
[50] Disraeli to Queen Victoria, 18 Jan. 1876, RA, Add. MS. A 50/18. 'Cabinet agree that a general support shall be given to the Austrian note, but you should not act until you receive further instructions' (Derby to Elliot, teleg., 5.30 p.m. 18 Jan. 1876, PRO FO 424/40, no. 96). Derby's telegram to Elliot went to all the British ambassadors and was known in London by all the foreign embassies. The opinion of Ponsonby, the Queen's private secretary, might have come from the pen of Derby. 'It is clear that

your Majesty's Government could allow no other course. . . . The danger of course arises as to what the next step may be, for if we too cordially supported Austria we might be led into a further action which would not approve itself to the nation' (Ponsonby to Queen Victoria, 19 Jan. 1876, RA, Add. MS. A 50/19).

[51] Beust's figure was two or three days (Beust to Derby, 24 Jan. 1876, PRO FO 424/40, no. 116).

[52] Derby to Buchanan, 24 Jan. 1876, ibid., no. 115.

[53] Harris, p. 207.

[54] Beust to Derby, 24 Jan. 1876, PRO FO 424/40, no. 116. Decazes was also unwilling to request a written Turkish reply. 'It would, he [Decazes] conceived, be an extraordinary solecism in diplomacy for a Foreign Ambassador to ask the Government to which he was accredited for a solemn written answer to a document neither emanating from his own Government nor addressed to himself.' Decazes favoured recommending the note to the Porte with a written Turkish reply to go to the powers but not to each ambassador individually (Lyons to Derby, 24 Jan. 1876, ibid., no. 117).

[55] Harris writes of a 37-page letter (Harris, pp. 208–9).

[56] Derby to Beust, F.O., 25 Jan. 1876, PRO FO 424/40, no. 119. Tenterden wrote a 20-page memorandum on Turkish reform from 1838 to the Andrássy note. He prepared it for the use of the Cabinet when it would meet to decide its response to the Andrássy note. There is no evidence that Derby showed the Cabinet this memo when it met, but his official reply to the note given above is lifted almost entirely, at times verbatim, from Tenterden's memorandum. It was printed for the use of the Foreign Office on 6 January. A copy is in RA H6/200.

[57] Derby to Elliot, teleg., 7.30 p.m., 25 Jan. 1876, ibid., no. 120. The dispatch of the same date repeats the telegram but at much greater length and in more detail (same to same, 25 Jan. 1876, ibid., no. 121).

[58] On the point of direct taxation for local purposes the Porte did not give a complete negative but promised that 'a sum shall be allotted to the two provinces for local purposes under the control of Provincial Councils' as provided for by the firman of December (Elliot to Derby, teleg., 13 Feb. 1876, ibid., no. 246). Elliot wrote that when the Turks found the Austrian proposals much more harmless than was feared there was a general feeling of relief. 'The credit for the moderation [of the proposals] is universally attributed to H.M. Govt. for people here are convinced that Count Andrássy modified what had first been intended only because he knew that he could not otherwise expect your support' (Elliot to Derby, private, 4 Feb. 1876, Derby Pap.).

[59] Elliot to Derby, 12 Jan. 1876, PRO FO 424/40, no. 49; same to same, 30 Jan. 1876, ibid., no. 239. Elliot telegraphed that if it were intimated that the consular commission would be withdrawn, if Turkey accepted the Andrássy note, it 'would have some weight with the Porte' (Elliot to Derby, teleg., 12 Jan. 1876. ibid. 78/2454, no. 41).

# CHAPTER FIVE

[1] Derby to Buchanan, 1 Mar. 1876, PRO FO 424/40, no. 332; Monson to Buchanan, 7 Mar. 1876, ibid., no. 395; same to same, 11 Mar. 1876, ibid., no. 401. The above, however, did not prevent Monson from reporting news of the insurrection derived from Stillman (same to same, 11 Mar. 1876, ibid., no. 405). Stillman was soon recalled by *The Times* and he departed for Britain on 28 March. He was the only representative of the British press in the area at that time. At Constantinople, *The Times* had Gallenga as a correspondent. He too was mis-spelt. Elliot reported that Ignatiev saw a 'good deal of Mr. Gallenger . . . whom he has to some extent imbued with his own views' (Elliot to Derby, 31 Dec. 1875, ibid., no. 80).

² Russell to Derby, 9 Feb. 1876, PRO FO 424/40, no. 224; Elliot to Derby, 5 Feb. 1876, ibid., no. 275; same to same, 28 Feb. 1876, ibid., no. 367.

³ Elliot to Derby, 15 Jan. 1876, ibid., 78/2454, no. 56. Tenterden described the address as a 'strange document apparently one of Mr. Urquhart's productions' (ibid.).

⁴ Queen Victoria to Derby, 20 Jan. 1876, RA H6/250; Derby to Ponsonby, 24 Jan. 1876, ibid. 260; same to same, 31 Jan. 1876, ibid. 272. According to the Spanish representative in Constantinople, who was not always a reliable reporter of events, Lady Strangford recently proposed to the Grand Vizier, reforms which would take as their base the creation of great schools to educate women (Conte to Calderon y Collantes, 3 Jan. 1876, Spanish Foreign Ministry, Madrid; hereafter cited as SFM).

⁵ Sandwith to Miss Irby, 16 Feb. 1876, F. Nightingale Papers, British Library, Add. MS. 45789, LI. Florence Nightingale wrote at the end of this letter the following: 'I could not have believed in the existence of such an idiot!' Hooray Florence.

⁶ Ponsonby to Queen Victoria, 16 Feb. 1876, RA H7/36.

⁷ Harcourt to Hartington, 11 Mar. 1876 (A. G. Gardiner, The Life of Sir William Harcourt, 2 vols., London, 1923, i. 302–3). Münster mentioned the open anti-Semitism of Disraeli's 'own colleagues and former ministers' who say that 'a British minister would never have done that'. The German ambassador wrote that this was the first time that he had heard Disraeli's Jewish descent mentioned by his own colleagues (Münster to Bismarck, 14 Mar. 1876, GFM, A1387). Queen Victoria thought 'it a mere attempt to injure Mr. Disraeli' (Queen Victoria to Theodore Martin, 14 Mar. 1876, G. E. Buckle (ed.). The Letters of Queen Victoria, 2nd ser., 2 vols., N.Y., 1926, ii. 450–1; hereafter cited as QVL). Thompson refers to it as 'the first instance in which Mr. Disraeli's Government showed any determination to withstand any strong expression of out-of-door opinion' (Thompson, i. 272). At the end of March, M. R. Grenfell wrote to Northbrook of the Government. 'The character of the administration has wholly given way. There is nothing left of it. Derby's qualifications of the intentions of the Canal purchase, Salisbury's temper, and the unblushing lies and incompetence of Dizzy, have completely neutralized any respect which Cross, Northcote, and Cairns may have won for the Government. ... The difficulty of getting rid of him [Disraeli] ... is his successor. ... Derby has not the courage to take the first place. And now I think Salisbury is openly bidding for it. Well!' (H. R. Grenfell to Northbrook, 31 Mar. 1876, India Office, Northbrook Papers, C 144/7; hereafter cited as Northb. Pap.).

⁸ Disraeli to Galway, 15 Mar. 1876, Galway Papers, Univ. of Nottingham Manuscripts Dept.

⁹ Salisbury to Duke of Buckingham, 7 Apr. 1876, Salis. Pap. C3.

¹⁰ Gladstone memorandum, n.d. [1876], Glad. Pap., Add. MS. 44763, DCLXXVIII.

¹¹ The German report of the conversation indicated Russell as saying things which are omitted from Russell's own report of the talk to Derby. 'He [Russell] made no concealment of the fact that England had fundamentally abandoned her traditional policy in this question. There were but very few Members of Parliament who would be still in favour of an adventure comparable with the Crimean War. ... Lord Odo suggested, as being perhaps least objectionable to England [to simplify complications], an occupation by Austria and inferentially the annexation of the insurgent provinces ...' (Bülow to Münster, confid., 4 Jan. 1876. GD i. 20–2).

¹² Russell to Derby, secret, Berlin, 2 Jan. 1876, PRO FO 64/850, no. 8; same to same, copy, 2 Jan. 1876, Derby Pap. Russell also telegraphed a much shorter version of the above (same to same, cipher, secret, teleg., 11 p.m., 2 Jan. 1876, PRO FO 64/850). There are discrepancies in the English and German versions of the Bismarck–Russell conversation, the German version omitting some of the things—especially German support for Ottoman territorial integrity—Russell reports Bismarck as saying, and the English version leaving out remarks of Russell contained in Bülow's report to Münster. Bülow's letter (Bülow to Münster, 4 Jan. 1876, GP ii. 29–31) leaves the impression that Bismarck wished merely to promote an Anglo-German exchange of ideas; Russell's

report indicates Bismarck as wishing for a more formal alliance. I believe the English version of the talk the more accurate, at least on the major point of Bismarck's intentions, for a number of reasons. Russell wrote his dispatch at once, the moment the discussion ended, and the following day, reading it at leisure, reported it to be accurate even if stylistically awkward. Bismarck's version was written by Bülow two days after the reported event. The meeting was not a chance one, nor were the Chancellor's words ones in a talk largely devoted to another subject. Bismarck was going to some trouble merely to elicit an exchange of ideas which could have been arranged easily enough by a letter to Münster. Finally, Bismarck repeated his offer of an understanding on 31 January to Russell. On the discrepancy in the British and German versions see W. N. Medlicott, 'Bismarck and Beaconsfield' in A. O. Sarkissian, *Studies in Diplomatic History and Historiography* (London, 1961), pp. 228–9. Harris is quite right in pointing out that Bülow's report to Münster was sent for his information 'rather than as an instruction to participate in subsequent negotiations' (Harris, p. 175). Bismarck's reasons for this last are not easy to discern. Like Disraeli, he thought little of most of his ambassadors and distrusted them as well. He may have wished to keep the negotiations in his own hands in Berlin. He also may have feared Münster's writing directly to William I of an anti-Russian scheme or plan.

¹³ Harris, p. 175; Medlicott, 'Bismarck and Beaconsfield', p. 232; Langer, pp. 80–1; Stojanovic, pp. 44–8; Taylor, p. 235.

¹⁴ Russell to Derby, secret, 3 Jan. 1876, PRO FO 64/850, no. 9. The reasons Russell thought this seem to me to be mistaken. He interpreted Bismarck's motives as revenge against Russia by using England to 'throw over his Northern Allies' and prevent Russia from gaining some of the Ottoman Empire (ibid.). Bismarck's wish was not to keep Turkish territory from Russia, but to prevent Russia from a war with Austria.

¹⁵ Derby to Russell, secret, teleg., 11.15 a.m., 6 Jan. 1876, ibid. 244/295. Derby's answer and his need to consult colleagues was in reference to Britain's reply to the Andrássy note. To the question of an Anglo-German understanding on the East, he returns a mere thank you and a meaningless assurance of his desire to co-operate with the German Government (same to same, 6 Jan. 1876, ibid., no. 16). Derby sent a copy of his telegram to Disraeli, who may never have seen the secret Russell dispatch which elicited it (Derby to Disraeli, 5 Jan. 1876, Derby Pap.).

¹⁶ Russell to Derby, 8 Jan. 1876, PRO FO 64/850, no. 15; same to same, private, 8 Jan. 1876, Derby Pap. Russell thought, and perhaps Derby did as well, that Bismarck was 'not in want of an immediate reply, for his offers of friendship are to come into play, when his present allies begin to quarrel and prepare to fight—perhaps next spring?' (Russell to Tenterden, private, 8 Jan. 1876, Tenterden Pap., PRO FO 363/3). If Derby did believe this, then it would at least partially explain his non-response to Bismarck's offer of an understanding. But for such an understanding Bismarck wished a preliminary exchange of ideas which Derby was not following up.

¹⁷ Lyons to Derby, 14 Jan. 1876 (Lord Newton, *Lord Lyons*, 2 vols., London, 1913, ii. 96–7); same to same, 14 Jan. 1876, Derby Pap.

¹⁸ Russell to Derby, private, 22 Jan. 1876, Derby Pap.

¹⁹ Russell to Derby, teleg., 31 Jan. 1876, PRO FO 424/40. Bismarck apologized for and explained his inability to delay further the delivery of the Andrássy note. The German Chancellor 'expressed great regret that your message through Münster asking for delay until your instructions to Elliot had reached Constantinople had not come a few days sooner, when he could have insisted at Vienna on the required delay but not hearing from you sooner he had been obliged to yield to the importunities of his Allies' (same to same, 1 Feb. 1876, Derby Pap.; same to same, secret, teleg., 26 Jan. 1876, PRO FO 64/850). 'He [Bismarck] liked to hope and believe that his present inability to comply with Your Lordship's request would not stand in the way of the cordial understanding he wished to establish with Her Majesty's Government in regard to Turkish affairs' (Russell to Derby, secret, 26 Jan. 1876, ibid., no. 41). Bülow brought

the above message to Russell from Bismarck (ibid.).

[20] Same to same, 26 Jan. 1876, ibid.

[21] Ibid.

[22] D. Harris, 'Bismarck's Advance to England, January, 1876', *Journal of Modern History*, iii (Mar.–Dec. 1931), 559.

[23] Russell to Derby, secret, 1 Feb. 1876, PRO FO 64/850, no. 56; same to same, 1 Feb. 1876, Derby Pap. He was reading Odo's reports even if he made no reply to them. On the back of no. 56 Derby wrote 'important'.

[24] Russell to Derby, private, 4 Feb. 1876, Derby Pap.

[25] Queen Victoria to Ponsonby, 7 Feb. 1876, RA H7/15. The Queen, recording in her journal her talk with Disraeli on 7 February, wrote that the Prime Minister had 'strongly urged' Derby to act (*QVL* ii. 443).

[26] Ponsonby to Queen Victoria, 7 Feb. 1876, ibid. 16.

[27] Queen Victoria to Derby, 9 Feb. 1876, ibid. 443–4. On the seventh the Queen wrote in her journal that she had talked with Disraeli who had strongly urged Derby to respond to Bismarck's overture. 'He [Disraeli] begged me also to urge, which I said I would, though of course one can never trust Bismarck . . .' (Queen's Journal, Windsor, 7 Feb. 1876, RA).

[28] Derby to Queen Victoria, 10 Feb. 1876, MB vi. 20–1. Ponsonby, who was sympathetic to Derby, after reading the latter's reply, wrote to the Queen that she had given Derby 'the spur that he required to move' (Ponsonby to Queen Victoria, 10 Feb. 1876, RA H7/19). Disraeli encouraged the Queen's pressure on Derby whom he acknowledged 'often seems ungenial, not to say morose'. He saw an understanding with Germany as enabling England once again to 'exercise that influence which, of late years, has so painfully and mysteriously disappeared' (Disraeli to Queen Victoria, 12 Feb. 1876, *QVL* ii. 444–5).

[29] Derby to Russell, 12 Feb. 1876, PRO FO 244/295, no. 115.

[30] Russell to Derby, private, 12 Feb. 1876, Derby Pap.

[31] Disraeli to Derby, 15 Feb. 1876, MB vi. 21–2; same to same, 15 Feb. 1876, Derby Pap.

[32] Derby to Russell, 16 Feb. 1876, PRO FO 64/846, no. 117; Derby to Disraeli, private, 15 Feb. 1876, MB vi. 22; same to same, 15 Feb. 1876, Derby Pap. Harris mistakenly dates Derby's no. 117 to Russell as 12 Feb. (Harris, 'Bismarck's advance to England', 451–2).

[33] Russell to Derby, 19 Feb. 1876, PRO FO 64/850, no. 76; same to same, private, 19 Feb. 1876, Derby Pap. Russell had come round to Derby.

[34] Taffs feels he did so when it became clear that Disraeli was not planning to take an active part in the East (Winifred Taffs, *Ambassador to Bismarck. Lord Odo Russell*, London, 1938, p. 125). Another possibility is his feeling that Andrássy's tenure in Vienna was no longer in danger, which Russell learned toward the end of February (Russell to Derby, 26 Feb. 1876, PRO FO 64/850, no. 88). Earlier in February and throughout January Bismarck had indicated that one reason he wished a British understanding was his fear of Andrássy's fall. In fact, he even asked Britain to speak in support of Andrássy at Vienna. It is not clear what caused his worry about Andrássy's position to disappear.

[35] Lee writes that Odo Russell was almost alone in believing Bismarck's sincerity for peace (Dwight Lee, *Great Britain and the Cyprus Convention Policy of 1876*, Cambridge, Mass., 1934, p. 12; hereafter cited as Lee). This is inaccurate. On the British side, of those who knew of Bismarck's offer, all except Derby thought he wished peace, and perhaps Derby did as well, merely not wishing to have to help him in preserving it.

# CHAPTER SIX

[1] Continual changes were made in the central administration as well as the provincial posts; Elliot complained that such action rendered government nearly impossible (Elliot to Derby, 11 Feb. 1876, PRO FO 78/2455, no. 198; same to same, 7 Mar. 1876, ibid., 424/40, no. 421).

[2] Elliot to Derby, 28 Mar. 1876, ibid., no. 523.

[3] Freeman to Derby, Sarajevo, 4 Apr. 1876, ibid., no. 636. In Bulgaria as well there was little change in the actual administration of the province as a result of proclaimed reforms (Brophy to P. Francis, Bourgas, 9 Par. 1876, ibid., no. 806).

[4] Holmes to Elliot, Mostar, 7 Apr. 1876, ibid., no. 607.

[5] On 9 March copies of a 'Manifesto of Moslem Patriots' were sent to some of the 'leading statesmen of Europe' asking for 'European understanding and patience' while the Sultan's deposition and the creation of a Parliament were being worked out (Robert Devereux, *The First Ottoman Constitutional Period*, Baltimore, 1963, pp. 31–3). There is a touch of irony in the fact that Midhat and Ignatiev, far from being friends or allies, were both working for the same means—decentralization—to attain nearly opposite ends. Ignatiev was pestering the Grand Vizier for more administrative decentralization which he hoped would raise the level of the Christian Slavs and give them the necessary experience required to eventually function satisfactorily in a state of independence. Midhat was vocal in criticizing both Turkish and Austrian reforms because they gave little voice to local inhabitants and offered no check or control on the arbitrary rule of a Sultan, whom he felt was leading the Empire to total ruin. Elliot was friendly with Midhat and had known for a considerable period of time of his intentions, dropping along the way unperceived hints to Derby that the root of all the trouble was the quixotic incompetence of the Sultan.

[6] Elliot to Tenterden, private, 6 Apr. 1876, Tenterden Pap., PRO FO 363/1; Ponsonby to Queen Victoria, 16 Mar. 1876, RA H7/160.

[7] Elliot to Derby, 1 Mar. 1876, PRO FO 424/40, no. 415. In Hercegovina one Wassa Effendi, a Roman Catholic Albanian and former follower of Garibaldi, was the agent appointed to carry out the above. Apart from the imperial firman of 12 December, the Porte promised additional reforms to Bosnia-Hercegovina toward the end of February. They included the sale of Government lands on easy terms, increased supplies for public works, religious liberty, no tax farming, and an amnesty and food to all insurgents who laid down their arms (Freeman to Derby, 2 Feb 1876, ibid., no. 341).

[8] Buchanan to Derby, 17 Mar. 1876, ibid., no. 432; Elliot to Derby, 13 Mar. 1876, ibid., no. 427.

[9] Freeman to Derby, 10 Mar. 1876, ibid., no. 446. Freeman further pointed out that 'although the Austrian government may refuse to afford them [the refugees] further assistance, they will probably be kept from absolute starvation by private charity, whereas were they to return, I really do not know how they would subsist . . .' (ibid.). Holmes estimated the cost of feeding alone the 300,000 people for fourteen months at £2,000,000 (Holmes to Elliot, 20 Mar. 1876, ibid., no. 491). Fourteen months was the duration of time to the next full harvest when it was assumed that relief would no longer be necessary.

[10] Buchanan to Derby, 24 Mar. 1876, ibid., no. 457.

[11] Same to same, 24 Mar. 1876, ibid., no. 460. At the end of January the British Government, together with the French, complained strongly at Constantinople that the Porte was £15,000 short in meeting the dividend due on 1 February on the guaranteed loan of 1855. The Turks were told to pay at once. So much for a new British loan (Lyons to Derby, 30 Jan. 1876, ibid. 27/2160, no. 68). By mid-March there

were already reports that the refugees, fearing violence and oppression at the hands of the Ottoman soldiers and native Muslims, refused to return to 'a state of corrupt administration and unbridled licentiousness and crime' (Freeman to Derby, 17 Mar. 1876, ibid., no. 486).

[12] Monson to Buchanan, Ragusa, 21 Mar. 1876, ibid., no. 488. It was said that the 'King of Trebigné' had diverted money, sent from Russia to succour the refugees, into the hands of the insurgents. In his defence, however, the line separating refugee and insurgent was often fine or non-existent.

[13] Taylor to Derby, Ragusa, 7 Apr. 1876, ibid., no. 586. The following terms were offered: refugees would be supplied with grain and their houses would be rebuilt at Government cost; those who returned would be exempt from taxation for at least one year and there would be a general amnesty for all who came back within four weeks from 24 March. Those who did not return would have their lands confiscated (ibid.). When Rodich met the representatives of the refugees, he was told they would not leave Dalmatia until the insurrection had ended, fearing that if they did, they would be hardly used by both the insurgents and the Ottomans (Buchanan to Derby, 8 Mar. 1876, ibid., no. 376).

[14] Holmes to Elliot, Mostar, 7 Apr. 1876, ibid., no. 607; Gonne to Buchanan, Ragusa, 25 Apr. 1876, ibid., no. 735; Paget to Derby, Rome, 20 Apr. 1876, ibid., no. 618.

[15] Freeman to Derby, 2 Mar. 1876, ibid., no. 375; Monson to Buchanan, 11 Mar. 1876, ibid., no. 403; Buchanan to Derby, 20 Mar. 1876, ibid., no. 414.

[16] There were also requests for land and further guarantees.

[17] Gladstone to de Lisle, 22 Apr. 1876 (E. S. Purcell, Life and Letters of Ambrose Phillipps de Lisle, 2 vols., London, 1900, ii. 152).

[18] When it was seen that Ottoman regular troops could not suppress the insurrection, the use of Bashi-Bazouks suggested itself. 'They [the Turks] argue that the trend of warfare carried on by the insurgents is one which cannot be fairly met but by similar tactics; that the daily perpetration of outrages and massacres ... justify the use of reprisals; and that even on philanthropical grounds, if the insurrection is to be stamped out, any hesitation at employing every practicable coercive measure is misplaced ...' (Monson to Derby, 14 Apr. 1876, PRO FO 424/40, no. 623).

[19] Derby to Buchanan, 10 Mar. 1876, ibid., no. 372.

[20] Buchanan to Derby, 9 Mar. 1876, ibid., no. 378.

[21] Monson to Buchanan, 11 Mar. 1876, ibid., no. 402.

[22] Monson to Derby, 25 Mar. 1876, ibid., no. 493.

[23] Buchanan to Derby, 9 Apr. 1876, ibid., no. 556.

[24] This was suggested by Holmes and strongly advocated by Ignatiev. Elliot interpreted the latter's advocacy as a desire to get the credit and stand well with the South Slavs. The British ambassador thought that at the present moment it was not 'possible to expect that the Turkish Government would come forward to make a gift of territory to the Prince of whom they had so much reason to complain' (Elliot to Derby, 20 Feb. 1876, ibid., no. 362). Elliot was generally negative on both a Turkish recognition of Montenegro's independence as well as a cession of territory to her.

[25] Derby to Buchanan, 26 Apr. 1876, ibid., no. 679.

[26] Buchanan to Derby, 2 May 1876, ibid., no. 742.

[27] Derby to Loftus, 27 Apr. 1876, ibid., no. 685; Derby to Elliot, 27 Apr. 1876, ibid., no. 683; Bourke memorandum, 27 Apr. 1876, ibid., no. 681; Loftus to Derby, 22 Apr. 1876, ibid., no. 671. On 20 April and again on the twenty-first Elliot had advised the Turks against any attack on Montenegro and it was his warnings which may have caused the Porte to draw back (Elliot to Derby, 20 Apr. 1876, ibid., no. 763; same to same, 21 April 1876, ibid., no. 766).

[28] Loftus to Derby, teleg., 26 Apr. 1876, ibid., no. 687.

[29] The opposite technique, that usually employed by Bismarck, left almost no

latitude to German ambassadors who were often kept in ignorance of the master's goals and were always restricted by his instructions.

[30] Elliot to Derby, private, 1 Mar. 1876, Derby Pap.

[31] White to Derby, 1 Mar. 1876, ibid., no. 386.

[32] Elliot to Derby, 27 Mar. 1876, ibid., no. 517. Mackenzie refers to the Austrian threat of occupation as 'Wrede's bomb' and says it was delivered on 16 March (Mackenzie, pp. 82–5). White, who talked with Wrede, puts the date of delivery as 17 March. Sumner indicates the sixteenth (Sumner, p. 182).

[33] Loftus to Derby, 26 Apr. 1876, ibid., no. 722. The French ambassador wired from St. Petersburg that the Austro-Russian entente continues despite some differences during the past few days (LeFlô to Decazes, 21 Apr. 1876, DDF ii. 49–50). Even in February there had been, as Harris points out, a divergence in Austro-Russian views on the procedure to be followed after the Porte accepted the note. Gorchakov wished the execution of the reforms as a preliminary step to pacification, while Andrássy desired pacification first, to be followed by the carrying out of reforms. Andrássy was urging strong Turkish military measures against the insurgents; Gorchakov pushed for a relaxation of them (Harris, p. 258).

[34] Derby to Buchanan, 4 May 1876, PRO FO 424/40, no. 755.

[35] Paget to Derby, 20 Apr. 1876, ibid., no. 654.

[36] Paget to Derby, 29 Apr. 1876, ibid., no. 705. The British action was in response to a circular addressed to all the Powers by the Porte, to influence Montenegro to cease the military role she was playing in the insurrection (Safvet Pasha to Musurus Pasha, Constantinople, teleg., 28 Apr. 1876, ibid., no. 696). The Italian Government acceded to the request of the British Government and the Porte. Gorchakov's reply to the Turkish circular was negative. 'He said that Russia had done already more than could be expected in causing Servia and Montenegro to remain neutral and that it now depended only on the Porte to obtain pacification by showing itself more disposed to make reasonable concession' (Elliot to Derby, teleg., 30 April 1876, ibid., no. 709). Gorchakov told Loftus that though he would not incite, no longer would he restrain Serbia or Montenegro from military action (Loftus to Derby, teleg., 20 Apr. 1876, ibid., 715). Major Gonne, who was attached to the British Embassy at Vienna, was making a tour of the Balkans, including the Montenegro-Hercegovinian border area. He wrote that 'to all intents and purposes Montenegro is fighting the Turk and the warriors complain that they receive little help from the Hercegovinians' (Gonne to Buchanan, Cettinje, 22 Apr. 1876, ibid., no. 724).

[37] Derby to Paget, 2 May 1876, ibid., no. 744.

[38] Derby to Disraeli, private, 27 Apr. 1876, Derby Pap. Shuvalov commented on the inertia of the British Cabinet, a view, he wrote, shared by the other ambassadors in London (Shuvalov to Gorchakov, 27 Apr. 1876, Seton Watson, Slav. Rev. iii. 661–2).


# CHAPTER SEVEN

[1] Bismarck wrote to the German Emperor on the same day that he told Andrássy that Germany would support any Austro-Russian agreement. 'Suggestions *of our own* would not be made in the German interest, and if we could further agreement on points of issue [between Austria and Russia] . . . our mediation would be guided by our friendly attitude for both' (Bismarck to William I, 10 May 1876, GFM, no. 108).

[2] On the origins of and the Berlin meeting itself see Taylor, p. 236; Stojanovic, pp. 59–63; Harris, pp. 288–301; Rupp, pp. 94–104; Sumner, pp. 161–5; Wertheimer, ii. 297–8; Bridge, *From Sadowa to Sarajevo*, pp. 74–6. Mackenzie using the Austrian archives indicates that Gorchakov also suggested, unsuccessfully, an Austro-Russian

occupation of Bosina-Hercegovina.

[3] During the very days of the Berlin talks, the softas, or theological students, rioted in Constantinople, and demanded the dismissal of the Grand Vizier and the Sheikh ul Islam (the Chief Mufti). Lewis feels these riots were organized by Midhat, or by those favourable to his interests. The significance of the demonstration by the theological students was that it had been prearranged to bring about a change of ministry, which after two days it was successful in doing (Bernard Lewis, *The Emergence of Modern Turkey*, London, 1968, pp. 160–3). See also Henry O. Dwight, *Turkish Life in War Time* (New York, 1881), p. 7. Davison, in his outstanding volume, writes of the impossibility of knowing how the overthrow of the Turkish Government was planned (Davison pp. 322–7). In the Jomini–Onou Papers is a copy of a letter (18 May 1876) describing the overthrow of Abdul Aziz. The writer and receiver of the letter are not indicated but it is probably from Onou to either Jomini or Giers (Eg. 3187, fos. 38–42). The letter contains the Russian date of 18 May, rather than the Western date of 30 May. Davison mentions 'that Elliot's dispatches indicate a general knowledge of Midhat's views but no intimate connection' (Davison, p. 322). The same is true of the ambassador's private letters to Derby and Tenterden.

[4] Apparently a Bulgarian girl had come to Salonica to embrace the Muslim faith. Upon her arrival she was carried off, ostensibly for her own protection, by some Greeks and taken to the American Consulate. This caused great Muslim excitement in the city and a Muhammadan mob demanded the girl's release to them, and during the commotion the two consuls were killed. Blunt, the British consul at Salonica, at once wired to the British minister at Athens for the dispatch of a ship to protect British subjects, as the deceased German consul was a British national. Elliot supported this request and sent another to that part of the British Mediterranean fleet at Beirut to station itself at Smyrna (Izmir) and along the Syrian coast so that 'some of our ships of war should be frequently seen at all parts of the coast' (Elliot to Derby, teleg., 7 May 1876, PRO FO 146/1873). The fury of the Muslim population continued and was intermixed with Muhammadan anger and discontent at the Ottoman Government at Constantinople. Fearing further outbreaks of 'fanaticism' against Christians, the ambassadors of the Powers at Constantinople, including Elliot, requested their governments to send an armed gunboat through the Straits to the capital. Elliot also telegraphed for the British Mediterranean fleet to come to Besika Bay, just outside the Dardanelles. The guilty were quickly executed by the Turkish authorities. The reaction of the European governments to this regrettable event was greater, especially on the part of the German and French governments, than the response to the massacre of great numbers of Bulgarians, going on simultaneously, when the news of the latter became known. It is true that European opinion outside the Government response was greater than the latter to the Bulgarian atrocities and, of course, was greatest of all in Britain.

[5] Gontaut-Biron to Decazes, Berlin, confid., teleg., 6.35 p.m., 13 May 1876, *DDF* ii. 59–60. Russell's report generally confirms that of the French ambassador but omits any reference to his own belief that Derby or his Government would support the note (Russell to Derby, 13 May 1876, PRO FO 424/41, no. 1). The Emperor and the Crown Prince of Germany both wrote of this meeting to the Empress Augusta. The Crown Prince described Andrássy's proposals as moderate and the Austrian minister as opposing all ideas of occupation or acquisition of territory. He is described as having said that neither the Turks nor the insurgents deserved any sacrifices on the part of the Great Powers. Gorchakov is pictured as seeing Balkan affairs in a very gloomy light and advocating active measures. The meeting of the representatives of all six Powers was said to have been of forty-five minutes duration. 'It must not be overlooked, however, that the Austrians assert that Russian agents were constantly at work to promote insurrection in the Slavonian provinces of Turkey, though it may be taken for granted that the Emperor Alexander is altogether unaware of this' (Crown Prince of Germany to Empress Augusta, Berlin, 13 May 1876, RA H7/134).

[6] Russell to Derby, 13 May 1876, PRO FO 424/41, no. 1. Russell further reported that Gorchakov and Andrássy expressed a hope that Britain, France, and Italy would be able to respond before they left Berlin on Monday the fifteenth. This allowed less than two days for the transmission of the memorandum from Berlin, its consideration at Rome, Paris, and London, and a reply to be communicated back to Berlin. The thirteenth was a Saturday, and in Britain there had begun, as foreigners disparagingly referred to it, 'le weekend'. The part of the memorandum referring to more 'efficacious measures' was Gorchakov's contribution.

[7] Russell to Derby, private, 13 May 1876, Derby Pap. Two days later Russell wrote again that 'I have no doubt H.M. Govt. will support the new 5 points with France and Italy at Constantinople'. He supported adherence to the Berlin note as the next best thing to permitting the Turks and Montenegrins to fight it out, which the Tsar would not allow (Russell to Derby, 15 May 1876, ibid.).

[8] Blake writes that the telegram arrived at 5 p.m. (Disraeli, p. 588). Derby told Disraeli that it did not arrive until late at night (Derby to Disraeli, private, 16 May 1876, Derby Pap.). Derby, however, may have been stretching the truth in order to clear his department with the Prime Minister from the charge of laxity.

[9] Tenterden mem., 13 May 1876, ibid.

[10] Ponsonby to Disraeli, 13 May 1876, RA H7/127. A similar note was sent Derby (no. 128). The Queen was also fearful that the calling of the British fleet to Besika Bay to be at hand if the necessity to protect Christians at Constantinople arose might be a dangerous step. She alluded to the 'drifting' into the Crimean War, which drifting she wished to avoid now.

[11] Ponsonby to Disraeli, 13 May 1876, Disraeli Papers, Hughenden Archives, XIX/B/504.

[12] Disraeli to Queen Victoria, 14 May 1876, RA H7/136. There seems to be no written evidence that, in fact, he did so. He may have, however, verbally communicated with the Foreign Secretary as Derby wrote a letter defending his department. 'You might have received it [telegram containing Berlin memorandum] the first thing on Sunday morning; and to that extent there has been negligence. I do not suppose you would have wished to be called up for it in the night.

Some loss of time must occur in the case of long telegrams. This one would probably take an hour and a half to decipher.

I do not think the resident clerk can be blamed for being out for a couple of hours. The same man is on duty for a week and close confinement to the office would be impracticable' (Derby to Disraeli, private, 16 May 1876, Derby Pap.).

[13] Ponsonby to Queen Victoria, 14 May 1876, RA H7/137.

[14] Disraeli to Derby, 15 May 1876, Derby Pap.

[15] Derby to Russell, 15 May 1876, PRO FO 424/41, no. 14.

[16] Derby to Loftus, 15 May 1876, ibid., no. 15. The Foreign Secretary, with an extraordinary excess of reticence, did not think it necessary to indicate to Loftus his response or non-response to Shuvalov's suggestion. The Russian ambassador did indicate to Derby his expectation that such an affirmative reply from Britain on the armistice alone would be acceptable to the Russian Government (ibid.). This last derives support in a letter from Jomini, who was at Ems, to Giers, who had been left in charge of the Foreign Ministry at St. Petersburg. Jomini wrote that if England could be brought to support the armistice demand, that would suffice, and then, later, she might go further and agree to more (Jomini to Giers, Ems, 16 May 1876, Charles and Barbara Jelavich (eds.), Russia in the East, Leiden, 1959, pp. 7–8). In his report of his meeting with Derby, Shuvalov wrote that when he saw the Foreign Secretary so hostile to the five points he tossed them aside in an effort to save the armistice. Derby then seemed to respond favourably and in spite of his first denunciation of the armistice he told Shuvalov that he would support it at the Cabinet meeting on the following day (Shuvalov to Gorchakov, 19 May 1876, Seton Watson, Slav. Rev. iii. 665–6).

[17] Elliot to Derby, teleg., 11.55 p.m., 15 May 1876, PRO FO 424/41, no. 24. The telegram reached the foreign office at 8.50 p.m. of the sixteenth.

[18] According to Shuvalov, Derby knew already that Disraeli and Salisbury opposed the memorandum, and the Russian ambassador anticipated Britain's negative response, which he attributed to the influence of the Prime Minister and the Secretary of State for India (Shuvalov to Gorchakov, 19 May 1876, Seton-Watson, *Slav. Rev.* iii. 664–7).

[19] Shuvalov to Gorchakov, 19 May 1876 (Seton-Watson, *Slav, Rev.* iii. 664–5). Disraeli's attempt at secrecy failed as the news spread throughout Europe, including London, of the heated conversation which transpired and the Prime Minister's reference to treating Britain like Bosnia and Montenegro.

[20] Disraeli memorandum, 16 May 1876, MB vi. 24–6. Harris makes a passionate but misdirected denunciation of Disraeli's position. He attacks the Prime Minister's memorandum and its author as totally lacking 'any sense of reality' and exhibiting insensibility to the issues at stake. Disraeli's honesty is impugned and his purpose described as off the mark (Harris, pp. 307–8). Blake divines more accurately when he maintains that Disraeli was more concerned with raising Britain's influence in Europe than with buttressing Turkey, as asserting Britain's position as a Great Power, rather than showing himself to be an unqualified friend of the Porte (*Disraeli*, pp. 588–9, 596). Of course, to the extent that he felt British prestige and Ottoman integrity to be consistent, he would support both. Taffs supports this contention as well, but criticizes Disraeli for not making a constructive proposal in place of the one he rejected (*Ambassador to Bismarck*, pp. 146–7). Disraeli and Derby recognized this, but also realized that European proposals, however, intended, were prolonging the insurrection by encouraging the rebels. Though both wished to see the Porte crush the rebellion, they appeared to consider mediation fruitless or worse as long as neither side in the struggle had been able to win a decided advantage.

[21] Disraeli to Queen Victoria, 16 May 1876, RA H7/156. Disraeli also enclosed his memorandum.

[22] Hardy diary, 17 May 1876, Hardy, i. 365; same to same, 17 May 1876, Cran. Pap., HA43/T501/296. A year after the Cabinet, Carnarvon, the Colonial Secretary, thought that 'with most of us there was, I think, a desire to resist what we considered insolent dictation, and there was also a sort of reaction against Derby's extreme irresolution . . .' (Hardinge, ii. 329–30). Over four years later Northcote, the Chancellor of the Exchequer, put down his memories of the meeting (Andrew Lang, *Life, Letters, and Diaries of Sir Stafford Northcote*, 2 vols., London, 1890, ii. 101; Northc. Pap., Add. MS. 50063A). On Sunday, 15 May Russell saw both Andrássy and Gorchakov and questioned them as to the meaning of 'measures efficaces'. Andrássy replied that it only meant that if the proposed plans failed, other measures would be necessary two months hence. Gorchakov answered that they would be measures arranged by all the guaranteeing Powers, such as stationing ships at Turkish ports (Russell to Derby, secret, 15 May 1876, PRO FO 424/41, no. 29).

[23] Queen Victoria to Ponsonby, 16 May 1876, RA H7/154–5. The Queen, of course, already had Disraeli's 'reasons' which were contained in the memorandum he read to the Cabinet, a copy of which he had sent to Her Majesty at Windsor. Ponsonby was favourably impressed with the Prime Minister's explanation, as indicated in a note he sent to the Queen. 'These arguments of Mr. Disraeli are most forcible. . . . The conduct of the 3 northern powers in conferring without the others is certainly not friendly' (Ponsonby to Queen Victoria, 16 May 1876, RA H7/158. The Queen had Ponsonby write Disraeli of her reaction to his memorandum. 'It is true that the three Emperors have acted without taking the other powers into their deliberations. But their interests are more intimately and more vitally connected with the welfare of Turkey than those of England, France and Italy' (Ponsonby to Disraeli, 16 May 1876, *QVL* ii. 453–4). Derby's full explanation to Berlin concerning Britain's refusal to adhere is in Derby to

Russell, 19 May 1876, PRO FO 424/41, no. 58. Menebrea, the Italian minister in London, thought that the Government had refused the memorandum because they had not been consulted beforehand, in order to maintain their freedom of action, and so not to antagonize Britain's own Muslim subjects. Menebrea reported that in London it was thought that the memorandum had been drawn up by Russia aided by Bismarck (Menebrea to Melegari, 18 and 26 May 1876, Italian Foreign Ministry Archives, Rome, 113, 5 and 8; hereafter cited as IFM).

[24] Russell to Derby, teleg., Berlin, 16 May 1876, PRO FO 64/852. Russell's telegram was received in London during the night.

[25] Derby to Disraeli, 17 May 1876, Derby Pap. MacDonnell was probably trying to protect his chief at Berlin by telling Derby that Russell was opposed to the Berlin proposals.

[26] Russell to Derby, teleg., 18 May 1876, PRO FO 424/41, no. 37. In a letter sent by Disraeli to reassure and mollify the Queen, the Prime Minister wrote, in reference to the above dangers feared by Russell, that 'there is nothing in Lord Odo's remarks of significance. . . . The Turks will feel . . . in a manner they cannot mistake, that Your Majesty is not going to rush into rash enterprises to prop up their falling power. . . . It will now all end in a Congress. . . . And before the Congress meets, the policy of England and Germany should be decided, and the same' (Disraeli to Queen Victoria, 18 May 1876, QVL ii. 454). Ponsonby thought Russell's 'reasons are certainly good. . . . What will happen because England does not join? Will the 5 powers apply their remedies at once, or will they consent to a Congress?' (Ponsonby to Queen Victoria, 18 May 1876, RA H7/168).

[27] Buchanan to Derby, teleg., 3.50 p.m., 17 May 1876, ibid., no. 31.

[28] Derby to Buchanan, 18 May 1876, PRO FO 424/41, no. 38. When he met Beust and wrote the above, Derby may have already received Elliot's telegram which reached the Foreign Office on the eighteenth, and which reported the Ottoman Foreign Minister, Raschid Pasha, as speaking 'with indignation of the resolutions come to at Berlin' (Elliot to Derby, teleg., 18 May 1876, ibid., no. 39).

[29] Disraeli to Derby, 18 May 1876, Derby Pap.

[30] Derby to Russell, 19 May 1876, PRO FO 424/41, no. 60. When Russell delivered this information to Bülow, the latter replied that the Berlin meeting had only been considered to be 'a preliminary discussion' to enable Austria and Russia to agree on measures (Russell to Derby, 27 May 1876, PRO FO 424/41, no. 136).

[31] Derby to Russell, secret, 19 May 1876, PRO FO 244/297, no. 386. In his telegram to Russell of the seventeenth, Derby instructed him to express to Bismarck 'our sincere desire to act as far as possible, with the German Government. I have given full explanations to Count Münster' (Derby to Russell, teleg., 5.10 p.m., 17 May 1876, PRO FO 424/41, no. 34).

[32] It was at Andrássy's request that Germany, France, and Italy attempted to win some kind of British adhesion. See Decazes to Harcourt, teleg., 23 May 1876, DDF ii. 63.

[33] Decazes, who felt the Berlin proposal was moderate and who was disappointed at the absence of a British counter-proposal, went even further and unsuccessfully attempted to get the Turks to ask London to join the other Powers, as the Porte had done with the consular mission and the Andrássy note (Elliot to Derby, teleg., 29 May 1876, PRO FO 424/41, no. 138). Decazes also favoured a European conference. Melegari, the Italian Foreign Minister, tried to obtain an English assurance that she would advise the Porte to accept the armistice (Paget to Derby, 22 May 1876, ibid., no. 121).

[34] Derby to Elliot, 25 May 1876, ibid., no. 106.

[35] Elliot to Derby, teleg., 23 May 1876, ibid., no. 83.

[36] Buchanan to Derby, Budapest, teleg., 9.30 p.m., 26 May 1876, ibid., no. 112; same to same, strictly private and confid., teleg., 26 May 1876, ibid., no. 113. When Disraeli

read that Russell had expressed his personal opinion at Berlin that Britain would accept the Berlin memorandum, he manifested great indignation and referred to it as 'an unheard of step!' (Disraeli to Derby, 29 May 1876, MB vi. 28). Derby jumped to Odo's defence and expressed doubt as to his saying what had been ascribed to him. 'Russians are not scrupulous, and Gorchakov may probably enough have told the French ambassador and others that he had ascertained that we were ready to join, on the mere speculation that such a statement would be useful, It is possible that Russell may have allowed his personal opinion to be guessed at, but without more proof I cannot believe that he has gone farther' (Derby to Disraeli, 29 May 1876, Derby Pap.). Russell made little attempt to hide his opinion from Derby. 'I rather thought and hoped H.M. Govt. could have given a general support to the united policy of the other great Powers in principle, and would have afterwards raised objections and proposed amendments according to circumstances' (Russell to Derby, 20 May 1876, ibid.). The evidence supporting Odo's serious indiscretion is the French ambassador's report of the Berlin meeting, Andrássy's words to Buchanan, and the personal and admitted desire of Russell that Britain adhere to the Berlin memorandum. The evidence against his having so rashly acted is his own denial given after he had read a copy of Buchanan's report of his talk with Andrássy on 26 May. 'I was particularly careful not to express any personal opinion or to commit Her Majesty's Government one way or the other during the Conference, which I was the first to leave as soon as it was over' (Russell to Derby, 9 June 1876, PRO FO 424/41, no. 329). Russell returned Disraeli's contempt and perhaps was informed of the Prime Minister's reaction to his reported behaviour. He told Ponsonby, while on leave in England that 'The Tsar wished for peace—but this split [Britain's refusal of the Berlin memorandum] made it impossible for him to restrain the Servians—and thus came the war. If we had adopted a dull steady policy working with the rest—there would have been no outbreak. But our Government preferred the brilliant stroke of genius which has undoubtedly been heartily supported by the English nation' (Ponsonby to wife, Osborne, 11 Aug. 1876, Arthur Ponsonby, *Henry Ponsonby*, London, 1943, pp. 344–5).

[37] Derby to Buchanan, 1 June 1876, PRO FO 424/41, no. 155.

[38] This was the very offer Bismarck had made to England in January and Derby's first real response to it was nearly five months too late. In the interval Bismarck committed himself to supporting an Austro-Russian arrangement which would avoid a war.

[39] Russell to Derby, very confid. and secret, 26 May 1876, PRO FO 64/852, no. 234. Bismarck asked that his words about Austria and Russia be kept secret (ibid.).

[40] Russell to Derby, 27 May 1876, Derby Pap.

[41] Russell to Derby, secret, 27 May 1876, PRO FO 424/41, no. 135.

[42] There are some details concerning the deposition in a conversation between Onou, the Russian dragoman, and the Turkish Grand Vizier in an unsigned letter in the Jomini–Onou Papers. The letter seems to have been one from Onou to Ignatiev written on 22 (30 Western style) June (e.g. 3187, fos. 43–50). Derby thought it 'a fortunate event. This misgovernment of the late Sultan had been notorious and extreme; and his success for whatever he might turn out to be, could hardly do worse, and would probably do better' (Derby to Paget, 1 June 1876, PRO FO 424/41, no. 156). For the joy the deposition created in Turkey see Blunt to Derby, Salonica, 31 May 1876, PRO FO 146/1873, no. 68. Five days after his deposition Abdul Aziz committed suicide. Both Elliot and Onou agreed that it was suicide and not murder. Abdul Aziz's death loosened further the already slender hold on reality that his successor, Murad, maintained.

[43] Little was known as yet about events in Bulgaria.

[44] Derby to Russell, 19 May 1876, PRO FO 424/41, no. 58.

[45] Disraeli memorandum, 16 May 1876, MB vi. 24–6. It was at Constantinople, of course, where most, if not all, of the Turkish fleet was anchored. The biographer of Lord Carnarvon several times indicates that Disraeli hinted to the Cabinet that he was

ready to seize Constantinople if it were necessary. Hardinge gives no proof or evidence for this (ii. 330).

[46] Disraeli wrote to Derby, 'don't you think we ought to ascertain the exact naval force of For. Powers in the Mediterranean, and consider about strengthening our own?' (Disraeli to Derby, 20 May 1876, Derby Pap.). Hunt quickly reported that there were 27 ironclads in the Turkish fleet, seven of which were incomplete, and of the remaining 20 there was uncertainty as to how many were in commission or fit to be commissioned. Britain had 7 ironclads in Turkish waters, 2 of which were not powerful. As to reinforcement, the *Monarch* could reach Besika Bay in eleven days, the *Sultan* in twenty-three days, and the *Rupert* in thirty-five days. This would leave 6 ships in the Channel fleet. Hunt then gave a list of the other Powers.

| France | 7 ironclads | Italy | 6 ironclads |
|--------|-------------|-------|-------------|
|        | 9 unarmoured |       | 7 unarmoured |
| Russia | 1 ironclad | Austria | 5 ironclads |
|        | 3 unarmoured |       | 4 unarmoured |

The Admiralty was in the process of ascertaining the figures for Germany (Hunt to Disraeli, 20 May 1876, Disraeli Pap. xx/HU/77, 78).

[47] Disraeli to Queen Victoria, 24 May 1876, *QVL* ii. 454–5; diary, Hardy, i. 365. Because of an attack of gout, this Cabinet was held at Disraeli's London home. Hunt, at the time, was suffering equally, or more so, from the same affliction.

[48] Jomini to Giers, 26 May 1876 (Jelavich, *Russia in the East*, pp. 9–10). Giers was told to keep Gorchakov's view on entry into the Straits a secret. The Minister of Marine was merely to be told that Alexander II desired to act exclusively within the Mediterranean and in concert with the other Powers (ibid.). Gorchakov envisioned a sort of floating Red Cross acting under the Geneva Convention.

[49] Tenterden memorandum, 26 May 1876, Derby Pap. In the earlier part of the memorandum the Under-Secretary rightly concluded that the Treaty of 1841 prohibited foreign warships from entering the Straits while the Porte was at peace, save for light vessels attached to the foreign embassies at Constantinople. The Treaties of 1856 and 1871 supported the above but the last added a clause that enabled the Sultan in time of peace to open the Straits to war vessels of friendly Powers in case the Porte judged it necessary in order to enforce the Treaty of Paris of 1856. The Treaty of 1841 had been twice infringed. In 1849 during complications over Hungary the British and French fleets at Besika Bay, owing to bad weather, entered the Dardanelles but quickly returned to their original anchorage outside when the weather permitted. In September of 1853 the two fleets were summoned from Besika to Constantinople to protect Christians. Russia protested, but France and Britain declared that Turkey was no longer at peace. As there is no mention of it, Tenterden apparently forgot the warning contained in the British answer to the Berlin memorandum about violating the treaty rights of the Porte.

[50] Decazes to Bourgoing, teleg., 26 May 1876, *DDF* ii. 64. The Queen tended to agree. 'She does not either quite see why we strengthen our fleet so much in the Dardanelles. All that would seem really necessary is a few ships in different parts to protect the Christians' (Queen Victoria to Derby, 27 May 1876, *QVL* ii. 455). Lyons, the British ambassador in Paris, a level-headed and stable son of an Admiral, thought the English naval demonstration a good idea. 'I trust more to the impression produced by our naval force in the Mediterranean than to anything else to bring the other powers into accord with us upon equitable grounds' (Lyons to Derby, 6 June 1876, Lyons Papers, West Sussex Record Office, RAI). In Constantinople itself the British show of force made a great impression. The Spanish minister interpreted the British naval demonstration as an indication that London would go to war, with or without allies, to preserve Ottoman integrity (Conte to Calderon y Collantes, 26 June 1876, SFM, no. 83).

[51] Derby to Adams, 27 May 1876, PRO FO 424/41, no. 116; Derby to Disraeli, 28 May 1876, Derby Pap. Disraeli's irritation with Derby can be seen in his report of the above to the Queen. 'Mon. r d'Harcourt [the French ambassador] saw Ld. Derby on Saturday, and offered the idea of a conference. Lord Derby listened and asked for time, as usual, to consider it, then went into the country. . . . On Sunday he wrote to Mr. Disraeli. . . . Mr. Disraeli telegraphed instantly to Yr Majesty' (Disraeli to Queen Victoria, 30 May 1876, RA H7/204). Disraeli, admittedly, had here an ulterior motive. He saw a conference as the arrangement which might effect a desirable solution, and knew that Derby would oppose any such meeting. He also knew that the pressure from the Queen could sometimes cause Derby to move, and so he was trying to win Her Majesty's favour for a congress in the event that royal intervention upon the Foreign Secretary became desirable. This was not straightforward conduct by the Prime Minister, but such conduct could not usually get the Foreign Secretary to move. Derby's position on conferences, slightly exaggerated, was that they were only useful when they were unnecessary. He believed that if disagreement could not be arranged otherwise, international meetings could offer no solution. Shuvalov also asked Derby if he would agree to a conference, and was told that there was no basis for one—'the powers were not agreed beforehand' (Summary of Foreign Office conversations, 30 May 1876, RA H7/300).

[52] Disraeli to Derby, 29 May 1876, Derby Pap. The first half only of this letter is in MB vi. 28. The Prime Minister wrote also to the Prince of Wales. 'My own opinion is that the Congress will be held. If we are firm as well as conciliatory—it may not only secure peace but increase and establish the influence of England' (Disraeli to Prince of Wales, 29 May 1876, RA T6/96).

[53] Russell's secret dispatch of 26 May to Derby reporting Bismarck's admission that Gorchakov had proposed autonomy but that Andrássy had successfully objected to it, could have reached London in two days from Berlin. Two to four days was probably normal time. Depending on where the Prime Minister was, a further one or two days were required for the Foreign Office to send him a copy of an incoming dispatch. Disraeli, when he wrote to Derby on 29 May, either had not yet received his copy of Russell's report, or if he had, had not yet been able to read it. Of course, even if Disraeli and Gorchakov agreed on autonomy, Russia favoured and Britain opposed territorial increase for Serbia and Montenegro. Further, autonomy for Russia was merely a resting-place on the road to Slavic independence, while for Disraeli it would have been a long-term solution to the Eastern Question. Disraeli again wrote on 31 May supporting a conference and autonomy. 'I feel convinced it [a Congress] is the only practical solution in the long run. Conference or Congress on the basis of status quo; administering creation of new vassal states but sine qua non, no increase of the territory of any existing vassal state. If Bismarck agrees to this, the affair is finished, and for a generation' (Disraeli to Derby, 31 May 1876, Derby Pap.).

[54] Disraeli to Derby, 28 May 1876, MB vi. 29–30; in the Derby Papers the above is given as a memorandum by Disraeli of the same date.

[55] Disraeli to Queen Victoria, 29 May 1876, QVL ii. 455–6.

[56] Disraeli to Queen Victoria, 2 June 1876, ibid.; same to same, 2 June 1876, RA H7/221. Elliot was instructed to 'be watchful lest, under cover of protecting the Christian population or on some similar pretext, a proposal may be made to summon the fleets to Constantinople. Should such a proposal be made Y. Ex. will at once inform H.M. Govt. in order that they may determine on the course wh so grave an event . . . may call upon them to adopt' (Derby to Elliot, confid., 31 May 1876, PRO FO 146/1871, no. 341).

[57] See p. 499 n. 22. At approximately this time, Disraeli wrote of Derby that he was cool enough, 'but I am not sure of his firmness as of his salutary apathy' (Disraeli to Lady Bradford, 6 June 1876, ii. 607).

[58] Jomini thought the British rejection stemmed from wounded pride and further

considered that treatment of England as a second-rate Power had been a mistake (Jomini to Giers, 11 June 1876, Jelavich, *Russia in the East*, pp. 13–15).

## CHAPTER EIGHT

[1] White to Elliot, Belgrade, 21 Apr. 1876, PRO FO 424/40, no. 405.

[2] White to Derby, Belgrade, 28 Apr. 1876, ibid., no. 804. According to White, Ignatiev held sway at Belgrade. 'I have every reason to believe that the Prince of Servia has not, during the last seven months, taken a single step of any importance here without consulting that Ambassador [Ignatiev] previously, and that both his negotiations with the Prince of Montenegro, and the military preparations carried on here have been regularly and strongly recommended by General Ignatiev' (White to Elliot, 10 May 1876, ibid., no. 164).

[3] Loftus to Derby, St. Petersburg, 30 Apr. 1876, ibid. 441, nos. 4, 6.

[4] Holmes to Derby, 5 May 1876, ibid., no. 20.

[5] Buchanan to Derby, secret, 30 May 1876, ibid., no. 189. Major Gonne, the British military attaché at Vienna, who had travelled throughout the Balkans, felt 'convinced that it will require months rather than weeks to make the armed strength of Serbia anything better than a mob; in truth . . . only as irregulars would they [the Serbians] in my opinion, be able to contend against the Turks' (Gonne to Buchanan, 3 June 1876, ibid., no. 263). Wrede, the Austrian consul at Belgrade, told his British opposite number in Hungary that 'nothing could now prevent Servia from attacking Turkey' (Harris-Gastrell to Buchanan, 4 June 1876, ibid., 41, no. 292).

[6] Derby to White, teleg., 6 June 1876, ibid., no. 256. Austria also made an urgent appeal to France, which was complied with, to press Serbia from war (Lyons to Derby, 6 June 1876, ibid., no. 264). Derby, in accepting the Austrian request, told Beust that 'Her Majesty's Government could scarcely expect that any advice which Great Britain could give would meet, under present circumstances, with the same attention at Belgrade as the counsels of the other Powers, and if those counsels were seriously pressed, the action of Her Majesty's Agent would scarcely be required' (Derby to Buchanan, 7 June 1876, ibid., no. 267).

[7] Lyons to Derby, 6 June 1876, ibid., no. 266. Almost simultaneously with the Turkish suspension of hostilities, Austria, Germany, and Russia officially announced the postponement of the execution of delivery of the Berlin memorandum.

[8] Derby to Disraeli, 2 June 1876, Disraeli Pap. xx/S/1136. Loftus confirmed Gorchakov's desire for an autonomous Bosnia-Hercegovina arranged by a European conference (Loftus to Derby, St. Petersburg, 7 June 1876, Derby Pap.); so did Odo Russell at Berlin (Russell to Derby, teleg., 5 June 1876, PRO FO 64/852). Decazes, who was presumed by London to be acting for Russia, suggested to the British a new version of the Berlin memorandum to which both England and the other five Powers might agree. Tenterden wrote a negative memorandum for Derby on the French suggestion, to which the Foreign Secretary entirely concurred (Lyons to Derby, 7 June 1876, ibid. 424/41, no. 286; Tenterden memorandum, 8 June 1876, ibid. 27/2164).

[9] Disraeli to Lady Bradford, 7 June 1876, MB vi. 31. Elliot was also quite happy. 'I cannot tell you the delight it has been to find H.M. Govt. adopting the independent line they have followed . . .' (Elliot to Tenterden, private, 9 June 1876, Tenterden Pap., PRO FO 363/1).

[10] Disraeli to Queen Victoria, 7 June 1876, *QVL* ii. 457–8.

[11] Queen Victoria to Duke of Edinburgh, Balmoral, 7 June 1876, RA H7/257; Queen Victoria to Disraeli, Balmoral, 8 June 1876, *QVL* ii. 458–60.

[12] This meeting took place, and in a note which is pure Disraeli, the latter refers to it.

'Schouvaloff was with Lord Derby, yesterday, as I had arranged. . . . I think things look as well as possible; but we must be prepared yet for strange vicissitudes and trials of our mettle. So much the better! These are politics worth managing' (Disraeli to Lady Bradford, 13 June 1876, Zetland, ii. 64).

[13] At the beginning of January 1875 Salisbury, with Disraeli's support, instructed Northbrook, the viceroy, to make arrangements to place a British agent at Herat or Kandahar in Afghanistan. The purpose of this step was to provide the Indian Government with reliable information, especially in view of Russian advances toward Afghanistan. Northbrook opposed his instructions and did not immediately act upon them. In the spring of 1875 there was an Anglo-Russian exchange of views on Afghanistan during which London indicated that it attached the highest importance to the integrity of Afghanistan and reserved to itself complete liberty of action to secure it. When Northbrook resigned his post, he was replaced as viceroy by Lytton. In February 1876, before leaving for India, the latter was given secret instructions from Salisbury to arrange for a British mission to go to Kabul. Upon his arrival in India, Lytton, as instructed, requested the ameer to receive a temporary British mission. Sher Ali refused to do so, but did agree to talk further about it.

[14] Shuvalov to Gorchakov, teleg., 10 June 1876 (Seton-Watson, *Slav. Rev.* iii. 669–70); Gorchakov to Shuvalov, Ems, teleg., 10 June 1876, ibid. 670; Shuvalov to Gorchakov, 10 June 1876, ibid. 670–1; same to same, 11 June 1876, ibid. 672–5; same to same, 11 June 1876, ibid. 675. Shuvalov puzzled over the motive for Disraeli's overture and gave Gorchakov a list of possibilities: a desire to separate Austria and Russia, a wish to take Austria's place in the concert of the three, simply an attempt to close with Russia so England would influence any subsequent decisions, or, as seemed most probable to Shuvalov, that after collecting the popularity from refusing the Berlin memorandum and making a fleet demonstration, England desires to return to a wiser policy for the ensurance of peace and chooses for that end a direct entente with Russia. There were more possibilities the Russian ambassador might have added. The Spanish representative at Constantinople believed as Disraeli did that the insurgents hoped only for independence (Conte to Calderon y Collantes, Constantinople, 13 June 1876, SFM, no. 77).

[15] Tenterden memorandum, 8 June 1876, Derby Pap. Sanderson, a clerk in the Foreign Office and private secretary to Derby, and who would become Permanent Under-Secretary, defended Russell but did agree with Disraeli that 'a reminder of the importance of a good understanding with Germany would no doubt do no harm' (ibid.).

[16] Jomini's contemporary reaction squares with that of Harris, who believed that Disraeli was merely trying to destroy the Dreikaiserbund. Jomini felt it was necessary to calm and flatter London in order to bring her back to the European concert and he refers to Gorchakov's not following up Disraeli's advances because of Britain's cutting policy toward Russia. Jomini interprets Disraeli's overtures as stemming from pure jealousy of the entente of the three Imperial courts and his desire to destroy it as it reduced the role of Britain (Jomini to Giers, Ems, 11 June 1876, Jelavich, *Russia in the East,* pp. 13–15). See Harris, pp. 357–9. Disraeli could have known of Austro-Russian differences at Berlin while producing the Berlin memorandum, and may have hoped to replace Austria as Russia's negotiating partner. 'I am told on very good authority that Prince Gorchakov wishes for a General Conference in the hope of getting his own plan adopted, which Count Andrássy had successfully resisted and rejected in the Berlin Conference. . . . [Gorchakov's plan] as far as I know it is based on the autonomy of the states under the suzerainty of the Sultan' (Russell to Derby, teleg., 5 June 1876, PRO FO 424/41, no. 235.

[17] Russell to Derby, private, 10 June 1876, Derby Pap. If Disraeli had been unaware of Bismarck's pro-Austrian sympathies, then when he learned of them, he might have decided to throw over any agreement with Russia. Of course, if the Prime Minister

knew of them previously, which was possible from Russell's private letters from Berlin, then he might have moved toward Russia in order to raise Britain's desirability in Bismarck's eyes by showing him that England had other options aside from isolation or a German understanding.

[18] Derby to Elliot, 13 June 1876, PRO FO 424/41, no. 334. Derby's last paragraph may have reflected information supplied by Elliot. 'Here I have to take pains to make the Turks feel that they must not expect too much, and to warn them from taking any course upon the assumption of receiving national support from us. Our present popularity amongst Turks ... is boundless and a word of advice from H.M. Govt. will have great weight' (Elliot to Tenterden, private, 9 June 1876, Tenterden Pap., PRO FO 363/1).

[19] Derby to Loftus, 14 June 1876, PRO FO 424/41, no. 341. To Decazes's proposal of a new European note to the Porte, Derby replied in the negative and added such effort could more usefully be used in restraining Serbia and Montenegro, in advising the insurgents to return home, and in refraining from proposals which seem to offer political advantages to them. (Derby to Lyons, 14 June 1876, ibid., no. 343). To Shuvalov, Derby explained that if the Turks failed to suppress the rebels they would have to grant an autonomous status to them, but if the Porte was successful then the insurgents would be forced to moderate their demands and accept an arrangement similar to the one given the Cretans after the revolt there in 1866–7 (Derby to Loftus, 14 June 1876, ibid., no. 341).

[20] Derby to Buchanan, confid., 22 June 1876, ibid., no. 430. Gorchakov informed both France and Austria of Disraeli's offer to Shuvalov. If Andrássy knew of it by 21 June, it may have produced his above appeal for Anglo-Austrian cooperation.

[21] Having received a report of Derby's talks with Shuvalov, Ponsonby made a suggestion to the Queen. 'We should endeavour if possible to avoid being held up as the protectors of the Turks against the insurgents, as the Turks are too anxious to do. As in that case the Russians will appear as the protectors of the oppressed Christians and will openly—as they even now do secretly—give them aid' (Ponsonby to Queen Victoria, Balmoral, 18 June 1876, RA H8/55). In response to this, the Queen had Ponsonby write to Derby of this danger and pointed out that Britain has 'no intention of making the state of the Ottoman Empire a cause of quarrel with Russia' (Ponsonby to Derby, 18 June 1876, QVL ii. 464–5; same to same, Balmoral, 19 June 1876, RA H8/57). This last, which was for the information of the Turks, was about the last thing that Derby needed to be told.

[22] See the Shuvalov–Gorchakov correspondence in Seton-Watson, Slav. Rev. iii. 669–81; Gontaut-Biron to Decazes, Ems, 15 June 1876, DDF ii. 71; Jomini to Giers, Ems, 15 June 1876, Jelavich, Russia in the East, pp. 15–16; same to same, Jugenheim, 29 June 1876, ibid., pp. 18–19. Shuvalov's charm had by this point won a friend in Lady Derby who was indiscreet enough to confirm the Russian ambassador's belief that Derby was upset and paralysed by Russia's willingness and expectation that England act with her (Shuvalov to Alexander II, 22 June 1876, Seton-Watson, Slav. Rev. iii. 678–9; Shuvalov to Gorchakov 27 June 1876, ibid. 681). Gorchakov's letter or dispatch proposed autonomy for Bosnia-Hercegovina, a port for Montenegro, and Little Zvornik to Serbia (Derby to Lyons, 21 June 1876, PRO FO 146/1873, no. 633). On 16 June Serbia and Montenegro signed an alliance to go to war, with the former obtaining Bosnia and the latter, Hercegovina, in the case of victory. Nicholas of Montenegro did not tell Russia of his negotiations with Serbia (Mackenzie, pp. 87–91).

[23] Disraeli to Derby, 24 June 1876, MB vi. 34–5. At this talk Shuvalov attempted to disarm British suspicions by emphasizing that autonomy would still leave sovereignty over Bosnia-Hercegovina with the Porte. For Montenegro, Shuvalov said, a port was not necessary, only 'a little garden to grow cabbages and potatoes' (ibid.). According to Lady Derby, Disraeli wrote to Derby after the former's talk with Shuvalov that he was satisfied with the Russian ambassador's explanations regarding autonomy (Shuvalov to

Gorchakov, 27 June 1876, Seton-Watson, *Slav. Rev.* iii. 681).

²⁴ Disraeli to Queen Victoria, 25 June 1876, RA H8/69.

²⁵ Shuvalov to Derby, 27 June 1876, PRO FO 424/41, no. 486 and enclosures.

²⁶ Shuvalov to Gorchakov, 27 June 1876 (Seton-Watson, *Slav. Rev.* iii. 681). I could find no corroborating evidence to back up Lady Derby's explanation. On 27 June, however, Beust called at the Foreign Office, directed by Andrássy, who was attempting to frustrate an Anglo-Russian deal arranging autonomy for Bosnia-Hercegovina. Beust gave Andrássy's opinion that the mixed population of Bosnia-Hercegovina made autonomy an impossible solution. Further, that if granted, other areas such as Bulgaria would demand it, and finally it would not restrain Serbia and Montenegro, who were preparing for war to annex Bosnia-Hercegovina, not to win autonomy for them (Derby to Buchanan, 27 June 1876, PRO FO 424/41, no. 482).

²⁷ Derby to Loftus, 28 June 1876, ibid., no. 487.

²⁸ Derby to Shovalov, 29 June 1876, ibid., no. 487A. Harris writes that the thought and phraseology of the letter were Disraeli's (Harris, pp. 365–6). This is incorrect. The letter reflected the observation and reactions of the Levantine consuls, Elliot and Tenterden, not Disraeli. The latter was more willing to grant autonomy than Derby.

²⁹ Jomini to Giers, Jugenheim, 29 June 1876, Jelavich, *Russia in the East*, pp. 18–19. Something close to this is Harris's conclusion. He argues that Disraeli only 'toyed with the Russians' and then, it seems to me, allows his feelings for Disraeli to overcome his judgement. He writes that Disraeli 'had terminated the sterile discussion by a letter [Derby to Shuvalov of 29 June, see p. 507 n. 25] of patent malice, brazen lies and studied insult' (Harris, p. 367). The meager evidence indicates that Disraeli favoured the proposals in Gorchakov's letter.

³⁰ Crown Princess of Germany to Queen Victoria, 13 June 1876, *QVL* ii. 464; Crown Prince of Germany to Queen Victoria, 13 June 1876, Disraeli Pap. xix/B/547; same to same, 13 June 1876, Derby Pap. The Queen sent a copy of the letters to Disraeli, who in turn gave one to Derby. In her answer to her daughter's letter, the Queen made reference to the lack of an active British policy beyond encouraging Turkey to reform and a disinclination 'to be excluded from all councils and discussions and then be asked to join' (Queen Victoria to Crown Princess of Germany, Balmoral, 13 June 1876, RA H8/21). The Italian minister in London thought that Britain's refusal of the memorandum had produced division among Austria, Russia, and Germany. Bismarck is described as moving closer toward London, Austria as abandoning the memorandum, and Russia as left in isolation, save for France (Menebrea to Melegari, 16 June 1876, IFM 113, 16).

³¹ Ponsonby to Disraeli, 16 June 1876, Disraeli Pap. xix/B/549; same to same, 16 June 1876, Derby Pap.; Queen Victoria to Disraeli, 16 June 1876, RA H8/41; same to same, teleg., 16 June 1876, ibid., no. 42.

³² Derby to Disraeli, secret, 17 June 1876, Derby Pap.

³³ Disraeli to Queen Victoria, 18 June 1876, RA H8/53. As this was the Queen's reply to her daughter and son-in-law, Ponsonby tactfully suggested the Queen only incorporate Disraeli's remarks in her reply rather than to communicate the Prime Minister's letter 'which would have the appearance of an official communication' (Ponsonby to Queen Victoria, 20 June 1876, RA H8/59).

³⁴ Derby and Tenterden memorandums, 17 June 1876, Derby Pap. This seemed to be partly true of Bismarck now, but was not the case in the previous January. But even presently Bismarck asked, not for a programme in advance, but an idea now. In her reply to the Crown Prince the Queen wrote that 'Mr. Disraeli hints, simply as a remark and not as a reproach, that considering Prince Bismarck's desire to maintain confidential relations with us, he is sorry that the Prince joined the Berlin note without even stipulating that England should have a voice in the matter. I must repeat that my ministers are most ready to act with Prince Bismarck' (Queen Victoria to Crown Prince of Germany, Balmoral, 29 June 1876, RA H8/99).

³⁵ See p. 506 no. 19.

³⁶ Derby to Ponsonby, 20 June 1876, RA H8/62; same to same, 20 June 1876, MB vi. 33–4.

³⁷ Derby, at Austria's request, directed White to warn Serbia against war.

³⁸ Elliot to Derby, 27 May 1876, PRO FO 424/41, no. 242. The British representative at Budapest reported that his Turkish colleague had told him that in a talk with Andrássy, the latter suggested that the Porte 'could easily settle with Montenegro and that then she should turn all her force immediately against Servia, which had, in spite of his excellency's counsels, armed to the teeth, and seemed determined to move' (Harris-Gastrell to Buchanan, Budapest, 2 June 1876, ibid., no. 248).

³⁹ Loftus to Derby, 7 June 1876, Derby Pap.

⁴⁰ Holmes to Elliot, Mostar, 1 June 1876, PRO FO 424/41, no. 389. Holmes's view influenced that of both Elliot and Derby. But while Holmes continued to believe what he wrote, Andrássy continued to affirm that real reforms, and not autonomy or independence, were the desire of the insurgents (Buchanan to Derby, teleg., 18 June 1876, ibid., no. 414). Andrássy believed that the mixed population of Bosnia-Hercegovina made it unfit for autonomy or independence (Ffrench to Derby, teleg., 20 June 1876, ibid., no. 417).

⁴¹ Monson to Derby, Ragusa, 14 June 1876, ibid., no. 428. Derby, after receiving this, instructed Buchanan to speak to Andrássy, and say that pacification was only possible if the Austrian frontier were sealed and the Pan Slavist committees suppressed (Derby to Buchanan, 24 June 1876, ibid., no. 451).

⁴² Elliot to Derby, teleg., 23 June 1876, ibid., no. 474. A telegram was therefore sent by the Porte (Elliot to Derby, teleg., 26 June 1876, ibid., no. 417). The Ottoman Government's offer to Montenegro was ambiguous in that no specific territorial concession was mentioned (same to same, teleg., 24 June 1876, ibid., no. 453). Derby apparently did not officially sanction Elliot's suggestion to the Porte but did send the following letter to Elliot. 'I recently mentioned to the Turkish Ambassador ... that Her Majesty's Government strongly advised the Turkish Government to endeavour to make terms with Montenegro. ... A slight rectification of the frontier might be promised in the event of the Prince of Montenegro exerting his influence to put an end to the insurrection' (Derby to Elliot, 27 June 1876, ibid., no. 479).

⁴³ Thompson, i 307–10. As Harris points out, there were fear and distrust of Disraeli. 'By the first of July those fears of the *Daily News* and *Spectator* as to what Disraeli might do had made a number of conquests among the periodical writers. Notable among those who expressed their misgivings were John Morley in the *Fortnightly Review* and Walter Bagehot in the *Economist*' (*Horrors*, pp. 94–6).

⁴⁴ Thompson, i 290–2.

# CHAPTER NINE

¹ Lytton to Corry, private, 10 July 1876, Disraeli Pap. xx/Ly/232. Dilke, after talking with Bourke, concluded that 'Dizzy is his own Foreign Secty' (Dilke to wife, [?] July 1876, Dilke Pap., Add. MS. 43903, xxx). All this leaves little room for Tenterden, which is a mistake, as the Permanent Under-Secretary was an able and perceptive individual. He knew Derby well enough, and for that matter Disraeli also, to guage and predict the Foreign Secretary's line. One's first reaction is to rate highly his influence, through his many memorandums, on the making of policy, but this is probably mistaken. Derby, by 1876, constantly asked his advice on matters great and small, and once given, invariably accepted it. His reactions to both the Andrássy note and the Berlin memorandum were not without their weight on Derby and Disraeli. But what he actually did was

to draw up, with skill and accuracy, the range of predictable reactions by the Foreign Secretary, saving the latter the time required to formulate reasons why something should not be done, and occasionally why something should. Derby came to lean more and more heavily on a man who could mirror and sound his own opinions, and then formulate them so well. The Foreign Secretary also trusted Tenterden, who was very discreet.

[2] Hardy diary, 12 July 1876, Cran. Pap., HA 43/T501/296. Eventually the solution reached was Disraeli's elevation to the House of Lords with Northcote replacing him as leader in the House of Commons.

[3] Blake, *Disraeli*, pp. 574–5.

[4] To this list, of course, could now be added the many Russian volunteers who flocked to Serbia as war approached, General Cherniaiev being the most important. Jomini wrote of him to Giers, that for legal form, the Russian Government rages against him, but that if war occurs, we would not be displeased to see a man of his ability at the head of the Serbian army. Officially, he wrote, we must condemn Cherniaiev's conduct, because what he has done violates the law (Jomini to Giers, 26 May 1876, Jelavich, *Russia in the East*, pp. 9–10).

[5] There was a two-year delay in the execution of the firman while the Porte attempted to win the concurrence of the Greek Patriarch to the change. According to Elliot, Ignatiev attempted to obtain the withdrawl of the 1870 firman in order to maintain his influence among the Greeks and create Bulgarian discontent with the Porte. When the firman was executed in 1872, Ignatiev openly proclaimed his joy for the Bulgarians and attempted to win the credit for the Turkish concession which he had tried to block (Elliot memorandum, 30 Mar. 1872, PRO FO 78/2216). Andrássy, apparently to counter Ignatiev, had favoured an independent Bulgarian church organization (Rumbold to Granville, Pera, 1 May 1872, ibid. 2217, no. 115).

[6] Gladstone to Granville, 2 Jan. 1873, Ramm, ii. 368–9.

[7] Sumner, pp. 108–116; *Horros*, pp. 13–15.

[8] Dupuis to Elliot, Adrianople, 20 Nov. 1875, PRO FO 424/39, no. 523.

[9] White to Elliot, Belgrade, 4 Dec. 1875, ibid., no. 565. After the insurrection of May 1876 had occurred, Elliot talked with the recently dismissed Ottoman governor of that district in Bulgaria. 'There is not, he said [the Ottoman governor] the shadow of a doubt that the Russian consul at Philippopoli was the prime mover and agent of the Revolutionary Committee by which the movement was directed, and his brother is at this moment a leader among the insurgents' (Elliot to Derby, 17 May 1876, ibid. 424/41, no. 173). Dwight describes the Bulgarian insurrection as the 'creation of the Servian agitators' (Dwight, *Turkish Life in War Time*, pp. 22–4).

[10] See *Horrors*, pp. 16–20; M. MacDermott, *A History of Bulgaria* (London, 1962), 259–86. Djordjević writes that the rising began in April (Djordjević, p. 134).

[11] *Horrors*, pp. 20–1. Dupuis at Adrianople was a little closer to the area of the insurrection than Brophy at Bourgas or Reade at Rustchuk. But Dupuis was nearly 100 miles from the scene of most of the Bulgarian rising and Ottoman suppression, and further, as Harris points out, he was a victim of paralysis and could not go easily himself to the scene of the troubles to substantiate the reports he received. Harris mentions that one of Dupuis's informants was a railway inspector and another a Jewish missionary, but the vice-consul's own dragoman also sent him news from Philippopolis (*Horrors*, pp. 29–30). In fact, later on in July Dupuis did go to Philippopolis and reported first hand.

[12] Elliot to Derby, 9 May 1876, PRO FO 424/41, no. 11.

[13] In Elliot's covering note of 12 May, enclosing Dupuis's of 9 May, the ambassador wrote that 'as soon as a Government is formed here [Constantinople] to which I can present representations, I shall not fail to communicate to it Mr. Kyriatzi's [Dupuis's dragoman] reports, and to point out the danger of allowing the local authorities to act as those of Eski Zagara [in arming irregulars] have apparently been doing' (Elliot to

Derby, 12 May 1876, ibid., no. 46). In Elliot's dispatch of 15 May is enclosed Dupuis's of 12 May in which the vice-consul refers in one line to unconfirmed accounts of Bashi-Bazouks laying waste to the country. But in the same report, Dupuis also writes of 'horrible cruelties' done to Turks by Bulgarians (Elliot to Derby, 15 May 1876, ibid., no. 80).

[14] Elliot to Derby, 24 May 1876, ibid., no. 179 with enclosures from Dupuis of 16 and 19 May 1876. These dispatches, as well as one from Reade at Rustchuk, were received at the Foreign Office on 2 June. 'There is a grave matter here which I should bring to your Excellency's knowledge, and that is the arming of the Mussulmans and Circassians in the vilayet—and the letting loose of the latter on the Bulgarians simply reported to be in revolt! The lawless character of these Circassians is notorious . . .' (Reade to Elliot, Rustchuk, 23 May 1876, ibid., no. 185). In a dispatch sent four days later, Reade repeated his warning that the arming and use of Circassians would drive peaceful people into open revolt. 'We are daily hearing of the grossest acts of violence on their part' (Reade to Derby, Rustchuk, 27 May 1876, ibid., no. 260). This dispatch was receive by the Foreign Office on 7 June.

[15] Derby to Elliot, 6 June 1876, ibid., no. 246. Again on 4 July Derby approved Elliot's repeated warning to the Grand Vizier about irregular cruelties in Bulgaria (Derby to Elliot, 4 July 1876, ibid. 424/42, no. 55). Until the end of June the Foreign Office had given Elliot no other indication of its views or wishes on Bulgaria.

[16] Elliot to White, private, 26 May 1876, White Papers, PRO FO 364/7; H. Sutherland Edwards, Sir William White (London, 1902), pp. 99–100.

[17] Elliot to Derby, 8 June 1876, PRO FO 424/41, mo. 365. On the back of this dispatch the Foreign Secretary minuted, 'Important D.'

[18] Elliot to Derby, 19 June 1876, ibid., no. 507; Reade to Derby, Rustchuk, 18 June 1876, ibid. 42, no. 1 and enclosure. There is no doubt that many of the Bulgarian and Turkish peasants in Bulgaria hated one another, and as Green, the American military attaché at Constantinople, has pointed out there was 'little to choose' between them 'in the matter of cruelty to the opposition race' (Greene to Stoughton, 29 Jan. 1878, enclosed in Stoughton to Evarts, 15 Feb. 1878, U.S. State Dept., no. 7).

[19] Harris writes that when Washburn and Long failed to draw a sympathetic response from Elliot, they approached Sir Philip Francis, the British consul-general and a man not particularly friendly with the ambassador. At Francis's suggestion, Long submitted the Bulgarian information to the correspondents of the Daily News and The Times (Horrors, pp. 42–3). This account is corroborated by a report from Maynard, the U.S. minister in Constantinople. Washburn and Long are described as having received letters and verbal reports from Bulgaria about the atrocities. When Elliot returned their information as not 'sufficiently authentic', Francis 'suggested an appeal through the press to the people of England'. Long's statement was given to Pears of the Daily News (Maynard to Fish, Constantinople, 21 Nov. 1876, U.S. State Dept., vol. 30, no. 108).

[20] Sir E. Pears, Forty Years in Constantinople (London, 1910), p. 16. Pears was both a lawyer and a correspondent. His account written from memory long after most of the events described is not a reliable narrative. Not following my own suspicions, I have used it here.

[21] Horrors, pp. 32–3; W. N. Medlicott 'Vice Consul Dupuis' 'Missing' Dispatch of 23 June 1876', Journal of Modern History, iv, no. 1 (Mar. 1932), 44–5. For Giers's reaction to events in Bulgaria see Jelavich, Russia in the East, pp. 16–17. No 'previous information' suggested that 60 villages had been destroyed and 12,000 old men, women, and children had been killed.

[22] Hansard, 26 June 1876, 3rd ser. 230, 385–8, 424–46.

[23] Derby to Elliot, 28 June 1876, PRO FO 424/42, no. 2. Number 2 is the Foreign Office confidential print number of this dispatch. The actual office number of the dispatch is given as 425. Medlicott in his article on Dupuis's missing dispatch gives the FO

number as 428 ('Dupuis', 46). Although the normal time for a dispatch to reach Constantinople from London was between nine and twelve days, Medlicott writes that this particular one only left London between 6 and 10 July and reached Constantinople on 20 July.

[24] Elliot to White, 29 June 1876, White Pap., PRO FO 364/7; same to same, 4 July 1876, ibid., Edwards, White, pp. 100–1. This seems to contradict Elliot's feelings as expressed in his private letter to White of 26 May. See p. 510, m. 16. Elliot's earlier concern was that irregulars might provoke insurrection. Here it is that their use might stamp it out. In both instances suppression of insurrection was paramount.

[25] Derby to Ponsonby, 3 July 1876, *QVL* ii. 467. Disraeli spoke of irregular activity as so far unauthenticated 'and that we must wait for further information' (Ponsonby memorandum, 8 July 1876, ibid. 470).

[26] *Hansard*, 3 July 1876, 3rd ser. 230, 873–83, 847, 852.

[27] Queen Victoria to Ponsonby, [? 4] July 1876, RA H8/116.

[28] Ponsonby to Derby, 8 July 1876, *QVL* ii. 470–1; Ponsonby to Queen Victoria, 8 July 1876, RA H8/127. On the point of English sympathy for Turkey, Ponsonby wrote that 'Many [in Britain] believe that the collapse of the Turkish empire is inevitable and imminent, and that it will be damaging to the prestige of England if we are put forward as the protectors of Turkey and it falls to pieces' (ibid.).

[29] Derby to Ponsonby, 10 July 1876, *QVL* ii. 471; same to same, 10 July 1876, RA H8/135. There were others who had little sympathy for the oppressed Christian Slavs. 'If this should end in a [Muslim] movement against the Christians, I fear the popular voice in this country [Britain] will be influenced by religious sympathy and people will deem the European Christians angels and martyrs instead of the vilest scoundrels in the world' (Hammond to Layard, 29 June 1876, Lay. Pap., Add. MS. 38955, xxv). In a Commons debate on 3 July, Dr. Kenealy, who was not a Turkish sympathizer, spoke of the Eastern Christians as 'about the worst specimens of humanity extant' (*Hansard*, 3 July 1876, 3rd ser. 230, 882–3).

[30] *Horrors*, p. 47.

[31] Derby to Elliot, 13 July 1876, PRO FO 424/42, no. 440 and enclosures.

[32] Ibid. Exaggerated figures have persisted to the present. Djordjević has estimated that 80 villages were burned, 200 pillaged, and 30,000 Bulgarians killed (Djordjević, p. 134).

[33] Derby to Elliot, teleg., 3.40 p.m., 13 July 1876, ibid., no. 141.

[34] *Hansard*, 10 July 1876, 3rd ser. 230, 1168–70, 1174, 1180–6; Mundella to Leader, 10 July 1876, Mundella Papers, Sheffield University Library. In the debate, Disraeli had said that in connection with the atrocities, the Government was in close communication with its consuls at Belgrade, Ragusa, and Cetinje. Britain had no consul at Cetinje and, as Ashley pointed out, all three places were remote from the affected district in Rumelia. Ashley then asked if the Government had any information from its consuls at Adrianople and Philippopolis. In the last-named place there was no British consul. Disraeli replied that from those places as well the government had received no reports confirming the particulars of specific atrocities which appeared in the *Daily News*.

[35] Hartington to Grant Duff, 12 July 1876, Grant Duff Papers, Orford, Suffolk.

[36] Derby to Disraeli, 13 July 1876, Derby Pap.; Queen Victoria to Disraeli, teleg., 13 July 1876, ibid.; Disraeli to Derby, 13 July 1876, ibid.; Disraeli to Lady Bradford, 13 July 1876, Zetland, ii. 69–70.

[37] Reade to Derby, Rustchuk, 18 June 1876, PRO FO 424/42, no. 1.

[38] Disraeli to Derby, 14 July 1876, MB vi. 44–5; same to same, 14 July 1876, Derby Pap.

[39] The same day Disraeli exploded to Derby, he wrote to Queen Victoria that 'Lord Shaftesbury is always ready to place philanthropy at the aid of faction' (Disraeli to Queen Victoria, 14 July 1876, *QVL* ii. 471–2).

[40] Disraeli to Derby, 14 July 1876, MB vi. 44–5.

[41] Derby to Disraeli, private, 14 July 1876, Disraeli Pap. xx/S/1139; Tenterden memorandum, 14 July 1876, ibid. 1139a; Derby to Tenterden, 14 July 1876, Derby Pap. In the Derby Papers the copy of the letter of explanation from Derby to Disraeli is dated 15 rather than 14 July.

[42] Thompson, i. 347–9; Wirthwein, pp. 56–7; *Horrors*, pp. 111–12. Among the signers of the memorial were Joseph Chamberlain, Joseph Cowen, A. J. Mundella, and Sir Wilfrid Lawson. Derby's reply to the second deputation introduced by Lewis Farley heading the 'League in aid of the Christians in Turkey' was a 'chilling and contemptuous [one]. . . . He met the suggestion for the adoption of a policy of emancipation [of the Balkan Christians] . . . as something that was not practical' (Thompson, i. 347–9).

[43] *Horrors*, pp. 111–12; R. Walling, *Diaries of John Bright* (New York, 1931), p. 383. Derby was also pleased with the effect of his words to the deputations. 'I hear that the line I took to the deputation has put out the plans of the opposition a good deal. They had got all ready for a declaration of [parliamentary] war on the Turks . . . and on the Cabinet. . . . I knew it would be so and meant to spoil their game' (Derby to Disraeli, 18 July 1876, Derby Pap.).

[44] Disraeli to Queen Victoria, 14 July 1876, *QVL* ii. 471–2.

[45] Elliot to Derby, 6 July 1876, PRO FO 424/42, no. 158 and two enclosures from Dupuis. On the day that his dispatch arrived in London, Elliot wrote a private letter to Tenterden, asking him to tell Derby that he had been ill for two days and though 'there were abominable atrocities committed . . . none of the particular cases of wholesale slaughter as given in the newspapers can in the least be accepted as trustworthy'. As to the *Daily News* accounts, Elliot wrote that they came from U.S. missionaries, who were good men, but 'ultra Bulgarian' and certain, therefore, to colour highly the suffering of their protégés (Elliot to Tenterden, private, 14 July 1876, PRO FO 78/2460). Musurus Pasha, the Turkish ambassador in London, attempted to mitigate and explain the atrocity reports (Ottoman minister for foreign affairs to Musurus Pasha, 17 July 1876, PRO FO 424/42, no. 233).

[46] Derby minute on Elliot's no. 158 of 6 July to Derby.

[47] Elliot to Derby, teleg., 14 July 1876, PRO FO 424/42, no. 183.

[48] Derby to Dupuis, teleg., 14 July 1876, ibid., no. 180. The next day Derby telegraphed to Elliot to send one of the secretaries of the Constantinople Embassy, or Wrench, the vice-consul, to accompany Dupuis (Derby to Elliot, teleg., 15 July 1876, ibid., no. 198). On 19 July Baring left Constantinople for Adrianople 'to inquire into the alleged atrocities in Bulgaria' (Elliot to Derby, teleg., 19 July 1876, ibid., no. 238). Baring was the second secretary at the Embassy, a man whom Harris describes 'as much a Turcophile as the ambassador from whom he allegedly absorbed opinions without question' (*Horrors*, pp. 144–5). This is unfair and incorrect. Harris seems willing to accept unconfirmed and unsigned Bulgarian evidence of atrocities without according equal suspension of disbelief to reports of them from non-Bulgarian sources.

[49] MacColl to Gladstone, [? 20 July 1876?], Glad. Pap., Add. MS. 44234, CLVII; Hammond to Layard, 19 July 1876, Lay. Pap., Add. MS. 38955, XXV. Gladstone had received earlier opinions, and at least one that he trusted more on the Bulgarian atrocities than MacColl's. 'I have had accounts of the Turkish atrocities in Bulgaria and am inclined to think them reliable enough to go before the public. I shall rejoice to be mistaken, but . . . the cloud no bigger at first than a human hand appears to be spreading into a storm of indefinite dimensions' (Stratford de Recliffe to Gladstone, 29 June 1876, Glad. Pap., Add. MS. 44450, CCCLXV).

[50] Davison suggests that Farley's sudden turn against his old employer may have been due to the stoppage of his salary as Turkish consul as a result of the economies forced on the Porte by coming bankruptcy. Farley had founded the League in the previous autumn, for the purpose, Harris writes, 'of a campaign against his erstwhile

employer' (*Horrors*, pp. 109–10). In October 1875 Farley had gone to Shuvalov for money for a press campaign and propaganda among the Protestant clergy in Britain in order to give a religious colour to anti-Turkish agitation (Shuvalov to Jomini, 14 Oct. 1876, Seton-Watson, *Slav. Rev.* iii. 430–1).

[51] Harris writes of him that he 'was unique in the violence of his language' (*Horrors*, pp. 109–10).

[52] Thompson, i. 360–1; Edwin Hodder, *The Life and Work of the Seventh Earl of Shaftesbury* (3 vols., London, 1887), iii. 374–5; F. M. Leventhal, *Respectable Radical George Howell and Victorian Working Class Politics* (London, 1971), pp. 191–3.

[53] *Horrors*, pp. 152–3; Elliot to Derby, 6 July 1876, PRO FO 424/42, no. 159.

[54] *Horrors*, pp. 148–9, 160–2; Schuyler to Miss King, 21 July 1876 (E. Schuyler, *Selected Essays*, N.Y., 1901, pp. 63–4).

[55] Dupuis to Derby, Philippopolis, teleg., 21 July 1876, PRO FO 424/42, no. 261. As to whether Baring, or a consul from the Embassy, would be sent to aid Dupuis in investigating the atrocities see, Elliot to Derby, teleg., 23 July 1876, ibid., no. 303. If Wrench, the consul, had been sent as was originally intended, the Embassy, some insinuated, would have had less control over his reports. Elliot, of course, denied the insinuation. Also preparing a trip to the Balkans were MacColl and his friend and fellow churchman, Liddon.

[56] Elliot to Derby, 14 July 1876, ibid., no. 360.

[57] Elliot to Derby, teleg., 23 July 1876, ibid., no. 304; Reade to Derby, Rustchuk, 22 July 1876, ibid., no. 381.

[58] Decazes to Bourgoing, 20 July 1876, *DDF* ii. 83; Russell to Derby, Berlin, 20 July 1876, PRO FO 424/42, no. 307.

# CHAPTER TEN

[1] Two books have been devoted to the Bulgarian atrocities and Britain. Harris, *Britain and the Bulgarian Horrors of 1876*, places the story firmly within a Christian context, too much so it seems to this reader. He adds a few things not in Thompson and stops his book in October 1876 when he feels the agitation in Britain is really over. I would submit that he allows his admirably humane feelings to warp his judgement. On p. 32 Harris writes that the Bulgarian students at Robert College in Constantinople were 'naturally . . . among the first to learn the truth'. On p. 35 he writes that 'Elliot was unable to weigh information objectively'. Bulgarian students first heard the news of slaughter in Bulgaria, but to equate this with the 'truth' is misleading. Harris's displeasure with Elliot was that he was not pro-Bulgarian. R. T. Shannon, *Gladstone and the Bulgarian Agitation, 1876* (London, 1963), focuses less on the diplomatic side and treats the story more from the angle of British domestic politics and opinion. He feels the life of the agitation extends from July to December 1876, and stresses the connection between religious Nonconformity in Britain and the agitation. The book emphasizes Gladstone's debt to the agitation and its effect on him. W. T. Stead and the North of England are given credit for bringing on the outburst which is described as the 'greatest and most illuminating revelation of the moral susceptibility of the High Victorian public conscience'. My main quibble with Shannon, apart from his general characterization of the agitation, is his statement that the agitation had no effect on Russia or on producing the Russo-Turkish war of 1877. He may believe this but he makes no attempt to prove it. One might also consult H. Temperley, 'The Bulgarian and Other Atrocities, 1875–8', and Robert J. More, *Under the Balkans* (London, 1877).

[2] For the Reichstadt meeting and 'agreement' see Stojanovic, pp. 74–7; Harris, pp. 432–8; Rupp, pp. 134–46; Mackenzie, pp. 105–12; Taylor, pp. 237–8; Sumner, pp. 172–5; Langer, pp. 92–3.

³ Thanks to Loftus and White, London was reasonably well informed as to the secret part of the agreement, and Andrássy fully informed Bismarck as to its contents. White wrote that 'one of the results of the meeting at Reichstadt was that the Czar would not consent to any modification of the *status quo* in Servia, even though the Turks succeeded in reconquering the Vassal Principality' (White to Derby, Belgrade, 25 Aug. 1876, PRO FO 424/43, no. 535). Loftus reported that 'some understanding was come to between Prince Gorchakov and Count Andrassy, which, in certain eventualities, implied the annexation by Austria of Bosnia . . . with the sanction of Russia' (Loftus to Derby, 29 Aug. 1876, ibid., no. 447). In other dispatches, Loftus refers to Austria's annexing three-quarters of Bosnia 'in certain eventualities' (Loftus to Derby, teleg., 6 Sept. 1876, ibid., no. 496; same to same, 2 Sept. 1876, ibid., no. 655; same to same 5 Sept. 1876, ibid., no. 656).

⁴ A great deal of the British Press, Liberal and Conservative, London as well as provincial, castigated the Serbian attack. *The Times, Standard, Globe, Birmingham Daily Gazette*, and *Sheffield Daily Telegraph* all referred to Serbian treachery. The Liberal *Daily Telegraph* and the *Pall Mall Gazette* did as well, and Russia was singled out as the real instigator of the war, using Serbia as her tool (Wirthwein, pp. 54–5).

⁵ 'There were many causes that contributed to delay to as late a day in the session as July 31st, the debate on the Eastern policy of the Government. Among the official leaders of the Parliamentary Opposition, there was the conviction that a victory was impossible if they challenged a regular party division, such as would decide the fate of the Cabinet' (Thompson, p. 363).

⁶ *Horrors*, pp. 130–1. Disraeli was pleased, as he wrote to Lady Bradford. 'Last night went off very well. It was to have been . . . a great attack on Ministers, but Granville and Hartington were too sensible to indulge Gladstone's vagaries . . . and the affair then collapsed, as I wd not, could not, give them another day, as they declined bringing forward a vote of censure. I did not speak at all to my own satisfaction, wanting energy, and therefore fluency . . .' (Disraeli to Lady Bradford, 1 Aug. 1876, MB vi. 37–8).

⁷ Elliot learned of Gladstone's slur on Baring's fitness and disposition to inquire into the atrocities, and he defended him to Derby. 'There is nothing in either Mr. Baring's disposition or history to justify the supposition that he will report otherwise than with strict impartiality' (Elliot to Derby, 9 Aug. 1876, PRO FO 424/43, no. 198). Elliot's sister was the second wife of Lord John Russell, and she, unlike her brother, wrote directly to Gladstone. 'A good deal of pain as well as surprise had been left from what you said in Parliament about Mr. Baring. . . . My brother [Elliot] at first selects Mr. W[rench], as it is difficult for the hard worked Embassy to spare Mr. B[aring], but find that Mr. W. cannot go [to Bulgaria] for several days, sends Mr. B. at once in spite of all inconveniences; Mr. B. is a man in whom the utmost confidence may be placed, whose bias is strongly anti-Turkish . . .' (Lady Frances Russell to Gladstone, 24 Aug. 1876, Glad. Pap., Add. MS. 44451, CCCLXVI).

⁸ Walter Baring, brother of Earl Cromer, was born in 1844 and educated at Eton and Oxford. He entered the Diplomatic Service in 1865 and married Helen Guarracino in 1875. He eventually became minister at Montevideo from 1893 to 1906. In 1876 Baring was a second secretary at the Constantinople Embassy.

⁹ Derby to Elliot, 3 Aug. 1876, PRO FO 424/43, no. 24; Baring to Elliot, Philippopolis, 20 July 1876, ibid., no. 2. This last dispatch was received at the Foreign Office on 1 Aug; Baring to Elliot, Philippopolis, 22 July 1876, ibid., no. 27, received at the Foreign Office on 4 August.

¹⁰ *Horrors*, pp. 144–5. When Derby decided to send another investigator to accompany Dupuis, it was at first decided to send Mr. Wrench from the consular establishment at the Constantinople Embassy. When he was not available to proceed, Elliot nominated Mr. Baring who was a member of the diplomatic staff of the Embassy, being a second secretary. Baring knew some Turkish but no Bulgarian, but this, rather

than causing him to fall in with the estimates of Bulgarian-speaking Ottoman officials, allowed him to give greater weight to non-Muslim Bulgarian guesses.

[11] Baring to Elliot, Philippopolis, 22 July 1876, PRO FO 424/43, no. 27, received at the Foreign Office on 4 August.

[12] Elliot to Derby, teleg., 9 Aug. 1876, ibid., no. 81.

[13] Same to same, teleg., 9 Aug. 1876, ibid., no. 85. In a conversation with the Grand Vizier about 20 July, Elliot was informed that a *Daily News* report of 1,300 killed in the village of Boyajikeui was incorrect, and that upon Turkish inquiry 'only 70 persons out of the village were still missing, many of whom were certainly not killed and would reappear' (Same to same, 23 July 1876, ibid., no. 106).

[14] Baring to Elliot, Philippopolis, 27 July 1876, ibid., no. 114, received at the Foreign Office on 11 August. Baring was accompanied to Klissoura and Singirli by Dupuis. The former was reported as burnt by Bashi-Bazouks on 8 May. At Singirli, 'one of the first to rise, a house being set on fire . . . by the priest of the village to compel the inhabitants to take up arms against the Turks, telling them that the Russians were advancing to their assistance. Some twelve Turks were killed by the Bulgarians in the beginning of the affair; it was then attacked by the Bashi-Bazouks, who completely gutted it' (Dupuis to Elliot, Philippopolis, 27 July 1876, ibid., no. 114). Dupuis's report almost exactly repeats Baring's.

[15] Ibid. Later in the year the Foreign Office appointed Mr. Calvert as acting consul at Philippopolis. At the end of October he visited Peroushtitza where Schuyler had given the dead as 1,000 and Baring 750. Calvert was told by the leading Bulgarian Christian of the village that the total number of dead was 313 (Calvert to Elliot, Philippopolis, 30 Nov. 1876, ibid. 424/46, no. 335).

[16] Baring to Elliot, Tatar-Bazardjik, 1 Aug. 1876, ibid. 43, no. 197; same to same, Philippopolis, 4 Aug. 1876, ibid., both received at the Foreign Office on 17 August. Baring estimated the dead at Batak and many other villages according to the measure of allowing ten Bulgarians for each house. Calvert, however, upon later investigation requested by Salisbury, when the latter was representing Britain at the Constantinople Conference, found that five to a house was more accurate in the 10 villages he visited on the slopes of Balkan Mountains. By this scale, Baring's estimate of 5,000 to 6,000 killed at Batak would be halved (Calvert to Salisbury, 11 Jan. 1877, PRO FO 424/37, no. 219).

[17] Ibid.

[18] Dupuis to Derby, Adrianople, 7 Aug. 1876, PRO FO 424/43, no. 239. Dupuis made a supplementary report on 19 August (Dupuis to Derby, 19 Aug. 1876, ibid., no. 337).

[19] Report of Baring on the Bulgarian insurrection of 1876, 1 Sept. 1876, enclosed in Elliot to Derby, 5 Sept. 1876, ibid., no. 602, received at the Foreign Office on 14 September.

[20] Harris writes that Washburn and Long, suspicious of Baring's mission as a Government attempt to whitewash the atrocities, went to Maynard, the U.S. minister, and arranged with him to send Schuyler, who had arrived recently, on a 'competing' mission of investigation. Schuyler was more than anxious to go to Bulgaria and probably needed little convincing to undertake the mission (*Horrors*, pp. 148–9). This is derived from Washburn himself. 'He [Elliot] was not only sending his youngest secretary, who knew but little of the country and none of the languages . . . but . . . was . . . to be in the country only two or three days. I protested in vain, although Mr. Baring agreed with me. . . . I begged him [Maynard, the U.S. Minister] to send Mr. Schuyler. . . . I found it easy to persuade Mr. Schuyler . . .' (George Washburn, *Fifty Years in Constantinople and Recollections of Robert College*, New York, 1909, pp. 109–10). Schuyler's final report of the atrocities of 20 November 1876 was transmitted to Washington by Maynard, the American minister. The following quotation is from Schuyler's report. 'Naturally much of what I [Schuyler] shall state rests on the authority

of the Bulgarians, who were often the only persons able or willing to tell what had happened. . . . As a general rule I have thought it needless to give the process by which I have arrived at my facts' (Maynard to Fish, 21 Nov. 1876, U.S. State Dept., vol. 30, no. 106).

[21] Schuyler to Maynard, Philippopolis, 10 Aug. 1876, enclosed in Elliot to Derby, 5 Sept. 1876, PRO FO 424/43, no. 602.

[22] Baring to Elliot, 5 Sept. 1876, ibid., no. 603.

[23] As far as I was able to ascertain there were two European consuls at that place during the insurrection and repression in May 1876. One was the Russian vice-consul, who, it was generally admitted, helped to organize the insurrection. The other was the Greek consul, whose reports in the Foreign Office papers are not sufficient to enable one to reach any conclusion. In one report the Greek consul writes that 'up to the present [24 May] approximately 25 villages have been burned in the district of Bazardjik, as many by the insurgents as by the Bashi-Bazouks' (Wyndham to Derby, 6 Sept. 1876, ibid., no. 633). Matalas was the Greek vice-consul at Philippopolis. Kofos has shown that the British Government requested from Athens copies of Matalas's reports on 19 August. The latter agreed with the figure of 15,000 Bulgarian dead (E. Kofos, Greece and the Eastern Crisis 1875–8, Thessalonika, 1975, p. 59). The Austrian consul was present for part of the month of May.

[24] MacGahan to Daily News, 28 July 1876 (J. A. MacGahan, The Turkish Atrocities in Bulgaria, London, 1876, p. 11).

[25] MacGahan to Daily News, 2 Aug. 1876, ibid., pp. 24–5. Schuyler estimated that 'fully six thousand people were massacred . . . after they had given up their arms' at Batak (Schuyler to Miss King, 3 Aug. 1876, Schuyler, Selected Essays, pp. 71–2). MacGahan's above report on Batak appeared in the Daily News of 7 August.

[26] Schuyler to J. Fiske, Philippopolis, Saturday evening, 5 or 12 or 19 Aug. 1876, ibid., pp. 73–4.

[27] Hansard, 11 Aug. 1876, 3rd ser. 231, 1078–146. One measure of the Government, after it had become clear that some atrocities had been committed, was the appointment of an acting vice-consul at Philippopolis. For this Elliot to Derby, 14 Aug. 1876, PRO FO 424/43, no. 179.

[28] Disraeli to Derby, 7 Aug. 1876, MB vi. 46; same to same, 7 Aug. 1876, Derby Pap. Medlicott has written that 'it is difficult to avoid the general conclusion that the main responsibility for Disraeli's denials in the commons rests partly with the foreign office and partly with the Prime Minister himself' 'Dupuis', 48).

[29] Tenterden memorandum, 9 Aug. 1876, Derby Pap. Tenterden wrote another memorandum of the same date (no. 2916, FO 78/2532), given by Harris. It is also a defence of Elliot and the Foreign Office, but is distinctly different from the memorandum quoted above. 'so far as the English Government was concerned, during the first period there was little, indeed nothing, which they could do to urge the repression of these outrages. Sir H. Elliot, although baffled for some time by the disorganization of the Turkish ministry, was continually pressing upon the Porte the necessity of disarming the volunteers and punishing the outrages. During the excitement arising from the stirring events then taking place at Constantinople, it may have been that his representations were not sufficiently heeded. . . . In doing this [making representations to the Porte on atrocities] the British Government and Embassy, have so far as is known, been alone, or, at all events, foremost, in remonstrating with the Porte . . .' (Horrors, p. 180).

[30] Hammond wrote that 'Elliot was certainly very unfairly dealt with in the debate; but after the complaint against him was, not that he omitted to remonstrate with the Porte, but that he did not believe and report home as if they were true, all the stories which our Correspondents palmed off on the gullibility of the public at home' (Hammond to Layard, 15 Aug. 1876, Lay. Pap., Add. MS. 38955, xxv).

[31] Bylandt to Willebois, London, 12 Aug. 1876, NA 289; Shuvalov to Gorchakov,

2 Aug. 1876 (Seton-Watson, *Slav. Rev.* iv (1925–6), 179, no. 109; Hanley to Gladstone, 10 Aug. 1876, Glad. Pap., Add. MS. 44451, CCCLXVI. The British press also blasted Elliot. *The Times* criticized the ambassador 'for his failure to report and for his closed mind'. *Vanity Fair*, *Punch*, the *Daily News*, and the *Spectator* all attacked him strongly, with the latter demanding his recall (*Horrors*, pp. 187–92). Werther, the German minister at Constantinople, did not think Elliot would be recalled. 'But I [Werther] have reason to assume that he [Elliot] feels himself that in some events, lately, he has compromised himself and has made errors' (Werther to Bülow, Constantinople, very confid., 30 Aug. 1876, GFM, A4830).

³² Elliot to Gallenga, 13 Aug. 1876 (Gallenga, *Two Years of the Eastern Question*, ii. 466–7).

³³ Disraeli to Derby, 15 Aug. 1876, MB vi. 48–9; same to same, 15 Aug. 1876, Derby Pap. Derby attempted to put the Premier off with 'be assured that what you say [about Elliot and Buchanan] will not be lost sight of' (Derby to Disraeli, 21 Aug. 1876, Derby Pap.). Derby, after much thought, considered it unwise to remove Elliot now, as he would be made a scapegoat and no one could now replace him adequately in the midst of such a crisis. 'Peace made, he might not be unwilling to retire' (Derby to Disraeli, 31 Aug. 1876, Derby Pap.).

³⁴ Temperley, 'The Bulgarian and other Atrocities', 124–5. A special Turkish tribunal under Edib Effendi, which conducted investigations during July, estimated 1,836 Bulgarian dead. No one was willing to accept this, as a second Turkish investigation was carried out in September and found that 3,100 Christians and 480 Muslims had died. Djordjević writes that the Bulgarian rebellion had been suppressed by the Ottomans by the end of May (Djordjević, p. 134).

³⁵ Dorothy Anderson, *The Balkan Volunteers* (London, 1968), pp. 70–1.

³⁶ As a result of Disraeli's initiative Britain attempted to moderate German demands on the Porte for reparation. 'I don't think we ought to let France and Germany bully the poor Turks with ultimatums about the Salonika compensation' (Disraeli to Derby, 2 Aug. 1876, Derby Pap.). As a result of this Derby instructed Odo Russell 'to urge [the German Government] that pressure for immediate payment should not be put upon the Porte in such a manner as to increase the difficulties of the present situation, but that a reasonable time should be allowed to permit the sum required to be procured' (Derby to Russell, 3 Aug. 1876, PRO FO 424/43, no. 22).

³⁷ Derby to Elliot, 21 Sept. 1876, ibid., no. 758; same to same, teleg., 22 Sept. 1876, ibid., no. 825. Bourke had written to Derby about 25 August. 'I continue to receive daily letters from members of Parliament recording the indignation of their constituents about Bulgarian atrocities. . . . Would it not be desirable to propose a commission of enquiry. . . . I wd plainly demand a Turkish Commission of enquiry. It would be a righteous act on the part of England; it wd be a most excellent political move' (Bourke to Derby, [?] Aug. 1876, Derby Pap.).

# CHAPTER ELEVEN

¹ Derby to Elliot, 11.55 p.m., 29 Aug. 1876, PRO FO 424/43, no. 381. Derby, as well as the governments of Italy and France, feared that any delay in mediation would allow more opportunity for an inflamed Russian public opinion to prevail over the pacific policy of the Russian Government. Derby's explanation above to Elliot was also given to the Turkish ambassador in London, Musurus Pasha. It got out, and reached Andrássy. 'He [Andrássy] expressed anxiety at the effect on public opinion in Russia if the report should become known there . . . that Great Britain would not oppose Russian armed intervention in Turkey' (Buchanan to Derby, teleg., Vienna, 2 Sept. 1876, ibid., no. 426). When Derby asked Buchanan the source of Andrássy's information, the

British ambassador replied that 'it originated with Count Shouvaloff who appears to have concluded, from an answer given to him' [by Derby] (Buchanan to Derby, teleg., 6 Sept. 1876, ibid., no. 494). Derby's request for an explanation of the leak was due to the Queen's having Ponsonby write to the Foreign Secretary for an explanation (Ponsonby to Queen Victoria, 4 Sept. 1876, RA H9/69; Queen Victoria to Ponsonby, 4 Sept. 1876, ibid., no. 71; Ponsonby to Derby, 4 Sept. 1876, ibid., no. 72). Derby's threat to Turkey became known as well to d'Harcourt, the French ambassador in London (d'Harcourt to Decazes, 10 Sept. 1876, *DDF* ii. 88–9). DeLisle apparently knew of the dispatch by Derby. 'The last dispatch from our Govt. to that of Turkey . . . [without the British atrocity outburst] would never have been transmitted. The Turks now know, that they can no longer count upon any British support' (DeLisle to Manning, 7 Sept. 1876, Purcell, *deLisle*, ii. 158–9). It is probable that Lady Derby told Shuvalov of the dispatch.

² Derby to Elliot, 6 Sept. 1876, PRO FO 424/43, no. 409.

³ Bourke to Derby, [25] Aug. 1876, Derby Pap. Bourke also sent a copy of his suggestion to Disraeli (Bourke to Disraeli, 26 Aug. 1876, Disraeli Pap. xxi/B/680, 680a). A letter from Bourke was read at an atrocity meeting on 31 August. It was an attempt on the part of the Under-Secretary to defend the conduct of the Government and to placate the public wrath over the atrocities. Bourke had not cleared his letter with Derby before sending it, and this drew a rebuke from the Foreign Secretary. 'It is not as a rule a good thing to fire off manifestoes like your letter of last week without previous consultation' (Derby to Bourke, 3 Sept. 1876, Derby Pap.).

⁴ Derby to Bourke, 28 Aug. 1876, Derby Pap.

⁵ 'And all because he is an invalid—probably has a torpid liver, and never sees anybody, and is obliged to be in bed' (Disraeli to Lady Bradford, 4 Sept. 1876, Disraeli–Bradford letters, Weston Park, Shifnal. Zetland dates this letter 24 September, but the original seems to be dated 4 September; Zetland, ii. 92–3).

⁶ Disraeli to Derby, 15 Aug. 1876, MB vi. 48–9; same to same, 15 Aug. 1876, Derby Pap.

⁷ Disraeli to Northcote, 2 Sept. 1876, MB vi. 51; Disraeli to Derby, 2 Sept. 1876, Derby Pap.

⁸ Disraeli to Salisbury, 3 Sept. 1876, MB vi. 51–2; same to same, 3 Sept. 1876, Salis. Pap.

⁹ Disraeli to Derby, 4 Sept. 1876, MB vi. 52–3; same to same, 4 Sept. 1876, Derby Pap. Derby indicated the difficulties of such a course in reply to the Premier. 'If once we raise the question of partition, the risk of war is great, for the Powers will all want something, and the division of the spoil is not likely to be made in an amiable manner. . . . I do not believe any territorial advantages on the frontier would reconcile Russia to seeing Constantinople in the hands of a great power' (Derby to Disraeli, 5 Sept. 1876, Derby Pap.).

¹⁰ Disraeli to Derby, 6 Sept. 1876, MB vi. 53–4.

¹¹ Disraeli to Queen Victoria, 10 Sept. 1876, *QVL* ii. 476–9. 'No member of the Government should countenance the idea that we are hysterically 'modifying' our policy, in consequence of the excited state of the public mind. If such an idea gets about, we shall become contemptible' (Disraeli to Northcote, 11 Sept. 1876, MB vi. 61–2).

¹² Elliot was designated as stupid; 'he has nearly destroyed a strong and popular government' (Disraeli to Derby, 2 Sept. 1876, Derby Pap.). Loftus 'was absurd in quiet times, but now that there is real business, he is not only absurd, he is mischievous' (Disraeli to Queen Victoria, 10 Sept. 1876, *QVL* ii. 476–9). Disraeli was furious with Russell for taking a holiday on the grounds that Bismarck was 'in hiding' and not seeing anyone (ibid.).

¹³ Disraeli to Salisbury, 3 Sept. 1876, MB vi. 51–2; same to same, 3 Sept. 1876, Salis. Pap.

[14] Disraeli to Queen Victoria, 1 Sept. 1876, RA H9/55. What Disraeli is probably referring to here—Derby's audacity—is the Foreign Secretary's threatening Turkey in order to force her to make peace.

[15] Hardy to Cairns, 29 Aug. 1876, Cairns Pap., PRO FO 30 51/7; Hardy diary, 29 Aug. 1876, Cran. Pap., HA 43/T501/296. Hardy was one of the few—Grant Duff, Lyons in Paris, and Tenterden were others—who felt Elliot was blameless. 'Our Ambassador did not realise to the full extent, but he constantly and emphatically remonstrated against what he believed was much less flagrant, and his ignorance of details was shared by all his colleagues, as I believe, without exception' (Hardy diary, 7 Sept. 1876, Hardy, i. 368–9).

[16] Northcote to Disraeli, 2 Sept. 1876, Disraeli Pap. xx/N/14; same to same, 2 Sept. 1876, Derby Pap. Northcote described as 'brutally stupid' the Porte's decorating rather than punishing the Bashi-Bazouks (Northcote to Cross, 3 Sept. 1876, Cross Papers, British Library, Add. MS. 51265, III). Derby admitted to Northcote the legitimacy of demanding securities against future Turkish misgovernment, but cautioned him against publicly favouring autonomy as a solution for Bulgaria since once granted to that province, it might be impossible to refuse it to any other. 'We have a right to ask for punishment of the chief offenders, for some compensation to the sufferers, and for security . . . against the recurrence of such excesses. I would keep clear of the autonomy question' (Derby to Northcote, 9 Sept. 1876, North. Pap., Add. MS. 50022, x; same to same, 9 Sept. 1876, Derby Pap.).

[17] Northcote to Carnarvon, 4 Sept. 1876, Hardinge, ii. 335–6. Northcote also wished the Turks to grant a quick and moderate peace to the Serbs (Northcote to Queen Victoria, 4 Sept. 1876, RA H9/73; same to same, 4 Sept. 1876, RA H86; 1 Sept. 1876, RA 9/108). Ponsonby also noted the censure which Disraeli's levity was exciting. 'Lord Beaconsfield is being severely criticised for having treated the subject so lightly' (Ponsonby to Queen Victoria, 31 Aug. 1876, RA H9/52).

[18] Carnarvon to Northcote, Guernsey, 30 Aug. 1876, Carnarvon Papers, PRO 30/6, 7; Carnarvon to Lytton, Guernsey, 31 Aug. 1876, Lytton Pap., Hertfordshire Record Office. 'I do not see my way at all' illustrates that the Prime Minister was as uncertain as to measures as Carnarvon (Disraeli to Lady Bradford, 4 Sept. 1876, Disraeli–Bradford letters).

[19] Carnarvon to Disraeli, 5 or 6 Sept. 1876, Disraeli Pap. xx/He/72. Disraeli forwarded this letter to Derby.

[20] Carnarvon to Hardy, 12 Sept. 1876, Carn. Pap., HA 43/T501/262; Carnarvon to Salisbury, 9 Sept. 1876, Salis. Pap., E. Disraeli's reply to Carnarvon was, of course, that the storm would blow over, and to modify our policy would be 'hysterical' and 'make us contemptible' (ibid.).

[21] Cairns to Hardy, 31 Aug. 1876, Cran. Pap., HA43/T501/262; Cairns to Disraeli, 31 Aug. 1876, Disraeli Pap. xx/Ca/186; A. Cross, A Political History (privately printed, 1903), p. 38. This was another bit of pressure on Derby to force the Turks to peace.

[22] Salisbury to Disraeli, 29 Aug. 1876, Disraeli Pap. xx/Ce/82.

[23] Salisbury to Lytton, 5 Sept. 1876, Salis. Pap., C3, letter-book; same to same, 5 Sept. 1876, Lytton Pap., India Office, D/x/203; Salisbury to Lytton, 6 Sept. 1876, ibid. 209. Salisbury desired some guarantee for the better government of Turkey's Christians. He regarded promises of the Porte in this sense to be no longer negotiable currency (Salisbury to Derby, 21 Sept. 1876, Salis. Pap., vol. 16).

[24] Derby to Disraeli, 8 Sept. 1876, Derby Pap.

[25] Derby to Bourke, 3 Sept. 1876, Derby Pap. Elliot believed exactly the opposite, that the protection of British interests 'is not affected by the question whether it was 10,000 or 20,000 persons who perished in the suppression. We have been upholding what we know to be a semi-civilized nation . . . [but this] cannot be sufficient reason for abandoning a policy which is the only one that can be followed with a due regard to our own interests' (Elliot to Derby, 4 Sept. 1876, PRO FO 424/43, no. 604).

[26] Derby to Disraeli, 31 Aug. 1876, Derby Pap. The Foreign Secretary asked Russell, who was home on leave, of the probability of Russian intervention. 'He [Russell] does not consider it great' (Derby to Disraeli, 13 Sept. 1876, ibid.).

[27] Elliot to Derby, teleg., 11 Sept. 1876, PRO FO 424/43, no. 577. Elliot referred to British influence with the Turkish ministers, 'within the last few weeks [as being] impaired by the tone of the debates in Parliament and of the public press' (Elliot to Derby, 3 Sept. 1876, ibid., no. 597). Shuvalov attributed Derby's co-operative efforts in part to the agitation movement in Britain (Shuvalov to Gorchakov, 3 Sept. 1876, Seton-Watson, *Slav. Rev.* iv. 183).

[28] Derby's dispatches to Elliot of 21 September which contained a proposal for a temporary Christian commissioner, as well as the above, were soon learned of by the public. Derby explained to Disraeli that *The Times* correspondent at Vienna or Constantinople 'seems to have got hold of the terms we propose—not certainly from any leakage here' (Derby to Disraeli, 22 Sept. 1876, Derby Pap.). Toward the end of September Derby read to a deputation the terms of his dispatch to Elliot of 21 September (Derby to Disraeli, 25 Sept. 1876, ibid.). Some, Mundella was one, thought Derby's dispatch a capitulation to the agitation (Mundella to Leader, 1 Oct. 1876, Mundella Pap.). Hayward, the well-known essayist, agreed that Derby's dispatch 'put an entirely new complexion on the Eastern Question. . . . It does him great credit, but in reality he has simply followed in the track which Gladstone marked out for him' (Hayward to Lady Waldegrave, 7 Oct. 1876, A. Hayward, *Selections From His Correspondence From 1834 to 1881*, 2 vols., London, 1886, ii. 265–6).

[29] Buchanan to Derby, teleg., 12 Sept. 1876, PRO FO 424/43, no. 584. Elliot informed Derby of his personal agreement with Andrássy's reaction. Derby then explained what he meant. 'You will understand that by the phrase "local or administrative autonomy," as applied to Bosnia and Herzegovina, nothing more is intended by Her Majesty's Government than a system of local institutions, which shall give the population some control over their own local affairs, and guarantees against the exercise of arbitrary authority. There is no question of the creation of a tributary state' (Derby to Elliot, teleg., 15 Sept. 1876, ibid., no. 623). Gorchakov tended to support Derby's conditions (Derby to Loftus, 13 Sept. 1876, ibid., no. 594), and Jomini reported official Russia as 'enchanted' with the British peace terms, though Austria was not (Jomini to Giers, Livadia, 13 Sept. 1876, Jelavich, *Russia in the East*, p. 24).

[30] Onou to [Jomini], 16 Sept. 1876, Jomini–Onou Pap., Eg. 3187, Fos. 90–1; ibid., fos. 92–3. There is also some evidence that the Turks feared the success of the agitation might alter London's traditional support of Turkey. Forster, the Liberal statesman, made a trip to the Balkans and wrote to his wife from Constantinople that 'there can be no doubt that the Turks are now seriously alarmed about the effect of the atrocities' (Forster to wife, 17 Sept. 1876, T. W. Reid, *The Life of the Rt. Hon. William Edward Forster*, 2 vols., London, 1888, ii. 126; hereafter cited as Reid).

[31] T. V. Lister, Assistant Under-Secretary at the Foreign Office, explained the difference between a suspension of arms and an armistice as the case 'that the former is easy to break and the latter difficult to make' (Lister to Ponsonby, 2 Oct. 1876, Ponsonby, *Henry Ponsonby*, p. 319; same to same, 2 Oct. 1876, PRO FO 800/3).

[32] The new Sultan, Abdul Hamid, told one of his doctors who happened to be the Germany Embassy physician, to inform the German ambassador that he very much desired a quick peace and he would rely on Britain and Germany to obtain it (Werther to Bülow, Constantinople, very confid., 14 Sept. 1876, GFM, A 5110). Loyd-Lindsay, who was leading a British relief mission to both the Serbs and the Turks, wrote from Belgrade that the former all wished for peace, but not their Russian 'friends' (Loyd-Lindsay to D. Galton, 29 Aug. 1876, H. S. L. Wantage, *Lord Wantage. A Memoir*, London, 1907, pp. 222–3). Lindsay did not like the Serbians and thought that in Western Europe, Milan and Ristich would have been fortunate 'if they obtained the posts of managers and markers in billiard saloons'. Nor did Loyd-Lindsay believe in the Ser-

bian war. 'The Serbian people have been made a catspaw by Russia. . . . The insurrection is a sham, it could not have existed without Russia. . . . Russia is finding the money and furnishing the officers' (Loyd-Lindsay to Lord Overstone, 4 Sept. 1876, ibid., pp. 228–9). Convinced that the Serbs were fighting against their will by the number 'of these poor peasants who have blown off their fingers on the battle field to avoid serving', Lindsay felt Britain should protest against so driving a people to war. He urged the Prince of Wales to write to the Tsar about this (Loyd-Lindsay to Prince of Wales, 5 Sept. 1876, RA H9/88). Loyd-Lindsay's letters to Lord Overstone, his wealthy father-in-law, were sent by the latter to Disraeli, Granville, and Stratford de Redcliffe (Wantage, pp. 230–2).

[33] Derby to Loftus, 27 Sept. 1876, PRO FO 424/43, no. 924. Shuvalov replied that because of Russian public feeling it would be difficult for the Tsar to check the emigration. 'The state of public feeling in Russia, his Excellency said, was something to which the excitement felt here [Britain] bore no comparison' (ibid.). Loftus had telegraphed of 10,000 people at a Moscow railway 'to witness the departure of persons charged to convey a Greek chapel and its sacred appurtenances to General Tchernaieff' (Loftus to Derby, St. Petersburg, 10 Sept. 1876, ibid., no. 571). White believed that while the majority of Serbians wished peace, the Russian volunteers with a few 'noisy patriots' prevented this.

[34] The Turks were willing to write a note promising the same things as would appear in a protocol. But they refused the latter because it had a kind of legal international validity, and they felt it to be both a humiliation and an acknowledgement of the right of foreign interference in Ottoman internal reforms.

[35] Derby to Eliot, teleg., 5 Oct. 1876, PRO FO 424/44, no. 99. Three hours later Derby sent another telegram to Constantinople. 'It is desired that your manner and language should be very earnest, for the consequences of a refusal by Turkey of these last overtures are incalculable. You may show this telegram also' (same to same, teleg., 5.08 p.m., 5 Oct. 1876, ibid., no. 104). Bismarck was angry when he learned of the instructions to Eliot to leave Constantinople as 'he could not well believe that Her Majesty's Government would take so serious a step without communicating their intention to the Guaranteeing Powers with whom they were acting in concert' (Russell to Derby, secret, 10 Oct. 1876, ibid., no. 356). Derby explained that no rupture of relations with the Porte were intended. 'It was thought better in that event [a Turkish refusal of the armistice] that Sir H. Elliot should retire for a time, and take no part in the negotiation, but the Secretary of the Embassy would have remained. The step was intended to show displeasure on the part of England, but it would not have been a diplomatic rupture. Her Majesty's Government are most anxious to act with the Government of Germany and . . . that Government could do much in the interest of peace if Germany would exert its influence to procure Russian acceptance of the armistice' (Derby to Russell, teleg., 16 Oct. 1876, ibid., no. 373). Derby, of course, was aware that Elliot's removal from Constantinople would have done much to propitiate the agitation in Britain. He apparently allowed Shuvalov to know that he was dissatisfied with Elliot over Bulgaria, but that if the ambassador were sacrified today, tomorrow the dismissal of the Foreign Secretary would be demanded (Shuvalov to Gorchakov, 15 Sept. 1876, Seton-Watson, *Slav. Rev.* iv. 193–4). The Foreign Secretary's decision to threaten the Porte with the withdrawal of Elliot was in part the result of a private letter from the ambassador, in which the latter wrote that unless it were possible to induce the Porte to accept peace conditions at once, Russia would probably attack (Elliot to Derby, 26 Sept. 1876, Derby Pap.). Elliot informed Derby privately that the threat to leave Constantinople 'was known to several of my colleagues . . . almost as soon as I received it' (Elliot to Derby, 9 Oct. 1876, Derby Pap.). The main explanation of the threat to remove Elliot was a decision of the Cabinet on 4 October to do so as a result of the assurance of Shuvalov that Russia would drop a proposal to occupy Ottoman territory. Derby had got this concession from the Russian ambassador on

3 October on the understanding that Britain 'peremptorily' press the Porte to accept an armistice. The Cabinet then agreed with Derby at a meeting on 4 October to threaten the removal of Elliot as pressure on Turkey to grant an armistice (Disraeli to Queen Victoria, 4 Oct. 1876, RA H10/17; Cairns to Queen Victoria, 7 Oct. 1876, ibid. 24).

[36] Derby to Elliot, teleg., 11 Oct. 1876, PRO FO 424/44, no. 248. Earlier Russia had pushed for a three-month armistice which the Porte had opposed. Derby must have felt vindication at this point, for there was even pressure within the Cabinet for Elliot's removal. Disraeli and Salisbury would have gladly assented to it, and they were now joined by Cairns, who thought the ambassador should be removed (Cairns to Disraeli, 10 Oct. 1876, Disraeli Pap. xix/D/181). Derby, of course, disagreed, and could now point to Elliot's success in obtaining an armistice, which forced even Disraeli to write that 'he [Elliot] seems to have managed the business in a masterly style' (Disraeli to Derby, 16 Oct. 1876, Derby Pap.; Derby to Disraeli, 14 Oct. 1876, ibid.; same to same, 14 Oct. 1876, Disraeli Pap. xx/S/1169).

[37] Derby to Russell, teleg., 13 Oct. 1876, PRO FO 424/44, no. 296. Disraeli probably deserves some credit for Derby's unusual energy. He periodically lauded the Foreign Secretary with expectations of success in order to raise his confidence. 'I am convinced myself, that Russia at the present moment, wd. be glad to wind up affairs, and apparently with us—I think you will succeed in yr undertaking, and gain glory' (Disraeli to Derby, 21 Sept. 1876, Derby Pap.). The Belgian minister noted both the 'surprise' and 'irritation' produced in London by Russia's refusal to accept the armistice of six months (Solvyns to d'Aspremont-Lynden, London, 16 Oct. 1876, BFM). Gladstone 'rejoiced' at Russia's refusal of the Turkish armistice (Gladstone to Acton, 16 Oct. 1876, Glad. Pap., Add. MS. 44093).

[38] Derby to Loftus, 13 Oct. 1876, PRO FO 424/44, no. 299. Russian opinion, as reported by Loftus, was hardly less tranquil than the British. 'Russian press is violent and unanimous against the acceptance of the proposed Turkish armistice. There is much fanatical excitement and a general feeling for war throughout the country. Position of the Emperor and Government very embarrassing . . . they may be forced by public opinion into action' (Loftus to Derby, teleg., 17 Oct. 1876, ibid., no. 425).

[39] There was some confusion as to whether the Turkish proposal was for five or six months.

[40] Derby to Russell, 18 Oct. 1876, ibid., no. 444; same to same, teleg., 19 Oct. 1876, ibid., no. 455. The Times, which had recently veered to support the Government, after having been pro-agitation, expressed a hope in its lead article of 16 October 'that Bismarck would counsel Russia' (Wirthwein, pp. 118–19).

[41] Elliot to Derby, teleg., 31 Oct. 1876, PRO FO 424/44, no. 697. The Tsar told Loftus that the reason for the ultimatum was the complete Serbian defeat and the fear that it might lead to Ottoman atrocities (Loftus to Derby, Yalta, teleg., 2 Nov. 1876, PRO FO 424/45, no. 46). When Ignatiev, who had been at Livadia, departed for Constantinople on 17 October, he took with him the ultimatum which he eventually delivered (Jomini to Giers, 5/17, 10/22, 11/23, 14/26 Oct. 1876, Jelavich, Russia in the East, pp. 31–4; Zichy to Andrássy, 24 Oct. 1876, Haus-, Hof- und Staatsarchiv, Politisches Archiv, Vienna, xii, 114; hereafter cited as HHSA). Bylandt, the Netherlands minister in London, thought that the success of the Russian ultimatum 'has produced a certain jealousy in England, much as there is an attempt to hide it by claiming that the principle of the armistice had already been accepted and that the Russian ultimatum only smashed in an open door' (Bylandt to Willebois, London, 6 Nov. 1876, NA 380).

[42] Besides the books of Harris and R. T. Shannon, the volumes of Wirthwein and Thompson deal with this subject. One should also consult Anderson, The Balkan Volunteers and Wantage, Lord Wantage (hereafter cited as Anderson and Wantage). The excellent volume by Anderson tells the story of the relief and charitable work done in the Balkans by British individuals and committees for the Bulgarians, Serbs, and

Turks. Wantage's volume has many interesting letters on the agitation.

[43] Within the last few days, however, we have witnessed a most astonishing phenomenon, an outburst of public feeling the like of which no man, perhaps ever beheld in this country' [Grant Duff in *The Times* of 11 Sept.]. 'On hearing of the terrible atrocities in Bulgaria, the mind and spirit of Englishmen were moved more than ever happened within any recollection' ([Lowe in speech at Bristol, in *The Times* of 14 Nov.] Thompson, i. 415–16).

[44] Thompson writes of the 'graphicness of detail and of description of the narratives of the two Americans'. Schuyler's official report appeared in the *Daily News* on 29 August, but Baring's was only published in the *London Gazette* on 19 September (Thompson, i. 334–6).

[45] The National Aid Society voted a sum of £20,000 for the relief of the Serbian and Turkish sick and wounded (Wantage, pp. 218–19). Loyd-Lindsay's father-in-law, Lord Overstone, had doubts. 'But I cannot say that I am an enthusiast in the cause of Neutral Aid to the Sick and Wounded of foreign armies. It is open to much question on the ground both of policy and humanity' (Lord Overstone to G. W. Norman, 22 Aug. 1876, D. P. O'Brien (ed.), *The Correspondence of Lord Overstone*, 3 vols., Cambridge, 1971, iii. 1291–2).

[46] Schuyler to Miss King, 2 Aug. 1876 (Schuyler, *Selected Essays*, pp. 71–2; Loyd-Lindsay to Derby, 4 Aug. 1876, PRO FO 424/43, no. 46.

[47] Anderson, pp. 13–15; Butler Johnstone, a Turcophile M.P., solicited appeals for a Turkish Wounded Soldiers' Relief Fund (ibid.). On 16 August, with Lord Harrowby presiding, a meeting was held in support of the Eastern War Sick and Wounded Relief Fund, at which a letter from Florence Nightingale, wishing it well, was read (Wantage, pp. 218–19).

[48] Wirthwein, pp. 74–6.

[49] *Horrors*, pp. 201–8.

[50] Ibid. Dilke, a Radical within the Liberals, was more anti-Russian than anti-Government, though he abhorred the Turkish barbarities. His opinion of the Montenegrins and Serbians was not high. Loyd-Lindsay and Lytton shared his low opinion of the Serbians.

[51] Shannon, *Gladstone and the Bulgarian Agitation*, pp. 67–9 (hereafter cited as Shannon). There were a few pro-Turkish letters written at this point. Admiral Slade wrote one to *The Times* and Hobart Pasha, the British commander of the Ottoman navy, sent an epistle published in the *Pall Mall Gazette* (*Horrors*, pp. 209–9).

[52] Ibid., pp. 216–17. 'The function of local agitation-making was eventually taken up, in the overwhelming majority of cases, by Nonconformist ministers and Anglican clergy' (Shannon, pp. 58–106).

[53] Ibid., pp. 49–50.

[54] Shannon describes him as 'psychologically incapable of balance and restraint, and almost everything he wrote is infected to some degree with hysteria' (Shannon, pp. 70–3). Under thirty, a convinced Slavophile, 'bursting with rather frantic energy, ambitious, able ... proud and intensely pious ... Stead in 1876 was ripe for just such a cause as the atrocities offered' (ibid.).

[55] Ibid. He provided a programme for the agitation 'in a series of useful heads of resolutions for the guidance of organisers of meetings' (ibid.).

[56] Ibid., pp. 74–6.

[57] *Horrors*, pp. 216–17; Wirthwein, pp. 80–1. Shannon writes that the Hackney meeting was 'the first public indication by Gladstone of his attitude to the agitation' (Shannon, pp. 76–8). He allowed a letter of his to be read and made a financial contribution.

[58] *Horrors*, pp. 224–6. By 1 September Stead counted 14 such meetings (Shannon, p. 76). It was at this point, at 11.55 p.m. on the evening of 29 August, that Derby sent his telegram to Elliot (see p. 517 n. 1) indicating that were Russia to attack Turkey, Britain

could not help the latter. Shannon misdates this telegram as 22 August, but he is correct, I think, in characterizing as exaggerated Temperley's view of Derby's telegram as a great change in British foreign policy (Shannon, pp. 68–9).

[59] See p. 519 n. 25.

[60] Liddon to Freeman, 24 Aug. 1876, Liddon Papers, Keble College Library.

[61] Shannon, pp. 85–6.

[62] Wirthwein, pp. 78–80.

[63] Freeman to Bryce, 27 Aug. 1876, Bryce Papers, Bodleian. Gladstone told Halifax that the motive for Disraeli's conduct 'was his judaism' (Halifax to Grey, 11 Oct. 1876, Hickleton Papers, Garrowby). Shannon argues that 'the anti-Semitic aspect of the atrocities agitation was prominent but superficial' as there was an absence 'of the substantial bulk of prejudice which in France produced the Dreyfus Affair' (Shannon, pp. 200–1). Disraeli described his opponent in non-religious terms. 'Posterity will do justice to that unprincipled maniac, Gladstone—Extraordinary mixture of envy, vindictiveness, hypocrisy, and superstition and with one commanding characteristic . . . never a gentleman!' (Disraeli to Derby, 12 Oct. 1876, Derby Pap.). Freeman's language can only be described as despicable. 'There is a nation [Russia] in the freshness of a new life, burning to go on the noblest of crusades and our loathsome Jew wants to stop them' (Freeman to Bryce, 23 Nov. 1876, Bryce Pap.).

[64] Shannon, pp. 81–5. Stead, of course, also lacked a sense of restraint.

[65] 'Gladstone has had the impudence to send me his pamphlet, tho he accuses me of several crimes. The document is passionate and not strong; vindictive and ill-written' (Disraeli to Derby, 8 Sept. 1876, MB vi. 60).

[66] Shannon, pp. 100–1. Harris denies Gladstone's political opportunism (*Horrors*, pp. 231–3). He is, I think, mistaken. Morley, Gladstone's biographer, sees 'humanity . . . at the root of the whole matter' (John Morley, *Gladstone*, 3 vols., London, 1903, ii. 551–2). Shannon takes something of a middle position, that Gladstone came to the agitation late and only when he saw 'that it restored the moral rapport between himself and the masses which the defeat of 1874 had snapped' (Shannon, pp. 91–2). 'It was the opportunism of very belated enlightenment of one standing absentmindedly at a bus stop, and then having to scramble hurriedly to catch the bus which has almost passed by' (ibid., pp. 109–12).

[67] MacColl to Gladstone, 21 Aug, 1876, Glad. Pap., Add. MS. 44243, CLVIII; deLisle to Gladstone, 22 Aug. 1876, (Purcell, *deLisle*, ii. 154). In reply to deLisle's letter Gladstone wrote that '"the defence of belief is the noblest . . . of all human enterprises"' (Gladstone to deLisle, 26 Aug. 1876, ibid. ii. 155).

[68] Gladstone to Granville, 27 Aug. 1876, Ramm, i. 2–3.

[69] Lady Strangford to Gladstone, 28 Aug. 1876, Glad. Pap., Add. MS. 44451, CCLXVI. It was not always easy to raise money and Lord Shaftesbury recorded in his diary that 'Money, the test of all truths, does not come in'. His great love of humanity was temporarily not elicited by the London poor when he wrote 'and yet one penny a piece from the rabble who roared in the Park [Hyde] and in the streets would have netted £50,000' (Snaftesbury diary, 9 October 1876, Hodder, *Shaftesbury*, iii. 375–6).

[70] Gladstone to Granville, 29 Aug. 1876, Ramm, i. 3–4. Granville replied that he did not object to a pamphlet (Granville to Gladstone, 31 Aug. 1876, ibid. i. 4). Liddon saw the need for the agitation to focus on the object or programme 'to be *enforced* upon the Government' (Liddon to Freeman, 31 Aug. 1876, Liddon Pap.). MacColl also wrote in this sense. 'It [the thoroughly roused country] wants guidance. The aspirations are all in the right direction, and all it requires is to have its ideas and wishes put into shape and order. I think immense capital might be made against Dizzy just now' (MacColl to Gladstone, 1 Sept. 1876, Glad. Pap., Add. MS. 44243, CLVIII). Cardinal Manning saw little good to be derived from public meetings 'which proposed no definite policy' (Wirthwein, pp. 83–4). As Harris informs us, the agitation remained leaderless until Gladstone spoke out. Until then 'no prominent Liberal expressed an opinion' except

for the party's two elder statesmen, John Russell and Bright. The former had contributed money to the agitation, and on 24 August, in a letter to *The Times*, demanded an autumn session of Parliament and united European action against Turkey. Bright at the beginning of September wished every town to hold a public meeting in order to force the Government to end its Turkish partnership (*Horrors*, pp. 227–30). Russell urged an autumn session and European action on Granville (John Russell to Granville, 23 Aug. 1876, Gran. Pap., PRO 30 29/26A). 'I [Granville] get letters as you [Hartington] probably do reproaching the leaders of the party for remaining mute—I have not answered them, and I think it very unlikely that I shall avail myself of any opportunity to speak on the matter' (Granville to Hartington, 1 Sept. 1876, Hartington Papers, Chatsworth, 340/672; hereafter cited as Hart. Pap.).

[71] Lady Strangford to Gladstone, 1 Sept. 1876, Glad. Pap., Add. MS. 44451, CCLXVI. From a letter from MacColl, it is evident that Gladstone suspected Lady Strangford's purity of motive, perhaps due to a recognition of his own mixed motives. 'I [MacColl] quite agree with you about Lady . . . 's Fund. She is a thorough Turk, and I don't trust her at all. . . . Her sympathy for the Bulgarians is artificial and for a purpose. Her sympathy for the Turks . . . is thoroughly genuine. Of course I should regard what you have said on that point as private' (McColl to Gladstone, 13 Oct. 1876, G. W. E. Russell (ed.), *Malcolm MacColl, Memoirs and Correspondence*, London, 1914, p. 55. One of the few things which Gladstone and Disraeli agreed on at this time was apparently Lady Strangford. 'Lady Strangford shrieks that her appeal [for money] is niggardly responded to. If the public knew as much about that Lady as Ld. Beaconsfield does, they would wonder she had got so much' (Disraeli to Queen Victoria, 2 Oct. 1876, RA H10/8).

[72] Shannon, p. 110. Granville attempted to dissuade Gladstone from proposing autonomy, as Derby did with Northcote, but failed (Gladstone to wife, 6 Sept. 1876, A. Tilney Bassett (ed.), *Gladstone to His Wife*, London, 1936, p. 218). On the same day of the pamphlet's publication, Stead wrote to Gladstone and proposed a national day of humiliation, 'a Bulgarian Sunday', during which collections would be taken 'for the sufferers whom we have been the unwilling means of destroying' (Stead to Gladstone, 6 Sept. 1876, Glad. Pap., Add. MS. 44303, Shannon, pp. 136–8).

[73] W. E. Gladstone, *Bulgarian Horrors and the Questions of the East* (London, 1876), p. 33. Gladstone wrote to his friend deLisle that 'the Turk now stands revealed in such a light, that it is dangerous to consort with him' (Gladstone to deLisle, 3 Sept. 1876, Purcell, *deLisle*, ii. 155–6). The Duke of Argyll shared Gladstone's feelings of guilt and anger. On 19 September he spoke at a meeting at Glasgow. 'I begin with this proposition, that the Turkish Government is bad, so execrably bad, that any and every rebellion against it on the part of its Christian subjects is presumably just and righteous. . . . I am one of the five survivors of the Cabinet which urged the Crimean War. . . . If I could imagine that this policy of Lord Derby had been the legitimate result of that Crimean War, I would sit in sackcloth and ashes for the part which I then took, as one of the greatest sins of my youth. . . . I labour under no such conviction. On the contrary, it was the Crimean War which specially lifted us above the level of such a cold and heartless and selfish policy as this' (Thompson, i. 392–3). Argyll wrote of this meeting to Granville, that 'the crowd swaying to and fro in a frightful way under the distant gallery' created a great row (Argyll to Granville, 20 Sept. 1876, Duke of Argyll, *Autobiography and Memoirs*, 2 vols., London, 1906, ii. 323).

[74] Ibid. 64. Morier, the British diplomat, thought a Government-sponsored loan of ten million pounds to rebuild Bulgaria would counteract Russian influence as the latter country, not having the credit could not compete (Morier to Lady Morier, 5 Oct. 1876, Ramm, *Morier*, pp. 55–71).

[75] See p. 525 n. 72. About three weeks later Bright wrote to ask Gladstone whether the proposal of his Birmingham friends for a national petition to the Queen was feasible and whether he would be willing to sign it (Bright to Gladstone, 23 Sept. 1876, Glad.

Pap., Add. MS. 44113, XXVIII). In reply Gladstone indicated that he did not wish to come forward any more than he had. 'My old Crimean responsibilities forced me forward: my position in the party as a leader who has abdicated holds me back. I desire therefore to leave the further prosecution of this great business, if I can, in the hands of others' (Gladstone to Bright, 27 Sept. 1876, Bright Papers, British Library, Add. MS. 43385, III).

[76] Wirthwein, pp. 88–9; Shannon, pp. 114–15, 126–9; Thompson, i. 398–9; *Horrors*, pp. 275–6.

[77] J. A. Giles to Granville, 21 and 23 Sept. 1876, Gran. Pap., PRO 30 29/26a. The Exeter Hall meeting on the evening of 18 September was jammed with working men who had been invited 'to express their horror'. That afternoon a meeting at the Guildhall rejected a motion expressing confidence in the Government and substituted one calling for an early reassembling of Parliament. On the next day an 'excited audience of over 3,000 workingmen' listened to the Duke of Argyll and the Earl of Shaftesbury at Glasgow (Wirthwein, pp. 90–2).

[78] Thompson, i. 408–12; Shannon, pp. 113–14; Wirthwein, p. 87; *Horrors*, pp. 248–50. Stratford's suggestion of a 'mixed commission', he later explained to Gladstone was to be composed of Turks, as well as Christians, the latter to be selected by the mediating Powers (Stratford deRedcliffe to Gladstone, 14 Sept. 1876, Glad. Pap., Add. MS. 44451, CCCLXVI).

[79] Froude to Lady Derby, 19 Sept. 1876 (H. Paul, *Life of Froude*, London, 1905, pp. 279–80); Queen Victoria memorandum, 13 Sept. 1876, RA H9/118; Salisbury to Carnarvon, 13 Sept. 1876, Salis. Pap., vol. 8; Disraeli to Lady Bradford, 12 Sept. 1876, Disraeli–Bradford letters; Disraeli to Derby, 12 Sept. 1876, Derby Pap.; Mallet to Lytton, 15 Sept. 1876, Lytton Pap., India Office, E218/517/2; Thompson, i. 419–22; *Horrors*, pp. 271–81, 284–5; Disraeli to Derby, 10 Sept. 1876, Derby Pap. Harris writes that 'the foreign secretary's speeches . . . did tend to cut the ground out from under the agitation. . . . Furthermore even had there been no explanation, it is doubtful if the agitation could have gone on in its full intensity much longer . . .' (*Horrors*, pp. 291–2). Lord Stanley of Alderley, diplomatist and Orientalist, and also a converted Muslim, agreed with Froude that except for Hartington the Liberal leaders were behaving badly. 'By expressing my regret that you [Salisbury] and your colleagues are the victims of such factious hypocrisy. . . . Gladstone is to get up an agitation for party purposes and accuse you all of complicity in massacres . . .' (Stanley of Alderley to Salisbury, 21 Sept. 1876, Salis. Pap., E).

[80] Hardy to Cairns, 14 Sept. 1876, Cairns Pap., PRO 30 51/7; Hardy to Derby, 15 Sept. 1876, Derby Pap.; Cairns to Hardy, 16 Sept. 1876, Cran. Pap., HA43/T501/262; Cairns to Disraeli, 16 Sept. 1876, Disraeli Pap. xx/Ca/188. Hardy agreed with Cairns that the agitation tied the Government's hands and gave Russia a clear field for mischief (Hardy to Cairns, 14 Sept. 1876, Cairns Pap., PRO 30 51/7). Cairns was especially anxious about Derby. 'I wish D. had a touch, even the slightest, of sentiment' (Cairns to Cross, 16 Sept. 1876, Cross Papers, British Library, Add. MS. 51268, VI). Hardy wished the Cabinet were more fully informed as to Britain's policy, and Cairns and Carnarvon were pushing for a Cabinet (Carnarvon to Hardy, 17 Sept. 1876, Cran. Pap., HA43/T501/262). Cairns favoured all the Powers forcing the Porte to create autonomous but tributary states which would be guaranteed.

[81] Derby to Queen Victoria, 19 Sept. 1876, RA H9/132; Derby to Disraeli, 12 Sept. 1876, Derby Pap. 'My [Derby] deputation went off well. There were two of them. The first respectable and sensible: the second a gathering of idiots who talked about doing away with war . . .' (ibid.). Derby received the Guildhall deputation at the Foreign Office on 27 September and spoke for his local or administrative autonomy. Without mentioning Gladstone by name, the Foreign Secretary characterized his proposals 'as outside the range of practical politics' (Thompson, i. 424–31; Wirthwein, pp. 96–8).

[82] Thompson, ii. 16–19; Shannon, pp. 123–4; Gladstone to Granville, 16 Sept. 1876,

Ramm, i. 8–9. On 16 September, five days after Derby's speech to the deputations, Northcote spoke at a Conservative meeting at Edinburgh. His personal desire was to 'try to get something better than the status quo as regards the administration of the [Turkish] provinces' (Northcote to Disraeli, 19 Sept. 1876, Northc. Pap., Add. MS. 50053, XLI); Thompson, i. 417–18; Wirthwein, pp. 89–90; Queen Victoria to Disraeli, 20 Sept. 1876, RA H9/135. Northcote wrote of his effort at Edinburgh that it was 'rather remarkable that the Edinburgh people have not held any atrocities meetings: I believe they don't mean to hold one' (Northcote to Richmond, 18 Sept. 1876, Goodwood Papers, West Sussex Record Office, 868; hereafter cited as Good. Pap.).

⁸³ Disraeli to Lady Bradford, 21 Sept. 1876, MB vi. 67; Thompson, ii. 19–22; Wirthwein, pp. 94–5; Ponsoby to Queen Victoria, 20 Sept. 1876, RA H9/136; Froude to Lady Derby, 22 Sept. 1876, W. H. Dunn, *James Anthony Froude*, 2 vols., Oxford, 1961–3, ii. 448; Shannon, pp. 130–1. In the last week of September the *Daily News* counted 262 agitation meetings since MacGahan's telegram of 7 August (*Horrors*, pp. 251–3). Disraeli's speech at Aylesbury occurred when 'the campaign for his vacated seat in the Commons was coming to an end. . . . There was a disposition throughout the country to regard the election as an important test of the ministry's strength' (ibid., pp. 314–20). In the Bucks election the anti-Turk and Liberal Carrington lost to the pro-Turkish Conservative Freemantle by 186 votes, 2,539 to 2,725. For an interesting discussion of the Bucks election see Richard W. Davis, *Political Change and Continuity 1760–1885* (Hamden, Conn., 1972), pp. 201–5. For a contemporary reaction to the Prime Minister's address at Aylesbury see W. Boyd Carpenter, *Some Pages of My Life* (London, 1911), pp. 233–4. For Disraeli's reaction to his own speech at Aylesbury see MB, vi 83–4. Cairns described the Bucks election as 'a narrow squeak' and Disraeli's speech as too 'defiant of public opinion'. He complained to Richmond that Derby and the Prime Minister put too little 'sentiment, & sympathy with public feeling into their speeches' (Cairns to Richmond, 23 Sept. 1876, Good. Pap. 868).

⁸⁴ Granville to Argyll, 24 Sept. 1876, Argyll, *Autobiography*, ii. 324.

# CHAPTER TWELVE

¹ Disraeli to Lady Bradford, 1 Sept. 1876, Zetland, ii. 84. There are in the PRO six volumes used by Shannon (FO 78/2551–6) which contain letters and notices of the public meetings, together with the resolutions these meetings passed, which were sent to the Foreign Office. The period covered is from the beginning of September to the end of December 1876. Volume 2551, which contains notices from 1 to 11 September, is the largest of the six volumes. Volume 2556, which goes from 10 October to the end of December, also contains the beginning of resolutions sent from gatherings which supported the Government and condemned the agitation meetings. Each meeting passed usually between two and five resolutions. The most popular type of resolution was the one which expressed outrage at the barbarities committed in Bulgaria; next were those which demanded the recall of Elliot and those requesting the taking of measures to prevent a reoccurrence of the atrocities. Then came those which favoured the removal of British support for Turkey, called for independence or self-government for Bulgaria and Bosnia, suggested reparations and relief aid for Turkey's Christians, called for an autumn session of Parliament, expressed thanks to the *Daily News*, and desired the removal of the fleet from Besika Bay.

² Lyons to Derby, 7 Sept. 1876, Derby Pap.

³ Derby's energy was not restricted to the Eastern Question. When Morier reported from Lisbon another of the stream of rumours regarding Iberian union, he was told by the Foreign Secretary that the independence of Portugal was important and that 'the

British government would not view with indifference any Spanish attempt to force Portugal into a union' (Derby to Morier, 23 Oct. 1876, PRO FO 244/299, no. 68).

⁴ Blake points out that Disraeli shared the widely accepted opinion that if Aberdeen had shown a readiness to go to war, the Tsar would have backed down and the Crimean conflict would have been prevented. Disraeli felt that peace and British interests could be upheld only if 'the credibility of the British threat to intervene on the side of Turkey' was evident (Blake, *Disraeli*, p. 607).

⁵ Disraeli to Derby, 21 Oct. 1876, MB vi. 99; same to same, 21 Oct. 1876, Derby Pap.; Disraeli to Hardy, 21 Oct. 1876, Cran. Pap., HA 43/T501/266; Disraeli to Derby, 22 Oct. 1876, MB vi. 99–100; same to same, 22 Oct. 1876, Derby Pap.; Hardy diary, 24 Oct. 1876, Hardy, i. 374; MB vi. 100. Northcote wrote to Hardy of the financial, Parliamentary, and diplomatic obstacles in the way of a British occupation of Constantinople (Northcote to Hardy, 24 Oct. 1876, Cran. Pap., HA 43/T501/271). The Foreign Office was informed by the War Office that Lieutenant-Colonels Home and Elphinstone had been ordered to Constantinople on special service. On 28 October Mr. Hertslet drew up for the Foreign Office a memorandum on the instructions given to Stratford deRedcliffe and Colonel Rose in 1853 and 1854 on the sending of a British fleet into the Dardanelles and Bosphorus (PRO FO 146/1884, Foreign Office confidential print, 2 Nov. 1876). As no secret was made of sending the British officers to Contantinople, the Russians were aware of their arrival and purpose (Onou to wife, 22 Nov. 1876, Jomini–Onou Pap., Eg. 3226). According to Zichy, the Austrian ambassador at Constantinople, the presence of four British engineer officers 'has not been well received by the Russians' (Zichy to Andrassy, teleg., 12 Nov. 1876, HHSA, PA xii, 114). Preston has done a solid and useful dissertation on British military and strategic planning during the years from 1876 to 1880. He points out that Colonel Home produced two secret memorandums which argued for a British occupation of Constantinople. They were delivered to Disraeli on the evening of 21 October. It was after this that the Prime Minister and Hardy decided to send officers to Constantinople to plan for the fortification of both the lines around the city and the Bulair ridges near Gallipoli (A. Preston, 'British Military Policy and the Defence of India', Univ. of London dissertation, 1966, pp. 127–33).

⁶ Derby to Disraeli, 29 Oct. 1876, Derby Pap.; Hardy to Disraeli, 30 Oct. 1876, Disraeli Pap. xx/Ha/133; Derby to Hardy, 31 Oct. 1876, Derby Pap.; Hunt to Derby, 24 Oct. 1876, ibid.; Derby to Hunt, 24 Oct. 1876, MB vi. 100; same to same, 24 Oct. 1876, Derby Pap.; Hunt to Disraeli, 24 Oct. 1876, Disraeli Pap. xx/S/1174.

⁷ Disraeli to Derby, 25 Oct. 1876, Derby Pap.; Derby to Disraeli, 25 Oct. 1876, ibid.; Tenterden to Derby, 26 Oct. 1876, ibid.; Tenterden to Derby, 28 Oct. 1876, ibid.; Derby to Disraeli, 28 Oct. 1876, ibid.; Disraeli to Derby, 29 Oct. 1876, ibid. Disraeli wrote to reassure the Queen. 'When a first rate Power [Russia] violates the conditions of a first rate treaty [Paris of 1856] the consequences must or at least, should be serious. They need not take the form of absolute warfare: they might be a blockade, or the occupation of some point of territory. . . . Their precise nature cd not be laid before Your Majesty until circumstances have more developed' (Disraeli to Queen Victoria, 21 Oct. 1876, RA H10/120).

⁸ Disraeli to Queen Victoria, 25 Oct. 1876, ibid.

⁹ Lytton to Morley, Simla, [?] Sept. 1876, Lytton Pap., India Office, E218/522/15; George Hamilton to Lytton, 1 Sept. 1876, ibid. 517/2; Lytton to Disraeli, 18 Sept. 1876, ibid. 518/1; Lytton to Queen Victoria, 4 Oct. 1876, *QVL* ii. 482–4; Lytton to Salisbury, 2 Oct. 1876, PRO FO 424/44, no. 30.

¹⁰ Salisbury to Disraeli, 29 Oct. 1876, Disraeli Pap. B/xx/Ce/273; Lytton to Salisbury, 25 Oct. 1876, Lytton Pap.; same to same, 25 Oct. 1876, Salis. Pap.; M. A. Khan, 'British *Attitudes to the Growth of Russian Influence in the Central Asian States 1867–78*, (McGill Ph.D., Montreal, 1962), pp. 287–8.

¹¹ Morley to Harrison, [?] Sept. 1876 (Francis W. Hirst, *Early Life and Letters of John*

*Morley*, 2 vols., London, 1927, i. 30); Granville to Hartington, 1 Sept. 1876, Hart. Pap. 304/672; Granville to Argyll, 18 Sept. 1876, Gran. Pap., PRO 30 29/22a; Shannon, p. 140.

[12] One obvious defector from the agitation cause in the beginning of October was *The Times*. Delane, its editor, feared unilateral Russian intervention into the Ottoman Empire if the agitation in Britain continued (Wirthwein, pp. 116–17; Gladstone to Hayward, 10 Oct. 1876, A. Hayward, *Correspondence*, ii. 267).

[13] Shannon, pp. 141–3; William T. Stead, *The M.P. for Russia* (N.Y., 1909), pp. 275–80. Shannon feels that the atrocities agitation began in late August and ended in early October. From then on it was 'got up' by committees (Shannon, pp. 144–6).

[14] Loftus to Derby, Yalta, teleg., 2 Nov. 1876, PRO FO 424/45, no. 46.

[15] Derby to Loftus, 3 Nov. 1876, ibid., no. 56.

[16] Hartington to Duke of Devonshire, 8 Oct. 1876, Hart. Pap. 340/476.

[17] Campbell to Salisbury, Constantinople, 17 Oct. 1876, Derby Pap. Elliot at this point was very depressed and near a breakdown from overwork, worry, and criticism.

[18] Salisbury to Disraeli, 23 Oct. 1876, Disraeli Pap. xx/Ce/181; Salisbury to Carnarvon, 13 Sept. 1876, Salis. Pap., vol. 8. Hartington thought that 'Dizzy's speeches and Sir H. Elliot's known antipathy to Russia make the Turks utterly disbelieve that we can ever leave them in the lurch and let Russia have her own way' (Hartington to Duke of Devonshire, 8 Oct. 1876, Hart. Pap. 340/676).

[19] Disraeli to Queen Victoria, 4 Oct. 1876, RA H10/17.

[20] Salisbury to Derby, 3 Nov. 1876, Derby Pap.; Derby to Salisbury, 3 Nov. 1876, ibid.

[21] Lady Derby to Salisbury, 3 Nov. 1876, Salis. Pap., E.

[22] Salisbury to Disraeli, 23 Sept. 1876, MB vi. 70–1; same to same, 23 Sept. 1876, Derby Pap.; same to same, 23 Sept. 1876, Disraeli Pap. xx/Ce/219. For Salisbury's explanation to others, see Salisbury to Carnarvon, 13 Sept. 1876, Salis. Pap., vol. 8 and Salisbury to Mallet, 23 Sept. 1876, ibid., vol. 12. Disraeli forwarded Salisbury's letter to Derby who described Salisbury's suggestion as 'large and new; it amounts to a new constitution for the Turkish empire. I hardly think we could get it adopted, or that if adopted it would work' (Derby to Disraeli, 26 Sept. 1876, Disraeli Pap. xx/S/1158; same to same, 26 Sept. 1876, Derby Pap.). Salisbury was not ready to let go completely of Ottoman integrity because Russia could not be trusted and also because the latter distrusted England. Otherwise, Salisbury would have been ready to join with Russia in turning the Turks out of Europe (Salisbury to Mallet, 23 Sept. 1876, Salis. Pap., vol. 12). A scheme similar to Salisbury's was advocated by Lord Grey, the former Colonial Secretary, in a letter in *The Times* on 18 November (Wirthwein, pp. 141–2).

[23] Elliot wrote strongly opposing Constantinople as the site for the conference because it would give undue influence to Ignatiev and be exceedingly humiliating for the Ottoman Government. The ambassador described European interference or foreign control, in order to guarantee administrative autonomy, as a mistake (Elliot to Derby, 20 Oct. 1876, PRO FO 424/45, no. 65). The British bases, which Derby put forward, had been suggested by Tenterden (Tenterden memorandum, 4 Oct. 1876, Derby Pap.; Tenterden to Derby, 29 Oct. 1876, ibid.). Tenterden also contacted the War Office to send British officers to help arrange the armistice between Serbia and Montenegro with Turkey. It is significant that in the above British bases and in instructions later drawn up for Salisbury as representative to the Constantinople conference, Bulgaria was distinctly kept separate from Bosnia. It would require more than a battalion of Philadelphia lawyers to explain the difference between administrative autonomy and similar guarantees against maladministration. Bulgaria crowded upon Constantinople geographically in a way that Bosnia did not. Local or administrative autonomy, whatever it meant, was therefore less dangerous to Britain in Bosnia-Hercegovina than it would have been in Bulgaria.

[24] Disraeli to Derby, 4 Nov. 1876, MB vi. 89; same to same, 4 Nov. 1876, Derby Pap.;

Buchanan to Derby, Vienna, teleg., 2.45 p.m., 5 Nov. 1876, PRO FO 424/45, no. 126.

[25] Buchanan to Derby, teleg., secret, 5.45 p.m., 5 Nov. 1876, ibid., no 129. In London, in the meantime, Corry, Disrael's private secretary, was discussing with Montgelas an Anglo-Austrian alliance treaty.

[26] Loftus to Derby, Yalta, teleg., 6 Nov. 1876, ibid., no. 161. Lyons interpreted a possible Russian occupation as a Russian scheme. 'It looks very much as if the Russians were simply scheming in order to get into Bulgaria without a war with Turkey—in short to paralyse at once Turkish armed resistance, and European opposition, by playing the part of the agents of the European Conference' (Lyons to Derby, 7 Nov. 1876, Derby Pap.). On the back of this letter Derby wrote 'No doubt this is their game' (ibid.).

[27] Derby had no intention of acquiescing in a Russian occupation. 'We cannot give way on that point' (Derby to Disraeli, 7 Nov. 1876, ibid.). He let Shuvalov know this as well. Germany accepted the conference 'in principle' on 10 November.

[28] The Queen was leaning the same way. 'Should not advantage be taken of Austria's inclination to go with us? Germany seems unmanageable, but Austria has shown much more disposition to agree with us' (Queen Victoria to Disraeli, 1–2 Nov. 1876, QVL ii. 493).

[29] There are a number of discrepancies regarding these talks as given by Stojanovic using the Austrian archives (Stojanovic, pp. 125–7) and the information in the Disraeli Papers (Corry to Disraeli, 5 Nov. 1876, Disraeli Pap. B/xvi/10; Montgelas to Corry, 5 Nov. 1876, ibid. xvi/C/162; Corry draft treaty, 7 Nov. 1876, ibid. xvi/C/164a–c; Montgelas to Corry, 7 Nov. 1876, ibid. xvi/C/165). Taylor is mistaken in writing that Disraeli only acquiesced in a conference when he failed to get an Austrian alliance (Taylor, pp. 241–2). Disraeli wished an understanding with Andrássy to strengthen Britain's hand at the meeting.

[30] Thompson, ii. 93; Gladstone to Granville, 8 Nov. 1876, Gran. Pap., PRO 30 29/29a; Gladstone repeated to Granville a bit of gossip told him by Olga Novikov. 'There is a story that the cabinet have decided to occupy Egypt if Russia occupies Bulgaria' (Gladstone to Granville, 8 Nov. 1876, ibid.; Olga Novikov to Gladstone, 7 Nov. 1876, Glad. Pap., Add. MS. 44268, CLXXXIII). Salisbury wrote to the Marquis of Bath minimizing the differences between the Government and its Bulgarian critics and also defending Derby for whom he had little respect and less liking (Salisbury to Bath, 10 Nov. 1876, Salis. Pap., D/xvii/84).

[31] Bylandt to Willebois, London, 11 Nov. 1876, NA 388. Florence Nightingale referred to Salisbury as 'a master of men' (Ponsonby to Queen Victoria, 11 Nov. 1876, RA H11/110).

[32] Lady Derby to Salisbury, 9 Nov. 1876, Salis. Pap., E. One might surmise that Count Shuvalov, with whom Lady Derby was on close terms, would have been at least equally 'glad to know' the British position.

[33] Queen Victoria to Disraeli, 10 Nov. 1876, QVL ii. 496. The Queen favoured independence and neutrality for Serbia and Montenegro as the best guarantee against future Russian interference in the Balkans and the raising of the Eastern Question. Ponsonby encouraged her in this Gladstonian idea of creating a barrier of free Christian states in the Balkans against Russian aggression. 'These rising countries would cling to us in gratitude' (Ponsonby to Queen Victoria, 6 Nov. 1876, RA H11/73).

[34] Disraeli to Queen Victoria, 8 Nov. 1876, RA H11/97; Disraeli to Queen Victoria, 11 Nov. 1876, QVL ii. 496–8.

[35] Derby to Musurus Pasha, 11 Nov. 1876, PRO FO 424/45, no. 229. Zichy, the Austrian ambassador, was informed by Safvet Pasha, the Ottoman, Foreign Minister, of the Porte's attempt to try to persuade London to abandon the conference. As Elliot was not informed of this attempt, Zichy attempted to persuade Safvet Pasha to repair this discourtesy. The latter sent an interpreter to Elliot to apologize. Zichy, considering the courage Elliot displayed in his 'warm advocacy of Turkish goals', found Ottoman

behaviour 'little encouraging' (Zichy to Andrássy, Constantinople, teleg., 9 Nov. 1876, HHSA, PAxii/114; Zichy to Andrássy, confid., 10 Nov. 1876, ibid.).

[36] Disraeli to Derby, 4 Nov. 1876, MB vi. 89; Thompson, ii. 94–7.

[37] Bylandt to Willebois, London, 11 Nov. 1876, NA 388. Menebrea, the Italian minister, also was drawn to comment on the much-quoted bellicose section of Disraeli's speech (Menebrea to Melegari, 11 Nov. 1876, IFM 114, 73). Lady Knightley thought the speech was 'pluckily dignified, and statesmanlike' (Lady Knightley's journal, 10 Nov. 1876, Knightley, *Journals*, pp. 309–10).

[38] The Tsar had been in the Crimea at Livadia from 9 September until 7 November. While there, he was converted or converted himself to a more forceful and warlike policy, apparently supported by Ignatiev and Gorchakov though opposed by Reutern, the Finance Minister. Still unsympathetic to his own Pan-Slavs, he was influenced by them and Russian opinion in general that the use of compulsion against Turkey was necessary. In September Bismarck was sounded as to Germany's position should Russia be forced to take isolated action. At the end of the same month Vienna was approached on a combined Russo-Austrian occupation of Bulgaria and Bosnia. Andrássy refused and Bismarck would not openly side with either St. Petersburg or Vienna against the other. In October the Tsar suggested to Francis Joseph a secret treaty, which Austria accepted, to be negotiated through Novikov. By the middle of October Alexander II approved of a plan of unilateral war, as Austria refused a joint campaign, if diplomacy failed, and partial mobilization was sanctioned for 13 November. At the end of October Serbian military defeat elicited the Russian ultimatum which Mackenzie interprets as the reassertion of official leadership and the relegation of Slav committees and the Press to the background. For all this see Sumner, pp. 196–228; Stojanovic, pp. 111–27; Mackenzie, pp. 134–53; Rupp, pp. 184–205, 210–30, 233–54; Taylor, pp. 238–9.

[39] Taylor, pp. 238–9; Doria to Derby, St. Petersburg, teleg., 12.30 p.m., 11 Nov. 1876, PRO FO 424/45, no. 222. The Tsar had not yet received news of Disraeli's speech at the Guildhall when he made his own. Giers attempted to explain away the menace of an appeal to arms as an attempt on the part of Alexander II 'to keep the initiative out of the hands of Slav Committees' (Doria to Derby, teleg., 3.30 p.m., 11 Nov. 1876, ibid., no. 224). The Queen did not like the speech of the Russian Emperor but wrote in her journal that 'I believe he was forced to make it, in order to appease the excitement of his people, who are most fanatical' (Queen's journal, 11 Nov. 1876, RA). Disraeli repeated Doria's opinion of the Tsar's address to the Queen (Disraeli to Queen Victoria, 17 Nov. 1876, RA H11/135).

[40] Thompson, ii. 102–3; Borthwick to Corry, 13 Nov. 1876, Disraeli Pap. xvi/c/24. The Queen was anxious about Russian war preparations and had Ponsonby telegraph Derby. The foreign secretary replied that Russia's purpose was 'to influence and intimidate the conference. . . . War is undoubtedly contemplated by Russia as a possible alternative but there seems no ground for supposing that it is decided on' (Derby to Ponsonby, teleg., 15 Nov. 1876, RA H11/121).

[41] Derby to Elliot, teleg., 16 Nov. 1876, PRO FO 424/45, no. 313. On 17 November Elliot enclosed to London a letter from Colonel Home on fortification outside and around Constantinople. On the back of Elliot's dispatch Tenterden wrote a minute. 'The result is that 100,000 men with 200 guns could defend the position with a week's preparation. In case of England supporting the defense 65,000 men wd. be wanted & 120 guns. The men could be raised in Turkey or India' (Elliot to Derby, secret, 17 Nov. 1876, PRO FO 78/2467, no. 1291).

[42] Lady Derby to Salisbury, 14 Nov. 1876, Salis. Pap. E. On 16 November Lord Camperdown dined at Lady Derby's and Salisbury and Shuvalov were present. 'Shouvaloff was making himself doubly extra agreeable to Lady Derby, who thinks him a sincere friend of peace' (Camperdown to Northbrook, 19 Nov. 1876, Northb. Pap., India Office, C 144/7).

[43] Bismarck informed Russell that he would come from the country to Berlin in order to see Salisbury (Russell to Derby, teleg., 17 Nov. 1876, PRO FO 424/45, no. 364). Disraeli encouraged Salisbury to see Europe's leaders on his way to the conference as 'there has been little real interchange of thought between the English Government & foreign powers' (Disraeli to Salisbury, 10 Nov. 1876, Salis. Pap., E 170–3).

[44] Tenterden memorandum, 14 Nov. 1876, Derby Pap.

[45] Gorchakov told Nigra, the Italian ambassador to Russia, that only a Russian occupation of Bulgaria would be satisfactory to his Government (Nigra to Melegari, 16 Nov. 1876, IFM 159, 44).

[46] Derby to Buchanan, confid., 16 Nov. 1876, PRO FO 424/45, no. 320.

[47] Derby to Disraeli, 18 Nov. 1876, Disraeli Pap. xx/S/1186, 1186a.

[48] Queen Victoria to Salisbury, 18 Nov. 1876, QVL ii. 500–1.

[49] Lady Derby to Salisbury, 18 Nov. 1876, Salis. Pap., E.

[50] Borthwick to Corry, 19 Nov. 1876, Disraeli Pap. xvi/C/26. Shuvalov complained that he could never extract anything from Derby (ibid.).

[51] Montenegrin military success and the influence of Monson who strongly supported territorial compensation for Montenegro account for this (Monson to Derby, 9 Nov. 1876, PRO FO 424/45, no. 392).

[52] Derby to Salisbury, 20 Nov. 1876, PRO FO 424/46, no. 1. Derby also explained to Elliot that there was no desire in London to impose any particular scheme of local autonomy. 'An International Commission' to replace the use of a diplomatic veto, was one variation which the Foreign Secretary mentioned (Derby to Elliot, 20 Nov. 1876, ibid., no. 9).

[53] Carnarvon to Salisbury, 20 Nov. 1876, Hardinge, ii. 345–6; Richmond to Cairns, 19 Nov. 1876, Cairns Pap., PRO FO 51/3; Derby to Disraeli, 19 Nov. 1876, MB vi. 95; same to same, 19 Nov. 1876, Derby Pap. The Cabinet which met on Thursday, 23 November agreed to the supplementary instruction which Derby sent privately to Salisbury (Derby to Salisbury, 24 Nov. 1876, Derby Pap.).

[54] Derby to Disraeli, 19 Nov. 1876, MB vi. 95; same to same, 19 Nov. 1876, Derby Pap.

[55] Disraeli to Derby, 20 Nov. 1876, MB vi. 96. Three and a half weeks later, however, the Prime Minister appealed to Derby in order to 'quiet' Cairns who was still arguing for occupation (Disraeli to Derby, 9 Dec. 1876, MB vi. 96).

# CHAPTER THIRTEEN

[1] Salisbury to Derby, teleg., 6 Dec. 1876, PRO FO 424/37, no. 20. One of the two French delegates to the conference reported that Salisbury was showing a conciliatory attitude and did not oppose an international gendarmery commanded by European officers. Bourgoing thought that an Anglo-Russian agreement was possible (Bourgoing to Decazes, 6 Dec. 1876, DDF ii. 123). Schuyler who was 'advising Ignatiev' thought so as well (Schuyler diary, 7 Dec. 1876, Schuyler, Selected Essays, p. 91; hereafter cited as Schuyler). Salisbury described Ignatiev's occupation proposal as designed to make Britain responsible for any further Turkish atrocities if they opposed it (Salisbury to Derby, 7 Dec. 1876, Salis. Pap., vol. 16; same to same, 7 Dec. 1876, Derby Pap.). After he read Salisbury's telegram of the sixth, Cairns wrote to Derby urging the acceptance of Ignatiev's suggestion 'that some force . . . should be provided to prevent the possibility of a massacre of Christians pending the inauguration of reforms'. Cairns's only reservation was that such a proposal should be 'properly guarded and qualified' (Cairns to Derby, 7 Dec. 1876, Derby Pap.). Richmond agreed with Cairns

and Salisbury that to break off the conference on Ignatiev's proposal would be 'awkward' for Britain (Richmond to Disraeli, 8 Dec. 1876, Disraeli Pap. xx/Le/120; same to same, 8 Dec. 1876, Good. Pap. 868). Cairns was even more strongly in favour of an occupation than Richmond, and thought that the Porte ought to be made to request one (Cairns to Richmond, 11 Dec. 1876, ibid.).

² Disraeli to Salisbury, secret, 1 Dec. 1876, Salis. Pap., E 186–90. On 5 December Disraeli telegraphed Salisbury that the above unofficial advice was on its way, and that, until he received it, he was to 'maintain a cordial reserve'. Salisbury telegraphed back that he had begun already to negotiate as it would be 'injurious' to delay (Disraeli to Salisbury, 5 Dec. 1876 and Salisbury to Disraeli, 6 Dec. 1876, Disraeli Pap. xx/Ce/185 and 186). Morier, the British diplomat, supported a plan for a joint Anglo-Russian occupation (Morier to Malet, 2 Dec. 1876, Morier Papers, Ramm, pp. 60–1). Salisbury very quietly and indirectly mooted an English occupation and found that the suggestion of it elicited great resentment (Salisbury to Disraeli, secret, 11 Dec. 1876, Disraeli Pap. xx/Ce/226).

³ Salisbury to Derby, teleg., 8 Dec. 1876, PRO FO 424/37, no. 21; same to same, 7 Dec. 1876, Derby Pap.; Calice to Andrássy, 7 Dec. 1876, HHSA, PA xii/115; Zichy and Calice to Andrássy, 7 Dec. 1876, ibid.

⁴ H. S. Northcote to Northcote, 7 Dec. 1876, Northc. Pap., Add. MS. 50032, xx.

⁵ Schuyler diary, 7 Dec. 1876, Schuyler, p. 91.

⁶ Onou to wife, 10 Dec. 1876, Jomini–Onou Pap., Eg. 3227. Later Onou admitted that Madame Ignatiev had succeeded in attracting the Salisburys (Onou to wife, 13 Dec. 1876, ibid.). Eleven days later Onou wrote that Ignatiev arranged with his wife to 'work on' both Chaudordy and Salisbury, and that they both had responded positively to her flirting (Onou to wife, 24 Dec. 1876, ibid.).

⁷ Shuvalov to Gorchakov and Ignatiev, 7 and 8 Dec. 1876 (Seton-Watson, *Slav. Rev.* iv. 452).

⁸ Lady Derby to Salisbury, 7 Dec. 1876, Salis. Pap., E.

⁹ Salisbury to Disraeli, secret, 11 Dec. 1876, Disraeli Pap. xx/Ce/226; Richmond to Disraeli, 8 Dec. 1876, ibid. xx/Le/120; Carnarvon to Derby, 10 Dec. 1876, Carnarv. Pap., PRO 30 6/8; same to same, 10 Dec. 1876, Derby Pap.; Cairns to Derby, 9 Dec. 1876, ibid.; Derby to Cairns, 8 Dec. 1876, ibid.; Richmond to Cairns, 12 Dec. 1876, Cairns Pap., PRO FO 30 51/3; Carnarvon to Cairns, 13 Dec. 1876, Cairns and Carnarv. Pap., PRO 30 51/8 and PRO 30 6/6. Manners thought that occupation was a Russian trap for Salisbury set by Ignatiev (Manners to Disraeli, 13 Dec. 1876, Disraeli Pap. xx/M/203).

¹⁰ Salisbury to Carnarvon, 11 Dec. 1876, Salis. Pap., vol. 8. Derby defended himself against any personal indiscretion and blamed the mischief on Shuvalov for attempting that 'old diplomatic dodge' of setting the Secretary of State against the ambassador. 'The truth is I have been cautious almost to excess' with Shuvalov (Derby to Salisbury, 14 Dec. 1876, Derby Pap.; Derby to Disraeli, 14 Dec. 1876, Disraeli Pap. xx/S/1192). No mention or suspicion of Lady Derby was put forward.

¹¹ Northcote to Derby, 14 Dec. 1876, Derby Pap.; Carnarvon to Derby, 14 Dec. 1876, ibid.; Northcote to Cross, 14 Dec. 1876, Cross Pap., Add. MS. 51265, iii. Northcote wrote also to the Prime Minister pressing the adoption of a 'national gendarmerie with a Belgian contingent', as he argued that the moment for a settlement and the averting of a war had come (Northcote to Disraeli, 15 Dec. 1876, Disraeli Pap. xx/N/20).

¹² Onou wrote to his wife that Ignatiev exaggerated the danger of a Muslim rising and further atrocities in order to win support for foreign occupation (Onou to wife, 3 Jan. 1877, Jomini–Onou Pap., Eg. 3227).

¹³ Since at least the fifteenth of November Schuyler had been busy 'getting up a constitution for Bulgaria' which Ignatiev was to present at the conference. By 5 December the plan for Bulgaria, which Tzeretelev assisted on, was almost finished (Schuyler to Mrs. Schaeffer, 15 Nov. 1876, Schuyler, pp. 85–6; Zichy to Andrássy, 5 Dec. 1876,

HHSA PA xii/115). Washburn and Long of Robert College were also at work and sent Elliot a 'Memoir of reforms in Turkey', which the ambassador forwarded to London (Elliot to Derby, 9 Nov. 1876, PRO FO 424/45, no. 346).

[14] Tenterden memorandum, 13 Dec. 1876, Foreign Office print, Foreign Office library, vol. 57, 2997. There was some British hesitation about the Russian proposal to restrict Ottoman troops to specific fortified places, as Derby thought that in such a case the Porte could not maintain order. Not surprisingly, Andrássy opposed Ignatiev's proposals as 'the first step towards the decomposition of Turkey. ... The whole scheme in his opinion goes too far ... whereas a more modest plan, accepting what exists and merely reforming abuses ... but leaving the Central Power sufficient authority to maintain order, would gradually bring about the civilization of the country' (Buchanan to Derby, teleg., 11 Dec. 1876, PRO FO 424/46, no. 280). Berlin approved Ignatiev's proposals (Russell to Derby, teleg., 13 Dec. 1876, ibid., no. 311).

[15] On 11 December Salisbury telegraphed that he was ready to accept the gendarmery proposal, and that if the Cabinet objected 'they must stop' him (Salisbury to Derby, teleg., 9.45 p.m., 11 Dec. 1876, PRO FO 424/37, no. 26).

[16] Zichy and Calice wrote of a 'significant rapprochement' between Russia and Britain (Zichy and Calice to Andrássy, telegs., 13 Dec. 1876, HHSA, PA xii/115). This 'rapprochement' concerned both Andrássy and Bismarck. The latter on 27 December told Russell that while he was happy to see Anglo-Russian harmony, he regretted that Salisbury was not showing more support and interest in Austria. The German statesman suggested that British sympathy for Austria would help maintain Andrássy in office and prevent those Austrian ministers who favoured a war against Russia from obtaining their opportunity (Russell to Derby, secret, 27 Dec. 1876, PRO FO 424/48, no. 20).

[17] Lady Derby to Cross, 14 Dec. 1876, Cross Pap., Add. MS. 51266, iv.

[18] Zichy and Calice to Andrássy, most secret, 12 Dec. 1876, HHSA, PA xii/115. Mackenzie writes that Austria opposed Montenegrin access to the Adriatic (Mackenzie, pp. 176–7). It seems that Austria opposed only some possible accesses to the sea for Montenegro. Andrássy, apparently, would have been happy to see Montenegro gain the sea to the south, through Albania.

[19] Derby to Salisbury, teleg., 12 Dec. 1876, PRO FO 424/37, no. 32. Disraeli discussed with Derby this reply and agreed with the Foreign Secretary 'that it would not be politic to be precipitate in entertaining the Russian proposals' (Disraeli to Queen Victoria, 11 Dec. 1876, RA H11/219). The Queen agreed with Salisbury as to the awkwardness of breaking off on this point, and wished to allow him the freedom 'to make some arrangement' (Queen Victoria to Disraeli, teleg., 9 Dec. 1876, RA H11/215).

[20] Salisbury to Derby, teleg., 13 Dec. 1876, PRO FO 424/37, no. 37.

[21] Salisbury to Derby, secret, teleg., 13 Dec. 1876, ibid., no. 39; same to same, teleg., 14 Dec. 1876, ibid., no. 51. Mackenzie implies that Russia abandoned her own occupation of Bulgaria because of Austrian objections, and that neither Austria nor England objected to a large Bulgaria on ethnic grounds (Mackenzie, pp. 175–6). This does not seem to have been the case. All the representatives at the conference opposed occupation by the Great Powers, and the opposition was led by Salisbury. Also Britain did object to a large Bulgaria on both ethnic and strategic grounds, and, again, it was Salisbury who suggested the longitudinal division of the province. 'It was in the first instance proposed that one province of Bulgaria should be constituted, extending from the Danube almost to Salonica. To this proposal there appeared to me to be insuperable objections. Under a system of self-government the province would have been in the hands of a Slav majority. ... I pressed therefore, for a subdivision of the district into two, and the dividing line I proposed was so drawn as to leave the eastern district in the hands of a non-Slav population ...' (Salisbury to Derby, 4 Jan. 1877, PRO FO 424/37, no. 168).

[22] Salisbury to Derby, teleg., 7.25 p.m., 14 Dec. 1876, ibid., no. 50; conference of 14 Dec. 1876, HHSA, PA xxii/115.

[23] Derby to Salisbury, teleg., 12.5 a.m., 15 Dec. 1876, PRO FO 424/37, no. 49.

[24] Salisbury to Derby, 15 Dec. 1876, Derby Pap. At this point, opinion in Russia favourable to war apparently subsided. A Russian diplomat, who had just returned to the Embassy at Constantinople from Odessa, reported that 'people' at the general headquarters of the Grand Duke were not enthusiastic about a war (Onou to wife, 17 Dec. 1876, Jomini–Onou Pap., Eg. 3227). Elliot was asking for a 'long leave' which Disraeli saw as the end of his embassy at Constantinople as 'his views . . . [were] entirely of the old school' (Queen's journal, 16 Dec. 1876, RA).

[25] When Ponsonby read this in a letter from Disraeli to the Queen, he contacted Sanderson, Derby's private secretary, who replied that Derby indicated that Shuvalov had never made any such proposal, and asked Ponsonby how he had got such an impression. Later Sanderson told Ponsonby 'that he had heard Schouvaloff had made the proposal in a very vague way to Lady Derby and Ld. B'[eaconsfield] (Sanderson to Ponsonby, 28 Dec. 1876, Sanderson Papers, PRO FO 800/3). The Prime Minister, apparently, was using some poetic licence.

[26] Derby to Salisbury, teleg., 8 p.m., 18 Dec. 1876, PRO FO 424/37, no. 26; same to same, teleg., 8.30 p.m., 18 Dec. 1876, ibid., no. 58; Disraeli to Queen Victoria, 18 Dec. 1876, RA H11/252; Hardy diary, 19 Dec. 1876, Cran. Pap., HA 43/T501/296; Salisbury to Derby, teleg., 1.20 a.m., 17 Dec. 1876, PRO FO 424/37, no. 56.

[27] Zichy and Calice to Andrássy, telegs., 19 Dec. 1876, HHSA, PA xii/115; sixth sitting of 19 Dec. 1876, ibid. On 27 December Bismarck indicated to Odo Russell that in his private opinion the use of Belgian troops was a 'dangerous experiment' and one likely to increase the difficulty of inducing the Porte to accept the whole scheme of reforms (Russell to Derby, secret, 27 Dec. 1876, PRO FO 424/48, no. 19).

[28] In reply to a question from Ignatiev on 26 November, Gorchakov answered that Alexander II preferred a pacific solution (Seton-Watson, pp. 126–7).

[29] Salisbury to Derby, secret, teleg., 1 a.m., 20 Dec. 1876, PRO FO 424/37, no. 66. Colonel Home also believed that the Russians would cross the Pruth on 7 or 9 January (Home to Simmons, 20 Dec. 1876, Simmons Pap., PRO FO 358/1, Lee, pp. 169–72).

[30] Salisbury to Derby, teleg., 11.15 a.m., 21 Dec. 1876, PRO FO 424/37, no. 71.

[31] Salisbury to Derby, teleg., 6 p.m., 21 Dec. 1876, ibid., no. 77; Werther to Bülow, private, 21 Dec. 1876, GFM, A7167. London, in spite of the desire of the special ambassador, had no intention of coercing the Turk to accept, and thereby playing Russia's game. Britain's strategy was to attempt privately to win Ottoman agreement (Queen Victoria to Ponsonby, 20 Dec. 1876, RA, Add. MS., A12/346).

[32] Salisbury to Derby, 21 Dec. 1876, Derby Pap. Elliot and Home believed the Turks were eager for war, but Salisbury, who presumably thought they were bluffing, did not (Home to Simmons, 20 Dec. 1876, Simmons Pap., PRO FO 358/1, Lee, pp. 169–72). According to Zichy, Salisbury told Midhat that the Porte could expect no longer the sympathy and support of England, and Midhat said he knew this, and that Turkey 'would have time enough to ponder the latest change in British policy over the graves of Turks' (Zichy to Andrássy, 22 Dec. 1876, HHSA, PA xii/115).

[33] Onou to Ignatiev, between 21 Dec. and 3 Jan. 1876–7, Jomini–Onou Pap. Eg. 3187; Zichy to Andrássy, teleg., 21 Dec. 1876, HHSA, PA xii/115. Ignatiev told Zichy that if the Turks refused he had been instructed to break off diplomatic relations (Zichy and Calice to Andrássy, telegs., 21 Dec. 1876, ibid.).

[34] Derby to Lyons, 21 Dec. 1876, PRO FO 424/46, no. 396; Derby to Loftus, 21 Dec. 1876, ibid., no. 395; Derby to Salisbury, 21 Dec. 1876, Derby Pap. Disraeli saw the Queen on 20 December, the day before Derby saw Shuvalov and d'Harcourt, and told her that if the Turks refused it would be impossible for Britain to coerce the Porte but that all the plenipotentiaries would leave Constantinople (Queen's journal, 20 Dec. 1876, RA).

[35] Disraeli to Derby, 21 and 22 Dec. 1876, MB vi. 108–9; same to same, 21 and 22 Dec. 1876, Derby Pap.; Derby to Disraeli, 22 Dec. 1876, Disraeli Pap. xx/5/194.

[36] Salisbury to Disraeli, 22 Dec. 1876, ibid. xx/Ce/227. Prophetically, Salisbury predicted that if the Porte refused, war would result in a Russian victory and a great 'scramble' for Ottoman territory (ibid.). 'A line . . . to express an earnest hope that you will strongly support, and if possible, get others to support, any request I may have to make for powers to squeeze the Turk—I believe we have got out of Russia all that it is possible to get. . . . She cannot concede more without danger to the Emperor's position. At all events, I am convinced she will not . . .' (Salisbury to Carnarvon, 22 Dec. 1876, Cecil, ii, 114–16). The Italians informed St. Petersburg that if Austria took Bosnia it would break the balance of power in the Adriatic and force Italy to grab the Trentino (Nigra to Melegari, St. Petersburg, 24 Dec. 1876, IFM 91/64).

[37] Derby to Salisbury, teleg., 8 p.m., 22 Dec. 1876, PRO FO 424/37, no. 80; Disraeli to Queen Victoria, 22 Dec. 1876, RA H11/272.

[38] Carnarvon to Salisbury, secret, 25 Dec. 1876, Salis. Pap., E; Hardy diary, 23 December 1876, Cran. Pap., HA43/T501/296. Carnarvon believed Disraeli was working for war and that he was dragging Derby with him (ibid.). Northcote was anxious about England's course were Turkey to refuse concessions and Russia to threaten force or go to war (Northcote to Cairns, 23 Dec. 1876, Cairns Pap., PRO FO 30 51/5).

[39] H. S. Northcote to S. Northcote, 21 Dec. 1876, Northc. Pap., Add. MS. 50032, xx. Derby wrote of Elliot to the Queen. 'I have no doubt that Sir Henry must have more than once felt his position disagreeable, not being able to say what he really thinks of some of the proposals, being officially bound to support what he does not personally approve of—It is an experience which everybody has to go through in affairs, and by no means a pleasant one' (Derby to Ponsonby, 25 Dec. 1876, RA H11/301).

[40] Elliot to Derby, teleg., 23 Dec. 1876, PRO FO 424/46, no. 406. For a description of the 'broken' Elliot see Onou to wife, 27/28 Dec. 1876, Jomini–Onou Pap., Eg. 3227, fos. 65–74. On 28 December H. S. Northcote wrote to his father, the Chancellor of the Exchequer. 'It is a pity that the Salisburys and Elliots have quarreled so desperately and the ladies on both sides have something to answer for. I so far, and so far only, sympathize with Elliot, that I think he realizes Ignatiev's incredible rascality better than Lord Salisbury. But his only counter plan is to play the Achilles in his tent game, and I fear that as a solution to his comparatively ignoble part, he allows the Turks to think that when their ships are burning he will rise in might . . . and demolish the Russians' (H. S. Northcote to S. Northcote, 28 Dec. 1876, Northc. Pap., Add. MS. 50032,xx).

[41] Disraeli to Queen Victoria, 22 Dec. 1876, RA H11/272; Salisbury to Derby, teleg., 1 a.m., 24 Dec. 1876, Derby Pap.; Tenterden minute, 27 Dec. 1876, ibid.; Derby minute, 27 Dec. 1876, ibid. Shannon feels that Disraeli and Derby counted on Elliot's 'being a hobbling ball and chain on Salisbury's restless leg' (Shannon, pp. 253–4). This was not the case. Salisbury was Disraeli's choice to go to Constantinople as special emissary. If he needed to be checked, it would have been far simpler to send a 'safer' delegate. Rather the opposite is nearer the truth. When Disraeli chose Salisbury he was disgusted with Elliot, and expected the India Secretary to push the ambassador aside, which is exactly what he did do upon arrival at Constantinople. Disraeli desired someone in Constantinople who would be able to force the Turks to dance in time to a British beat. He felt that Elliot could no longer do that, but that Salisbury might be so able.

[42] Salisbury to Queen Victoria, 23 Dec. 1876, QVL ii. 505–7; Devereux, The First Ottoman Constitutional Period, pp. 92–3; C. de Moüy, Souvenirs et causeries d'un diplomate (Paris, 1909), p. 51; Salisbury to Derby, teleg., 26 Dec. 1876, PRO FO 424/37, no. 93. For the Turkish constitution see Devereux, pp. 55–62, 80–93, Davison, pp. 360–75, 380–7, and B. Lewis, The Emergence of Modern Turkey (2nd edn., London, 1968), pp. 165–6. Salisbury's reaction to the new constitution was to press Zichy and Calice to

exert more pressure on the Porte to give way on the conference proposals (Zichy and Calice to Andrássy, telegs., 23 Dec. 1876, HHSA, PA xxii/115).

[43] Hammond, who was not anti-Turkish, thought the constitution 'a crafty device, for those Powers who are governed constitutionally can hardly deny that the sole safeguard for just administration is to be found by such an institution. The Porte therefore may justly urge that in this Constitution will be found the guarantees required for the carrying out of the administrative reforms which will precede or flow from it' (Hammond to Layard, 27 Dec. 1876, Lay. Pap., Add. MS. 38955, xxv).

[44] Elliot to Salisbury, 26 Dec. 1876, Salis. Pap., E; Salisbury to Carnarvon, most secret, 25 Dec. 1876, ibid., vol. 8; Salisbury to Derby, 26 Dec. 1876, Derby Pap.

[45] Salisbury to Derby, teleg., 26 Dec. 1876, PRO FO 424/37, no. 93; Zichy and Calice to Andrássy, telegs., 27 Dec. 1876, HHSA, PA xii/115; Salisbury to Derby, teleg., 25 Dec. 1876, PRO FO 424/37, no. 91. Zichy felt that Salisbury had hoped to detach the Sultan from his ministers in order to win his personal acceptance for the proposals of the Powers (Zichy to Andrássy, 29 Dec. 1876, HHSA, PA xii/115).

[46] The Greek Government periodically chaffed at possible lack of British sympathy lest their Balkan interests suffer with the gains of the Slavs. Britain's Jewish community, wishing to take advantage of the Constantinople Conference, organized a deputation which saw Derby in order to urge equality for Jews with their Muslim and non-Muslim fellow subjects in Serbia and Romania. J. M. Montefiore was president of the Anglo-Jewish Association which the deputation represented. Derby instructed Salisbury to 'take such steps as you may think advisable in dealing with this matter . . . [either] to lay the memorial before the Conference, or to make such other use of it as you may think proper' (Derby to Salisbury, 28 Dec. 1876, PRO FO 424/37, no. 95).

[47] Onou to wife, 27/28 Dec. 1876, Jomini–Onou Pap. Eg. 3227, fos. 65–74.

[48] Salisbury to Derby, teleg., 28 Dec. 1876, PRO FO 424/37, no. 99; Salisbury to Disraeli, 28 Dec. 1876, Disraeli Pap. xx/Ce/188. It was at this point that the Prime Minister began to express irritation with Salisbury, feeling that he had been duped by Ignatiev (Disraeli to Derby, 28 Dec. 1876, MB vi. 111; same to same, 28 Dec. 1876, Derby Pap.). Mackenzie suggests that the armistice was extended because of Russian pressure (Mackenzie, p. 179). If so, very little was required, as the Turks seemed most happy to do it. I believe Smith is correct in brilliantly describing the effect of Salisbury's religious beliefs on his political views and 'his fierce hostility towards those who denied Christianity itself. It was his belief that Christianity could not co-exist with, but must destroy, civilizations which rejected it. . . . Because it was so essential to the security of Salisbury's mind, religion furnishes the most important example of the sub-ordination of his intellectual powers to needs and feelings arising at the deepest level of his being' (P. Smith (ed.), *Lord Salisbury on Politics*, Cambridge, 1972, p. 17). Consequently, as he showed at the Constantinople Conference and as he later admitted to Lytton, he 'would in no way have discouraged the obliteration of Turkey' (Salisbury to Lytton, 15 June 1877, Salis. Pap., C4, letter-book). Even Münster, the German ambassador, thought that Salisbury was 'one of the few English statesmen who would go so far as to share the booty [of a partition of Turkey] with Russia' (Münster to Bülow, London, very confid., 2 Apr. 1878, GFM, A 2172). Salisbury's contempt for the Turks rarely wavered and, as a result of the Bulgarian massacres, it increased. In 1878 he would agree to an association with the Porte [the Cyprus Convention] in order to contain Russian expansion in Asia. His opposition to Russia in 1878 was probably necessary if he expected to succeed Beaconsfield as leader of the Conservative party.

[49] Elliot to Tenterden, 29 Dec. 1876, Tenterden Pap., PRO FO 363/1; Salisbury to Derby, 29 Dec. 1876, Salis. Pap., vol. 16; same to same, 29 Dec. 1876, Derby Pap.; Gallenga to Delane, 29 Dec. 1876 (A. I. Dasent, *John Thadeus Delane*, 2 vols., N.Y., 1908), ii. 329–30). Ignatiev was doing all he could to arrange for Elliot's recall (Ignatiev to Shuvalov, 29 Dec. 1876, Seton-Watson, *Slav. Rev.* iv. 456; Derby memorandum, 30 Dec. 1876, Derby Pap.). Derby read Salisbury's letter about Elliot to a Cabinet meeting

held on 8 January. 'You [Salisbury] seem to anticipate the probable breaking up of the Conference. They [Cabinet] think it therefore inexpedient to come to a decision today as to the step which you suggest which would be a serious one and might give rise to misconception. This telegram has been read to and approved by the Cabinet' (Derby to Salisbury, teleg., 8 Jan. 1877, Derby Pap.).

[50] Disraeli to Derby, 31 Dec. 1876, Derby Pap.; same to same, 30 Dec. 1876, MB vi. 111–12; same to same, 31 Dec. 1876, Derby Pap.; Salisbury to Disraeli, 30 Dec. 1876, Disraeli Pap. xx/Ce/189. Derby telegraphed Salisbury in the sense requested by Disraeli, that Turkey was willing to compromise and that Russia, ill prepared for war, would make concessions (Derby to Salisbury, 30 Dec. 1876, Derby Pap.). Loftus had reported that the Russian enthusiasm for war had 'almost entirely subsided' owing to financial difficulties, disenchantment with Serbia, and the Tsar's desire for peace (Loftus to Derby, 19 Dec. 1876, PRO FO 424/46, no. 428). In December Russia dispatched a mission to Serbia under General Nikitin to report on Serbia's war potential and to reorganize the Serbian army. Arriving in Belgrade on 24 December, Nikitin wrote that the Serbian military could not be made into an effective army and he left the city on 10 January (Mackenzie, pp. 165–70).

[51] Salisbury to Derby, teleg., 11.50 p.m., 30 Dec. 1876, PRO FO 424/37, no. 111: Salisbury to Disraeli, teleg., 30 Dec. 1876, Disraeli Pap. xx/Ce/190; Salisbury to Derby, teleg., 2.15 p.m., 31 Dec. 1876, PRO FO 424/37, no. 113; same to same, teleg., 31 Dec. 1876, Derby Pap. Onou described the third sitting as a clash between the Ottoman representatives and Salisbury and Chaudordy, with Ignatiev sitting back and appearing moderate (Onou to wife, 31 Dec. 1876, Jomini–Onou Pap., Eg. 3227, fos. 75–87). The Spanish minister reported that at the end of this sitting, in an attempt to impress the Porte with unity between the Great Powers, all the foreign representatives rose simultaneously and walked out (Conte to Calderon y Collantes, 5 Jan. 1877, SFM, no. 1).

[52] Elliot to Derby, teleg., 28 Dec. 1876, PRO FO 424/46, no. 456. Midhat also objected to the confinement of Turkish troops to certain specified fortresses or towns, and the assignment of one-third of the revenue of the provinces to imperial purposes (ibid.). Disraeli thought, but Derby did not, that Elliot never communicated to Salisbury his talk with Midhat (Disraeli to Derby, 30 Dec. 1876, MB vi. 111).

[53] Salisbury to Derby, teleg., 31 Dec. 1876, PRO FO 424/37, no. 114; Salisbury to Disraeli, teleg., 31 Dec. 1876, Disraeli Pap. xx/Ce/193; Zichy and Calice to Andrássy, 2 Jan. 1877, HHSA, PA xii/118.

[54] Salisbury to Derby, teleg., 1 Jan. 1877, PRO FO 424/37, no. 117. Salisbury, who was described by the correspondent of the *Daily Telegraph* as 'bitter' toward Turkey, informed Carnarvon that if Elliot could be recalled, ostensibly to advise the Cabinet, the effect on the Porte would be 'immense' (Borthwick to Corry, 2 Jan. 1877, Disraeli Pap. xvi/C/30; Salisbury to Carnarvon, teleg., 1 Jan. 1877, Salis. Pap., vol. 8).

[55] At this meeting Elliot made a plea, that for the purpose of winning Ottoman acceptance, the proposals of the Powers should be modified (Elliot to Derby, 5 Jan. 1877, PRO FO 424/48, no. 220).

[56] Salisbury's interpretation of Ignatiev's motivation was not shared by Onou, who thought that Ignatiev was working only for a personal diplomatic success.

[57] Salisbury to Derby, teleg., 7 Jan. 1877, PRO FO 424/37, no. 135; Salisbury to Derby, 4 Jan. 1877, Salis. Pap., vol. 16; same to same, 4 Jan. 1877, Derby Pap.; Salisbury to Carnarvon, 5 Jan. 1877, Cecil, ii. 120; Salisbury to Disraeli, most secret, teleg., 5 Jan. 1877, Disraeli Pap. xx/Ce/195. When the Cabinet meeting of the eighth would not approve Elliot's recall, Salisbury telegraphed to Derby. 'Sir H. Elliot's unconscious attitude, still more the conduct and attitude of those around him, have done enormous evil, but it may not be reparable now' (Salisbury to Derby, teleg., 9 Jan. 1877, Derby Pap.).

[58] Derby to Ponsonby, 6 Jan. 1877, Derby Pap.; Zichy to Andrássy, teleg., 8 Jan.

1877, HHSA, PA XII/118.

[59] Tenderden memorandum, 8 Jan. 1877, Derby Pap.

[60] Salisbury to Derby, teleg., 8 Jan. 1877, PRO FO 424/37, no. 140. The Andrássy note's mixed Christian-Muslim commission to watch over the execution of reforms was far different from the commission of control proposed by the Powers at Constantinople. The former was to be appointed by the Porte and to be completely under its control.

[61] Disraeli to Salisbury, [8] Jan. 1877, Disraeli Pap. xx/Ce/196; Derby to Salisbury and Elliot, 10 Jan. 1877, PRO FO 424/37, no. 147; Devereux, *The First Ottoman Constitutional Period*, pp. 94–5. Both Derby and, apparently, Disraeli were strongly supporting Salisbury, in so far as they could, from London. 'I [Derby] do not see that we can say or do more than has been said or done to strengthen Lord Salisbury's position: I have told Musurus, again and again in the plainest terms that the Turks have no help to expect from England' (Derby to Ponsonby, 9 Jan. 1877, Derby Pap.; Queen's journal, 10 Jan. 1877, RA; Ponsonby to Queen Victoria, 9 Jan. 1877, ibid., no. 57; Derby to Salisbury, teleg., 9 Jan. 1877, PRO FO 424/37, no. 142). Even Elliot was dragged in; the ambassador appealed to the Sultan on 10 January to accept the proposals of the Powers (Elliot to Derby, teleg., 11 Jan. 1877, ibid., no. 151). On 2 January Midhat intimated to Sandison, the British dragoman, that if Britain and France left Turkey to face Russia alone, the Porte would either fight, or if necessary, come to an arrangement with Russia (Elliot to Derby, teleg., 3 Jan. 1877, PRO FO 424/48, no. 38).

[62] Disraeli to Queen Victoria, 4 Jan. 1877, RA H12/19. Salisbury himself believed, as he wrote after his return to London, that the Cabinet had 'supported me most kindly and readily' (Salisbury to Richmond, 6 Feb. 1877, Good. Pap. 869).

[63] On 11 January Salisbury telegraphed a Russian list of minimum proposals which included some for local government and local autonomy. Holmes, consul at Sarajevo, had for over a year been urging some of the reforms on the Russian list as a solution for Bosnia, but he had no faith in autonomy or local government for so primitive and mixed—both racially and religiously—an area. On the other hand, he considered that modification of the old arrangements, where administrative power remained with the native Muslim Slavs, was bound to fail, and that only a new system had any chance of success. He felt the basis for any new departure would be a competent governor chosen with the consent of the Powers and guaranteed a six-year term of office (Holmes to Derby, 30 June 1876, PRO FO 424/42, no. 115; same to same, 14 Sept. 1876, ibid. 43, no 877; same to same, 27 Oct. 1876, ibid. 45, no 132; Salisbury to Derby, teleg., 3 p.m., 11 Jan. 1877, ibid. 37, no. 152).

[64] Salisbury to Derby, teleg., 6.30 p.m., 11 Jan. 1877, ibid., no. 153.

[65] Salisbury to Carnarvon, teleg., cipher, 13 Jan. 1877, Salis. Pap., vol. 8. Derby, of course telegraphed back authorization, once it was approved by the Cabinet, 'to accept the modified proposals' (Derby to Salisbury, teleg., 13 Jan. 1877, PRO FO 424/37, no. 175).

[66] Salisbury to Derby, teleg., 7 p.m., 11 Jan. 1877, ibid., no. 154.

[67] Salisbury to Derby, teleg., 9 p.m., 12 Jan. 1877, ibid., no. 173. Disraeli had described this meeting as one on which 'all depended' (Disraeli to Prince of Wales, 13 Jan. 1877, RA T7/5).

[68] Salisbury to Derby, teleg., 14 Jan. 1877, PRO FO 424/37, no. 178.

[69] Augustus Charles Hobart was the third son of the Earl of Buckinghamshire. He entered the navy and served during the Crimean War. He afterwards retired from active service, but hired himself out to the southern states during the American Civil War as a blockade-runner. In 1867 he entered Ottoman employ and was sent to Crete to stop Greek blockade-runners. His success in Crete brought him promotion to full admiral with the rank of Pasha. At the outbreak of the Russo-Turkish War Hobart was put in command of the Turkish Black Sea fleet.

[70] Salisbury to Derby, secret, teleg., 15 Jan. 1877, ibid., no. 180.

[71] Salisbury to Derby, teleg., 15 Jan. 1877, ibid., no. 183; Salisbury to Disraeli, teleg., 14 Jan. 1877, Disraeli Pap. xx/Ce/198, received 9 p.m. Salisbury telegraphed to Disraeli that war would not necessarily follow the failure of the conference. 'Our going will probably convince the Turks to negotiate' (Salisbury to Disraeli, teleg., 14 Jan. 1877, ibid., no. 197, received 1.40 a.m.). Ignatiev described Salisbury's performance at this sitting as magnificent (Ignatiev to Shuvalov, 15 Jan. 1877, Seton-Watson, *Slav. Rev.* iv. 459).

[72] Derby to Salisbury and Elliot, 19 Jan. 1877, PRO FO 424/37, no. 193. Salisbury suggested to Derby that the best course for Britain to follow now that the conference had failed was to come to terms with Austria and Russia for a temporary occupation of Bulgaria and Bosnia (Salisbury to Derby, 19 Jan. 1877, Derby Pap.). Before the foreign representatives left Constantinople, Salisbury indicated to Calice that he favoured occupation and hoped that a rumour about the conclusion of an Austro-Russian arrangement for it would turn out true (Calice to Andrássy, 22 Jan. 1877, HHSA, PA xii/118).

[73] Conte to Silvela, Constantinople, 23 Jan. 1877, SFM, no. 7.

[74] Duke of Argyll, *The Eastern Question* (2 vols., London, 1879), i. 336–7. *The Edinburgh Review* of January 1877 also considered the conference proposals as a denial of Ottoman sovereignty.

[75] He was a rabid Turcophile M.P. for Canterbury.

[76] On Lady Salisbury's foolish rudeness and 'insolence' see Home to Simmons, 16 Jan. 1877, PRO FO 358/1 (Lee, pp. 172–4). Zichy and Calice thought that when the Turks sensed that Russia appeared no longer bent on war, they interpreted this as weakness. The Austrian representatives also reported Salisbury's 'great surprise' at the apparent Russian shift away from war (Zichy and Calice to Andrássy, 23 Jan. 1877, HHSA, PA xii/118).

[77] Elliot to Derby, 22 Jan. 1877, Derby Pap. Wolseley's estimate of Salisbury at this time he gave to his brother. 'He is a clever fellow but of a curiously inexpressive disposition that has no friends or even very intimate acquaintances. He forms his opinions too quickly without listening to the views of others, and is therefore often wrong in his estimate' (G. Wolseley to R. Wolseley, 15 Jan. 1877, Wolseley Papers, Hove Central Library). Derby showed Elliot's letter to Disraeli and wrote 'that S[alisbury] has misarranged the matter and affronted him [Elliot] in a quite unnecessary way' (Derby to Disraeli, 3 Feb. 1877, Disraeli Pap. xx/S/1208). Layard, based on information he received from the Sultan, Edhem Pasha, and Safvet Pasha, who of course hated Salisbury as a result of the conference, believed that the special ambassador had been duped by Ignatiev into feeling that the only way to deal with Turkey was by 'addressing them in peremptory language and by threatening them with violent measures'. Layard also thought that the Ignatievs' had succeeded by influencing Salisbury against any reasonable relationship with Elliot. 'Lord Salisbury's somewhat impetuous character, his ignorance of the country [Turkey] and people . . . his impatience with diplomatic forms and control, and his eager desire to prove that he was not unduly influenced by a suspicion of Russia, rendered his employment on this occasion especially undesirable and dangerous' (Layard Memoirs, 3–6 Apr. 1877, John Murray, London; hereafter cited as Lay. Mem.).

[78] Werther to Bülow, 14 Jan. 1877, *GD* i. 46–7.

[79] Northcote to Salisbury, 22 Jan. 1877, Salis. Pap., E, 108–11.

# CHAPTER FOURTEEN

[1] The two together are referred to as the Budapest Convention. The political agreement, which was reached on 18 March, was antedated to coincide with the signing of

the military contract reached on 15 January.

[2] For the Budapest Convention see, Taylor, pp. 242–3; Mackenzie, pp. 170–4; Sumner, pp. 273–88; Rupp, pp. 265–304; Langer, p. 114.

[3] At the close of Parliament in August 1876 a number of M.P.s formed a committee to watch Eastern events. Mundella became the group's leader. This Parliamentary committee then nominated a conference committee.

[4] Thompson, ii. 110–12. Mundella's conference committee included W. Morris, E. A. Freeman, J. A. Froude, J. W. Probyn, Professor Bryce, C. Hopwood, G. Boing, A. Herbert, Denton, H. Richard, Bryce, Chesson, and H. Broadhurst.

[5] Shaftesbury to Gladstone, 2 Nov. 1876, Glad. Pap., Add. MS. 44300, CCXV. Liddon hoped the conference would prevent Britain from going to war for Turkey, and also lend itself towards securing religious and civil liberty for Turkey's Christians (Liddon to Pusey, 4 Dec. 1876, Pusey Papers, Pusey House, Oxford).

[6] Wirthwein, pp. 130–1.

[7] Hammond to Layard, 4 Nov. 1876, Lay. Pap., Add. MS. 38955, XXV.

[8] Ponsonby to Dean of Windsor, 6 Nov. 1876 (Ponsonby, *Henry Ponsonby*, pp. 158–9). The fifth Earl Spencer, another sympathizer of Gladstone's, also thought the latter had gone too far, and that 'his last war with the *Pall Mall* [was] exceedingly unjudicious' (Earl Spencer to Hartington, 16 Nov. 1876, Hart. Pap. 340/688).

[9] Gladstone to Broadhurst, 23 Nov. 1876, Broadhurst Papers, London School of Economics.

[10] Mundella to Gladstone, 25 Nov. 1876, Glad. Pap., Add. MS. 44258, CLXXIII. Carlyle's letter of 24 November to George Howard extolled the Russians and berated the Turks. It was published in *The Times* on 28 November (Wirthwein, p. 143). Mundella showed Courtney, a columnist and leader writer for *The Times*, Carlyle's letter, and apparently the latter arranged for its publication (Mundella to Gladstone, 26 Nov. 1876, Glad. Pap., Add. MS. 44258, CLXXIII).

[11] Mundella to Gladstone, 2 Dec. 1876, ibid.; same to same, 26 Nov. 1876, ibid.

[12] Hartington to Granville, 26 Nov. 1876, Gran. Pap., PRO 30 29/22A; B. Holland, *Life of Spencer Compton, Eighth Duke of Devonshire* (2 vols., London, 1911), i. 183–4.

[13] Gladstone to Disraeli, 4 Dec. 1876, Disraeli Pap. XVI/C/73; Mundella to Leader, 3 Dec. 1876, Mundella Pap.

[14] Bright to Hayward, 7 Dec. 1876 (Hayward, *Correspondence*, ii. 276–7); Gladstone to wife, 6 Dec. 1876, Glad. Pap., St. Deiniol's; Gladstone to Granville, 6 Dec. 1876, Ramm, i. 25–6.

[15] Shannon writes that in most cases the local Liberal Associations nominated the representatives to the conference (Shannon, pp. 258–61). He refers to the conference as 'undoubtedly the most brilliant array of intellectual figures ever brought together to intervene in a question of politics in England' (ibid., p. 25).

[16] His support of Gladstone was strongly attacked by his mother and by his cousin, the third Duke of Sutherland (G. Huxley, *Victorian Duke*, London, 1967, p. 107). On 12 December the Duke of Sutherland invited friends to his London home in order to consider what steps might be taken to alleviate the suffering of the Turkish soldiers. From this group the Stafford House Committee was formed. It was named after the Duke's home, and it was to be a relief organization as well as a gesture of British and Conservative faith in Turkey. It absorbed the Turkish Wounded Soldiers' Relief Fund established three months earlier by Butler-Johnstone (Anderson, p. 46).

[17] W. H. G. Armytage, *A. J. Mundella* (London, 1951), pp. 174–5. Such a gesture by Gladstone was not typical as he wished his association with Madame Novikov to be unknown to the public.

[18] *The Times*, 9 Dec. 1876.

[19] The Duke of Westminster was its president and among its officers were Shaftesbury, Mundella, F. W. Chesson, and J. W. Probyn (Wirthwein, pp. 149–50).

[20] In September 1876 Liddon and MacColl were travelling on the Sava river and

claimed they saw on the Turkish Bosnian shore a man impaled on a pole next to other poles free of bodies. On their return to England they gave to the Press what they thought they saw, and the authenticity of their account was challenged. Both men's gullibility was ridiculed (Anderson, pp. 44 ff.). Holmes, upon investigation, denied the possibility of impalement, and signified that what may have been seen was the fixing upon pikes of heads cut off from the dead (Holmes to Elliot, 5 Oct. 1876, PRO FO 424/44, no. 410; same to same, 3 Nov. 1876, ibid. 45, no. 284).

[21] Ponsonby to Queen Victoria, 11 Dec. 1876, RA H11/220. Ponsonby thought that 'the evident object of the assemblage [the conference] was to express indignation against Lord Beaconsfield' (Ponsonby to Lytton, 11 Dec. 1876, Lytton Pap., India Office, E218/517/2).

[22] Hartington to Granville, 18 Dec. 1876, Gran. Pap., PRO 30 29/22A; same to same, 18 Dec. 1876, E. Fitzmaurice, *Life of Granville*, 2 vols., London, 1905, ii. 167–8; Granville to Gladstone, 11 Dec. 1876, Ramm, i. 26–7; Hammond to Layard, 11 Dec. 1876, Lay. Pap., Add. MS. 38955, xxv.

[23] F. Cavendish to Hartington, 22 Dec. 1876, Hart. Pap. 340/691.

[24] Lady Fullerton to Gladstone, 25 Dec. [1876], Glad. Pap., Add. MS. 44452, CCCLXVII. The following appeared in the *Quarterly Review*. 'It is difficult to understand how men, calling themselves Liberals, should advocate injustice and persecution against a whole race, merely because that race is not Christian; or that, because horrible cruelties have been inflicted upon Christians, therefore even more horrible and wholesale cruelties should be inflicted upon Mussulmans ... Russian despotism is more organized and ruthless than Turkish oppression, and her cruelty more systematic than Moslem cruelty. ... Turkey has cruelty enough to answer for; but she has neither a Poland nor a Siberia.

If this pressure [of popular opinion] ... is to be had recourse to every time popular sentiment and emotion are excited by cruel deeds and foreign misgovernment, England would be rarely without a war on her hands. ... In fact, there is scarcely a country in Europe with which England would not have been at one time or other at war, if her foreign policy had been guided by spasmodic outbursts of emotion at acts of cruelty and wrong.

No nation [Turkey] has ever been treated by civilised nations with a more reckless contempt of justice, right and international law. ...' (*Quarterly Review*, CXLIII (Jan. 1877), 276–320).

[25] Madame Novikov to Gladstone, 1 Jan. [1877], Glad. Pap., Add. MS. 44268, CLXXXIII; same to same, 2 Jan. [1877], Ibid.

[26] Gladstone to wife, 3 Jan. 1877, Glad. Pap., St. Deiniol's.

[27] Madame Novikov to Gladstone, 3 Jan. 1877, Glad. Pap., Add. MS. 44268, CLXXXIII. 'Pce Gortchakoff has thanked me [Madame Novikov] very much for the letter wh. I was allowed to forward and wh. has been sent to our Emperor' (Madame Novikov to Gladstone, 30 Jan. 1877, Glad. Pap., Add. MS. 44268, CLXXXIII).

[28] Gladstone to Madame Novikov, 2 Jan. 1877, ibid.

[29] Gladstone to Granville, 2 Jan. 1877, Ramm, i. 28.

[30] Thompson, i. 76–9. Thompson's work on British opinion was published in 1886.

[31] Ibid. i. 392–3.

[32] Ponsonby to Prince Leopold, 25 Aug. 1876, RA, Add. MS. A12/316.

[33] Shannon, pp. 161, 169, 13–15, 23–5, 28–30, 30–5, 147–50, 226–31.

[34] Thompson, i. 31–3, 383–4.

[35] Anderson, pp. 8–9.

[36] Stead, shortly after this in 1877, met and carried on an affair with Olga Novikov (J. W. Robertson Scott, *The Life and Death of a Newspaper*, London, 1952, pp. 99–108). The pain which this caused his wife troubled him deeply. For Stead's recognition of the force of female honour to stir indignation see R. L. Schults, *Crusader in Babylon* (Lincoln, Nebraska, 1972), p. 12.

[37] Shannon, pp. 33–5. Though William Morris, Freeman, Froude, and others were sometimes violently anti-Semitic, Shannon will only permit anti-Semitism a 'superficial' position in the agitation as there 'was nothing of the substantial bulk of prejudice' evidenced in France during the Dreyfus affair. Apart from the fact that Dreyfus was a Jew who was believed by many to have sold his country's secrets and the absence of any Jewish murders of Bulgarians, this is a little like describing Mt. Blanc as smallish superimposed upon Mt. Everest.

[38] F. Villiers, *His Five Decades of Adventure* (London, 1921), pp. 64–5, 69. See also id., *Pictures of Many Wars* (London, 1902).

[39] Thompson, i. 392–3, 400–1.

[40] Anderson, pp. 8–9. One of the first, if not the first, of the relief organizations was Lewis Farley's League in Aid of the Christians in Turkey. It had received much in the way of public donations but produced no assistance for the suffering which was the point of the contributions. Apparently only Farley himself benefited financially and the atrocitarians were forced to repudiate Farley and his League. One of Farley's main detractors was another agitation leader, Freeman, the historian. The latter's style of general scurility reached such lengths that Hill and the *Daily News* dropped him as being, in Shannon's words, 'too violent and extravagant'.

[41] Ibid., pp. 10–11. Anderson notes with surprise that, compared to the numerous British visitors to Serbia, 'few Englishmen' went to Bulgaria (ibid., pp. 49–50).

[42] Ibid., p. 51.

[43] Blake, *Disraeli*, p. 693.

[44] At the end of 1877 Gladstone again attempted to convince Granville that agitation enthusiasm was still alive in the hope of drawing the official Liberal leadership to associate itself with the atrocities movement (Gladstone to Granville, 28 Jan. 1877, Gran. Pap., PRO 30/29/29a, Ramm, i. 29).

[45] Frederic Harrison, *Autobiographic Memoirs* (2 vols., London, 1911), i. 311–12.

[46] Loftus to Derby, teleg., 4 Feb. 1877, PRO FO 424/49, no. 55. The Russian Government made little attempt to mask their probable intentions. Reutern, the Finance Minister, told Loftus that if 'no solution is arrived at by the month of April, we [Russia] shall be no longer able to remain inactive, even though we may be obliged to act alone' (Loftus to Derby, 27 Jan. 1877, ibid., no. 63).

[47] Wirthwein, pp. 171–3.

[48] Disraeli to Derby, 9 Feb. 1877, MB vi. 126; same to same, 9 Feb. 1877, Derby Pap. The Italian reaction to the Russian circular was that the latter Power must have 'succeeded in securing the concurrence of Austrian designs against Turkey' (Paget to Derby, teleg., 4 Feb. 1877, PRO FO 424/49, no. 65). Disraeli's position on the circular and the need for Turkish reform to enable Russia to retreat was taken from Salisbury who had returned from Constantinople (Lady Derby to Cross, 16 Feb. 1877, Cross Pap., Add. MS. 51266, IV).

[49] Derby to Loftus, 9 Feb. 1877, PRO FO 424/49, no. 114. On 5 February Midhat Pasha, the Grand Vizier and anti-Russian Ottoman constitutionalist, was dismissed by the Sultan and sent into exile. See Davison, pp. 395–401. Andrássy thought that Midhat's dismissal was a 'suicidal act' since he was 'the only man who appeared to have the ability and energy required to save his Empire' (Buchanan to Derby, 8 Feb. 1877, PRO FO 424/49, no. 144).

[50] Derby to Jocelyn, teleg., 11 Feb. 1877, ibid., no. 126; Jocelyn to Derby, teleg., 13 Feb. 1877, ibid., no. 164.

[51] Derby to Monson, teleg., 14 Feb. 1877, ibid., no. 168.

[52] Lady Derby to Cross, 16 Feb. 1877, Cross Pap., Add. MS. 51266, IV. Lady Derby wrote to Salisbury of this success in persuading Disraeli to his opinion. 'You [Salisbury] appear to have exercised some magical art over the Chief. Before 2 o ck. yest. y there came a letter wh you might have dictated & it was well received at F.O.' (Lady Derby to Salisbury, 10 Feb. 1877, Salis. Pap., E).

[53] Ibid. Salisbury arrived back in England on the evening of 6 February and saw Lady Derby before conferring with any of his colleagues. He told her that unilateral Russian action against Turkey would produce a great explosion in Britain. Shuvalov had asked Lady Derby to tell Salisbury of his desire to see him and to compliment him on his performance at Constantinople. Salisbury thanked Shuvalov through Lady Derby and indicated it would be better to meet after the excitement caused by the fall of Midhat had subsided in England (Shuvalov to Gorchakov, 7 Feb. 1877, Seton-Watson, *Slav. Rev.* iv. 740–1). Shuvalov waited a few days and on the evening of 11 February sought out Salisbury and pressed 'for some bridge on which the Russians might retreat. ... I [Salisbury] am not very sanguine of a bridge being found—especially with Derby's dislike to pledge himself' (Salisbury to Lady Salisbury, 11 Feb. 1877, Cecil, ii. 127). Shuvalov reported Salisbury as saying that Britain would not support coercion against Turkey (Shuvalov to Gorchakov, 12 Feb. 1877, Seton-Watson, *Slav. Rev.* iv. 742–4).

[54] Derby to Loftus, teleg., 6.15 p.m., 15 Feb. 1877, PRO FO 424/49, no. 179.

[55] Salisbury to Derby, private, 15 Feb. 1877, Derby Pap.

[56] Tenterden to Derby, 16 Feb. 1877, ibid. When the Turkish commissions, which were sitting to pass sentence on those guilty of committing the atrocities in Bulgaria, exonerated some of those who appeared most guilty, Baring, who was attending the sessions as an observer, was ordered to withdraw. Strong representations were also made to the Porte by the British Head of Embassy (Jocelyn to Derby, teleg., 7 Feb. 1877, PRO FO 424/49, no. 88).

[57] Russell to Derby, 27 Jan. 1877, Derby Pap. Lyons reported Decazes's belief that Bismarck was 'annoyed by the cordiality which had subsisted between the Comte de Chaudordy and General Ignatiev at the Conference' (Lyons to Derby, 9 Feb. 1877, PRO FO 424/41, no. 118). Bismarck did give the same reply to the Russian circular as Britain had given (Russell to Derby, teleg., 16 Feb. 1877, PRO FO 424/49, no. 191).

[58] Russell to Derby, 3 Feb. 1877, Derby Pap. Decazes learned of Bismarck's overtures and reported them to his London Embassy (Decazes to d'Harcourt, 7 Feb. 1877, *DDF* ii. 144–5). The apprehension felt in Germany concerning a Franco-Russian alliance was not limited to Bismarck (Russell to Derby, most confid., 9 Feb. 1877, PRO FO 64/876, no. 59).

[59] Queen's journal, 11 Feb. 1877, RA; Salisbury to Lady Salisbury, 11 Feb. 1877, Cecil, ii. 127; Hardy, ii. 15. Salisbury's misappreciation of Bismarck and his policy placed him in a large club along with Derby, Shuvalov, Decazes, and the Queen. The India Secretary felt he was only waiting for a Russo-Turkish war in order to attack France, therefore, if Russia could be kept at peace for one year, France would be strong enough to make Bismarck behave (Salisbury to Lytton, 2 Mar. 1877, Salis. Pap. D/X/330).

[60] Derby to Queen Victoria, 13 Feb. 1877, RA H12/127; same to same, 13 Feb. 1877, Derby Pap.

[61] Russell to Derby, 17 Feb. 1877, ibid.

[62] Shuvalov to Gorchakov, 21 Feb. 1877 (Seton-Watson, *Slav. Rev.* iv. 747–9). Gorchakov's reply to Disraeli's words was the necessity for Russia to have a formal reply to her circular (Gorchakov to Shuvalov, teleg., 22 Feb. 1877, ibid.).

[63] Disraeli to Derby, 9 Feb. 1877, MB vi. 126. Odo Russell ably summed up the situation. 'The friends of peace believe that the coming Turco-Russian war might be averted if the Powers built Russia a golden bridge to help her out of her present dilemma, that the Powers are willing to follow the lead of England in answering the Russian Circular, and that England is waiting to see what Turkey will do before answering it, so that Russia unanswered and isolated, and therefore unable to demobilize without even the semblance of a national satisfaction to uphold her honour, will be compelled to go to war, however much she would prefer peace' (Russell to Derby, 24 Feb. 1877, PRO FO 424/49, no. 304).

[64] Derby to Jocelyn, teleg., 18 Feb. 1877, ibid., no. 218. Derby also warned the Porte of his unhappiness that insufficient punishment was being meted out to those guilty of the Bulgarian massacres (Derby to Jocelyn, teleg., 20 Feb. 1877, ibid., no. 254).

[65] Derby to Loftus, 21 Feb. 1877, ibid., no. 262. A proposal similar to Shuvalov's had been made earlier at the conference by Midhat Pasha to Elliot (ibid.).

[66] Derby to Jocelyn, teleg., 23 Feb. 1877, ibid., no. 285.

[67] Shuvalov feared that Ignatiev's coming to England would create a negative British outburst. At the ambassador's suggestion, the public reason given for Ignatiev's trip was the necessity to consult an occulist (Shuvalov to Gorchakov, 28 Feb. 1877, Seton-Watson, *Slav. Rev.* iv. 751; Gorchakov to Shuvalov, 1 Mar. 1877, ibid. 752). On Ignatiev's mission see Sumner, pp. 257–60.

[68] Shuvalov to Gorchakov, 1 Mar. 1877 (Seton-Watson, *Slav. Rev.* iv. 753); same to same, 1 Mar. 1877 (ibid.).

[69] Lady Derby to Salisbury, 23 Feb. 1877, Salis. Pap. E; same to same, 2 Mar. 1877, ibid. Lady Derby by her own estimation thought she was acting independently of Shuvalov. In this she was probably mistaken, but Derby now considered his wife to be completely in Shuvalov's camp. 'I [Lady Derby] tell you [Salisbury] all this and try to leave it in your hands, because—because—well—Ld. D. thinks always I am under Schou's influence' (Lady Derby to Salisbury, 9 Mar. 1877, Salis. Pap., E).

[70] Herbert to Andrássy, Constantinople, 27 Feb. 1877, HHSA, PAxii/118.

# CHAPTER FIFTEEN

[1] Derby to Russell, secret, 6 Mar. 1877, PRO FO 424/50, no. 63; Russell to Derby, secret, teleg., 7 Mar. 1877, ibid., no. 66. The French ambassador in Berlin reported that the Russian protocol allowed Turkey two months to comply with the reforms of the Constantinople Conference, and that if satisfaction were not given by the Porte, coercive measures were to be taken against it (Gontaut Biron to Decazes, Berlin, teleg., 7 Mar. 1877, *DDF* ii. 145–6). This was confirmed also by the Italian ambassador at Berlin (Derby to Lyons, teleg., 9 Mar. 1877, PRO FO 424/50, no. 83). Disraeli objected to Gorchakov's equation of the Porte's refusal of European mediation with an 'offence to the dignity of Europe' (Disraeli to Derby, 2 Mar. 1877, MB vi. 126–7).

[2] Journal, 8 Mar. 1877, Prince C. Hohenlohe-Schillingsfürst, *Memoirs* (2 vols., London, 1906), ii. 188–9; Lyons to Derby, 9 Mar. 1877, PRO FO 424/50, no. 93.

[3] Wirthwein, pp. 200–2.

[4] Queen Victoria to Derby, 10 Mar. 1877, RA H12/155; Queen's journal, 6 and 9 Mar. 1877, RA.

[5] Salisbury to Lytton, 9 Mar. 1877, Salis. Pap. D/xi/337.

[6] Salisbury to Disraeli, 12 Mar. 1877, Disraeli Pap. xx/Ce/202. On the same day Salisbury invited Ignatiev to Hatfield (Salisbury to Ignatiev, 12 Mar. 1877, Salis Pap. G/6).

[7] Disraeli to Queen Victoria, 11 Mar. 1877, RA H12/161.

[8] Disraeli to Queen Victoria, 12 Mar. 1877, ibid., no. 162.

[9] Disraeli memorandum enclosed to Queen Victoria, 13 Mar. 1877, RA H12/166. Derby told Münster, the German ambassador, that assurances regarding demobilization must be binding, and that nothing smacking of coercion must appear in the protocol (Münster to Bülow, 13 Mar. 1877, GD i. 49–50). See also Hardy diary, 14 Mar. 1877, Cran. Pap., HA 43/T501/297.

[10] Derby to Loftus, 13 Mar. 1877, PRO FO 424/50, nos. 156, 158.

[11] Lady Derby to Disraeli, 14 Mar. 1877, Disraeli Pap. xx/S/1467. For Derby's proposed changes in the wording of the protocol see Münster to Ger. For. Office,

teleg., 13 Mar. 1877, *GD* i. 49–50.

[12] Disraeli to Queen Victoria, 16 Mar. 1877, RA H12/170; Disraeli to Lady Bradford, 16 Mar. 1877, Zetland, ii. 137.

[13] Tenterden memorandum, 20 Mar. 1877, Derby Pap., with Derby minutes (ibid.).

[14] Tenterden to Derby, Hatfield, 20 Mar. 1877, ibid. Derby told the Queen that the failure to agree on the protocol was now a real possibility as the Russians wished to back out of demobilization. They were, he said, 'very slippery people'. The Queen replied that she 'hoped they [the Government] would on no account give way to the Russians' (Queen's journal, 20 Mar. 1877, *QVL* ii. 524). See also Derby to Disraeli, 20 Mar. 1877, Disraeli Pap. xx/S/218; Corry to Disraeli, 20 Mar. 1877, ibid. xvi/B/19. Bylandt, the Dutch ambassador, was the only member of the London ambassadorial corps invited to Hatfield to receive Ignatiev. He reported the ambassador as saying that Russia did not wish to make war at present as the fall of the Ottoman Empire was only a few months distant (Bylandt to Willebois, 21 Mar. 1877, NA 97).

[15] Salisbury to Derby, 21 Mar. 1877, Salis. Pap., vol. 16; same to same, 21 Mar. 1877, Derby Pap.; Northcote to Derby, 21 Mar. 1877, ibid.; Forster diary, 20 Mar. 1877, Reid ii. 167–71.

[16] Tenterden to Derby, 21 Mar. 1877, Derby Pap. The three Russian conditions appeared in the *Daily News* on the same day (Ponsonby to Queen Victoria, 21 Mar. 1877, RA H12/190).

[17] Disraeli to Queen Victoria, 21 Mar. 1877, ibid. 192.

[18] Queen Victoria to Ponsonby, 21 Mar. 1877, 193; Queen Victoria to Disraeli, 21 Mar. 1877, MB vi. 130.

[19] Disraeli to Queen Victoria, 21 Mar. 1877, RA H12/192.

[20] Derby to Loftus, 21 Mar. 1877, PRO FO 424/50, no. 295. To Bylandt, Shuvalov praised Disraeli's 'superiority of spirit and clarity of judgment', but complained of 'the hesitations and tergiversations' of Derby (Bylandt to Willebois, 23 Mar. 1877, NA 100).

[21] Disraeli to Queen Victoria, 22 Mar. 1877, RA H12/194. In a letter to Derby, Northcote made reference to growing Cabinet disunity. 'As regards the internal difficulties which threaten the Cabinet, I am sure I need not say anything to you. They are becoming very serious' (Northcote to Derby, 19 Mar. 1877, Derby Pap.).

[22] Ponsonby To Queen Victoria, 22 Mar. 1877, RA H12/190. The Queen did so. 'Talked pretty strongly to Ld Carnarvon, who is frightened about the Eastern Question & will not take the proper view about it' (Queen's journal, 24 Mar. 1877, RA).

[23] Disraeli to Queen Victoria, 23 Mar. 1877, RA H12/200; same to same, 23 Mar. 1877, *QVL* ii. 524–6; Carnarvon memorandum, Hardinge, *Carnarvon*, ii. 353; Hardy diary, 24 Mar. 1877, Cran. Pap., HA43/T501/297. Hardy remarks that the Cabinet was 'rather alarmed . . . at one point' when Disraeli urged Cabinet unanimity (ibid.). See also Queen's journal, 23 Mar. 1877, RA. Both the German Emperor with Queen Victoria, and Bismarck with Odo Russell, appealed to Britain to relent on the demand for Russian disarmament as it is 'difficult for the Czar to appear to yield to dictation in a matter affecting national dignity' (Russell to Derby, 24 Mar. 1877, Derby Pap.; William I to Queen Victoria, 24 Mar. 1877, RA H12/202). It is not completely clear why Disraeli made such a point of Cabinet unanimity. There is a report from the Italian ambassador in London that Ignatiev had plotted with Salisbury while in England concerning the formation of a new Cabinet without Disraeli and Derby (Menebrea to Melegari, very confid., 25 Mar. 1877, IFM 114 (1356, 356)). Carnarvon was seized at this moment by a fit of paranoia, and wrote to Salisbury that Disraeli intended the resignation of the two High-Churchmen and that the Queen was ready for a war with Russia. Salisbury replied to Carnarvon that he did not think the Premier was planning anything so violent (Carnarvon to Salisbury, most private, 25 Mar. 1877, Salis. Pap., E 294–7; Salisbury to Carnarvon, 26 Mar. 1877, Cecil, ii. 138). The Colonial Secretary also thought, from an article in the *Pall Mall* of 29 March, that Disraeli and Derby were advertising Cabinet disunity in the newspapers (Carnarvon to Northcote, 30 Mar.

1877, Northc. Pap., Add. MS. 50022, x).

[24] Derby to Loftus, 23 Mar. 1877, PRO FO 424/50, no. 346. Ignatiev arrived in Paris on the evening of 22 March and left for Vienna the following evening. While in Paris he gave Lyons a message for Derby which repeated the arguments he used while in Britain (Lyons to Derby, 23 Mar. 1877, ibid., no. 350).

[25] Derby to Loftus, 24 Mar. 1877, ibid., nos. 357, 358.

[26] Loftus to Derby, 21 Mar. 1877, ibid., no. 384.

[27] Derby to Loftus, 26 Mar. 1877, ibid., no. 395.

[28] Derby to Loftus, teleg., 27 Mar. 1877, ibid., no. 417; same to same, 27 Mar. 1877, ibid., no. 428. Shuvalov appears to be trying very hard for peace and the protocol, partly, no doubt, to garner a triumph where Ignatiev had failed. After their talk on 26 March, Derby sent the following telegram to Constantinople. 'Telegraph to Consular Officers throughout Turkish dominions to be especially careful in investigating and reporting any cases of disturbances or outrages . . . and authorize them to charge in their public accounts the expense of visiting any places where such occurrences are reported to have taken place' (Derby to Jocelyn, teleg., 8 a.m., 27 Mar. 1877, ibid., no. 409).

[29] Loftus to Derby, teleg., 1 a.m., 28 Mar. 1877, ibid., no. 437.

[30] Derby to Loftus, teleg., 28 Mar. 1877, ibid., no. 442. Disraeli believed that Russia desired peace, despite Ignatiev and the fact that the Russian decision would depend on the 'capricious' will of the Tsar. The Prime Minister wished the Government's answer to reach St. Petersburg before Ignatiev's return there. He attributed Derby's suspiciousness, for which he admitted there were grounds, partly to the influence of Tenterden, 'who is a most able public servant, with unrivalled capacities for labour, but prejudiced & contracted in his views' (Disraeli to Queen Victoria, 29 Mar. 1877, RA H12/206; same to same, 28 Mar. 1877, ibid., no. 204). The Queen did not especially like Shuvalov's compromise proposal (Queen Victoria to Disraeli, 29 Mar. 1877, ibid., no. 207).

[31] Lady Derby to Cross, Keston, 30 Mar. 1877, Cross Pap., Add. MS. 51266, IV. For her information to Cross, Lady Derby expected a return. 'I shd so very much like to know if that last Cabinet was a very uncomfortable one—I am afraid it was & I cannot make it all out. I promise to throw your letter straight into the fire!' (ibid.).

[32] Derby to Loftus, teleg., 1.50 p.m., 31 Mar. 1877, PRO FO 424/50, no. 493; same to same, teleg., 3 p.m., ibid., no. 494; The last paragraph above was not part of the Russian declaration but formed part of a British one which Derby annexed to the protocol. A copy of the latter is in Derby to Loftus, 31 Mar. 1877, ibid., no. 264. The protocol itself indicated the interest of all the Powers in an improved state for the Christian inhabitants of Bulgaria and Bosnia-Hercegovina. If such reform was not carried out by the Porte, the Powers reserved the right to collectively advise Turkey of the means to ensure the well-being of the Christians (ibid.). It was on the thirtieth, the day before the protocol was signed, that it was learned that Layard was to go to Constantinople as interim ambassador. Shuvalov, according to Münster, was annoyed at the appointment of a known Turcophile (Münster to Bülow, 31 Mar. 1877, GD i. 50).

[33] Derby to Queen Victoria, 2 Apr. 1877, QVL ii. 526–7; same to same, 2 Apr. 1877, Derby Pap.

[34] Russell to Derby, 27 Mar. 1877, ibid. Taffs gives the German version of the above talk in a memorandum by Bülow. It is much different from the version given in Russell's private letter to Derby. See Taffs, Ambassador to Bismarck, pp. 185–6.

[35] Andrássy to Herbert, teleg., 3 Apr. 1877, HHSA, PA XII/122. Andrássy was also working hard to bring peace between Turkey and Montenegro (Buchanan to Derby, 2 Apr. 1877, PRO FO 424/51, no. 131; Derby to Buchanan, 9 Apr. 1887, ibid., no. 144).

[36] Loftus to Derby, teleg., 6 Apr. 1877, ibid., no. 89; Jomini to Onou, [?1877], Jomini–Onou Pap., Eg. 3211, fos. 32–3; Jomini to Onou, 2 Apr. 1877, ibid., fos. 36–7.

[37] Derby to Jocelyn, teleg., 9 Apr. 1877, PRO FO 424/51, no. 141.

[38] Derby to Jocelyn, 9 Apr. 1877, ibid., no. 147. The ninth article of the Treaty of Paris recorded the Porte's promise to execute Christian reforms and its expectation that the European Powers would not interfere in the internal administration of the Ottoman Empire. The protocol explicitly indicated the intention of the Powers through their diplomatic agents at Constantinople to observe whether the Porte was executing its promises of Christian reform. If, in the opinion of the Powers, such was not the case, they reserved 'to themselves to consider in common as to the means which they may deem best fitted to secure the well-being of the Christian population' (Edward Hertslet, *The Map of Europe by Treaty*, London, 1875–91, ii. 2564–5). It was this last, as Safvet Pasha told Onou, that the Turks found so humiliating. The Ottoman minister described it as a second edition of the Berlin memorandum. Onou found the Turks believing that a war with Russia was inevitable (Onou to Jomini, 11 Apr. 1877, Jomini–Onou Pap., Eg. 3187, fos. 181–2).

[39] Derby to Jocelyn, 12 April 1877, PRO FO 424/51, no. 188. When the circular dispatch was delivered to Derby by the Ottoman ambassador, the Foreign Secretary expressed his regret at the Porte's reaction (ibid.). Gorchakov felt that if the Turks had been unaware of the British declaration attached to the protocol—that the latter would be considered by Britain to be null and void should Turko-Russian disarmament fail—then the Porte might not have refused to send a delegate to Russia to discuss demobilization. As it was the Turks knew that if they did not agree to send an agent to St. Petersburg, Britain would consider the protocol not binding as far as she was concerned. This last the Porte could not have found displeasing. The Ottoman officials, according to the Austrian chargé, still counted on the material support of England as they believed that the interests of the latter would not allow Russia to gain significant victories in European Turkey (Herbert to Andrássy, Constantinople, 13 Apr. 1877, HHSA, PA XII/119).

[40] Loftus to Derby, 6 Apr. 1877, PRO FO 424/51, no. 183.

[41] Derby to Paget, 18 Apr. 1877, ibid., no. 296; deMartino to Melegari, London, 14 Apr. 1877, IFM 114 (1356), 125. Shuvalov now considered war inevitable, and hoped that it would be short and limited, Russia not advancing beyond the Balkan Mountains, so that the results of it would be acceptable to Britain and Austria (Corry to Disraeli, confid., 15/16 Apr. 1877, Disraeli Pap. XVI/13/21). The Spanish minister in St. Petersburg reported his belief that the Ottoman refusal of the protocol enabled the Tsar to overcome his scruples against going to war (Bedmar to Silvela, St. Petersburg, 21 Apr. 1877, SFM, no. 69).

[42] Before Layard left London for Constantinople he had a number of talks with Disraeli, Derby, and Salisbury who gave him to understand that the main object of his mission was to prevent the impossible, a Russo-Turkish war. He was to intimate to the Sultan that in the event of hostilities he was not to expect any military aid from Britain and that British sympathy for the Ottoman Government could be regained only if Christian reforms were executed. Layard inferred from his talk with the Prime Minister that Disraeli felt that it would be impossible for Britain to aid Turkey in a war with Russia, though he was not prepared to witness a downfall of the Ottoman Empire if it meant an extension of Russia into European Turkey. Salisbury told him that Turkey could not resist Russia militarily, and that the ambassador's main object should be to obtain personal influence over the Sultan in order to induce Turkey to make concessions and reform (Lay. Mem., 3–6 Apr. 1877). It was while in Paris on his way to Constantinople that Decazes suggested to Layard an appeal to the eighth article of the Treaty of Paris (Lyons to Derby, teleg., 14 Apr. 1877, PRO FO 24/2237).

[43] Herbert, the Austrian chargé, interpreted Layard's being sent to Constantinople as a significant step which marked a divergence of the British from the Continental governments (Herbert to Andrássy, Constantinople, 20 Apr. 1877, HHSA, PA XII/119).

[44] Lay. Mem., 20 Apr. 1877; Layard to Derby, teleg., 21 Apr. 1877, PRO FO 424/51,

no. 343; Herbert to Andrássy, teleg., 23 Apr. 1877, HHSA, PA XII/119. The ambassador explained to the Foreign Secretary that 'not having specific instructions from your Lordship on the subject, I did not press strongly appeal to VIII Article of Treaty of Paris. I should be glad to know . . . [what you] wish me to do' (Layard to Derby, 21 Apr. 1877, PRO FO 424/51, no. 343). After consulting Disraeli, Derby instructed Layard that England would favour mediation if the other Powers accepted it including Russia, which would, of course, have made its proposal unnecessary. Derby felt it was too late to prevent hostilities (Derby to Disraeli, 21 Apr. 1877, Derby Pap.; Derby to Layard, teleg., 21 Apr. 1877, PRO FO 424/51, no. 345). Tenterden was as pessimistic as Derby about the use of an appeal for mediation under the Treaty of Paris. 'There seems no prospect that any practical result wd. come. . . . If they [Russia and Turkey] failed to come to an agreement at the conference what better prospect is there now that the two armies are preparing for battle?' (Tenterden minute, 16 Apr. 1877, on back of Lyons to Derby, teleg., 14 Apr. 1877, PRO FO 27/2237). Granville, in a note wishing the ambassador success in his new post, wrote 'do not get us into another Crimean War' (Granville to Layard, 19 Apr. 1877, Lay. Pap., Add. MS. 39012, LXXXII). Layard himself admitted to Derby that he had little hope of effecting successful mediation, but had pressed the Porte to make such an appeal for several reasons. One was a play to the gallery of European opinion; another, to loosen the hold of the Ottoman war party over the Sultan; and finally, that an appeal to mediation by the five Powers now might lead to their coming forward in the future to put a stop to the war (Layard to Derby, 30 April 1877, Lay. Pap., Add. MS. 39130, letter-book).

⁴⁵ Lay. Mem., 21 Apr. 1877; Layard to Derby, teleg., 21 Apr. 1877, PRO FO 424/51, no. 356, 357. Ironically, it was about this time that considerable opinion in London questioned the extent of the Bulgarian massacres. 'There is a very strong feeling in the House of Commons and elsewhere, that the number of persons massacred as given by Mr. Baring is greatly in excess of the truth' (Lister memorandum, 28 Feb. 1877, Derby Pap.).

⁴⁶ Layard to Derby, teleg., 23 Apr. 1877, PRO FO 424/51, no. 400; Herbert to Andrássy, Constantinople, 24 Apr. 1877, HHSA, PA XII/119. The ambassador also talked with the Austrian chargé of ways to avoid war (Herbert to Andrássy, Constantinople, 24 Apr. 1877, HHSA, PA XII/119). The latter viewed Layard's effort to get the Porte to request mediation by the Great Powers mainly as an attempt 'to make Russia appear as the aggressor' (Herbert to Andrássy, 27 Apr. 1877, ibid.).

⁴⁷ Lay. Mem., 24 Apr. 1877, I; Layard to Derby, teleg., 24 Apr. 1877, PRO FO 424/51, no. 440. Loftus had seen Gorchakov on the evening of 23 April. 'He [Gorchakov] observed in regard to appeal to VIIIth Article of Treaty of Paris, that it had been already exhausted by Protocol of London, and he considered the Turkish Circular in reply to it as a declaration of war. His Highness added that sending an [Ottoman] Ambassador to Kischeneff [to see the Tsar as was suggested by the Italian government] was useless' (Loftus to Derby, teleg., 23 Apr. 1877, ibid., no. 501).

⁴⁸ Reid, ii. 165. The readiness of the Liberal leaders, if necessary, to coerce Turkey pleased Chamberlain and the Radicals except for Cowen (Chamberlain to Bunce, 9 Feb. 1877, Chamberlain Papers, University of Birmingham Library, JC 5/8/24). Northcote got wind of the Liberal decision and wrote to the Queen. 'Sir Stafford has heard privately that Mr. Gladstone has said to a political friend that, if no one else does so, he shall propose a Resolution to the effect that this country ought to join with the other Powers in making an identic representation to the Porte, and in threatening, if it is not complied with, to follow it up with stronger measures' (Northcote to Queen Victoria, 12 Feb. 1878, RA B28/3).

⁴⁹ Cairns to Disraeli, 25 Jan. 1877, Disraeli Pap. xx/Ce/201.

⁵⁰ Disraeli to Derby, 25 Jan. 1877, Derby Pap.

⁵¹ Northcote to Derby, 4 Feb. 1877, Northcote Pap., Add. MS. 50022, X ; Disraeli to Derby, 29 Jan. 1877, MB vi. 116–17; same to same, 29 Jan. 1877, Derby Pap.

Northcote alerted the Attorney-General to be ready to speak in Parliament as 'there may probably be certain questions of international law which will be raised in the coming debates on the Eastern Question' (Northcote to Holker, 3 Feb. 1877, Northc. Pap., Add. MS. 50053, XLI ). There is an interesting discussion of the independence and integrity of the Ottoman Empire in a letter from Nelidov to Jomini, [?] May 1877, Jomini–Onou Pap., Eg. 3173, fos. 116–49.

[52] Bylandt to Willebois, 9 Feb. 1877, NA 53.

[53] Thompson, ii. 156–7. Münster, the German ambassador, thought the position of the Liberals was weak and impractical and that the Government had nothing to fear from them (Münster to Bülow, very conf., 14 Feb. 1877, GFM, A1000).

[54] Northcote to Queen Victoria, 16 Mar. 1877, RA B28/28; Northcote to Salisbury, 16 Mar. 1877, Salis. Pap., E, 112–13. Forster and Gladstone, the latter partly for personal reasons, were intent upon Elliot's not returning to Constantinople (Gladstone to Granville, 17 Mar. 1877, Ramm, i. 33–4; Gladstone to Elliot, 26 Feb. 1877, Glad. Pap., Add. MS. 44453, CCCLXVIII ). Northcote answered in Parliament that after consultation with Derby it had been the latter's wish that Elliot should return to his post, but that as a result of poor health the ambassador would remain on leave in England. 'The general feeling among the supporters of the government was one of satisfaction that Sir Henry was not going back' (Northcote to Queen Victoria, 19 Apr. 1877, RA B28/30). Granville heard that Layard was to be sent to Constantinople, which he did not oppose as 'he is a very strong man with Orientals' (Granville to Gladstone, 20 Mar. 1877, Ramm, i. 34).

[55] Hartington to Gladstone, 18 Mar. 1877, Glad. Pap., Add. MS. 44144, LVIX; Granville to Gladstone, 18 Mar. 1877, Ramm, i. 34; Gladstone wrote to Hill, editor of the *Daily News*, that he could safely state that an announcement of Elliot's return by the Government 'would have been challenged from the Liberal side' (Gladstone to Hill, 19 Mar. 1877, Glad. Pap., Add. MS. 44453, CCCLXVIII ).

[56] Dilke to Hill, 20 Mar. 1877, Dilke Pap., Add. MS. 43898, XXV ; Hartington to Granville, 22 Mar. 1877, Gran. Pap., PRO 30 29/22A; Hartington to Gladstone, 22 Mar. 1877, Glad. Pap., Add. MS. 44144, LVIX ; Forster diary, 23 Mar. 1877, Reid, ii. 171–2.

[57] Here, as Wirthwein has indicated, the debate might have ended had not Gladstone risen to speak to give it new life (Wirthwein, pp. 205–6).

[58] Northcote spoke sarcastically of the opposition taunting and implying censure of the Government, yet fearing to bring on a vote. The Liberals used various subterfuges to escape a division (ibid., pp. 206–7).

[59] Northcote to Queen Victoria, 23 Mar. 1877, RA B28/33; Thompson, ii. 162–3, 171–2.

[60] Criticism of Elliot brought on debate on 27 March. Anticipating the attack, Derby wrote to Northcote. 'Speak strongly for him [Elliot]. Even if you say more than you think, allowance is made for a minister defending a subordinate' (Derby to Northcote, 27 Mar. [1877], Northc. Pap., Add. MS. 50022, X ; Thompson, ii. 163–4; Northcote to Queen Victoria, 28 Mar. 1877, RA H12). The Queen was furious with the attack on Elliot, and wanted it clearly understood that Layard was only temporary and that Sir Henry would be returning to Constantinople (Queen Victoria to Disraeli, Osborne, 29 Mar. 1877, RA H12/207).

[61] Disraeli to Queen Victoria, confid., 31 Mar. 1877, RA H12/209; Northcote to Salisbury, 16 Mar. 1877, Salis. Pap., E 112–13.

[62] See p. 550 n. 54 and pp. 269–70.

[63] Wirthwein, pp. 208–10; Borthwick to Corry, 2 Apr. 1877, Disraeli Pap. XVI /C/32. Freeman was his usual scurrilous self to Bryce. 'Along with Layard and such filth. Can anything be more defiant than sending that *advocatus diaboli* to C[onstantinop]le? And the Tories are crying out that it shows their superiority to party. I should say it showed the Jews allegiance to the Devil' (Freeman to Bryce, 8 Apr. 1877, Bryce Pap.).

[64] Disraeli to Queen Victoria, 7 Apr. 1877, RA H13/10; *Hansard*, 9 Apr. 1877, 3rd ser. 233,778.

[65] Northcote to Queen Victoria, 9 Apr. 1877, RA B28/39; Hartington to Granville, 9 Apr. 1877, Gran. Pap., PRO 30 29/22A. 'We were inclined yesterday to a motion of censure; but I [Hartington] think that today it looks more like a debate only; with a formal motion for papers' (Hartington to Duke of Devonshire, 10 Apr. 1877, Hart. Pap. 340/703).

[66] Hartington to Gladstone, 11 Apr. 1877, Glad. Pap., Add. MS.; 44144, CCXXXIII ; Hartington to Granville, 10 Apr. 1877, Gran. Pap., PRO 30 29/26a.

[67] Dilke to Hill, 13 Apr. 1877, Dilke Pap., Add. MS. 43898, xxv. The Liberals seemed to place more importance on the Russian declaration attached to the protocol (that the Porte would send an agent to St. Petersburg to discuss mutual disarmament), and interpreted this as an ultimatum which would bring on war.

[68] Northcote to Queen Victoria, 13 Apr. 1877, RA B28/42. Northcote thought that the Government had come out of the debate very well (ibid.). Hartington admitted as much to Granville. 'I thought the debate last night decidedly flat especially on our side. I was not much cheered & Harcourt hardly at all. . . . I am sure a vote of censure would have been a great failure' (Hartington to Granville, 14 Apr. 1877, Gran. Pap., PRO 30 29/26a). Part of the Conservative's success in the discussion was due to Hartington's manner of speaking, 'that sing-song intonation', and Hardy's enthusiastic and buoyant reply (Henry W. Lucy, *A Diary of Two Parliaments*, London, 1885, pp. 205–6; Hardy, ii. 18). One interesting side light of the debate was the speech of Kenealy, who regarded English concern over Turkish misrule as her Christians as 'hypocritical cant', while humanitarian feeling was conveniently silent on the question of misrule in Ireland (*Hansard*, 13 Apr. 1877, 3rd ser. 233, 1133–5). The Queen was furious that the opposition would criticize the Government in the midst of serious negotiations (Sir T. Biddulph to Queen Victoria, 14 and 16 Apr. 1877, RA H13/18, 23). Disraeli wrote that 'the great whig reconnaissance ended very disastrously for its concocters' (Disraeli to Lady Bradford, 14 Apr. 1877, MB vi. 136).

[69] *Hansard*, 16 Apr. 1877, 3rd ser. 233, 1180–1208. Safvet Pasha, the Ottoman Foreign Minister, agreed with Granville. See p. 548 n. 38. Disraeli expressed a little surprise at the very effective answer Derby made to Granville (Disraeli to Lady Bradford, 17 Apr. 1877, MB vi. 136–7).

# CHAPTER SIXTEEN

[1] Disraeli to Queen Victoria, secret, 17 Apr. 1877, RA H13/24.

[2] Ibid.; Hardy diary, 17 Apr. 1877, Cran. Pap., HA43/T501/297. Gallipoli is a town on a peninsula of the same name which guards the European side of the entrance from the Mediterranean into the Sea of Marmora. It is about 130 miles from Constantinople. It, and the Asiatic shore of Anatolia opposite, control the coming and going of vessels through the Dardanelles, which stretches about 37 miles between the Aegean and the Sea of Marmora. The Dardanelles is about three-quarters of a mile to four miles wide, and just outside its Mediterranean entrance lies Besika Bay on the Anatolian shore.

[3] Disraeli to Queen Victoria, secret, 17 Apr. 1877, RA H13/24.

[4] Salisbury to Carnarvon, 18 Apr. 1877, Cecil, ii. 139–40. It was at this point that Shuvalov reported home that London was considering the occupation of Gallipoli and Crete (Shuvalov to Grochakov, 18 Apr. 1877, Seton-Watson, *Slav. Rev.* v (1926–7), 414). He also considered that Derby was the only British minister opposed to any interference in the war (same to same, 20 Apr. 1877, ibid. 416–19).

[5] Disraeli to Queen Victoria, secret, 23 Apr. 1877, RA H13/36; same to same, 23 Apr. 1877, *QVL* ii. 529–31.

[6] Ibid.

[7] Ibid.

[8] Disraeli to Hardy, 18 Apr. 1877, Cran. Pap., HA43/T501/266; same to same, 19 Apr. 1877, ibid. The Queen, though reassured by Richmond, was anxious because news of Cabinet disharmony, if it became known, would prevent the Government from upholding British interests. As she wrote to Disraeli, 'it is not a question of upholding Turkey—it is the question of Russian or British supremacy in the world!' (Queen Victoria to Disraeli, 19 Apr. 1877, RA L14/24; Duke of Richmond to Queen Victoria, 19 Apr. 1877, RA H13/29). Disraeli thanked the Queen for her 'memorandum', which he informed her he planned to read to the Cabinet because it would 'strengthen Lord Beaconsfield's hands' (Disraeli to Queen Victoria, 20 Apr. 1877, ibid., no. 30). The Queen recorded in her journal 'that we [Britain] would not tolerate being subservient to her [Russia] & that we must be prepared for a bold policy' (Queen's journal, 18 and 19 Apr. 1877, RA). General Sir J. L. A. Simmons was asked by Hardy to prepare for the Cabinet's use a memorandum on the seizure and occupation of Gallipoli, which the former sent to Hardy on 19 April (Simmons memorandum to Hardy, 19 Apr. 1877, PRO FO 358/2).

[9] The Foreign Office had received a number of requests for aid from British business and financial interests around the Black Sea. One such came from the Odessa Water Works Company, a British concern which supplied the city's water, asking the Government to prevent the bombardment of Odessa by the Turkish fleet. There were similar requests from other representatives of British capital (F. Head to Derby, 14 Apr. 1877, PRO FO 424/51, no. 272; Messrs. Ransomes, Sims, and Co. to Derby, 20 Apr. 1877, ibid., no. 501). In the anxiety created by the outbreak of war, rumours, unfounded as it turned out, that a Russian fleet was sailing for the Mediterranean were given credence in Britain. Loftus reported that seven ironclads at Cronstadt to be joined with a Russian squadron in American waters would proceed to the Mediterranean (Loftus to Derby, teleg., 28 Apr. 1877, ibid., no. 603). Derby spoke to Shuvalov of a report of 'a possible' Russian blockade of Egypt. He said that such an action would block the Canal and interrupt communication with India. 'It was not necessary to point out the inconveniences which would follow, or the state of feeling which would be produced in this country.' Shuvalov described such a Russian intention as 'pure invention' (Derby to Loftus, 24 Apr. 1877, ibid., no. 426).

[10] Disraeli to Queen Victoria, secret, 23 Apr. 1877, RA H13/34–6; same to same, 23 Apr. 1877, *QVL* ii. 529–31.

[11] Northcote to Disraeli, confid., 21 Apr. 1877, Disraeli Pap. xx/N/26; same to same, 21 Apr. 1877, Northc. Pap., Add. MS. 50018, vi; Carnarvon memorandum, 21 Apr. 1877, Hardinge, ii. 353; Hardy diary, 22 Apr. 1877, Hardy, ii. 19. Hunt, who headed the Admiralty, reported to Disraeli on the disposition of the Mediterranean fleet, and in doing so indicated that Russia's Baltic fleet was presently only capable of coastal defence in home waters (Hunt to Disraeli, 21 Apr. 1877, Disraeli Pap. xx/HU/92). Disraeli did not read 'directly' the Queen's letter or memorandum to the Cabinet (Queen's journal, 22 Apr. 1877, RA).

[12] Disraeli to Queen Victoria, 25 Apr. 1877, RA H13/40; Northcote to Cairns, confid., 24 Apr. 1877, Cairns Pap., PRO FO 30 51/5; Münster to Bülow, confid., 24 Apr. 1877, *GP* ii. no. 289; same to same, 24 Apr. 1877, *GD* i. 51–3. Gorchakov's 'circular', which was communicated to all the Powers on the outbreak of war, was a Russian attempt to neutralize any adverse reaction by assuming that Russia was invading Turkey in the name of Europe in order to force the Porte to grant Christian reform. Münster was encouraged by Bismarck to influence London, if the occasion arose, in the direction of taking Egypt as a material pledge rather than to engage in war (Herbert Bismarck to Bülow, 27 Apr. 1877, *GD* ii. 149). The sending of the fleet to

Besika was apparently either not agreed upon or subsequently dropped.
[13] Salisbury to Lytton, 27 Apr. 1877, Salis. Pap., India Office, D/xi/379; same to same, 27 Apr. 1877, letter-book, C4; Queen's journal, 25 Apr. 1877, RA; Disraeli to Queen Victoria, 26 Apr. 1877, RA H13/42.
[14] Northcote to Disraeli, 27 Apr. 1877, Disraeli Pap. xx/N/28.
[15] Disraeli to Queen Victoria, secret, 28 Apr. 1877, RA H13/50; same to same, 28 Apr. 1877, QVL ii. 532–4; Hardy diary, 29 Apr. 1877, Hardy, ii. 20; same to same, 29 Apr. 1877, Cran. Pap., HA 43/T501/297. Hardy spoke at the Cabinet meeting 'of the need of steady preparation, and am free to take more action' (ibid.). He wrote the following to Ponsonby. 'Steps have therefore been taken to prepare as far as possible with a peace establishment an Army Corps for the field. A Military Committee . . . sits daily to consult upon all necessary details and keep themselves in communication with the Admiralty on the subject of transport' (Hardy to Ponsonby, 4 May 1877, RA E23/59). This was sent in reply to a letter from Ponsonby expressing the desire of the Queen to learn whether all had been readied to dispatch a British expeditionary force should that prove necessary (Ponsonby to Hardy, 4 May 1877, ibid., no. 58).
[16] Northcote to Derby, confid., 29 Apr. 1877, Derby Pap.; Carnarvon to Northcote, confid., 30 Apr. 1877, Northc. Pap., Add. MS. 50022, x; Salisbury to Northcote, confid., 29 Apr. 1877, ibid. 50019, vii.
[17] This article of the Treaty of London gave the Porte the right to invite foreign warships through the Straits during peacetime, if he judged it necessary in order to uphold the Treaty of Paris of March 1856. Layard sent this telegram before the Russian declaration of war had been publicly communicated.
[18] Layard to Derby, secret, teleg., 27 Apr. 1877, PRO FO 424/51, no. 552; same to same, secret, teleg., 29 Apr. 1877, ibid., no. 440; Derby to Layard, secret, teleg., 25 Apr. 1877, ibid., no. 486; Lay. Mem., 30 Apr. 1877, ii; Shuvalov to Gorchakov, secret, 28 Apr. 1877 (Seton-Watson, Slav. Rev. v. 420); Preston, 'British Military Policy and the Defence of India', p. 192; hereafter cited as Preston.
[19] Disraeli to Queen Victoria, 2 May 1877, RA H14/7; same to same, 2 May 1877, QVL ii. 535–6; Carnarvon to Salisbury, 29 Apr. 1877, Salis, Pap., E 300–1; Preston, p. 189. At this meeting General Simmons advised that a force of men much larger than 60,000 would be required in order to hold the Gallipoli Peninsula for any length of time. This and the opposition of Carnarvon, Northcote, Derby, and Salisbury to Disraeli's desire for a bold strike at Gallipoli temporarily shelved the matter (Simmons memorandum, 2 May 1877, Simmons Pap., PRO FO 358–4).
[20] Derby to Loftus, 1 May 1877, PRO FO 424/53, no. 18. Loftus communicated this dispatch to Gorchakov on the morning of 6 May. The latter 'not wishing to commence a polemical discussion' refrained from making any reply to the ambassador (Loftus to Derby, teleg., 6 May 1877, ibid., no. 133a). This dispatch was communicated to the German Government which published it, causing a sensation in Berlin 'because it is understood to indicate the intention of England to go to war with Russia' (Russell to Derby, 9 May 1877, ibid., 53, no. 382).
[21] Münster thought that Shuvalov was returning to Russia as Gorchakov's replacement. He reported that as the Tsarina favoured the move, Alexander II was considering it (Münster to Bülow, teleg., 10 May 1877, GFM, A 2897).
[22] Disraeli to Queen Victoria, 5 May 1877, RA A51/40. Hardy has described this cabinet as 'very unanimous and cordial & we could only laugh at the reports of dissension and disunion—Resignation of S[alisbury] & C[arnarvon] had been rumoured on no grounds at all' (Hardy diary, 6 May 1877, Cran. Pap., HA43/T501/297). The Government also decided 'to ask only Austria to join us, as we could not rely on France and Italy' (Queen's journal, 4 May 1877, RA).
[23] Derby to Shuvalov, 6 May 1877, PRO FO 424/53, no. 140. Hicks-Beach, Secretary for Ireland, now came forward to help draft the above dispatch of conditional neutrality (Beach to Derby, 5 May 1877, Derby Pap.). The note to Shuvalov of 6 May

was also communicated to Beust and Andrássy (Derby to Buchanan, teleg., 9 May 1877, PRO FO 424/53, no. 266). On 10 May Decazes and de Lesseps presented Derby with a proposal to neutralize the Suez Canal, which the latter rejected. Derby communicated this rejection to both the Porte and the Khedive, with the expectation that they too would refrain from obstructing navigation through the water-way. Layard was instructed to acquaint the Porte with Britain's 'intimation' to Russia about the Canal contained in the above note (Derby to Layard, 16 May 1877, ibid., no. 432; Derby to Lyons, 16 May 1877, ibid., no. 433). Northcote influenced Derby's replies to de Lesseps and the Porte (Northcote to Derby, 10 May 1877, Northc. Pap., Add. MS. 50022, X).

²⁴ Derby memorandum of talk with Shuvalov, 8 May 1877, Derby Pap.; ibid., Disraeli Pap., XX/S/1228 and 1228a. Shuvalov's 'satisfaction' with the note and his expectation of receiving Russian assurances about the enumerated British interests were, as the ambassador told the Foreign Secretary, only to be considered as his personal observations and not the official answer of his Government (ibid.). When Andrássy learned of the contents of the British note, he told Buchanan that he like Shuvalov thought that Russia would claim the freedom of the navigation of the Straits. 'He also apparently feared that your Lordship's [Derby's] reservation might be interpreted by Russia as leaving her more free action than is desirable' (Buchanan to Derby, teleg., confid., 18 May 1877, PRO FO 424/53, no. 478).

²⁵ Derby to Loftus, confid., 11 May 1877, ibid., no. 313. According to Disraeli the Cabinet at its meeting on 25 April had approved sending the fleet to Alexandria, and then to Besika Bay, just outside the entrance to the Dardanelles. Either the order was afterwards changed, or Disraeli was too optimistic in his report to the Queen.

²⁶ Shuvalov left London about 11 May and stopped off in Germany on the thirteenth for a talk with Bismarck, who had telegraphed to the ambassador before he left London that he desired to talk with him (Bismarck to Münster, teleg., 10 May 1877, GFM, A 2895). The ambassador arrived in St. Petersburg on the evening of 16 May.

²⁷ Beust to Derby, confid., 7 May 1877, Derby Pap.; Simmons memorandum, 11 May 1877, Simmons Pap., PRO FO 358/2; Derby memorandum [?] May 1877, Derby Pap. On 14 May the Queen recorded having seen Disraeli who told her that the Cabinet 'now really sees the necessity for taking a strong attitude. He [Disraeli] thought they would all keep together & that Ld. Carnarvon would remain, if Ld. Salisbury did, though he must be prepared, if necessary, to lose them, rather than let the Govt. be broken up' (Queen's journal, 14 May 1877, RA). The Austrian documentation for the Anglo-Austrian discussions is in Stojanovic, pp. 164–73.

²⁸ According to the Queen's journal, this Cabinet probably met between 14 and 16 May (Queen's journal, 16 May 1877, RA).

²⁹ Derby memorandum 17 May 1877, Derby Pap.; Northcote to Derby, 16 May 1877, ibid.; Derby to Northcote, 16 May 1877, Northc. Pap., Add. MS. 50022, X; same to same, 16 May 1877, Derby Pap. Disraeli had seen Derby's draft before it was commented on by the other ministers.

³⁰ Derby memorandum confid., [?] May 1877, Derby Pap.; Derby to Disraeli, 18 May 1877, ibid. Disraeli at this point, during the month of May, was incapacitated by a severe attack of gout. On 1 June Andrássy's reply to Derby's invitation 'to discuss a plan of joint action' in case Russia marched on Constantinople was communicated by Beust. As the Government had already informed Austria of the enumerated British interests it was hoped that Russia would respect, the Austrian minister listed seven possible results of the war which his Government would not accept. Among these were the creation of a large Slavic state, a Russian occupation of Constantinople, or an incorporation by her of Romania, or Russian acquisition of territory on the right bank of the Danube. Andrássy underlined to Derby the importance of keeping their overtures secret (Derby to Beust, confid., 19 May 1877, PRO FO 424/64 no. 2; Andrássy to Beust, 29 May 1877, communicated to Derby on 1 June 1877, ibid., no. 6).

[31] This last was true, as the Russians largely owing to the level of the Danube, were not able to effectively bridge it until June. In Armenia as well the weather and geography of the area were causing obstacles to Russian advances.

[32] Derby to Northcote, 19 May 1877, Northc. Pap., Add. MS. 50022, x; same to same, 19 May 1877, Derby Pap.; Derby to Disraeli, 20 May 1877, Disraeli Pap., xx/S/1233; same to same, 20 May 1877, Derby Pap.; Northcote to Derby, 26 May 1877, ibid.; same to same, 26 May 1877, Northc. Pap., Add. MS. 50022, x. Disraeli wrote to the Queen that only Cairns was up to the mark. 'There is among the leading members [of the Government] too great a fear of responsibility! This is not the way . . . to maintain empires' (Disraeli to Queen Victoria, 18 May 1877, RA H51/45).

[33] Salisbury to Carnarvon, 27 May 1877, Salis. Pap., vol. 8; Cairns to Disraeli, 24 May 1877, Disraeli Pap., xx/Ca/213; Carnarvon to Salisbury, 23 May 1877, Salis. Pap., E 304–5; Disraeli to Derby, 22 May 1877, Derby Pap.; same to same, 22 May 1877, MB vi. 140. Montgelas wrote to Corry that 'shilly shallying propositions seem to me to be only a waste of my precious time. Propositions . . . would come with a very different force if supported by an English corps of occupation already established or enroute for Gallipoli' (Montgelas to Corry, 28 May 1877, Disraeli Pap. xvi/c/171).

[34] Salisbury to Lytton, 25 May 1877, Salis. Pap., C4; same to same, 25 May 1877, ibid., India Office, D/xi/404; Carnarvon memorandum, August 1879, Hardinge, ii. 355–6; Disraeli to Derby, 25 May 1877, Derby Pap.; same to same, 25 May 1877, MB vi. 141; Derby to Disraeli, 24 May 1877, MB vi. 140–1; same to same, 24 May 1877, Disraeli Pap. xx/S/1234; same to same, 24 May 1877, Derby Pap.

[35] Cairns to Richmond, 31 May 1877, Good. Pap. 869.

[36] Chamberlain to Gladstone, 16 Apr. 1877, Glad. Pap., Add. MS. 44125, xL; G. M. Trevelyan, Life of John Bright (London, 1913), p. 420; Forster diary, 26 Apr. 1877, Reid, ii. 172–3; Bright diary, 27 Apr. 1877 (The Diaries of John Bright, N.Y. 1930, p. 390); Gladstone to Granville, 23 Apr. 1877, Ramm, i. 34. Gladstone wrote to Hill of the Daily News that 'it would harmonize very well with the purpose of my motion were you to show what great danger may arise to the interests of this country, from leaving the matter to be fought out or adjusted by the exclusive action of Russia and Turkey' (Gladstone to Hill, 27 Apr. 1877, Glad. Pap., Add. MS. 44454, CCCLXIX).

[37] Argyll to Hartington, 30 Apr. 1877, Hart. Pap. 340/707; Dilke diary, 29 Apr. 1877 (S. Gwynn and G. M. Tuckwell, Life of Sir Charles Dilke, 2 vols., London, 1917, i. 220); Chamberlain to Collings, 28 Apr. 1877, Chamberlain Pap., JC5/16/65; Argyll to Gladstone, 27 Apr. 1877, Glad. Pap., Add. MS. 44104, xix. Harcourt was furious with Gladstone because he felt that the latter's 'move will give Dizzy a decisive advantage over his peaceful colleagues' (Harcourt to Hartington, [?] Apr. 1877, Gardiner, Harcourt, i. 318). Bath told Granville that Salisbury had told him that Gladstone's motion would be ' "fatal to peace, and will place the ball at Beaconsfield's feet" ' (Granville to Gladstone, 27 Apr. 1877, Ramm, i. 35).

[38] Northcote to Queen Victoria, 30 Apr. 1877, RA B28/53; Forster to Lady Ely, 1 May 1877, QVL ii. 534–5; Hartington to Granville, 1 May 1877, Gran. Pap., PRO FO 30 29/26a; Brand diary 30 Apr. 1877, Brand Pap.; Hansard, 30 Apr. 1877, 3rd ser. 234, 101–3; Wirthwein, pp. 219–20. There was an attempt, partly successful and quite temporary, to stir up out-of-doors opinion by Radical groups and the Eastern Question Association. Thompson refers to it as 'a second outburst of acute agitation' with public meetings occurring again in great profusion. But it lacked the intensity, duration, and spontaneity of the agitation of the previous September (Thompson, ii. 191–2, 195–6). The phrasing of the resolutions was partly due to an attempt not to alienate the peace party in the Liberal camp, as well as those who believed that Gladstone was ready to go to war in order to coerce Turkey.

[39] Reid, ii. 174–5; Harcourt to Granville, 5 May 1877, Gran. Pap., PRO 30 29/29a; Morley, Gladstone, ii. 564–5; Brand diary, 4 May 1877, Brand Pap.; Stratford de Redcliffe to Gladstone, 3 May 1877, Glad. Pap., Add. MS. 44454, CCCLXIX;

Chamberlain to Stead, 3 May 1877, Cham. Pap.; Dilke diary, 3 May 1877, Gwynn, i. 221; Granville to Gladstone, 2 May 1877, Ramm, i. 36; Northcote to Cairns, 7 May 1877, Cairns Pap., PRO 30 51/5. Part of the Liberal front-bench opposition to the resolutions was due to a belief that no attempt should be made to embarrass the Government at the critical juncture of the outbreak of a Russo-Turkish war.

⁴⁰ *Hansard*, 7 May 1877, 3rd ser. 234, 366–476; Northcote to Queen Victoria, 7 May 1877, RA B28/57; Lady F. Cavendish, *Diary*, 7 May 1877 (2 vols., N.Y., 1927), ii. 205–6; Morley, *Gladstone*, ii. 563–8; Forster diary, 7 May 1877, Reid, ii. 175; Brand diary, 7 May 1877, Brand Pap.; Thompson, ii. 197–8; Castellanos to Silvela, 8 May 1877, SFM, no. 182; Hardy diary, 9 May 1877, Hardy, ii. 21–2; Aberdare to daughter, 9 May 1877 (*Letters of H. A. Bruce*, 2 vols., Oxford, 1902, ii. 51–2). Granville was convinced that some, at least, of the Radicals cared not for the Eastern Question, but saw an opportunity of breaking up the Liberal party, and this 'really excites them' (Granville to Gladstone, 8 May 1877, Ramm, i. 37). Chamberlain's correspondence tends to support this view (Chamberlain to Collings, 10 May 1877, Chamberlain Pap., JC 5/16/66). Cross's speech enumerated Britain's imperial interests involved in the war and was a Parliamentary version of Derby's dispatch to Shuvalov of 6 May (Wirthwein, pp. 220–2).

⁴¹ Northcote to Queen Victoria, 8 May 1877, RA B28/58; *Hansard*, 8 May 1877, 3rd ser. 234, 501–82.

⁴² *Hansard*, 10 and 11 May 1877, 3rd ser. 234, 623–708, 728–827; Northcote to Queen Victoria, 10 and 11 May 1877, RA B28/59, 60; Mundella to Leader, 11 May 1877, Mundella Pap.

⁴³ *Hansard*, 14 May 1877, 3rd ser. 234, 864–978; Northcote to Queen Victoria, 14–15 May 1877, RA B28/61; Forster diary, 14 May 1877, Reid, ii. 176; Wirthwein, pp. 222–4; Seton-Watson, pp. 185–8; Brand diary, 14 May 1877, Brand Pap. A foreign observer of the debates, the Dutch minister, commented on 'what little dignity . . . a great country like England manifested, by exhibiting such panic and fear of Russia' (Bylandt to Willebois, 15 May 1877, NA 184). During the course of the debate over 50 speeches were made, and when a division was taken, it was found that 25 members of the opposition had voted with the Government in what was essentially a party vote. Of the 25, about 20 were Irish home rulers (Selborne to A. H. Gordon, 16 May 1877, Selborne Pap., Lambeth Palace Library, MS. 1873). In the Lords on 14 May there transpired a short debate on the efficacy of the Tripartite Treaty of April 1856, Rosebery wishing to abrogate it.

⁴⁴ Currie to Layard, 17 May 1877, Lay. Pap., Add. MS. 39012, LXXXII; Granville to Gladstone, 16 May 1877, Ramm, i. 37; Brand diary, 14 May 1877, Brand Pap.; Seton-Watson, p. 185; Wirthwein, pp. 222–4; Bath to Gladstone, 18 May 1877, Glad. Pap., Add. MS. 44454, CCCLXIX. Anti-Russian sentiment was running strong. Corry informed Disraeli that at a London music-hall he attended, one song was wildly cheered for the sake of its refrain. ' "We'll give the Russian bear" "A taste of what we are" "and first to keep our empire" "of the seas" ' (Currie to Disraeli, 21 May 1877, Disraeli Pap. XVI/B/25).

⁴⁵ Hartington to Granville, 25 May 1877, Hart. Pap., 340/710; same to same, 25 May 1877, Gran. Pap., PRO 30 29/22a; Hartington to John Fell, 18 May 1877 (Holland, *Devonshire*, i. 200); Gladstone to Arthur Gordon, 16 May 1877, Glad. Pap., Add. MS. 44321; CCXXXVI; Gladstone to Granville, 17 and 23 May 1877, Ramm, i. 38–9, 41–2; Granville to Gladstone, 18 and 27 May, ibid. 39–40, 42–3. On 24 May the Queen recorded in her journal that upon receiving a telegram from the German Emperor blaming the war on Turkish obstinance, she 'replied it was as much due to the ambition of Russia and that we [Britain] should preserve neutrality . . . as long as possible' (Queen's journal, 24 May 1877, RA).

⁴⁶ J. A. Godley, who earlier had been one of Gladstone's private secretaries, examined the resolutions passed by town meetings and the letters from individuals,

and reported to Granville that about 80 per cent supported Gladstone's resolutions and about 10 per cent favoured neutrality (Godley to Granville, 5 June 1877, Gran. Pap., PRO 30 29/26a).

[47] Thompson, ii. 212–13, 221–5; Wirthwein, pp. 227–8; Hicks Beach to Queen Victoria, 2 June 1877, Hicks Beach Pap., Gloucester Record Office; R. Spence-Watson to wife, 1 June 1877, Spence-Watson Pap., House of Lords Record Office; Gladstone to Granville, 1 June 1877, Ramm, i. 43; J. E. Ellis to J. Rowntree, 1 June 1877 (A. T. Bassett, *Life of the Rt. Hon. John Edward Ellis*, London, 1914, pp. 47–8).

[48] Loftus to Derby, teleg., 21 May 1877, PRO FO 424/53, no. 521; Derby to Loftus, 23 May 1877, ibid., no. 556; Loftus to Ponsonby, 23 May 1877, RA H4/39; Russell to Derby, secret, 27 May 1877, PRO FO 64/878, no. 221. Bismarck praised the note of 6 May and told Russell the only touchy Anglo-Russian points were Constantinople and the navigation of the Straits. Bismarck said he agreed with Shuvalov that a first attempt at peace should be made before Russia crossed the Balkan Mountains, and should this fail, a second effort should be made before Russia reached Adrianople. If this also failed, he advised Britain to occupy the Dardanelles in order to stop the Russians short of Constantinople and prevent the spread of the war (ibid.).

[49] Kemball was the British military attaché observing and reporting on the war in Armenia. He was with the Turkish army.

[50] Derby to Ponsonby, 29 May 1877, Derby Pap.; Layard to Derby, telegs., secret, 5 and 5.15 p.m., 24 May 1877, PRO FO 424/53, nos. 575, 614.

[51] Layard to Derby, 30 May 1877, Derby Pap.; 'My [Layard] position is an extremely difficult and delicate one. I have much to ask and nothing to offer in return.—I must avoid giving cause to the Turks to think that we, too, are disposed to treat them with injustice. There is already a very bitter feeling springing up against England. . . . It must be my endeavour to make them understand that, tho we cannot help them, we are not disposed to deal with them unjustly' (Layard to Derby, 6 June 1877, ibid.).

[52] Disraeli to Queen Victoria, 4 June 1877, RA H14/62; Beach to Queen Victoria, 4 June 1877, ibid., no. 60; Disraeli to Queen Victoria, teleg., 2 June 1877, ibid., no. 55; Loftus to Derby, teleg., 3 June 1877, PRO FO 425/55, no. 65. The Queen, unlike Beach and the Cabinet, considered Austria's answer 'barely satisfactory' (Queen's journal, 4 June 1877, RA). For Andrássay's seven points see p. 558 n. 58.

[53] Gorchakov to Shuvalov, 30 May 1877, PRO FO 424/55, no. 129; memorandum of a confidential conversation between Shuvalov and Derby, 8 June 1877, ibid., no. 130. The British note of 6 May and the Russian answer brought by Shuvalov, though not the Russian peace terms, were known and commented on by the Press and Parliamentary M.P.s (Wirthwein, pp. 244–5; Hansard, 26 June 1877, 3rd ser. 235–60). As a result of the Russian refusal to restrict her military operations beforehand by promising to bypass Constantinople, the Foreign Secretary asked Beust on 13 June whether Austria would join Britain in preventing a temporary Russian occupation of that city. Andrássy's reply delivered by Beust on 16 June was evasive but friendly. London, interpreting Vienna's refusal to prevent a temporary Russian occupation as a desire to have Britain protect Austrian interests alone, informed Andrássy 'that England would be reluctant to enter into a second Crimean War without an ally', and that 'an Austrian refusal to co-operate might . . . lead to, and justify, inaction on our [English] part'. Andrássy replied that, heretofore, there was no reason to suspect Russia to renege on promises made to Austria. 'I . . . cannot imagine any period at which a joint mediation of Austria-Hungary and England could not compel Russia to evacuate Constantinople in the very shortest time.' The Austrian minister, in his letter to Beust of 22 June, did clearly indicate his desire for an English 'understanding', and his willingness to adopt the 'English reservations [interests] . . . as our own' (Andrássy to Beust, 22 June 1877, communicated to Derby on 25 June 1877, PRO FO 424/64, no. 57; Derby to Buchanan, most confid., 13 and 19 June 1877, ibid., nos. 26 and 48).

[54] Disraeli to Queen Victoria, secret, 12 June 1877, RA H1●/78; same to same, secret,

10 June 1877, ibid., no. 74. The Queen described Shuvalov's communication as one of 'endless traps & sly dodges, as well as most dangerous pretensions' (Queen's journal, 10 June 1877, RA'. On 6 June the Prime Minister, perhaps anticipating the resignation of Derby, secretly wrote to Layard asking the ambassador if it would be possible to obtain the Sultan's consent to a British occupation of Gallipoli and the dispatch of the fleet to Constantinople. Layard did not receive Disraeli's communication until 16 June, and replied in a very long letter on 20 June that, though it would be difficult, he thought he could get the Sultan's consent (Layard to Disraeli, private and secret, 20 June 1877, Lay. Pap., letter-book).

[55] Queen Victoria to Disraeli, 7 June 1877, MB vi. 143–4; Queen Victoria to Derby, 8 June 1877, QVL ii. 539–41; Queen's journal, 10 June 1877, RA; Derby to Queen Victoria, 11 June 1877, QVL ii. 541–2; same to same, 11 June 1877, Derby Pap.; Northcote to Disraeli, 9 June 1877, Disraeli Pap. xx/N/36; Manners to Disraeli, 12 and 13 June 1877, ibid. xx/M/216,220. The Queen found Derby's reply to her 'annoying & dissatisfactory' (Queen's journal, 12 June 1877, RA). Both Derby and Salisbury spoke on 11 June at a dinner at the Merchant Taylor's School. Both men deprecated the necessity for going to war (Thompson, ii. 214–15).

[56] Montgelas to Corry, confid., 10 June 1877, Disraeli Pap. xvi/C/174; Disraeli to Derby, 11 June 1877, Derby Pap.; Layard to Derby, 13 June 1877, Lay. Pap., letter-book; same to same, 13 June 1877, Derby Pap.; Derby to Layard, teleg., 12 June 1877, PRO FO 424/55, no. 256; Disraeli to Layard, secret, 6 June 1877, MB vi. 142–3.

[57] Derby to Layard, 14 June 1877, Lay. Pap., Add. MS. 39013, LXXXIII; Derby to Layard, teleg., 14 June 1877, PRO FO 424/55, nos. 294, 300; Derby to Loftus, 18 June 1877, ibid., no. 357; Jomini to Giers, 9 and 11 June 1877, Jelavich, pp. 37–9. Disraeli informed Derby that he would never approve the Russian peace terms 'except with much modification' (Disraeli to Derby, 14 June 1877, Derby Pap.). Manners was even more strongly opposed to them (Manners to Disraeli, 14 June 1877, Disraeli Pap. xx/M/217).

[58] Disraeli to Derby, 14 June 1877, Derby Pap.; same to same, memorandum, ibid.; Disraeli to Salisbury, 14 June 1877, Salis. Pap., E 244–5. Andrássy had enumerated seven things which were unacceptable to Austria. They were as follows: any one Christian Power acquiring exclusive control over the Balkans; a peace settlement without the participation of the guaranteeing Powers; Russian acquisition of territory on the right bank of the Danube; Romania incorporated into or made dependent upon Russia; an Austrian or Russian secundogeniture in Bulgaria, Romania, or Serbia; Russian occupation of Constantinople; and the creation of a large Slavic state in the Balkans.

[59] Disraeli to Hardy, 18 June 1877, Hardy, ii. 24; Manners to Queen Victoria, 19 June 1877, RA H14/92; Derby to Disraeli, 17 June 1877, Disraeli Pap. xx/S/1242; Disraeli to Derby, 17 June 1877, Derby Pap.; same to same, 17 June 1877, MB vi. 145–6; Salisbury to Lytton, 15 June 1877, Salis. Pap., India Office, D/xi/420; same to same, 15 June 1877, Salis. Pap., C4, letter-book; Disraeli to Queen Victoria, teleg., 16 June 1877, RA H14/90; same to same, 14 June 1877, ibid., no. 83. Disraeli's words to Hardy may have been in part due to having received Layard's reply to his secret telegram of the sixth. The ambassador emphasized 'the gravity of the situation', and raised the possibility, at least, that he might not be able to induce the Sultan to appeal to Britain to occupy Gallipoli (Layard to Disraeli, private and secret, teleg., 18 June 1877, Disraeli Pap. xvi/C/116a, b, c; same to same, 18 June 1877, Lay. Pap., Add. MS. 39136, ccvi).

[60] Hertslet memorandum 27 June 1877, Disraeli Pap. xvi/D/56; Queen Victoria to Disraeli, 25 June 1877, MB vi. 147; Disraeli to Queen Victoria, 26 June 1877, ibid. 148; Queen's journal, 22 June 1877, RA; Disraeli to Queen Victoria, teleg., 20 June 1877, RA H14/194; same to same, 23 and 25 June 1877, RA B52/1,2; same to same, 25 June 1877, MB vi. 146–7. The technicality Disraeli indicated to the Queen apparently was

that, while Britain remained neutral, a vote of money and men could not be requested until the war estimates had been passed by Parliament, which had not yet occurred (Disraeli to Queen Victoria, 28 June 1877, MB vi. 149). The Queen was extremely anxious and excited and urged Disraeli to take bold measures without delay or else lose prestige and influence (Queen Victoria to Disraeli, 27 June 1877, ibid. 148–9).

[61] Disraeli to Queen Victoria, confid. and secret, 28 June 1877, ibid. 149.

[62] Bylandt to Willebois, London, 20 June 1877, NA 239; Münster to Bülow, 18 June 1877, GFM 64, xi (Bjork, 'Münster and Anglo-German Relations' p. 127); Shuvalov to Gorchakov, very secret, 27 June 1877 (Seton-Watson, Slav. Rev. v. 428–9).

[63] For Shuvalov's relationship with the Derbys see Rupp, pp. 372–3. Disraeli told Currie in the Foreign Office that Derby was 'the greatest cynic in the world—he believes every action in life to be a blunder—& therefore is always in favour of doing nothing' (Currie to Layard, 28 June 1877, Lay. Pap., Add. MS. 39013, LXXXIII).

[64] The ambassador did not think Derby was sufficiently alive to the dangers facing British interests. On 27 June he wrote to the Foreign Secretary that rather than permit Russia to break up European Turkey and create vassal states which she would control, such autonomous states should be represented in the Ottoman Parliament (Layard to Derby, 27 June 1877, Derby Pap.; same to same, 27 June 1877, Lay. Mem.).

[65] When Kaufmann, the Russian Governor-General in Turkestan, attempted to establish communication with the Ameer of Afghanistan, Britain sent a warning to Russia at the beginning of October 1876, reminding the latter of her repeated assurances that Afghanistan lay outside the Russian sphere of influence. Gorchakov denied that Kaufmann had any instructions to interfere in Afghanistan, and said that there was no Russian intention of making any move on Merv. By the beginning of 1877 Lytton had become more Russophobe, but Salisbury, affected by the Bulgarian massacres and the failure of the Constantinople Conference, had become even more Turcophobe and acted to restrain his viceroy. Lytton, with some justice, felt he had been thrown over and that Salisbury had gone back on the instructions he had initially given to the viceroy. The sending of an envoy by the Porte to Afghanistan only increased the tension between the two men. On 15 June, in answer to remarks made in Parliament by Argyll, Lawrence, and Northbrook, Salisbury made a reply which seemed to deny any attempt to place a British mission in Afghanistan. In the same month, however, Russia was again warned against any attempt to occupy Merv. At the heart of the disagreement between Lytton and Salisbury was the latter's hope that Turkey was dying, and that rather than fight Russia to prevent this, Britain should join her in partitioning the Ottoman remains. The viceroy attempted unsuccessfully to convince Salisbury that Turkey was still sustainable and that it was in Britain's interest to support her. In the autumn of 1877 Lytton produced a pamphlet which attacked what he described as London's pro-Russian policy.

[66] Layard to Derby, private and most confid., teleg., 29 June 1877, PRO FO 424/55, no. 575. Hardy noted in his diary that 'the Russian crossing so easy & complete makes our position now critical' (Hardy diary, 30 June 1877, Cran. Pap., HA43/T501/296).

[67] Richmond to Queen Victoria, 1 July 1877, RA H15/1; Disraeli to Queen Victoria, 30 June 1877, RA H14/115; Hardy diary, 1 July 1877, Cran. Pap., HA43/T501/296. The Queen recorded in her diary that 'Ld. Salisbury & Ld. Derby had made no difficulty about the Fleet, indeed the former had been strongly for it' (Queen's journal, 1 July 1877, RA). Münster believed that Disraeli's continuing bad health was causing a decline in the determination of the cabinet (Münster to Bismarck, 2 July 1877, GFM, A 4238).

[68] Derby to Layard, confid., teleg., 30 June 1877, PRO FO 424/55, no. 576.

[69] Derby to Disraeli, 30 June 1877, Disraeli Pap. xx/S/1248. In part the strengthening of the fleet was due to several dispatches from Lyons indicating that the French had considerably increased the size of their Mediterranean force. Lyon's reports were based on consular information and the observations of a naval attaché, Captain Nicholson.

In the latter's opinion 'the French Squadron now in the Mediterranean is stronger than the English' (Lyons to Derby, secret, 27 June 1877, PRO FO 27/2239, no. 552; same to same, 21 and 26 June 1877, ibid., nos. 523,542). Derby brought this information before the Cabinet (Tenterden memorandum and Derby minute, 29 June 1877, Derby Pap.). The British Mediterranean fleet was reinforced by the addition of four ironclads (Queen's journal, 1 July 1877, RA).

[70] More might have been made of French co-operation though Decazes was plainly Russian. He suggested a plan to Lyons to counteract the opening of the Dardanelles to Russian fleets. His proposal, which Lyons discouraged, was for an Anglo-French protectorate over Egypt and Syria with Crete and Cyprus thrown in (Lyons to Derby, secret, 7 June 1877, PRO FO 424/55, nos. 196, 197).

# CHAPTER SEVENTEEN

[1] Lyons to Derby, confid., 4 July 1877, PRO FO 424/57, no. 77; same to same, very confid., 6 July 1877, ibid., no. 131. Paget reported Italy's main desire to be the maintenance of neutrality but thought that there were 'circumstances in which her active cooperation with England' was 'possible' (Paget to Derby, 30 June 1877, ibid., no. 154).

[2] Russell to Derby, secret, 6 July 1877, ibid., no. 163. Russell noted the change Bismarck's opinions had undergone. Previously the German statesman thought that peace might be made before the Russians reached the Balkan Mountains. 'As the belligerants now stand it is . . . he says . . . too soon to interfere with advantage.' As to the newspaper reports indicating an Anglo-Austrian alliance against Russia, Bismarck said that such a combination 'would be useless at present' and that for Austria an increase of territory was safer than a quarrel with Russia (Russell to Derby, secret, 9 July 1877, ibid., no. 275). Derby agreed with Bismarck that mediation was premature, when asked about it by the French ambassador. The Foreign Secretary referred to the fact that 'no decisive advantage . . . [had] been obtained on either side' (Derby to Lyons, 18 July 1877, ibid., no. 350).

[3] Wellesley to Derby, most confid., 3 July 1877, ibid., no. 265.

[4] Queen Victoria to Disraeli, 5 July 1877, RA H15/7. Disraeli informed the Queen that 'the "Russian Atrocities"' would be brought before the country 'in a popular form' (Disraeli to Queen Victoria, 6 July 1877, ibid., no. 8). Simmons on 5 July produced another memorandum on Gallipoli read by the Prime Minister (Simmons memorandum, 5 July 1877, Simmons Pap., PRO FO 358/2). Shuvalov reported that he learned from a good source that the Queen was inclining toward war. Further, that the British ministers resented the conspiracy of Disraeli and the Queen which the ambassador described as an alliance between a half-crazed woman and a political clown (Shuvalov to Gorchakov, confid., 10 July 1877, Seton-Watson, *Slav. Rev.* v. 430–1).

[5] Northcote to Queen Victoria, 6 July 1877, RA B28/85; *Hansard*, 3 July 1877, 3rd ser. 235, 663; Disraeli to Derby, 3 July 1877, Derby Pap.; Hartington to Gladstone, 4 July 1877, Glad. Pap., Add. MS. 44144, LVIX.

[6] Queen's journal, 8 July 1877, RA. Hunt, dying of gout at a spa in Germany, was bitterly disappointed at giving up the vote of credit. He thought, as he wrote to Northcote, that such an appeal would have been carried in Parliament 'by an overwhelming majority' (Hunt to Northcote, Homburg, 13 July 1877, Northc. Pap., Add. MS. 50040, XXVIII).

[7] Disraeli to Queen Victoria, 10 July 1877, RA H15/14. At the end of June the Foreign Secretary, as agreed in Cabinet, proposed to Austria the signing of a protocol to record 'the understanding' arrived at by Britain and Austria. Vienna at first refused

to sign a protocol, which led London to suspect a secret Austro-Russian agreement, the existence of which Andrássy denied (Derby to Buchanan, confid., 30 June and 16 July 1877, PRO FO 424/64, nos. 61 and 87; Buchanan to Derby, very confid., teleg., 7 July 1877, ibid., no. 75).

[8] But, as Hardy reported to the Prime Minister, the confidential committee of military experts sitting at the War Office concluded that nothing would be gained by sending troops to Malta and Gibraltar unless supplies and transport were kept in readiness at those two places (Hardy to Disraeli, 12 July 1877, Disraeli Pap. xx/Ha/141).

[9] As a result of this telegram Disraeli asked Richmond, who was deputizing for Hunt, how many marines were presently with the Mediterranean fleet, and whether their number could be augmented (Disraeli to Richmond, 12 July 1877, Good. Pap. 865).

[10] Disraeli to Queen Victoria, 12 July 1877, RA H15/18; Queen's journal, 13 July 1877, QVL ii. 547; Layard to Disraeli, private and secret, teleg., 10 July 1877, Disraeli Pap. xvi/C/119–20; same to same, 10 July 1877, Lay. Pap., Add. MS. 39136, ccvi; Queen's journal, 11 July 1877, RA. Carnarvon maintains that at the Cabinet meeting on 11 July Manners, supported by Beach, made a proposal to send the fleet to Constantinople if Russia crossed the Balkan Mountains (Hardinge, ii. 358). Disraeli, I think, underestimates Salisbury's following in both the country and Parliament.

[11] Currie to Layard, 12 July 1877, Lay. Pap., Add. MS. 39103, lxxxiii.

[12] Cairns to Queen Victoria, 15 July 1877, RA H15/21–2; Disraeli to Queen Victoria, 14 July 1877, RA B52/5. Monypenny and Buckle misdate Disraeli's letter as twelve, instead of as it should be, fourteen July (MB vi. 150–1). It was Cairns and Manners who made the proposal to send the fleet to Constantinople (Queen's journal, 14 July 1877, RA). On the same day as the Cabinet meeting Hardy was informed by Sir H. Yelverton, a former commander of the Mediterranean fleet, that the fleet could not prevent a land assault on Constantinople; also, 'that if Gallipoli were taken by Russia, ships might run the gauntlet unless very heavy guns were in position' (Hardy to Disraeli, 14 July 1877, Disraeli Pap. xx/Ha/142).

[13] Queen Victoria to Disraeli, 16 July 1877, MB vi. 152–3; same to same, teleg., 16 July 1877, Disraeli Pap. xix/B/7818; Disraeli to Queen Victoria, 16 July 1877, RA B52/7; same to same, 16 July 1877, MB vi. 151–2; Queen Victoria to Disraeli, 15 July 1877, QVL ii. 547–9; Disraeli to Derby, 16 July 1877, Derby Pap. At the meeting Richmond, who like Cairns had generally supported the Prime Minister, was won over by the Lord Chancellor to oppose the casus belli warning to Russia (Corry memorandum, 17 July 1877, Disraeli Pap. xix/C/284). Grey thought that the Cabinet would not be able to continue on much longer and that the Ottoman Empire would soon be at the point of breaking up as well (Grey to Halifax, 2 July 1877, Hickleton Pap.).

[14] Derby to Disraeli, 14 July 1877, Derby Pap.

[15] Derby to Russell, secret and confid., 17 July 1877, PRO FO 424/307, no. 259.

[16] Queen's journal, 16 July 1877, RA; Hornby to Hunt, 18 July 1877, Hornby Papers, National Maritime Museum, PH1/126; Disraeli to Salisbury, 18 July 1877, Salis. Pap., E 246–7; Queen's journal, 17 July 1877, QVL ii. 550–1. The British, apparently, did not know where on the European side of the Dardanelles the Ottoman heavy guns were positioned, or, whether they were 'actually manned' (Derby to Layard, teleg., 28 July 1877, PRO FO 424/64, no. 105). This may have been part of the reason why the military disagreed on the necessity to control these guns, should the fleet be ordered to Constantinople. In reply to Derby's request for information about these batteries, Layard reported that it would be difficult to obtain this information as the Porte 'maintained the greatest secrecy on the subject' (Layard to Derby, secret, teleg., 29 July 1877, ibid., no. 109).

[17] Gladstone to Shuvalov, 20 July 1877, Glad. Pap., Add. MS. 44454, ccclxix; Hansard, 19 July 1877, 3rd ser. 235, 1517; Bylandt to Willebois, 19 July 1877, NA 281. Selborne agreed with Gladstone that 'the inevitable horrors of war' were distinct from

the 'wanton barbarities' of the Turks in Bulgaria in 1876 (Selborne to Granville, 18 July 1876, Gran. Pap., PRO 30 29/26a). A declaration testifying to Russian outrages on inoffensive Muslims was signed by 20 correspondents of leading British and European newspapers (Layard to Derby, teleg., 21 July 1877, PRO FO 424/57, no. 414). Gladstone also appealed to Madame Novikov for the 'severe and prompt punishment of some offenders' (Gladstone to Madame Novikov, 24 Aug. 1877, O. Novikov, *The M.P. for Russia*, 2 vols., N.Y. 1909, i. 75–6]). The Whig section of the Liberal party, represented below by Grey, were almost as unhappy with Gladstone's behaviour as were most Conservatives. 'Of course there is nothing to be hoped from Gladstone—his utter want of judgment & his recklessness of the public interest, & readiness to do anything to gratify his own vanity and ambition become more conspicuous every day' (Grey to Halifax, 28 Aug. 1877, Hickleton Pap.).

¹⁸ Disraeli to Queen Victoria, 22 July 1877, RA B52/11; same to same, 22 July 1877, MB vi. 154–5; same to same, teleg., 21 July 1877, Disraeli Pap. xix/B/821; Carnarvon memorandum, Hardinge, ii. 359; Queen's journal, 21 and 22 July 1877, RA; Layard to Derby, teleg., 19 July 1877, PRO FO 424/57, no. 383; Wellesley to Derby, 11 July 1877, ibid., 65/985, no. 5; Sumner, pp. 614–15. On the same day as the Cabinet meeting, Shuvalov called upon Derby, and not yet having received his Government's reply to Britain's warning of 17 July, expressed his personal opinion of 'the difficulty of giving any pledge not to march on Constantinople' (Derby to Lyons, very confid., 21 July 1877, PRO FO 446/1959, no. 291).

¹⁹ Salisbury to Lytton, 6 July 1877, Salis. Pap., C4, letter-book; same to same, 6 July 1877, ibid., India Office, D/xi/436.

²⁰ Manners to Disraeli, 22 and 24 July 1877, Disraeli Pap. xx/M/224–5; C. Whibley, *Lord John Manners and his Friends* (2 vols., London, 1925), ii. 190–2; Disraeli to Manners, 24 July 1877, MB vi. 156; Queen's journal, 28 July 1877, RA.

²¹ Hardy diary, 24 July 1877, Cran. Pap., HA43/T501/297; Hardy to Disraeli, 22 July 1877, Hardy, ii. 25–6. Earlier, Salisbury had overcome Hardy's objections by indicating at the Cabinet meeting on 14 July that India ships were available to transport the men once they were in Malta.

²² On 21 July the British again questioned Andrássy as to his distinction between a permanent and temporary Russian occupation of Constantinople, only the former of which had Vienna promised to resist. On 26 July the Austrian minister, having refused Derby's protocol, sent Beust a 'declaration' which the ambassador communicated to the Foreign Secretary on 30 July. It stipulated that 'if any one of the common interests of the two countries, as they have been defined, should be attacked, or even seriously menaced, an agreement as to the means of defending it could be arrived at without difficulty or delay'. Beust was instructed to leave a copy of the 'declaration' with the Foreign Secretary, providing the latter sent a corresponding document to Vienna, and would maintain the secrecy of the communication from both Parliament and other governments. Nothing was said about wives. On 15 August Derby forwarded to Buchanan the equivalent British 'declaration' which went along with the Austrian preference for 'parallel but independent action' by the two Powers until their common interests were threatened or attacked. If and when this occurred, 'the Austrian Government would be ready to join with that of Her Majesty in considering the further measures which might be necessary for the defence and material preservation of such of our reciprocal interests as might be menaced'. What the British Government had obtained finally from the protracted and ambiguous negotiations with Austria was that both 'would act independently of each other in protecting their separate and joint interests against injury from certain possible consequences of the war between Russia and Turkey, but should reserve the right of joint action should necessity for it arise' (Derby to Buchanan, 14 Aug. and 1 Sept. 1877, PRO FO 424/64, nos. 134 and 145; Andrássy to Beust, 26 July 1877, read to Derby on 30 July 1877, ibid., nos. 116, 117; Derby to Buchanan, confid., 21 July 1877, ibid., no. 94).

[23] Disraeli to Derby, 23 July 1877, Derby Pap. One of the obstacles which the Austrians put forward as an excuse that prevented an alliance was the unfavourable reaction to it of Francis Joseph. The latter told Lord Denbigh, who had a long talk with him in July, that Austria was not tied to Russia and might be forced to occupy Bosnia-Hercegovina. Denbigh indicated that Britain wished an alliance with Austria. According to Wertheimer, Denbigh had been sent to Vienna by Disraeli (Rupp. p. 397). There are references to Denbigh's mission in Buchanan to Derby, 28 July 1877, Derby Pap., and in [?] memorandum, 28 July 1877, RA H15/64.

[24] Queen Victoria to Disraeli, 26 July 1877, MB vi. 156–7; Buchanan to Derby, 26 July 1877, RA H15/55; Derby to Disraeli, 24 and 25 July 1877, Derby Pap.; Queen's journal, 24 and 25 July 1877, RA.

[25] Queen's journal, 28 July 1877, RA; Layard to Derby, teleg., 27 July 1877, PRO FO 424–57, no. 493. Simmons had sent Hardy a memorandum in answer to a request for information from the War Secretary. He argued that in order to keep the Dardanelles open to a British fleet it would be necessary to destroy the guns and batteries along the Dardanelles. He also suggested the importance of obtaining or destroying the Turkish fleet to keep it from Russia (Simmons to Hardy, 26 July 1877, Disraeli Pap. xviii/A/12). Colonel Home also advised destroying the guns along the European side of the Dardanelles, and, with the fleet in the Dardanelles, an occupation of Chanak on the Asian side of the water-way was feasible. He also felt it was possible to force the Bosphorus in order to seize the Turkish fleet (Home memorandum, 29 July 1877, RA H15/70). The Cabinet meeting on 28 July authorized the sending of Captain Fraser along with a carpet-bag of gun-cotton to Constantinople in order to personally destroy the guns at Gallipoli (Preston, pp. 263–4). Layard and the British attachés had been urging the Porte to improve and ready the Bulair lines at Gallipoli so that, if necessary, they might be used to prevent the Russian army from occupying the Gallipoli Peninsula and controlling the Dardanelles. Salisbury now explained to Lytton that if Russia permanently occupied Constantinople, the Government would go to war, but the Austrian promise to oppose Russian occupation, though it might not be kept, made the India Secretary feel that war was 'not at all a probable contingency' (Salisbury to Lytton, 25 July 1877, Salis. Pap., C4, letter-book; same to same, 25 July 1877, India Office, D/xi/452).

[26] Richmond to Cairns, 31 July 1877, Cairns Pap., PRO 30 51/4; Hardy diary, 31 July 1877, Hardy, ii. 26. The confidential communication given to Shuvalov on 28 July indicated a British hope and readiness for peace, and an intention to remain neutral so long as her interests were not threatened. 'But they do not consider that they would be departing from this neutrality . . . if they should find themselves compelled to direct their fleet to proceed to Constantinople, and thus afford protection to the European population against internal disturbance' (Confidential memorandum to Shuvalov, 28 July 1877, PRO FO 424/64, no. 108).

[27] Queen Victoria to Derby, 29 July 1877, MB vi. 158–9; Disraeli to Queen Victoria, 29 July 1877, ibid. 158; Derby to Queen Victoria, 28 July 1877, ibid. 157–8; same to same, 28 July 1877, Derby Pap.

[28] Disraeli to Queen Victoria, teleg., 1 Aug. 1877, RA H15/85; Queen Victoria to Disraeli, 1 Aug. 1877, RA B52/17; same to same, 1 Aug. 1877, Disraeli Pap. xix/C/289; Disraeli to Layard, personal and most confid., 29 July 1877, Lay. Pap., Add. MS. 39136, ccvl; Derby to Layard, confid., teleg., 28 July 1877, PRO FO 424/57, no. 507.

[29] Plevna was a town and fortress about 85 miles north-east of Sophia which had been occupied by the able Ottoman commander, Osman Pasha. He defeated a Russian force there on 20 and again on 30 July. After this second defeat, Russian troops reinforced by a Romanian army attempted to surround the town and starve Osman's force into surrender.

[30] Layard to Disraeli, 1 Aug. 1877, Lay. Pap., Add. MS. 39130, cc; Layard to Derby, 1 Aug. 1877, ibid.; same to same, teleg., 2 Aug. 1877, PRO FO 424/59, no. 61.

[31] Disraeli to Queen Victoria, 6 Aug. 1877, RA B52/20; same to same, 6 Aug. 1877,

Disraeli Pap. XIX/C/293; Queen's journal, 8 Aug. 1877, RA H15/111; same to same, 8 Aug. 1877, *QVL* ii. 560–1; Disraeli to Queen Victoria, 8 Aug. 1877, RA B52/21; Queen Victoria to Disraeli, 9 Aug. 1877, *QVL* ii. 561–2; Ponsonby to Queen Victoria, 9 Aug. 1877, RA H15/114; Wellesley to Queen Victoria, 9 Aug. 1877, Disraeli Pap. XIX/C/297; same to same, 9 Aug. 1877, RA H15/116; Disraeli to Queen Victoria, secret, 9 Aug. 1877, RA H15/117; Ponsonby to Queen Victoria, 10 Aug. 1877, RA H15/120; Lady Derby to Halifax, 12 Aug. 1877, Hickleton Pap.; Queen Victoria to Disraeli, 14 Aug. 1877, *QVL* ii. 563–4; same to same, 14 Aug. 1877, Disraeli Pap. XIX/C/300, 301; Derby draft for Wellesley, 14 Aug. 1877, RA H15/139; Queen Victoria to Wellesley, 14 Aug. 1877, RA H15/141; Ponsonby to Queen Victoria, 15 Aug. 1877, RA H15/143; same to same, 15 Aug. 1877, Disraeli to Queen Victoria, 1877, Disraeli Pap. XIX/C/301, 302; Queen Victoria to Disraeli, teleg., 15 Aug. 1877, RA H15/145; Queen's journal, 16 Aug. 1877, *QVL* ii. 564–5. It was assumed by Disraeli that the fighting would stop once winter had set in and begin again, if it did at all, the following spring. The secret message was Disraeli's, though completely agreed to by the Queen. The latter had merely wished to inform the Tsar that if Russia went to Constantinople, Britain would declare war.

³² Confidential memorandum for Colonel Wellesley, PRO FO 424/64, no. 135.

³³ Queen Victoria to Disraeli, 14 Aug. 1877, Disraeli Pap. XIX/C/300, 301; same to same, 14 Aug. 1877, *QVL* ii. 563–4. See pp. 310 and 316 for Disraeli's warning to the Foreign Secretary and the Queen's letter of 1 August. Further confirmation of the realization of the relationship of the Derbys with Shuvalov is contained in a private note from Ponsonby to his wife on 16 August (Ponsonby, *Henry Ponsonby*, pp. 164–5). When Ponsonby asked the Queen why Derby should not be told of the secret communication to the Tsar, Her Majesty answered 'how can we—he tells Lady D—and she tells all to Schouvaloff' (ibid.).

³⁴ See p. 316.

³⁵ For Salisbury's relationship with the Queen see the latter's letter to Disraeli of 25 July in *QVL* ii. 554–5.

³⁶ Northcote to Corry, 15 Aug. 1877, Disraeli Pap. xx/N/41; Disraeli memorandum on meeting of 15 August 1877, RA B52/24; same to same, 15 Aug. 1877, MB vi. 171–2; Queen's journal, 16 Aug. 1877, RA; Disraeli to Queen Victoria, 8, 10, 13 Aug. 1877, RA B52/21, 22, 23; same to same, 8, 10, 13 Aug. 1877, MB vi. 171; Disraeli to Cross, 10 Aug. 1877, Cross Pap., Add. MS. 51265, III. Salisbury's feelings about the opposition within the country to an alliance with Turkey is borne out by the American minister in London. 'If tomorrow the Cossack shall stable his horses in the Mosques of the Bosphorus not a British sword will be drawn to dislodge them. The increased intelligence and improved morality of Great Britain makes longer continuance of . . . [Ottoman preservation to restrain Russia] impossible. . . . Depend upon it, no British ministry could last a month which should decide to embroil England in a war for the preservation of the Moslem Empire' (Pierrepont to Fish, 15 Aug. 1877, U.S. State Dept., J4, no. 219).

³⁷ Gladstone had written privately to Derby about the atrocities the war was bringing about, and suggested to him the usefulness of having Blunt make an on the spot investigation of them. The Foreign Secretary and the Cabinet refused to do so because hostilities were still in progress (Gladstone to Derby, 1 Aug. 1877, Glad. Pap., Add. MS. 44141, LVI; Derby to Gladstone, 16 Aug. 1877, ibid.).

³⁸ Disraeli to Queen Victoria, 4 Oct. 1877, Disraeli Pap. XIX/C/326, 327; Wellesley to Queen Victoria, 30 Aug. 1877, ibid. 310, 311; same to same, 30 Aug. 1877, *QVL* ii. 565–7. Argyll was one of those who felt that Russia could not accept defeat at the hands of Turkey alone, and that for the sake of her reputation must continue to fight until the Ottomans had been crushed. 'Therefore I look to a prolongation of the war, and in the end to a more complete revolution in the status quo than wd. have resulted from an easier victory. On the other hand if it were possible to suppose that Turkey shd assert successfully equality in military strength with Russia, her arrogance wd be intolerable,

and I sh expect that Europe wd. find itself compelled to interfere both by policy & by sentiment. Thus in either case . . . the final defeat, and I hope the destruction of Turkey as a government' (Argyll to Halifax, 9 Oct. 1877, Hickleton Pap.).

[39] Queen Victoria to Disraeli, teleg., 12 Sept. 1877, QVL ii. 569; Disraeli to Queen Victoria, teleg., 11 Sept. 1877, ibid. 568–9; same to same, 11 Sept. 1877, RA H16/31; Queen Victoria memorandum, 7 Sept. 1877, QVL ii. 567–8; Queen Victoria to Disraeli, 5 Sept. 1877, RA B52/30; Hardy to Cairns, 3 and 6 Sept. 1877, Cairns Pap., PRO FO 51/7; Hardy to Derby, 3 Sept. 1877, Derby Pap.; Hardy to Disraeli, 5 Sept. 1877, Disraeli Pap. XIX/B/887.

[40] After the Russian defeat at third Plevna, Ignatiev who had been with the Tsar at army headquarters was dismissed, and returned to his estates near Kiev. Gorchakov and Jomini continued to remain in Bucharest, and the military and Alexander II continued to ignore them and the Foreign Ministry. Military and diplomatic decisions were made by the Tsar and the Grand Duke advised by the generals. Finding his advice scorned, Gorchakov gave himself over to pleasurable pursuits.

[41] Cross knew Lady Derby well and corresponded with her.

[42] Disraeli to Queen Victoria, 24 Sept. 1877, Disraeli Pap. XIX/C/318; Disraeli to Derby, 13 and 17 Sept. 1877, Derby Pap.; same to same, 17 Sept. 1877, MB vi. 178–9; Disraeli to Cross, 16 Sept. 1877, Cross Pap., Add. MS. 51265, III; Hardy to Cross, 10 Sept. 1877, ibid. 51267, V; Wirthwein, pp. 264–5. It had just been decided to retire Buchanan and replace him at Vienna with Elliot. This meant Layard's position could be made a permanent one as was always intended by Beaconsfield, if not Derby.

[43] Queen Victoria to Disraeli, confid., 4 Oct. 1877, Disraeli Pap. XIX/C/326; Disraeli to Queen Victoria, 4 Oct. 1877, ibid., no. 327; Seton-Watson, Slav. Rev. vi (1927–8), 425—6; Disraeli to Queen Victoria, secret, 3 Oct. 1877, Disraeli Pap. XIX/C/325, 326; Disraeli to Salisbury, 3 Oct. 1877, ibid. XX/Ce/205; same to same, 3 Oct. 1877, Salis. Pap., E 253–6; Cairns to Disraeli, 1 Oct. 1877, Disraeli Pap. XX/Ca/220; Northcote to Disraeli, 1 Oct. 1877, ibid. XX/N/42; Manners to Disraeli, 30 Sept. 1877, ibid. XX/M/228; Disraeli to Richmond, 30 Sept. 1877, Good. Pap. 865; Derby to Disraeli, 29 Sept. 1877, Derby Pap.; same to same, 29 Sept. 1877, MB vi. 182–3; Hardy diary, 29 Sept. 1877, Hardy, ii. 32–3; Queen's journal, 2 and 3 Oct. 1877, RA; Disraeli to Queen Victoria, 16 Sept. 1877, RA B52/32; Disraeli to Queen Victoria, most confid., 24 Sept. 1877, RA B53/3; same to same, 28 and 29 Sept., 3 and 4 Oct. 1877, RA B53/9, 10, 14, 16.

[44] Richmond, Cairns, Hardy, Manners, and Beach assented, and Salisbury, Cross, Smith, and Northcote raised objections (Cairns memorandum, 5 Oct. 1877, RA B53/18). There is also a copy of this memorandum in the Disraeli Papers, XIX/C/328.

[45] Ibid.; Disraeli to Queen Victoria, teleg., 5 Oct. 1877, RA H16/103; Carnarvon memorandum, 5 Oct. 1877, Hardinge, ii. 362–3; Hardy diary, 6 Oct. 1877, Cran. Pap., HA43/T501/297; Hardy diary, 6 Oct. 1877, Hardy, ii. 33. Salisbury agreed that Russia 'should be called upon to give an absolute about Constantinople, and that, if she refused, we should act as we thought fit' (Manners to Disraeli, 8 Oct. 1877, Disraeli Pap. XX/M/229).

[46] Disraeli to Queen Victoria, secret, 6 Oct. 1877, RA B42/19; same to same, 6 Oct. 1877, MB vi. 183–4; Lady Derby to Carnarvon, 8 Oct. 1877, Hardinge, ii. 363; Carnarvon to Salisbury, 8 Oct. 1877, Salis. Pap., E 314–15. Salisbury replied to Carnarvon that Derby would prevent any 'pledge of assistance' or forward policy and that in his opinion, though anti-Russian feeling in Britain was strong, the country would not sanction an increase in taxation in order to help Turkey. Russophobia, he wrote, 'nowhere rises nearly to income-tax point' (Salisbury to Carnarvon, 14 Oct. 1877, Salis. Pap., vol. 8).

[47] Disraeli to Queen Victoria, teleg., 8 Oct. 1877, RA H16/110; Disraeli to Queen Victoria, secret, 6 Oct. 1877, RA B53/19; Derby to Ponsonby, 18 Sept. 1877, RA H16/50; Ponsonby to Derby, 14 Sept. 1877, RA H16/41; Queen Victoria to Disraeli,

22 Sept. 1877, RA B53/2.

**48** Shuvalov talked of this to Disraeli at Brighton as a 'real victory but "not in the right place"'. The Russian ambassador also informed Disraeli, as he had previously told Derby on numerous occasions, that a written Austro-Russian convention, which he had seen, existed. Beust, under instruction from Andrássy, had always denied to the British that any formal Austro-Russian treaty existed. Beust had not been told of the Budapest Convention. Andrássy did admit to London that there was an informal understanding with Russia. Ironically, in September and October, after long, tortuous, and inconclusive negotiations with Austria, Derby and Disraeli talked of an informal understanding between Britain and Austria. At his talk with Shuvalov at Brighton, Disraeli told the Russian ambassador that if there were a second campaign, Britain could not remain neutral (Disraeli to Queen Victoria, secret, 10 Oct. 1877, MB vi. 185–6). At the beginning of December, Crowe, a British consul, informed Odo Russell that at Reichstadt Austria and Russia had signed a political alliance (Crowe to Russell, confid., 10 Dec. 1877, Odo Russell Pap., PRO).

**49** The party ready to go to war now to assist Turkey was 'headed by Hardy, supported' by Manners and Beach. A second group—Cross, Cairns, Smith, and Richmond—was prepared for war only after Russia had refused not to occupy Constantinople. Salisbury is described as the third party agreeable to war only after peace had been made and a Russian refusal to evacuate Constantinople had been declared. Derby, of course, wanted peace at any price, and Northcote was designated as party number five, and opposed to standing up for 'selfish British interests'. Number six was the little Carnarvon, whom Disraeli characterizes as desiring a permanent Russian occupation of Constantinople, Beaconsfield and the Queen were the seventh party favouring the written promise from Russia (Disraeli to Queen Victoria, secret, 3 Nov. 1877, RA B53/35; same to same, 3 Nov. 1877, MB vi. 193/5).

**50** Ibid.; Northcote to Disraeli, confid., 3 Nov. 1877, Disraeli Pap. xx/N/43; Derby to Disraeli, 1 Nov. 1877, ibid. xix/B/935; same to same, 1 Nov. 1877, Derby Pap.; Queen's journal, 3 and 4 Nov. 1877, RA; Hardy diary, 29 Oct. 1877, Cran. Pap., HA43/T501/297; Disraeli to Queen Victoria, 23 and 26 Oct. 1877, RA, B53/27, 29; Disraeli to Queen Victoria, 1 Nov. 1877, MB vi. 193.

**51** Carnarvon memorandum, 5 Nov. 1877, Hardinge, ii. 363; Disraeli to Queen Victoria, teleg., 5 Nov. 1877, Disraeli Pap. xix/C/343; same to same, 5 Nov. 1877, RA B53/36; Queen Victoria to Disraeli, 5 Nov. 1877, QVL ii. 569/70; same to same, teleg., 6 Nov. 1877, RA H17/16; Disraeli to Queen Victoria, 7 Nov. 1877, QVL ii. 571–2; same to same, 7 Nov. 1877, Disraeli Pap. xix/C/345. On the morning of the Cabinet meeting of 5 November Layard, who had sounded the Porte on its readiness for peace and its terms as a step leading to their communication by Britain to Russia, reported the Porte's reaction. The Grand Vizier and Ottoman Foreign Minister were willing to grant the reforms of the London Protocol, a frontier rectification for Montenegro, restoration of Bessarabia to Russia, Romania to Austria, and Batum made a free port (Layard to Derby, secret, teleg., 5 Nov. 1877, PRO FO424/62, no. 49).

**52** Derby to Loftus, 17 Nov. 1877, ibid., no. 193; Wirthwein, pp. 270–2; Thompson, ii. 262–4; Ollier, *History of the Russo-Turkish War*, i. 484–5 (hereafter cited as Ollier); Münster to Bülow, 8 and 10 Nov. 1877, GFM, A6731, A6740; Queen Victoria to Disraeli, 6 Nov. 1877, QVL ii. 570–1. Gladstone responded to Beaconsfield's speech by one of his own at Holyhead on 12 November, in which he described Disraeli as representing 'Turkism in a very developed form' (Ollier, i. 485–6). On 6 December he advised Hill, editor of the *Daily News*, that the point to work in print was that Disraeli was still capable of a dangerous stroke (Gladstone to Hill, 6 Dec. 1877, Glad. Pap., Add. MS. 44455, CCCLXX). Layard thought that the Prime Minister's speech was 'excellent as far as it went', and reported the Turks to be greatly satisfied with it (Layard to Lyons, 21 Nov. 1877, Lay. Pap., Add. MS. 39130, CC).

**53** This excuse for not formally asking for a Russian promise was Derby's, and he apparently convinced Disraeli of its validity because the latter informed the Queen that it was the reason why no communication was made to Russia (Disraeli to Derby, 25 Nov. 1877, Derby Pap.).

[54] Disraeli to Queen Victoria, 16 Nov. 1877, MB vi. 197–8; Queen Victoria to Disraeli, 16 Nov. 1877, Disraeli Pap. XIX/C/350; same to same, 15 Nov. 1877, ibid.; same to same, 15 Nov. 1877, RA B53/47; Mansfield to Derby, teleg., 14 Nov. 1877, PRO FO 424/62, no. 121; Layard to Derby, secret, teleg., 13 Nov. 1877, ibid., no. 110; Disraeli to Queen Victoria, secret, 14 Nov. 1877, QVL ii. 574; same to same, 14 Nov. 1877, RA B53/146; Queen Victoria to Disraeli, 13 Nov. 1877, QVL ii. 573; Disraeli to Queen Victoria, 12 Nov. 1877, ibid. 347; Disraeli to Queen Victoria, 12 Nov. 1877, ibid. 346; same to same, 12 Nov. 1877, RA B53/42; Queen Victoria to Ponsonby, teleg., 9 Nov. 1877, Disraeli Pap. XIX/C/346. Beaconsfield's explanation to the Queen as to why the Cabinet did not, as agreed, ask Russia for a promise on Constantinople sounds like a scheme hatched by Derby and Shuvalov, which Beaconsfield temporarily bought. It was Derby who delayed sending a note to Russia, putting forth as an excuse Russian peace terms on Bulgaria (Disraeli to Derby, 25 Nov. 1877, Derby Pap.).

[55] Derby to Disraeli, 26 Nov. 1877, Derby Pap.; Disraeli to Derby, 25 Nov. 1877, ibid.; same to same, 25 Nov. 1877, Disraeli Pap. XIX/B/903; Derby to Disraeli, 24 Nov. 1877, ibid. XIX/B/962; same to same, 24 Nov. 1877, Derby Pap.; Disraeli to Derby, 23 Nov. 1877, ibid.; Derby to Disraeli, 19 Nov. 1877, ibid.; same to same, 19 Nov. 1877, Disraeli Pap. XX/S/1276; Queen Victoria to Ponsonby, 21 Nov. 1877, ibid. XIX /C/352; Queen Victoria to Disraeli, 19 Nov. 1877, ibid. 351; Cairns to Disraeli, 19 Nov. 1877, Derby Pap.; Northcote to Queen Victoria, 16 Nov. 1877, RA H17/41.

[56] Cowley to Layard, 29 Nov. 1877, Lay. Pap., Add. MS. 39016, LXXXVI; Lay. Mem., 28 Nov. 1877, VI, VII; Cairns to Disraeli, 30 Nov. 1877, Disraeli Pap. XX/Ca/224; Hardy to Disraeli, 28 Nov. 1877, ibid., Ha/14a; Manners memorandum, 26 Nov. 1877, ibid., M/234. Cowley who informed Layard that he thought the Government would probably break up, gave his opinion that there was strong sympathy for Turkey in Britain, but no real desire to assist her militarily (Cowley to Layard, 29 Nov. 1877, Lay. Pap., Add. MS. 39016, LXXXVI). On 28 November Derby asked Beust again the same question the British had been putting to the Austrians periodically for the previous six months. 'What course [would] Andrassy be prepared to pursue if a Russian army should approach' Constantinople. The Austrian minister replied on 1 December that he would not interfere in the operations of the war, but that a permanent Russian occupation of Constantinople would elicit an Austrian declaration of war (Derby to Buchanan, most confid., 28 Nov. 1877, PRO FO 424/64, no. 203; Buchanan to Derby, most confid., teleg., 1 Dec. 1877, ibid., no. 206; memorandum communicated by Beust on 3 Dec. 1877, ibid., no. 207).

[57] Manners to Disraeli, 2 Dec. 1877, Disraeli Pap. XIX/B/966; Wirthwein, pp. 277–9; Thompson, ii. 264–5; Currie to Layard, 29 Nov. 1877, Lay. Pap., Add. MS. 39016, LXXXVI. Though Derby's speech to the deputations had a calming—because anti-war—effect generally on the public, it was strongly resented by the Queen and Disraeli. The Queen asked Disraeli to speak to the Foreign Secretary, and the Prime Minister replied that 'he expressed himself the other day . . . in such severe terms to Ld. Derby, that he feels he cannot revert to the subject. Lord Derby even expressed his regret, that he had made the speech' (Disraeli to Queen Victoria, 21 Dec. 1877, RA B54/22).

[58] Tenterden memorandum, 7 Dec. 1877, Derby Pap.; Derby draft, 4 Dec. 1877, ibid.; Derby to Disraeli, 4 Dec. 1877, Disraeli Pap. XX/S/1280; Manners to Queen Victoria, 4 Dec. 1877, MB vi. 198–9; same to same, 4 Dec. 1877, RA B54/6; Disraeli to Queen Victoria, teleg., 4 Dec 1877, RA H17/89; same to same, 4 Dec. 1877, Disraeli Pap. XIX/B/968.

[59] See p. 324.

[60] Hardy diary, 6 Dec. 1877, Cran. Pap., HA43/T501/297; Disraeli to Derby, 5 Dec. 1877, Derby Pap.; same to same, 5 Dec. 1877, MB vi. 199.

[61] Disraeli to Queen Victoria, 8 Dec. 1877, RA B54/7; same to same, 8 Dec. 1877, Disraeli Pap. XIX/C/357.


# CHAPTER EIGHTEEN

[1] Wirthwein, pp. 281–3; Giers to Jomini, 11 Dec. 1877, Jelavich, p. 146. Opinion in Britain was turning against Russia, and many admired what they saw as a gallant Ottoman struggle against a more powerful foe. Derby described to Layard the change in opinion. 'The neo Russian party headed by Gladstone scarcely exists except among a few ecclesiastically minded persons to whom the Greek Church is worth all risks' (Derby to Layard, 13 Dec. 1877, Lay. Pap., Add. MS. 39017, LXXXVII). The historian and M.P., G. O. Trevelyan, in a speech at Galashiels described a division in British opinion little due to religious or theological inclination. 'The division is not, as is generally described, one of class, but of personal habits and character. If you meet a man who does an honest stroke of work on every week day, whether he be manufacturer, or artisan, or tradesman, or barrister, it is ten to one that he wishes his country to leave this quarrel to be fought out by those whom it concerns. If you meet a man who amuses himself for fifteen hours in the twenty-four and sleeps the rest, it is ninety-nine to one but he thinks we should send an ultimatum to Russia as soon as she crosses the Balkans' (Thompson, ii. 254).

[2] Anderson, pp. 106–13.

[3] The peace terms the Porte was willing to give or accept tended, naturally, to reflect the fortunes of the war. on 11 October, when Turkey was more than holding her own, Server Pasha, the Foreign Minister, listed the following acceptable: a return to the separation of Moldavia and Wallachia, Turkey to be given fortified positions on the Pruth river, the fortress of Belgrade to be restored to the Porte, and a favourable rectification of the Armenian frontier with Russia. On 5 November after Plevna had been invested Layard was given the following bases: the Porte to execute the concessions of the Constantinople Conference and the London Protocol reforms, *status quo ante* for Serbia and Montenegro with a possible frontier rectification for the latter, Bessarabia to Russia, Romania to Austria providing she consented to Turkey's unrestricted use of the Adriatic port of Klek, and Batum to be declared a free port (Layard to Derby, secret, telegs., 11 Oct. and 5 Nov. 1877, PRO FO 424/64, nos. 150, 180).

[4] Layard to Derby, secret, teleg., 11 Dec. 1877, ibid. 63, no. 107; Derby to Layard, teleg., 12 Dec. 1877, ibid., no. 109; Derby to Layard, 13 Dec. 1877, Lay. Pap., Add. MS. 39017, LXXXVII; same to same, 13 Dec. 1877, Lay. Mem., 13 Dec. 1877, VII.

[5] Layard to Derby, very secret, teleg., 13 Dec. 1877, PRO FO 424/63, no. 167. Derby wrote back that any reply would need to wait for the next meeting of the Cabinet (Derby to Layard, 14 Dec. 1877, ibid., no. 181).

[6] Memorandum communicated to Shuvalov, 13 Dec. 1877, ibid., no. 128; Derby to Loftus, secret and confid., 13 Dec. 1877, ibid., no. 155; Loftus to Derby, teleg., 13 Dec. 1877, ibid., no. 135.

[7] Cowley to Layard, 13 Dec. 1877, Lay. Pap. Add. MS. 39017, LXXXVII; Bylandt to Kell, London, 11 Dec. 1877, NA 495; Disraeli to Queen Victoria, 11 Dec. 1877, RA B54/9; Hardy to Disraeli, 11 Dec. 1877, Disraeli Pap. XIX/B/973; Queen's journal, 12 Dec. 1877, RA; Queen Victoria to Disraeli, 11 and 13 Dec. 1877, ibid., no. 10; same to same, 13 Dec. 1877, Disraeli Pap. XIX/C/358; same to same, 13 Dec. 1877, QVL ii. 575–6; Borthwick to Corry, 13 Dec. 1877, Disraeli Pap. XVI/C/33; R. Lucas, *Lord Glenesk and The Morning Post* (N.Y., 1910), pp. 259–60.

[8] Disraeli memorandum on the meeting of 14 Dec. 1877, secret, MB vi. 201–2; memorandum, 14 Dec. 1877, RA B54/13; Queen's journal, 15 Dec. 1877, RA; MB vi.

200; extract from Queen's journal, 15 Dec. 1877, *QVL* ii. 576–7. Beaconsfield thought that Carnarvon and Salisbury would eventually assent to his proposals (Disraeli to Queen Victoria, teleg., 14 Dec. 1877, RA H18/3; same to same, 14 Dec. 1877, *QVL* ii. 576). Before the next Cabinet met, the Queen, accompanied by Princess Beatrice, journeyed to Hughenden to visit and lunch with Beaconsfield. It was a calculated and highly unusual mark of affection by the monarch for her minister. Buckle tells us that no other minister while in office was paid such an honour by the Queen save for Melbourne in 1841 (MB vi. 202–3). Though the royal visit publicly conveyed support for the Prime Minister, the Queen was as much concerned with the spirits of Beaconsfield, which she wished to buoy, as with marking for the public, which was already aware, her confidence in the Prime Minister. At this time the third volume of the *Life of the Prince Consort,* which included the events of the Crimean War, was published. The Queen sent Granville a copy, as he was a member of a former Government which 'stood up *manfully* and loyally for the honour and interests of this country, and resisted the *aggression, ambition* and *duplicity* of Russia' (Queen Victoria to Granville, 26 Dec. 1877, *QVL* ii. 580–1). She also wrote to the wife of Odo Russell in an attempt to undercut Derby and influence the ambassador and perhaps Bismarck (Queen Victoria to Emily Russell, very confid., 1 Jan. 1878, RA H18/66).

⁹ Salisbury to Northcote, confid., 15 Dec. 1877, Northc. Pap., Add. MS. 50019, VII; same to same, 15 Dec. 1877, Salis. Pap., India Office, D/XIV/133; Tenterden memorandum, 14 Dec. 1877, Derby Pap.; Northcote to Salisbury, confid., 14 Dec. 1877, Salis. Pap., E 123–4.

¹⁰ Northcote to Salisbury, 16 Dec. 1877, Salis. Pap., E 127–9; Salisbury to Northcote, confid., 16 Dec. 1877, Northc. Pap., Add. MS. 50019, VII; Carnarvon to Northcote, 15 Dec. 1877, ibid. 50022, X. In his letter to Lady Derby the Colonial Secretary made reference to the Queen's warning about Cabinet leaks to wives and foreign ambassadors (Carnarvon to Lady Derby, 15 Dec. 1877, and Lady Derby to Carnarvon, 15 Dec. 1877, Hardinge, ii. 364–5).

¹¹ Disraeli to Queen Victoria, 17 Dec. 1877, MB vi. 204; same to same, 17 Dec. 1877, RA B54/18; same to same, teleg., 17 Dec. 1877, Disraeli Pap. XIX/B/980; Hardy diary, 17 Dec. 1877, Hardy, ii. 40; Hardy diary, 17 Dec. 1877, Cran. Pap., HA43/T501/297; Carnarvon memorandum, 17 Dec. 1877, Hardinge, ii. 366–7.

¹² Disraeli memorandum on the meeting of 18 Dec. 1877, MB ii. 206–7; memorandum, 18 Dec. 1877, RA B54/21; Disraeli to Queen Victoria, 18 Dec. 1877, ibid., no. 19; same to same, 18 Dec. 1877, *QVL* ii. 577–8; Northcote to Disraeli, most confid., 17 Dec. 1877, Disraeli Pap. XX/N/46; Manners to Disraeli, secret, 17 Dec. 1877, ibid., N/235; Northcote to Salisbury and Salisbury to Northcote, 18 Dec. 1877, Northc. Pap., Add. MS. 50019, VII. Carnarvon has described his disappointment with the results of the Cabinet meeting somewhat eloquently. "The courage of one man [Salisbury] failed, the manœuvres of some succeeded, the fears of many prevailed. The question of *casus belli* was staved off and it was decided as a matter of compromise to summon Parliament for the 17th January' (Carnarvon memorandum, 18 Dec. 1878, Hardinge, ii. 367).

¹³ Gladstone to Stead, 21 Dec. 1877, Glad. Pap., Add. MS. 44303, CCXVIII; Gladstone to F. Schnadhorst, 21 Dec. 1877, ibid. 44295, CCX; Mundella to Leader, 20 Dec. 1877, Mundella Pap.; Solvyns to d'Aspremont-Lynden, 19 Dec. 1877, BFM, no. 242; Thompson, ii. 277–8; Currie to Layard, 20 Dec. 1877, Lay., Add. MS. 39017, LXXXVII. Cowley thought that 'no war is the universal cry' (Cowley to Layard, 20 Dec. 1877, ibid.).

¹⁴ Granville to Gladstone, 20 Dec. 1877, Ramm, i. 62–3. Gladstone and Granville agreed that the best way to block Disraeli and the latter's suspected desire for war was to create a non-party agitation which would strengthen the peace party in the Cabinet (Gladstone to Bright, 22 Dec. 1877, Glad. Pap., Add. MS. 43385, III). Consequently, they encouraged Mundella and others to create activity on the part of Chambers of

Commerce, such groups being already very anxious about the industrial depression which had struck the country (Mundella to Gladstone, 22 Dec. 1877, ibid. 44258, CLXXIII; Mundella to Leader, 22 Dec. 1877, Mundella Pap.).

[15] Andrássy to Beust, secret, 22 Dec. 1877, PRO FO 424/64, no. 248; same to same, teleg., 21 Dec. 1877, ibid., no. 246; Buchanan to Derby, secret, teleg., 20 Dec. 1877, ibid., no. 242; Derby to Buchanan, secret, teleg., 19 Dec. 1877, ibid., no. 232; Derby to Layard, confid., teleg., 19 Dec. 1877, ibid., 63, no. 256c. In case there were any doubt, Derby told the Ottoman ambassador on 21 December 'that no such [British] intervention [into the war] was to be expected' (Derby to Layard, confid., 21 Dec. 1877, ibid., no. 301).

[16] Derby and Tenterden mistakenly believed, owing to the inability of Beust and Montgelas to understand German or their own cipher, that Andrássy favoured a British appeal to the Tsar. Before the mistake could be remedied the British appeal had been made (Beust to Derby, 23 Dec. 1877, Derby Pap.; Tenterden to Ponsonby, 24 Dec. 1877, RA H18/39). Tenterden was not unhappy that the mistake had been made because he strongly favoured the British appeal to Russia, and feared Andrássy's proposal of allowing Turkey to deal directly with Russia, Austria, and Britain, interfering only after the terms had been reached by the belligerents, to be a dangerous one. He did not trust Andrássy and was disinclined 'to abandon the Porte to Russia' (Tenterden memorandum, 23 Dec. 1877, Tenterden Pap., PRO FO 363–5). Layard was another who opposed allowing the Porte to negotiate directly with St. Petersburg, equating such an occurrence as a great defeat for Britain.

[17] Loftus to Derby, teleg., 29 Dec. 1877, PRO FO 424/64, no. 276; Derby to Loftus, teleg., 27 Dec. 1877, ibid., no. 265; Layard to Derby, teleg., 25 Dec. 1877, ibid., no. 257; Derby to Layard, teleg., 24 Dec. 1877, ibid., no. 253; Derby to Buchanan, 23 Dec. 1877, ibid., no. 249 The Porte circularized the Powers that owing to the lack of result from its appeal for collective mediation, it had asked Britain to mediate with Russia (Layard to Derby, teleg., 29 Dec. 1877, ibid., no. 277).

[18] Derby to Disraeli, 22 Dec. 1877, Derby Pap.; Disraeli to Derby, confid., 21 Dec. 1877, ibid.; same to same, 21 Dec. 1877, Disraeli Pap. xx/S/1287a and b; Disraeli to Queen Victoria, 21 Dec. 1877, ibid. xix/C/372; Disraeli to Layard, 20 Dec. 1877, Lay. Pap., Add. MS. 39136, CCVL. Cairns, as well as Disraeli, was pleased that Britain's intention to mediate had the unintended effect of drawing Andrássy, they thought, slightly closer to London. The Lord Chancellor took the credit for modifying the draft to Russia, omitting the latter's June peace terms, out of consideration for Vienna (Cairns to Richmond, confid., 25 Dec. 1877, Good. Pap. 869; Cairns to Northcote, 24 Dec. 1877, Northc. Pap., Add. MS. 50021, ix). Beaconsfield, leaving little to chance, told Musurus, the Ottoman ambassador, to get the Porte to appeal for British mediation (Lay. Mem., 20 Dec. 1877, VII). The Sultan asked Layard on 24 December to transmit his thanks to the Prime Minister for the latter's communicating to Musurus the suggestion of an appeal to England (Layard to Disraeli, private and confid., 26 Dec. 1877, Lay. Pap., Add. MS. 39130, CC).

[19] Derby to Salisbury, secret, 23 Dec. 1877, Salis. Pap., E; same to same, 23 Dec. 1877, Cecil, ii. 170–1. Lady Cecil in her biography of her father indicates that she has quoted the above letter in full. In fact she omitted, not feeling the necessity for elipses, the entire last sentence of the above quotation. Disraeli was making an effort to keep scattered colleagues informed of any action taken (Corry to Richmond, confid., 24 Dec. 1877, Good. Pap. 865; Corry to Carnarvon, confid., 24 Dec. 1877, Carnarvon Pap., PRO 30 6/11).

[20] Salisbury to Disraeli, confid., 26 Dec. 1877, Disraeli Pap. xix/B/996; same to same, 26 Dec. 1877, MB vi. 211; Disraeli to Salisbury, confid., 24 Dec. 1876, Salis. Pap., E 263–5. The copy of Disraeli's letter to Salisbury of 24 December is undated in the Disraeli Papers but the enclosed letter from Wellesley to Disraeli is dated 7 December. There are a number of discrepancies, apart from the date against which Buckle places a

question mark, in the text of the original at Christ Church and the copy at Hughenden (Disraeli to Salisbury, very private, [?] Dec. 1877, Disraeli Pap. xix/B/969 and 969a; same to same, [?] Dec. 1877, MB vi. 210). I am indebted to Mr. C. R. St. Q. Wall and the staff at the Hughenden archives for their help in dating and explaining the above letter.

²¹ Colonel Wellesley to Derby, confid., 24 Dec. 1877, PRO FO 424/64, no. 280; Buchanan to Derby, secret, 26 Dec. 1877, ibid., no. 288; Blake, Disraeli, p. 635. The correspondence concerning Lady Derby's indiscretions and the unsuccessful attempt to put a stop to them is in the Windsor Archives (Dean of Windsor to Queen Victoria, 27 Dec. 1877, RA H18/52; same to same, 29 Dec. 1877, ibid., no. 57; same to same, 7 Jan. 1878, ibid., no. 68 and enclosure; Lady Derby to Dean of Windsor, 29 Dec. 1877, ibid.; Disraeli to Queen Victoria, 3 Jan. 1878, RA B54/42).

²² Hardy diary, 3 Jan. 1878, Cran. Pap., HA43/T501/297. Colonel Wellesley returned to England after the fall of Plevna and in January talked with the Queen. 'Col. Wellesley told me how dreadfully difficult his position had been for when he had really got the Emperor [of Russia] to see & feel alarmed at our being in earnest he would suddenly receive news from Schouvaloff to say the Peace Party had prevailed, nothing need be feared—& the Emperor's tone and conduct altered entirely' (Queen's journal, 13 Jan. 1878, RA).

²³ See p. 346. Derby to Disraeli, 27 Dec. 1877, Derby Pap.; Disraeli to Queen Victoria, 27 Dec. 1877, RA B54/29; same to same, 27 Dec. 1877, QVL ii. 581-2. Italy, in view of the Russian response, felt she could do nothing; the French Government, with Waddington now heading the Foreign Ministry, while not associating itself officially with the British representation, was willing through its ambassador in St. Petersburg 'to impress privately upon the Emperor the earnest desire of the French Government that the war may be ended at once' (Lyons to Derby, teleg., 31 Dec. 1877, PRO FO 424/64, no. 290; Paget to Derby, teleg., 1 Jan. 1878, ibid., no. 298; Lyons to Derby, 28 Dec. 1877, Lyons Pap.). Disraeli was not the only one who thought that Britain was mediating. Musurus, the Porte, and perhaps Layard as well were under this mistaken impression (Layard to Derby, teleg., 4 Jan. 1878, PRO FO 424/64, no. 316). The Foreign Secretary explained the distinction between mediation and non-mediation to the unhappy and bitter Turks (Derby to Layard, teleg., 7 Jan. 1878, ibid., no. 338; Layard to Derby, teleg., 9 Jan. 1878, ibid., no. 356). The Porte was confused by the disparity between Derby's official and cold neutrality and Disraeli's growing sympathy. Corry was sent regularly at the beginning of January to see and advise the Ottoman ambassador (Corry memorandum, 7 and 10 Jan. 1878, Disraeli Pap. xvi/B/36 and 37). The Porte naturally allowed its lingering hope for British aid to exaggerate the significance of the Prime Minister's intentions (Lay. Mem., 8 Jan. 1878, viii).

²⁴ Harcourt to Granville, private and confid., 31 Dec. 1877, Gran. Pap., PRO 30 29/29a; Harcourt to wife, [31] Dec. 1877, Harcourt Papers, Stanton Harcourt; Granville to Selborne, 27 Dec. 1877, Selborne Pap., MS. 1866. Granville replied to Harcourt's communication that he found it 'deeply and painfully interesting. I will send it to Hartington at once with a hint not to let it be known that any of us are in confidential communication with Schouvaloff. You seemed to have sucked him dry' (Granville to Harcourt, 1 Jan. 1878, Harcourt Pap.; Granville to Harcourt, 7 Jan. 1878, Gardiner, Harcourt, i. 323).

²⁵ Ollier, ii. 9; Bath to Granville, 30 Dec. 1877, Gran. Pap., PRO 30 29/26a; Thompson, ii. 290-2; Wirthwein, pp. 291-2. At the same time, the Italian ambassador in Russia reported a division in that country's opinion between those who were ready for peace and others who wished the war's continuation (Nigra to Depretis, St. Petersburg, 31 Dec. 1877, IFM 159 (1401), box 171).

²⁶ Gorchakov to Shuvalov, 16 Dec. 1877, PRO FO 424/64, no. 299 and enclosed memorandum. Gorchakov told Loftus 'that the sudden convocation of the English Parliament might reanimate . . . [Ottoman] hopes, and thus indispose the Porte to

those concessions on which alone peace could be obtained. Prince Gortchakow further observed that no peace could be desirable without efficient guarantees for the future government of the Christian provinces, for which, in his opinion, the Turkish Constitution did not suffice' (Loftus to Derby, confid., 29 Dec. 1877, ibid., no. 329).

²⁷ Derby to Layard and Loftus, telegs., 8 Jan. 1878, ibid., nos. 342, 343; Derby to Queen Victoria, 7 Jan. 1878, RA 18/98; Disraeli to Queen Victoria, 7 Jan. 1878, RA B54/51; same to same, 7 Jan. 1878, MB vi. 215; Loftus to Derby, teleg., 5 Jan. 1878, PRO FO 424/64, no. 320; Derby to Loftus, teleg., 4 Jan. 1878, ibid., no. 305; Disraeli to Queen Victoria, 2 Jan. 1878, RA B54/39; same to same, 2 Jan. 1878, MB vi. 212; Harcourt to Granville, 1 Jan. 1878, Gran. Pap., PRO 30 29/29a; Harcourt to Lady Harcourt, 1 Jan. 1878, Harcourt Pap.; Disraeli to Queen Victoria, 1 Jan. 1878, Disraeli Pap. xix/C/384. At the meeting on the seventh 'after some feeble opposition from Lord Derby' the ministers decided to ask Parliament for a vote of £5 million. The Cabinet's acceptance of direct Russo-Turkish negotiation was reached on 7 January before a telegram of the same date arrived from Layard depicting a deteriorating military situation for Turkey and the Porte's critical need of an armistice (Layard to Derby, teleg., most secret, 7 Jan. 1878, PRO FO 424/64, no. 340). Harcourt, Hartington, and Granville, through information supplied by Shuvalov, interpreted the Cabinet's support for direct Russo-Turkish negotiation as a defeat for Disraeli and the ascendancy of those ministers who desired peace (Harcourt to Hartington, 8 Jan. 1878, Harcourt Pap.; Harcourt to Granville, 8 Jan. 1878, Gran. Pap., PRO 30 29/29a).

²⁸ 'I [Mundella] think it will interest you [Gladstone] to know something of the Carnarvon episode.... My friend Mr. Archibald Hamilton who stood for West Kent in '74 ... was the spokesman for the deputation.... Before going to the Colonial Office he received a visit from Froude [a close friend of Carnarvon] who intimated to him that Lord Carnarvon would not be unwilling to say something ... about the war in the East if the opportunity were afforded him.... So far from Lord Carnarvon making an impromptu [sic] reply, every word was written down, and carefully corrected; he saw the MS. and the corrections in a different handwriting. So you see the whole scheme was carefully prepared, and acted out' (Mundella to Gladstone, 9 Jan. 1878, Glad. Pap., Add. MS. 44258, CLXXIII). In his memorandum printed in Hardinge's Life of Carnarvon, the Colonial Secretary admitted that he was wrong, but that what he did was excusable. 'I am however now [August 1879] inclined to doubt whether even all these considerations did afford me an absolute justification for departing from ... the regular and approved course which a minister is bound to pursue' (Carnarvon memorandum, Aug. 1879, Hardinge, ii. 370–1).

²⁹ Thompson, ii. 294–8; Wirthwein. pp. 290–1; Ponsonby to Carnarvon, 4 Jan. 1878, Carnarvon Pap., PRO 30 6/13; Tenterden to Carnarvon, 3 Jan. 1878, ibid.; Childers to Clarke, 4 Jan. 1878 (S. Childers, Life and Correspondence of H. C. E. Childers, 1827–96, 2 vols., London, 1901, i. 250–1); Mundella to Leader, 3 Jan. 1878, Mundella Pap.; Gladstone to Chamberlain, 3 Jan. 1878, Glad. Pap., Add. MS. 44125, XL; Hartington to Granville, 4 Jan. 1878, Gran. Pap., PRO 30 29/29a; Bylandt to Kell, 3 Jan. 1878, NA 6; Münster to Bülow, 3 Jan. 1878, GFM 14128; Crown Princess of Prussia to Queen Victoria, 7 Jan. 1878, Disraeli Pap. xix/C/395; Hammond to Layard, 10 Jan. 1878, Lay. Pap., Add. MS. 38956, XXVI.

³⁰ Hardy diary, 6 Jan. 1878, Cran. Pap., HA43/T501/297; Disraeli to Queen Victoria, 6 Jan. 1878, RA B54/49; same to same, 6 Jan. 1878, Disraeli Pap. xix/C/393; Ponsonby to Lady Ely, 4 Jan. 1878, RA H18/84; Carnarvon to Queen Victoria, 4 Jan. 1878, ibid., no. 79; Ponsonby to Queen Victoria, 4 Jan. 1878, ibid., no. 83; Disraeli to Queen Victoria, teleg., 3 Jan. 1878, ibid., no. 76; Paget to Wharncliffe, 6 Jan. 1878, Paget Papers, British Library, Add. MS. 51232, XXVII; Disraeli to Lady Bradford, 6 Jan. 1878, Zetland, ii. 198; Carnarvon to Disraeli, 8 Jan. 1878, Disraeli Pap. xx/He/87; Carnarvon to Derby, 5 Jan. 1878, Carnarvon Pap., PRO 30 6/13; Smith to Carnarvon, 5 Jan. 1878, ibid.; Salisbury to Carnarvon, 4 Jan. 1878, ibid.; same to same, 4 Jan.

1878, Salis. Pap., vol. 8; Cecil, ii. 174–6 (Lady Cecil misdates this letter as 8 January); Northcote to Salisbury, 4 Jan. 1878, Salis. Pap., E 131–3; Carnarvon to Salisbury, 4 Jan. 1878, ibid., E 324–5; Northcote to Carnarvon, 4 Jan. 1878, Carnarvon Pap., PRO 30 6/13; Queen Victoria to Carnarvon. 4 Jan. 1878, QVL ii. 588–9; Disraeli to Queen Victoria, 4 Jan. 1878, ibid. 587–8; Hardy diary, 4 Jan. 1878, Cran. Pap., HA43/T501/297; diary, 4 Jan. 1878, Hardy, ii. 43–4; Queen Victoria to Disraeli, 4 Jan. 1878, Disraeli Pap. XIX/C/392; Queen's journal, 3 Jan. 1878, RA; Carnarvon to Salisbury, 3 Jan. 1878, Salis. Pap., E 318–20; Northcote to Carnarvon, 3 Jan. 1878, Carnarvon Pap., PRO 30 6/13; Carnarvon memorandum, Hardinge, ii. 367–71; Disraeli to Queen Victoria, 3 Jan. 1878, RA B54/41; same to same, 3 Jan. 1878, MB vi. 213–14; Northcote to Disraeli, 4 Jan. 1878, Disraeli Pap. xx/N/48. Grey and Halifax were both sceptical about the wisdom of granting the Government any money after it had failed to prevent the outbreak of war. 'But I [Grey] do not see what they [the Government] are to do now with increased force if they get it. . . . Now . . . anything we wd. do wd. be insufficient to prevent the Russians from doing almost what they please. . . . I think the Govt. blundered terribly in not taking a more decided line before, & that the mischief done by their mistake will be only aggravated by vain attempts now to correct it. . . . I believe that now the best thing both for the Turks and for us wd. be that the Turks shd. at once make peace on the least bad terms they can get from Russia without our interfering' (Grey to Halifax, 29 Dec. 1877, Hickleton Pap.).

[31] Disraeli to Queen Victoria, 7 Jan. 1878, RA B54/51; same to same, 7 Jan. 1878, MB vi. 215; Derby to Carnarvon, [6 or 7] Jan. 1878, Carnarvon Pap., PRO 30 6/13. Carnarvon's memorandum, which he read to the Cabinet, was an attempt at reconciliation without a complete loss of face (Carnarvon memorandum for Cabinet, Jan. 1877, Carnarvon Pap., PRO 30 6/13). The temper of opinion may be gauged by a speech which Mundella made in Sheffield on 7 December, indicating that a British declaration of war would not be justified by a Russian entry into Constantinople (Thompson, ii. 279), and the charge of the Duke of Sutherland on 10 January at a meeting at St. James's Hall, that Gladstone was a 'Russian agent' (Wirthwein, pp. 298–300). When Gladstone heard of this, he wrote to his wife. 'I am astonished at the Duke of Sutherland. He must have lost his head, which is not so very much' (Gladstone to Mrs. Gladstone, 12 Jan. 1878, Bassett, Gladstone to His Wife, pp. 221–2). Gladstone's relationship with Madame Novikov was being unfavourably noticed. 'He is in constant communication with that Russian woman, Mme. De Novikoff is I think her name . . . [a] pretty companion for a respectable character' (Hammond to Layard, 16 Jan. 1878, Lay. Pap., Add. MS. 38956, XXVI).

[32] Carnarvon memorandum, Hardinge, ii. 371; Disraeli to Queen Victoria, 9 Jan. 1878, MB ii. 216–17; same to same, 9 Jan. 1878, RA B54/60; same to same, teleg., 9 Jan. 1878, RA H18/107.

[33] F. V. Green, The Russian Army and Its Campaign in Turkey, 1877–78 (N.Y., 1879), pp. 367–9. Gladstone grew more ecstatic with each Russian victory (Gladstone to Mrs. Gladstone, 11 and 12 Jan. 1878, Bassett, Gladstone to His Wife, pp. 221–2).

[34] Layard's positive feeling and compassion for Turkey did not prevent him from carrying out his official instructions of neutrality, and repeatedly he found himself informing the Porte that it could not expect British military support. He had convinced himself that Ottoman defeat could also destroy or threaten important British interests, and continually pressed Derby on the necessity of occupying and protecting Gallipoli, as well as the great danger to the Euphrates Valley route to India if Russia annexed Armenia. He pointed out to London that a sunken ship or a few pounds of dynamite could effectively block the Suez Canal, making an alternate route to India absolutely necessary. Apparently the ambassador considered the sea route round the African Cape inadequate. To his credit, even before the fall of Plevna, he urged Derby to mediate in order to end a war, which it was not then clear that Turkey must lose. After Plevna he feared that, in lieu of British indifference, the Porte would be driven into a

direct understanding with Russia to the disadvantage of Britain. Consequently, he repeatedly pressed Derby for specific instructions, which the latter refused to give, in the hope of encouraging the Sultan in order to maintain his personal influence in Constantinople. He realized that this last was necessary, so that when London did wish to move, he would be in a position to carry the Porte with him. The difference in language between Disraeli's secret letters to him and Derby's official dispatches, was both frustrating and slightly hopeful from his point of view. His secret letter to Disraeli of 12 December, in answer to Beaconsfield's question as to the possibility of convincing the Porte to cede territory to Britain for money, the latter enabling the Turks to undertake a second campaign, is interesting. In it the ambassador argues the importance of Batum in Armenia and Mohammerah near the Persian Gulf, as well as the necessity of abandoning 'at once a hesitating and undefined policy'. He desired a British fleet in the Straits and a British army corps at Gallipoli (Layard to Disraeli, secret, 12 Dec. 1877, Lay. Pap., Add. MS. 39130, CC). On 9 January the ambassador wrote to Disraeli that the latter's language 'to Musurus keeps up the courage of the Sultan & his Ministers to a certain extent' (Layard to Disraeli, private and secret, 9 Jan. 1877, ibid.).

    35 'Turkish Minister for Foreign Affairs authorized me [Layard] to tell Your Lordship [Derby] most secretly that if the Grand Duke Nicholas asks for conditions of too onerous a nature he will prolong or break off negotiations, should there be any hope of England assisting Turkey. . . . He will leave for Russian head-quarters tonight or tomorrow morning, but I have arranged means of communicating with him if I receive immediate reply from you' (Layard to Derby, most secret, teleg., 14 Jan. 1878, PRO FO 424/64, no. 407). As a result of both London's and Vienna's communicating to Gorchakov and the Porte their expectation that any Russo-Turkish treaty which affected the treaties of 1856 and 1871 would require the assent of all the Powers party to the two earlier treaties, Turkey attempted to negotiate with Nicholas on the basis of the Treaty of Paris of 1856. The Grand Vizier informed Layard that great effort would be made by Turkey to avoid any engagement with Russia 'without previous consultation' with Britain (Layard to Derby, teleg., 15 Jan. 1878, ibid., no. 420; Derby to Loftus, teleg., 14 Jan. 1878, ibid., no. 413; Layard to Derby, teleg., 15 Jan. 1878, ibid., no. 418; Moüy to Waddington, teleg., 15 Jan. 1878, DDF ii. 236–7).

    36 Sumner, pp. 340–53. As part of the Ottoman campaign of delay, their two delegates to the Grand Duke were instructed to negotiate for an armistice only, and any political terms were to be referred to Constantinople (Layard to Derby, teleg., 10 Jan. 1878, PRO FO 424/64, no. 372). Nicholas informed the Porte that any armistice negotiations would only follow an agreement on the bases of peace. On 11 January Musurus left with Derby an Ottoman appeal for the Queen to do something to save them from destruction (Derby to Queen Victoria, 11 Jan. 1878, RA H18/118). Ponsonby thought that the Sultan's appeal to the Queen to intercede with the Tsar was 'somewhat weakened . . . by alluding to the conditions on which he [Sultan] hopes peace may be established' (Ponsonby to Queen Victoria, 12 Jan. 1878, RA H18/125). The Queen with Cabinet sanction appealed to the Tsar on 14 January to accelerate the conclusion of an armistice, which drew a cool reply from Alexander (Queen's journal, 12 and 14 Jan. 1878, RA; journal, 12, 14 Jan. 1878, MB vi. 220; Queen Victoria to Alexander II, teleg., 14 Jan. 1878, RA B55/8).

    37 Layard to Derby, teleg., 10 Jan. 1878, PRO FO 424/64, no. 378; same to same, secret, teleg., 11 Jan. 1878, ibid., no. 380; Disraeli to Queen Victoria, 11 Jan. 1878, RA B54/67; same to same, 11 Jan. 1878, Disraeli Pap. XIX/C/409. The Queen and the Prime Minister were agreed that it was desirable to instruct the Press to support a spirited policy. Beaconsfield assured Victoria 'that Mr. Corry sees the Editors of Telegraph, M. Post, & Pall Mall, every day, & guides, instructs, & inspires them. And the Standard also, tho the writers of that print are very dull' (ibid.). The Queen was keeping up her side. Her relations with Ponsonby were now a bit awkward owing to the latter's

personal opinions and those of his wife, who was very Gladstonian. She asked Lady Ely to request Ponsonby to write to Lord Halifax, who was the uncle of Ponsonby's wife, and urge him to prevail with the Liberal party leaders to suspend any 'factious opposition' to the policy of the Government. Ponsonby sent the requested letter, but as he explained to Halifax there was a difficulty. 'My chief difficulty is in explaining to you ... what the policy of the Govt. is to which the Q. hopes no factious opposition will be made. I cannot tell you what I do not know' (Ponsonby to Halifax, 5 Jan. 1878, Hickleton Pap.; Ponsonby memorandum, Ponsonby, *Henry Ponsonby*, p. 169; Ponsonby to Halifax, 5 Jan. 1878, *QVL* ii. 590–1). Halifax's reply to the Queen was found by the latter to be less than satisfactory, but as he explained to Ponsonby Her Majesty apparently desired 'support ... [for] some warlike policy which Dizzy has put into her head.... Certainly she has no cause for complaining of the thwarting of Her Govt. by the Opposition so far' (Halifax to Ponsonby, 13 Jan. 1878, Hickleton Pap.). Shuvalov reported home that the Queen's 'daily and persistent intervention in all details of the present crisis ... is disapproved even by Ministers, who find that Her Majesty is leaving the limits prescribed by the constitution' (Shuvalov to Gorchakov, 8 Jan. 1878, Seton-Watson, p. 267). The ambassador cited no proof for his charges.

[38] Derby to Layard, teleg., 12 Jan. 1878, PRO FO 424/64, no. 390; Derby to Loftus, teleg., 12 Jan. 1878, ibid., no. 393; Disraeli to Queen Victoria, 12 Jan. 1878, RA B54/69; same to same, 12 Jan. 1878, MB vi. 219–20; Carnarvon memorandum, Hardinge, ii. 371–3; Hardy diary, 13 Jan. 1878, Cran. Pap., HA43/T501/297; Queen Victoria to Disraeli, 10 Jan. 1878, MB vi. 217; memorandum by Queen, 11 Jan. 1878, ibid., Queen Victoria to Ponsonby, 11 Jan. 1878, RA, Add. MS. A/12, 422/3.

[39] Ponsonby to Carnarvon, 13 Jan. 1878, Carnarvon Pap., PRO 30 6/13; Delane diary, Dasent, *Delane*, ii. 332; Smith to Northcote, 12 Jan. 1878, Northc. Pap., Add. MS. 50021, IX. On the same day as the Cabinet meeting, the Ottoman ambassador appealed to Derby for British help, to which the Foreign Secretary replied negatively that 'we were not prepared to give military assistance to Turkey' (Derby to Layard, teleg., 13 Jan. 1878, PRO FO 424/64, no. 403).

[40] Tenterden described Derby's prostration as 'an attack of diarrhoea', and 'a regular internal upset' which allowed the former to handle all routine Foreign Office business, consulting Derby 'for really important telegrams' (Tenterden to Layard, 17 Jan. 1878, Lay. Pap., Add. MS. 39137, CCVII). Halifax described Lady Derby as 'flourishing' despite her reporting her husband as 'very ill & ... suffering now from cramps in the limbs' (Halifax to Lady Halifax, 17 Jan. 1878, Hickleton Pap., H2/43). Hammond was told that Derby was 'in a very unsatisfactory state of worry and anxiety, and this I can well conceive, as he is not with all his ability, a man of very decided opinion of his own. Formerly his faith was entirely pinned on Lord Beaconsfield, and there is certainly no love between him and Salisbury, or their respective families; but between the two rivals, and his own want of self reliance and decision, I can well understand his being in great perplexity' (Hammond to Layard, 16 Jan. 1878, Lay. Pap., Add. MS. 38956, XXVI). Cowley reported Derby's being 'ill with a sort of cholera attack' (Cowley to Layard, 16 Jan. 1878, ibid. 39017, LXXXVII). Halifax reported to Grey that Derby had been very ill with an 'attack of dysentary and cramps. Lady Derby does not think that he will be fit for work for some days' (Halifax to Grey, 19 Jan. 1878, Grey Papers, Durham University).

[41] See p. 574 n. 36.

[42] Carnarvon to Derby, 14 Jan. 1878, Derby Pap.; same to same, 14 Jan. 1878, Carnarvon Pap., PRO 30 6/13; Disraeli to Queen Victoria, 14 Jan. 1878, RA B55/10; Hardy diary, 14 Jan. 1878, Cran. Pap., HA43/T501/297; Shuvalov to Gorchakov, 14 Jan. 1878 (Seton-Watson, *Slav. Rev.* XXV (Nov. 1946), 225–7); Queen Victoria to Disraeli, very confid., 14 Jan. 1878, RA B55/5; same to same, 14 Jan. 1878, Disraeli Pap. XIX/C/415; Carnarvon explained to the Foreign Secretary the reasons for his opposing the sending of the fleet even though 'the request was guarded by a statement that we

shd. go there as neutrals'. He saw it as unsafe for the fleet to go unless the Gallipoli Peninsula were militarily occupied; he feared it might be 'a step to something further', and that if it were merely demonstration, Russia would not be deceived and Turkey would be encouraged to continue her resistance. Finally, he felt that news of this step, on top of the money for which Parliament was to be asked, would alarm and convince the country that the Government intended war.

⁴³ Northcote to Disraeli, 15 Jan. 1878, Disraeli Pap. xx/N/52; Smith to Northcote, 15 Jan. 1878 (H. Maxwell, *Life and Times of W. H. Smith*, 2 vols., London, 1893, ii. 317). Carnarvon to Disraeli, 15 Jan. 1878, Disraeli Pap. xx/He/88; same to same, 15 Jan. 1878, Carnarvon Pap., PRO 30 6/13; Disraeli to Queen Victoria, teleg., 15 Jan. 1878, RA B55/12 and 13; Hardy diary, 15 Jan. 1878, Cran. Pap., HA43/7501/297; Carnarvon memorandum, Hardinge, ii. 373–4; Tenterden memorandum, 15 Jan. 1878, Derby Pap.; Derby to Disraeli, 15 Jan. 1878, ibid.; same to same, 15 Jan. 1878, Disraeli Pap. xx/S/1293. Apparently an attempt to hold the Cabinet meeting of 15 January at Derby's London residence failed (Northcote to Brand, 15 Jan. 1878, Brand Pap., no. 180). Bylandt, the Netherland's minister, was surprised that in light of the emergency Cabinet meetings were not held in the Foreign Secretary's residence (Bylandt to Kell, London, 16 Jan. 1878, NA, no. 32). Beaconsfield complained to Lady Bradford that 'the confusion is so great that it seems the end of the world' (Disraeli to Lady Bradford, 15 Jan. 1878, Zetland, ii. 201).

⁴⁴ Carnarvon memorandum, 16 Jan. 1878, Hardinge, ii. 374–5; Northcote to Derby, 16 Jan. 1878, Derby Pap.; Disraeli to Queen Victoria, 17 Jan. 1878, Disraeli Pap. xix/C/423; same to same, 17 Jan. 1878, RA B55/19; Layard to Derby, teleg., 15 Jan. 1878, PRO FO 424/64, no. 421; Loftus to Derby, teleg., 15 Jan. 1878, ibid., no. 427; Derby To Disraeli, 16 Jan. 1878, Disraeli Pap. xx/S/1295, 1296.

⁴⁵ Thompson, ii. 266–9, 280–5, 293–4; Wirthwein, pp. 292–4; Liddon to Pusey, 13 Jan. 1878, Pusey Pap.; Cowley to Layard, 16 Jan. 1878, Lay. Pap., Add. MS. 39017, LXXXVII; Liddon to [?], 15 Jan. 1878 (J. O. Johnston, *Life and Letters of Henry Parry Liddon*, N.Y., 1904, pp. 222–3). Of the days before the convocation of Parliament, Seton-Watson wrote that 'rarely, if ever, has opinion been so keenly roused, and so deeply divided, on a question of foreign policy' (Seton-Watson, p. 272). There are four volumes of memorials and petitions urging the Foreign Office to maintain the British neutral position. They were sent largely in January by working-class groups, Liberal associations, town meetings, and Nonconformist organizations, and are in PRO FO 78/2930–3.

⁴⁶ *Hansard*, 17 Jan. 1878, 3rd ser. 237, 7–122; Ponsonby to Queen Victoria, 18 Jan. 1878, RA B55/25; Northcote to Queen Victoria, 17 and 18 Jan. 1878, RA B29/2, 4; Wirthwein, pp. 308–9; Hammond to Layard, 17 Jan. 1878, Lay. Pap., Add. MS. 38956, XXVI; Münster to Bülow, teleg., 17 Jan. 1878, GFM, A320; Northcote to Queen Victoria, 10 Jan. 1878, RA H18/115; Queen's speech, 17 Jan. 1878, RA H19/4. The Belgian minister thought the Queen's speech was a compromise, and that it exhibited proof of Cabinet differences. Solvyns described it as neither a belligerent nor pacific address (Solvyns to d'Aspremont-Lynden, 19 Jan. 1878, BFM, no. 15). Halifax agreed that the Government's behaviour was a compromise (Halifax to Grey, 19 Jan. 1878, Grey Pap.). Disraeli gave a favourable report to the Queen of the Parlimentary reaction to the Government (Disraeli to Queen Victoria, 18 Jan. 1878, MB vi. 225).

⁴⁷ Northcote to Queen Victoria, 19 Jan. 1878, RA H19/14. According to Reuss, who was a wild Turcophobe, the effect on the Turks when they learned of the Parliamentary events of 17 January was a strong and depressing one (Reuss to Bülow, Constantinople, 22 Jan. 1878, GFM, A641). The Spanish minister at Constantinople agreed that the Queen's speech dispelled any Ottoman illusion of British help (Conte to Silvela, Constantinople, 23 Jan. 1878, SFM, no. 11).

⁴⁸ Layard was telegraphing to London that most of the Muslim population were fleeing before the Russian advance—'some hundred thousand women and children

are in the open fields dying of hunger and cold'. The ambassador was requested by the Porte 'in the name of humanity' to induce Russia to proclaim protection for all civilians. Derby instructed Loftus to 'make a suitable representation without delay to the Emperor, for the sake of the general population, Christian and Mohammedan' (Derby to Loftus, teleg., 20 Jan. 1878, PRO FO 424/66, no. 151; Layard to Derby, teleg., 19 Jan. 1878, ibid., no. 144).

⁴⁹ Disraeli to Queen Victoria, teleg., 20 Jan. 1878, Disraeli Pap. XIX/C/431; Disraeli to Queen Victoria, 20 Jan. 1878, ibid., no. 429; same to same, 20 Jan. 1878, RA B55/30; Layard to Derby, secret, teleg., 19 Jan. 1878, PRO FO 424/64, no. 474; Buchanan to Derby, secret, teleg., 18 Jan. 1878, ibid., no. 467. When Beaconsfield wrote that he despaired of keeping the Cabinet together and the probability of a war with Russia, the Queen attempted to buoy up the spirits of the Premier and took the occasion to offer him the Garter. Though Her Majesty admitted that she thought that war with Russia was inevitable, it is difficult not to respect her spirit and fire (Disraeli to Queen Victoria, 19 Jan. 1878, QVL ii. 596–7; Queen Victoria to Disraeli, 20 Jan. 1878, ibid. 597–8).

⁵⁰ Buchanan to Derby, secret, teleg., 22 Jan. 1878, PRO FO 424/64, no. 518; Borthwick to Corry, 22 Jan. 1878, Disraeli Pap. XVI/C/35; Corry to Disraeli, secret, 22 Jan. 1878, ibid. XVI/B/39; Buchanan to Derby, very confid., teleg., 22 Jan. 1878, PRO FO 424/64, no. 511; Derby to Buchanan, secret, teleg., 21 Jan. 1878, ibid., no. 500; same to same, secret, teleg., 21 Jan. 1878, ibid., no. 497; Disraeli to Queen Victoria, 22 Jan. 1878, Disraeli Pap. XIV/C/433; same to same, 22 Jan. 1878, RA B55/38; same to same, 21 Jan. 1878, ibid., no. 36; same to same, 21 Jan. 1878, MB vi. 227; Hardy diary, 22 Jan. 1878, Cran. Pap., HA43/T501/297; Carnarvon memorandum, Hardinge, ii. 375. Stojanovic, using the Austrian archives, writes that Disraeli saw Beust on the evening of 21 January and offered a defensive alliance to Vienna. Beust reported the Prime Minister's saying that 'if I have a treaty of alliance I can obtain ten million pounds from Parliament' (Beust to Andrássy, teleg., 21 Jan. 1878, HHSA, no. 24, Stojanovic, pp. 195–6).

⁵¹ Seton-Watson, p. 298; Derby to Disraeli, 23 Jan. 1878, MB vi. 228; same to same, 24 Jan. 1878, RA H19/32; Disraeli to Derby, 24 Jan. 1878, Derby Pap.; Carnarvon to Disraeli, 24 Jan. 1878, RA H19/33–4; Smith to Hornby, most secret, teleg., 7 p.m., 23 Jan. 1878, ibid. 36; Disraeli to Queen Victoria, telegs., 23 Jan. 1878, Disraeli Pap. XIX/B/1096, 1097; Queen Victoria to Disraeli, teleg., 23 Jan. 1878, ibid. 1094; same to same, 23 Jan. 1878, RA B55/40; Smith to Carnarvon, 23 Jan. 1878, Carnarvon Pap., PRO 30 6/13; Carnarvon memorandum, Hardinge, ii. 375–7; Manners to Disraeli, 23 Jan. 1878, Disraeli Pap. XX/M/239; Hart-Dyke to Disraeli, 23 Jan. 1878, ibid. XXI/D/471. Once the decision was made to send the fleet, Northcote appealed to Salisbury that both needed to be on guard lest 'some expression or other' by Disraeli might compromise British neutrality (Northcote to Salisbury, 23 Jan. 1878, Salis. Pap., E 135–6). Solvyns, the Belgian ambassador, confirms the role of Lady Derby mentioned by Seton-Watson. 'It was through an indiscretion of Lady Derby that Ct. Shuvalov was informed of the plan to send the English fleet to Gallipoli. He immediately sent the news to St. Petersburg and received the order to communicate the peace preliminaries to the English cabinet. This communication . . . caused the recall of the fleet' (Solvyns to d'Aspremont Lynden, London, 2 Feb. 1878, BFM 51, no. 126). Layard's efforts enabled his telegram with the peace terms to reach London on 24 January and this caused the Cabinet's decision to recall the fleet. Shuvalov communicated the Russian terms to Derby on 25 January.

⁵² Hornby to Admiralty, Vourla, 6.10 p.m., 24 Jan. 1878, RA H19/36; Admiralty to Hornby, 7.25 p.m., ibid.; Hornby to Admiralty, 5.45 p.m., 25 Jan. 1878, ibid.; Northcote to Queen Victoria, 24 Jan. 1878, RA B28/7; Derby to Layard, confid., teleg., 4.50 p.m., 24 Jan. 1878, PRO FO 424/64, no. 553a; same to same, 7.15 p.m., 24 Jan. 1878, ibid., nos. 553b, 553c. Layard's telegram number 102, upon which the fleet was

stopped, listed six Russian peace conditions: a pecuniary indemnity with Bayazid, Kars, Ardahan, and Batum to be held as a guarantee for payment, Romania to be independent, Serbia to be a kingdom with an increase of territory, Bulgaria to be given the status which Serbia had previous to the war, additional territory for Montenegro, and 'the question of Bosphorus and Dardanelles to be settled between the Sultan and the Emperor of Russia' (Layard to Derby, teleg., 24 Jan. 1878, PRO FO 424/64, no. 543). Gladstone informed Stead of his hopes for the Russian peace terms. The former desired that St. Petersburg 'make a clean job of the Slav redemption . . . be unkind to the Hellenes . . . secure an ample recompense for good, gallant, glorious Montenegro . . . and not mar a glorious immortal work by taking back the little Danubian bit of Bessarabia' (Gladstone to Stead, 20 Jan. 1878, Glad. Pap., Add. MS. 44303, CCXVIII). Hornby was 'not sorry' at the cancellation of the order to proceed to Constantinople because the Gallipoli Peninsula was not secured (Hornby to Layard, 26 Jan. 1878, Lay. Pap., Add. MS. 39018, LXXXVIII).

[53] Queen Victoria to Disraeli, teleg., 25 Jan. 1878, RA B55/51; Layard to Derby, most secret, teleg., 26 Jan. 1878, PRO FO 424/64, no. 577; same to same, teleg., 25 Jan. 1878, ibid., no. 572; Derby to Her Majesty's Embassies, teleg., 25 Jan. 1878, ibid., nos. 567, 568; Russian peace conditions, communicated by Beust, 27 Jan. 1878, ibid., no. 584.

[54] Northcote to Queen Victoria, 25 Jan. 1878, RA B29/8; Richmond to Queen Victoria, 25 Jan. 1878, ibid., no. 9; Thompson, ii. 324–5; Wirthwein, pp. 316–19; Disraeli to Queen Victoria, 25 Jan. 1878, RA B55/50; same to same, 25 Jan. 1878, Disraeli Pap. XIX/C/440–1. The Spanish minister reported that on 26 January there were fifteen 'peace meetings' in England (Laiglesia to Silvela, London, 27 Jan. 1878, SFM, no. 41). Stead was organizing an Anti-War Tax League to prevent the collection of taxes in case Parliament granted the Government's vote of credit (Stead to Gladstone, 27 Jan. 1878, Glad. Pap., Add. MS. 44303, CCXVIII).

[55] Disraeli, as he wrote to the Queen, credited Salisbury's separation from the political position of Derby and Carnarvon as the main factor in uniting the Cabinet in a policy of resistance to Russian pretensions. The Prime Minister suggested to the Queen on 24 January that Salisbury would be an excellent replacement for Derby as Foreign Secretary. The Queen, needless to say, was thrilled by the probability of Derby's retirement (Disraeli to Queen Victoria, 24 Jan. 1878, MB vi. 229; Queen Victoria to Disraeli, ibid. 229–30). Lady Cecil tells us that Beaconsfield had informed Salisbury 'immediately after Lord Derby's resignation that he already had "in his pocket" the Queen's acceptance of himself [Salisbury] as Foreign Secretary' (Cecil, ii. 194).

[56] 'It is represented to me, by all the great authorities on these matters, that the retirement of Lord Derby is producing disastrous results on the Conservative party. . . . A general disintegration is taking place. The vote of Monday next, which would have originally been carried by a large majority, and on which I depended as exercising a great influence on Austria and Russia, is, with the disruption of the Cabinet, not only endangered, but even problematical. . . . Almost every member of the Cabinet, has pressed strongly on me to advise your Majesty to retain him. . . . The Lord Chancellor and others seem to think that Lord Derby regrets his withdrawal. . . . Lord Beaconsfield has had no communication with him, and his resignation in the House of Lords last night was not announced, because it is believed, he did not wish to connect that act with the resignation of Lord Carnarvon' (Disraeli to Queen Victoria, 26 Jan. 1878, MB vi. 234). Disraeli was being dishonest with the Queen as may be seen by his note to Derby on 24 January asking the latter to delay any announcement of his resignation until he had received the Queen's assent. The Foreign Secretary, though emotionally and physically ill, did not wish to resign. He informed Northcote on 25 January that if Beaconsfield desired him to withdraw his letter of resignation, he was willing to do so. On the same day he used Disraeli's letter of 24 January as an excuse to Carnarvon in not announcing his resignation to the House of Lords as the Colonial

Secretary intended to do (Derby to Carnarvon, 3.30 p.m., 25 Jan. 1878, Carnarvon Pap., PRO 30 6/13; Derby to Northcote, 25 Jan. 1878, Northc. Pap., Add. MS. 50022, x; same to same, 25 Jan. 1878, Derby Pap.). The Queen was sorely disappointed at Derby's return.

[57] Tenterden to Derby, 24 Jan. 1878, Derby Pap.; Disraeli to Derby, 24 Jan. 1878, ibid.; Northcote to Disraeli, 25 and 26 Jan. 1878, Disraeli Pap. xx/N/62, 63; Hart-Dyke to Disraeli, 25 Jan. 1878, ibid. xx/S/1308; Derby to Northcote, 25 Jan. 1878, Northc. Pap., Add. MS. 50022, x; same to same, 25 Jan. 1878, Derby Pap.; Derby to Carnarvon, 25 Jan. 1878, Carnarvon Pap., PRO 30 6/13; Northcote to Queen Victoria, 26 Jan. 1878, QVL ii. 598–9; Hardy diary, 26 Jan. 1878, Cran. Pap., HA43/T501/297; Disraeli to Salisbury, 27 Jan. 1878, Salis. Pap., E 270–1; Northcote to Ponsonby, 27 Jan. 1878, RA B55/57; Disraeli to Queen Victoria, 27 Jan. 1878, ibid., no. 60; Salisbury to Disraeli, 27 Jan. 1878, Disraeli Pap. xx/Ce/229; Disraeli to Derby, 27 Jan. 1878, Derby Pap. The Queen was unhappy about Derby remaining but gave way. She recorded in her journal that 'almost all Ld. Beaconsfield's colleagues had urged that Ld. Derby should be persuaded to remain' (Queen's journal, 27 Jan. 1878, RA).

[58] Disraeli and Northcote informed both Houses on 25 January of the orders to the fleet. As Carnarvon indicated on the same evening that the sending of the fleet was largely the reason for his resignation, the Government attempted to present the naval movement in a very favourable light (Hansard, 25 Jan. 1878, 3rd ser. 237, 435–54, 464–72).

# CHAPTER NINETEEN

[1] Carnarvon was replaced as Colonial Secretary by Beach. On 28 January Beaconsfield asked the Duke of Somerset, a Liberal, to join his Government. The latter refused (Duke of Somerset to Disraeli, 29 Jan. 1878, Disraeli Pap. xxi/S/368).

[2] Lady Cecil in her biography of her father has given a convincing explanation of Salisbury's behaviour even if only a partial one. 'Lord Salisbury was compelled by circumstances to trust his chief—and found in fact that he could do so with impunity. Collaboration was the cause and not the result of the change of sentiment. . . . Lord Salisbury was not a good hater [I think he was]. . . . [Disraeli] was an old man, declining in physical strength, faced with a task of extreme difficulty for dealing with which he lacked both the expert knowledge and the energy to aquire it. . . . Salisbury became the only man in the Cabinet upon whom he could rely for effectual assistance. He accepted the fact with unqualified candour. The appeal of this dependence . . . [elicited from Salisbury] an answering chivalry of support. He had come into touch for the first time with that generosity of personal confidence, that unstinted recognition of services rendered, which forms such a recurrently attractive feature in the story of Lord Beaconsfield's life. The Prime Minister was only too willing to leave to his subordinate that free hand in initiation and action which his [Salisbury's] temperament required . . . [and Salisbury] was equally ready to profit by the prolific ingenuity of suggestion, the gleams of insight, amounting almost to inspiration, which characterized his leader's genius. . . . But the strongest cement to the understanding was the courage for which both men were preeminent' (Cecil, ii. 200–4).

[3] Elliot to Derby, teleg., 31 Jan. 1878, PRO FO 424/64, no. 676; same to same, teleg., 29 Jan. 1878, ibid., no. 646. Elliot interpreted Andrássy's reply as an offer of Austrian support for Constantinople in return for a British promise to back up Austria in Bulgaria. It was Derby's indication to Beust that 'without some stipulation of reciprocity on the part of Austria-Hungary', Parliament would not sanction a war for Bulgaria, that caused Andrássy to ask if England had thrown over the understanding of

14 August (Derby to Elliot, most confid., 1 Feb. 1878, PRO FO 424/67, no. 30; Elliot to Derby, secret, 29 Jan. 1878, ibid., no. 55). Shuvalov believed that an Anglo-Austrian understanding was being formed and was quite disturbed by this expectation. Münster could neither affirm nor deny the Russian ambassador's belief (Münster to Bülow, 29 Jan. 1878, GFM, A 614).

[4] According to Childers, he, Hartington, and Goschen were 'reluctant' to refuse the £6 million, Forster adopted a middle position, and opposed to the request for funds were Granville, Harcourt, Gladstone, Bright, and Argyll (Childers to Sir A. Clarke, 1 Feb. 1878, Childers, *Life and Correspondence of Childers*, i. 251–2). According to Goschen, at a meeting of Liberal front-benchers at Granville's on the twenty-ninth everyone save Hartington and himself wished to fight the Government's request for funds (A. D. Elliot, *Life of G. J. Goschen*, 2 vols., London, 1911, i. 183). Hartington felt that Gladstone was attempting to oust him as leader and was on the verge of resigning that post (ibid.; O. W. Hewett, *Strawberry Fair. A Biography of Francis, Countess Waldegrave, 1821–79*, London, 1956, pp. 250, 255–6). Hartington explained to Granville that to oppose the Government now would be unpatriotic and, further, that he agreed generally with the policy ministers were following. He wrote of Gladstone that 'he must be aware that it is he who has formed and guided the Liberal Party' (Hartington to Granville, 29 Jan. 1878, Gran. Pap., PRO 3 29/22A). For the Liberal meeting at Granville's which determined on Forster's amendment see Trevelyan, *Bright*, p. 421.

[5] *Hansard*, 31 Jan. 1878, 3rd ser. 237, 689, 722, 729–813; Disraeli to Queen Victoria, 31 Jan. 1878, RA B55/68; same to same, 31 Jan. 1878, Disraeli Pap. xix/C/452–3. Northcote described Forster's speech to the Queen as 'laboured and ineffective' and Cross's reply as 'excellent'. The Chancellor of the Exchequer thought 'the debate has been wanting in interest; and it seems difficult to understand how it is to be kept up, as proposed, for four nights' (Northcote to Queen Victoria, 31 Jan. 1878, RA, B29/14). For Richmond's report of proceedings in the House of Lords see Richmond to Queen Victoria, 1 Feb. 1878, ibid., no. 16. Brand describes Forster's speech as 'sensible' but 'dull' and Cross's reply as 'excited'. Bright's speech is described as 'very fine' (Brand diary, 31 Jan. 1878, Brand Pap.). Sandon received a report from Lancashire that most Conservatives at both ends of the social scale favoured a firm 'and determined' anti-Russian policy. 'Very many regret the fleet's recall and many more are disappointed at Derby's want of courage attributing it to his idleness' (Forwood to Sandon, 30 Jan. 1878, Harrowby Papers, Sandon Hall, Stafford, E. J. Feuchtwanger, *Disraeli, Democracy and the Tory Party* Oxford, 1968, p. 217).

[6] Shuvalov believed the Cabinet was ready again to send the fleet through the Dardanelles, and that even Derby, who opposed this, was being moved by the anti-Russian outburst of opinion in Britain (Shuvalov to Gorchakov, 31 Jan. 1878, Seton-Watson, *Slav. Rev.* XXV (Apr. 1947), 538–41).

[7] Thompson, ii. 361–3; Disraeli to Derby, secret, 1 Feb. 1878, Derby Pap.; Derby to Disraeli, 1 Feb. 1878, Disraeli Pap. xx/S/1315; same to same, 1 Feb. 1878, Derby Pap. The Guildhall demonstration occurred on 31 January; on 2 February 'stormy meetings' transpired at Bermondsey and Peckham and a large pro-Government meeting of over 20,000 people was held at the Pomona Gardens in Manchester. Simultaneously in that city a group of ten to twelve thousand in Stevenson Square passed resolutions protesting against the 'war vote' (Thompson, ii. 361–3). On 29 January a pro-Government meeting at Sheffield caused Mundella to write 'it is the worst news since I have been an M.P. for Sheffield' (Mundella to Leader, 29 Jan. 1878, Mundella Pap.).

[8] Elliot, *Goschen*, i. 183–5. Wirthwein writes of this night's speeches as mechanical. For his description and the *Examiner's* interesting account see Wirthwein, pp. 324–6.

[9] The recall of the fleet and the debate on the vote of credit caused foreign observers, such as the Spanish minister, to comment on the 'timidity' and irresolution of the British Government (Casa Laiglesia to Silvela, London, 29 Jan. 1878, SFM, no. 44).

[10] Andrássy's assertion, and Britain's as well, that any European clauses in a Russo-Turkish peace would require European consent for their validity, implied the calling of a meeting of all the Great Powers for the above purpose. Bismarck, apparently, was willing to follow Andrássy's lead, as Odo Russell reported on 1 February 'that he [Bismarck] now thinks a conference at Vienna of the Powers interested in the pacific settlement of that question should follow the conclusion of an Armistice between the beligerents' (Russell to Derby, secret, 1 Feb. 1878, PRO FO 64/902, no. 71). On 31 January Andrássy told Elliot that Russia had agreed 'that all European questions . . . shall be submitted to a conference' (Elliot to Derby, secret, 31 Jan. 1878, ibid., 424/67, no. 60).

[11] Disraeli to Queen Victoria, 2 Feb. 1878, RA B55/76; same to same, 2 Feb. 1878, Disraeli Pap. xix/C/547; Derby to Queen Victoria, 2 Feb. 1878, RA H20/5; same to same, 2 Feb. 1878, Derby Pap.; Paget to Derby, teleg., secret, 1 Feb. 1878, PRO FO 424/67, no. 21; Disraeli to Derby, secret, 1 Feb. 1878, Derby Pap. France was also sounded on a combined naval action, and Italy was told that Austria could 'be relied on' (Derby to Paget, teleg., 2 Feb. 1878, PRO FO 424/67, no. 78; Derby to Lyons, ibid., no. 79).

[12] Layard to Derby, teleg., 31 Jan. 1878, PRO FO 424/67, no. 11; Derby to Layard, teleg., 30 Jan. 1878, ibid., 66, no. 261; Reade to Layard, Varna, 3 Feb. 1878, Lay, Pap., Add. MS. 39018, LXXXVIII; Wirthwein, pp. 328–9; Wyndham to Derby, 21 Jan. 1878, PRO FO 424/67, no. 38; Wyndham to Derby, teleg., 2 Feb. 1878, ibid., no. 73; Derby to Wyndham, teleg., 5 Feb. 1878, ibid., no. 180, Anglo-French pressure succeeded in inducing Greece to withdraw her troops from Ottoman territory on 6 February (Wyndham to Derby, teleg., 6 Feb. 1878, PRO FO 424/67, no. 270).

[13] Paget to Derby, very confid., teleg., 3 Feb. 1878, ibid., no. 122; Derby to Elliot, teleg., 2 Feb. 1878, ibid., no. 80; Andrássy to Beust, teleg., 3 Feb. 1878, ibid., no. 147; Lyons to Derby, teleg., 4 Feb. 1878, ibid., no. 157; Derby to H.M. Embassies, teleg., 4 Feb. 1878, ibid., no. 165; Paget to Derby, teleg., 5 Feb. 1878, ibid., no. 182; Lyons to Derby, 4 Feb. 1878, ibid., no. 199.

[14] Selborne to Hartington, 2 Feb. 1878, Hart. Pap. 340/744; Liddon to Freeman, 2 Feb. 1878, Liddon Pap.; Muller to Noire, 3 Feb. 1878 (F. M. Muller, *Life and Letters of F. M. Muller*, 2 vols., London, 1902, ii. 43–4). In his speech at Oxford Gladstone said the following. 'I tell you plainly that if the House of Commons is to make large votes of money without a proof of the necessity of the charge, your liberties are gone. . . . It depends at this moment on the action of the people. . . . We are a minority [in Parliament]. Nothing can give effect to our views but your support and the support of the country' (Thompson, ii. 326–8). Only the Radical journals approved Gladstone's two speeches at Oxford. '*The Times*, questioned the "opportuneness" of his railings, suggesting that it was not "worthy" of the great statesman' (Wirthwein, pp. 322–3).

[15] Northcote to Queen Victoria, 4 Feb. 1878, RA B29/19; Wirthwein, p. 330; *Hansard*, 4 Feb. 1878, 3rd ser. 237, 911–21, 926–7. Brand gives the following account. 'He [Gladstone] made a fine speech, temperate clear and forcible. . . . Hardy followed, who, however, scarcely noticed his olive branch of a joint address. Hardy spoke with force, but too much excited' (Brand diary, 4 Feb. 1878, Brand Pap.). 'Gladstone opened the debate last night in a carefully studied delusive speech. . . . I [Hardy] . . . was somewhat puzzled at the change of front' (Hardy diary, 5 Feb. 1878, Cran. Pap., HA43/T501/297). Lyon Playfair thought Gladstone's effort 'one of the most eloquent speeches I have ever heard . . . but I fear it will have little effect in producing harmony' (Playfair to Edith Russell, 6 Feb. 1878, W. Reid, *Memoirs and Correspondence of Lyon Playfair*, London, 1899, pp. 264–5).

[16] Goschen diary, 6 Feb. 1878, Elliot, *Goschen*, i. 185–6; Chamberlain to Bunce, 6 Feb. 1878, Chamberlain Pap., JC5/8/32; Northcote to Queen Victoria, 5 Feb. 1878, RA B29/20; Stead to Gladstone, 5 Feb. 1878, Glad. Pap., Add. MS. 44303, CCXVIII; Gladstone to Stead, 5 Feb. 1878, ibid. On 7 February, Forster, Hartington, Granville,

Frederick Cavendish, Gladstone, and Bright met and agreed that Forster should withdraw his amendment challenging the Government on its motion for supplies (Forster diary, 7 Feb. 1878, Reid, ii. 192–4). Münster, the German ambassador, attributed the growing British public exasperation with Russia as due to the suspicion that the latter Power had not played 'fair', using sly diplomacy instead of frank and open conduct (Münster to Bülow, London, 11 Feb. 1878, GFM, A1066).

[17] Wirthwein, pp. 331–3; Layard memoirs, 5 Feb. 1878; Layard to Derby, teleg., 5 Feb. 1878, PRO FO 424/67, nos. 209, 210, 211; Lyons to Derby, telegs., 5 Feb. 1878, ibid., nos. 208, 215. While Lyons was telegraphing to the Foreign Secretary the news of differences over the site of the conference, the latter asked the ambassador if he would be prepared to represent Britain at the conference (Derby to Lyons, 6 Feb. 1878, Newton, *Lyons*, ii. 125). Gorchakov had indicated as early as 1 February his objection to either Vienna or London for the conference (Schweinitz to Bülow, St. Petersburg, teleg., 1 Feb. 1878, GD i. 61). Bismarck considered that public knowledge of the Russo-Turkish conditions was as important as the site of the conference (ibid. 63–4). Before Russia permitted the Porte and the rest of Europe to receive an official copy of the above terms, terms which gave her the right to occupy Tchataldja, the Grand Duke's forces occupied the aforementioned place and also required the Turks to abandon the last good defensive position guarding Constantinople—the Buyuk Chekmedje, a fortified range of hills about 25 miles distant from the capital. This range the armistice left in a neutral zone between the Russians at Tchataldja and the Ottoman forces between it and Constantinople (Thompson, ii. 330–2). As London only learned of the official terms on 7 and 8 February, it appeared until then that the Russian army was advancing in defiance of the armistice which it was known had been signed on 31 January (Layard to Derby, 6 Feb. 1878, Lay. Pap., Add. MS. 39131, CCI). Later the ambassador would attribute the delay in communicating the terms signed on 31 January in part to the treachery of Server Pasha, one of two negotiators sent by the Porte to meet Grand Duke Nicholas. 'Server Pasha simply informed the Porte of the fact [the signing on 31 January], leading it to believe that military operations were suspended, and that belligerents were to occupy positions held at the time of the signature of the armistice. Russians were then only at Tchorlu [Corlu, about 50 miles from Constantinople]. He did not inform the Porte the lines of Constantinople were to be abandoned, and that Tchataldja was to be occupied by Russians. Consequently, when Russia advanced on that place, Porte believed there was a violation on their part of the Armistice, and requested me to telegraph as I did [on 5 February] to your Lordship. The Protocol of Bases of Peace and Convention of Armistice were sent by a servant of Server Pasha, who left Adrianople on the morning of the 2nd instant. . . . He did not reach Constantinople until 6th and it was only on that day that Porte was made aware of the fact that the lines of Constantinople were to be abandoned under the terms of the armistice. . . . Server Pasha excuses himself for not having sent terms of armistice by telegraph, as the Convention was of so great a length' (Layard to Derby, teleg., 17 Feb. 1878, PRO FO 424/67, no. 752).

[18] Queen Victoria to Disraeli, Osborne, 6 and 7 Feb. 1878, Disraeli Pap. XIX/C/462, 464–5; Currie to Layard, 7 Feb. 1878, Lay. Pap., Add. MS. 39018, LXXXVIII; Salisbury to Northcote, 7 Feb. 1878, Salis. Pap. D/XIV/141; same to same, 7 Feb. 1878, Northc. Pap., Add. MS. 50019, VII; Salisbury to Disraeli, 6 Feb. 1878, Disraeli Pap. XX/CE/231; Disraeli to Salisbury, 6 Feb. 1878, Salis. Pap., E 274; Derby to Disraeli, 6 Feb. 1878, Derby Pap.; Disraeli to Derby, 6 Feb. 1878, ibid.; Layard to Hornby, 6 Feb. 1878, Lay. Pap.; Add. MS. 39131, CCI.

[19] Derby to Lyons, teleg., 12.45 p.m., 7 Feb. 1878, PRO FO 424/67, no. 278; Derby to Elliot, 7 Feb. 1878, ibid., no. 279; Derby to Loftus, teleg., 3.30 p.m., 7 Feb. 1878, ibid., no 281; Hardy diary, 8 Feb. 1878, Hardy, ii. 51; Derby to Queen Victoria, 7 Feb. 1878, Derby Pap.; same to same, 7 Feb. 1878, RA H20/32; Disraeli to Queen Victoria, Teleg., 1.30 p.m., 7 Feb. 1878, RA B56/32; Disraeli to Queen Victoria, 7 Feb. 1878,

ibid., no. 15. The French answer to the British request for a joint fleet movement was telegraphed by Lyons at midnight on 7 February. It was in the negative. 'French Minister for Foreign Affairs does not consider that the information received up to this time from their own agents would, taken by itself, warrant the dispatch of the ships to Constantinople' (Lyons to Derby, Paris, teleg., 7 Feb. 1878, PRO FO 424/67, no. 309).

[20] Thompson, ii. 353–7; Northcote to Queen Victoria, 7 Feb. 1878, *QVL* ii. 601–2; Brand diary, 7 Feb. 1878, Brand Pap.; Wirthwein, pp. 333–7; *Hansard*, 7 Feb. 1878, 3rd ser. 237, 1198–1205, 1211–1313. Partly out of spite at the Conservatives who were not anxious for him to speak, Randolph Churchill suggested to the Liberal Dilke that he would be willing to propose 'an address to the Crown praying H.M. to use her influence at the Conference in favour of the widest possible freedom to Bulgaria, Bosnia & Hercegovina, & Thessaly & Epirus, & in favour of totally and finally putting an end to all direct Turkish Govt. in those provinces' (Churchill to Dilke, [7 Feb. 1878], Dilke Pap., Add. MS. 43893, xx). Dilke told Granville, who was willing to consider Churchill's suggestion but doubted whether the latter could obtain any Conservative support for it. Without such support it could only result in another Liberal defeat (Granville to Dilke, 13 [Feb.] 1878, Dilke Pap., Add. MS. 43878, v). Hartington, whom Dilke also informed on the suggestion of Granville, expressed no 'distinct opinion either way' on Churchill's proposal (Dilke to Granville, 14 Feb. 1878, Dilke Pap., Add. MS. 43878, v).

[21] *Hansard*, 8 Feb. 1878, 3rd ser. 237, 1315–51; Northcote to Queen Victoria, 8 Feb. 1878, *QVL* ii. 602–4; Smith to Queen Victoria, teleg., 8 Feb. 1878, Hambleden Papers, W. H. Smith, London, PS 6/15; Derby to Queen Victoria, 8 Feb. 1878, *QVL* ii. 604; same to same, 8 Feb. 1878, Derby Pap.; Derby to Loftus, Lyons, and Layard, telegs., 5.10, 5 and 4.45 p.m., 8 Feb. 1878, PRO FO 424/67, nos. 322–4; Northcote to Salisbury, 8 Feb. 1878, Salis. Pap., E 139—40; Northcote to Derby, confid., 8 Feb. 1878, Derby Pap.; Casa Laiglesia to Silvela, London, 8 Feb. 1878, SFM, no. 60.

[22] Four days earlier a Foreign Office memorandum by C. M. Kennedy pointed up the value for Britain of Black Sea trade. The value of it was estimated at six and three-quarter million pounds for the year 1876, whereas for the same year the value of British trade with European Turkey totalled only one and a half million additional pounds (Foreign Office confidential print, 4 Feb. 1878, 3479). For 1877 the value of British trade with Black Sea ports almost equalled the value of British trade with all of European Turkey (Board of Trade statistics, 14 Feb. 1878, *Hansard*, 3rd ser. 237, 1621).

[23] Northcote to Queen Victoria, 8 Feb. 1878, RA B29/22; Hardy diary, 9 Feb. 1878, Hardy, ii. 51; *Hansard*, 8 Feb. 1878, 3rd ser. 237, 1352–1420; Wolseley to Richard Wolseley, 8 Feb. 1878, Wolseley Pap.; Wirthwein, pp. 338–9; Northcote to Queen Victoria, 8 Feb. 1878, *QVL* ii. 602–4. Lady Knightley recorded in her journal that 'Lord Hartington and Mr. Gladstone have apparently entirely broken with each other, and they say Schouvaloff is constantly with Lady Derby, and gets everything out of her' (Lady Knightley's journal, 8 Feb. 1878, Knightley, p. 321). Shannon gives an excellent description of Gladstone's political motivation and activity. 'Gladstone's politics had become, in fact, sublimely self-centered. ... He found that he could employ mass enthusiasm in a righteous cause. ... His politics, however, became essentially personal, almost idiosyncratic and in a strict sense irresponsible, to an extent incompatible with the usages of English political life. As a rule, nothing is more useless in studying Gladstone than the assumption that normal and conventional criteria of judgment will be adequate.' (Shannon, pp. 12–13).

[24] Hewett, *Strawberry Fair*, pp. 255–6. On the ninth Hartington again indicated to Granville his desire to retire from party leadership in the Commons (Hartington to Granville, 9 Feb. 1878, Fitzmaurice, *Granville*, ii. 175). The Spanish minister in London reported to his Government the fear expressed in England that 'Gladstone would be the object of unpleasant manifestations of disapproval because of his attitude and conduct' (Casa Laiglesia to Silvela, 9 Feb. 1878, SFM, no. 64). For Chamberlain's attitude

to Gladstone and the Liberal leadership see Chamberlain to Collings, 18 Feb. 1878, Chamberlain Pap., Jc5/16/76.

[25] *Hansard*, 11 Feb. 1878, 3rd ser. 237, 1421–54. Northcote described Cowen's speech as 'most eloquent and interesting', marred only by his thick accent making it 'often difficult to understand him' (Northcote to Queen Victoria, 11 Feb. 1878, RA B29/23).

[26] Casa Laiglesia to Silvela, London, 11 Feb. 1878, SFM, no. 66. Smith attributed the Liberal collapse before the Government's vote of credit as 'due very much to the strong expression of feeling out of doors' (Smith to Hornby, 9 Feb. 1878, Hambleden Pap., PS/19). On Derby see p. 580 n. 5.

[27] Tenterden memorandum, 11 Feb. 1878, Derby Pap. The inner Cabinet myth probably arose from Dilke's wandering among the Tunis papers in 1881 when Under Secretary for Foreign Affairs. The story is related in his biography (Gwynn, i. 248–9).

[28] Admiralty to Tenterden, 9 Feb. 1878, PRO FO 424/67, no. 385, 386, 387; Layard to Derby, telegs., 6.45 and 10.15 p.m., 9 Feb. 1878, ibid., nos. 389, 392; Lay. Mem., 9 Feb. 1878; Hornby to Layard, 9 Feb. 1878, Lay. Pap., Add. MS. 39018, LXXXVIII; Smith to Disraeli, 10 Feb. 1878 (Maxwell, *Smith*, pp. 322–3). In his private communications with Hornby, Smith, First Lord of the Admiralty, asked the Admiral 'to avoid' giving 'offense to either side' as 'good judgment' was necessary 'if Europe is to keep as I hope she will out of war' (Smith to Hornby, Admiralty, 9 Feb. 1878, Hambleden Pap., PS/19).

[29] According to Sumner, the Tsar and the Russian Press were furious with Britain's unjustified and unprovoked naval action. The Tsar desired and apparently ordered a Russian occupation of Constantinople in retaliation, but the Grand Duke Nicholas, the Russian commander, and his staff hesitated owing to military uncertainties and the contradictions of the instructions coming from Alexander II in St. Petersburg (Sumner, pp. 373–8).

[30] Ponsonby to Paget, 11 Feb. 1878, Paget Pap., Add. MS. 51205, x; Lay. Mem., 10 Feb. 1878; Layard to Derby, teleg., 7 p.m., 10 Feb. 1878, PRO FO 424/67, no. 425; Shuvalov to Derby, 10 Feb. 1878, ibid., no. 422; Nigra to Depretis, St. Petersburg, confid., 9 Feb. 1878, IFM 159 (1401), no. 122; Layard to Derby, teleg., 10.50 a.m., 10 Feb. 1878, PRO FO 424/67, no. 393. Layard reported that 'according to railway authorities the total number of Russian troops . . . south of the Balkans [Balkan Mountains] does not exceed 65,000 men, who are in bad condition' (Layard to Derby, teleg., 11 Feb. 1878, ibid., no. 469).

[31] Derby to Loftus, teleg., 11 Feb. 1878, PRO FO 424/67, no. 438; Derby to Layard, 6.15 p.m., 11 Feb. 1878, ibid., no. 437; same to same, 3.40 p.m., 11 Feb. 1878, ibid., no. 433; Smith to Queen Victoria, teleg., 11 Feb. 1878, RA H20/46; Cross to Queen Victoria, confid. 11 Feb. 1878, ibid., no. 47; Salisbury to Disraeli, confid., 10 Feb. 1878, Disraeli Pap. xx/Ce/232. Salisbury felt the Turkish refusal of the firman the 'most critical moment we have yet passed through' (ibid.). Derby explained to the Ottoman ambassador that the need to have the fleet nearer to Constantinople was due to the delay in the issuing of orders for passage of the Straits, the possible interruption of telegraphic communication, and the distance of the Dardanelles from Constantinople (Derby to Musurus Pasha, 12 Feb. 1878, PRO FO 424/67, no. 465).

[32] Ollier, ii. 118–19; Casa Laiglesia to Silvela, London, 13 Feb. 1878, SFM, no. 69; Derby to Grote, 12 Feb. 1878, Grote Pap., Add. MS. 46691; Hardy diary, 12 Feb. 1878, Hardy, ii. 52; Forster to Byles, 12 Feb. 1878, Reid, ii. 194–7; Hartington to Duke of Devonshire, 12 Feb. 1878, Hart. Pap. 340/746; Wirthwein, pp. 344–5; Thompson, ii. 338–9.

[33] Elliot to Derby, confid., 13 Feb. 1878, PRO FO 7/928, no. 114; Moüy to Waddington, Constantinople, teleg., 13 Feb. 1878, *DDF* ii. 251; Lay. Mem., 13 Feb. 1878; Server Pasha to Musurus Pasha, Constantinople, telegs., 12 Feb. 1878, PRO FO 424/67, nos. 512–15; Zichy to Andrássy, Constantinople, teleg., 13 Feb. 1878, HHSA, PA XII/126; Lay. Mem., 11–13 Feb. 1878; Dwight, *Turkish Life in War Time*, pp. 240–1.

It was felt, especially by the Porte, that if the British fleet, was not anchored within the Bosphorus itself, Russia might be persuaded against sending troops into Constantinople. According to the registers of the consulate in Constantinople there were only '1,482 registered British subjects in Constantinople'. The remainder of the figure of 3,000 British subjects was made up of registered (629) and unregistered Maltese (Layard to Derby, 31 Jan. 1878, PRO FO 424/67, no. 593). When questioned in Parliament as to the number of British subjects in Constantinople for 1876, 1877, and 1878, Bourke answered disingenuously and asked for a postponement of the question as the Government, he said, did not yet have this information (*Hansard*, 18 Feb. 1878, 3rd ser. 237, 1847).

³⁴ Northcote to Queen Victoria, 14 Feb. 1878, RA B29/25; Aberdare to wife, 15 Feb. 1878 (*Bruce Letters*, ii. 64–5); Shuvalov to Gorchakov, 14 Feb. 1878 (Seton-Watson, *Slav. Rev.* XXV (Apr. 1947), 545–8; Turnor to Corry, 14 Feb. 1878, Disraeli Pap. XVI/C/304; Cameron to [Disraeli], 14 Feb. 1878, ibid. XIX/C/479; Derby to Loftus, teleg., 9.45 p.m., 13 Feb. 1878, PRO FO 424/67, no. 542; Derby to Loftus, teleg., 9.15 p.m., 13 Feb. 1878, ibid., no. 541. On 14 February Abdul Hamid used the crisis as an occasion to dissolve the Ottoman Parliament, which never would meet again.

³⁵ Smith to Hornby, teleg., 15 Feb. 1878, Hambleden Pap., PS 6/25; Smith to Queen Victoria, teleg., 15 Feb. 1878, RA B56/76; Smith to Disraeli, 15 Feb. 1878, Disraeli Pap. XVI/F/9; Smith to Northcote, 15 Feb. 1878, ibid. XX/N/66a; Hardy to Queen Victoria, 15 Feb. 1878, RA E24/3; Disraeli to Queen Victoria, teleg., 15 Feb. 1878, RA B56/75; Derby to Loftus, teleg., 5.05 p.m., 15 Feb. 1878, PRO FO 424/67, no. 661; Derby to Layard, most secret, teleg., 14 Feb. 1878, Lay. Pap., Add. MS. 39137, CCVII; same to same, teleg., 8.10 p.m., 14 Feb. 1878, PRO FO 424/67, no. 582; Currie to Layard, 14 Feb. 1878, Lay. Pap., Add. MS. 39018, LXXXVIII; Brand diary, 15 Feb. 1878, Brand Pap.; Childers to Layard, 14 Feb. 1878, Lay. Pap., Add. MS. 39018, LXXXVIII. The orders to the fleet above had been first suggested by Hornby to the Admiralty on 14 February (Hornby to Admiralty, teleg., 14 Feb. 1878, enclosed in Admiralty to Tenterden, secret, 15 Feb. 1878, PRO FO 424/67, no. 669).

³⁶ Ribera to Silvela, St. Petersburg, 16 Feb. 1878, SFM, no. 23. In London the Belgian minister reported the opinion of two financial magnates as optimistic as long as Derby and Andrássy remained in control of their respective foreign policies (Solvyns to d'Aspremont-Lynden, London, 16 Feb. 1878, BFM, no. 42). The Spanish minister indicated that speculation in London focused on 'the probability of dragging Austria into the British orbit of action' (Casa Laiglesia to Silvela, London, 16 Feb. 1878, SFM, no. 71).

³⁷ Loftus to Derby, teleg., 2 p.m., 15 Feb. 1878, PRO FO 424/67, no. 689. London received Loftus's telegram on the morning of the sixteenth causing much excitement and the immediate calling of a Cabinet. Shuvalov may have saved the peace at this point. Upon hearing that the Cabinet was near a decision for war, he went at once to Derby and announced that Gorchakov's telegram, which contained his version of his talk with Loftus, was undecipherable (Shuvalov to Gorchakov, 17 Feb. 1878, Seton-Watson, *Slav Rev.* XXV [Apr. 1947], 548–52). The ambassador indicated, however, that the general purport of Gorchakov's telegram on Gallipoli was 'satisfactory' and in order to clarify its content he had 'telegraphed [St. Petersburg] for fuller explanations' which he hoped to give the Foreign Secretary on 18 February (Derby to Loftus, most confid., 16 Feb. 1878, PRO FO 424/67, no. 716). See also Sumner, pp. 382–3.

³⁸ According to the Spanish minister in London, the English public saw the movement of the fleet to Mondania Bay as 'a new and painful humiliation' (Casa Laiglesia to Silvela, 18 Feb. 1878, SFM, no. 73).

³⁹ Layard to Derby, teleg., 8 p.m., 17 Feb. 1878, PRO FO 424/67, no. 758; same to same, most secret, teleg., 1 p.m., 17 Feb. 1878, ibid., no. 753; Hornby to Admiralty, teleg., 8 p.m., 17 Feb. 1878, enclosed in Admiralty to Tenterden, 18 Feb. ibid., no. 750; same to same, 17 Feb. 1878, Maxwell, p. 326; Layard to Derby, most secret, teleg.,

15 Feb. 1878, PRO FO 424/67, no. 697; same to same, 8 p.m., 15 Feb. 1878, ibid., no. 694; same to same, most secret, teleg., 1 p.m., 15 Feb. 1878, ibid., 78/2810; Lay. Mem., 14–15 Feb. 1878, Dickson's plan for a combined Anglo-Turkish defence of the Bulair lines and the Gallipoli Peninsula was a temporary measure until troops could be brought from Britain to reinforce the 20,000 odd Ottoman army already there (Layard to Derby, teleg., 8 p.m., 17 Feb. 1878, PRO FO 424/67, no. 758). When the Ottoman ambassador requested Derby to define Britain's position or attitude now that she had sent the fleet through the Dardanelles, the Foreign Secretary after reaffirming England's neutrality gave the following reply. 'We [H.M's Government] might find ourselves forced into hostilities against our will. Under these circumstances, I [Derby] thought it was undesirable that the Sultan should ask us to define more distinctly the position which we took up. His Majesty [the Sultan] might be well assured that it was not with any unfriendly designs towards him or his Empire that the British fleet had gone up to the Sea of Marmora' (Derby to Layard, most confid., 16 Feb. 1878, ibid., no. 718).

⁴⁰ Shuvalov to Gorchakov, 17 Feb. 1878 (Seton-Watson, *Slav. Rev.* XXV [Apr. 1947], 548–52); Derby to Loftus, most confid., 16 Feb. 1878, PRO FO 424/67, no. 716; Sumner, p. 383; Seton-Watson, pp. 319–20. Upon being questioned by Russell, Bismarck answered that Germany would be neutral in an Anglo-Russian war. He further mentioned that while Andrássy sincerely supported England, Francis Joseph would not allow Austria to make war on Russia (Russell to Derby, secret, teleg., 17 Feb. 1878, PRO FO 424/67, no. 727). Disraeli had continued his secret negotiations outside the Foreign Office with Andrássy. On 12 February the Prime Minister told Beust that if left in isolation England would see to her own interests in Egypt and at the Dardanelles, but that with Austrian co-operation Britain was prepared to fight for Austria's interests as well as her own. It was necessary, Beaconsfield added, that London and Vienna reach agreement before the conference and request Russia not to occupy Constantinople (Beust to Andrássy, secret, 12 Feb. 1878, Stojanovic, pp. 215–16). Andrássy replied that he was prepared to insist that Russia should not remain in Constantinople, but that a 100 to 150 million subsidy was necessary for Austrian mobilization (Andrássy to Beust, 14 Feb. 1878, ibid., p. 217). Stojanovic's conclusion appears correct. Disraeli desired Austrian military support to threaten Russia away from Constantinople, and Andrássy was only ready to consider active military co-operation with London if Austrian interests were violated, not for the object of mere pressure on Russia (ibid., p. 218). Andrássy was prepared to use the conference to check Russia in Bulgaria and Serbia in Bosnia; Disraeli's concern was more immediate and involved the safety of the fleet and the non-entry of Russia into Constantinople.

⁴¹ Derby to H.M. Ambassadors, teleg., 19 Feb. 1878, PRO FO 424/67, no. 804; same to same, teleg., 5 p.m., 18 Feb. 1878, ibid., no. 770; Beaconsfield to Queen Victoria, teleg., 2.40 p.m., 18 Feb. 1878, RA B56/85; Elliot to Derby, teleg., 18 Feb. 1878, PRO FO 424/67, no. 773; Lyons to Derby, teleg., 11.35 a.m., 18 Feb. 1878, ibid., no. 767; Paget to Derby, teleg., 6.30 p.m., 17 Feb. 1878, ibid., no. 760; Derby to H.M.'s Embassies, teleg., 4.30 p.m., 16 Feb. 1878, ibid. no. 709; Seton-Watson, p. 319. There is some indirect proof that Derby or Lady Derby informed Shuvalov both of England's attempt to buy the four Ottoman ironclads and to convince the Sultan of the desirability of Britain's occupying the forts on the Asiatic side of the Dardanelles (Layard to Derby, most secret, teleg., 1 p.m., 17 Feb. 1878, PRO FO 424/67, no. 753; Lay. Mem., 17 Feb. 1878). According to Layard information concerning the attempt to buy the four ironclads had to have leaked out from London as he never communicated the arrangement in Constantinople upon learning indirectly that the Sultan would not make such a sale (ibid.). Having learned of the British intention to embark men on the Asiatic side of the Dardanelles, the Russians then promised to leave Gallipoli alone if London foreswore the landing of men on either side of the Straits. It is very possible that Server Pasha, Ottoman Foreign Minister, was the informant for Russia. For this

see Sumner, p. 385.

[42] For this see Sumner, pp. 371–2, 375–8.

[43] Odo Russell, who was not without energy, sometimes misled his chief on important points. 'It is believed here [Berlin] by the best informed persons that Germany would desert Austria if the alliance of the three Emperors should ever break up' (Russell to Derby, secret, teleg., 20 Feb. 1878, PRO FO 424/67, no. 840). Odo did report the following. 'Prince Bismarck replied that I was wrong in supposing him to be more favourable to Russia than to Austria; the object of the strictly neutral position he wished to observe was to be able to give his support to a peaceful issue at the first favourable moment. At Gastein he had promised Count Andrassy that he would "befriend" him to the end, and that promise was sacred. Besides which the sympathies of the people of Germany were for Austria and in opposition to the Russian sympathies of the reigning families in Germany' (Russell to Derby, secret, 17 Feb. 1878, PRO FO 424/68, no. 997).

[44] Layard to Lytton, 20 Feb. 1878, Lay. Pap., Add. MS. 39131, CCI ; Layard to Derby, 20 Feb. 1878, ibid.; Derby to H.M.'s Embassies, teleg., 9.15 a.m., 21 Feb. 1878, PRO FO 424/67, no. 869; Loftus to Derby, private and confid., teleg., 20 Feb. 1878, ibid., no. 867; Layard to Derby, teleg., 1.20 p.m., 20 Feb. 1878, ibid., no. 837; Hornby to Admiralty, teleg., 6 p.m., 20 Feb. 1878, Disraeli Pap. XVI/F/13; Tenterden memorandums, 18 and 20 Feb. 1878, Derby Pap.; Tenterden to Derby, 21 Feb. 1878, ibid.; Layard to Derby, confid., teleg., 19 Feb. 1878, PRO FO 424/67, no. 822; same to same, most secret, teleg., 19 Feb. 1878, ibid., no. 821; Shuvalov to Gorchakov, 18 Feb. 1878 (Seton-Watson, *Slav. Rev.* XXV [Apr. 1947], 522–3); Elliot to Derby, secret, teleg., 19 Feb. 1878, PRO FO 424/67, no. 829; Elliot to Derby, secret, 18 Feb. 1878, ibid. 7/928, no. 127; Queen's journal, 16 Feb. 1878, RA.

[45] On Sunday, 24 February an anti-Russian meeting in Hyde Park carried some resolutions and then attacked and dispersed another meeting organized by Auberon Herbert, Bradlaugh, and working men's leaders before the latter could pass their resolutions for peace. The mêlée was witnessed by over 60,000 observers who saw gangs of medical students attempt to injure the peace group. The patriotic group, having been victorious at the Marble Arch, marched to Downing Street and cheered Beaconsfield before departing for Trafalgar Square to give vent to their exuberant spirits. A portion of the mob made for Harley Street where they stoned the windows of Gladstone's residence (Thompson, ii. 365–8; Wirthwein, pp. 346–7; H. B. Bonner, *Charles Bradlaugh*, London, 1908, pp. 82–5).

[46] Russell to Derby, secret, 25 Feb. 1878, no. 142, enclosed in Derby to Layard, secret, 14 Mar. 1878, PRO FO 195/1167, no. 360; Saint Vallier to Waddington, confid., 24 Feb. 1878, *DDF* ii. 258–61; Admiralty to Hornby, teleg., 21 Feb. 1878, enclosed in Admiralty to Tenterden, secret, 22 Feb. 1878, PRO FO 424/67, no. 939; Currie to Layard, 21 Feb. 1878, Lay. Pap., Add. MS. 39018, LXXXVIII ; Derby to Loftus, teleg., 21 Feb. 1878, ibid., no. 870; Derby to H.M. Embassies, teleg., 9.15 a.m., 21 Feb. 1878, ibid., no. 869; Hammond to Layard, 23 Feb. 1878, Lay. Pap., Add. MS. 38956, XXVI ; Casa Laiglesia to Silvela, London, 22 Feb. 1878, SFM, no. 88; Wirthwein, pp. 342–5.

[47] Currie to Layard, 28 Feb. 1878, Lay. Pap., Add. MS. 39018, LXXXVIII ; Cowley to Layard, 27 Feb. 1878, ibid.; Derby to Northcote, 28 Feb. 1878, Northc. Pap., Add. MS. 50022, X; same to same, 28 Feb. 1878, Derby Pap.; Disraeli to Queen Victoria, 28 Feb. 1878, Disraeli Pap. XIX/C/490; Northcote to Disraeli, 27 Feb. 1878, ibid. XX/N/69; Northcote to Derby, 27 Feb. 1878, Derby Pap.; Derby to Loftus, confid., 26 Feb. 1878, Derby Pap., not sent. Tenterden, suspecting a partition of European Turkey, argued for the occupation of the Suez Isthmus rather than for the taking of an island, and to remain 'so long as the Russians remain in Bulgaria' (Tenterden memorandum, 27 Feb. 1878, ibid.).

[48] Derby to Layard, teleg., 6 p.m., 27 Feb. 1878, PRO FO 424/67, no. 1045; Disraeli to Derby, 28 Feb. 1878, MB vi. 249–50; same to same, 28 Feb. 1878, Derby Pap. After

receiving Derby's warning, Shuvalov urged Gorchakov to communicate Russia's terms (Shuvalov to Gorchakov, teleg., 27 Feb. 1878, Seton-Watson, *Slav. Rev.* XXV [Apr. 1947]).
[49] Thompson, ii. 352–3; Smith to Disraeli, 1 Mar. 1878, Hambleden Pap., PS6/38; Salisbury to Lytton, 1 Mar. 1878, Salis. Pap., C4, letter-book; Derby to Disraeli, 1 Mar. 1878, Disraeli Pap. xx/S/1326; same to same, 1 Mar. 1878, Derby Pap.; Münster to Bülow, 1 Mar. 1878, GFM, A 1490. Alexander II was apparently not impressed with the British threat to remove Loftus if Constantinople were occupied without the Porte's consent. Gorchakov indicated that the Tsar 'intended to do what was necessary;—"L'Angleterre fera ce qu'elle voudra"' (Bülow memorandum, 23 Feb. 1878, *GD* i. 66–7). Münster reported the existence of a political party truce. 'No one turns even the worst driver off the box, when the carriage is on the edge of a precipice' (Münster to Bülow, London, 25 Feb. 1878, ibid. 68).
[50] Layard to Hornby, 2 Mar. 1878, Lay. Pap., Add. MS. 39131, CCI.

# CHAPTER TWENTY

[1] A plan was put forward at Constantinople to raise money for the relief of the thousands of Muslims who had fled Bulgaria by raising the Ottoman duty on the importation of foreign goods from 10 per cent to 25 per cent. This humanitarian plan was refused by the Continental powers and the United States, though initially approved by London when the added duty amounted to 2 per cent only. Many in England were fearful of its implementation. The Manchester Chamber of Commerce appealed to Salisbury. 'The proposal has created grave apprehension amongst merchants in this city, whose trade with Turkey would, under so large an increase of duty, be nearly destroyed' (Mr. Browning to Salisbury, 3 June 1878, PRO FO 424/71, no. 86D). It should be said that Manchester had not opposed the original scheme of adding only 2 per cent to Ottoman duties.
[2] Sumner writes that Gorchakov had intended a protocol instead of a treaty with Turkey, which would contain only general and provisional agreement pending the reaction of the European Powers to it in congress. The fact of a treaty, therefore, is interpreted as a victory for Ignatiev (Sumner, p. 417). News of the treaty was greeted wildly by Russian opinion, but Andrássy's objections to it caused Ignatiev to leave for Russia on 10 March to fight for his creation and also to reap the plaudits of satisfied Pan-Slav feeling. Jomini describes the ambassador's spirits and energy at this time as immense (Jomini to Onou, 15 Mar. 1878, Jomini–Onou Pap., EG. 3211, fos. 59–60). British opinion reacted to the treaty in mixed fashion ranging between satisfaction and execration. Most found some of the terms faulty and even the pro-Bulgarian *Daily News* 'criticized the fact that Russia had seemingly "sacrificed every Christian population, with the exception, perhaps of Montenegro, to the Bulgarians"' (Wirthwein, pp. 351–2; Thompson, ii. 380–2).
[3] Tenterden memorandum, 5 Mar. 1878, Derby Pap.; Northcote to Queen Victoria, 2 Mar. 1878, MB vi. 253; Disraeli to Queen Victoria, 2 Mar. 1878, ibid. 253–4; Mundella to Leader, 5 Mar. 1878, Mundella Pap. One of the most widespread rumours concerning Derby was that excessive drinking made it impossible for him to fulfil the functions of his office. Shuvalov denied the validity of these reports in the second week in March (Shuvalov to Gorchakov, 12 Mar. 1878, Seton-Watson, *Slav. Rev.* xxvi [Apr. 1948]. 554).
[4] *Hansard*, 7 Mar. 1878, 3rd ser. 238, 851–6; Duke of Richmond to Queen Victoria, 7 Mar. 1878, RA B29/38; Wirthwein, pp. 352–4; *Hansard*, 8 Mar. 1878, 3rd ser. 238,

949–50; Russell to Bülow, 8 Mar. 1878, *GP* ii. no. 336; Stolberg to Bülow, 4 Mar. 1878, ibid., no. 333; Bülow to Stolberg, teleg., 3 Mar. 1878, ibid., no. 332. Münster reported the following from London on Britain's reaction to a congress. 'The knowledge that the proposal originated with Prince Gorchakoff has revived the distrust of Russia. There has been such deep suspicion that the three Empires have come to a preliminary understanding and that British interests will not be sufficiently safe guarded at the Congress, that until yesterday morning it was generally assumed that the answer would be unfavourable. . . . The feeling against the Congress exists in both the Parliamentary parties and even in a section of the Ministry—notably in Lord Beaconsfield himself' (Münster to Bülow, 9 Mar. 1878, *GD* i. 71–3); Bülow memorandums, 9 Mar. 1878, *GD* i. 74–5. When Beust gave Derby the official congress invitation, he reiterated Andrássy's adherence to the Anglo-Austrian agreement of 14 August 1877 (Derby to Elliot, 7 Mar. 1878, PRO FO 424/68, no. 158). The Tsar told Loftus on 10 March that he hoped the conference would lead to a 'satisfactory arrangement' as he would 'deeply regret any rupture with England, with whom he had always wished to maintain friendly relations' (Loftus to Derby, teleg., 10 Mar. 1878, PRO FO 424/68, no. 221). Bismarck had Bülow inform Russell that if Britain declined to accept a conference Germany 'would withdraw from it also' (Russell to Derby, secret, teleg., 11 Mar. 1878, PRO FO 424, no. 267).

⁵ Layard to Disraeli, private and secret, 6 Mar. 1878, Lay. Pap., Add. MS. 39131; Lyons memorandum, 12 Mar. 1878, Foreign Office print 3529 (434), Foreign Office library.

⁶ The largely illusory idea of a Mediterranean league was partly encouraged and kept alive by Paget, the British representative at Rome, who informed London, with more hope than perhaps accuracy, that Depretis was favourable to such a combination. Before a formal proposal could be made to Italy the Government fell and Paget was forced to wait until a new Government was formed before transmitting the memorandum from the Foreign Office given below. 'In view of the changes which the recent war . . . may bring about . . . as to the communications between the Mediterranean and the Black Sea, the Governments of [England, Italy, France, Austria, and Greece] agree to consider the maintenance . . . of their commercial and political interests in the Mediterranean and the Straits . . . as questions of general concern; and they will from time to time . . . come to an understanding as to the measures which may be necessary for the maintenance of these interests' (Derby to Paget, most confid., teleg., 7.30 p.m., 13 Mar. 1878, PRO FO 424/68, no. 307). Eventually the new Italian Government politely refused the British proposal.

⁷ Disraeli to Queen Victoria, 8 Mar. 1878, MB vi. 254–6; Disraeli to Derby, 12 Mar. 1878, Derby Pap.; Derby to Disraeli, 9 Mar. 1878, Disraeli Pap., xx/S/1327 a and b; Tenterden memorandum, 9 Mar. 1878, PRO FO 363/5, Tenterden Pap.; Hardy diary, 8–9 Mar. 1878, Cran. Pap., HA43/T501/297; Disraeli to Queen Victoria, teleg., 7 Mar. 1878, Disraeli Pap. xIX/B/1205. The Cabinet also suggested the admission of Greece to the congress; this met with little support from Andrássy, Bismarck, or Gorchakov (Stolberg to Bülow, Vienna, teleg., 12 Mar. 1878, *GD* i. 78). The Government's action reflected a desire to inflate a Mediterranean league, use the Greeks to contain the Slavs and end the insurrection in Thessaly.

⁸ Brand diary, 12 Mar. 1878, Brand Pap.; Reeve to Layard, 13 Mar. 1878, Lay. Pap., Add. MS. 39019, LXXXIX; Thompson, ii. 387–8; Lay. Mem., 12 Mar. 1878; Northcote to Queen Victoria, 12 Mar. 1878, RA B29/43; *Hansard*, 12 Mar. 1878, 3rd ser. 238, 1156–1217. Reference was made in the debate to Gladstone's pamphlet published in Russia urging the latter to forcefully coerce the Porte (ibid. 1192).

⁹ Disraeli to Queen Victoria, 16 Mar. 1878, RA B57/11; Salisbury to Temple, 15 Mar. 1878, Temple Pap., F86/16, Ind. Office; Disraeli to Queen Victoria, 13 Mar. 1878, RA B57/6; Tenterden memorandum, 16 Mar. 1878, Foreign Office Library

3526; Casa Laiglesia to Silvela, 13 Mar. 1878, SFM, no. 143. The British fleet reinforced from the Channel was in force throughout the eastern Mediterranean. The following ironclads or capital ships were in the following numbers: in the Sea of Marmora, 9; at Gallipoli, 4; in the Gulf of Zeros, 3; at Besika Bay, 4; at Malta, 10; one each at Corfu, Piraeus, Port Said, Gibraltar, and Beyrout (Admiralty print, 20 Mar. 1878, Disraeli Pap. xvi/F/19). Of the 13 vessels at Gallipoli and within the Sea of Marmora, 6 were ironclads. For Britain's two congress conditions see Derby to Beust, 9 Mar. 1878, PRO FO 424/68, no. 213. In the Commons debate on 14 March several references were made to the inadvisability of having either Lyons or Derby represent Britain in the anticipated congress (*Hansard*, 14 Mar. 1878, 3rd ser. 238, 1336–70).

¹⁰ At the end of March there was an attempt, unsuccessful, to reach a Russo-Turkish agreement or alliance (B. Jelavich, *The Ottoman Empire, the Great Powers, and the Straits Question, 1870–1887*, Bloomington, 1973, pp. 108–9).

¹¹ Münster to William I, London, 20 Mar. 1878, GFM, A 1909; Disraeli to Derby, 19 Mar. 1878, Derby Pap.; Derby to Disraeli, 19 Mar. 1878, ibid.; same to same, 19 Mar. 1878, Disraeli Pap. xx/S/1331; Tenterden memorandum, 19 Mar. 1878, Derby Pap.; Northcote to Lyons, 19 Mar. 1878, Northcote Pap., Add. MS. 50053, xli; Derby to Her Majesty's Embassies, teleg., 20 Mar. 1878, PRO FO 424/68, no. 471; Shuvalov to Derby, 19 Mar. 1878, ibid., nos. 448–9; Disraeli to Queen Victoria, 18 and 19 Mar. 1878, RA B57/12 and 13; Disraeli to Salisbury, secret, 18 Mar. 1878, Salis. Pap., E 277–8; Münster to Bülow, 17 Mar. 1878, GP, no. 58. It is not unlikely that Disraeli's secret informant concerning Shuvalov's intentions was Lady Derby.

¹² Münster to Bülow, teleg., 22 Mar. 1878, GP ii. 236–7, no. 366; Derby to Her Majesty's Embassies, teleg., 4.45 p.m., 21 Mar. 1878, PRO FO 424/68, no. 489; Disraeli to Queen Victoria, 20 Mar. 1878, RA B57/14; Hardy diary, 21 Mar. 1878, Hardy, ii. 55; Münster to Bülow, telegs., 21 Mar. 1878, GP ii. 234–6, nos. 363–5. Andrássy did not support what he considered Britain's unnecessary congress conditions (Elliot to Derby, teleg., 6 p.m., 24 Mar. 1878, PRO FO 424/68, no. 560). Beust communicated Andrássy's views to Derby on 25 March. 'It seems to me [Andrássy] that it would be better to stand firm about the Conditions of Peace than to make difficulties about the meeting of the Congress' (Andrássy to Beust, [?] Mar. 1878, ibid., no. 575).

¹³ Disraeli to Queen Victoria, 22 Mar. 1878, RA B57/15; *Hansard*, 21 Mar. 1878, 3rd ser. 238, 1731–5; Malet to mother, London, 22 Mar. 1878, Malet Pap., bundle A; Salisbury to Disraeli, confid., 21 Mar. 1878, Disraeli Pap. xx/Ce/233; memorandums, [?] Mar. 1878, RA E24/8, 17. Hornby had largely convinced Smith that should war occur the fleet should force the Bosphorus into the Black sea in order to cut Russian sea communications between Bulgaria and Odessa—this despite the expectation that Russia would plant the Bosphorus with floating torpedoes (Smith to Hornby, secret and confid., 23 Mar. 1878, Hornby Pap, PH 1/118B).

¹⁴ Playfair to Edith Russell, 24 Mar. 1878, Reid, pp. 273/4; Seton-Watson, pp. 348–50; Wirthwein, pp. 357–9; Disraeli to Lady Bradford, 24 Mar. 1878, Disraeli–Bradford letters; Chamberlain to Stead, 27 Mar. 1878, Chamberlain Pap.; Tenterden memorandum, 23 Mar. 1878, Derby Pap.; Thompson, ii. 161–2. The Cabinet meeting held on 23 March appointed a committee to compose the official reaction to the Treaty of San Stefano. The committee's report was written on the twenty-seventh and suggested that objection should be made to extending Bulgaria to the Aegean, to the method of choosing a governor for the new principality, and to the length of Russian occupation there, arguing for a shorter occupation and even a joint Austro-Russian one. An international commission representing all the Powers was suggested to superintend the administration of Bulgaria, as well as Rumelia, Thessaly, Epirus, Armenia, and Crete. As for the Straits, the committee recommended that all forts and batteries should be removed and that warships as well as those of commerce should be permitted through them. Objection was made to restoring Bessarabia to Russia, to the amount of the indemnity, and to the method of payment to be made by

Turkey and to the size and extent of Armenia claimed by Russia (Disraeli to Queen Victoria, teleg., 2.10 p.m., 23 Mar. 1878, RA B57/16; report of committee on San Stefano, 27 Mar. 1878, Cabinet print, Foreign Office library, 3548; H. Temperley and L. M. Penson, *Foundations of British Foreign Policy*, New York, 1966, pp. 367–72).

[15] Elliot to Derby, Vienna, teleg., 12.05 p.m., 28 Mar. 1878, PRO FO 424/68, no. 621; same to same, teleg., 27 Mar. 1878, ibid., no. 620; Sanderson to Ponsonby, 28 Mar. 1878, Ponsonby Pap., PRO FO 800/3; Andrássy to Beust, [?] Mar. 1878, ibid., no. 585, communicated to Derby on 26 Mar.; Layard to Derby, secret, teleg., 25 Mar. 1878, ibid., 78/2818, no. 329; Disraeli to Queen Victoria, most secret, 24 Mar. 1878, MB vi. 260; Queen's journal, 24 Mar. 1878, RA. Beaconsfield's report to the Queen of the arrival of the Russian answer and that it was a refusal of British conditions was probably given to him by Lady Derby. Münster thought Russia was being unreasonable in not accepting Britain's congress conditions (Münster to Bülow, London, 22 Mar. 1878, GD i. 82–4). In answer to an English request for his position on Bulgaria, Andrássy told Elliot that he favoured restricting Bulgaria north of the Balkan Mountains, limiting Russian occupation to six months there, and favouring a European instead of a Russian commission to help organize the administration of the new principality (Elliot to Derby, teleg., 6.30 p.m., 27 Mar. 1878, PRO FO 424/68, no. 605). San Stefano extended Bulgaria to the Aegean and allowed for a Russian occupation of two years.

[16] Disraeli had long been advocating increased arms.

[17] Disraeli to Queen Victoria, secret, 27 Mar. 1878, RA B57/21; same to same, 27 Mar. 1878, MB vi. 262–3; same to same, 26 Mar. 1878, ibid.; Gorchakov to Shuvalov, teleg., 28 Mar. 1878, Seton-Watson, pp. 373–4; same to same, teleg., 31 Mar. 1878, ibid., p. 378; Disraeli to Hardy, 27 Mar. 1878, Hardy, ii. 56; Queen's journal, 26 Mar. 1878, RA; Derby to Queen Victoria, teleg., 12.40 p.m., 27 Mar. 1878, RA H21/45; Münster to Bülow, 27 Mar. 1878, GP i. 85–6; Shuvalov to Derby, 26 Mar. 1878, PRO FO 424/68, no. 601; Derby to Loftus, teleg., 3.50 p.m., 27 Mar. 1878, ibid., no. 604. Buckle gives an account of the Cabinet meeting of 27 March which Derby left in a note and in his diary (MB vi. 264–6). Ignatiev would later tell Wellesley that the written answer which Shuvalov gave Derby on 26 March, which led the Cabinet to call out the reserves and to initiate an Indian expedition, was a misinterpretation by Shuvalov of the Russian position (Wellesley to Loftus, 17 Apr. 1878, enclosed in Loftus to Salisbury, secret, 17 Apr. 1878, PRO FO 424/69, no. 620).

[18] Malet to mother, 28 Mar. 1878, Malet Pap., bundle A; same to same, 26 Mar. 1878, ibid.; Disraeli to Queen Victoria, 27 Mar. 1878, MB vi. 262–3; Shuvalov to Gorchakov, 29 Mar. 1878 (Seton-Watson, *Slav. Rev.* xxviii [Nov. 1949], 226); same to same, very secret, 27 Mar. 1878, ibid. 220; same to same, 28 Mar. 1878, ibid. 221; Seton-Watson, pp. 365–8. Lady Derby maintained that her husband's resignation was due to his firm convictions 'which his colleagues do not share' (Lady Derby to Halifax, 29 Mar. 1878, Hickleton Pap.). Derby, as may be seen in a letter he wrote to Cross, also believed that his firm desire to avoid war led to his resignation. 'Where . . . both sides act from strongly-felt convictions, there need be, and there is no break of private friendship' (Derby to Cross, 29 Mar. 1878, Cross Pap., Add. MS. 51266, IV; same to same, 29 Mar. 1878, Derby Pap.).

[19] Solvyns to d'Aspremont-Lynden, London, 31 Mar. 1878, BFM, no. 104; Russell to Derby, 30 Mar. 1878, Derby Pap.; Currie to Layard, 28 Mar. 1878, Lay. Pap., Add. MS. 39019, LXXXIX; Casa Laiglesia to Silvela, London, 30 Mar. 1878, SFM, no. 172; Forwood to Sandon, 30 Mar. 1878, Harrowby Pap., L/90 (Feuchtwanger, *Disraeli, Democracy and the Tory Party*, pp. 217–18); Münster to Bülow, London, 29 Mar. 1878, GD i. 88–90; Wirthwein, pp. 361–2; Childers to Sir Andrew Clarke, 29 Mar. 1878, Childers, *Correspondence*, i. 253; Münster to Bülow, teleg., 28 Mar. 1878, GD i. 86; Hammond to Layard, 28 Mar. 1878, Lay. Pap., Add. MS. 38956, XXVI; Derby to Hardy, 30 Mar. 1878, Hardy, ii. 57; Casa Laiglesia to Silvela, 28 Mar. 1878, SFM, no.

167; Malet to mother, 29 Mar. 1878, Malet Pap., bundle A; Cross, *A Political History*; Disraeli to Derby, 28 Mar. 1878, Derby Pap.; Cross to Derby, 28 Mar. 1878, ibid.; Manners to Derby, 29 Mar. 1878, ibid.; Hardy to Derby, 29 Mar. 1878, ibid.; Derby to Cross, 29 Mar. 1878, ibid.; same to same, 29 Mar. 1878, Cross Pap., Add. MS. 51266, IV; Derby to Northcote, 28 Mar. 1878, Northc. Pap., Add. MS. 50022,X; same to same, 28 Mar. 1878, Derby Pap.; MB vi. 271; Richmond to Queen Victoria, 29 Mar. 1878, RA B29/62. Beaconsfield offered Derby the Garter, and the latter though very touched by the offer did not accept it. Even the Queen parted kindly from their official relationship. MacColl learned at the Russian Embassy and so wrote to the editor of the *Daily News* that Derby had resigned owing to the Government's decision to grab a strategic point belonging to Turkey, possibly Gallipoli or Mitylene (MacColl to editor of *Daily News*, 30 Mar. 1878, Malcolm MacColl, *Memoirs and Correspondence*, London, 1914, p. 57). The reaction of Earl Grey to Derby's resignation was not untypical. 'I cannot say that I have the slightest confidence in Derby or think him any loss to the F.O., on the contrary I think he has mismanaged the whole Eastern business from first to last most grossly' (Grey to Granville, [28] Mar. 1878, Gran. Pap., PRO 30, 29/26a).

²⁰ Salisbury to Loftus, 3 Apr., 1878, Salis. Pap., A/31/1; Commerell to Admiralty, 10 Apr. 1878 (Arthur J. Marder, 'British Naval Policy in 1878', *Journal of Modern History*, xii [Sept. 1940], 371); Hornby to Admiralty, 2 Apr. 1878, Disraeli Pap. XVI/F/26; Hornby to Layard, 31 Mar. 1878, Lay. Pap., Add. MS. 39109, LXXXIX; Layard to Tenterden, secret, teleg., 9.30 p.m., 30 Mar. 1878, ibid. 39137, CCVII; Layard to Derby, most secret, teleg., 31 Mar. 1878, PRO FO 78/2810, no. 341. Smith and the Admiralty refused, unless directed by the Cabinet, to order Hornby into the Black Sea if the Bosphorus forts fell to Russia (Hornby to Disraeli, 1 Apr. 1878, Disraeli Pap. XVI/F/23). Colonel Home advised Tenterden to instruct Layard to ascertain the number of Russian troops south of the Balkan Mountains (Home to Tenterden, 10 Apr. 1878, Lay. Pap., Add. MS., 39137, CVII). Home in London and General Dickson in Constantinople tended to minimize the number of Russian troops and along with Layard emphasized the effects of sickness within the Russian forces. Sumner writes that 90,000 Russians faced 80,000 Turks before Constantinople (Sumner, p. 471). These numbers represent only a rough guess and are probably more accurate for Russia than Turkey whose forces were probably considerably less than 80,000. Hornby reported that Layard had informed him that the Russians had 83,000 men around Constantinople and Gallipoli and 129,000 men south of the Balkan Mountains (Hornby to Admiralty, Ismid, teleg., 18 Apr. 1878, enclosed in Admiralty to Tenterden, 18 Apr. 1878, PRO FO 424/169, no. 407).

²¹ Thompson, ii. 408–9; Salisbury to H.M. Embassies, 1 Apr. 1878, PRO FO 146/2027, no. 243. For reactions to Salisbury's circular see the following: Seton-Watson, pp. 381–2; Ponsonby to Queen Victoria, 1 Apr. 1878, Disraeli Pap. XIX/C/517; Münster to Bülow, very confid., 2 Apr. 1878, GFM, A2172; same to same, 2 Apr. 1878, GD i. 91; Gordon to Sandon, 3 Apr. 1878, Harrowby Pap., vol. 39; Burne to Lytton, 4 Apr. 1878, India Office, Lytton Pap., E 218/517/5; Crown Princess Victoria to Queen Victoria, 5 Apr. 1878, *QVL* ii. 611–12; Reeve to Layard, 5 Apr. 1878, Lay. Pap., Add. MS. 39019, LXXXIX; Disraeli to Queen Victoria, 2 Apr. 1878, RA B57/33. The content of 'Salisbury's' circular contains almost nothing new. Almost all the argument may be found in a memorandum by Tenterden of 23 March and the report of the unnamed committee appointed by the Cabinet dated 27 March (Committee report, 27 Mar. 1878, Cabinet print, Foreign Office library, 3548; Tenterden memorandum, 23 Mar. 1878, Derby Pap.). Salisbury's contribution was the straightforward language of the circular which required a certain amount of both courage and coolness. The reason for the popularity of the circular was due to its simultaneous communication to all the Powers and the public. The pluck and reasonableness of the circular appealed to much of the British public which was inflamed with anti-Russian feeling in the midst of crisis, and which found the articulation of the reasons for their

anger satisfying. Temperley and Penson write that the committee which prepared the report of 27 March was the so-called 'inner Cabinet' of Cairns, Disraeli, and Salisbury, but there is no proof for this and they give none (*Foundations*, p. 363).

[22] Elliot to Salisbury, Vienna, 5 Apr. 1878, PRO FO 424/69, no. 181; Salisbury to Loftus, 4 Apr. 1878, ibid., no. 98; Salisbury to Queen Victoria, 3 Apr. 1878, *QVL* ii. 611; Reeve to Layard, 5 Apr. 1878, Lay. Pap., Add. MS. 39019, LXXXIX; Derby to Disraeli, 3 Apr. 1878, MB vi. 270; same to same, 3 Apr. 1878, Derby Pap.

[23] Salisbury to Russell, 10 Apr. 1878, Salis. Pap., A/27/2; Cecil, ii. 242–3; Schweinitz to Bismarck, St. Petersburg, 10 Apr. 1878, *GP* ii. 263, no. 338; Russell to Salisbury, teleg., 9 Apr. 1878, *QVL* ii. 613–14; Salisbury to Queen Victoria, 9 Apr. 1878, ibid. 614–15; Bismarck to Münster, teleg., 9 Apr. 1878, *GD* i. 91–2; Russell to Salisbury, private and secret, teleg., 7 Apr. 1878, Salis. Pap., E; same to same, 7 Apr. 1878, *QVL* ii. 613–14; Salisbury to Russell, personal and most secret, teleg., 6 Apr. 1878, ibid. 612–13; Salisbury to Queen Victoria, 3, 4, and 5 Apr. 1878, RA H21/54, 55, and 56; Salisbury to Russell, 4 Apr. 1878, PRO FO 244/315, no. 198; Salisbury to Layard, 4 Apr. 1878, Salis. Pap., A/32/1; same to same, 4 Apr. 1878, Lay. Pap., Add. MS. 39137, CVII; Salisbury to Elliot, teleg., 6.30 p.m., 1 Apr. 1878, PRO FO 7/923, no. 229; Salisbury to Ponsonby, 1 Apr. 1878, *QVL* ii. 610–11. The Turks had previously asked London to agree to a simultaneous withdrawal, but Salisbury had to explain that Britain could only consider such a proposal from Russia but not suggest it herself 'as it would be misconstrued both by Russia and elsewhere' (Derby to Layard, teleg., 10.15 a.m., 1 Apr. 1878, PRO FO 424/69, no. 30; Layard to Derby, secret, teleg., 28 Mar. 1878, ibid. 68, no. 622). For Münster's estimate of Salisbury see Münster to Bülow, 2 Apr. 1878, *GD* i. 90. Some still remembered what they considered Salisbury's misdirected conduct as special emissary to the Constantinople Conference (Malet to mother, 4 Apr. 1878, Malet Pap., bundle A).

[24] Grey to nephew, 8 Apr. 1878, Grey Pap.; Dilke diary, 7 Apr. 1878, Gwynn, *Dilke*, i. 250–1; Northcote to Hartington, 5 Apr. 1878, Hart. Pap. 340/751; Chamberlain to Collings, 5 Apr. 1878, Chamberlain Pap., JC5/16/87; Thompson, ii. 420–4; Herbert to wife, 4 Apr. 1878, Harris, pp. 199–200; Wirthwein, pp. 362–3.

[25] *Hansard*, 8 and 9 Apr. 1878, 3rd ser. 239, 858–942, 964–1041; Northcote to Queen Victoria, 5 and 8 Apr. 1878, RA B29/72, 73; Wirthwein, pp. 368–70; Thompson, ii. 412–14; Hardy diary, 9 Apr. 1878, Hardy, ii. 62–3. Forster, as he explained to his wife, was torn between 'letting the country get committed to a war policy without a protest and fear of encouraging Russia not to concede' (Forster to wife, 8 Apr. 1878, Reid, ii. 203). Gladstone thought that the Liberal party had been hurt by 'the alarm of some members for their seats', but was encouraged because he felt the effect of the debates in both houses was favourable 'to the cause of peace' (Gladstone to Stead, 9 Apr. 1878, W. T. Stead, *Truth About Russia*, London, 1888, pp. 485–6). Granville felt the debates to have been 'one of the heaviest blows to the discipline of a party I had ever remembered' (Granville to Hartington, 10 Apr. 1878, Fitzmaurice, *Granville*, ii. 175–6). For the Radical's plan to oppose the calling out of the reserves see Courtney to Margorit, 10 Apr. 1878, Courtney Papers, London School of Economics. Apparently even the Radicals had decided against presenting an amendment but Lawson acted despite this, forcing the Radicals and a few Liberals to vote for it (Mundella to Leader, 14 Apr. 1878, Mundella Pap.). Gladstone did not withdraw and voted for Lawson's amendment with the minority. He explained his reasons for doing so to Granville. 'On this occasion . . . I was by no means led into the lobby by my mere concurrence with Lawson's words, but by my relation to the mass of feeling & opinion out of doors, in concert with which I have worked all along, & which would have been utterly bewildered by my not voting' (Gladstone to Granville, 12 Apr. 1878, Ramm, i. 70–1).

[26] Casa Laiglesia to Silvela, London, 11 Apr. 1878, SFM, no. 203; Burne to Lytton, 12 Apr. 1878, India Office, Lytton Pap., E 218/517/5; *Hansard*, 8 Apr. 1878, 3rd ser. 239, 760–853; Northcote to Queen Victoria, 8 Apr. 1878, RA B29/73; Richmond to

Queen Victoria, 9 Apr. 1878, ibid., no. 74; Disraeli to Queen Victoria, 9 Apr. 1878, MB vi. 272; Granville to Gladstone, 9 Apr. 1878, Ramm, i. 69. Bylandt, the Netherland's minister, thought the speeches of both Derby and Granville were good, referring to the former's as an 'expression of the true patriotism of good sense'. Disraeli's speech is described as an 'expression of English Chauvinism' (Bylandt to Kell, 9 Apr. 1878, NA, no. 172). Malet, Hammond, and Halifax thought with most that Derby's speech was 'wrong' and 'indiscreet' (Malet to mother, 9 Apr. 1878, Malet Pap., bundle A; Halifax to Lady Wood, 11 Apr. 1878, Hickleton Pap.; Hammond to Layard, 10 Apr. 1878, Lay. Pap., Add. MS. 38956, xxvi). The queen thought Derby's speech was 'ungentlemanlike . . . indiscreet, & inaccurate'. As he had made very un-flattering remarks about Austria and France in his speech, the diplomatic corps in London was astonished and Beust and d'Harcourt presented official complaints about Derby's remarks (Queen's journal, 11 Apr. 1878, RA; Salisbury to Queen Victoria, 9 and 10 Apr. 1878, RA H21/67, 70; Richmond to Queen Victoria, 10 Apr. 1878, ibid., no. 71). The usual Continental complaint about British indiscretion was the informa-tion given to Parliament in blue books containing reports of diplomatic negotiations. Derby's remarks in his Parliamentary speech cast aspersions on the reliability of the Austrian army in a war in the Balkans due to the Slavic portions of her forces. As Gladstone habitually denounced Vienna in and out of Parliament, Derby had eloquent company.

²⁷ Salisbury to Elliot, teleg., 15 Apr. 1878, PRO FO 424/69, no. 337; Layard to Salisbury, secret, teleg., 14 Apr. 1878, ibid., no. 333; Same to same, teleg., 14 Apr. 1878, ibid., no. 332; same to same, secret, teleg., 14 Apr. 1878, ibid., no. 307; same to same, secret, teleg., 11 Apr. 1878, ibid., no. 266; same to same, teleg., 9 Apr. 1878, ibid., no. 206; Elliot to Salisbury, secret, teleg., 3 Apr. 1878, ibid., no. 74; Bülow to Reuss, teleg., 11 Apr. 1878, GP ii. no. 434; Layard to Salisbury, most secret, 8 Apr. 1878, PRO FO 78/2784, no. 459; same to same, most secret, teleg., 6.30 p.m., 7 Apr. 1878, ibid., 2812, no. 357.

²⁸ In an interesting and revealing debate in the Commons on 22 March to consider extending or altering the Declaration of Paris of 1856 on maritime rights, Harcourt made reference to the probability of Russia, should war occur, using U.S. ships as privateers against British commerce. Most speakers in the debate assumed that Britain generally was more likely to be neutral than a belligerent in future European wars, and that giving up the right of blockade, some argued, in the interest of making private property at sea free from capture could only benefit Britain as she had more ships and goods at sea than anyone else (Hansard, 22 Mar. 1878, 3rd ser. 238, 1842–1909).

²⁹ Salisbury to Russell, confid., teleg., 17 Apr. 1878, PRO FO 424/69, no. 370; Bismarck to Schweinitz, teleg., 16 Apr. 1878, GP ii. no. 394; Münster to Bismarck, very confid., 15 Apr. 1878, ibid., no. 392; Münster to Bülow, teleg., 15 Apr. 1878, ibid., no. 391; Münster to Bismarck, very confid., 14 Apr. 1878, ibid., no. 390; Bismarck to Münster, teleg., 14 Apr. 1878, ibid., no. 389; Schweinitz to Bismarck, teleg., St. Petersburg, 14 Apr. 1878, ibid., no. 388; same to same, teleg., 13 Apr. 1878, ibid., nos. 387, 385; Lytton to Temple, very secret, 12 Apr. 1878, India Office, Temple Pap., F86/15; Disraeli to Queen Victoria, 12 Apr. 1878, RA B57/45; same to same, 12 Apr. 1878, MB vi. 285–6; Salisbury to Russell, secret, teleg., 13 Apr. 1878, PRO FO 424/69, no. 295; Salisbury to Queen Victoria, 12 Apr. 1878, QVL ii. 614–15; Münster to Bülow, teleg., 12 Apr. 1878, GP ii. no. 386. When Loftus informed London of Russia's intention to purchase U.S. steamers to prey upon British commerce, a circular was ad-dressed to all British consuls in the U.S.A. to be on watch for any such transactions (circular to H.M. consuls in the U.S., 5 Apr. 1878, enclosed in Thornton to Salisbury, Washington, confid., 8 Apr. 1878, PRO FO 424/69, no. 419). Salisbury kept the Queen fully informed of the withdrawal negotiations (Salisbury to Queen Victoria, 13, 15, and 16 Apr. 1878, RA H21/74, 78, and 79).

³⁰ Salisbury to Queen Victoria, 20 Apr. 1878, RA H21/85; Elliot to Salisbury, 18

Apr. 1878, Salis. Pap., A/4/2; Andrássy to Beust, secret, 14 Apr. 1878, communicated to Salisbury on 19 Apr., PRO FO 244/315, Cabinet confid. print, no. 3580; Andrássy to Beust, teleg., 18 Apr. 1878, ibid.; Salisbury to Loftus, 17 Apr. 1878, Salis. Pap., A/31/2; Salisbury to Russell, 17 Apr. 1878, Salis. Pap., A/27/4; Salisbury to Russell, teleg., 11.45 a.m., 20 Apr. 1878, PRO FO 424/69, no. 432; Schweinitz to Bismarck, St. Petersburg, teleg., 17 Apr. 1878, GP ii. no. 395; Salisbury to Elliot, 16 Apr. 1878, PRO FO 7/923, no. 260; ibid. 424/69 no. 390; Salisbury to Queen Victoria, 17 Apr. 1878, RA H21/80; Andrássy to Beust, 14 Apr. 1878, communicated to Salisbury 17 Apr. 1878, PRO FO 244/315; Salisbury to Elliot, 16 Apr. 1878, PRO FO 424/69 no. 359; Salisbury to Russell, teleg., 25 Apr. 1878, ibid., no. 540; same to same, 25 Apr. 1878, ibid., no. 530; Salisbury to Russell, 26 Apr. 1878, Salis. Pap., A/27/7; Salisbury to Disraeli, 25 Apr. 1878, Disraeli Pap. xx/Ce/235; Münster to Bismarck, 20 Apr. 1878, GD i. 92–5. Argyll was alarmed and angered at news of Indian troops coming into the Mediterranean, regarding it as the latest 'trick of the great trickster [Disraeli]'. He was right in thinking that it would 'be cheered by the idiots who like anything which is called a spirited policy' (Argyll to Grey, 17 Apr. 1878, Grey Pap.). Most of the Conservative Press applauded the move. The Times and most opposition journals complained that Parliament 'had not been taken into the confidence of the Government' (Wirthwein, pp. 372–4). On Bright's speech at Rochdale on 19 April and Gladstone's in London on 18 April see Ollier, ii. 149. Derby referred to 'the tone of reckless rowdyism among what ought to be the educated classes' (Derby to Grote, 19 Apr. 1878, Grote Pap., Add. MS. 46691). Hartington thought the India expedition of 7,000 men 'rather audacious' (Hartington to Granville, 20 Apr. 1878, Gran. Pap., PRO 30/29/22a). Münster thought that the reason for the dispatch of Indian troops was 'political rather than military; and . . . calculated to produce a deep impression on India' (Münster to Bismarck, 20 Apr. 1878, GD i. 93–4).

³¹ Salisbury to Queen Victoria, 24 Apr. 1878, RA H21/88; Salisbury to Northcote, 28 Apr. 1878, Salis. Pap., D/XIV/147; Elliot to Salisbury, Vienna, teleg., 23 Apr. 1878, PRO FO 424/69, no. 496; Salisbury to Elliot, 25 Apr. 1878, PRO FO 7/923, no. 280; Elliot to Salisbury, 24 Apr. 1878, Salis. Pap., A/4/3; Andrässy to Beust, 21 Apr. 1878, GP ii. no. 400; Malet to mother, 26 Apr. 1878, Malet Pap., bundle A; Elliot to Salisbury, teleg., 23 Apr. 1878, PRO FO 424/69, no. 503; Salisbury to Layard, secret, teleg., 23 Apr. 1878, ibid., no. 500; Salisbury to Layard, secret, 23 Apr. 1878, PRO FO 195/1168, no. 516; Layard to Salisbury, secret, teleg., 22 Apr. 1878, PRO FO 78/2810, no. 391; Smith to Hornby, private and confid., 20 Apr. 1878, Hornby Pap., PHI/118B; same to same, 20 Apr. 1878, Hambleden Pap., P36/83; Queen's journal, 18 Apr. 1878, RA. On 17 April Wellesley had an audience with Alexander II and came away from it with the impression 'that the Emperor is sincerely anxious for the maintenance of peace' (Wellesley to Loftus, St. Petersburg, 17 Apr. 1878, enclosed in Loftus to Salisbury, secret, 17 Apr. 1878, PRO FO 424/69, no. 620). Part of Salisbury's difficulty in assessing the diplomatic terrain was Odo Russell's inability to accurately gauge Bismarck's intentions. For this see Russell to Salisbury, secret, 22 Apr. 1878, PRO FO 64/904, no. 282. For the impasse in Anglo-Austrian negotiations see Elliot to Salisbury, PRO FO 244/315, nos. 117–18 of 27 Apr. 1878 and telegs., Salisbury to Elliot, 29 Apr. 1878, ibid.

³² For Austro-Russian negotiations and their failure during April see Mackenzie, pp. 272–7, and Bülow to H. Bismarck, 7 May 1878, GP ii. no. 104.

³³ Apart from remaining resolute, Salisbury felt it was necessary to 'show no inclination to inflict any gratuitous humiliation upon Russia' (Salisbury to Cross, 30 Apr. 1878, Cecil, ii. 253–4).

³⁴ In his memoirs Layard would take credit for having influenced the Grand Duke from entering and occupying Constantinople. 'I have little doubt that reports of my resolve [to call the fleet to the Golden Horn without orders from London should the Russians advance on the city] had reached Russian headquarters' (Lay. Mem., 29 Apr. 1878).

[35] Salisbury to Queen Victoria, 1 May 1878, RA H22/1; same to same, 29 Apr. 1878, RA H21/96; Münster to Bülow, 29 Apr. 1878, *GD* i. 95; Queen's journal, 28 Apr. 1878, RA. When asked by Shuvalov for the 'English view', Salisbury avoided any positive recommendations and gave only six objects: Russian preponderance in Asia to be diminished, 'securing English rights of blockade, removing the Slav state from the sea, securing greater independence for Turkey, keeping the Greek race from absorption, putting the indemnity into a shape in which it cannot take the form of territorial annexation' (Salisbury to Queen Victoria, 1 May 1878, RA H22/1). For the absence of direction and the situation in St. Petersburg see Jomini to Onou, 29 Apr. 1878, Jomini–Onou Pap., Eg. 3211, fos. 74–5. According to Shuvalov, Salisbury had requested Russia to indicate which parts of San Stefano she would insist upon. 'You are joking my dear Marquis [Shuvalov replied] in making such a proposal. You know what we want since you have the treaty in your hands. It is for you to say what you do not want. . . . One can't demand of us indiscreet confessions, or to annul our work by abjuring it ourselves. . . . It is for you, then, to formulate your *sine qua non* and for us to examine it and reply' (Shuvalov to Gorchakov, 30 Apr. 1878, Seton-Watson, pp. 411–12). Surprisingly, during all the earlier negotiations for military withdrawal Salisbury had not consulted the advice of General Dickson and Admiral Hornby, both at Constantinople. Only when the Queen, suspicious of Russian intentions, suggested such a step did Salisbury telegraph Constantinople and receive back a reply that no military advantage would be sacrificed by the contemplated withdrawal (Salisbury to Layard, secret, teleg., 5 a.m., 1 May 1878, PRO FO 424/70, no. 10; Layard to Salisbury, teleg., 3 May 1878, ibid., no. 90).

[36] Disraeli to Queen Victoria, 7 May 1878, Disraeli Pap. XIX/C/544; same to same, 7 May 1878, RA B57/59; Salisbury to Queen Victoria, 6 May 1878, RA H22/16; same to same, 5 May 1878, *QVL* ii. 617–18; Cabinet memorandum, 3 May 1878, Foreign Office library, confid., print, 3596; Salisbury to Russell, 4 May 1878, Salis. Pap., A/27/10; Münster to Bülow, 2 May 1878, *GD* i. 96; Sumner, pp. 481–5; Seton-Watson, p. 412. On the Cabinet meeting called to consider the memorandum of British conditions given to Shuvalov, Hardy expressed satisfaction with Salisbury's departure from secrecy. 'I am not sorry to hear of a cabinet for I was sadly afraid of errors of ignorance. We are hardly kept sufficiently well instructed' (Hardy to Cross, 2 May 1878, Cross Pap., Add. MS. 51267, v).

[37] Layard to Salisbury, 1 May 1878, Lay. Pap., Add. MS. 39131; same to same, 17 Apr. 1878, ibid.; Salisbury to Layard, 2 May 1878, Salis. Pap., A/32/4; Salisbury to Elliot, 4 May 1878, ibid. 23/7; Salisbury to Queen Victoria, 4 May 1878, RA H22/2. Salisbury's advice to the Porte was to avoid giving Russia any pretexts for military action. At the same time Britain attempted to end the insurrection in Thessaly and bring about a Greco-Ottoman accommodation. To bring slight pressure on Vienna for an agreement, Salisbury telegraphed the following to Elliot. 'If Count Andrássy should renew his question about assistance in raising a loan from here, say that the [British] Government . . . [could only offer] a guarantee [for a loan] . . . which . . . is never offered by Parliament except to allies who are in arms on our side' (Salisbury to Elliot, secret, teleg., 6 May 1878, PRO FO 424/70, no. 152). For Anglo-Austrian negotiations see the following: Andrássy to Beust, 29 Apr. 1878, communicated to Salisbury on 3 May, PRO FO 244/315, no. 1; same to same, 1 May 1878, ibid., no. 2; Elliot to Salisbury, teleg., 2 May 1878, ibid.; Salisbury to Elliot, 4 May 1878, enclosed in Salisbury to Lyons, 11 May 1878, PRO FO 146/2031, no. 313. In the foregoing letter to Elliot, the ambassador was instructed to read the dispatch to Andrássy, and, if requested, to leave him a copy of it. In an effort to induce Andrássy to agree with England upon a southern boundary for Bulgaria, Salisbury indicated that Britain was willing to consider with Austria other boundaries than the Balkan Mountains. Andrássy had been putting England off with the excuse that he could not agree to the Balkan Mountains as Bulgaria's southern border because he had agreed to another

boundary in his previous negotiations with Ignatiev.

[38] Thompson, ii. 427–9; Wirthwein, pp. 376–80; S. Maccoby, *English Radicalism, 1853–1886* (London, 1938), p. 232; Seton-Watson, pp. 391–3; Ollier, ii. 162–5. Both Anglican and Nonconformist clergy made protests in the Press and through petitions against what seemed like the Government's intention to go to war. One such Nonconformist effort elicited a newspaper petition signed by more than 200,000 people during the month of May (ibid.).

[39] Hartington to Gladstone, 9 May 1878, Glad. Pap., Add. MS. 44144, LVIX; Childers to Clarke, 10 May 1878, Childers, i. 253–4; *Hansard*, 9 May 1878, 3rd ser. 239, 1592; Hartington to Harcourt, 8 May 1878, Harcourt Pap.; Gladstone to Hartington, 8 May 1878, Hart Pap. 340/756; Northcote to Disraeli, 8 May 1878, Disraeli Pap. xx/N/76; Northcote to Hartington, confid., 7 May 1878, Hart. Pap. 340/755; Hartington to Granville, 6 May 1878, Gran. Pap., PRO 30 29/26a; Hammond to Layard, 2 May 1878, Lay. Pap., Add. MS. 38956, xxvi; *Hansard*, 6 May 1878, 3rd ser. 239, 1420–49; Northcote to Queen Victoria, 6 May 1878, RA B29/88. Gladstone had not been quiet. On 3 May at a conference at Liverpool letters were read from him and Bright. Gladstone pleaded for peace and pointed out that 'we [Britain] are not united, but a divided people. . . . It is then high time for you to bestir yourselves . . . to control the Government' (Thompson, ii. 418–19). On 8 May Gladstone received a deputation at Hawarden whom he addressed. He questioned the desirability of the Indian expedition (Ollier, ii. 166–7). For a discussion of the Liberal plan to criticize the Indian expedition on constitutional grounds see Harcourt to Selborne, 10 May 1878, Selborne Pap., MS. 1866. On May 13 a debate on the expedition to Malta resulted in a division which gave the Government a majority of 111 to 19. On 20, 21, 23, and 27 May there would be lengthy Parliamentary debates on the expedition from India, the Liberals arguing that such an act was unconstitutional 'because previous Parliamentary consent was necessary for any forces in addition to those voted for the year and mentioned in the Mutiny Act to be employed in peacetime except in India whether they were Indian troops or not' (Ollier, ii. 167–77).

# CHAPTER TWENTY-ONE

[1] Layard to Salisbury, teleg., 6 p.m., 10 May 1878, PRO FO 78/2819; Bismarck to Bülow, teleg., 10 May 1878, *GP* ii. no. 406; Stolberg to Bülow, teleg., 9 May 1878, *GP* ii, no. 405. Andrássy naturally wished to know what proposals Shuvalov was taking to Russia. Salisbury, upon being questioned by Beust, replied, with less than complete sincerity, that Austria was familiar already with the British 'propositions—the line of the Balkans, & a reduction in the duration of the Russian occupation, & that these were rather communicated as suggestions than as proposals' (Salisbury to Queen Victoria, 10 May 1878, RA H22/11). While Shuvalov was in Berlin Bismarck told him to inform his Government that an understanding with Austria would be more useful for Germany than one with British (Bismarck to Stolberg, teleg., 21 May 1878, *GP* ii, no. 410). This is borne out by what Shuvalov told Salisbury of his interview with Bismarck (Sandon Cabinet journal, 24 May 1878, C. Howard and P. Gordon (eds.), supplement no. 10 of the *Bulletin of the Institute of Historical Research*; hereafter cited as HG).

[2] Salisbury and the Cabinet were not prepared to accept completely official Russian explanations. Salisbury sent out the following telegram for naval additions. 'Ascertain, confidentially, whether Chinese Government are disposed to sell to Her Majesty's Government the four gun-vessels built in England for them, which left this country for China in the years 1876 and 1877' (Salisbury to Fraser, secret, teleg., 17 May. 1878,

PRO FO 424/70, no. 439). The Chinese declined to sell but promised to give Britain the right of first refusal should they decide to do so (Fraser to Salisbury, secret, teleg., Peking, 27 May 1878, ibid. 71, no. 31). There would soon be further Anglo-Russian tension over Central Asia as a result of Russian activity there. Though Lytton had been unable in 1877–8 to convince Sher Ali to receive a temporary British mission at Kabul, he hesitated to push the Afghan leader too hard lest he shove him into the hands of Russia. When a Russo-British war seemed likely between January and May 1878, Russian authorities in Central Asia made military and political preparations to cause London trouble there should it become desirable to do so. Britain learned at the beginning of July of the sending of a Russian mission which was received at Kabul. London then supported Lytton in demanding that Sher Ali receive a British mission, which the latter refused to do. In September 1878 the viceroy ordered a British force into Afghanistan which led to the Second Afghan War of 1878–9.

³ Though Sandon, a new addition to the Cabinet, thought that the giving way to Russia was a throwing over of Austria, Salisbury put a good face on it for Queen Victoria who was pro-Austrian. 'I caused all our previous communications with Austria to be carefully examined in order to ascertain whether the assurance asked of us by Russia was in any degree inconsistent with our language with Austria, & I satisfied myself that in that respect we were perfectly free' (Salisbury to Queen Victoria, 17 May 1878, RA H22/12; Sandon Cabinet journal, 15 May 1878, HG).

⁴ Elliot to Salisbury, secret, 16 May 1878, PRO FO 7/931, no. 398; same to same, 16 May 1878, Foreign Office library, no. 3614; Salisbury to Queen Victoria, teleg., 6 p.m., 15 May 1878, RA H22/15; Sandon Cabinet journal, 15 May 1878, HG; Loftus to Salisbury, teleg., 14 May 1878, PRO FO 424/70, no. 235; Schweinitz to Bülow, St. Petersburg, 19 May 1878, GP ii, no. 407. Layard had been supporting Austria's attempt with the Porte to gain its acquiescence to an Austrian 'occupation' of Bosnia. Zichy, the Austrian ambassador at Constantinople, reported to Andrássy of Layard's loyalty (Layard to Salisbury, most confid., 17 May 1878, PRO FO 78/2788, no. 634; Zichy to Andrássy, teleg., 16 May 1878, HHSA, PA xii/127).

⁵ Sandon Cabinet journal, 18 May 1878, HG; Salisbury to Layard, 19 May 1878, PRO FO 195/1168, no. 632; Lay. Mem., 18 May 1878; Layard to Salisbury, secret, teleg., 18 May 1878, PRO FO 78/2811, no. 483; Hornby to wife, 17 May 1878 (F. Egerton, Sir Geoffrey Phipps Hornby, Endinburgh, 1896, p. 271); Salisbury to Smith, 16 May 1878, Hambleden Pap., PS 6/108; Salisbury to Layard, secret, 16 May 1878, Salis. Pap., A/32/6; Sandon Cabinet journal, 11 May 1878, HG. Jomini thought that Britain's readiness to reach an agreement with Russia and avoid war was due to the Parliamentary disapproval of the Indian expedition and the industrial depression existing throughout the country (Jomini to Onou, 20 May 1878, Jomini–Onou Pap., Eg. 3211, fos. 76–8). Onou attempted to reassure Layard that the forward movement of Russian troops did not indicate 'the slightest intention on the part of Todleben to attack Constantinople or to advance upon the Bosphorus' (Layard to Hornby, 18 May 1878, Lay. Pap., Add. MS. 39131). It is possible that the forward move by Todleben was designed by Russia to pressure the Porte to evacuate Shumla, Varna, and Batum. On 28 May Lobanov, the new Russian ambassador, informed the Porte that if it would give Varna and Shumla to Russia, the latter's army would be withdrawn from the vicinity of Constantinople (Layard to Salisbury, teleg., 28 May 1878, PRO FO 424/70, no. 681).

⁶ Shuvalov told Loftus in St. Petersburg that before he left London he had discussed with Salisbury a formula by which a congress might be called. 'The difficulty with regard to the "submission" of the Treaty of San Stefano is to be turned by a guarantee to be expressed in the invitation by Bismarck that there shall be a full and free discussion of the treaty. This formula Shuvalov tells me [Loftus] was known to Ld. Salisbury before he left and was said to be acceptable. This is a profound secret' (Loftus to Russell, St. Petersburg, 22 May 1878, Odo Russell Pap., PRO).

[7] Salisbury to Queen Victoria, 22 May 1878, RA H22/23; same to same, 22 May 1878, *QVL* ii. 620–1; Salisbury to Russell, 22 May 1878, Salis. Pap., A/27/13; Salisbury to Elliot, 22 May 1878, ibid., A/23/10; Bülow to Stolberg, 22 May 1878, *GP* ii, no. 412; Stolberg to Bismarck, teleg., 21 May 1878, ibid., no. 411; Bismarck to Stolberg, 21 May 1878, ibid., no. 411; Bismarck to Stolberg, 21 May 1878, ibid., nos. 409–10; Bülow to Bismarck, 20 May 1878, ibid., no. 408; Schweinitz to Bülow, 19 May 1878, ibid., no. 407.

[8] Sandon Cabinet journal, 22 May 1878, HG; Vivian to Salisbury, Alexandria, 11 May 1878, Salis. Pap., A/6/2; Lyons to Salisbury, confid., 22 May 1878, PRO FO 26/2309, no. 430; same to same, secret and confid., 14 May 1878, ibid., no. 412. In an attempt to use the Greeks against the Slavs, London had intervened and tried to mediate between Turkey and Greece in order to end insurrection and unrest in Thessaly and Crete. Further, Salisbury asked Layard whether the Porte might agree to a cession of some of Thessaly and Epirus to Greece for the purpose of creating a common Ottoman-Greek front against the Slavs. The ambassador favoured such an alliance, though he did little to hide his anti-Greek feelings.

[9] Münster to Bismarck, London, teleg., 23 May 1878, *GP* ii, no. 414; Disraeli to Queen Victoria, secret, 23 May 1878, RA B57/64; Salisbury to Queen Victoria, teleg., 23 May 1878, *QVL* ii. 621–2; Sandon Cabinet journal, 24 May 1878, HG; Wylde to Layard, 23 May 1878, Lay. Pap., Add. MS. 39020, xc; Sumner, pp. 487–91; Salisbury to Loftus, 23 May 1878, PRO FO 244/315, no. 332 and enclosures. Andrássy like Beaconsfield objected to the Russian prohibition against any Turkish troops in the southern portion of Bulgaria. The Austrian minister, while accepting the invitation to the congress, asked Bismarck to delay its opening so that Austria might obtain 'a more advantageous position *vis-à-vis* Russia'—which presumably was intended by him to allow for the necessary time to conclude agreement with London as well as one with Turkey which would give Vienna Bosnia-Hercegovina (Stolberg to Bülow, secret, Vienna, teleg., 23 May 1878, *GP* ii, no. 413). Andrássy further wished a short delay in order to arrange for an appropriation from the legislature so that, if necessary, at the congress she could threaten to send her army into Novibazar as well as Bosnia generally (same to same, confid., 25 May 1878, ibid., no. 418).

[10] Layard was instructed that his communications on the convention with Turkey were to go to Salisbury personally and not to the Foreign Office, a procedure of questionable value but characteristic of Salisbury. A small group composed of his private secretary and a few others closely attached to him shielded the negotiation from the staff at the Foreign Office, which deeply resented this new system (Lay. Mem., night of 24–5 May 1878). Cowley, the retired veteran diplomat, confirmed the existence of the new system. 'The change in the F. O. has brought with it, I hear, a complete change of system. Lord S. does everything himself, tells nothing to his undersecretaries, in short consults nobody. Cyphers even are concocted in his own room. We shall see the result' (Cowley to Layard, 29 May 1878, Lay. Pap., Add. MS. 39020, xc). Balfour incorrectly suggests that Salisbury initiated this new departure only after and as a result of Marvin's leak of the Anglo-Russian agreement of 30 May to *The Globe* (A. J. Balfour, *Retrospect*, N.Y., 1930, p. 109). The change came well before 30 May and it obviously did not affect all Foreign Office business, most of which continued to be handled in the old way, but only a few vital negotiations.

[11] Lay. Mem., 24–5 May 1878; Salisbury to Layard, personal and most confid., teleg., 24 May 1878, Lay. Pap., Add. MS. 39137, ccvii; Salisbury to Queen Victoria, 24 May 1878, RA H22/35; Salisbury to Elliot, 24 May 1878, PRO FO 244/315, no. 348; Salisbury to Queen Victoria, teleg., 7.15 p.m., 24 May 1878, *QVL* ii. 622–3; Salisbury to Loftus, 24 May 1878, PRO FO 244/315, no. 334; Salisbury to Layard, personal and most secret, teleg., 25 May 1878, Lay. Pap., Add. MS. 39137, ccvii. Salisbury felt that Russian insistence upon no Ottoman troops in southern Bulgaria was for the sake of domestic opinion. 'It is more apparently for the purpose of boasting to the Russian

people that he [Tsar] has attained the emancipation of the Bulgarians, than with any great solicitude as to the practical working of the institutions proposed, that the Emperor insists so strongly on the withdrawal of the Turkish troops in principle' (Salisbury to Queen Victoria, 24 May 1878, RA H22/35). Shuvalov had indicated to Salisbury that if the principle of excluding Ottoman troops from southern Bulgaria were granted, 'any number of exceptions' to it could be raised in congress (ibid.; Sandon Cabinet journal, 25 May 1878, HG).

[12] Ibid.

[13] Salisbury to Elliot, most secret, teleg., 27 May 1878, PRO FO 244/315; Herbert Bismarck to Bülow, Friedrichsruh, 25 May 1878, GP ii, no. 415; Münster to Bülow, very confid., 25 May 1878, ibid., no. 417, GD i. 96–7; Salisbury to Russell, 25 May 1878, PRO FO 244/315, no. 294; Salisbury to Queen Victoria, 25 May 1878, RA H22/36.

[14] Layard to Salisbury, most secret and confid., 27 May 1878, PRO FO 78/2789, no. 692; Salisbury to Layard, teleg., 27 May 1878, Lay. Pap., Add. MS. 39020, XC; Lay. Mem., 25 and 26 May 1878; Layard to Salisbury, most confid., teleg., 26 May 1878, Salis. Pap., A/3/3; Layard to Salisbury, personal and secret, teleg., 7.30 p.m., 25 May 1878, PRO FO 78/2820, no. 506; Queen's journal, 8 May 1878, RA; Disraeli to Queen Victoria, 5 May 1878, MB vi. 291. The agreement provided that if Batum, Ardahan, or Kars were retained by Russia, and if the latter made any attempt to obtain Ottoman territory to be fixed by the final treaty, England engaged to support the Sultan militarily against such an attempt. The Sultan in return gave the traditional promise to reform—specific provisions for which were to be decided later—and assigned Cyprus to be occupied and administered by Britain. Though he had not mentioned Cyprus, Salisbury had warned Shuvalov of the necessity for Britain to take steps to secure Asiatic Turkey. The Foreign Secretary also gave the plan for an Asian protectorate to *The Times* 'to prepare opinion in this direction'. *The Times* did so in articles on 25 and 27 May (Sandon Cabinet journal, 27 May 1878, HG).

[15] Anglo-Russian memoranda, 29 May 1878, PRO FO 244/315; Münster to Bülow, 29 May 1878, GP ii, no. 423; Salisbury to Loftus, 29 May 1878, Salis. Pap., A/31/5; Salisbury to Russell, 29 May 1878, ibid. 27/14; Salisbury to Layard, secret, 29 May 1878, PRO FO 195/1168, no. 659; Salisbury to Loftus, 28 May 1878, PRO FO 244/315, no. 341; Sandon Cabinet journal, 29 May 1878, HG; Münster to Bismarck, teleg., 28 May 1878, GP ii, no. 421; Münster to Bülow, teleg., 28 May 1878, ibid., no. 420; Münster to Bismarck, 27 May 1878, ibid., no. 419, GD i. 97; Seton-Watson, pp. 416–17; Queen's journal, 27 May 1878, RA; Disraeli to Queen Victoria, 26 May 1878, RA B57/65; same to same, 26 May 1878, MB vi. 294–5. Salisbury, worried by both the possibility of an incident at Constantinople and the growing instability of the Sultan, suggested to Layard that it might help the Sultan if he had some trusted western officer on whom he could depend. He mentioned the name of a British officer in Ottoman service, Baker Pasha, who might be attached to the person of the Sultan 'with a small Varangian guard' (Salisbury to Layard, 30 May 1878, Salis. Pap., A/32/7).

[16] Salisbury explained to the Queen that the Cabinet felt it could not refuse the congress on this point, especially as it was in southern Bulgaria where the atrocities had occurred, and to do so would be to court Parliamentary defeat. 'All those who know the House of Commons as it is were certain that a defeat would have been the result. But in Congress there is good hope that sufficient precautions will be taken, by admitting the Ottoman troops to guard the passes of the Balkans' (Salisbury to Queen Victoria, 31 May 1878, RA H22/50).

[17] Anglo-Russian memorandums, 29 May 1878, PRO FO 244/315; Sumner, pp. 493–5. The second memorandum reserved Britain's liberty of action on six points: European rather than merely Russian participation in the administrative organization of Bulgaria, the duration and manner of Russian occupation of Bulgaria and of her passage through Romania, the name to be given to southern Bulgaria, the navigation

of the Danube, all questions touching on the Straits, and the rights of non-Slavic monks on Mount Athos. A third document was signed on 31 May by which Russia promised not to extend her conquests in Asia beyond those stipulated in the San Stefano Treaty as modified by the retrocession of the Alashkert Valley. Salisbury appealed for Bismarck's support for the Sultan's right to station Ottoman troops on the borders of the southern Bulgarian province (Münster to Bismarck, 2 June 1878, *GP* ii, no. 427).

[18] In order to save the congress Shuvalov was ardently pressing, without success, for St. Petersburg to agree to withdrawing its forces before the congress would meet. Münster thought that the acceptance of the congress by the Cabinet in the face of the Russian refusal of a military withdrawal was obvious proof that Britain did not desire war and was being more accommodating than 'Count Shuvalov and I could assume'. Salisbury informed the German ambassador that if the Tsar did not yield, he would bring up the question 'at the beginning of the Congress and count upon the support of the other powers and Your Excellency [Bismarck]' (Münster to Bismarck, 2 June 1878, *GP* ii, no. 426). Apparently Salisbury implied to Münster that he had given way to Russia out of 'consideration for Count Schuvalov and the desire to see him step to the head of the Foreign Office in St. Petersburg' (Münster to Bismarck, 2 June 1878, ibid., no. 427). Münster further explained on the tenth that 'Lord Salisbury told me he is departing from his earlier declaration … only because he feels that everything depends above all on Count Shuvalov retaining his influence in St. Petersburg, and this threatens to be lost, if the negotiations over the meeting of the Congress are protracted and Shuvalov's trip to and presence in St. Petersburg delayed any longer' (Münster to Bismarck, 10 June 1878, *GP* ii, no. 431).

[19] Sandon Cabinet journal, 1 June 1878, HG; Hardy diary, 2 June 1878, Hardy, ii. 71; Disraeli to Queen Victoria, 1 June 1878, RA B57/75; Münster to Bismarck, 2 June 1878, *GP* ii, nos. 426–7; Münster to Bülow, teleg., 1 June 1878, ibid., no. 425; Bülow to Bismarck, 1 June 1878, ibid., no. 424; Salisbury to Queen Victoria, 31 May 1878, RA H22/50. Not surprisingly, Vienna was very concerned about the content of the Anglo-Russian agreement (Elliot to Salisbury, Vienna, 2 June 1878, PRO FO 7/932, no. 448). Salisbury explained to the Queen that the Cabinet's acceptance of a congress before Russia had agreed to military withdrawal from Constantinople was in part due to a promise of Shuvalov's, the ambassador again returning home to St. Petersburg, 'that he would do his utmost to procure the withdrawal' while in Russia. The Cabinet also informed Berlin that if withdrawal had not occurred before the congress 'England would raise it as the first question before any other business was discussed' (Salisbury to Queen Victoria, teleg., 6.17 p.m., 3 June 1878, RA H22/57).

[20] Münster to Bülow, 27 May 1878, GFM, A 3205; Northcote to Queen Victoria, 20, 21, and 24 May 1878, RA B29/100, 104; *Hansard*, 20–1 May 1878, 3rd ser. 237, 187–253, 264–348, 362–438; ibid., 23 May 1878, 237, 499–610; Knightley, *Journals*, 20 May 1878, pp. 323–4; Goschen diary, 20 and 23 May 1878, Elliot, i. 190–2; Brand diary, 20 and 23 May 1878, Brand Pap.; Ollier, ii. 167–77; Mundella to Leader, 22 May 1878, Mundella Pap.; Wirthwein, pp. 380–1; Thompson, ii. 439–45. Halifax explained to Granville his objection to the use of Indian troops. 'If they were brought into action and were found wanting against the Russians, it wd. weaken our dependence on them, in the improbable event of a Russian invasion of India. If they did well it wd. probably make them bumptious in India' (Halifax to Granville, 26 May 1878, Gran. Pap., PRO 30 29/26a).

[21] Derby to Granville, 2 June 1878, Gran. Pap., PRO 30, 29/26a; Taffs, *Ambassador to Bismarck*, p. 232; *Hansard*, 3 June 1878, 3rd ser. 240, 1061; Salisbury to Elliot, secret, teleg., 1 June 1878, PRO FO 424/71, no. 22; Sandon Cabinet journal, 5 June 1878, HG; Salisbury to Layard, teleg., 31 May 1878, Lay. Pap., Add. MS. 39137, CCVII; Wirthwein, pp. 388–9; Chamberlain to Bunce, 28 May 1878, Chamberlain Pap., JC5/8/37; Reeve to Lytton, 28 May 1878, Lytton Pap., E 218/517/5, India Office;

Brand diary, 27 May 1878, Brand Pap.; Hansard, 27 May 1878, 3rd ser. 240, 747–812; ibid. 721–2; Northcote to Queen Victoria, 27 May 1878, RA B29/106. The agreement signed on 31 May as distinct from the two Anglo-Russian memorandums of 30 May did not appear in the *Globe* revelation which was printed on the evening of the thirtieth. Derby wrote of the Anglo-Russian agreement as a complete Russian victory and English capitulation, which could have been obtained 'without pressure or intimidation' (Derby to Granville, 2 June 1878, Gran. Pap., PRO 30 29/26a). Just after the Congress of Berlin opened the *Globe* published the full text of the Anglo-Russian agreement of 30 May and Salisbury was rightfully criticized for having misled the public on the authenticity of the journal's original report on 30 May.

²² The congress boded to be a geriatric disaster. Disraeli's bronchial difficulties and gout, Bismarck's shattered nervous system, and Gorchakov's ills, which caused Jomini as late as 3 June to assume his master's inability to go to Berlin, created the possibility of an uninvited plenipotentiary in the form of the grim reaper (Jomini to Onou, 3 June 1878, Jomini–Onou Pap., Eg. 3211, fos. 39–40).

²³ Northcote to Queen Victoria, 3 June 1878, RA B29/113; *Hansard*, 3 June 1878, 3rd ser. 240, 1055–60, 1076–86; Brand diary, 3 June 1878, Brand Pap.; Hammond to Layard, [?] June 1878, Lay. Pap., Add. MS. 38956, XXVI; Münster to Bülow, 3 June 1878, *GP* ii, no. 428, *GD* i. 97–8; Queen's journal, 1 June 1878, RA.

²⁴ Zichy to Andrássy, strictly secret and personal, teleg., 9 June 1878, HHSA, PA XII/128; Salisbury to Layard, most secret, 30 May 1878, PRO FO 244/315, no. 675. Salisbury's dispatch to Layard may have been composed with a view to its presentation to Parliament at the appropriate time. The Foreign Secretary assumed that moment would be when Russia made an absolute refusal at the congress to give up Batum, Ardahan, or Kars (Salisbury to Northcote, 6 June 1878, Northc. Pap., Add. MS. 50019, VII). It was further stipulated in the convention with the Porte that should Russia surrender that part of Armenia assigned to her by the Treaty of San Stefano, the convention would cease to be in effect and Cyprus would be evacuated by England.

²⁵ See p. 440.

²⁶ Salisbury to Elliot, Berlin, 12 June 1878, Salis. Pap., A/23/12; Ponsonby to Queen Victoria, 6 June 1878, RA H22/69–70; Salisbury to Elliot, 3 June 1878, Salis. Pap., 14/23/11. For Anglo-Austrian negotiations during April and May see Stojanovic, pp. 245–54, 260–2.

²⁷ Salisbury to Elliot, 3 June 1878, Salis. Pap., A/23/11.

²⁸ Sandon Cabinet journal, 5 June 1878, HG. At least part of Salisbury's desire to strengthen the Greeks by the addition of territory in Thessaly and Epirus was the hope that for such gains Athens would support Turkey against the Slavs.

²⁹ Stojanovic, p. 273.

³⁰ Grote to Layard, 10 June 1878, Lay. Pap., Add. MS. 39020, XC; Tenterden memorandum on Eastern Question and congress instructions, 7 June 1878, Foreign Office confid. print, Foreign Office library, 3638; Sandon Cabinet journal, 5 and 7 June 1878, HG.

# CHAPTER TWENTY-TWO

¹ Hertslet memorandum, 22 Apr. 1878, Foreign Office confidential print 3626, Foreign Office library.

² Salisbury wrote to Carnarvon of his conversation with Beaconsfield. 'I objected to this proposal [of the Prime Minister's to ask the Porte's consent to an English occupation of Gallipoli until the end of the Russo-Turkish war] very strongly—insisting that such a course would be in effect an alliance with Turkey . . . that even if she [Russia] did

reach Constantinople we could shell her out of it with ease; and that by deferring our action till Russia had manifested a resolution to attack Constantinople, we should run no risk, and should clear ourselves from the suspicion of using our military force to maintain the Turk in Bulgaria. I added that I doubted Russia's intention to attack Constantinople' (Salisbury to Carnarvon, 18 April 1877, Cecil, ii. 139–40).

³ Salisbury to Northcote, 15 Dec. 1877, Cecil, ii. 163–4.

# INDEX

Abdul Aziz, Sultan, 76, deposed, 101; 165
Abdul Hamid II, Sultan, appeals for British mediation, 336; suggests British alliance, 394
Afghanistan, 302, 505 n.13, 559 n.65, 597–8 n.2
Alexander II, Emperor, 31, 87, 146, 195, Moscow speech, 202; 298, talks with Wellesley, 306; 387, 531 n.38
Ali Pasha, 75, 78
Anderson, Dorothy, characterizes agitation, 242; 335
Andrássy, Count Julius, 3, 16, 18–19, on Serbians, 21; 23–4, 30, on Turkish integrity and Ignatiev, 31–2, 43; 37, 41–2, reform proposals, 44; 48, on pacification, 77, opposes rebel conditions, 79, 84; on Austrian frontiers, 80; opposes Montenegrin expansion, 81; Berlin meeting, 87ff; seeks British support for Berlin armistice, 96; on Berlin Memorandum, 98–9; presses Serbia from war, 108; 146–7, opposes Bosnian autonomy, 173; 199 opposes Russian military occupation, 204; on Balkan territorial change, 232; vetoes port for Montenegro, 260; presses Turkey on London Protocol, 262–3; refuses British protocol, 307; advises against British mediation, 344–5; refuses British alliance offer, 365–6; 372–3, 397, 412, 426, decides to treat with Britain, 434; 482 n.46, 496 n.33, 558 n.58, convention with Britain, 562 n.22; 567 n.56, negotiates with Disraeli, 586 n.40
Andrássy note, 44ff., execution of, 74
Anglo–Austrian Treaty, 447–8
Anglo–Russian memoranda, 441–3, 600–1 n.17
Argyll, Duke of, 130, 229, 240, advises Gladstone, 286; 525 n.73
Austria–Hungary, military–annexationist party, 16, 31; Croatia and Dalmatia, 13–18, 76, 80, 118–19; 22, 34, Andrássy note, 54–5; warns Serbia, 84; 107,

146, 265, secret negotiations with Britain, 282, 294–5; 562 n.22

Baring, Walter, sent to investigate atrocities, 144, 148–55; 157, 162, 514 n.7 and 8
Bashi–Bazouks, 24, 30, 38, 39ff., 125ff., 144, 152, 162–3, 265, 486 n.1
Batak, 152–3, 155–6, 157–8
Berlin Memorandum, 87ff., proposals of, 88; accepted by France and Italy, 92; 101
Beust, Count F., 48–9
Bismarck, Prince Otto von, 2, 3, offers understanding to Britain, 49; on Eastern Question, 61; seeks British entente, 61ff., 491–2 n.12; on Ottoman partition, 63–4, 72–3; on delaying Andrássy note, 66; repeats entente offer, 67; suspicion of, 69–72; offers exchange of ideas, 72–3; Berlin meeting, 87ff; asks Britain to support Andrássy, 99–100, 112, 534 n.16; desires to follow British lead, 115–16; contempt for Gorchakov, 146; approaches Britain, 249–50; anxiety over Britain, 262; on movement of fleet to Besika Bay, 305–6; his neutrality, 397; suggests Britain take Egypt, 399; attempts to mediate military withdrawal, 419–23; refuses sealing off of Austria–Hungary, 433; 439–40, 577 n.48, 560 n.2
Blake, Robert, 5, 121, 349, 499 n.20
Borthwick, Algernon, talks with Shuvalov, 202; 205
Bosnia, 16, 18, insurrection, 30, 480 n.21; twelve-day armistice, 78; 146, 229, Austria attempts to acquire, 422
Bourke, Robert, 8, 158–9, 164, 166–7, 518 n.3
Brand, Henry Bouverie, on Gladstone, 392
Bright, John, speech against Ottoman integrity, 132; 419–20, 430
Buchanan, Sir Andrew, 37, 160
Budapest Convention, 232–3, 566 n.48

Bulair lines, 311, 394–5, 399
Bulgaria, insurrection, 15, 124ff., 162; massacres, 123, 125ff; atrocities exaggerated, 140, 155 n.15 and 16; 146, myth of the atrocities, 161–3; estimates of killed, 162; 214, 226, 229
Bulgarian Peasant Relief Fund, 177
Bulwer, Sir Henry, 20
Butler–Johnstone, H. A. M., 59

Cabinet, of 16 May 1876 considers Berlin Memorandum, 94; on Derby's indecision, 105; of 4 October 1876, 191; of 19 November 1876 on Salisbury's instructions, 206; of 18 December 1876 on Belgian gendarmery, 216; opposes coercion of Turkey, 219–20, 231; of 13 March 1877 on Russian protocol, 256; 258, of 23 March 1877, 258–9; on London protocol, 259–60; of 21 April 1877, 275–6; orders fleet to Besika Bay, 277; disunity of, 279; on defending Constantinople, 283–4; 299, leaks, 300, 310, 333–4, 348–9; of 30 June 1877, 303; 307, of 14 July 1877, 308–10; 311, of 21 July 1877, 312–13; of 28 July 1877, 315; 320–2, of 5 October 1877, 325; 326, of 5 November 1877, 328; of 4 December 1877, 333; of 14 December 1877, 338–40; of 17–18 December 1877, 341–3, 349; of 2–3 January 1878, 352, 354–5; of 7 January 1878, 355; of 9 January 1878, 356; of 12 January 1878, 357–9; of 15–16 January 1878, 360–1; of 21 January 1878, 365; of 23 January 1878, 366–7; asks Parliament for money, 369; united, 372; of 7 February 1878, 380; of 8 February 1878 sends fleet to Constantinople, 382; of 11 February 1878, 388; of 21 February 1878 warns against occupation of Constantinople, 399, objects to Derby's dispatch, 400; of 7 March 1878 on a Mediterranean League, 405–6; of 27 March 1878, 412–13; reconstruction of, 415; of 11 May 1878, 434; of 24–5 May 1878, 437–8; accepts congress, 442–3; of 5–7 June 1878, 451; 566 n.49
Cairns, Earl, on Derby, 121, 186–7; on atrocities, 171; 206, 267, 275, on the Dardanelles, 278; cabinet mediation, 342; 532–3 n.1

Canning, George, 1
Carnarvon, Earl of, 8, 9, disgust with Turks, 170–1; 206, 219–20, concern for Christians, 258–9; believes Disraeli desires war, 276; criticizes Derby's offer to Austria, 283–5; opposes Turkish alliance, 340–1, 343; speech to deputation and conflict with Disraeli, 353–5; resignation, 360–1, 367, 369–70; 572 n.28, 575–6 n.42
Chamberlain, Joseph, invites Gladstone to speak, 286; 378, 419–20, 430
Chernaiev, General, 108
Churchill, Randolph, 583 n.20
Congress, 376, 379, 395–6, 404–5, British conditions for, 407–8, 411–12; Russian refusal of British conditions for, 408–9, 412; 415, 424, 435, 442–3, 598 n.6, 601 n.18 and 19
Constantinople Conference, 208ff., preliminary conference, 213ff.
Consular Commission, 19ff., 22–3
Corry, Montagu, 205
Cowen, Joseph, opposes agitation, 241; on agitation and Turkey, 385
Cross, Assheton, on atrocities, 171; replies to Gladstone, 288–9; 430
Currie, Philip, 208
Cyprus, 11, Convention, 600 n.14

Daily News, 129–30, 143, 332, 369
Davison, Roderic, 15
Decazes, Duc, 27, on Andrássy note, 47; suggests a congress, 103; on British fleet movement, 305; 490 n.54, 500 n.33
De La Warr, Earl, 377
Derby, fourteenth Earl of, 4, 5
Derby, fifteenth Earl of, 4, education, personality and career, 4ff; Luxemburg guarantee, 6; political views, 7; illness, 9; wife's political indiscretions, 7; 10, resignation, 11; on Ottoman Empire, 6, 8, 9; on insurrection in Bosnia, 18–19, 24; warns Serbia, 19; on consular commission, 19–20; on Ottoman bankruptcy, 27–8; 29–30, 34, on intervention within Ottoman Empire, 35; on Ottoman reform, 36, 112–13; 37, 41, 48, reaction to Andrássy note, 48–9, 51–7; on Bismarck, 49; on Ottoman integrity, 52, 105; 59, reply to Bismarck's entente offer, 65,

68–71; on Ottoman territorial *status quo,* 70; on territorial cession to Montenegro, 81; on collective warning to Porte, 82; urges neutrality on Montenegro, 85–6; reaction to Berlin Memorandum, 91–2, 97; refuses Berlin armistice, 96; tells Porte Britain can only offer moral support, 98; refuses French congress proposal, 103; attitude toward Turks, 105; on understanding with Russia, 113–15; on autonomy for Bosnia–Hercegovina, 114–15; on understanding with Germany, 116–17; suspiciousness, 117; feels mediation premature, 122–3; initial reaction to Bashi-Bazouks, 126; on atrocity reports, 130–1; requests atrocity information, 131–2, 134–5; on use of irregular troops, 132–4; replies to Disraeli's criticism, 138–9; replies to deputations, 139, 332–3; urges Porte to end atrocities, 141; instructs Dupuis to visit area of the atrocities, 141; reaction to Baring's report, 163–4; urges armistice on Porte, 165–6; fears a Russian war, 169; on atrocities agitation, 172–3; on peace conditions, 173; threatens the Porte, 174; receives two deputations 185–6; favours autonomy for Bosnia, 187, 198–201; effect of agitation on, 188; seizes the initiative, 190; opposes Disraeli and military preparations, 191–2; warning to Russia, 192–3; invites powers to Constantinople Conference, 198; warns the Porte, 202–3; opposes occupation of Ottoman Empire, 207; against coercion of Turkey, 218; on reduced terms for Turkey, 225; presses Turkey to avoid war, 227; asks Porte to accept reform, 247, 252; reaction to Russian protocol 254–6; requests Russian demobilization, 256–7; suspicious of Russia, 261–2; on Russian occupation of Constantinople, 264, 274; on occupation of Gallipoli, 275, 315; dispatch of 6 May 1877 on conditions for neutrality, 281; obstructs Austrian alliance offer, 282–3; defends inaction and policy, 319–20; objects to Disraeli's mediation attempt, 324; differs from Disraeli on proposal to Russia, 330–2; differs from Disraeli on

Constantinople, 333; objects to war for Constantinople, 338; warns Salisbury about Disraeli 347; nervous breakdown, 359–60, 575 n.40; opposes sending fleet inside Dardanelles, 360; resignation and return, 367, 370, 578–9 n.56; on sending fleet to Constantinople, 380–1; criticized, 386–7, 389, 401; warns Russia about moving upon Gallipoli, 391–3; unpopularity, 391–2, 404; suggests a conference, 395–6; on taking an Ottoman island, 400–1, 404; 409–10, resignation, 413–15; defends resignation in Parliament, 421; 452ff., 475 n.8 and 11, 476 n.18, on joining the Liberals, 477 n.26; speech in Parliament, 593–4 n.26

Derby, Countess of, 7, 10, 171, 197, 200, 203, 205, relationship with Shuvalov, 211; 213, 248, 253, 256, 298, 326, warned by the Queen, 348–50; 404, 410, 506 n.22, 544 n.53, 545 n.69, 577 n.51

Dilke, Sir Charles, 8, 178, opposes agitation, 241

Disraeli, Benjamin, 3, 5, 9–10, relationship with Derby, 4–5, 11, 52, 73, 90–1, 121–2; 16, 20, Guildhall speech, 29; on Andrássy note, 52–3, 488–9 n.41; 54, Empress of India controversy, 60; on German entente, 69, 71; becomes critical of Derby, 90, 192; health, 93; talks with Shuvalov on Berlin Memorandum, 93–4, 105; on Berlin armistice, 96; on a congress, 103–4; favours autonomy for Bosnia, 104–6; on the straits, 104; prestige and empire, 105–6; policy toward Germany and Russia, 106; on British influence, 108; on understanding with Russia, 109–10, 113–15; handling of Derby, 111–12, 168–9, 503 n.51; influence on policy, 121; on isolation, 123; on Bulgarian revolt and massacres, 131; Parliamentary answer on atrocities, 135–6; on atrocities exaggeration, 136–7, 141; explodes at Derby, 137–8, 158–9; defends Government on atrocities, 158–9; criticizes Elliot, 158–9; suggests Ottoman partition, 168, 247, 265–6, 274; reaction to

Disraeli (*contd.*)
  agitation, 168; speech at Aylesbury, 187–8; suggests occupation of Constantinople, 191; surveys Constantinople, 192; initiates talks with Austria, 199; suspicious of Russia, 200–1; Guildhall speech, 201–2; suggests a British occupation of Turkey, 209; opposes coercion of Turkey, 219; critical of Salisbury, 223; advises acceptance of conference proposals, 227; motives for action, 245; offers accord to Russia, 251–2; on Salisbury and Carnarvon, 258; on war and Ottoman integrity, 267–8; suggests occupation of Gallipoli, 274–5; reaction to Russian terms, 296; asks Queen to stir Derby, 297; personal diplomacy, 297; presses Austrian alliance, 298–9; asks for vote of credit, 299–300; proposes increase in Mediterranean garrisons, 307; sends secret warning to Tsar, 318; unwilling to ask for Derby's resignation, 319; relationship with Queen, 327; disagrees with Derby on proposal to Russia, 330–2; purchase of Ottoman territory, 332; differs with Derby on Constantinople 333; proposes to send fleet inside the Dardanelles and occupy Bulair, 357–8; critical of Derby, 359; proposes Austrian alliance, 365; 376, on Constantinople, 380; 453ff., 491 n.7, 511 n.34, negotiates with Andrássy, 586 n.40

Dupuis, Consul H., 24, 39–40, urges a consul at Philippopolis, 129; dispatch of 23 June 1876, 133; on Turkish barbarism, 140; reports atrocities exaggerated, 144; investigates atrocities, 148–54

Eastern Question, definition of, v, 1ff
Eastern Question Association, 236, 351, 369
Edinburgh, Duke of, 3
Elliot, Henry, 19, 20, on Ottoman integrity, 20–21, 35; on Andrássy, 21; on Austria, 22; 24–26, on Ottoman bankruptcy, 27; on Ottoman reform, 33; warning to Serbia, 33–4; 39, on control of Ottoman irregulars, 40–1; 42, 44, on Andrássy note, 46, 53, 57,

487–8 n.25; 59, on territory for Montenegro, 119; remonstrates on use of Bashi–Bazouks, 126–7; information on atrocities, 128–9; on use of irregulars, 131; 153, criticized, 159–61, 195–6; 210, 219–20, 270–1, 372, 519 n.15, removal of, 521–2 n.35; 536 n.40
Esher, Viscount, 7
Evans, Arthur, 13

Farley, Lewis, 141, 543 n.40
Forster, W. E., on Bulgarian atrocities; 131, talks with Ignatiev, 257; 373–4
France, on Andrássy note, 47; 60–1, on Berlin Memorandum and Britain, 97; 173, 265
Francis, Sir Philip, 133, 160
Francis–Joseph, Emperor, 16, 146, 563 n.23
Fraser, Bishop, 179
Freeman, Consul, 41
Freeman, E. A., 39, 59, urges Slavic independence, 142–3; 179, 181
Fullerton, Lady Georgianne, 237–8

Gallenga, J., 127–8, 133, 160
Gallipoli, 358–9, 393, 551 n.2
Gathorne–Hardy, G., 9, on Berlin Memorandum, 94; on atrocities, 169; on Derby, 186–7, 315; 274—5, 332, becomes India Secretary, 415; 429–30
Germany, refuses Ottoman mediation appeal, 344
Gladstone, W. E., 2–3, on Ottoman bankruptcy, 27; 79, 124, 148, and agitation, 181–4, 188–9, 194; pamphlet on Bulgarian horrors, 183–4; Blackheath speech, 185; 187, 234, encourages Mundella, 235; appeals to Disraeli, 235; speaks at St. James's Hall, 236; favours policy of Canning, 237; writes to Russian government, 238–9; on Disraeli's Judaism, 245; moral idiosyncracy, 245–6; Parliamentary resolutions of, 286ff; speaks in Parliament, 288; agrees to speak at Birmingham, 291–2; appeals to Shuvalov on Russian atrocities, 311–12; 343, speech at Oxford, 376–7, 581 n.14; 377–8, opposes vote of money, 383; on morality and policy, 384–5; denounces Austria,

392; on Treaty of San Stefano, 411; 524 n.66, 525–6 n.75, 583 n.23

*Globe,* the, publishes Anglo – Russian agreement, 443; 444–5, 601–2 n.21

Gorchakov, Prince Alexander, 21, 31, 43, on Ottoman reform, 44; 48, on pacification, 78; disapproves Andrássy's opposition to rebel conditions, 79, 84; warns against Ottoman attack upon Montenegro, 82; Berlin meeting, 87ff; on Serbia and Montenegro, 107; suspicious of Britain, 109; suggests autonomy for Bosnia–Hercegovina, 113; 146, proposes armistice, 174; presses Derby on a conference, 195; occupation of Ottoman Empire, 199; circular of, 247, 277, 552 n.12; announces occupation of Constantinople, 387–8; promises not to occupy Gallipoli, 396; 406–7, 421, 482 n.46, 496 n.33

Grant Duff, M. E., 8

Granville, Earl, 185, on agitation, 188; 194; 237, 343–4, 419–20

Great Britain, and Crimean War, 1; Ottoman reform, 1–2; Treaty of Paris, 2; central Asia, 4; Suez Canal, 30; accepts Andrássy note, 54–6; 60–1, refuses Berlin Memorandum, 94–5; fleet sent to Turkish waters, 101–2, 305; public meetings, 179ff., 43–4, 343, 351; 241, change in British policy, 190, 246; charitable relief, 244, 335; suspicion of Bismarck, 251; press, 254, 335, 379, 398; Turkish bankruptcy effect, 265; answer to Gorchakov's circular, 280; secret negotiations with Austria, 282ff., 313–4; warning to Russia on occupation of Constantinople, 310; warning to Russia, 336–7; asks if Russia will consider armistice, 346; Gallipoli and Dardanelles, 358–9; fleet ordered to Constantinople, 366–7; attempt to buy four Ottoman ironclads, 392

Greece, incites rebellion, 327; invades Turkey, 375

Guarracino, 149

Hamilton, Lord George, 185

Hammond, Lord, E. 10, 142, 237

Harcourt, Sir William, talks with

Shuvalov, 350; on Ottoman integrity, 378

Harris, David, 15–16, 21, 63, 67, on Elliot, 128; on Pears, 143; 147–8, 149–50, 239, on Disraeli, 499 n.20; 513 n.1

Hartington, Marquis of, 136, 185, on agitation, 188; opposes conference, 235; on St. James's Hall conference, 237; angry with Gladstone, 287; speech in Parliament, 290; speaks at Glasgow, 329; 343–4 383, 580 n.4

Herbert, Auberon, 420

Hercegovina, insurrection, 13ff., 480 n.21; 18, 30, twelve–day armistice, 78; rebel conditions, 79; 146

Hofmann, Baron, 37

Holmes, William, 13, 15, 17, 18, 20, 22, 40, on Ottoman reform 76; 478 n.3

Home, Colonel, 274, 563 n.25

Hornby, Admiral, wishes to occupy, Gallipoli, 311; 367, 369, 387–90, suggests Ottoman understanding, 394

Howell, George, 143

Ignatiev, Count Nicholas, 18, 19, 21–4, 30–1, opposes Andrássy, 32–3; on territory for Montenegro, 81; on occupation of Turkey, 208–9, 214–15; flattery of the Salisburys, 211; 229, 253, mission to Germany and Britain, 254ff; conditions for disarmament, 257; 395, 484 n.20, 486 n.11, 504 n.2, 565 n.40

Italy, on Andrássy note, 47; 61, exchange of ideas with Britain, 85–6; 173, 265, 374–5

Jelavich, Barbara, 14, 15, 454–5

Jomini, Baron, 34, 36–7

Kartsov, M., 31

Langer, William L., 15, on Anglo-German entente, 64

Layard, Henry Austen, 10, 160, 220–1, attempts to save peace, 264–5; requests British officers, 279; relationship with Sultan, 293–4; deprecates Russian peace terms, 297; urges occupation of Gallipoli, 314; transmits a version of Russian armistice terms, 368; telegram on Russian advance, 379; 380, on fleet

Layard (contd.)
to Constantinople, 388; moves fleet away from Constantinople, 394; 398, on Treaty of San Stefano, 402; on railroad to Persian Gulf, 405; 406–7, 429, negotiates Cyprus Convention, 440–1; 548–9 n.42 and 44, 573–4 n.34
Liberal party, 147ff; disunity of, 194; 267, 269, 272, 286ff; 349–50, challenges cabinet's request for money, 373–4
Liddon, Canon, 179–181, 541–2 n.20
Loftus, Lord Augustus, 36, 117–8, 204, excited by Russia, 279; warns of Russian duplicity, 293
London Protocol, 257ff.
London, Treaty of 1827, 1; Treaty of 1871, 2 102, 416, 502 n.49
Long, Dr. Albert, 127, 133
Loyd–Lindsay, Colonel, 177
Lyons, Lord, on Andrássy note, 53; 65–6, 197, 405
Lytton Earl, on war with Russia, 193; 559 n.65

MacColl, Malcolm, appeals to Gladstone on atrocities, 142, 181; 531–2 n.20
MacGahan, J. A., goes to Rumelia, 143–4; reports on atrocities, 156–8; 178
Mackenzie, David, 16, 480 n.18, 534 n.21
Mahamoud Pasha, 31, 46
Malet, Edward, 10, 425
Manners, Lord John, on Andrássy note, 50; resignation of, 312–13; 332
Medlicott, W. N., v, 63–4, on Elliot, 128
Melegari, M., 85
Midhat Pasha, 76, 217–18, 224–6, opposes foreign commission, 228
Milan, Prince, 18–19, 84, leans toward war, 107
Mollinary, General, 78, 80
Montenegro, 13, 15–18, 22, 81, 108, 117–18, goes to war, 119; 147, negotiates for peace, 260
Morier, Sir Robert, 5, 220
Mosse, W. E., 2
Mundella, A. J., on atrocities, 135; 233, appeals to Gladstone on conference, 234–5; 343
Münster, Count, 3, 28, 60
Murad V, Sultan, 108, 165
Musurus Pasha, 42

National Federation of Liberal Associations, 351, 369
National Society for Aid to the Sick and Wounded, 177
Nationalism, Balkan, 2; Serbian, 15–16, 17–18
Negroponte Affair, 406–7
Nevesinje, 13,
Nicholas, Grand Duke, 357, 397
Nicholas, Prince, 18, 25, 81, 248
Nigra, ambassador, 387
Nonconformity, 239, 241
Northcote, H. S., 208
Northcote, Sir Stafford, on atrocities, 169–70; advocates seizure of Suez Canal, 276–8; advises Derby on policy, 278–9; 339, on Derby's lethargy, 339; 342, explains changed British opinion, 362–3; on sending fleet to Constantinople, 382; on British objectives, 383
Novikov, E., 25, 31, 46
Novikov, Olga, appeals to Gladstone, 238

Ollier, E., 351
Onou, M. K., 31, 484 n.17
Osman Pasha, 327, 334, 563 n.29
Ottoman Empire, Christian disabilities, 16; tax farming, 13–14; 16, requests British support, 18; imperial irade of October 1875, 26; 33, bankruptcy, 27; use of Circassians, 39; firman of 12 December 1875, 43, 46–7; asks English acceptance of Andrássy note, 53; Porte's acceptance of Andrássy note, 57, 73; announces amnesty, 77; Sultan deposed, 101; suppression of Bulgarian revolt, 125; refuses armistice, 173; orders suspension of hostilities, 173–4; accepts armistice, 175; defeats Serbia, 176; opposes autonomy, 201; accepts Constantinople Conference 203; constitution for, 221–2; offer to execute Andrássy note, 227–8; grand council refuses conference proposals, 228–9; rejects London Protocol, 263–4; appeal for European mediation, 336; signs Russian terms at Adrianople, 371, 582 n.17; refuses permission for the fleet, 387; attempts to prevent coming of the fleet, 390; refuses cession of Bosnia, 422

Palmerston, Viscount, 1–2

Paris, Treaty of 1856, 2, 47, 102, 192, 250, 264, 436, 502 n.49, 548 n.38, 594 n.28

Parliament, 59, on Bulgarian atrocities, 130–3, 135–6; 141–2, 147ff., 157–8, 269–73, five days debate, 288–90; defeat of Gladstone resolution, 290; early meeting of, 343; 363–4, 366, 377–8, 381, 382–3, 406, 420–1, 431–2

Parnell, Charles S., on rate of money, 385–6

Paulovich, Peko, 25

Pears, E., 127–8, 129–30, 133–4, 143

Plevna, 316, 323, 334–5, 563 n.29

Pomaks, 150–1, 162

Ponsonby, Henry, 2, 20, 59, 236–7, 506 n.21, 574–5 n.37

Public opinion,
    Continental, 163
    Great Britain, 1, 4, 119, 163–4, 166, 175, 176ff., 190, 233, on Turkey, 240; 267ff., desire for peace and suspicion of Russia, 361–2; 374, 398–9, 568 n.1, 576 n.45, 580 n.7, 587 n.45
    Ottoman, 29, 38
    Russia, 147

Reform, Ottoman, 1–2, 33, 38, 42–3, tax in lieu of military service, 74; 74–6, and British opinion, 239–40; 487 n.16

Refugees, Bosnian, 58, 76–8, 327, 494 n.9; Ottoman, 376, 576–7, n.48, 588 n.1

Reichstadt meeting, 146

Renouvin, P., 17

Richard, Henry, 420–1

Richmond, Duke of, on Derby, 315

Rodich, Baron, 15, 78–9, 80–1

Roebuck, J. A., Parliamentary speech, 289

Rogers, Thorold, 8

Rupp, G., 15, 146

Russell, Odo, 49, on Andrássy note, 52; talks with Bismarck, 61ff., 65, 68, 70, 491–2 n.12; advises acceptance of Berlin Memorandum, 88, 95; reassures Bismarck, 250–1; on Bismarck, 262; 500 n.36, misleads Derby, 587 n.43

Russia, 2, Balkan consuls, 16, aids insurrection, 18; 23, agrees to Andrássy reforms, 44; double policy of, 83; naval power, 102; 146, volunteers for

Serbia, 174; ultimatum to Porte, 176; favours war, 263; declaration of war, 265; reply to Derby's dispatch of 6 May, 295–6; peace terms, 295–6; alteration of peace terms, 298; reply to British request on peace, 346; reply to British good offices and Constantinople, 351

Safvet Pasha, 221, 265

St. James's Hall Conference, 233ff.

Salisbury, Marquis of, 4, 7–8, 12, on Andrássy note, 50–1, 54; on Ottoman Empire, 172, on Elliot, 196; asked to go to Constantinople, 195–6; opposes Palmerstonian policy, 197–8, 255; approval of, 199–200; instructions for Constantinople Conference, 203, 206–7; journey to conference, 208; unites with Ignatiev, 210, 213; establishes secret cypher with Carnarvon, 212; on military occupation of Turkey, 214–15; ready to put pressure on Turkey, 216–17; 219, sees Sultan, 222, 228; urges Elliot's recall, 233; attempts to scare Porte, 224; 227–8, duped by Ignatiev, 230; poor treatment of Elliot, 230; on Turkish partition, 230, 255; criticizes Derby, 249; bad judgement, 253; 274, objects to alliance with Turkey, 275, 321, 338, 340; no fear of Russia, 277–8; criticizes Derby's offer to Austria, 282–3; 285, switches sides in cabinet, 356; on changed British opinion toward Turkey, 363–4; supports Disraeli, 372; on fleet to Constantinople, 388; 410, becomes Foreign Secretary, 415; circular of, 416–8, 592 n.21; implements policy, 418–9; suggests mediation by Bismarck, 419; on Turkish occupation of Shumla, Varna, and Batum, 425; gives British conditions to Shuvalov, 427–8, 596 n.35; on alliance with Turkey, 428, 434, 437–8, 440–1, 446–7; tells Shuvalov of Cyprus Convention, 437; reaction to Russian concessions, 437–8; offer to Austria, 440; denies *Globe* story, 444; explains Cyprus Convention, 446–7; policy of, 448–50; 453ff., 477 n.22, 489 n.44, 536 n.36, 537 n.48, 540 n.77, 579 n.2, secrecy at the Foreign Office, 599 n.10

Salonica, murder of French and German consuls, 101, 163, 497 n.4

San Stefano, Treaty of, 402, 404, 410–11, 588 n.2

Sandison, Alfred, 38

Sandon, Lord, replies to Gladstone, 289; enters cabinet, 415

Sandwith, Humphrey, 59

Schuyler, Eugene, travels to Rumelia, 143–4; investigates atrocities, 155–7; 178, preliminary report, 180; 515–16 n.20, 533–4 n.13

Selborne, Earl of, 377

Serbia, 13, 15–18, 22, warned against war, 33–4, military preparations, 84; 107, goes to war, 119; 147, requests an armistice, 165; concludes peace, 253; declares war on Turkey, 338; 520–1 n.32

Seton–Watson, R. W., v, 15

Sever Pasha, 22, 397

Shaftesbury, Lord, speaks at atrocity meeting, 143; 233

Shannon, R. T., 164, on MacGahan, 178; 180–1, 239, characterizes the agitation, 240–4; 513 n.1

Shuvalov, Count Peter, 10, 28, 36, 48, pleas for armistice, 92; talks with Disraeli, 93–4; presses autonomy for Bosnia–Hercegovina, 108; talks on Anglo – Russian understanding, 109–10, 113–15; 202, 205, relationship with Lady Derby, 211; 248, 252, compromise suggestion, 260; departs for Russia, 281–2; on cabinet dissension, 337–8; talks with Harcourt, 350; delivers Russian peace terms, 369; works for peace, 395, 585 n.37; puts pressures on Derby, 400; 417–18, direct negotiations with Britain, 426ff; gives Russian concessions on Treaty of San Stefano, 436

Sidgwick, Henry, 180

Simmons, Sir L., military memorandum, 282; on Gallipoli, 311; 563 n.25

Smith, W. H., 402

Stanley, Frederick, appointed war secretary, 415

Stead, W. T., 179, 523 n.54

Stillman, William J., 13, 16–17, 19, 25, 58

Stojanovic, M. D., 15, 64, 450–1, 586 n.40

Stoney, estimates of Bulgarians killed, 162

Straits Convention, 1, 105, 502 n.49

Strangford, Lady, 59, 177, appeals unsuccessfully to Gladstone, 182–3

Stratford de Redcliffe, 2, 288

Stratheden and Campbell, Lord, 58–9

Summer, B. H., 15–16, 23, 427

Sutorina meeting, 79, 81–2

Taylor, A. J. P., 15–16, 64, 415, 460

Tchertelew, Prince, 156

Temperley, H. W. V., 15–16

Tenterden, Lord, 20, on Andrássy note, 49–50, 490 n.56; on German entente, 66; reaction to Berlin Memorandum, 89–90; memorandum on the Straits, 102–3; on Bismarck, 116–17; 138, 159, 225–6, favours putting pressure on Turkey, 249; talks with Ignatiev, 257–8; presses Derby on Turkish armistice request, 339–40; 360, suspicious of Russia, 397–8; 508–9 n.1

Thompson, G. C., 119, 239–40, characterizes agitation, 242; 268–9, 271–2, 351, 402, 417, 420

*Times, The,* 178, 381–2, 389, 430–1, 529 n.12

Todleben, General, 327, 427

Tripartite Treaty of 1856, 2, 166, 191

Vassilitsky, M., 77–8

Victoria, Queen, 29, 59, Empress of *India* controversy, 59–60; on a German entente, 69–70; on British isolation, 91; on Berlin Memorandum, 95; warns Tsar of Ignatiev, 109; favours cooperation with Germany, 116; outrage with atrocities, 132, 137; 200, opposes Russian occupation, 204–5; angry at St. James's Hall Conference, 236–7; suspicious of Russia and Bismarck, 254–5; advises Derby, 297; 301, anger with Gladstone, 306; desires to oppose Russia, 309–10; impatience with Derby, 313–14; on the Derbys, 316; secret warning to Alexander II, 318; attempts to end war, 323; relationship with Disraeli, 327; presses for mediation, 329–30, 338; warns Lady Derby, 349; ashamed, 380; 568–9 n.8, 574–5 n.37

Villiers, F., sends Bulgarian skulls to London, 243

Vogüé, M. de, 47

Waddington, W. H., 435–6
Ward Hunt, G., 102
Washburn, Dr. George, 127, 133, 144
Wellesley, Colonel F., 301, mission to Britain, 317ff; takes secret message to Tsar, 322
Werther, Baron, 22

White, Sir W., 19, 33–4
William I, 100
Wirthwein, W. G., 377
Wolseley, Sir Garnet, 383–4

Yonin, Alexander, 15, 31
Yriärte, Charles, 13

Zichy, Count, 22